Making Dictionaries

Making Dictionaries

Preserving Indigenous Languages of the Americas

EDITED BY

William Frawley
Kenneth C. Hill
Pamela Munro

UNIVERSITY OF CALIFORNIA PRESS

Berkeley   Los Angeles   London

This book is dedicated to Ken Hale (1934–2001),
mentor, colleague, and friend.

University of California Press
Berkeley and Los Angeles, California

University of California Press, Ltd.
London, England

© 2002 by the Regents of the University of California

Library of Congress Cataloging-in-Publication Data

Making dictionaries : preserving indigenous languages of the Americas / edited
  by William Frawley, Kenneth C. Hill, Pamela Munro.
p. cm.
Includes bibliographical references and index.
ISBN 0-520-22995-9 (cloth : alk. paper) — ISBN 0-520-22996-7 (pbk. : alk.
  paper)
1. Indians—Languages—Dictionaries. 2. Indians—Languages—Lexicography.
  I. Frawley, William, 1953- II. Hill, Kenneth C. III. Munro, Pamela.
PM136 .M35 2002
497—dc21

2001053046

Manufactured in the United States of America
10 09 08 07 06 05 04 03 02
10 9 8 7 6 5 4 3 2 1

The paper used in this publication meets the minimum requirements of
ANSI/NISO Z39.48-1992 (R 1997) (*Permanence of Paper*).

CONTENTS

Making a Dictionary
Ten Issues

William Frawley, Kenneth C. Hill, and Pamela Munro

Lexicographic war stories are a special genre of tales of impossibility and thanklessness. Get a few dictionary veterans around a table, and you will hear

- how difficult it was even to know where to begin;
- how, after finally beginning, the work was both glacially incremental and wildly circuitous;
- how the funding was precarious, if there was agency support at all;
- how the project went on and on and the book kept expanding from a modest list of words and glosses to something like a cultural encyclopedia—what must be the lexicographic version of Congress's feared "mission creep";
- how some things turned out to be absolutely inachievable, no matter how clever the lexicographer;
- how, for some at least, the project had back-burner status because those who promoted and rewarded employees wanted more short-term and ostensibly theoretical results;
- how, when the work was finally completed and published, some people were unimpressed, and even mean-spirited and critical—"What! You forgot to include . . . ???"

The funny thing about these war stories is that not one of them is a fish story.

A reasonable person might then naturally ask, Why do it? One way to read the contributions to this volume is as personal answers to this question.

But a more general response can be discerned in all the chapters and, indeed, in the work of every lexicographer. There is something at once both marvelous and practical about producing a guide to the mind, world, and behavior of a group of people. The benefits that accrue from such a handbook—literacy, preservation, history, discovery—only add to the excitement of seeing the published dictionary standing upright on the bookshelf.

The intrinsically daunting task of dictionary making has been mitigated in recent years by the appearance of excellent comprehensive studies of the decisions and procedures involved in putting a dictionary together. Ladislav Zgusta's (1971) manual is the classic, but other important works are Sidney Landau's (1984) and Bo Svensén's (1993) surveys, the three-volume handbook of the field (Hausmann et al. 1990–91), journals devoted to problems in dictionary making (e.g., *Dictionaries, International Journal of Lexicography, Lexicographica, Lexikos*), and any number of more specialized studies on all phases of the development and production of dictionaries.

These mounting resources ease the lexicographer's perceived burden that he or she has not only to do the dictionary work proper but also to invent the method on the fly. But because the resources are mostly from the European-American tradition, they directly address the small portion of the world's languages with a long and documented history of literacy and lexical recording (indeed, one of the first texts in Hittite inscription is a rudimentary dictionary: Frawley 1987). The remainder of the world's languages, of course, do not have such extensive lexicographic and literate traditions. Admittedly, many nuts-and-bolts issues of lexicography cross all languages and so make these European-American resources valuable to those working outside that tradition. But many problems specific to non-Western languages either go unconsidered in these works or are addressed tangentially or vaguely. How, for example, do you even write down the entry in a language that has no writing system? This situation has engendered a parallel world, where lexicographers outside the European-American tradition have wrestled unassisted with problems particular to their languages and sometimes inadvertently repeated the theoretical lexicographic work established elsewhere.

We hope to productively unite these traditions by looking at ten issues raised by the compilation of dictionaries of the indigenous languages of the Americas and the ways the chapters in this volume come together over these issues. The list below is representative, not exhaustive, and characterizes some of the crucial points—often flash points—at which European-American lexicography, with its philological roots and sympathies, makes contact with linguistically and anthropologically oriented American Indian lexicography.[1]

1. The indigenous languages of the Americas are widely referred to as "American Indian languages." In the United States, "American Indian languages" is traditional and is still the

One distinct absence in the list below must be acknowledged. Cultural aspects of the indigenous languages that affect lexicography are not given separate treatment but discussed throughout each of the ten sections below. This is not to say that cultural factors are unimportant: on the contrary, they are so important in matters of American Indian lexicography that they appear everywhere in the discussion.

1. ENTRIES.   What forms does the lexicographer choose to define or have point to other forms for definition? This question is quickly complicated by some simple observations. In a dictionary of contemporary English, are *link* 'loop of a chain, usually metal' and *link* 'hypertext code for automatic transferral to another URL' separate words deserving separate entry status? Is the latter too new even to be in the dictionary?

Traditional lexicographic practice distinguishes a variety of entries, forms that go into the dictionary to be defined or to direct or anchor search. Headwords (often referred to generally as "entries") begin a dictionary article and are the object of definition, usually with subentries nested under them. Blind entries are headwords with no definition but which merely point to other headwords for definition. Cross-references are forms within entries that point to other entries.[2]

Consider just the selection of headwords. The rule of thumb for a headword is that it is a basic form, but what counts for basic is clear neither in lexicographic principle nor, especially, in practice with American Indian languages. Ideally, a headword is a lemma—an abstraction that subsumes other forms related both morphologically and semantically—and so is basic in the way a superordinate concept is. Hence *link* 'chain loop' and *link* 'hypertext code' cluster under the lemma LINK. But note how this makes the headword not a word at all but an abstract pointer. Such a lemmatization would get very complex with American Indian languages.

---

term of choice for many scholars and tribal members, but some consider "Native American languages" to be more appropriate. In Canada, the expression "First Nations languages" covers most indigenous languages of that country. Complicating the use of "Indian" (adjective or noun) is the fact that in much of Latin America the Spanish *indio* (or Portuguese *índio*) 'Indian' is a term of racial disparagement while *indígena* 'indigenous, indigenous person' is relatively neutral in tone. Furthermore, languages of the Eskimo-Aleut group, such as Inuit and Yupik, are normally counted neither among "American Indian languages" nor among "First Nations languages," but they are clearly indigenous. To avoid terminological complications, we use the neutral expression "indigenous languages of the Americas" in the title of this book. Because several terms are acceptable usage, we have allowed authors to use their term of choice.

2. Caveat emptor. When you read on the dust jacket of a commercially produced dictionary that it has a half million entries, check to see what "entry" means: anything in the dictionary in boldface type? just the highest-level headword? something in between? These yield significantly different counts.

Jonathan D. Amith and Una Canger note the difficulties that Nahuatl poses in this regard. Incorporation and reduplication are widespread in the language and produce lexicalizations with different degrees of productivity and hence relatedness. *Teki* 'cut in one act' and *teteki* 'cut repeatedly' might be nested under a single headword, but what about *no:tsa* 'call to' and *no:no:tsa* 'give advice', where the morphological lemmatization is clear but the semantic relatedness begins to stretch?

Pamela Munro observes how what counts as the basic form for a verb varies by and even within language, a point echoed by Catherine A. Callaghan and William Pulte and Durbin Feeling. Uninflected forms, bare stems, stems with affixes, or even lemmas with variables might take the role of basic or neutral. In Chickasaw, for example, some verbs are best entered under a headword that is a non-person-marked, infinitive-like form while others are entered under the applicative prefix. The latter choice is a natural and logical solution that is sensitive to the morphological and semantic productivity of the language, but it nonetheless engenders the famous "clumping problem": uneven distribution of headwords across the phonology or orthography. Because the Chickasaw applicative prefix, *aa-*, is part of the headword, you get a lot of *aa-* entries. Clumping, of course, is not peculiar to the American Indian languages. Munro notes the feared *un-*, *re-*, and *dis-* lists of English-language lexicographers, and the same issue arises in Swahili dictionaries, some of which clump headwords under the animate and inanimate prefixes.

As if issues in relatedness were not enough, changes in the goal of a dictionary from general to special purpose affect what counts as a headword. Thus, William Bright notes how his dictionary of American Indian placenames poses unique issues of headword selection. While headword choice and lemmatization correspond in a general-purpose dictionary, in a placename dictionary, the lemma does not seem to apply. Is there an abstract ANGELES headword subsuming *Los Angeles, Port Angeles,* and so on? One strategy is to choose by source language: European derivative? indigenous derivative? But this method then runs into its own problems, such as false-Indian words. For example, *Itasca,* which sounds Indian, is actually a shortened form of the ungrammatical Latin *veritas caput* 'true head(waters)'.

In addition to relatedness, another strategy in headword choice is quantity—*basic* as the simplest and shortest form—and so the lexicographer might seek the quantitatively minimal form as the headword. The problem with this strategy is what lexicographers know as multiword lexical units, relatively fixed collocations, or multiple forms with high transitional probabilities and thus single-word function (see Mel'čuk's 1988 work on these expressions in his explanatory-combinatorial dictionaries of French and Russian). Indeed, Pulte and Feeling struggle with this very problem in their Cherokee dictionary, where headwords for verbs are complex units of stems plus aspect and person markers. They acknowledge, however, that such units complicate the nesting of subentries and indicate that these complex Cherokee headwords could be supplemented with a more analytical appendix of stems to capture forms chosen via the basic-as-minimal strategy.

These sorts of language- and purpose-specific difficulties in determining relatedness to help choose lemmas ultimately make a dictionary a tradeoff between the pressures for maximal explicitness and the desire to match the users' minds to facilitate their inferences as they fill in what must be left implicit. This tension leads to another typical heuristic in headword choice—the citation form. You can point to an object and ask a speaker, "What is the name of this?" You do this with the hope that you will elicit a neutral expression. Generally, this works well for nouns denoting things, but think of the intrinsic difficulty of eliciting citation forms for events or states. You approach an English speaker and ask her to name the event of a boy moving rapidly over the ground with arms and hands outstretched and pumping. She says, "Running." You ask the same for slower movement. She says, "Walking." Should the citation form for verbs in English be the gerund or present participle? Now imagine suggesting to English-language lexicographers that they change every verb lemma from the infinitive—the tradition inherited from Latin influence—to the gerund or present participle because the latter are the natural citation forms of the event. Rebellion! But this is the very pressure that lexicographers of American Indian languages face. The method of elicitation of citation forms interacts with the linguistic sophistication of the speakers and the context of elicitation. Pulte and Feeling observe that, in their work, the third-person singular form is the natural way Cherokee speakers refer to events in the abstract. Shouldn't this natural match to the minds of the users guide lemma selection?

In the end, entries are a wager that the tension between the way the dictionary ought to look to the compiler and the way it feels to the user will not be too great. Headwords come in many forms, and their selection reflects the influence of both lexicographic practice and the structure of the language under description.

2. THEORY. How much linguistics should be in lexicography? How theory driven is a dictionary?[3] The traditions of European-American and

3. Here we speak of linguistic theory but recognize that other theoretical pursuits affect dictionary making. Social and cultural theory might guide decisions about representing human relations and worldview, visual design theory might guide decisions about dictionary format, and so on.

American Indian lexicography seem to come to theory from opposite directions. Originating in the philological, literary, and etymological view of language, the former is often suspicious of theory—even defiantly atheoretical (although some of this attitude is changing; see, e.g., the forum on theory and practice in *Dictionaries:* Frawley 1992–93). In the European-American tradition, exhaustiveness is always secondary to minimal accuracy and usability, making a dictionary, to borrow and modify something Chomsky once said about pedagogical grammars, a collection of hints. In contrast, the latter tradition, arising out of field data and exhaustive analysis, often begins with theory and faces the daunting task of reducing details and predictions to a manageable collection of hints.

This uneasy alliance of theory and practice can be seen in all the chapters that follow. Callaghan argues that it is to the lexicographer's advantage to make a theory-neutral dictionary because such a work can more readily serve other purposes and a broader readership.[4] In contrast, Joseph E. Grimes observes that the embrace of a particular theory—in his case, the theory of formal lexical relations—can be a great advantage in making a dictionary and even drive discovery by uncovering the structure of the lexicon. For Grimes, then, the line between theory and practice is usefully porous.

The various subfields of linguistics provide a shopping list of the interactions of theory and practice in dictionary construction. Keren Rice and Leslie Saxon, discussing dictionaries of Dogrib, Slave, and Kaska, note the difficulties caused by trying to represent as much phonetic variation as possible to capture the range of dialects, yet, at the same time, seeking to be sensitive to sociolinguistic pressures and having the conservative speech forms of the elders taken as standard. Given phonological neutralizations in dialects, the user of a dictionary with headwords based on older varieties might not be able to infer the headword spellings from his own speech. An alternative is to include every possible phonetic variant in the dictionary and mark each for use. This strategy runs the risk not only of unchecked expanse but also of rejection by the very individuals whom the lexicographer is trying to appease, since speakers often react negatively to the presence of what they perceive as deviations from the standard.

Similar observations can be found in the use of morphological and syntactic theory. Ken Hale and Danilo Salamanca's study of the lexical argu-

4. This is also the traditional view in European-American lexicography. But it should be pointed out that neutrality is also a kind of theory. Frequently, the ostensibly theory-neutral dictionaries of the European-American tradition implicitly embrace a sociolinguistic commitment to upper-middle-class literate speech and so reproduce an ideology of presumed neutrality.

ment patterns of transitive alternating verbs in the Misumalpan languages is a case in point of how syntactic theory might be a good arbiter of lexicographic choice. In Ulwa, for example, the predicate *sang* 'green' can be intransitive (*wâlang baska sangdai* 'the foliage of the savanna is greening up') or transitive (*kahlu âka sangputing* 'I am going to green (dye) this shirt'). Dozens of predicates exhibit similar alternations, while some others do not. Hale and Salamanca show that a single semantic account of these alternations is not sufficient, and purely grammatical factors must be taken into account in representing the relatedness of alternating forms.

These theoretical observations on argument structure affect the organization of dictionaries of these languages because they split verbs into a variety of classes, depending on the cause of the alternation. This in turn can guide the nesting or cross-referencing of entries on the basis of shared structural properties or the explicit listing of entries because of unpredictability. These insights, in fact, would be a good lesson for compilers of current dictionaries of American English, which has experienced a spurt of new or modified transitives: *he (the magician) will disappear the dove* (new use), *they tasked us* (resurgence of older use), *Greenspan grew the economy* (selectional restriction change). Should these be explicitly listed at their headwords or left unsaid because they are (semantically or grammatically) predictable?

Semantics and pragmatics come readily to mind as bearing on lexicography. After all, a dictionary is mostly a list of truths (meanings), and with this there comes the whole problem of the tools we use to describe and explain the way a group of people construes the world. In his study of lexical structure in Huichol, Grimes makes an important point when he observes that there is a significant difference between glosses and definitions. Lexicography, he argues, begins after systematic data analysis. As he says, "we define senses of lexical items," not lexical items themselves. Defining is thus a second-order pursuit, an attempt to redescribe our initial descriptions (glosses), and so it is necessarily theoretical because redescription requires a theoretical viewpoint.[5]

Richard A. Rhodes's work on meaning-form relations and the line between semantics and pragmatics in the description of Ojibwe further underscores the interaction between semantic theory and lexicographic practice. His retrospective look at his 1985 dictionary reveals three places where it (and other dictionaries, it should be added) could be improved:

---

5. In this regard, it is worth considering dictionaries that claim to be doing new things with their definitions—COBUILD (Sinclair 1987), for example. What makes COBUILD different is that it approaches the problem of definition with a new semantic theory and applies it consistently.

the recognition of many-to-many form/meaning mappings in multiform units, the determination of purely constructional meanings, and the characterization of Ojibwe-specific pragmatic implications of lexical items.

There are lots of other ways that semantic and pragmatic theory impinge on the practical aspects of dictionary construction. For instance, Amith (Nahuatl) and Rice and Saxon (Kaska) note how lexical lists can be either organized or supplemented by semantic fields, yielding conceptually based dictionaries and search procedures. In the end, the lesson is that theory can retain its claim to fine-grained analysis and subtle insight while still serving the practical lexicographic purpose of usable accuracy.

3. LITERACY. What could be more of a truism than to say that dictionaries are tied to literacy? Headwords, definitions, and various lexicographic notations are written; users are readers; entries are sequenced alphabetically; a major source of evidence for lexicographic decisions, especially in the European-American tradition, is citation from printed sources. Dictionaries, by definition, are books.

This tie to literacy is not, however, a necessary one. Imagine a not-so-far-off, ultra-high-tech world with advanced speech processing technology and the compression of hardware and data to nanoform. Why couldn't a dictionary be a wallet-sized accessory, Velcro-attached to your belt, with completely oral output? You speak your word queries into it, or show its scanner some print, and it speaks back a definition and range of use. The only nonoral part would be the graphics, and they, too, could take up part of the burden of the printed word, in the useful and interesting ways that pictorial dictionaries now do. So who needs the dictionary-as-book?

Thrilling as this cut at the hegemony of the printed page may be to the imagination, it is unlikely to surface in practice. There are great social, cultural, and political pressures surrounding printed lexicons. Tradition, schooling, and the connection of literacy to economic advance continue to loom large on dictionaries, no matter what the advance in technology. These pressures are especially clear in the making of dictionaries of American Indian languages.

Many of the languages have no written tradition until the dictionary itself is compiled. The chapters by Leanne Hinton and William F. Weigel, Callaghan, Pulte and Feeling, and Rice and Saxon highlight the well-known and controversial issues in the selection of an orthography. Should the orthography use phonetic symbols or a Roman alphabet? The representational capacities of the former can capture not only the range of segmental distinctions typical of the Indian languages but also aspiration, length, tones, accents, and other prosodic features. These things can sometimes be missed in an alphabetic orthography. But the advantage of a traditional Roman alphabet is that it has a recognizable tie to literacy: frequently the users of the new alphabet are bilingual and so have been exposed to the alphabets of other languages in their communities.

If the orthography is rendered in phonetic symbols, another concern arises: should the representation be phonetic or phonemic? Answers to this question require answers to other questions about level of detail, variation, attitudes of the community toward written forms, and even the predictions of phonological theory. For example, is any orthography sufficient to allow the reader to infer pronunciation, and if not, what sorts of descriptions should supplement the orthography to aid the reader?

Alphabetization is the traditional basis of entry order (although Hinton and Weigel note attempts to sequence entries by articulatory position of the initial sound), but alphabetic sequencing from *a* to *z* is not a self-evident principle. Although the users' literacy in their second language can limit the sense of the arbitrariness of *a* to *z* alphabetization, more specific worries arise. As Hinton and Weigel ask, does *p'* precede or follow *p*? Should the sequence of *ch* be treated as one unit or two, and if one, does it precede *ci*? These questions again bring to light the hegemony of print. In an electronic dictionary, intrinsic order is not an issue. If a user wants an alphabetical printout, then the machine can do that, but in the machine, it makes little difference if a *p'*-word is physically near a *p*-word.

Many of the authors of chapters in this volume participated in the development of orthographies for the languages in the dictionaries they describe. Orthography development is always a difficult issue because orthographic traditions vary according to the tradition of the language in which definitions are written. For example, the expected phonetic value of the letter *j* is different for those literate in English, Spanish, French, or German. If the orthography is a new one, it is especially important for the dictionary to have a section in which it is clearly explained and related to the sounds of the language. Often, though, it is difficult to persuade users that the dictionary's orthography follows different rules from the alphabet they are most used to. English-speaking users expect *oo* to be pronounced as in *boot* or *foot,* for instance.

In addition to orthography choice per se, there is the larger and thornier issue of standardization and its connection to schooling and language maintenance. As Rice and Saxon and Paul V. Kroskrity observe, the European-American tradition in lexicography buys heavily into the ideology of one word/one best form. This kind of hierarchical standardization, where one form comes out on top of the pecking order, is often counter to what communities of speakers may believe. Rice and Saxon argue that the one-to-one strategy may be good in principle but must be abandoned in practice, given the stratification of the speech varieties to be represented. Indeed, their work shows that standardization is not a prerequisite to literacy, either in American Indian languages or in the languages that have served the Western tradition in lexicography.

In Mono, as Kroskrity notes, this tendency toward diversity is very significant. The Mono ideology of the value of variation and individual speech usage makes a single standard entirely counter to the culture's beliefs. For the Mono, the dictionary should include everything, high forms, slang, and all other varieties. Such a belief has even proved a bit treacherous for Mono itself, since the speakers have allowed English to overtake the language, accepting English, too, as another perfectly fine variety!

A final issue concerning literacy, orthography, and standardization—not explicit in the chapters but crucial to them all—is the connection of written representation to research on these languages. Comparative work and the evaluation of evidence can be affected by orthography and font choice. Consider the common practice of data passing and file sharing among researchers. This procedure is essential to the cooperative work that often characterizes research on American Indian languages. But it quickly turns into a nightmare when written representations do not transfer from one computer system to another. Certainly part of the problem is the technology (and business practice) that hinders cross-platform transfer, but also at issue are the representations themselves, which are, first and foremost, in the hands of the researchers.

4. GRAPHICS.   Writing is not the only kind of representation in a dictionary. Photographs, halftones, line drawings, and other sorts of graphical representations also play a significant role, though not equally either across dictionaries or within any single one. Some dictionaries—and not just those for children or learners—are almost entirely visual. The Oxford-Duden pictorial dictionaries, for example, are focused on adult native speakers, and they pay a high price for it. They are so packed and complicated, with every nook, cranny, and micro-part labeled, that they are often difficult to use. The usual lexicographic model is a judicious combination of graphics and words, but even this desire is put into practice unevenly. The *American Heritage Dictionary*, for instance, is famously overloaded with graphics.

While the exact reason why a graphic is selected or inserted at a point in the text can sometimes be baffling—why an elephant but not a dog?—there are a number of standard motivations for the use of nonlinguistic representations: increase authenticity, typify because of unusualness, reduce complexity (Landau 1984).[6] These motivations surface readily in

6. Another compelling reason is tradition. Dictionaries have pictures because they have always done so. Michael Hancher (1996) notes the extremes to which this tradition can push lexicographers. In the nineteenth century, editors sometimes inserted pictures for things they had never seen under the belief that the item simply had to be illustrated graphically.

American Indian language dictionaries. Haruo Aoki notes that the lexicographer can let pictures stand alone for either the headword or the definition. "What is a mushroom? That!" This is an especially useful strategy when the item to be defined is unusual with respect to the user. The graphic can provide a visual substitution for the referent or gloss.

But different graphical choices carry their respective problems (Landau 1984). Photographs are authentic but very busy informationally. Line drawings and halftones are cogent but idealized. Consider again Aoki's concern. Would a photograph of a mushroom, given that it would also represent all sorts of information about the mushroom ancillary to the user's ostensible need, be better than a line drawing? The latter might cause the opposite problem: in scaling down the mushroom to a schematic, it would transfer the burden onto the user again to make the inference of what the object is.

Diagrams, graphs, charts, and other sorts of data-driven representations run the risk of what Edward Tufte (1983, 1990, 1997) sees as letting the design variation rule the data variation. If you give every piece of data its own explicit representation, you produce a representational monster. Graphics need maximal data compression (as Tufte says, "Less is bore!"), but this is a tricky strategy to effect. Consider the immense illustration problem that David S. Rood and John E. Koontz face in their comparative Siouan dictionary, the front matter of which must capture in a cogent way the (still-disputed) genetic relationships across the subfamilies. Alternative names, structural and geographic overlaps, and disputed derivations make the ideal of a smooth, branching graphic for the Siouan family a challenge indeed. The problem also shows that different types of dictionaries pose their own graphical problems: a comparative dictionary, like Rood and Koontz's, would have markedly different illustrations from a placename dictionary, like Bright's.

All these issues come together in Kroskrity's work, which shows how advanced technology provides portable multimedia dictionaries with huge data capabilities that can do many things at once and serve all kinds of users' and designers' needs in virtually a single package. One of the true benefits of this technology is complex and immediate cross-referencing. In a printed book, the user turns and turns pages to follow the pointers and, as we know from user studies, may give up in the end. But a CD makes several data sets and formats available at once: as Kroskrity shows, the meanings and the forms can not only co-occur, but the user can also have input into the interaction, and the information can take a variety of forms, both visual and oral.

Graphics in dictionaries are thus like the SAT and GRE examinations: they often do not tell you much, but you'd better require them or you'll be looked on strangely.

There is no doubt that multimedia dictionaries are the wave of the future, despite their enormous technical demands. But even as they perch on the cutting edge, they pose the age-old graphics questions: who is using this dictionary, for what purpose, and how?

5. ROLE OF THE COMMUNITY.   The role of the community of users and native speakers in the European-American tradition stands in marked contrast to its role in the compilation of American Indian language dictionaries. There is perhaps no clearer symptom of this matter than the difference between the intellectual sources of these lexicographic approaches.

Dictionaries of Western languages are generally made by teams of trained lexicographers who principally rely on their own intuitions as speakers and who use data and evidence from a citation file and from other dictionaries published by their employers and their competitors. This work is always supplemented by selective editing by area experts, usage panels, and, increasingly, corpus data. The community of users and speakers is taken into account especially when the dictionary is targeted for a specialized group. But it is one of the axioms of lexicography that users have quite particular reasons for opening a dictionary—usually just to check spelling or definition of unknown words, not to browse. And given the commercial pressures on dictionaries, community sensitivity often is equivalent to market sensitivity, with the business side of a press exerting great influence on the editorial side. In the end, the community in the European-American tradition is a kind of mild abstraction, a group to be satisfied, but at a distance from the book itself.[7]

In contrast, in American Indian-language dictionaries, the community has active and necessary involvement in the development of the dictionary. The direction of community pressures can affect the direction of the work as a whole.

These pressures and the significant role of the community surface in at least three ways. First there is the matter of consultants, those from the speech community who provide data to the lexicographer and/or advise on selection, illustration, and accuracy. (Indeed, these two groups need not be the same individuals, given their different roles.) Who should serve in these roles? And when you ask certain individuals to be consultants

---

7. A sociology of the workplace of lexicographers would be a revealing study in this respect. The pool of lexicographers for dictionaries of English is quite small, given the enormity of the task. Some lexicographers stay at certain publishing houses for their entire careers, thereby establishing and maintaining the traditions; others switch from house to house, bringing their histories with them. What this means is that the community as an abstraction in these dictionaries is heavily constrained to remain faithful to past practice—because there are so few new lexicographers.

or advisers, whose language are you choosing as the language of the dictionary, and what commitments are you thereby entering into? Rice and Saxon note the age and geographic variables affecting the answers to these questions: some members of the community might want older forms with less variation, which would serve the purpose of preservation, but other groups might want more current forms and wider variation to aid language renewal and maintenance. Indeed, some lexicographers are lucky enough to find that some members of the community have been trained in linguistics to a certain extent, which can help the compilation of the dictionary enormously.

Second, how do you work with the consultants and advisers? The answer seems to be: closely, continuously, patiently, and honestly (see Aoki's description of his work with the Nez Perce). Grimes notes that teaching consultants an ordinary-language version of technical linguistic questions can facilitate the discovery of lexical patterns and even turn the dictionary into a kind of community activity. The speakers then own the tools for insight into their speech. Kroskrity argues for the value of constant interchange between the community and the lexicographers to ensure not only accuracy but also a sense of the work as a genuine cooperative venture. Community-based lexicography and the continual back-and-forth work that is essential to it are difficult and time consuming. Amith, in arguing for this activity in the development of a Nahuatl dictionary, notes how the adaptability of electronic dictionaries facilitates this interchange because of the absence of space constraints and the possibility for interactive consultation.

Overall, the issue in how to work with dictionary consultants and advisers is the standard one that guides the ethics of fieldwork. Mere data extraction can suggest a throwback to colonialism; consultant or (better) community involvement is preferable. Kenneth C. Hill and Hinton and Weigel note the inestimable advantages of having the community feel ownership of the dictionary. Without such close work, the lexicographer would not only run the risk of producing a book that has the feel of a foreign artifact to the community, but would also simply miss basic and important facts—for example, that for some groups personal names of the dead, a typical inclusion in a dictionary, are taboo or that certain forms can be spoken by a restricted group and so cannot be represented in the dictionary.

The third and final issue emerges only after the dictionary has been compiled and printed. What does the community think of this book? Usually, the dictionary is viewed as an important, cooperatively produced resource. But even after the dictionary has been developed with community-based lexicography, objections to the work and tensions about intellectual property rights are not uncommon. Aoki describes how some members of the Nez Perce community thought that his dictionary was full of errors because of their feeling that he did not work with the right consultants. Hill's experience with the Hopi is a striking example of how a community can exercise legal pressures to influence—even delay—the production of a dictionary by claiming that the language is the intellectual property of a group.

These aftereffects can have serious consequences in the context of American Indian language lexicography because decisions about these languages and cultures can be politically charged. But such aftereffects are actually quite common in the European-American tradition. Corporate attorneys, aides to elected officials, and other individuals of influence frequently contact the editorial offices of dictionaries to complain about trademark infringement—"You can't put XX in the dictionary! We own that word!"—and to seek to have words and definitions modified or deleted because they offend the sensibilities of constituents (see Landau 1984: 296–302). Sometimes these lobbying efforts are successful. But the lesson is that intellectual-property wars are hardly the province of the American Indian lexicographic community. They are widely fought, with legal saber rattling the usual case. This is precisely because of the power that a dictionary can have over the community that not only is the source of the dictionary itself, but the ultimate ratifying body.

6. E PLURIBUS UNUM.   How many dictionaries should a lexicographic project produce? To those working in the European-American tradition, the answer is straightforward—one for now, but as many as possible, so make the database that underlies the one for now general enough to be widely used and adaptable to a variety of specialized products (or spinoffs, as they are called). From a good general dictionary, you can produce thesauri, subject-area dictionaries, learners' dictionaries, dictionaries of roots and prefixes, slang dictionaries, and all sorts of reference and resource books. Of course, it is easier to say this than to actually produce the derivatives, since no dictionary is blithely "spun off," but the basic issue is unchanged. Because commercial dictionaries are compiled by teams and market driven and because there are many markets, the overall strategy in European-American dictionary production is multiple-product development.

To those working on dictionaries of American Indian languages, this strategy must seem a noble goal but a quite distant practice. With a small group of workers (some of whom may be transient, as graduate students can be), modest financial and technological resources, and a unique and demanding relationship with the community, the directors of such lexicographic projects are thrilled to produce a single word book. The problems with such development constraints are well known. The data compression needed to capture multiple uses in a single work can be daunting (see Rice and Saxon and Callaghan). The different kinds of communities and interest groups that will ultimately use the book mean that a single multipurpose dictionary will fall short of expectations for some users and exceed them for others. Consider Hale and Salamanca's point that the lower you are on the social hierarchy, the more languages and varieties you need to know. How do you make a single, full-service dictionary for a community that lives under this kind of sociolinguistic pressure?

Technology can perhaps rise again to the occasion. The storage problems posed by multipurpose-multilanguage-multidialectal dictionaries are at least mitigated by electronic forms. But two kinds of access problems are exacerbated. First, what does the user interface look like? That is, how does a member of the community access a dictionary that is otherwise everything to everybody? The kludgey solution of just putting in a huge, long list of headwords—that is, everything—will be off-putting. A single, full-service dictionary has to have an intelligent user interface, one that can anticipate a range of access strategies and demands (see, e.g., Amith's Nahuatl Learning Environment). This problem, moreover, is not tied to technology per se, since a printed full-service book faces the same challenging access issues.

Second, how do you get enough technology to the users so they can have access to begin with? While the issues surrounding access to technology are more fully treated below, we will just point out here that packing large amounts of information in a single, multipurpose dictionary shifts some burdens to the user—for example, training in the use of such a complex resource and costs for the acquisition of technology to use the resource.

In the grand scheme of things, one dictionary is obviously not enough. But the scheme of practical action makes a single dictionary more than enough for now.

7. HISTORY.   How much does history affect the construction of a dictionary? How much historical information should be included in a dictionary, and, if any, where should it be placed? History has a bearing on lexicography both as a backdrop to a dictionary project itself and as lexicographic content—for the latter, perhaps most obviously in etymology. Are words like fossils, things that cannot be understood without essential reference to their history? Or are they found objects, things that can be perfectly well understood and explained in the clothes they appear in?

Those outside the European-American lexicographic tradition might be surprised to learn that fierce intellectual battles have been waged over etymologies. Some dictionaries have cut back or eliminated etymology altogether—either from design (e.g., desk dictionaries lack the space) or from the high moral ground (e.g., etymologies are curios and not often used). Others have retained etymology—again, either from design (e.g., etymological dictionaries or *Webster's,* where the senses are historically ordered) or from the high moral ground (e.g., history provides the true context of the meaning and form). Indeed, one of the great challenges to the dominance of the *Webster* regime in American dictionaries came at the turn of the last century when competitors, like *Funk and Wagnall's,* made the then-radical decision to put the etymology at the end of the entry rather than at the beginning (Landau 1984).

The determination of the historical origin of forms and the inclusion of this information in the dictionary surface in American Indian language lexicography in a number of ways. One is the relation between historical reconstruction and the dictionary itself. Indigenous American languages continue to be the subject of intense debate over classification and genetic grouping. Dictionaries of these languages are ineluctably bound up in this research problem, and they often contain substantial amounts of historical background, including cultural background, in their prefaces. This sense of history is an essential problem of Rood and Koontz's work, one of the goals of which is to use comparative morphological and lexical analysis to reconstruct the ancestor of the modern Siouan languages.

But entries themselves are often the site where historical facts are explicitly represented or expressly motivate the analysis. Callaghan and Canger argue that a historically plausible analysis is an important pressure in the choice of stems and roots—even if it forces one to override consistency—because a dictionary whose entries are historically accurate can serve long-term work on reconstruction outside of lexicography proper. Munro's work on Maricopa shows that we can understand why the -*k* and -*m* aspectual suffixes appear on Maricopa verbs if we understand that these suffixes reflect historically earlier forms of Yuman.

Another way that history bears on lexicography—different from either historical backdrop or etymology—is through archiving and preservation. As is well known, many American Indian languages have very small and declining numbers of speakers and are on the verge of extinction. Pulte and Feeling's observation about this situation poignantly captures the role of lexicography: making dictionaries of such endangered languages can be the last best shot at preserving them or intervening in their rapid disappearance. Indeed, successful and thorough archiving—"tabulating of the past"—can have substantial influence on the future: dictionaries can take preservation one step further and be instruments of revitalization. Hinton and Weigel observe that a dictionary is a teaching tool and "a repository of tribal identity" and so is vital to language maintenance and reproduction. Because dictionaries are open-ended, they can help the creation of new words as a language seeks to adapt its vocabulary to the changing conditions under which it is spoken. Pushing beyond even functional literacy, dictionaries can assist what Kroskrity calls, in the case of Mono, postliteracy. Dictionaries in CD form provide one of many new resources for literate technology in the service of language renewal.

A final issue involving history and which cuts across all the issues discussed above concerns old recordings of words that are no longer in use. Many dictionaries may turn out to be the only record of the languages they treat, so if their coverage is to be as full as possible, it often makes sense to include recordings from previous scholars, even if these cannot be confirmed with living speakers. But such recordings usually reflect older transcriptions or spelling systems. Should they be included as is? Should they be included in both the earlier recording and with a guess as to the probable phonemic (orthographic) form? Should they, perhaps, only be listed in an appendix? All these questions can be perplexing, and they underscore the fact that the interactions between lexicography and history are quite complicated.

8. TECHNOLOGY.   Technology has completely changed lexicography. In the European-American tradition—though less so in the American Indian tradition—what was once the tedious practice of file-card sorting, the painstaking recording and cross-referencing of forms, and the protracted and worrisome task of transmission of data from project to project have mercifully given way to on-line incoming files, automated citation, and remote password-secure access to ongoing projects with automatic storage of editing histories. This is not to say that the watchful human eye and hand have been eliminated. Data and cross-references need to be inputted and checked, but very many of the tedious and time-intensive activities of the past have become automated. Johnson's harmless drudge now often deserves a more modern epithet—"techie" or "Unix geek."

The lexicographic benefits of technology are not just in the obvious—organization, storage, and format. The computer has also aided in uncovering new facts that dictionaries ought to capture. Corpus development and search, now at the vanguard of lexicography and even pushing into linguistic theory through statistical approaches, affords rapid access to massive contextual data for words. Corpora show, for example, that in current English, the complement of *cause* is most likely negative: *cause the destruction of the beach, cause more problems, cause us to worry,* not, generally, *cause increased happiness* (reported at the Dictionary Society of North America symposium on corpus tools, University of California, Berkeley, 1999). This finding would suggest that the verb itself is undergoing a change in selectional restrictions and usage that should be notated in the dictionary. Indeed, it is this instrumental use of technology as a discovery tool—not automation as a goal in itself—that Grimes shows is relevant to the construction of dictionaries of American Indian languages. The Summer Institute of Linguistics has developed a free tool, *Shoebox*, one component of which can build a working lexical data list from text input. *Shoebox's* technology is thus a way to begin a lexicographic project, not to augment it.

More general issues in the influence of technology on American Indian language dictionaries have been discussed previously. Here we look at some of the more technical matters. Perhaps the most obvious ones are database organization, formatting, and character design. Rood and Koontz's chapter is in many ways a testimony to the difficult and long-term struggle with these issues. The fields in a lexical database have to be chosen judiciously so as to capture the correct semantic and grammatical categories without undue expansion or ad hoc classification. Rhodes notes this pressure in his examination of the database structure of the Ojibwe dictionary, which used early and rudimentary database code that often lacked adequate space in the fields to represent semantic information fully. The database must be searchable in a variety of ways and in a format that allows easy file sharing. The phonetic properties of the languages pose a major challenge to character design. Given the way programs run (or don't!) on different platforms, even ingenious solutions to character coding might fail as files are passed. Many solutions to these issues can be found in Amith's work on the Nahuatl dictionary. Semantic, grammatical, and even cultural information can be matched to database fields for a variety of search and discovery procedures and for using the corpus to check accuracy. The cautions of Tufte (1983, 1990, 1997) return: do not let design variation determine data variation; massive data compression is possible with a good plan.

Another technical issue is interactivity. A significant benefit of automation is the relative ease of change, updating, and access. Canger's work on the Copenhagen Nahuatl Dictionary Project is representative in this regard. The dictionary and text corpus that her group has been developing allow access to multiple forms at once—word, root, text—precisely because storage is not alphabetic. Moreover, the technology allows interactive comments on the entries and outputs throughout project development, and so editorial procedures and decisions can be tracked, and any member of the group can view the editorial record for a guide to updating.

One of the most striking benefits of technology for lexicography is its multimedia capability. With a variety of visual and auditory outputs, the electronic dictionary can be a truly multipurpose reference work. This goal is very much behind the work of Amith, whose dictionary can serve both scholarly and pedagogical purposes at once. It also motivates Kroskrity's work on the Mono dictionary, which, in integrating speech, grammar, narrative, and visual illustration, is multitask in a single compact form. A significant consequence of Kroskrity's multimedia project is that it helps the Mono see that their language is contemporary—that is, can be computerized—and thereby affects their attitudes to language maintenance and renewal.

A final issue is portability. The precipitous drops in cost and size of technology, with the simultaneous increase in computing power, potentially put technology and the information it carries in the hands of many. In some ways, members of American Indian language communities are in a better position to take advantage of electronic dictionaries than are the members of the communities that surround them. The compilers of these dictionaries appreciate better than those in the European-American tradition the need to make an electronic product and deliver it directly to the user; they are also subject to fewer countervailing business pressures and traditions that apotheosize the cumbersome printed book.

These rosy tales of technology in dictionary making should, however, be tempered with some cautions. The prevalence of computerization has also engendered an increased feeling in American Indian communities that the only good type of knowledge transmission is via CD-ROM. Perhaps most discouraging is the fact that technological advance always runs speedily ahead of any practice, lexicographic or otherwise. Sometimes a lexicographer has to be an amateur software engineer just to keep up. And even doing so, it is not uncommon to see years of effort spent on solving technological problems suddenly solved in a downloadable package—of course, at the cost of lost time. Rhodes's description of his early work with the Ojibwe dictionary is a good example of the barriers of technology. A retrospective look at his initial lexical database for the language shows how problematic thirty-year-old Fortran code was for access, use, and modification.

Technology has thus been both a bull and a bear for dictionary makers. But no one would turn down the benefits of the bull.

9. LEXICOGRAPHIC TRADITION.   One of us (Frawley) was driving his eight-and-a-half-year-old son to school one day when the boy—who was very much concerned with clocks, time, and measurement—asked in a child's out-of-the-blue-like way: "When somebody set the first clock, what clock did he use to see what time to set?" Indeed! What better illustration of a lexicographer's worry than his puzzlement about infinite expanse and the starting point for what you now have in front of you? When you have decided to do a dictionary and, full of energy, sit down to start, where do you start? What dictionary do you use to see what dictionary you have to write? Who wrote the first dictionary?

Often, if you are working in indigenous American lexicography, you suddenly and frighteningly realize that you are writing the first dictionary. Certainly, this observation is not without exceptions. As Amith, Canger, and Mary Clayton and R. Joe Campbell point out, Nahuatl has a centuries-old lexicographic tradition. Indeed, the striking lesson of Clayton and Campbell's detailed study of the practices of Alonso de Molina, the sixteenth-century Spanish-Nahuatl lexicographer, is that his work is surprisingly sophisticated and modern. For example, Molina saw his task as the explanation of Nahuatl lexis—not just the recording of translational equivalence between source and target language—and often structured the entries to achieve this end, much the way that a conceptually oriented dictionary might take judicious liberties with headword choice in order to meet the encyclopedic demands on lexical description. Still, even with these remarkable and early successes, overall there is a sense in American Indian language lexicography that the tradition has to be substantially invented with the project.

Such is manifestly not the case in European-American lexicography, where techniques, decision procedures, and even judicious ways to fudge have been debugged and passed down for generations. Written in-house guides spell out everything: definition, headword selection, illustration, cross-reference, etymology, abbreviation, font choice, and formatting. Dictionary houses have substantial training programs through which they inculcate both the general and the local tradition. These activities are supplemented by substantial editorial folklore and legend, often retold at professional conferences and kept in the practitioner's consciousness: true trade secrets. In short, when the Western lexicographer sits down to do a dictionary, there is a "first clock" to look at.[8]

The general absence of this kind of lexicographic apparatus in indigenous language lexicography leads to some serious challenges to getting the work done. One is the problem of turning to the Western tradition to borrow techniques. As Canger notes, the European style of lemmatization and word-based entry crashes hard when tried on Nahuatl. Roots, stems, affixes, and such—not easily or practically lemmatized—drive head-"word" selection. Similarly, the tradition in European-American lexicography of choosing a kind of moderately conservative standard as the speech represented in the dictionary—and marking deviations therefrom as *colloq., slang, dial.,* and so on—runs against what is found in many Indian communities. Both Rice and Saxon and Kroskrity describe how their need to be faithful to the attitudes of the community required them

---

8. In Chinese lexicography, there is a tradition of copying directly from the past. It is a sign of respect and responsibility for a contemporary lexicographer to directly reproduce definitions from earlier dictionaries (Creamer 1989).

to move away from such a standard and seek maximal variation in the speech represented.

Another challenge might be called the jack-of-all-trades problem. In the European-American tradition, dictionaries are typically made by teams of workers overseen by one or more directors with editorial, managerial, and business skills. Everyone on the team is capable in both the general and the in-house procedures, but all assume a specialty as a particular project develops: an etymology editor with experience in historical-comparative work, a pronunciation editor with experience in phonetics and variation, and so on. These in-house specialists are supplemented by dozens of out-of-house experts, contracted on a need basis and assigned all or part of a subject area to check accuracy and coverage.

The contrast of this tradition of the well-oiled team with that in indigenous lexicography is stark indeed. This is not to say that there are no teams or that cooperative work has not led to excellent dictionaries. But financial resources are limited, and it is often the case that the groups working on these dictionaries are small and have to be expert at everything. Aoki's description of the challenges he faced in defining everyday artifacts for the Nez Perce is typical. And all the chapters are testimony to the fact that the lexicographer is not only simultaneously a phonetician, morphologist, syntactician, and semanticist but also a sociologist, anthropologist, biologist, diplomat, therapist, mediator, and salesman.

Making a huge general-purpose dictionary of English or French is unquestionably difficult but assuaged, at least, by the machinery of tradition. Making a dictionary of an indigenous language in the absence of—or with a parallel or orthogonal—tradition poses its own sorts of difficulties, often transferring the burden directly onto the one or two individuals who remain dedicated to seeing the task through to completion.

10. RULES SHALL BE KNOWN BY THEIR VIOLATION. While the discussion in the previous section underscores the differences between the European-American tradition and that of American Indian lexicography, there is at least one point on which they both agree completely. Every principle, heuristic, or technique designed to maximize consistency will be violated in the compilation of the dictionary. These transgressions, moreover, will not be random sins of omission but sins of commission, and lexicographers are repeat offenders—of necessity, it turns out.

Any dictionary is a very tricky juggle. In one hand are water-tight principles of analysis, representation, and documentation: the perfect world; in the other are practical accuracy, use, and the pressure just to get the thing done. Each wins at the other's expense, although the violations of the watertight principles seem always to call more attention to themselves than any impracticalities introduced. Canger notes how practical decisions about Nahuatl morphology override desires for analytical consistency. Munro similarly acknowledges the need to violate rules for the optimal verb entry in order to get both coverage and accuracy. Rood and Koontz confess to failing to adhere to their own standards in database design. Bright notes that typologies for headword inclusion are "never carved in stone" and that some forms will be omitted. Fighting these pressures to omit forms, Pulte and Feeling advise: if in doubt, include everything, because exclusion may mean that a form will be lost forever. The best defense is sometimes a strong offense.

This mix of high ideals and judicious sinning (McCawley 1992–93) makes lexicography an odd profession indeed. In few other lines of work can you say: I tried to get it right. But I have to admit that there are dozens of places where I have in fact gone completely against what I promised I was going to do. I know it sounds crazy, but I did so on purpose.

A dictionary is a thousand pages of ideas and history, a guide to the mind and world of a people. No book—except for, perhaps, religious documents, themselves guides to the mind and world of a people—has a shelf life longer than a dictionary. Surely that must be worth something.

ONE

Form and Meaning in the Dictionary

CHAPTER ONE

Theoretical and Universal Implications of Certain Verbal Entries in Dictionaries of the Misumalpan Languages

Ken Hale and Danilo Salamanca

1. INTRODUCTION. The lexicon is traditionally seen as the repository of what is idiosyncratic in a language. And this is to an extent accurate, inasmuch as the relation between a lexeme and the concept it names typically respects Saussurian arbitrariness (setting aside sound symbolism). Furthermore, and importantly, the lexicon is where irregularities (suppletions, unpredictable alternations, etc.) are registered. But there is another aspect of the lexicon, of course, which gives it the character of an entirely lawful system, like grammar—or, more specifically, like syntax and the semantic interpretations determined by syntactic structure. This is the aspect of the lexicon known as "argument structure."

In the discussion to follow, some material from recent work in Misumalpan dictionary making is discussed. The focus is narrow, being restricted to argument structure and, further, to aspects of argument structure that are to some degree "active" in the lexicon and grammar of the languages. When they are completed, years from now in all likelihood, the Misumalpan dictionaries will be expected to serve many purposes, including, for example, those served by such impressive and exceptional

We are indebted to the members of UYUTMUBAL/CODIUL (the Ulwa Language Committee) for their work on the Ulwa dictionary, to Jorge Matamoros for his work on the Miskitu dictionary, and to CIDCA for its support of the Miskitu dictionary project and, in general, for logistical support for linguistic work in Nicaragua. (CIDCA is the acronym for the Centro de Investigaciones y Documentación de la Costa Atlántica, established in three locations: Managua, Bluefields, and Puerto Cabezas [Bilwi].) And we are indebted to the National Science Foundation for financial support for research on Ulwa (Grant no. SBR-9308115) and for support of work on the comparative grammar of the Misumalpan languages (Grant no. SBR-9615545).

resources as the recently published Hopi dictionary (Hopi Dictionary Project 1998) and the justly renowned Navajo dictionary of barely more than a decade earlier (Young and Morgan 1987). Like these works, the Misumalpan dictionaries, if successful, will contribute to the general linguistic database for the scientific study of regular and recurrent principles of grammar as projected from the lexicon. Predicate argument structure is one aspect of the lexicon governed by recurrent cross-linguistically valid principles. And the present discussion is intended as an introduction to some of the Misumalpan forms that might help in reaching an understanding of these principles and the parameters implicated in their variable expression in the languages of the world. As indicated, our focus here is narrow—in particular, it is on the grammatical factors involved in the lexical distribution of the well-known transitivity alternation exemplified, for example, by the labile Misumalpan (Ulwa) verb *birhdanaka* (intransitive) and *birhnaka* (transitive) and its similarly labile English equivalents *tear* and *rip*.

2. ARGUMENT STRUCTURE.   Before introducing material from Misumalpan, we outline a general framework for the formulation of argument structure regularities, beginning with a definition of what we mean by the term. Here the examples come primarily from English.

By "argument structure," we mean the syntactic configuration projected by a lexical item. Argument structure is the system of structural relations holding between heads (nuclei) and the arguments linked to them, as part of their entries in the lexicon. While a full lexical entry is clearly more than this, argument structure in the sense intended here is this alone. Departures from this simplifying assumption would have to be strongly motivated.

The following three examples can be used to illustrate the nature of the problems we are concerned with. They represent three distinct and productive classes in the English verbal inventory.

(1) (a) The colt sneezed.
    (b) The sky cleared.
    (c) This factory bottles water.

The verbs of these sentences have readily distinguishable syntactic characteristics, and we assume that their syntactic behavior is correlated in some precise way with their associated argument structure configurations, that is, with the syntactic structures they project.

The properties that must be accounted for are the following at least. The verb *sneeze* in (1a) is "unergative." It is therefore superficially intransitive and moreover lacks a transitive counterpart of the type popularly termed "causative":

(2) *The alfalfa sneezed the colt.

This property is shared by all canonical unergatives, including other evidently denominal verbs—*laugh, cough, smile, pup, cub, foal,* and so on. By contrast, the verb *clear* in (1b) is "unaccusative." It is intransitive and has a transitive counterpart:

(3) The wind cleared the sky.

The same is true of other unaccusatives, quite systematically those that are evidently deadjectival—*narrow, thin, widen, redden,* and so on. Finally, the verb *bottle* in (1c) has the property that it is transitive and has no intransitive counterpart (apart from the middle):

(4) *The water bottled.

This verb belongs to a large class of denominal location and locatum verbs sharing this property—*box, bag, shelve; saddle, harness, clothe* (for these and other denominal verb types, see Clark and Clark 1979).

To account for these observations, we make certain assumptions about argument structure, of which the principal ones are expressed informally in (5):

(5) Argument structure is defined in reference to two possible relations
    between a head and its arguments, namely, the
    head-complement relation and the head-specifier relation.

For a given configuration, a complement is the unique sister of the head—for example, B in (6), where H is the head. And a specifier is the unique sister of the first branching projection of the head—for example, A is the specifier in (6), where H dominating [H B] is the first branching projection of the head H:

(6)

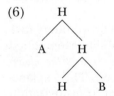

A given head may enter into one or both or neither of these relations. These are its argument structure properties, and its syntactic behavior is determined by these properties, insofar as its syntactic behavior can be attributed to argument structure as defined.

With reference to the verbs of (1), our proposals are as follows, starting with the unergative type exemplified by *sneeze*. First, we assume that this, and other verbs of its type, involves a process of "conflation," involving a bare nominal root and a phonologically empty verb; we assume the process is a morphophonologically motivated concomitant of Merge. The nominal is the complement of the verb. The process of conflation (a restrictive variant Head Movement, adjoining the nominal to the verbal head) fuses the two items into a single word: its effects are visible at Phonological Form (PF) only, not at Logical Form (LF). At conflation, the verb is no longer "empty," as it shares the overt phonological matrix of the noun. This is our theory of denominal verb formation—and correspondingly of deadjectival (e.g., *clear*) and deverbal (e.g., transitive *grow*) verb formation as well, since these too involve the same fusion of a head with that of its complement.

Abstracting away from the conflation process itself, the argument structure of *sneeze* of (1a) is as follows:

(7)

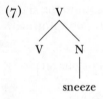

The essential property of the verbal head here is that it projects a structure that contains a complement, its sister, but it projects no specifier. This is characteristic of unergative verbs in general. They project no specifier. Their sentential syntactic subjects are EXTERNAL arguments and, thus, excluded from the argument structure configuration itself.

It is to this essential property that we trace the inability of unergative verbs to enter into the transitivity alternation, an inability exemplified in this case by (2) and by countless other cases, such as *the clown laughed the child, *the medicine slept the patient, and so on. The explanation depends on another assumption, namely, that transitivization involves embedding a verbal projection as the complement of another verb, a free and unavoidable possibility within a system that recognizes the head-complement relation. Transitivization will be successful, or not, depending on the nature of the embedded verbal projection. Consider (8), a result of the Merge process, defining a structure in which (7) appears as the complement of V_1:

(8)

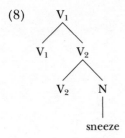

sneeze

Conflation would fuse V_2 and its nominal complement *sneeze*, and this derived verb would then conflate with V_1, giving a putative transitive verb *sneeze*, as in (2). But this is not a successful transitivization: transitive *sneeze* cannot result from this, since there is no position in (8) for a sentential syntactic object, that is, no place for *the colt* in this case. This is the desired result, because transitive *sneeze*, in this use, does not exist.

Many explicitly transitive verbs also share this property. Consider, for example, the verb *give* in (9):

(9) The cow gave birth.

Abstractly, this verb projects the same V+complement structure as does the empty verb of (7):

(10)

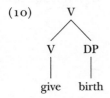

give   birth

It is the result of Merge alone. The verb of (1a), on the other hand, represents the "synthetic" type, so called because it is the result of both Merge and concomitant conflation. The synthetic and analytic forms share the property that the head projects no specifier, and, as a consequence, neither can undergo transitivization in our sense. Thus, just as (2) is ungrammatical, so also is (11) ungrammatical:

(11) *An injection gave the cow birth early.

If this has an interpretation, it is not the simple causative of (9); that is, it is not "an injection brought it about that the cow gave birth early." The insertion of (10) in the complement position of a matrix empty verb leads to the same transitivity failure as that noted for (8) above:

(12)

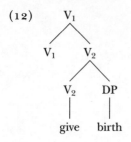

This is an abstract representation of the relations defined by Merge; the surface form would have V_1 and V_2 conflated, of course. Since the subject of V_2, that is, *the cow,* is an external argument, it will not appear as a specifier in the lexical argument structure of that verb, by hypothesis. It will therefore not be possible for it to function as the sentential syntactic object of the derived verb. Whatever the fate of (12), it will not give rise to the putative transitive *give the cow birth.* The DP *the cow* simply cannot appear in the object position of *give.* And this is accounted for under the assumption that the verb that heads the complement—*give*—does not project a specifier, just as the empty verb of (7) does not.

The behavior just noted contrasts with that of the deadjectival verb *clear,* the relevant syntactic behavior of which is illustrated in (1b) and (3). We assume that the intransitive variant of *clear* is identified with the following structure:

(13)

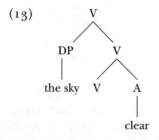

Again, this is an abstraction, indicating only the relations defined by Merge, not the conflation that gives rise to the actual deadjectival verb *clear.* The property we are interested in is this: the head V together with its complement A (*clear*) force the projection of a specifier (*the sky* in (13)). This is a consistent characteristic of deadjectival verbs, which are classic unaccusatives (see Levin and Rappaport Hovav 1995 for these and their opposites, the unergatives), and it is this property that permits transitivization. If (13) appears as the complement of a higher verb, the latter will locally c-command the specifier *the sky.* This specifier is thus in the position required for it to function, without further ado, as the sentential syntactic object of the derived verb, that is, of the verb *clear*, arising through conflation first with V_2 and finally with the higher verb, V_1:

(14)

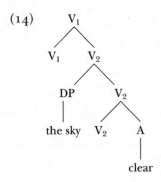

Deadjectival verbs such as *clear, narrow, thin,* and *redden* are synthetic representatives of their argument structure type. Analytical representatives abound, of course:

(15) (a) The cloth turned red.
      (b) The lake froze solid.
      (c) The safe blew open.

These have precisely the same dyadic structure as their synthetic counterparts:

(16)

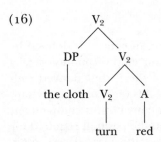

And like their synthetic counterparts, they participate in the transitivity alternation, unavoidably, so to speak, since Merge applies freely and the specifier projected by these verbs presents a DP in the required position, shown in (18), corresponding to (17a), abstracting away from conflation (of V_2 with V_1):

(17) (a) The ocher turned the cloth red.
      (b) The arctic air froze the lake solid.
      (c) The charge blew the safe open.

(18)

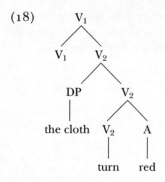

Finally, let us consider the argument structure configuration associated with *bottle* in (1c):

(19)

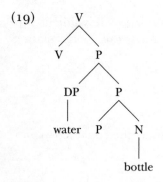

The actual surface form related to this structure, of course, is defined by conflation of the noun *bottle* with its sister, P, an empty (phonologically null) preposition, and subsequent conflation of the P thus derived with the governing V, also empty. The complement of this verb is a P-projection, which, by the very nature of that category, contains both a complement (*bottle*) and a specifier (DP, *water*). The latter is in the position required for it to function as the sentential syntactic object of the derived verb *bottle*, resulting from conflation. Denominal location and locatum verbs—such as *bottle* and *saddle*, respectively—are synthetic. Analytical counterparts include *put (water in bottles)*, *fit (the horse with a saddle)*, and so on.

The necessary transitivity of denominal location and locatum verbs (see (4) above) follows from their argument structure. Unaccusative verbs alternate because both the inner head and the outer head are verbs; the intransitive is simply the inner projection unmerged with another verb. Location and locatum verbs, by contrast, are built on a prepositional projection, by hypothesis. That is to say, the inner head is a preposition, not a verb; in the absence of the outer verbal structure, we are left not with an intransitive verbal projection but with a prepositional phrase.

3. THE MISUMALPAN LANGUAGES. The Misumalpan languages of Nicaragua and Honduras form a small and well-defined family whose name, devised by John A. Mason (1939, 1940), incorporates the initial syllables from the names of three of its members, that is, Miskitu, Sumu, and Matagalpa. The unity of the family was established by the extraordinarily prolific Walter Lehmann (1920), who also assembled in his work most of the Misumalpan linguistic data available in his time. To our knowledge, the first serious comparative work seeking to reconstruct aspects of the putative protolanguage is that of Adolfo Constenla Umaña (late 1980s, n.d.).

Misumalpan predominates among the indigenous languages remaining in present-day Nicaragua, the only other living indigenous Nicaraguan language being Rama, of Chibchan affiliation, with approximately two dozen speakers remaining (Craig 1985). Misumalpan is comparatively widespread in the region, with representatives both in Nicaragua and in Honduras. Nevertheless, it is a small family. The languages still spoken go under the names Miskitu and Sumu, the former having by far the most speakers, with estimates ranging from 70,000 to 90,000, of whom some 17,000 are in Honduras (see CIDCA 1985). Miskitu is clearly the indigenous lingua franca of the Autonomous Atlantic Regions of Nicaragua. Sumu has a much smaller number of speakers, by comparison, though it is still strong in some areas. It is said to have between 6,000 and 8,000 speakers, some 2,000 of whom live in Honduras (see Constenla Umaña n.d.). But these Sumu figures represent the estimate for what we will refer to as Northern Sumu (see Heath 1950). Southern Sumu, or Ulwa, which we take to be a separate though closely related language, is confined today to the town of Karawala, near the mouth of the Rio Grande de Matagalpa. The population of Karawala is approximately 935, and the majority is ethnically Ulwa (Green and Hale 1998). Linguistically, however, the town is effectively Miskitu, although 350 people are still able to speak Ulwa.

The western branch of Misumalpan, called Matagalpan following Daniel Brinton (1895), comprises the extinct Matagalpa and Cacaopera. These are closely and obviously related, and they were recognized as such by Brinton, who was appropriately cautious in his assessment of linguistic relationships. We believe that this entity forms a subfamily with Sumu (in agreement with Lehmann's intuition in this regard), and we refer to that grouping as Sumalpan. And we believe that this entity excludes Miskitu, an isolate within the larger Misumalpan family. Our assumptions concerning the relationships within the family as a whole are embodied in figure 1.1.

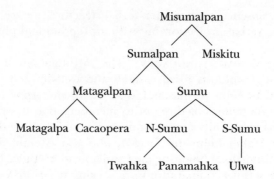

FIGURE 1.1. Misumalpan Family of Languages.

The Northern and Southern branches of Sumu, like the two forms of Matagalpan, are very closely related. However, there are certain systematic morphosyntactic differences between them whose cumulative effect is substantial enough to impede easy mutual intelligibility. A learning period of some months would be required in order for a Northern Sumu speaker to acquire a reasonable command of Southern Sumu. The reverse is true as well, though many Southern Sumu speakers are incidentally also speakers of some variety of Northern Sumu. In addition to the SYSTEMATIC differences between the two branches of Sumu, there are also RANDOM lexical differences. Of a sample of one hundred basic vocabulary items, Northern and Southern Sumu share between 61 and 71 percent, depending on whether judgments of cognation are, respectively, conservative or liberal (Hale and Lacayo 1988; but see Constenla Umaña n.d. for a higher estimate). In any event, we are inclined to say that Ulwa and its northern relatives are different languages, though closely related. By contrast, the division indicated within Northern Sumu is of quite a different nature. Twahka and Panamahka are clearly sister dialects of a single language, a fact that was recognized by the first travelers who took an interest in such matters, not to mention sophisticated investigators like Lehmann (1920) and Edward Conzemius (1929).

Internal relations in the Misumalpan family are reasonably secure, though the precise nature of the genetic relation of Miskitu to Sumu is still a matter of investigation, as it is obscured somewhat by the existence in Miskitu of a large body of (Northern) Sumu loans, many of an intimate nature; and substantial back borrowing from Miskitu into Sumu in the modern period also clouds the picture, though to a lesser extent. Furthermore, the syntactic structures of the present-day Misumalpan languages exhibit the characteristics of grammatical "merger," not uncommon in well-defined "linguistic areas" (see Campbell,

Kaufman, and Smith-Stark 1986) and particularly in regions of extensive bilingualism. This circumstance renders syntax of little use here in the effort to establish a Miskitu-Sumu genetic connection. Nonetheless, once the effects of relatively recent historical processes are identified and set aside, deep-seated aspects of Miskitu morphology can be brought forth in support of the linguistic family posited by Lehmann and his successors.

Although Misumalpan is in geographic proximity to two Chibchan languages, Paya (Pech) to the north and Rama to the south, it is not obviously related to them. Chibchan is, however, the external connection generally accepted for the Misumalpan languages, which are held to belong to a larger linguistic entity termed Macro-Chibchan by Mason (1939) (see also Holt 1975 and Campbell 1979 for discussion and references). If Misumalpan is in fact related genetically to Chibchan, the relation may be too distant to establish. Certainly, it cannot be established on the basis of shared lexicon, in our opinion, and the evidence from morphology is weak as well (see Craig and Hale 1992 for a study of one putative morphological etymology).

For many years the modern Misumalpan languages have been spoken in a situation of intense bilingualism, even multilingualism. While there are monolingual speakers of Misumalpan, to be sure, there are large areas in eastern Nicaragua where no one who speaks a Misumalpan language is monolingual. Of course, it is not surprising to learn that many, perhaps most, speakers of Miskitu, say, also speak either Spanish or English, the two Indo-European languages of the Atlantic Coast. But what is especially relevant here is that many, perhaps most, people who speak Sumu (Northern *or* Southern) also speak Miskitu, another Misumalpan language. As Susan Norwood (1993) has pointed out, a person's position in the eastern Nicaraguan ethnoeconomic hierarchy determines the number of languages he or she speaks: the farther down you are in the hierarchy, the more languages you speak. In general, people learn the languages that are higher in the hierarchy, not those that are lower. Thus, people whose first language is Sumu tend to know more languages than other people do, and their first "second" language is normally Miskitu.

While the observed linguistic capabilities of members of most Sumu communities can be understood in terms of the social and economic circumstances on the Atlantic Coast of today, it is evident to us that Sumu-Miskitu bilingualism itself is a matter of considerable historical depth and complexity. Most important for our purposes here, long-term bilingualism is part and parcel of a linguistic development that has resulted in a degree of structural isomorphism that permits us to say, setting certain details aside, that the three modern Misumalpan languages "share the same grammar."

Consider the following simple sentence (from Hale 1994) in which the three lines are respectively Miskitu, Northern Sumu, and Ulwa:

(20)	Witin	raks	wal	sula	kum	ik-an.
	Witing	arakbus	kau	sana	as	î-na.
	Alas	arakbus	karak	sana	as	î-da.
	he	gun	with	deer	one	kill-PAST

'He killed a deer with the gun.'

The Misumalpan sentences exemplify a number of things immediately, including the general head-final phrase structure of the languages: the verb is final in the clause, the instrumental phrase is P-final, as expected, and the indefinite determiner *kum/as* is final in the DP. The definite determiner is also phrase-final, as illustrated in (21), an example that presents an apparent exception to the general head-final character of Misumalpan phrase structure, that is, in the postnominal placement of attributive adjectival modifiers.

(21)	Sula	tara	ba	ai-kaik-an.
	Sana	nuhni	kidi	yâ-tal-na.
	Sana	sikka	ya	yâ-tal-da.
	deer	big	the	me-see-PAST3

'The big deer saw me.'

It has been shown, however, that this is not exceptional within the head-final grammar of Misumalpan. The N+A structure exemplified in (21) is a reduced relative clause and the adjective is in its expected clause-final position, that is, predicate position (Green 1992, on Miskitu, though the analysis extends to the Sumu languages as well). In fact, this modificational structure is supremely consistent with the general principles of phrase structure in the family, inasmuch as it follows straightforwardly from the structure of the relative clause. The Misumalpan relative clause is "internally headed," like that of Lakhota (Williamson 1987) or Navajo (Platero 1974, 1982). In surface form, the relative is simply a clause functioning as the complement of the definite determiner, as can be seen in (22).

(22)	[[Yang	sula	kum	kaik-ri]	ba]	plap-an.
	[[Yang	sana	as	tal-na-yang]	kidi]	k-îra-na.
	[[Yang	sana	as	tal-ikda]	ya]	îr-ida.
	I	deer	one	see-PAST1	the	run-PAST3

'The deer which I saw ran (away).'

The relative NP argument, 'the deer' in this example, is INTERNAL to the clause. This is the only OVERT representative of the semantic "head." It appears in the position the argument would occupy within the clause under ordinary circumstances, in object position in the case at hand.

Thus, since adjectives function as predicates, their final position in N+A modificational constructions follows from the analysis according to which these are relative clauses.

While these examples serve to illustrate certain shared structures of the family, it is the extent to which the structures MATCH that has held our attention for some time. In the case of the Sumu languages, this is perhaps expected, being a result no doubt of their close relationship. In the case of Miskitu, however, it must be explained in other terms. Although Miskitu and the Sumu languages are probably related, at something like the "family" or "stock" level, the relationship is not a particularly close one. One cannot simply look at lists of vocabulary items to decide the nature of the relationship—far too much borrowing has gone on. Even such normally reliable items as the pronouns are of no use here, as the entire set of Miskitu personal pronouns has almost certainly been borrowed from Sumu. We can even be relatively sure that Northern Sumu, as opposed to Southern Sumu, was the source of the pronouns—and of the bulk of the other Sumu-derived items in modern Miskitu. The situation is further complicated by the fact that modern Miskitu is now the source of hundreds of borrowings into Northern Sumu, including items that were originally Sumu to begin with. When all of the borrowed items are removed from consideration, what remains is a form of Miskitu that is quite different from Sumu. Very little vocabulary remains in common, and the evidence for a genetic relationship between the two is found almost exclusively in shared morphology. The evidence includes the construct state and possessive morphology in the nominal system (found not only in Sumu and Miskitu but in Matagalpan as well) and a number of rather specific details of verbal derivation. The evidence is certainly strong enough to support a genetic relationship, but, we repeat, it is not a close relationship.

In view of the foregoing, we feel compelled to attribute much of the structural isomorphism within contemporary Misumalpan, as represented by Miskitu and Sumu, to contact and intensive bilingualism over a long period. To attribute all of it to common ancestry would severely strain credulity, in our judgment.

The parallels revealed by the examples we have seen so far are primarily in the realm of phrase structure: phrases are consistently head-final in the family as a whole. And all of the languages employ the internally headed relative clause, though all have an externally headed alternative as well. The examples also exemplify the fact that all members of the family have subject agreement expressed morphologically in association with the clause-final inflectional apparatus that also marks tense; and all three languages have object agreement realized prefixally on the verb.

Modern Misumalpan structural isomorphism extends to two grammatical subsystems that have assumed particularly important roles in the languages, to an extent that encourages us to say that they are now "hallmarks" of the family. They are not unheard of elsewhere, of course, but their presence within Misumalpan is especially prominent and pervasive. One of these grammatical features has been mentioned in passing: it is the so-called construct state (Heath 1927; listed systematically in Marx and Heath 1961). This is the form a noun assumes under specific grammatical conditions, one of which is illustrated in the following Misumalpan nominal construction:

(23) naha   waitni-ka
     âdika   al-ni
     âka   al-ka
     this   man-CNSTR

In general, when a noun is preceded by another element within a larger nominal construction that it heads, the noun appears in the construct—as here, where the noun is preceded by a demonstrative. The construct is also used in the possessive construction, in the right-headed relative clause construction, and autonomously (i.e., without prenominal accompaniment) where the nominal is referentially dependent on prior discourse. The grammatical principles governing the use of the construct are identical in the three languages.

The second prominent feature in Misumalpan is the extensive use of clause-sequencing constructions involving the system of subject obviation commonly known by the term "switch-reference" (Jacobsen 1967; Finer 1985a, 1985b). Misumalpan is not alone in the Americas in its use of switch-reference morphology, of course, but switch-reference is nevertheless a notable and extraordinarily important feature of the family, being used there in simple clause chaining (cf. Longacre 1985; Craig and Hale 1992), in one kind of complementation (cf. Kang 1987; Hale 1991a), in the serial verb construction (cf. Hale 1991a, 1992; Salamanca 1988), and in the causative (cf. Avilés, Hale, and Salamanca 1988; Hale 1989; Li 1991). Although there are morphological differences among the Misumalpan languages, the grammar and use of switch-reference are the same in all. The following sentences illustrate clause chaining.

(24) Waitna   ba   plap-i   kauhw-an.
     Al   kidi   k-îr-i   buk-na.
     Al   ya   îr-i   wauhd-ida.
     man   the   run-PROX   fall-PAST3
     'The man ran and fell.'

(25) Yang   waitna ba   kaik-ri   kauhw-an.
     Yang   al   kidi   tal-ing   buk-na.
     Yang   al   ya   tal-ing   wauhd-ida.
     I   man   the   see-OBV1   fall-PAST3
     'I saw the man and he fell.'

The head-final character of Misumalpan is reflected here not only in the verb-final order internal to the individual clauses but also in the relative ordering of the dependent and matrix inflectional morphologies and, consequently, of the clauses themselves. The latter are related structurally in approximately the manner in which a conditional is related to a main clause, with the inflection of the second commanding that of the first (as in the corresponding structure in West Greenlandic Inuit: Bittner 1994). The inflections glossed PROX(imate) and OBV(iative) are morphological portmanteaus representing TENSE and OBVIATION. They are dependent in that both of the grammatical categories they realize are interpreted (partly or wholly, depending on the particular form) in relation to the inflection of the matrix verb. The tense of the dependent verb is bound to that of the matrix. And the obviation (or switch-reference) category, which determines in part the referential possibilities of the subject, is likewise interpreted in relation to the matrix clause. The subject of the PROX clause is necessarily coreferential with the subject of the matrix, while the subject of the OBV clause is necessarily distinct from that of the matrix.

These observations are expected and quite ordinary for a switch-reference system, given the typological position and general typological consistency of Misumalpan. But the use of the switch-reference construction in expressing the causative gives rise to a circumstance that is far from ordinary. An example of the causative is given in (26), whose surface form is essentially identical to that of (25), a typical obviative clause-chaining construction. The arrangement of clauses expresses an ICONIC feature, commonly observed in clause-sequencing constructions cross-linguistically, according to which the cause precedes the effect. But this fact, together with the typologically expected ordering of the dependent clause before the matrix clause, results in a causative construction strikingly different from the causative as it is known elsewhere. In complete reversal of the usual situation, the Misumalpan languages have the cause predicate morphologically and syntactically SUBORDINATE to the effect predicate:

(26)	Yang	waitna	ba	yab-ri	kauhw-an.
	Yang	al	kidi	yamt-ing	buk-na.
	Yang	al	ya	ât-ing	wauhd-ida.
	I	man	the	cause-OBV1	fall-PAST3
	'I made the man fall.'				

It is as if one said, in Misumalpan, "When I did (something to) the man, he fell." And if this were all there was to the matter, there would be nothing much to say about it: it would simply be the case that Misumalpan does not really USE the canonical causative construction to express these ideas. But that is NOT all there is to it. For certain syntactic parameters (e.g., control and the imperative), it is possible to show that in (26), but not in (25), the subject of the FIRST clause is the subject of the construction as a whole, as expected in a CONVENTIONAL causative construction. So far, this remains a true contradiction, and its proper documentation, and analysis, is of some interest theoretically.

Turning now to argument structure and the lexicon, we will be referring to two Misumalpan dictionaries (actually, these are dictionaries in the making and thus unpublished). One of these is the Ulwa dictionary, now in its third version, cited as CODIUL/UYUTMUBAL (1998) in the references, after the Spanish and Ulwa acronyms for the Ulwa Language Committee, whose members compiled the first two versions of the dictionary under the direction of Ken Hale and the much-expanded current version under the direction of Thomas Green. This represents the Sumu branch of the family.[1] The second is the CIDCA Miskitu Dictionary (CIDCA 1998) being compiled by Jorge Matamoros and Danilo Salamanca.[2]

4. THE MISUMALPAN TRANSITIVITY ALTERNATIONS: ULWA (SOUTHERN SUMU).   Another pervasive feature of the Misumalpan languages is the existence of transitivity alternations marked by corresponding alternations in verbal morphology. Most verb themes in Ulwa—all but a handful, in fact—consist of a root and a thematic suffix. This suffix varies with transitivity, for verbs that participate in the standard "causative/inchoative alternation."[3] Essentially the same is true of Miskitu, as we will see, although that language possesses a very large number of verbs lacking any overt theme marker.

---

1. We choose Southern Sumu (Ulwa) for this discussion primarily because we have enough information on it to illustrate the lexical principles of interest to us. We do not have that information for Northern Sumu (Mayangna), at least not in an appropriately organized format. We know, however, that Mayangna has essentially the same system as Ulwa (although the *ta*-theme marker has spread to all *pa*-themes and to some Ø-themes as well; see below).

2. An early version of the Ulwa dictionary is on the Internet at http://members.tripod.com/~ulwa/index.html, and the current version of the Miskitu dictionary is at http://members.tripod.com/~ulwa/miskdict.html.

3. The term "causative" is used here merely to follow tradition. The alternation of interest here is a mere transitivity alternation and does not imply anything like the productive syntactic causative construction found in many languages. The derived transitives at issue here are constrained in the manner suggested earlier, that is, as in (14) and the like, in which, by hypothesis, the lexically headed complement projects a specifier locally commanded by the matrix, transitivizing, verb. By contrast, the sentential syntactic causative, like that involving the English verbs *have, cause, force* or *make*, for example, is not restricted in this way. Thus it permits a complement containing an external subject; while **laugh the child* is impossible in English, *make the child laugh* is, of course, perfect. The Misumalpan transitivity alternation is of the restricted type, the causative construction being utterly different (see Hale 1989, 1991a, 1992a).

The sentences of (27) through (29) illustrate a common Ulwa transitivity alternation, in which the intransitive alternant is marked by the thematic suffix -*da* (glossed -DA) and the transitive alternant by -*pa* (glossed -PA).

(27) ULWA:
  (a) Kuring   abuk-d-ida.
      canoe   capsize-DA-PAST3
      'The canoe turned over.'

  (b) Kuring   abuk-pa-h.
      canoe   capsize-PA-IMPER2
      'Turn the canoe over!'

(28) ULWA:
  (a) Kuring   batirh-da-rang (yataihdaram laih).
      canoe   tip-DA-FUT3
      'The canoe will tip (if you lean sideways).'

  (b) Turum   ya   waya   batirh-p-am (was ya utuhdangh).
      drum   the   little tip-PA-OBV2
      'Tip the drum a little (and let the water pour out).'

(29) ULWA:
  (a) Wâlang   bas-ka   sang-da-i.
      savanna   foliage-CNSTR   green-DA-PRES3
      'The foliage of the savanna is greening up.'

  (b) Kahlu   âka sang-p-uting.
      shirt   this green-PA-IMMEDFUT1
      'I am going to make (dye) this shirt green (or blue).'

As mentioned, Ulwa verbs are typically bipartite in the sense illustrated by these examples. So, for example, the verb *sang-da-* 'become green' (also 'become blue, alive') consists of a root element *sang-* and the intransitive verb formative, or thematic suffix, -*da-*. It is the latter, we must assume, that functions as the head of the lexical projection in which it appears. It is the "true verb," so to speak, like the nonovert verbal head postulated for the English deadjectival verb *clear* in (13) above. It is not surprising—and not an accident presumably—that the root elements in some of the alternating *da*-themes of Ulwa also enter into the formation of adjectives in the language. The derivation of adjectives involves the use of the construct-state morphology, though with syntactic consequences very different from those seen in the syntax of nominals. The root is morphologically nominal, but it functions as a stative predicator in the derived form to which we have applied the term "adjective." The verbs of (27) through (29) are based on roots that participate in this adjectival use, as shown in (30), where -*ka* is the construct morphology.

(30) ULWA:

(a) abuk-ka   'overturned, capsized, face down'
(b) batirh-ka   'leaning, tipped'
(c) sang-ka   'green, blue; alive'

We say it is not surprising that roots of this type are involved in the formation of Ulwa alternating verbs, because this type quite generally and cross-linguistically has the lexical property that it must appear in a structural configuration that permits it to satisfy its "attributive" or "predicative" character, that is, the fundamental and defining characteristic of adjectives. This requirement is satisfied in the argument structure configuration assumed for the intransitive verbs of (2) through (29):[4]

(31)

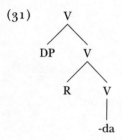

We take the head of the projection to be -da, claiming this to be the verbal nucleus. The root element, R, corresponding here to *abuk-, batirh-, sang-,* is perhaps of indeterminant or neutral category. But it has a lexical property of consequence: it has the lexical property that it must be in an appropriate structural position in relation to a nominal, to satisfy its attributive character. In (31) this requirement is satisfied by the projection of a DP in specifier position, as shown. We claim that the root element in these structures "forces" the head V (i.e., -da) to project a specifier. And it is this property that accounts for the transitivity alternation. The root elements force the appearance of a specifier. Verbs, in and of themselves, do not project a specifier—verbs canonically take external, not internal, subjects.

It is the lexical projection of a specifier, of course, that accounts for the transitivity alternation, the intransitive alternant being that whose structure is depicted in (31). Like other syntactic "constructions," the transitive arises as the result of Merge, according to which any syntactic

---

4. The linear order shown here is arbitrary, head-final being chosen here solely in conformity with the general head-final character of the Misumalpan languages. At this level, it has no linguistic significance.

object—for example, (31)—can appear as the complement of another head, say, a verb, as V_1 in (32).

(32)

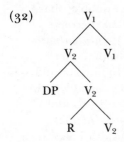

As in the parallel English case (e.g., *clear*), so also in the case of these alternating verbs of Ulwa, this formation is successful as a transitive precisely because of DP, the specifier of V_2. This is appropriately situated in relation to V_1, its governor and potential case assigner in sentential syntax. Moreover, this view of the matter correctly expresses the fact that the subject of the intransitive corresponds to the object of the transitive. In both cases, the argument functioning in these roles is the DP in the specifier position projected by V_2.

The structures (31) and (32) are abstractions, representing just the syntactic relations involved, not the morphology. Conflation applies to these structures, of course, resulting in the observed affixation of verbal nuclei to root elements. In (31) the verbal head is realized as the suffix *-da*. In (32), however, the conflation process is more complex. In accordance with the strict sisterhood principle of conflation, the root R conflates first with V_2, the resulting complex conflates with V_1, and the verbal heads are realized as the single suffix *-pa*.

The following is a sample listing of Ulwa *da*-theme verbs alternating with *pa*-theme transitives. The verbs are given in the infinitive (as in the dictionary), with the intransitive theme marker in square brackets [ ]; the corresponding transitive infinitive is obtained by deleting *-da;* the transitive theme marker *-pa* drops out in the infinitive, thus intransitive *abukdanaka*, transitive *abuknaka*, listed here as *abuk[da]naka*.

(33) ULWA ALTERNATING *DA*-THEME VERBS, WITH CORRESPONDING
    PA-THEME TRANSITIVES:
    abuk[da]naka (capsize, turn face down); *alh[da]naka* (develop a
    hole; perforate); *asah[da]naka* (spread legs; hold astraddle);
    asal[da]naka (be embarrassed; embarrass, shame); *baras[da]naka*
    (blacken, darken); *batirh[da]naka* (tip, lean); *birh[da]naka* (tear,
    rip, shred); *birik[da]naka* (cover self; cover); *dara[da]naka*

(spread—of plant growing; spread out evenly—e.g., rice for drying); *didiu[da]naka* (stretch, extend); *dim[da]naka* (extend to full length); *dut[da]naka* (come out; extract, pull out—as tooth, uproot—as plant); *isik[da]naka* (shudder, shake, wobble; shake, make shudder); *kara[da]naka* (melt); *king[da]naka* (become clogged; plug up); *kubit[da]naka* (bend at joint); *kuru[da]naka* (become unstitched; unstitch); *luhus[da]naka* (froth, lather, become foamy; lather, make foam); *rî[da]naka* (unfurl, unfold—as sail); *sang[da]naka* (become green; make green); *sayak[da]naka* (dislocate—as knee, joint); *suih[da]naka* (break off—as limb); *tah[da]naka* (drip, dribble—as water, medicine); *tak[da]naka* (peel—as skin, paint); *tarak[da]naka* (tangle—as fish line, vines); *tulu[da]naka* (revolve, turn; make turn, revolve); *turu[da]naka* (flake off—as skin, shell, husk); *uluh[da]naka* (come loose, come untied; untie, let loose); *utuh[da]naka* (spill—liquid); *warin[da]naka* (bend crooked); *wiri[da]naka* (swivel, turn around, twist); *wirih[da]naka* (mix—as medicines); *wiring[da]naka* (inflate, bloat— as stomach); *yaih[da]naka* (approach, come near; bring near, place near); *yûh[da]naka* (become long, tall—as person; lengthen, heighten—building); *yurah[da]naka* (open—of mouth).

Given that all the verbs of (33) participate in the transitivity alternation, we assume that they have the relevant properties attributed to the verbs of (27) through (29). Accordingly, their intransitive alternant is of the form shown in (31), and their transitive alternant takes the form shown in (32). The key to this is the circumstance that, in each case, the root element (R) has the lexical property of forcing the verbal head to project a specifier, internal to the lexical projection, which functions ultimately as sentential syntactic subject (of the intransitive) or object (of the transitive). While this is a fundamental characteristic of adjectives, given their attributive and predicative functions, the root elements in the verbs of (33) are not always attested independently in an adjectival use. Many are (*sangka* 'green, blue, alive'; *yûhka* 'long, tall'; *baraska* 'black'; *asalka* 'embarrassed'; etc.), but many are not. We do not know at this point in which cases the missing use is principled and in which cases it is simply a gap in the record. In fact, this illustrates one of the reasons why the sort of theoretical speculation we are engaging in here is appropriate even at this relatively adolescent stage of dictionary making. In this instance, our theoretical speculations tell us that we must, at some point, determine for every verb the full range of lexical projections in which the root (R) may appear. For example, we must know whether the root element in all of the verbs of (33) appears independently in the adjectival form and partakes of the corresponding adjectival syntax. If not, why not? This sort of question crops up constantly when a particular theoretical perspective is consistently applied, even if that perspective proves ultimately to be in error in some respects—as most theories do, that being the engine which drives the field forward. The dictionary must, it seems to us, be a resource that, to the extent possible, purports to answer questions of this nature. We return to this topic at a later point.

The verbs of (33) share the semantics traditionally referred to as "change of state," and this is consistent with the fact that they are alternating verbs. Given the generality of the grammatical and lexical principles involved here, it is not surprising, therefore, that many of these Ulwa verbs translate into English as verbs that are alternating verbs in that language as well (e.g., *lengthen, blacken, tip, break, tear, capsize, extend, clog, bend, peel*). In both languages, the root elements share the property of forcing the verb to project a specifier, the sine qua non of the simple "causative/inchoative" transitivity alternation at issue here. And we expect the principles observed in Ulwa to be replicated to a degree in the other Misumalpan languages.

The *da*-theme alternating verbs of Ulwa are not always paired with *pa*-theme transitives. Some are paired with members of the large *ta*-theme class instead, as in the sentences of (34), illustrating uses of intransitive *nû-da-* and corresponding transitive *nû-ta-* 'hide.'

(34)   ULWA:

(a) Yang   bikiska   balna   kaupak   nû-da-ring.
      I   children   PL   from   hide-DA-FUT1
    'I will hide (myself) from the children.'

(b) Yang   lih-ki-wan   man   kaupak   nû-ta-ring.[5]
      I   money-CNSTR1   you   from   hide-TA-FUT1
    'I will hide my money from you.'

While *ta*-theme verbs, both transitive and intransitive, are extraordinarily abundant in Ulwa (and in Northern Sumu as well, where *-ta* has supplanted *-pa* altogether), the favored transitive counterpart of Ulwa intransitive *da*-theme verbs is evidently the *pa*-theme, themes in *-ta* being relatively less frequent in this usage. Some of the latter are listed in (35). Here, again, the verbs are given in the infinitive with *-da* in brackets (like *-pa*, the *-ta* thematic element deletes in the infinitive, hence *nûdanaka* 'to hide (intr.)', *nûnaka* 'to hide (tr.)', jointly *nû[da]naka*).

(35)   ULWA ALTERNATING *DA*-THEME VERBS, WITH CORRESPONDING *TA*-
         THEME TRANSITIVES:
    dak[da]naka (snap, break; cut, chop off—as rope, limb);

---

5. Construct morphology (e.g., possessive *-ki* 1, *-ma* 2, and *-ka* 3, and *-ka* plain CNSTR) is suffixed not to the word but to the first metric foot—hence *lih-ki-wan* 'my money', not **lihwan-ki*.

mî[da]naka (stay, dwell; stop, detain); *muh[da]naka* (wake up);
nû[da]naka (hide; secrete, conceal, and, in a related sense, steal,
purloin); *pat[da]naka* (pop, burst; puncture—as blister);
pil[da]naka (chip—as plate); *pui[da]naka* (cool—as food);
pusing[da]naka (swell—as lip, hand); *tap[da]naka* (fall down;
lower—as trousers); *tulup[da]naka* (peel off whole or in large
pieces—as skin); *yam[da]naka* (become—as rich, a better person,
a doctor, etc.; make, create).

In relation to their essential grammatical properties, these verbs belong
to the same category as the verbs of (33). They project the same configu-
rational structures—namely, (31) for the intransitive, (32) for the transitive. A question we will not attempt to answer at this point is whether the
choice of *-pa* or *-ta* in the transitive is something significant and regular, as
opposed to an "archaic residue" and a mere matter of "spelling" in the synchronic grammar of Ulwa. This is another among many matters that remain
to be dealt with properly. In any event, we assume for present purposes that
the verbs of (35) are not fundamentally different from those of (33).

Not all Ulwa labile verbs have intransitive themes based on *-da*. Another
prominent intransitive verbal nucleus, defining a significant number of
Ulwa intransitive themes, is *-wa* (glossed -WA). This element is of some
historical interest for Misumalpan, given that it has an apparent cognate
in Miskitu, as we will see in due course. It is exemplified in (36) by the
verb *ala-wa-* 'grow', paired with the transitive *ta*-theme *ala-ta-* 'grow, raise.'

(36)   ULWA:

    (a) Baka-ki   itukwâna   ala-w-ida.
        child-CNSTR1   large   grow-WA-PAST3
        'My child has grown large.'

    (b) Alas   baka-ka   yam-ka   ala-t-ang.
        she   child-CNSTR3   good-CNSTR   grow-TA-REMPAST3
        'She raised her child well.'

Other verbs of this category are the following (listed in the infinitive, in
the now-familiar manner):

(37) ULWA ALTERNATING *WA*-THEME VERBS, WITH CORRESPONDING *TA*-
    THEME TRANSITIVES:
    ala[wa]naka (grow; raise—as child, plant); *â[wa]naka* (enter, go
    in: insert, put in); *bah[wa]naka* (break); *dâ[wa]naka* (burn);
    dis[wa]naka (go out; extinguish, put out—as fire); *il[wa]naka* (go
    up, ascend; raise, hoist); *î[wa]naka* (die; kill); *kah[wa]naka* (smear
    self, anoint self; smear, anoint, paint); *lah[wa]naka* (boil, cook);
    lak[wa]naka (lower, descend, go down; lower, let down, put down);
    lâ[wa]naka (pass, go across; move, transfer); *mah[wa]naka* (become

sated, full; fill—as food fills stomach); *pura[wa]naka* (get wet; wet); *râ[wa]naka* (be in the sun to dry; put in the sun, spread in the sun—as seeds to dry); *sah[wa]naka* (split—as wood); *sing[wa]naka* (heal, get well; heal, cure).

A small number of *wa*-theme verbs are paired with *pa*-theme transitives; these are generally verbs of putting and stance.

(38) ULWA ALTERNATING *WA*-THEME VERBS, WITH CORRESPONDING *PA*-THEME TRANSITIVES:
balah[wa]naka (put on self, don—as hat; put on—as hat); *kut[wa]naka* (lie down; lay down); *lau[wa]naka* (sit down; seat, put in sitting position); *muk[wa]naka* (lie down; lay down); *sak[wa]naka* (stand up; put in standing position); *sih[wa]naka* (move, change location; send).

Ulwa alternating verbs in -*wa* evidently project the same lexical syntactic structure as those in -*da*. The unifying feature of both types of verbal themes considered here is presumably to be found in the lexical character of the root (R). In both cases, the lexical requirement that the root element be appropriately positioned in relation to a nominal constituent (a "subject" of which it can be predicated) forces the head verb (V) to project a specifier, permitting transitivization, as in (32).

Part of the theoretical interest in labile, or alternating, verbs is in the CONTRAST between these and another large class of verbs, namely the non-alternating verbs. As we have seen, many Ulwa intransitives in -*da* have transitive partners. But many do not. The verb *ai-da-* 'cry' does not alternate, for example.

(39) Ai-da-yang (sûkilu îwida bahangh).
cry-DA-PRES1
'I am crying (because my dog died).'

This nonalternating behavior is not random among Ulwa *da*-theme verbs. The following verbs, we suspect, are correctly classified as nonalternating—that is to say, their lack of a transitive partner is almost certainly not a gap in the record but a true linguistic fact.

(40) ULWA NONALTERNATING *DA*-THEME INTRANSITIVE VERBS:
ahdanaka (moan); *aidanaka* (cry); *amatdanaka* (grieve); *âmhdanaka* (yawn); *âudanaka* (belch); *baladanaka* (rumble, make vibrating sound); *bârhdanaka* (snore); *bilamhdanaka* (blink eyes); *bisakdanaka* (make smacking sound); *bîsdanaka* (make a click or kissing sound); *buihdanaka* (twitch, have muscle spasm); *isamhdanaka* (sneeze); *isdanaka* (play); *nanadanaka* (tremble); *pisitdanaka* (do somersaults); *pitukdanaka* (kick, flail); *rikdanaka* (crawl—as of

baby); *sutdanaka* (jump); *tikahdanaka* (pontificate); *tisdanaka* (spark, sparkle, crackle—as fire); *tumhdanaka* (swim); *uhdanaka* (cough); *umitdanaka* (dive); *urukdanaka/urupdanaka* (breathe); *wamhdanaka* (travel); *wapdanaka* (growl); *wâtdanaka* (walk); *yaradanaka* (stagger, totter, reel); *yuputdanaka* (twitch, stir).

These are basically verbs of sound production, bodily movements, bodily responses, and manner of motion. They belong semantically to the category now generally referred to by the term "unergative," a fact that is immediately evident, for example, by comparing these meanings with David Perlmutter's (1978) excellent semantic classification, predating the term now current for verbs of this type. Like these Ulwa verbs, their English translations also fail to alternate as a rule, permitting only the intransitive use in sentential syntax. Thus, for example:

(41)   ULWA:
  (a) *Baka   ya   ai-t-ikda.
      child   the   cry-TA-PAST1
      *I cried the child.
      (Cf. 'I made the child cry.')

  (b) *Aitak   ya   yâ   âmh-t-ida.
      book   the   me   yawn-TA-PAST3
      *The book yawned me.
      (Cf. 'The book made me yawn.')

  (c) *Sumaltingka   ya   bikiska   balna   is-ta-i.
      teacher   the   children   PL   play-TA-PRES3
      *The teacher is playing the children.
      (Cf. 'The teacher has the children playing.')

The intended ideas here are perfectly easy to express in Ulwa, using the productive causative construction (e.g., *baka ya âting aidida* 'I made the child cry'), but they are not expressed using simple transitivization involving the structure depicted in (32). The same is true in English.

What is the reason for this? Given the striking meaning correlation between English and Ulwa, it is tempting to lay the entire business at the feet of semantics. And at some deep, as yet largely inaccessible, level of linguistic form this is quite probably where the matter resides. But at the level at which we are now able to operate, semantics is too unreliable, partly because we simply cannot say what the meanings of words are. Good reason for being cautious here comes from cross-linguistic considerations, ironically the very area that inspires optimism much of the time. In Hopi, the verbs that translate many of the unergatives of English and Ulwa do indeed participate in the very transitivity alternation we have been examining here (Jeanne and Hale 1998). Given our limitations, we cannot simply say that the Hopi roots involved are semantically different from their English and Ulwa counterparts, any more than we can say that they are the same.

We are stuck then with what is observable, namely, the syntactic behavior—some verbs alternate, others do not. And we have an elementary framework within which this difference can be expressed in a manner that is straightforwardly consistent with general syntactic principles relating to such matters as the argument structure of predicators, (abstract) case assignment, grammatical and thematic relations, and agreement.

Assuming that we are correct in assigning the structures (31) and (32) to Ulwa alternating verbs, we can express the phenomenon of nonalternation in a simple and straightforward manner. The root elements (R) of nonalternating (i.e., unergative) verbs have the lexical property that they do not force the verbal head to project a specifier. Thus, the argument structures of the verbs of (40) have fundamentally the following form:

(42)

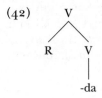

Affixation of -*da* to R is effected by conflation, as usual, respecting phonological requirements of the language. Transitivization is impossible, of course, since the unergative structure lacks a specifier (and potential sentential syntactic object)—that being the defining characteristic of unergatives. The subject of an unergative, like that of a transitive (e.g., (32)), is an external argument, in keeping with the general default principle according to which a verb does not project a specifier unless its complement, by virtue of its lexical properties, forces it to do so.

We have given a partial account of the alternating and nonalternating verbs of Ulwa. We have not yet looked at the phenomenon of nonalternation from the standpoint of verbs in -*ta* and -*pa* (both transitive and intransitive nonalternating verbs are found with these thematic elements), nor have we studied members of the small but rather important class of Ø-theme verbs (*talnaka* 'see', *dahnaka* 'hear', *watnaka* 'seize', *wânaka* 'come', *yawanaka* 'go', *kasnaka* 'eat', *dînaka* 'drink', *kawaranaka* 'laugh', *wasaranaka* 'bathe', *îranaka* 'run', *înaka* 'get', *atnaka* 'be', *amanaka* 'sleep', *duihnaka* 'carry', *kuihnaka* 'achieve'), all nonalternating.[6] We set these

---

6. Tom Green (pers.com.) suggests that the nonalternating verbs in -*ra* represent a class defined by an archaic thematic element. His evidence for this comes from the prosody of Ulwa verb roots, according to which each constitutes an iamb. If -*ra* were a part of the root in these cases, these verbs would be exceptions to this prevailing pattern.

matters aside for another occasion and turn now to a consideration of Miskitu transitivity alternations.

5. THE MISUMALPAN TRANSITIVITY ALTERNATIONS: MISKITU.   If there is indeed a Misumalpan family that includes Miskitu, then the evidence for it is probably to be found in the domain under investigation here. For it is in this domain that deep-seated and systematic commonalities are found, in a form sufficiently altered in appearance to suggest an antiquity far exceeding that of the overwhelming and beguiling more recent sharings resulting from intensive contact and bilingualism.

Although it is difficult to establish regular phonological correspondences at the level we suspect truly represents the common roots of Miskitu and the Sumu languages, we cannot help but be impressed by the fact that Miskitu transitivity alternations (with certain explicable exceptions noted in Salamanca 1998) are consistently marked by the element -*w* in the intransitive member of the alternation, recalling Sumu intransitive themes in -*wa*, illustrated by (36), (37), and (38) for Ulwa. Miskitu lacks anything corresponding to the Sumu intransitive -*da*. Instead, -*w* (glossed -W) is the standard Miskitu intransitive formative in all alternating verbs, as exemplified in (43).

(43)   MISKITU:

    (a) Windar   glas-ka   ba   bai-w-an.
          window   glass-CNSTR the   break-W-PAST3
          'The window glass broke.'

    (b) Lapta   ba   glas   bai-k-isa.
          heat   the   glass   break-K-PRES3
          'Heat breaks glass.'

These verbs represent the class of transitivity alternations in which the transitive member is marked by the thematic element -*k* (glossed -K). This is evidently felt by bilingual speakers to be the Miskitu equivalent of Sumu -*ta* (see Ulwa (35) and (37) above), hence such relatively recent comparisons as Sumu *sumal-ta-* 'teach' and Miskitu *smal-k-* and Sumu *pih-ta-* 'whiten' and Miskitu *pih-k-*. Other verbs participating in this alternation are listed in (44) in the infinitive and in the intransitive only. Thus *bai-waia* abbreviates intransitive *baiwaia* and transitive *baikaia*.[7]

---

7. Two phonological remarks should be made here: (i) when thematic -k- is added to a k-final root, degemination occurs, thus **blakkaia > blakaia;* and in certain roots ending in a peripheral nasal N (whose exact nature is not known, though it is probably /m/), the following takes place in interaction with the thematic elements: N+w > mm > m, N+k > ngk, as in *amaia, angkaia* 'burn', *dimaia, dingkaia* 'enter, insert'; but compare *sruhmaia, srumhkaia* 'bounce' (see Salamanca 1998); -w deletes after root-final /p/, as in intransitive *swapaia,* beside transitive *swapkaia.*

(44) MISKITU INTRANSITIVE *W*-THEMES, WITH TRANSITIVE *K*-THEMES:
amaia (burn); *âwaia* (float; set afloat); *banghwaia* (fill—as with
water); *blakwaia* (tangle, coil, roll up—as of thread, rope); *bulwaia*
(twist); *buswaia* (get wet; wet); *bûwaia* (raise up, stand up); *daiwaia*
(come out—as hair; pull out—as nail); *daswaia* (go out—as of
fire; extinguish—as fire); *dimaia* (enter; insert); *dîwaia* (get erased;
erase—as blackboard); *ilingwaia* (open—as book, sack, umbrella);
îwaia (sit down, get lower; set, lower—as baby from bed);
kakahwaia (get stuck; hook, snag); *kâwaia* (get toasted, lightly
burned—as face in sun; toast, roast—as coffee beans); *klakwaia*
(get cut; cut—as flesh); *klaswaia* (coagulate, thicken, solidify—as
liquid); *kriwaia* (break—as stick); *kwâwaia* (open—as door, earth
in quake); *laiwaia* (spill, pour—of liquid); *lapaswaia* (get
squashed; squash); *langhwaia* (come undone, unstitched; loosen,
unstitch); *lâwaia* (dry); *lûwaia* (cross to other side; take across);
nuhwaia (get fat; fatten); *palhwaia* (extend—as of wing); *pâwaia*
(grow; raise—as child); *pihwaia* (whiten, bleach—as clothes, hair);
prâwaia (close—as door, eyes, road); *pyawaia* (cook, boil); *raswaia*
(slither—as snake; drag on ground); *râwaia* (heal, wake up; heal,
cure, waken); *ratwaia* (cook until soft); *sirang îwaia* (become
frightened; frighten); *slilwaia* (melt); *sruhmaia* (bounce—as ball);
swapaia (soften, get tired; soften, tire); *tahwaia* (drip—as water,
medicine); *tîwaia* (get lost; lose); *tuhwaia* (burn, scorch); *ubulwaia*
(get stirred up, agitated—as water; stir up, agitate); *yamalwaia*
(release gas, air; fan, ventilate); *yukuwaia* (hide).

It is quite clear that the alternating verbs listed here represent the
same resultative and change of state semantic categories as the corresponding alternating verbs of Ulwa, and, accordingly, the same structures are assumed for them. Abstracting away from conflation, the structures are (45) for the intransitive, (46) for the transitive—the transitive
structure being defined by the operation Merge applied to (45) and V
(V$_1$ in (46)):

(45)

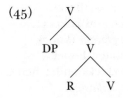

(46)

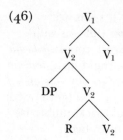

In the phonological representation of (45), R conflates with V and the latter is realized as the suffix -*w*. In (46) R conflates V_2 creating a verb form that is subsequently conflated with V_1; the two verbal elements are realized as the single suffix -*k*. This accounts descriptively for the morphophonological distribution of these elements in alternating verbs: the intransitive member is marked by -*w*, the transitive by -*k*.

While the intransitive partner of alternating verb pairs is consistently marked by -*w*, the transitive is not necessarily marked by -*k*; many alternating transitives are marked by -*b*, a thematic element we presume to be cognate with Ulwa -*pa* and, thus, part of the small body of relatively strong evidence supporting the generally accepted view that a Misumalpan family including Miskitu is real. The following sentences illustrate the -*w*/-*b* transitivity alternation.

(47)   MISKITU:

(a) Dûs   ba   pâsa   wal   yah-w-isa.
    tree   the   wind   with   shake-W-PRES3
    'The tree is shaking in the wind.'

(b) Pâsa   ba   dûs   târa   nani-ra   yah-b-isa.
    wind   the   tree   big   PL-ACC   shake-B-PRES3
    'The wind is shaking the big trees.'

Other verbs conforming to this pattern are listed in (48), in the infinitive, as before, and listing the intransitive alone, so that *yahwaia* abbreviates the pair intransitive *yahwaia*, transitive *yahbaia*.

(48) MISKITU INTRANSITIVE *W*-THEMES, WITH TRANSITIVE *B*-THEMES:
    dakwaia (break—as rope, string); *drâwaia* (stretch—as rubber); *drîwaia* (lean, incline, tilt—as tree in wind); *dringhwaia* (knock down, topple—as tower); *druwaia* (extend—as water, honey, thread); *dungwaia* (gather together, huddle—as chicks under hen's wings); *ilihwaia* (swarm, scatter—as ants, seeds); *kalhwaia* (dislodge—as riverbank, bone); *karhwaia* (move, rock—as waves rock boat); *kitwaia* (move, shift—as table, chair); *krukwaia* (become

disjointed; loosen); *klikwaia* (click); *krunghwaia* (splash, slosh—as water); *lakatwaia* (fold over, double over); *lahwaia* (lower—as price, bucket into well); *lalalwaia* (slip, slide); *lingwaia* (resound; make resound); *liswaia* (split—as wood); *plinghwaia* (peel, flake, skin—as skin, husk, bark); *wilwaia* (turn—as propeller); *yahwaia* (shake—as tree in wind); *yakawaia* (scatter; toss out—as garbage).

Given their participation in the simple transitivity alternation, we assume that these verbs project the same structures as do the alternating *w*-themes of (44). Within the conception of argument structure with which we are working, the structures projected are (45) for the intransitive member, (46) for the transitives. Miskitu clearly corresponds closely to Ulwa.

As in the case of Ulwa *da*-themes, so also for Miskitu *w*-themes, there are many that do not alternate, having only an intransitive use in sentential syntax. Some of these are listed in (49).

(49) MISKITU NONALTERNATING *W*-THEME INTRANSITIVE VERBS:
atakwaia, atwaia (limp—as lame person, horse); *atangwaia* (duck down); *birhwaia* (swing, hang—as monkey); *blahwaia* (quarrel—as heirs over land); *bubukwaia* (break out—as skin in sores); *byunghwaia* (emit sparks—as fire, short circuit); *dikwaia* (beat, pulsate—as heart); *irwaia* (dodge—as to avoid blow); *itikwaia* (crawl—as baby); *kilwaia* (fork, turn off—as road); *kratwaia* (snore); *lakwaia* (shine—as stars, newly shined shoes); *mutwaia* (squeeze in, squeeze through—as person in crowded space); *nawaia* (twist, warp—as wood with heat); *piswaia* (bubble—as water poured); *pitwaia* (pulsate—as arteries, heart); *puswaia* (wade, walk in water); *riswaia* (bristle—as when hair stands on end); *rutwaia* (breathe noisily—as child with cold); *sarhwaia* (trot, jog—as horse, person); *srutwaia* (jump—as person, animal).[8]

Since our focus here is on the aspects of argument structure that determine syntactic behavior, the behavior of these Miskitu verbs leads us to believe that they belong together in that they share the structural property that their verbal nucleus (i.e., -*w*) does not project a specifier. Presumably, therefore, their root components are of a type that does not require the projection of a specifier. Like their Ulwa counterparts in (40), these Miskitu verbs have the following simple structure:

(50)

8. Given that thematic -*w* is normally lost after root-final bilabials, the following are probably to be included here: *plapaia* (run); *wapaia* (walk); *yapaia* (sleep).

It follows, then, that hypothetical transitives of the type exemplified in (51) are not possible (shown with -*k*, but -*b* would also be impossible).

(51)   MISKITU:

(a) *Syahka   ba   ai   krat-k-isa.
     catarrh   the   me   snore-K-PRES3
     *The cold snores me.
     (Cf. 'The catarrh makes me snore.')

(b) *Aras-ki   sarh-k-amna.
     horse-CNSTR1   trot-K-FUT1
     'I will trot my horse.'

The semantic categories represented in (49) include manner of motion, bodily movements and responses, and emissions (sparks, light). These are meanings associated with canonical unergative verbs. However, although they are consonant with our semantic expectations, semantics cannot be relied on at this point to predict the behavior. The latter is itself more reliable. Thus, for example, at least two Miskitu verbs of sound production or sound emission (i.e., *klikwaia* 'click'; *lingwaia* 'resound') are alternating verbs (with *b*-theme transitives), though their English and Ulwa counterparts are nonalternating. Similarly, while Miskitu *sarhwaia* 'trot' cannot transitivize in the manner shown, its English translation (and those of other manner of motion verbs as well) do have transitive partners—with special semantics, to be sure (thus, **I jumped my horse when I slammed the door*, as compared to *I broke the mirror when I slammed the door*), and, in all probability, with a syntactic structure distinct from that of the alternating verbs we have been considering.

Unlike the Sumu languages, Miskitu has many nonalternating verbs (some intransitive, some transitive) that lack any overt thematic marker. Some representative examples are given in (52) and (53).

(52) MISKITU INTRANSITIVE Ø-THEME VERBS:
     aisaia (speak); *apaia* (lack, fall short—as food); *âpaia* (lay eggs); *balaia* (come); *kaia* (be); *inaia* (cry); *ipaia* (blink—of eye); *kikaia* (laugh); *klipaia* (blink—as in sunlight); *kwasaia* (crawl—as baby); *lamaia* (die down—as wind); *lipaia* (shine, flash—as lightning); *pâlaia* (fly); *plapaia* (run); *plupaia* (flutter—as flame, flag); *plimaia* (zigzag); *pristaia* (do somersaults in play); *snipaia* (break, fracture—as bone); *srimaia* (become numb—of extremities); *sripaia* (go down—of swelling; deflate—as tire); *takaia* (exit); *tamaia* (butcher, cut up—as carcass); *ulaia* (climb, ascend; see transitive below); *umaia* (swarm—of insects); *upaia* (doze); *waia* (go); *wapaia* (walk); *yapaia* (sleep).

(53) MISKITU TRANSITIVE Ø-THEME VERBS:
bapaia (put on—as hat; found—as organization; raise, hoist—as flag); *bikaia* (bury—as corpse, money); *briaia* (have, get); *diaia* (drink); *kapaia* (grope for—as under water; thresh—as rice); *klamaia* (squeeze—as to extract juice); *(s)mamaia* (weave—as hammock); *mâyunaia* (praise); *munaia* (do, cause); *pamaia* (hang); *piaia* (eat); *sâbaia* (stab, spear, shoot); *sâkaia* (get, extract, find); *samaia* (bite); *sapaia* (palpate—as doctor does to patient); *sipaia* (sew, caulk); *sunaia* (put in higher place—as load on horse; hoist—as flag); *swiaia* (leave, discontinue); *taibaia* (press, oppress, exploit); *tumaia* (envy—as another's possessions); *ulaia* (ride—as horse); *wâlaia* (hear); *wiaia* (say); *winaia* (call); *wipaia* (whip); *yâbaia, yaia* (give); *yuwaia* (distribute, share—as gifts).

While Ø-theme verbs are more numerous in Miskitu than in Ulwa, their number is not particularly great. The number might even be smaller than is evident on the surface, inasmuch as some *k*-final, *p*-final, *m*-final, and *w*-final roots may derive from themes in -*k*, -*b*, or -*w* (see Salamanca 1998); the implied phonological reductions are known to occur independently—labial assimilation and degemination; and final /k/ or /w/ could actually be the thematic element itself in some cases. Setting aside verbs that might be dismissed on these grounds, there remains a small set of what appear to be true Ø-theme verbs, including vowel final themes (*bri-, di-, pi-, swi-, wi-, aisa-, wa-*) and apical final themes (*bal-, in-, kwas-, mâyun-, mun-, pâl-, prist-, sun-, ul-*). It is possible, therefore, that the number of true Ø-theme verbs is more in line with the smaller total found in the Sumu languages. In any event, the observed Ø-theme verbs are nonalternating, and the intransitive members of the reduced set include *aisa-* 'speak', *in-* 'cry', *kwas-* 'crawl', *pâl-* 'fly', *prist-* 'do somersaults in play', items that correspond semantically to unergatives in many languages. We do not address here the question of whether the element referred to informally here as "zero" (Ø) is a genuine thematic element (i.e., a verbal nucleus V) or whether, alternatively, the overt verb itself is the verbal nucleus in the argument structures projected by these verbs. This latter is a very likely story for the vowel final verbs, which would then be verbs taking phrasal (i.e., XP) rather than bound root (R) complements.

6. FURTHER CONSIDERATIONS.   As mentioned earlier, a motive for this inquiry has been the questions it forces on the lexicographer and the gaps and imperfections it reveals in a dictionary in the making. Although the focus of this investigation is narrow in the extreme, it nonetheless indicates the necessity for extensive review of the preliminary entries we have at this point. An obvious question, of course, is whether verbs for which

no transitivity alternation is recorded are in fact nonalternating. This can be done systematically with relative dispatch. More demanding, however, is the establishment of argument structure properties beyond formal transitivity. For example, if a verb refers to the removal of a part from a whole (e.g., 'to skin, peel'), what is the direct object—the part, the whole, or either? This kind of information is not systematically recorded in the Misumalpan dictionaries so far. And in the case of formal intransitives, what is the nature of the phrases that appear to function as their complements—are they complements, adverbial adjuncts? And what is the grammatical function of the nominal components of phrasal verbs such as Miskitu *bîl-a kaik-aia* (road-CNSTR see-INF) 'to wait for x' (lit. 'watch x's road') and its identically glossed Ulwa co-calque *tâ-ka tal-naka?* And what is the grammatical function of the "genitive" argument corresponding to x in these phrasal verbs? These are issues partly for the grammar and partly for the dictionary, but, in any event, they must be acknowledged in the latter. They go beyond the matter of transitivity narrowly defined and well beyond the restricted domain of the transitivity alternation that has been the main focus here.

An interesting question that we will not be able to deal with adequately in this chapter is that of the semantic character of the thematic elements that are such a prominent feature of Misumalpan verbs. Ulwa and Miskitu intransitives of alternating verbs are fairly consistently associated with change of state or position, suggesting that this semantic feature is to be attributed to the presence of the thematic markers *-da, -wa* (Ulwa) and *-w* (Miskitu).

A more interesting and challenging problem is that presented by the thematic elements appearing in the transitive members of alternating pairs, that is, *-pa* and *-ta* of Ulwa and *-b* and *-k* of Miskitu. Is there a semantic basis for the selection of one or the other of these elements? A study of this matter has been initiated (Salamanca 1998), focusing primarily on the semantics of Miskitu *-b*, including not only *b*-theme verbs with intransitive partners but also nonalternating transitive and intransitive verbs having this thematic element. Although the study is in its initial phases, certain statistical tendencies have been observed, for instance, the frequent occurrence of *-b* in Miskitu verbs of sound production, as in *ihbaia* 'neigh', *akbaia* 'bark', *kakbaia* 'cackle', *lingbaia* 'ring (as bell)', *kinghbaia* 'knock (on door)', *ahbaia* 'moan, wail', *wasbaia* 'whistle'. Not surprisingly, these verbs are sometimes (but not always) translated by *pa*-themes in Ulwa, *ih-pa-* 'neigh', *auh-pa-* 'bark', *wiu-pa-* 'whistle'. The possibility that there may be a greater than chance correlation between theme type and meaning and the fact that the correlation extends across languages to some extent are, of course, suggestive. But to determine whether there is more to this than a slight statistical bias, possibly the product of changes from an earlier system that was more reliably rule governed, is a question whose answer will require an investigation that goes beyond the restricted scope of the present study. It will also require dictionaries that are more nearly perfect than the ones we have available now.

As a final remark, we return to the matter of labile, or alternating, verbs. These present us with at least two questions, one empirical, the other theoretical. Both have to do with nonalternating verbs, in fact. We have only looked at two types of these, leaving others for a later study, but the point can be made quite well with what we have. The empirical question—more accurately, the data question—is simply this: are the recorded nonalternating verbs truly nonalternating? Or have we simply failed to find one of the members in some alternating verb pairs? To answer this question, we have to check each apparent case—a relatively simple matter for a native speaker. A verb either alternates or it does not.[9] We will need to check apparent nonalternating verbs systematically until the time comes when we are so completely sure of the principles that govern Misumalpan verbal diathesis that it is no longer necessary to ask of a given verb whether it alternates or not. Our suspicion is that that time will never come, though it may very nearly come, as anyone can attest who has managed to get a feel for a language and for a grammatical phenomenon such as this.

In our earlier remarks about this issue (e.g., in relation to the ill-formed sentences of (41)), we noted merely that our conception of argument structure accounts in a natural way for the observed behavior of alternating and nonalternating verbs. Alternating verbs have the property that their verbal nuclei project a specifier, as in (45), a small clause configuration, repeated here as (54).

(54)

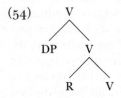

By contrast, nonalternating intransitives have the property that their verbal nuclei do not project a specifier.

---

9. We oversimplify, of course, but for the most part, speakers have clear and strong intuitions about this. Thus, for example, while some English speakers may be unclear about a verb like *disappear*, no one, so far as we know, is unclear about *appear, arrive,* or *arise.* Nor is anyone in doubt about unergatives like *cough, sneeze, cry,* or *laugh,* even though their conventional translations into some languages are in fact alternating verbs.

(55)

As noted in previous sections, if (55) is embedded in the complement relation to another verb, no interpretable verbal construction emerges; in particular, no transitive verb emerges, there being no specifier present in the inner verbal projection and hence no sentential syntactic object. On the other hand, if (54) is embedded as the complement of a verb, the construction that emerges is one of the major transitive types, that is, that in which the sentential syntactic object governs, and assigns case to, the specifier (and subject) of a small clause.

This is hypothesis, and it may or may not turn out to be right. But it is necessary in order to frame the real question, which is this. How does the first-language learner of Miskitu or Ulwa acquire a grammar in which some verbs are classified as nonalternating? Or, to rephrase the question in terms of the hypothesis itself: how does the child figure out which verbs contain roots that force the verbal nucleus to project a specifier and which verbs do not.[10]

The answer to this question is trivial in some languages, where unergative verbs are explicitly built on nominal roots—for example, Basque, with unergatives conforming to the pattern *barre egin* (laugh do) 'to laugh'; and Tanoan, with similarly constructed unergatives (but with incorporation of the nominal), as in *híínl-'e* (laugh-V) 'to laugh'; and even English is arguably transparent in this regard, with its denominal unergatives like *laugh*. Once we determine that these verbs have nominal roots, we can suggest an explanation for their inability to transitivize in the standard manner: being nominal, and hence substantive as opposed to predicative, the roots of unergatives do not (and presumably cannot) force the projection of a specifier. In this respect unergatives contrast with labile deadjectival verbs—*clear, redden,* for example—in which the root component is predicative in character and necessarily forces the verbal nucleus to project a specifier. The ability of deadjectival verbs to alternate follows straightforwardly, by hypothesis.

This is quite reasonable where the makeup of verbs is categorically perspicuous. In Misumalpan, however, the situation seems to us to be anything but perspicuous. Some alternating *da*-theme verbs in Ulwa might be built

---

10. We will not consider here the "easy answer," namely, that according to which the default is nonalternating, the alternating verbs being learned as they appear in the data available to the learner. This would deny that any interesting principles are at work, principles strongly suggested by the cross-linguistic correlations observed in this matter.

on adjectives, as we have seen, and this is of course compatible with our expectations, based on English and other languages that have deadjectival verbs of clear composition. But the status of roots in Ulwa is by no means clear; adjectives are themselves nominal in morphological category, and there is little that would lead us unerringly and unswervingly to any conclusion other than that "roots are simply roots." While it may be encouraging that some Ulwa alternating verbs are deadjectival, on the whole the morphological makeup of a verb does not tell us what its syntactic behavior is going to be.

The Misumalpan case is very interesting for this very reason. It presents the standard classification of verbs—unergatives and unaccusatives, the latter being the intransitive variants of verbs participating in the familiar causative/inchoative alternation. The verb classes are not in doubt, and the syntactic behavior is completely ordinary. But where does the evidence for the classification come from? How does the child learn the system? The answer surely involves semantics, the meanings of the verbs. But we are back at the beginning. Our reasoning is properly circular, because the meanings are themselves partly a result of the structure we hope to establish. Moreover, as linguists our understanding of verbal meanings is too primitive to lead us straight to the principles. We are stuck with observable syntactic behavior and lists, neither of which we can predict fully as yet. But the kids get it right somehow, so something must be working for them. We will have to do our best to ensure that the dictionary contain the information (the behavior and the lists) that will enable us ultimately to understand the principles behind it all.

CHAPTER TWO

Morphology in Cherokee Lexicography
The Cherokee-English Dictionary

William Pulte and Durbin Feeling

1. INTRODUCTION. The morphology of Cherokee is extremely rich and complex. In this chapter we discuss some of the decisions that we made about the treatment of morphology in the *Cherokee-English Dictionary* (Feeling and Pulte 1975). We hope that our discussion will be helpful to compilers of dictionaries for other languages who must decide how much morphological information to include in the dictionary entries.

We would like to preface our discussion with a brief history of the events that led to the development of the dictionary, in recognition of those members of the Cherokee Nation who made the dictionary project possible.[1] We also provide an outline of the process employed in constructing entries for Cherokee verbs.

The *Cherokee-English Dictionary* was made possible primarily by the efforts of the late Anna Gritts Kilpatrick. Anna Kilpatrick was proficient in Cherokee and a highly skilled translator from Cherokee to English. She and her husband, Jack Kilpatrick, conducted extensive research on Cherokee folklore and on other aspects of Cherokee culture. The Kilpatricks coauthored a number of books and articles (e.g., Kilpatrick and Kilpatrick 1965, 1966a, 1966b).[2]

During her years of research, Anna Kilpatrick had come to realize that the Cherokee language was receding and that measures had to be taken if it were to retain its vitality. One of these measures, in her view, was the development of a Cherokee dictionary. She envisioned the dictionary as an aid in language learning for Cherokees who did not speak

---

1. The Cherokee Nation was formerly known as the Cherokee Nation of Oklahoma.
2. The Kilpatricks' work has been continued by their son Alan (see Kilpatrick 1997).

their ancestral language and for non-Cherokees who might want to study Cherokee. She believed that the availability of a dictionary would increase pride in their language among Cherokee speakers, especially young people whom she hoped would continue to speak their native language.

Kilpatrick took every opportunity to discuss the need for a dictionary with W. W. Keeler, Chief of the Cherokee Nation during the 1960s and early 1970s. A number of meetings over a period of years eventually led to success. The Tribal Council, on the Chief's recommendation, allocated funds for a dictionary project, the first language project ever funded by the Cherokee Nation.

Wesley Proctor was employed in 1971 to begin work on the dictionary, and William Pulte's services were provided on a part-time basis by the Cherokee Bilingual Education Program, a federally funded project. The director, Herbert Bacon, had also been convinced of the need for a Cherokee dictionary by Anna Kilpatrick and obtained permission from the U.S. Office of Education for his staff to assist in its development.[3] The resulting partnership between the Cherokee Nation and the Cherokee Bilingual Education Program was a major factor in the project's success.

Unfortunately, Wesley Proctor became ill and was unable to continue his work. He was succeeded by Durbin Feeling in summer 1972.[4]

2. DICTIONARY DEVELOPMENT.   The initial stage in the development of the dictionary was to obtain audiotape recordings of speakers from various areas of the Cherokee Nation. The recordings provided samples of natural Cherokee speech from a number of communities and served as the major source of vocabulary for the dictionary; they also provided important information about dialect variation. The audiotapes were transcribed, and each word was entered on a 4 × 6 file card. Other sources of vocabulary included the Cherokee translation of the New Testament, other written materials, and Feeling's knowledge of Cherokee semantic domains.

Words were entered on the cards in the practical orthography adapted for use in the dictionary. As entries were developed, the file cards were

3. A major goal of the Cherokee Bilingual Education Program was to develop materials in Cherokee for elementary school students. The completion of a Cherokee dictionary was viewed as an important tool to be employed in achieving this goal.

4. Wesley Proctor was a former Cherokee language radio broadcaster who took great pride in speaking the language. When Proctor realized that he would not be able to continue his work because of ill health, he strongly recommended Durbin Feeling as his successor, and Feeling was subsequently employed. We wish to take this opportunity to recognize the late Wesley Proctor for his love for the Cherokee language and for his efforts on behalf of the dictionary project.

reviewed at least seven times before manuscript preparation began. Steps included representing pitch, marking vowel length, entering subentries for verbs and plurals for nouns and adjectives, providing Cherokee syllabary equivalents for all forms entered in the practical orthography,[5] writing an illustrative sentence for each entry, and providing cross-references to related entries.

Pamela Munro (pers. com.) has pointed out that the *Cherokee-English Dictionary* was perhaps the last dictionary of its scope to be developed for an American Indian language without the use of a computer. In the early 1970s, the computer facilities of the Cherokee Nation were used exclusively for administrative tasks, and computers were not in use by the Cherokee Bilingual Education Program.

As the work progressed, a problem was encountered. The amount of information entered on the file cards gradually filled the available space. The remaining space had to be allocated carefully, in a standard format, to avoid problems later during the typing of the manuscript.

What would have been different if modern computer processing had been employed? Obviously, the typing of the manuscript would have been easier and faster, and corrections would have been immensely simpler. Most important, the space limitations imposed by the use of file cards would not have been a factor. Without the use of a computer, the lack of space eventually made it difficult to add more information, tending to preclude expansion of entries.

3. ISSUES IN ENTRY CHOICE AND FORM IN THE DICTIONARY. Three aspects of the entries are likely to be noticed by someone looking at the dictionary for the first time. These are the use of superscript numbers to represent the complex surface pitch contours of Cherokee words, the representation of Cherokee forms in both a practical orthography and in the Cherokee syllabary, and the large number of subentries included for each verb.

Perhaps the most striking feature of the entries is the superscript pitch notation. We chose superscript numbers to represent pitch after we had the opportunity to examine some of Floyd Lounsbury's field notes on Cherokee, which were made available to us by Bill Cook, a student of Lounsbury who was working with speakers of Cherokee in North Carolina during the early 1970s.

Lounsbury had transcribed pitch phonetically using the superscript numbers 1–4. Before we saw his system, we had marked pitch as low, mid, or high. We realized that the three-pitch system was inadequate, however,

---

5. A table showing the complete Cherokee syllabary is provided at the end of this chapter.

and after working with Lounsbury's four-pitch system for a short time concluded that it represented Cherokee pitch perfectly. At that point we began to use Lounsbury's system and continued to employ it throughout the project.[6]

Another unusual feature of the entries is the use of two distinct orthographies to represent all Cherokee entries and subentries. Each Cherokee word appears both in a practical orthography and in the Cherokee syllabary.

The inclusion of the syllabary, the traditional Cherokee writing system developed by Sequoyah in the early nineteenth century, was intended for dictionary users literate in the syllabary. It was also intended as an aid to students learning the syllabic system.

The choice of the particular practical orthography used in the dictionary was dictated by two considerations. The Carnegie Cross-Cultural Education Project had carried out a literacy project for speakers of Cherokee during the 1960s, using a practical orthography developed by Willard Walker (see Walker 1969 for further discussion). We adapted Walker's orthography by adding Lounsbury's pitch notation and by using underdots to mark short vowels, instead of marking long vowels.

The Carnegie project had disseminated literacy materials widely throughout the Cherokee Nation, and we felt that introducing another practical orthography would have been confusing to Cherokee speakers accustomed to the Carnegie system. In addition, the Carnegie orthography seemed near-optimal for speakers of Cherokee who were literate in English but not in Cherokee.

Another striking aspect of the dictionary entries is the inclusion of five subentries for each verb. Many American Indian languages have a complex verb morphology, and Cherokee has a morphological system perhaps as complex as that of any language of North America. We decided to include enough information about morphology in the dictionary and its accompanying "Outline of Cherokee Grammar" (Pulte and Feeling 1975) to enable users to construct entire verb paradigms. This decision required the inclusion of a number of subentries for each verb.[7]

The third-person singular form was used as the main entry for each verb. We chose this form because it is the natural citation form for verbs

---

6. We are responsible, of course, for any inconsistencies in applying Lounsbury's superscript notation. In the dictionary, 4 represents the highest pitch, and 1 represents a fall in pitch from 2, which is the lowest-level pitch.

7. The minimal Cherokee verb consists of an obligatory personal pronoun prefix, a verb stem, and a tense/aspect suffix. Several prefixes may precede the pronoun prefix, and several suffixes may precede and/or follow the tense/aspect suffix, resulting in verb forms that are long and semantically complex. These elements of the verb complex are all bound: they never occur alone.

in Cherokee, that is, the form by which Cherokee speakers refer to a verb in the abstract. Corresponding to an English speaker's use of uninflected verb forms, Cherokee speakers say the equivalent of "he/she speaks," "he/she goes," and so on, in naming verbs in situations analogous to those in which an English speaker might say "speak" or "go."

An alternative, listing verbs alphabetically by their stems, would have made use of the dictionary extremely difficult for persons without training in linguistics. As Doris A. Bartholomew and Louise C. Schoenhals(1983:32) note, "Linguists sometimes find it convenient to catalogue lexical items according to the underlying form of the stem, which serves as a base for predicting all the forms of the paradigm. Even though an abstract stem is useful for such purposes, dictionaries designed for more general use normally list full words as citation forms for lexical items."

A workable solution is available to dictionary makers who wish to serve both groups of users. Without changing the organization of the dictionary proper, an alphabetical list of verb stems can be included as an appendix and cross-referenced to the main entries listed by their citation forms. This arrangement should serve the needs of linguists who would like to have a catalog of abstract stems, without lessening the utility of the dictionary for native speakers and language learners.

After determining the form to be used in main entries, we had to decide how many additional forms to include as subentries. As we attempted to answer this question, it was obvious that a great deal of additional information was needed to enable a dictionary user to predict a complete paradigm for any Cherokee verb. To provide this information, we included five subentries in each verb entry. The forms were selected because they could not be predicted from the main entry or because they were needed to predict other forms.[8]

Consider the dictionary entry for $a^1 di^2 ta^3 sg$ 'to drink', shown in (1) below (Feeling and Pulte 1975: 11).[9]

(1) a^{1}di^{2}tạ^{3}sga **DꞭWꭲS** v.t. he's drinking it
     gạ^{2}di^{1}tạ^{3}sga **SꞭWꭲS**
     u^{1}di^{2}tạ^{2}hv^{23}ʔi **ꝌꞭWꭹT**

---

8. For some verbs, it may be possible to predict one or more of the subentries from the main entry and from the other subentries. The rules required would be difficult to apply, however, for users without a background in linguistics. Omission of some subentries for some verbs, because they are predictable, also would have led to confusing inconsistencies in the format for verb entries. For practical purposes, we considered "unpredictable" to mean anything that cannot be predicted in a straightforward fashion.

9. Here, we represent Cherokee forms in the practical orthography of the dictionary. Word-final pitch is not marked because it is a predictable fall from pitch 4.

a¹di²tạ²sgo³ʔi **DJWⱺAT**
hạ²di²³ta **ⱵJW**
u²di²tạ²sdi **ᏫJWⱵWJ**
Kemili tsgwisdi ama *anaditasgoʔi*. **ⱵHⱢ Ᏼ-Ꮩ⍥ᏂJDᏘ**
DⱺJWⱺAT. Camels *drink* a lot of water. cf. aditasdi

The first subentry is the first-person singular form, which cannot be predicted from the third-person singular main entry, as shown in (2–3). The first- and third-person singular forms together enable the dictionary user to construct the entire verb paradigm by consulting the sample paradigms included by Pulte and Feeling (1975).

(2) (a) a¹hnị²gị³ʔa   he/she is leaving
     (b) ga¹nị²gị³ʔa   I am leaving

(3) (a) a¹hu²dị³ʔa   he/she is putting a long object in liquid
     (b) jị²ʔu²dị³ʔa   I am leaving

In examples (2–3), the third-person singular prefix is *a*- in both instances, but the first-person singular is *g*- in (2b) and *jị*- in (3b); the present tense suffix is -*a*. These examples show that first-person singular forms cannot be predicted from third-person singular forms.

The second subentry is the third-person singular remote past tense form, shown in (4b–5b).

(4) (a) a¹gị³ʔa   he/she is eating it
     (b) u¹gv²³ʔi   he/she ate it

(5) (a) a¹gị³ʔa   he/she is picking it up
     (b) u¹gị³sv²³ʔi   he/she picked it up

The pronoun prefix for the past tense forms in (4b–5b) is *u*-; note that the stems cannot be predicted from the main entry forms in (4a–5a).

The third subentry is the third-person singular habitual, shown in (6b–7b).

(6) (a) gạ²we³hlị²ha   he/she is joking
     (b) gạ²we³hli²sgo³ʔi   he/she habitually jokes

(7) (a) gạ²hlv³ʔị²ha   he/she is tying him/it up
     (b) gạ²hlv³ʔị²ho²ʔi   he/she habitually ties him/it up

The habitual suffix in (6b–7b) is -*oʔi*. Once again, the differences in the stems in (6b–7b) cannot be predicted from the main entries in (6a–7a).

The fourth subentry is the second-person singular imperative form, shown in (8b–9b).

(8) (a) ga̧^{2}ne^{3}ʔa   he/she is getting it (flexible object)
    (b) hi̧^{2}na̧^{2}gi   get it (flexible object)

(9) (a) ga̧^{2}lv^{3}sga   he/she is putting it (flexible object) in a container
    (b) hi̧^{1}y^{2}ʔv^{1}ga   put it (flexible object) in a container

The imperative prefix is *h-* in (8b–9b). The imperative stems in (8b–9b) cannot be derived from the main entries, and the imperative suffix is *-i* in (8b) but *-a* in (9b).

The fifth and last subentry is the infinitive form. Compare the main entry forms in (10a–11a) with the infinitives in (10b–11b).

(10) (a) ga̧^{2}wo^{3}ni̧^{2}ha   he/she is speaking
     (b) u^{2}wo^{1}ni^{23}hi̧^{3}sdi   for him/her to speak

(11) (a) ga̧^{2}we^{3}hli̧^{2}ha   he/she is joking
     (b) u^{2}we^{1}h^{1}vh^{3}di   for him/her to joke

The third-person singular prefix used with infinitive forms is *u-*. Infinitive stems vary greatly and must be listed separately for each verb.

The subentries, as the examples show, enable the dictionary user to determine the correct form for the first-person singular present, third-person singular remote past, third-person singular habitual, singular imperative, and infinitive. As we noted previously, these forms help the dictionary user to generate an entire verb paradigm by consulting the sample verb conjugations in the grammar sketch.

4. IMPROVEMENTS, IN RETROSPECT.   As we review our work almost twenty-five years after the completion of the dictionary, we would, of course, do some things differently. For example, we would provide an English gloss for all subentries. We did not do this initially because of the complexity of adding five additional English glosses to each verb entry, given the constraints imposed by manual processing of the manuscript. Providing English translations for the subentries should not present a problem in a possible future edition of the dictionary, however, given the current advanced state of the art in desktop publishing.

A future edition of the dictionary should also be expanded by including additional entries, particularly entries for nouns derived from verbs. Computer processing of the data can make expansion of the dictionary a relatively simple task. For example, the agentive suffix *-i* derives nouns from verbs, as in (12).

(12) (a) ga̧^{2}wo^{3}ni^{2}sgo^{3}ʔi   he/she is speaking
     (b) ga̧^{2}wo^{1}ni^{4}sgi   speaker

The agentive is formed by replacing the habitual suffix -*o* (shown in the third subentry for each verb) with the agentive suffix -*i*. This is a productive process, and agentive forms for all verbs in the dictionary can be generated by computer and checked by the dictionary compiler for possible inclusion as new main entries.

The Cherokee instrumental suffix also derives nouns from verbs, as in (13).

(13) (a) ga^{2}wo^{3}ni^{2}ha   he/she is speaking
      (b) u^{2}wo^{1}ni^{23}hi^{3}sdi   for him/her to speak
      (c) ga^{2}wo^{1}ni^{23}hi^{2}sdoh^{2}di   instrument to speak with

Instrumental forms such as (13c) have the third-person singular prefix, as in (13a), the infinitive stem, and the instrumental suffix -*dohdi*, as in (13b). A list of all instrumental forms can also be generated by computer, checked for exceptions, and considered for possible inclusion as main entries.

There are additional processes for deriving nouns from verbs, for deriving nouns from adjectives and from other nouns, and for deriving other parts of speech. All of these derivational processes can yield a number of additional main entries as we have just described for agentive and instrumental nouns.

5. MORPHOLOGY IN DICTIONARIES.   We have been focusing on the treatment of Cherokee verb morphology in the *Cherokee-English Dictionary*. Because Cherokee has an extremely complex morphology, we saw that a considerable amount of information about each verb has to be provided by subentries in order to generate all forms of a verb paradigm. To make this possible, a great deal of information about morphology was also included in "Outline of Cherokee Grammar" (Pulte and Feeling 1975).

Many other indigenous languages of North America have similarly complex morphologies. Compilers of dictionaries for these languages in the future will want to ask the same questions that we asked in deciding what kind of information to include in each entry, particularly entries for verbs.

For many languages, both subentries and an accompanying grammar will be required to make it possible for users to determine all the forms of a particular paradigm. This goal should have high priority because of the importance of morphology in the grammatical systems of these languages. The additional time and effort required to accomplish this goal is not as great as it might seem in this age of computer compilation of dictionaries. In making decisions about how much information to present, dictionary makers should consider a disturbing fact.

Tragically, the Native languages of North America seem to be disappearing at a rapidly accelerating rate. Twenty-five years from now, it is likely that many of the languages currently spoken will have no remaining speakers, and some estimate that no Native American language will be spoken by the end of the twenty-first century.

Because of these bleak prospects, the development of additional dictionaries takes on a real sense of urgency. In some instances, if dictionary development projects do not begin soon, the opportunity will be lost. In other cases, as the number of speakers becomes smaller, it may still be possible to construct a dictionary but with significant loss of information, including data on dialect variation and specialized vocabulary.

Dictionaries for individual languages should therefore be developed as soon as possible, and the compilers should realize that their work may well be the last major effort to document the language. This fact has implications for decisions regarding the content of the dictionaries.

Compilers of future dictionaries will inevitably have to decide what to include in entries. This will likely include the kind of information about morphology that we have focused on here. Whatever information is considered for inclusion, a basic principle suggests itself, given the rapid loss of languages. The principle is, simply, if in doubt, include.

Any information that is not already available elsewhere and is not included is likely to be lost forever. Decisions about what to include, or what not to include, thus take on great importance. We hope that our discussion will encourage future dictionary makers to include subentries in their dictionaries and sample paradigms in accompanying grammar sketches to enable users to generate complete verb paradigms. In doing so, they will document and preserve for posterity what is perhaps the most unique aspect of American Indian languages: the fascinating complexity of their morphological patterns.

APPENDIX: The Cherokee Syllabary

	-Ø	-a	-ah	-e	-i	-o	-u	-v
Ø-		Ꭰ		Ꭱ	Ꭲ	Ꭳ	Ꭴ	Ꭵ
d-		Ꮣ		Ꮥ	Ꮧ	Ꮩ	Ꮪ	Ꮫ
t-		Ꮤ		Ꮦ	Ꮨ			
dl-		Ꮬ		Ꮮ	Ꮯ	Ꮰ	Ꮱ	Ꮲ
tl-		Ꮭ						
g-		Ꭶ		Ꭸ	Ꭹ	Ꭺ	Ꭻ	Ꭼ
k-		Ꭷ						
gw-, kw-		Ꮖ		Ꮗ	Ꮘ	Ꮙ	Ꮚ	Ꮛ
h-		Ꭽ		Ꭾ	Ꭿ	Ꮀ	Ꮁ	Ꮂ
j-, ch-		Ꮳ		Ꮴ	Ꮵ	Ꮶ	Ꮷ	Ꮸ
l-		Ꮃ		Ꮄ	Ꮅ	Ꮆ	Ꮇ	Ꮈ
m-		Ꮉ		Ꮊ	Ꮋ	Ꮌ	Ꮍ	
n-		Ꮎ	Ꮐ	Ꮑ	Ꮒ	Ꮓ	Ꮔ	Ꮕ
hn-		Ꮏ						
s-	Ꮝ	Ꮜ		Ꮞ	Ꮟ	Ꮠ	Ꮡ	Ꮢ
w-, hw-		Ꮹ		Ꮺ	Ꮻ	Ꮼ	Ꮽ	Ꮾ
y-, hy-		Ꮿ		Ᏸ	Ᏹ	Ᏺ	Ᏻ	Ᏼ

CHAPTER THREE

Lexical Functions as a Heuristic for Huichol

Joseph E. Grimes

1. DICTIONARIES ARE NOT WORD LISTS. The idea of comparing languages seems to have influenced much of the work done on dictionaries in the Americas. One gets the impression that for von Humbolt, Nimuendajú, Rivet, and others the first priority in learning something about a language was to get a word list so as to classify the previously unrecorded languages they came across, then, if possible, some texts and grammatical notes. A word list with glosses and part of speech information filled in and some examples looks much like a dictionary even though it is not one. My own early work is similar (McIntosh and Grimes 1954).[1]

One problem, which I come back to later, is that word lists are built around glosses, not definitions. As a result, word lists collected for comparative purposes are filtered data. The investigator creates a word list based on thinking in his or her language, not the language being studied. Word list entries are not things that a linguist interested in how meaning is expressed would take to be conclusions that were arrived at by study of the inner logic of meaning in that language. Instead, somebody who is at the word list collecting stage—still needed for many languages—is likely to take the glosses in the word list as given: a mountain is a mountain, isn't it?

As comparativists grow older and wiser, they become more aware of how the meanings of forms slither around in semantic space over time. Indeed, they are the ones who have taught the rest of us how much

---

1. Out of print. Most of the entries had the form "quí, -te n. house, roof" with inaccurate tone and length information and no further elaboration on grammar or meaning. Grimes et al. 1981 is much closer to what I am talking about here; its entry for the same form contains close to a page of information.

semantic displacement language is capable of over time.[2] They are the ones who make it clear that the meanings habitually expressed in a language at any one time may or may not be reflected in the initial collection of data within a word list framework.

So, assuming we want to present meaning in a way that reflects what native speakers do, how do we go about it? Besides the tried and true method of trying to account for as much as possible in massive amounts of text and picking up fragmentary but unelicited material in its behavioral context, a large enough body of theory finally has grown up in that most atheoretical of sciences, lexicography, that some principled heuristics have emerged that are usable in the field. I will refer to them as LEXICAL FUNCTIONS. The appendix contains examples of a variety of them.

2. LEXICAL DATA FROM TEXT.   A sensible way to decide what goes into a dictionary is to ignore word lists developed outside the language and observe what speakers of the language actually say and in some cases write to each other. On occasion I have referred to this perspective as taking the semantic inventory of a language.

This is related to the technical notion of TEXT, which is usually taken as whatever linguistic material you get under any circumstances other than a direct question of the type, "How do you say X?" where X comes from a different linguistic system than the mother tongue of the person being asked. Text takes in monologues and dialogues, fragments, and interchanges. The idea is that influences from outside the speaker's ordinary patterns of speech are at a minimum in text. This does not mean that a linguist merely records passively what people are saying; he or she may set the topic or trigger the speech, but it is the speaker who determines the form.

From wax cylinders to digital disk, linguists have profited from sound recordings of speech in its natural setting.[3] Video recording now helps to synchronize nonverbal signals with speech and shows some of the physical setting. Most of what linguists currently want to know about a language is obtainable from TRANSCRIPTIONS of recorded texts, assuming that the transcriptions are made consistently. Texts represented in alphabetic, syllabic, or ideographic form can be entered into computers, scanned, and manipulated to help in their analysis.

2. Buck 1949 is a classic example.

3. That the linguist is there is of itself a source of disturbance but can often be minimized to the extent that its effect is more like background noise than a major disruption of communication. Milroy (1987: chap. 2) discusses ways of collecting data with the linguist off the scene, with the help of trained assistants from the same speech community who can fill the linguist in privately about the social and behavioral context of what is being said. We cannot eliminate interference with the data, but we can minimize it.

One of the most widely useful manipulations of text transcriptions for study of the lexicon is some variation of a CONCORDANCE. A concordance takes every word or morpheme in a text and redisplays it on a separate line for each instance, surrounded by its immediate context and accompanied by a reference to where that instance is found in case the display of the immediate context is not enough to show what is going on.[4]

Another presentation of data that helps to sort out lexical matters is INTERLINEARIZATION. Something like it has been done for years, either written out and set in type by hand or run on like the "multiple stage translation" advocated by Carl Voegelin in the 1960s as a format for examples in the *International Journal of American Linguistics*.[5]

A typical interlinearization begins with a numbered clause or sentence of the transcription that represents as accurately as possible what was actually said or written. The second line is a LEMMATIZATION of the words and morphemes that make up the text, giving the dictionary entry under which the information for each element is to be found (*feet*, for example, would be lemmatized under the name forms *foot* and *PLURAL*). The third line gives the part of speech and perhaps subclass information for the usage at that point in the text. A last line, needed when the language being studied is not the same as the language in which the study is presented, is a concise GLOSS in the language of explanation that gives a general idea of the meaning of each interlinearized element. There could be other lines for such things as semantic domains or discourse functions. Spaces or frames are juggled to make the elements line up vertically, and a free-form translation of the whole clause or sentence into the language of explanation (a real meaning-oriented translation, not a string of glosses) ends the set.

The reason for going into detail about interlinearization is that computer programs that are available now have made interlinearized text the tool of choice for broad coverage of the lexicon from the point of view of the language being studied. They also make it unnecessary to

4. Some of us remember when everything was copied out by hand or typewriter on file slips. Then the slips were sorted into piles and copied here and there. A concordance to the works of Shakespeare or the Bible was the work of a lifetime. I do not brag about the good old days, as if we had men of iron in ships of wood, because even then I was sure there had to be a better way to do our work. In 1963 I set up a ten-year project at the University of Oklahoma, partially supported by the National Science Foundation, that made it possible for any U.S. linguist working anywhere in the world to submit a collection of texts, have it punched on IBM cards, made into a concordance, and have a printout returned to the linguist. More than a quarter of a century later I still run into linguists who found these computer-produced concordances a major aid in their published research.

5. Voegelin suggested that when a phrase or sentence was used as an example, it would help the reader if it were followed by a morpheme-by-morpheme gloss, matching spaces with spaces and morpheme boundaries with hyphens. The final stage was a rendering in good English that highlighted what the example meant in its context.

waste time with extrinsic criteria for selection of words. We include things in the dictionary, not because they are mandated by some word list in English or any other language of explanation, but because we have observed speakers of the language using them in situations that we do not control.[6]

The most straightforward way I know to start a dictionary that is not shaped by some other language is to interlinearize texts using computer software that builds dictionary entries in order to guide the interlinearizer program.[7] The procedure snowballs on itself, in that the more the computer knows, the more text it can go through successfully without needing assistance from the linguist.

We start with a "dictionary" computer file with no entries in it. The computer looks at the first word of the text and of course does not find it in the dictionary. We can fill in a new entry for the first word, giving our current guess about its grammatical status, a short gloss to put on the last line of the interlinearization, and whatever other information can be filled in at that stage. Or we can take the word chunk by chunk and make multiple entries for prefixes, infixes, roots, and suffixes as we recognize them.[8] When all the pieces of information needed for interlinearizing are in the dictionary, the interlinear analysis appears on the screen.

6. There is a place for looking at word lists or dictionaries in other languages as a source of ideas to work toward completeness, but it comes later in the process, not at the beginning. Mere quantity of text is no guarantee that the language has been covered. I once consulted on a lexicography project that started with a million-word concordance of texts. When enough entries had been written that the million word instances were squeezed dry, the native speakers on the project started saying things like "This word reminds me that we haven't put in this other one" or "We've accounted for 129 examples of this word, but none of them illustrates this sense of it." At this point a look at what other languages express could trigger questions that might lead to filling in gaps.

7. For some time I have been using Shoebox, currently in Version 5 (JAARS, Inc. 2000) from www.sil.org on the World Wide Web. The current version includes the ability to handle moderately complex morphologies and morphophonemic systems, audio clips of examples, and a formatter (Coward and Grimes 1995) that sets up publishable pages with a variety of fonts, including IPA and some right-to-left writing systems. For more complex morphologies such as that of Huichol, I use an interacting combination of Shoebox to organize the results and Ample (Weber, Black, and McConnel 1988) to decompose words into their constituent morphemes and disentangle the morphophonemics. Shoebox is not the only dictionary-based parser available, but it is the one I am most familiar with, and the approach of the others is equivalent.

8. I now work with separate dictionary files on the computer for affixes, ordinary vocabulary, names, and sometimes specialized terms in the language. Shoebox asks for the order in which it should consult them; once that is determined, the fact that separate files are involved requires no further attention from me unless there are homographs in different files, like a name "Pat" and a verb "pat." In that case the computer asks which dictionary file I want to put the current form into.

At this stage we are not doing lexicography yet; we are only finding out what we will be doing lexicography on later as our knowledge builds up to a more sophisticated level. There is far more information yet to be compiled about the words in the computer dictionary than the small amount we need to produce a useful interlinearization. But tying the dictionary totally to texts means that its entries represent usage in a way that is not artificial.

When forms are already in the dictionary file, more and more of them get taken care of automatically. Inevitably, however, there comes an "oops!" interlinearization: we see that the way the computer has analyzed some new material is wrong. It is based on what we have told the literal-minded computer about the language up to that point, and that turns out to be incomplete; now we have to add other information the computer can use to get the analysis right. We may need to distinguish homographs, or parts of speech, or recognize different senses, or recognize senses that are limited to certain grammatical or lexical contexts. In this way a picture of the lexical stock and the grammar builds up simultaneously and is constantly being refined. All the minute details we have come across have at least been tallied somewhere, though not necessarily in their final form. If we change our minds about any part of the analysis, we pull up the dictionary file and make the change on the spot, then quickly reanalyze the whole corpus up to that point in terms of the new analysis.

When we can zip through texts with the interlinearizer and our mean time between failures gets to be on the order of a couple of hundred words at a stretch and all the analyses make good linguistic sense the way the computer lays them out, we can be fairly sure that our understanding of the function words and affixes, and the more common kinds of stems, is well along. Now the heavy lexicography can begin.

3. THE HEART OF THE LEXICON.   DEFINITIONS are the key to lexicography. A real definition is not a gloss in another language. For a definition to hold, it needs to be restricted to terms that Aristotle in the *Topics* characterized as "prior" and "more intelligible." To be prior, it may not be circular (a classical circular definition is one like "sugar is white *sweet* stuff," matched with "*sweet* means it tastes like sugar"). I would emphasize also that the defining words are in the same language as the words being defined, not in the language of explanation, because most of the words employed in definitions must themselves be defined.[9]

I use the word "most" advisedly, because obviously the process of noncircular definition has to stop somewhere. There are two proposals for stopping it. The most highly articulated proposal has been elaborated by Anna Wierzbicka

---

9. Definitions may of course be translated into the language of explanation for various purposes, but the result is not another definition but a translation of a definition.

(1972, 1996) and summarized by Cliff Goddard (1998). Wierzbicka finds evidence to suggest that the most elementary level of terms for definitions, the "primes" of her 1996 book, may well be universal to all languages.

The alternative, proposed by Uriel Weinreich (1966), is that it is simply impossible to eliminate circularity in defining, so what we want to do is to restrict it to the smallest set of terms possible. The terms that must be defined circularly or not at all are considered Level 0, or primitive terms for defining the rest; Level 1 terms are those that are defined noncircularly using only Level 0 terms, and so on up the ladder, with terms from levels 0 to n-1 accessible for making definitions at every level n > 0.[10]

We do not actually define words; we define senses of words.[11] Each sense in which a word is used has its own definition. It may have much in common with the definitions for other senses of the same word, but in its totality no definition covers accurately any of the other senses.[12]

At any rate, a presentation of lexical information that lacks a real definition for each sense ought to be kept separate from one that attempts serious defining. The former is an annotated word list, properly referred to as a GLOSSARY, but it is not yet a work of lexicography.

4. LEXICAL DATA FROM UNELICITED FORMS IN CONTEXT.   Not all the useful data come in connected text. The anthropological orientation of much American linguistics makes it likely that we will do most of our analysis on narratives, prayers, coherent conversations, songs, exhortations, attempts to convince people, and other well-structured pieces, especially set pieces. All these are clearly text. But there are unelicited things in great quantities that we pick up in context whenever we are in a community where the language we are looking into is spoken.[13]

10. When we consider lexical functions, it will be seen that some of them appear to lock on to part but not all of the meaning of their headwords—in other words, they relate to part of the definition but not all of it. Assuming that Wierzbicka's primitive terms enter into lexical functions, this could lead to the paradox (or duality) that they also must have definitions (Grimes 1996). That would be compatible with Weinreich's suggestion, but nobody has yet probed its implications.

11. As a matter of fact, it is not senses of words but senses of lexical items, which may be parts of words, full words, or phrases.

12. If it proves impossible to write definitions for two senses with enough in common to show the meaning connection between them, it is likely that we are dealing with homographs rather than polysemy.

13. In concentrating on the stance of an outsider as lexicographer, I hold strongly that the best strategy is to train fully one or more native speakers of the language in lexical theory and turn them loose. It will be some time, however, before this happens for very many languages, and outsiders in the meantime do have a contribution to make. And in my experience, native speakers as lexicographers are not immune to falling into the same difficulties outsiders have encountered.

Often these utterances are short, minimal even. Sometimes they are quite complex. The main thing about them is that they are observed in circumstances that we do not control but in which we are aware of what is going on at the time (provided we have a decent understanding of the speakers' culture). This gives us insight into the speaker's intended meaning and sometimes into the meaning perceived by the addressee. Within a community framework we sometimes have the opportunity to follow up by asking for explanations of things we miss.[14]

For years I have carried a surveyor's notebook and immediately jotted down such utterances and notes about the circumstances surrounding them. I sometimes use shorthand when events happen fast, but then I have to take time immediately afterward to transcribe it. I now use a Pocket PC for such notes, because I can transfer the results directly into my computer.[15] A substantial proportion of the examples in the dictionary I am now working on comes from such chance encounters. They are especially important for picking up new senses of words and spotting new grammatical environments.

Another twist on directing the acquisition of data without eliciting on the basis of another language is to come up with a form out of the clear blue sky and ask about the range of contexts in which the form might be used. I discovered this with Huichol when, for example, I had recorded the stem *zuríkí* and been told it matched Spanish *pecado* 'sin'. Since that put it within a nonnative conceptual framework, I later asked what I might be talking about if I were to say *pükázuu.ríkí*, the negative. Without blinking, my associate replied *wázá* 'a cornfield'. He then went on to explain that it referred to a cornfield that had not been picked, or a forest that had not been cut (like English "virgin forest"), or a woman who had not had sexual relations. Pragmatically it t rns out to have the latter as its basic meaning, plus an extension to a very short no-no list including murder, theft, adultery, and not much else. Since that time I have used ZERO-CONTEXT QUESTIONS freely and learned a lot of surprising things in the process.

5. LEXICAL DATA FROM LEXICAL FUNCTIONS.   Not only do the different senses of a polysemous word share meaning; distinct words also

---

14. With today's urgency to document endangered and moribund languages, it is not uncommon for the speech community to have disappeared and the language consultant not to have actually said anything to anybody in the language for years. Situations like that cannot produce state-of-the-art lexicography no matter how qualified the linguist investigating them is; the necessary data simply are not there, and one does what one can.

15. Living in a Pidgin-dominant area, my current fieldwork is on Hawaii Pidgin (Hawaii Creole English in some linguists' usage), so I refer to it freely even in a chapter on Huichol because I have learned a bit since I last lived with the Huichol and would certainly use what I have learned if I were there now.

share meaning. Even antonyms have in common the scale on which they differ.

This works in two ways. Some words, including antonyms and synonyms and other types that will come up later, are incompatible in some contexts: the weather cannot be called "cold" and "hot" at the same time without special comment; the "remainder" in your bank account is your "balance," but it would be questionable style to use both "remainder" and "balance" together; once you have called something "jet black" you do not immediately call it "very black," and so on. Some words and phrases are thus in some sense mutually exclusive in context.

Other words seem to attract semantically related words in context and co-occur with them by preference. You can ask the "driver" to "drive" you home, or the "pilot" to "fly" you there; you "pump" the "tire" with a "tire pump" and "cut" fish on a "cutting" board. "Wind" cannot do anything but "blow" (or "die down"), and "fire" cannot do anything but "burn" (or "smolder" or "go out" or "flare up"). You can "report" to your superiors, or you can "make a report" to them.

We are all familiar enough with the notion of a thesaurus that we can readily imagine a vast web of associations among words. Lexical function theory suggests that these associations are of different kinds and have more structure than one might suspect, enough that we can use the associations themselves to track down other words and other senses. They can be specified more precisely than the "have something to do with each other" relation that is behind the typical thesaurus. We now recognize that the entire vocabulary of a language is tied together by many different but identifiable kinds of ties—lexical functions—into a highly structured superthesaurus.[16]

These conventional relations among lexical items are part of every language, a standard feature of the lexicon that every native speaker knows implicitly. They should at least be reported, and the dictionary is the logical place to do that.

In addition to just reporting values of lexical functions when we stumble across them, we can turn them around and use them to search out other things about the lexicon of a language. We could say that every word in a language has other words in its close lexical neighborhood. Once we have roughed out what lexical functions a language uses, we can explore the lexical neighborhood of words by trying out those functions on every word. I was recently checking on boat termi-

---

16. The lexical relations are uniform enough that the scholars who first developed the idea christened them "lexical functions" by analogy with certain kinds of discrete mathematical functions (Mel'čuk and Žolkovsky 1984; Mel'čuk et al. 1984). Each function has a domain, consisting of the words it applies to, and a range, consisting of the nonunique and sometimes many words that stand in that relation to each member of the domain. To make it easier to tie in with the existing literature, I will use "lexical function" from this point forward.

nology in Hawaii Pidgin in order to pinpoint the difference between physically making a boat change direction and deciding when and which way it should change direction. It came out clearly as soon as I probed the nomenclature for the person whose regular job it was to do one and the other—the S_1 lexical function, on the order of English *steersman* versus *captain*.

But might not lexical functions simply be another importation from outside a language? A Westerner's idea of how language ought to be, little different in spirit from an arbitrary gloss list?

I think not. For starters, conventional collocations are fairly frequent in text, as are lexical substitutions and antitheses within single topics. It is impossible to prove that every language has them, but the crucial example of a language in which no words relate in ways that match our understanding of lexical functions has not turned up yet either. One could speculate that every language has to have lexical functions as a mechanism for extending its lexical stock to cover new situations and to make room for flexibility of expression.

Next, in the few dozen languages that have been looked at with care to investigate their use of lexical functions, the set found seems to be the same, though not all of the functions found in one language are necessarily made use of by another. The sameness might, of course, be an artifact of training or common association with the developers of the lexical function idea; but the relationships might really be there.

The clincher for me is the way linguistically untrained, and for that matter totally uneducated, speakers of a language (in the sense of never having studied in any school) catch on to the idea and use it. Granting that some of the functions are abstruse and require practice to recognize, many of them can be identified by just about anybody.

When I began to work on lexical functions in Huichol,[17] it was in a refugee community that had been displaced as a result of bandit activity.

17. Huichol is a southern Uto-Aztecan language spoken in the Sierra Madre Occidental of western Mexico, northwest of Guadalajara and northeast of Tepic. I began the study of Huichol in 1952; in 1978–79 when the research reported here was done under a grant from the National Science Foundation, there were between 12,000 and 20,000 first-language speakers of all ages. Consonants are given here as *p, t, c* [ts], *k, k^w*, '[glottal stop], *z* [retroflex voiced in the west, unvoiced in the east], *r* [reverse flap, often lateral in the east], *w, y, h* [homorganic voiceless vocoid, lenis], and vowels *a, e* [ɛ ~ æ], *i, u* [close to o], *ü* [high back unrounded]. They are written *p, t, s, c/qu, cu, ', x, r, v, y, h, a, e, i, u, ü* by many literate Huichols, and other writings are in use as well. Syllables always begin with C (i.e., a single consonant) and have as coda V or VV (long or diphthongal) in careful speech. Tones attach to the syllable and are high *á, é, í, ú, û* and low *a, e, i, u, ü*. A period in the middle of the word indicates rhythmic foot boundary, as does word space. Ordinary writing does not include tone, length, or rhythmic boundaries. Verb morphology is complex; it is covered in some detail in Grimes 1964 and from other angles by a group of linguists at the University of Guadalajara under the leadership of José Luis Iturrioz.

I had lived for several years in the mountain community from which they were displaced and knew nearly everybody there already. They were networked with other refugee communities and with most of the people who had stayed in the mountains or returned there after the danger had dissipated. There were daily comings and goings. The Huichol language was in constant use at all age levels, with pride.

I began to explain to the people I was working with how words lined up in groups with regular associations. They saw the point immediately, and it became a kind of game. At one time I remember having about twenty people standing around the table where I was making notes, coming up spontaneously with lexical function values faster than I could write them down. At other times two or three of us would ponder details of more difficult functions together, or in the middle of a conversation one of them would wink at me and say in Huichol, "Got that one?"

This is not the place to go into a long explanation of the lexical functions. The introductions to the works by Igor' A. Mel'čuk and Aleksandr K. Žolkovsky (1984) and Mel'čuk and colleagues (1984) are enough to give an orientation to a growing body of literature. I have, however, included an appendix of functions with examples, organized as suggested by Grimes (1990) to highlight relationships among some of the functions themselves. But it is instructive to have a few examples of the lexical function idea in action, being used as a heuristic for getting into previously unexplored areas of a language, especially in sense discrimination.

Sense 1 of the adverb *zaücíe*, 'not in the place we are talking about; somewhere else', has one antonym, *[NP] heecíe* 'in [an identifiable place-NP]' and another *'úuzéi.kûa* 'in the same place as some identified person or thing, and close to the orientation point'. The second sense of *zaücíe*, 'to some other place', is the conventional locative of *pátá* 'change location' and has as its antonym *'áazéi.kûa* 'in the place we are talking about'.[18]

The adjective *ce'íi*, multiple *cée.cé'íi* 'hard', also has different antonyms for two of its senses. In the sense 'hard to bend or make a depression in', the antonym is *yuméeni*, multiple *yuu.mémééni*, 'soft, squishy'; in the sense 'immobile, firmly set', the antonym is *yua* 'move'. *Yua*, in turn, has another antonym, a full word and not a stem— *'ací.púkaa.tíyúurienee* 'is not doing anything' (its stem is *yúurie*)—and overlapping synonyms *pátá* 'change location' (already mentioned as being in the lexical neighborhood of *zaücíe* 2), *yûü.yûaka* 'move the body multiple times, shake', *tûü.tûríi* 'tremble', and *tûü.tûpíi* 'be trembly'. The substantival form for *yua* is *yuaríiya* 'motion' and the causative is a morphologically regular form *yúitüa* 'cause

---

18. For most examples of verbs, I cite only the bare nonperfective stem to keep things simple. Normally there is an aspectual choice of stems and at least one prefix, usually more than one.

to move, operate'. That causative with a back-and-forth orientation prefix *ku-* has its own synonym, *kacée* 'shake', and its own finals, *nûtüa*, which is also a causative 'calm down', and táatua, not a causative, 'release'.

Examples such as the ones just given are the product of interaction with a group of linguistically unsophisticated speakers of Huichol, many more than the ones listed as coauthors. Even chance visitors would listen to what we were doing, catch on to the idea of related words, and come up spontaneously with suggestions that the others found acceptable and interesting. It became a kind of community game to fill in the dictionary as fully as possible. The coauthors then worked with me in more detail to pin down some of the less obvious lexical functions and flesh out the grammatical information.

Beyond that, there was a time bomb effect. People who had been brainstorming on lexical functions would wake up in the night with an idea or get one while walking along a trail. Often what they came up with in a noninteractive situation was more like a function of a function, but it was never irrelevant or confused. The wheels turned without an outsider there to tell them how. Furthermore, the whole idea was exciting to the community, far more than anything I have ever seen when pursuing syntactic constructions or phonology.

APPENDIX: The Lexical Functions

Read formulas such as S_0(travel) = trip *as "the substantival expression that corresponds to 'travel' is 'trip'."*

Category Functions		
S_0	Concept as substantive	S_0(travel) = trip
V_0	Concept as verb	V_0(flight) = fly
A_0	Concept as adjective	A_0(fire) = fiery
Adv_0	Concept as adverb	Adv_0(good) = well
Copula	Specific equivalent of "be"	Cop(example) = serve as
Predicative	Portmanteau with "be" + N or V	Pred(near) = to neighbor

Inverse Functions		
Simple Inverses		
Synonym>	More inclusive synonym	Syn>(refinement) = culture
		Syn>(balance) = remainder
Synonym<	Less inclusive synonym	Syn<(culture) = refinement
		Syn<(remainder) = balance
Antecedent	Prior state	Ante(dead) = die
Consequent	Resulting state (also Res)	Cons(die) = dead

Causative	Someone brings about a state of affairs	Caus(die) = kill
Event	State of affairs that someone brings about	Event(kill) = die
Permissive	Allows a state of affairs to come about	Perm(fall) = drop
Event	State of affairs that someone allows	Event(drop) = fall
Liquidative	Action that makes state no longer in effect	Liqu(mistake) = correct
State	State no longer in effect	State(correct) = mistake
Symptom	Part of body and state that manifests condition	Symptom(cold, nose) = runny
Manifest	Condition manifested by a state of a body part	Manifest(runny, nose) = cold
Leader	Dominant member of organization (also called Cap)	Leader(committee) = chair
Organization	People who relate to a leader	Org(commander) = regiment
Group	People necessary for a complex behavior pattern	Group(gun) = crew Group(cloister) = monks
Function	Behavior pattern that requires various people	Function(crew) = gun, ship, plane Function(monks) = cloister
Unit	Smallest scope of manifestation	Unit(violence) = act Unit(fury) = fit
Mass	Manifestation that can have unit scope	Mass(act) = violence Mass(fit) = fury
Multiple	Aggregate of individuals	Mult(sheep) = flock Mult(cow) = herd
Individual	Individuals that aggregate	Indiv(flock) = sheep Indiv(herd) = cow

---

Symmetric Inverses (own inverse)

Synonym	Exact synonym (rare)	Syn(Mearns' Quail) = Fool's Quail
Synonym^	Overlapping synonym	Syn^(magnificent) = grand Syn^(help) = aid
Conversive	Same situation, actants rearranged	$Conv_{1,2}$(buy) = sell $Conv_{1,2}$(sell) = buy $Conv_{2,3}$(instruct) = teach $Conv_{2,3}$(teach) = instruct
Complementarity	Polar opposites, no middle ground, a kind of antonym	Complem(male) = female Complem(female) = male

Antonym	Opposite ends of a scale that has a middle, antonym proper	Ant(hot) = cold Ant(cold) = hot
Reversal	Unwinding of a process	Rev(open) = shut Rev(shut) = open

Clustered Inverses

Species	Species with differentiated members	Species(ewe) = sheep Species(ram) = sheep Species(lamb) = sheep
Female	Female of a species	Female(sheep) = ewe
Male	Male of a species	Male(sheep) = ram
Young	Young of a species	Young(sheep) = lamb

The clustered inverses are rare enough that they might not qualify as lexical functions. Some species also have terms for castrated males like gelding, *subadults like* yearling *(for cattle), and extremely young offspring like* foal. *The lack of generality is an argument against treating these as lexical functions.*

Hierarchical Inverses (one to many; not true inverses)

Generic	Kind of thing this is an instance of	Gener(wrench) = hand tool Gener(hand tool) = tool
Specific	One thing of a particular kind	Spec(hand tool) = hammer, wrench, . . . Spec(tool) = hand tool, power tool, . . .
Whole	Something that has parts	Whole(sole) = shoe
Part	A functional part of something	Part(shoe) = sole, upper, tongue, . . .
Sequence	A culturally recognized sequence	Seq(insert needle) = inject
Phase	One event in a sequence	$Phase_1$(inject) = prepare syringe $Phase_2$(inject) = cleanse site $Phase_3$(inject) = insert needle $Phase_4$(inject) = inject 2

Detail Functions (part of meaning of head)

Actant Functions

S_1, S_2, S_3, S_4	Substantive denoting typical actant	S_1(type) = typist S_2(type) = paper
A_1, A_2, A_3, A_4	State of actant	A_1(know) = aware A_2(know) = known, familiar
$Able_1$, $Able_2$, . . .	Habilitative: property of actant that makes it capable of being that kind of actant	$Able_1$(burn 1) = combustible $Able_2$(eat) = edible

$Qual_1$,	Quality that entails	$Qual_1$(surprise) = unusual
$Qual_2$, ...	Able1, Able2, ... (rare)	[$Able_1$(surprise) = surprising]
Adv_1,	How the actant relates	Adv_1(accompany) = along with
Adv_2, ...	to its situation	
Positive	Praise for one actant	Pos_2(review) = favorable
		Pos_1(review) = competent

Peripheral Functions (nonargument)

Location	Conventional relator for position	Loc(school) = in Loc(home) = at
LocFrom	Conventional relator for motion away	LocFrom(height) = down from LocFrom(town) = out of
LocTo	Conventional relator for motion towards	LocTo(foe) = against LocTo(battle) = into
LocTime	Conventional relator for time	LocTime(Sunday) = on LocTime(May) = in LocTime(moment) = in the course of
SLoc	Conventional place where action occurs	SLoc(battle) = field SLoc(crime) = scene
Instrument	Conventional relator for instrument	Instr(radio) = by Instr(pen) = with Instr(computer) = on
S_{Instr}	Conventional instrument	S_{Instr}(communication) = means S_{Instr}(convince) = argument
S_{Mode}	Conventional way to carry out action	S_{Mode}(write 1) = handwriting S_{Mode}(write 2) = style
S_{Means}	Conventional thing that must be available in order for the action to be carried out	S_{Means}(shoot) = ammunition
S_{Res}	Conventional outcome of a situation	S_{Res}(catastrophe) = aftermath S_{Res}(hunt) = bag

---

Factives (S0 is normally the operational word)

$SubjFact_0$,	Subject tells what is	$SubjFact_0$(silence) = reign
1, ...	happening with subject (0) or subject's actant 1, 2, ... Also called $Func_0$, $_1$, ...	$SubjFact_0$(wind) = blow $PerfSubjFact_0$(dream) = come true $SubjFact_1$(anxiety) = gnaws at 1 $PerfSubjFact_2$(experiment) = work out for 1 $SubjFact_2$(blow 3) = falls on 2

		PerfSubjFact$_2$(hypothesis) = be in accord with 2
ObjFact$_{1, 2, \ldots}$	Object tells what is happening, its actant 1, 2, . . . is subject. Also called Oper$_{1, 2, \ldots}$	ObjFact$_1$(support) = lend PerfObjFact$_1$(program) = adopt ObjFact$_2$(support) = receive PerfObjFact$_2$(program) = carry out ObjFact$_1$(sacrifice) = make
Adjunct-Fact$_1$, . . .	Adjunct tells what is happening. Its actant 1 is subject, another is object. Also called Labor$_{ij(k)}$	AdjunctFact$_{1,2}$(consider) = 1 takes 2 into consideration PerfAdjunctFact$_{1,2}$(cannon) = 1 hit 2 with a cannon AdjunctFact$_{1,2}$(test) = 1 puts 2 to the test PerfAdjunctFact$_{1,2}$(dinner) = 1 has 2 [to eat] for PerfAdjunctFact$_{1,3}$(dinner) = 1 has 3 [as guest] for

Aspect Functions (internal to time frame)

Inceptive	Beginning of state of affairs. Usually combined with another function	IncepCop(victim) = fall IncepSubjFact$_0$(war) = break out
Continuative	Continuation of state of affairs. Combined	ContObjFact$_1$(silence) = preserve
Central	Culminating phase of state of affairs	Centr(life) = prime Centr(crisis) = peak Centr(flood) = crest
Degradatory	Loss of optimal state	Degrad(teeth) = decay Degrad(egg) = go bad
Final	End of state of affairs	FinSubjFact$_0$(sound) = die away FinObjFact$_1$(patience) = lose
Perfective	Process carried through to its end	Perf(die) = have died

Aspect Functions (external to time frame)

Preparatory	Make ready for normal	Prepar(gun) = load Prepar(pencil) = sharpen
Proximate	Immediately before the main situation	ProxIncepSubjFact$_0$(storm) = gather
Antecedent	Logical prerequisite (also under inverse)	Anteced(know) = learn
Consequent	Logical outcome (also under inverse)	Conseq(study) = know

Degree Functions		
Magn	Superlative degree English has many of these	Magn(important) = vitally Magn(black) = jet Magn(joy) = sheer
Increase	Greater extent than former state of the situation. Also called Plus	Increase(tension) = mount
Decrease	Lesser extent than former state of the situation Also called Minus	IncepDecrease(value) = shrink
Bon	Praiseworthy instance of the state of affairs, equivalent to Positive$_0$	Bon(aim) = lofty Bon(aid) = valuable Bon(chance) = happy
Veridical	Meeting an intended requirement	Ver(reason) = valid Ver(pride) = justifiable Ver(demand) = legitimate

Miscellaneous		
Imperative	Special command not using the head word	Imper(shoot) = fire! Imper(silence) = shut up! Imper(talk) = go ahead, over
Figurative	Standard, frozen figures of speech that everybody knows but no poet would use	Figur(passion) = flame Figur(misery) = abyss
Involve	Peripheral involvement	Conv$_{2,1}$Involv(wind) = be out in
Sound	Characteristic noise	Son(grass) = rustle Son(sheep) = bleat Son(Spaniard) = Spanish?

CHAPTER FOUR

Entries for Verbs in American Indian Language Dictionaries

Pamela Munro

1. INTRODUCTION.   This chapter presents a survey of some of the problems inherent in writing dictionary entries for verbs of languages that are often polysynthetic, with verbs frequently able to convey all the information in a very complex sentence. I examine some of the approaches that have been used by authors of dictionaries of a number of languages in an attempt to evaluate some of the strategies that may be useful to makers of dictionaries for such languages, particularly dictionaries that will be accessible to laypeople as well as scholars.

Minimally, a verb's entry in the dictionary should contain the verb itself and a definition. In addition, a full entry may need to contain inflectional information, irregular forms, examples, an etymology, and cross-references to related forms or other items of interest. Each of these

There is no way that I can thank all the people who have contributed to this chapter, which presents a current snapshot of some of my ideas about dictionary entry structure worked out over many years of making dictionaries for languages with very different structures. First, of course, I must thank the speakers of the languages I refer to here: particularly Catherine Willmond (for Chickasaw), the late Molly Fasthorse (for Tolkapaya Yavapai), Anita Martinez and Maurice Lopez (for Garifuna), the late Pollyanna Heath (for Maricopa), the late Nellie Brown (for Mojave), Virginia Carey (for Cherokee), Felipe Lopez (for San Lucas Quiaviní Zapotec), Katherine Siva Saubel (Sauvel) (for Cahuilla), and the late Hannah Fixico and Mary Iron Teeth (for Lakhota), as well as the other speakers listed in the sources I refer to below. I am also grateful to colleagues and teachers who have helped to shape my view of dictionary structure and morphological analysis, including, but certainly not limited to, William Bright, Kenneth C. Hill, Ronald W. Langacker, Margaret Langdon, and William Frawley. Many other linguists who I cannot acknowledge by name have contributed to the development of my views of particular languages.

A few of the issues I discuss in this chapter were treated in Munro 1996.

sections of the entry presents its own problems, but here I am concerned only with the selection of the entry and its definition; I touch only peripherally on how the dictionary entry form itself might be useful in specifying the type of inflection a word takes—something that might also be specified in other parts of the entry that I do not survey here, such as examples or explicit features of some type. I am considering only bilingual dictionaries whose main section goes from a target language (here the American Indian language being described) to a base language (usually English, in the examples I discuss).[1] Monolingual dictionaries may share some features with such bilingual dictionaries, but constructing them is quite a different matter, which I cannot address here. Certainly, definitions in monolingual dictionaries are quite different from those in bilingual dictionaries, as bilingual dictionary definitions might also be considered translations.

An important question for the maker of a dictionary of a polysynthetic or highly inflected language (like the majority of indigenous languages of the Americas) is whether to restrict dictionary entries to actual words or whether a dictionary can, or should, include roots or stems that are unpronounceable alone. I return to this question again and again throughout this chapter.

Athabaskan provides the best-known example of a language group for which many (probably most) dictionaries list roots or stems rather than full words. The reason for this is clear: a language like Navajo, in which ten or more separate prefixes may often be added to a root to produce a pronounceable verb, has so many possible words that the decision of how to list them in the dictionary raises innumerable problems for the lexicographer. Neither the root approach nor the fully inflected approach seems to be fully satisfactory,[2] as can be seen by comparing the two very different Navajo dictionaries produced by the eminent lexicographic team of Robert Young and William Morgan (Young and Morgan 1987; Young, Morgan, and Midgette 1992). Since I have not worked on an Athabaskan dictionary, however, I will not consider these further here.

The remainder of this chapter is somewhat autobiographical, though not organized chronologically. Although I will mention how various problems concerning verb entries have been handled by dictionary makers

---

1. Most, but not all, bilingual dictionaries of this type also have a section that goes from the base language to the target language. Definitions in this section, which is often called an "index," are usually shorter and less explicit than those in the first section. These certainly present their own interesting problems, but I do not consider them here.

2. I am extremely grateful to Siri Tuttle for helpful discussion of this issue and to everyone else who has taught me about Navajo.

other than myself, I will be primarily concerned with decisions I have made or participated in concerning the best form of a verb to give as a main verb entry and how such entries should be translated. Not all of these decisions may have been optimal, unfortunately, but I have learned from each one.

I begin by considering languages in which the entry word is a (relatively) uninflected stem (§2). Next I consider cases in which some affixes must appear on even some relatively simple entry words and others in which inclusion of an affix may assist in presentation of inflectional information (§3). Then I survey a number of languages whose verbs are always inflected, in which an inflected form must serve as the basic dictionary entry (§4). In these first three sections I translate cited verb entries with simple *to*-less infinitival glosses such as 'sleep' or 'be stingy', but in section 5 I specifically address the translation of all the different types of dictionary entry words that I have presented.[3]

2. UNINFLECTED ENTRY WORDS.   Usually the dictionary entry is a form that the compiler feels is "simple" or "basic." For some languages (which share this structural feature at least with English), selection of the verb form to be entered in the dictionary is an easy matter: every verb, or nearly every verb, has a single base form that all speakers will agree is the "name" of the verb.

I do not think there is any single defining feature of such basic forms. In English, for example, the basic entry form is generally taken to be the form of the verb that can be used alone as an imperative or that can follow *to* in a sentence like *I want to . . . ;* for every English verb except *be,* this form is identical with the form used with any non-third-person singular subject in the present tense.[4] In other languages, however, the basic entry form is the form of the verb used precisely with a third-person singular subject in the present tense. In all languages where an uninflected base verb is used as a dictionary entry, that entry word appears completely unaffixed in some parts of the verb paradigm.

2.1. In the Muskogean language Chickasaw (see Munro and Willmond 1994) the basic form of a verb can be interpreted either as a full present

3. There are many other issues concerning verb entries that I cannot address here, including the problems of how to present entries for multiword verbs and how to enter idioms in the dictionary.

4. I believe all English speakers would agree that the name of the verb *be* is indeed *be* and not *are*, but this intuition is somewhat difficult to access, given how much we have been trained to expect dictionary entries of a particular sort.

tense sentence with an elliptical third-person subject (1a)[5] or (depending on intonation) as an imperative (1b); the same form is used as an "infinitival" complement of verbs like 'want', regardless of their subject (1c, d). Thus the dictionary form of the Chickasaw verb 'sleep' is *nosi:*

(1) (a) *Nosi.*   'He sleeps', 'She sleeps', 'It sleeps', 'They sleep.'
    (b) *Nosi!*   'Sleep'!
    (c) *Nosi banna.*   'He wants to sleep.'[6]
        sleep want
    (d) *Nosi sa-banna.*   'I want to sleep.'[7]
        sleep 1sII-want

2.2. In the Yuman language Tolkapaya Yavapai (see Munro and Fasthorse in preparation), the basic form of a verb can also be used as a full present tense sentence with a third-person subject (2a), but this subject must be singular, since a plural suffix appears on a verb with a plural subject (2b). However, the basic form of a Tolkapaya verb cannot be used as an imperative (the imperative carries a second-person prefix) (2c) or as the complement of a 'want' verb with a non-third-person subject; such a complement must agree with the subject of 'want' (expressed idiomatically with 'say') and be marked irrealis (2d, e).

---

5. I could say much more about these examples or the others given for other languages below. For example, "present" here refers to the actual present or immediate past; the same sentences may usually be translated with the English progressive. Pronouns can be added to sentences like (1a), but they usually are emphatic. As shown in (1a), such sentences may be translated with either singular or plural third-person subjects, except in the case of certain verbs whose subject's number is restricted to singular, plural, dual, or "triplural" (three or more), all of which exist in Chickasaw. Space limitations prevent me from giving such information in other cases here except where specifically relevant to the discussion.

6. In general, I will not comment on multiple translation possibilities unless it is relevant. This sentence could also have a subject 'she', 'it', or 'they'. Of the languages discussed below, only Garifuna has a European-like gender system.

7. The following abbreviations are used in glosses in this chapter: abs = absolutive suffix (Tolkapaya), acc = accusative, anim = animal, asp = aspect suffix (Maricopa), aux = auxiliary, B = base stem (Garifuna), D = D-series inflection (Garifuna), ds = different subject, form = formal, hab = habitual, I = I-series inflection (Chickasaw), II = II-series inflection (Chickasaw), instr = instrumental, irr = irrealis, loc = locative, m = masculine singular (Garifuna), neg = negative, obj = object, P = prefixable stem (Garifuna), pl = plural, pres = present, Q = interrogative, R = R-series inflection (Garifuna), sg = singular, T = T-series inflection (Garifuna). Person and number are indicated with 1, 2, 3 for person and s and p for singular and plural. A period is used to separate elements of certain complex glosses. The use of "&" in the glosses in §3.5 is explained in the text.

Except as explicitly indicated, all citations are in the orthography of the cited reference.

(2) (a) *Smáa.*   'He sleeps', 'She sleeps', 'It sleeps.'
        sleep
    (b) *Smáa-ch-i.*[8]   'They sleep.'
        sleep-pl-abs
    (c) *M-smáa!* 'Sleep!'
        2-sing
    (d) *Smáa-ha 'i.*   'He [etc.] wants to sleep.'
        sleep-irr say
    (e) *M-smáa-ha m-i.*   'You want to sleep.'
        2-sleep-irr 2-say

The dictionary form of the Tolkapaya verb 'sleep' is the unmarked *smáa.* But while this seems superficially similar to Chickasaw *nosi* (§2.1), the meanings of these two unmarked verbs are quite different. An unmarked Tolkapaya verb is really a third-person form; an unmarked Chickasaw verb, though it can be used as with third-person reference, is more similar to a neutral, non-person-marked, infinitive. (In other words, one could argue that Tolkapaya has a zero third-person morpheme, while this does not seem so clearly true of Chickasaw.) I will return to Tolkapaya verb entries in section 3.3 below and to the definitions of dictionary verb entries in section 5.

2.3. The Arawakan language Garifuna is rather different from Chickasaw, Tolkapaya, and other languages of the same type, in that a subject agreement affix must appear on the verb of almost all types of simple sentences. There are eight pronominal subject categories in Garifuna, all of which are always overt, marked by one of seven series of prefixed, infixed, or suffixed affixes in different constructions (see, e.g., Munro 1997).

All Garifuna verbs have two fundamental stems, the base stem and the prefixable stem, which may be identical, somewhat similar, or suppletive.[9] Base stems like *hóu* 'eat' and *hangi* 'be stingy'[10] are used, for

---

8. I return in §3.3 below to the question of the *-i* 'absolutive' suffix in plural verbs like that in (2b).

9. Other stem types (perhaps derivable from these) are used in other constructions and should certainly be listed in a complete dictionary. A weakness of Cayetano 1993 is that it does not list even both of these fundamental stems for all verbs and does not fully identify the type of the stems it does list. There are certainly some general heuristics for stem identification: for example, all prefixable stems are vowel-initial. However, it is not the case, for instance, that all vowel-initial stems are prefixable.

10. In Garifuna, the syntax of active and nonactive intransitive and transitive verbs (at least) is different in different constructions. With the examples above, using one active transitive and one nonactive intransitive verb, I exemplify only some possibilities.

example, in simple sentences like (3a, b), in which suffixed agreement follows the stem.

(3) (a) *Hóu-tina aba fáluma.*   'I ate a coconut.'
        eat.B-1sT one coconut
    (b) *Hángi-tina.*   'I'm stingy.'
        be.stingy.B-1sT

Prefixable stems like *éigi* 'eat' and *angi* 'be stingy' are used, for example, in negative sentences (4).

(4) (a) *M-éigi-tina aba fáluma.*   'I didn't eat a coconut.'
        neg-eat.P-1sT one coconut
    (b) *M-ángi-tina.*   'I'm not stingy.'
        neg-be.stingy.P-1sT

However, bare (unaffixed) base and prefixable stems are used in certain other constructions. For example, unaffixed base stems are used when followed by certain auxiliary verbs (5), and unaffixed prefixable stems are used in subject Wh questions (6).[11]

(5) (a) *Hóu ba-dina aba fáluma.*   'I will eat a coconut.'
        eat,B aux-1sD one coconut
    (b) *Hangi ba-dina.*   'I will be stingy.'
        be.stingy.B aux-1sD

(6) (a) *Ka éigi be-i aba fáluma?*   'Who [known to be masculine]
        wh eat.P aux-3mR one coconut ate a coconut?'
    (b) *Ka angi be-i?*   'Who [known to be masculine]
        wh be.stingy.P aux-3mR   is stingy?'

Probably because all Garifuna verb stems may occur in constructions like those in (5) and (6), E. Roy Cayetano (1993) lists uninflected verb stems like *hóu* and *éigi* 'eat', *hangi* and *angi* 'be stingy', and speakers are happy to accept these entry forms as independent words.[12]

3. AFFIXES AND OTHER ADDED MATERIAL IN ENTRY FORMS OF VERBS.
It is often difficult for the dictionary maker to decide which affixed verb stems merit inclusion in the dictionary. Often only derivational affixes

---

11. The mysterious Garifuna auxiliary *ba* (glossed here simply as 'aux'; *ba* becomes *be* before *-i*, as in (6)), which indicates future in sentences like (5), is also used in Wh constructions like those in (6).

12. A further problem that I will not address here, however, is that when speakers are asked for the "name" of a verb (e.g., with a question like *How do you say 'eat'?*), they often respond with a citation stem that is only sometimes like the base or prefixable stem. I am not sure how these citation stems are used grammatically.

(those whose meaning is sometimes unpredictable) appear on verbs listed in the dictionary. Some English dictionaries, for example, include simply lists of verbs with prefixes such as *un-*, without definitions, reflecting a tacit assumption that the meanings of such verbs are so predictable that they need not be given explicitly. Still, the verbs themselves are included because not all basic verbs accept the *un-* prefix; only certain potential *un-* verbs are in fact attested. In other languages, however, it seems appropriate to include verbs with inflectional markers in the dictionary.

3.1. A few American Indian languages have true "infinitive" forms, comparable to those in familiar European languages. In Creek (see Loughridge and Hodge 1890), for example, there is an infinitive suffix *-ita* (*-etv* in Loughridge and Hodge's orthography) that occurs on verbs in certain standard infinitival contexts, such as complements of 'want' and derived nominalizations, and that is felt by speakers to be the "name" of the verb—all of which makes these verbs comparable to European infinitives. Loughridge and Hodge's decision to list the *-etv* form of all verbs in the dictionary thus seems fully comparable to (and doubtless is motivated by) the decision of the makers of German or French dictionaries to list verbs with infinitive endings like German *-en* or French *-er, -ir,* or *-re.*

3.2. Many languages present problems quite similar to that of English *un-*, concerning which derived verbs must be listed in the dictionary. In Chickasaw, for example, there are no adpositions: relational ideas that are expressed in most languages with pre- or postpositions are conveyed by Chickasaw derived verbs with added (applicative) arguments. Thus in (7), *hilha* 'dance' is an intransitive verb; a locative argument may appear in a sentence with this verb only when licensed by the appearance on the verb of the locative applicative prefix *aa-*; in (8), *apa* 'eat' is a transitive verb; an instrumental argument of this verb must be licensed by the instrumental applicative prefix *isht-*.

(7) (a) *Hilha-li.*   'I dance.'
        dance-1sI
    (b) *Chokk-a͟ aa-hilha-li.*   'I dance at the house.'
        house-acc loc-dance-1sI

(8) (a) *Pishof-a͟ apa-li.*   'I eat pishofa (hominy and pork
        pishofa-acc eat-1sI   stew).'
    (b) *Folosh-a͟ pishofa isht-apa-li.*   'I eat pishofa with a spoon.'
        spoon-acc pishofa instr-eat-1sI

There are only two cases in Chickasaw, nominative and accusative (though sentences may have an unmarked second object, like *pishofa* in

(8b)); any noun phrase in a Chickasaw sentence must be licensed by a verb's original subcategorization or by *aa-*, *isht-*, or any of five other added applicative markers.[13]

Although the system of Chickasaw applicatives expresses semantic notions ('dance in', 'eat with') that would certainly not be included in most dictionaries, this system is clearly derivational rather than inflectional. The interaction of many applicatives with verbs must be lexically specified: some verbs occur only with certain applicatives, and others cannot take applicatives that seem semantically justified; the meaning of many applicative-plus-verb combinations is semantically unpredictable; and many such combinations have an exceptional phonological form. For these reasons, I decided to list in the Chickasaw dictionary (Munro and Willmond 1994) all applicative-verb combinations encountered.[14]

This treatment of Chickasaw applicatives is similar to that of English *un-* in another way as well. Whenever the morpheme chosen for inclusion in the dictionary is a prefix, it results in a skewed distribution of verb entries. Thus all locative applicative verbs in the Chickasaw dictionary begin with *aa-*, just as all English *un-* verbs begin with *u-*. This is useful for people who want to find examples of verbs containing these morphemes but tends to clump verbs together in certain parts of the dictionary (though both Chickasaw and English generally distribute their verbs fairly evenly throughout the alphabet). The skewing problem intensifies, as we will see in sections 4.1 and 4.2, in languages in which all verb entries begin with a very small number of sounds.

3.3. In some languages, some or all verbs never occur without some inflection. In a number of American Indian languages, this statement applies to all verbs, as I discuss in section 4 below. In others, it is true only of certain verbs.

For instance, in section 2.2 we saw that Tolkapaya Yavapai verbs like *smáa* 'sleep' can be listed in the dictionary in the unmarked stem form,

---

13. I have simplified this description. For instance, possessors of other arguments are not (in their most basic form) verbally licensed, and time phrases need not be licensed at all. Instrumental *isht-* is actually a clitic whose morphology is rather different from that of the other applicatives, though the same comments I make concerning its analysis apply. For more details, see Munro and Willmond 1994 and Munro 2000.

14. Although this was my plan, I know that I actually did not list many common ones whose meaning and form are entirely predictable. Boring locative and instrumental verbs like those in (7b) and (8b) tend not to appear in the dictionary, although I believe I listed all verbs encountered with dative *im-*, for example. It is never completely clear what the best solution to such a problem is.

the same form that can be used as one type of simple sentence with a third-person singular subject.

However, Tolkapaya verbs are not all so uncomplicated. Tolkapaya plural stems containing the plural subject suffix -*ch*, as in (2b) (repeated below), and all other Tolkapaya verb stems ending in consonants, such as *swáar-i* 'sing' and its plural, as in (9), occur in citation and simplest form with the "absolutive" suffix -*i*,[15] which is dropped before any consonantal suffix, as (9b) shows:

(2) (b) *Smáa-ch-i.*   'They sleep.'
         sleep-pl-abs

(9) (a) *Swáar-i.* 'He sings.'
         sing-abs
     (b) *Swáar-ch-i.*   'They sing.'
         sing-pl-abs

One could certainly list only stems in the dictionary, with *smáach, swáar,* and *swáarch*[16] alongside *smáa.* I made the decision to include absolutive -*i* in verb entries because it presents very little cost in terms of added space and because speakers do not consider *smáach, swáar, swáarch,* and the like, to be words (even though the language allows other consonant-final words, including some ending in *r* and *ch*). Thus Tolkapaya is different from the other languages considered so far, in that the form of Tolkapaya verb entries cannot be specified morphosyntactically (as the form used in a given construction) but differs according to the phonological shape of the verb stem.

3.4. Given a choice between several possible entry forms of a verb, dictionary makers often choose one that conveys useful inflectional information. This is true, for example, of the Romance infinitive forms referred to earlier: the information that the infinitive of an unfamiliar French verb ends in -*er,* -*ir,* or -*re* provides a guide as to how to inflect that verb.

In the Yuman language Maricopa, any verb may appear completely uninflected as the complement of a third-person subject sentence containing the uninflected auxiliary verb *v'ar* 'used to', such as (10a, b).

(10) (a) *Ashvaar v'ar-k.* 'He used to sing.'
         sing used.to-asp

---

15. The term and analysis are from Hardy 1979; this suffix and the comparable -*a* absolutive (citation) suffix on nouns bear no connection to absolutive case in an ergative system.

16. In fact, regular plural stems formed only by suffixation of -*ch* to the stem do not have separate entries in Munro and Fasthorse in preparation (they are listed, however, in the main entries for the nonplural verbs), although all plurals that are formed less regularly have their own entries.

(b) *Shmaa v'ar-k.*   'He used to sleep.'
sleep used.to-asp

But in almost all other constructions, verb stems such as *ashvaar* 'sing' and *shmaa* 'sleep' must be followed by one of two pervasive realis aspectual suffixes, *-k* or *-m* (Gordon 1986), as in

(11) (a) *Ashvaar-k.*   'He sings.'
sing-asp
(b) *Shmaa-m.*   'He sleeps.'
sleep-asp.m

The choice of *-k* versus *-m* is not based on phonological or semantic criteria (Gordon 1986) but seems to be an archaic feature dating back at least to Proto-River, Maricopa's branch of Yuman (see Munro and Gordon 1990; Munro 1981). Knowing whether a Maricopa verb is a *-k* verb or an *-m* verb is vital for construction of almost all sentences in the language: not only are *-k* or *-m* themselves used in the majority of constructions, but there are many other simple and complex constructions in which *-k* verbs behave differently from *-m* verbs (Gordon 1986). Consequently, in the Maricopa dictionary (Gordon, Heath, and Munro in preparation) either *-k* or *-m* is included in the dictionary entry of all verbs.[17]

3.5. Other devices can sometimes be used in dictionary entries to convey useful information about inflection. Tolkapaya Yavapai verbs, for example, can display a further complication. Most verbs affix pronominal prefixes like second-person *m-* at the beginning of the verb stem, as in (12) (cf. (2c)).

(12) *M-smáa.*   'You sleep.'
2-sleep

However, many Tolkapaya verbs include a procliticized element before the pronominal prefix. Consider the 'you' subject forms of the verbs in (13).

---

17. I believe this is absolutely the right decision for any dictionary of Maricopa or a similar language. Regrettably, I did not realize the importance of ascertaining the *-k* or *-m* form of Mojave verbs when doing my fieldwork on Mojave, a language in which the syntactic facts seem to be a bit murkier than in Maricopa (see Munro 1981). Both Judith Crawford and I recorded and checked verbs for our Mojave dictionary (Munro, Brown, and Crawford 1992) in the unsuffixed stem form, which in Mojave can be used in many more syntactic contexts than in Maricopa. Although I was able to retrieve a considerable amount of *-k* vs. *-m* data from my notes, some verbs in the dictionary unfortunately had to be listed without a final suffix.

(13) (a) *Ha-m-thpúy-i.*   'You swim.'
&-2-swim-abs
   (b) *'ich-m-wíiy-i.*   'You are rich.'
&-2-be.rich-abs
   (c) *Ya-m-páa.*   'You believe.'
&-2-believe
   (d) *'ar-m-yé.*   'You are happy.'
&-2-be.happy

Stress and other prosodic phenomena show the items in (13a–d) to be single phonological words, yet in these verbs, unlike *smáa* 'sleep', inflectional prefixes like second-person *m-* do not appear at the beginning of the verb word but rather before the second part of the verb. The sequences *ha . . . thpúyi, 'ich . . . wíiyi, ya . . . páa,* and *'ar . . . yé* mean 'swim', 'be rich', 'believe', and 'be happy'; without the initial proclitic elements, the verbs do not have these meanings, so in the glosses above I have written "&" as a gloss of these initial elements.

Such verbs have different analyses. The *ha* of *ha . . . thpúyi* 'swim' (13a) is clearly a shortened, incorporated form of the independent noun *'há* 'water', but this word is not pronounced in isolation wihout its initial glottal stop in Tolkapaya, and *thpúyi* has no meaning without *ha*. With many transitive verbs, *'ich* indicates an unspecified object 'something'. By itself, the verb *wíiyi* means 'have'. But *'ich . . . wíiyi* (13b) does not have the expected 'have something' meaning; the meaning 'be rich' is lexical or idiomatic. *Ya* is an initial proclitic element on complex verbs in many Yuman languages, almost certainly connected with the independent word *iiyá* 'mouth'. But although some proclitic *ya* verbs have a connection with the mouth, many are clearly very old formations (some reconstructable in this form for Proto-Yuman). The Tolkapaya verb *páa* means only 'lie in ambush for': clearly, the combination *ya . . . páa* 'believe' (13c) has an independent lexical status. Finally, neither of the two parts of *'ar . . . yé* 'be happy' (13d) occurs alone or indeed elsewhere in Tolkapaya.

In the Tolkapaya dictionary (Munro and Fasthorse in preparation), a * is used to mark the position of pronominal and other inflectional prefixes in complex verbs such as *ha*thpúyi* 'swim', *'ich*wíiyi* 'be rich', *ya*páa* 'believe', and *'ar*yé* 'be happy'. This usage was originated by Abraham Halpern (1947) for the presentation of verbs in the Yuma language (he called the material before the * an "adhering prefix").[18]

---

18. Similar information about Yuman complex verb structure is conveyed with the use of ellipses (. . .) by Shaterian (1983, for Yavapai generally) and by Gordon, Heath, and Munro (in preparation, for Maricopa). In this style, for example, the dictionary entry for the Tolkapaya verb 'swim' would be *ha . . . thpúyi.*

This style of presenting inflectional information constitutes a departure from the strict requirement that dictionary entries be ordinary words, since "*" is not a pronounceable word element. There would be other ways to present the information, of course. For example, along with third-person entry forms like *hathpúyi* or *'aryé* (which could just as easily be prefixed as infixed),[19] the entry might contain second-person subject forms like those above (i.e., *hamthpúyi* and *'armyé*). This approach would not be possible for all verbs, since not all verbs can be used with second-person subjects, so a better second form to include in such an entry might be, for example, a subordinate form containing *nya-* 'when', which also goes at the * position (before pronominal prefixes, if these are present) but which also requires final switch-reference marking (here, for different subject):

(14) (a) *ha-nya-thpúy-ma* . . .   'when he swam [different subject] . . .'
&-when-swim-ds

(b) *'ar-nya-yé-ma* . . .   'when he was happy [different
&-when-be.happy-ds   subject] . . .'

Such an approach could be used if the target community for the dictionary was unhappy with the appearance of * in dictionary entries, but might present its own problems.

4. VERB ENTRIES THAT MUST BE AFFIXED.   In this section, I consider three languages in which verbs never occur bare or unaffixed, in which, if the entries-are-words principle is to be followed, an inflected form must serve as the basic dictionary entry, plus a fourth language in which a large percentage of verbs present similar problems.

4.1. In the Iroquoian language Cherokee there are no zero pronominal markers, just as in Garifuna; moreover, the pronominal markers are prefixes, and there are to my knowledge no constructions at all in which verbs appear without pronominal marking. In their dictionary of Cherokee, Durbin Feeling and William Pulte (1975) list verbs like ga^2ti^3ha 'stab', $a^3go^2ni^3ha$ 'target practice', u^1dlv^3ga 'be sick', and ka^2ne^3ga 'speak' with

---

19. The verb *wa*hávi* 'be stingy', for example, which contains a proclitic *wa* (derived from *iiwá* 'heart', similarly to the *ya* in (13c)), can also appear as *wahávi*. Thus 'You are stingy' can be either *Wamhávi* or *Mwahávi*. There are reasons for believing that the second form is innovative (in particular, Yuman *w* really only occurs immediately before a stressed vowel or a vowel that was once stressed, as in the independent source for these proclitics), but synchronically both forms are acceptable, so given a third-person subject verb like *wahávi* it is not possible to predict the position of inflection.

third-person singular subject marking, in the form that these verbs appear in the following present tense examples:[20]

(15) (a) *Ga²tị³ha.*   'He's stabbing him.'
    (b) *A³go²nị³ha.*   'He's target practicing.'
    (c) *U¹dlv³ga.*   'He's sick.'
    (d) *Kạ²ne³ga.*   'He's speaking.'

Cherokee has a complicated inflectional system with two sets of pronominal markers, generally called A and B: in typical simple sentences, A prefixes usually mark active intransitive and transitive subjects, while B prefixes mark nonactive intransitive and some transitive subjects. The usual forms of the third-person A and B prefixes are *g(a)-* or *a-* and *u-*, respectively; these three prefixes are seen in (15a–c). In many Cherokee words, it is difficult to clearly represent phonemic analysis because of the operation of a pervasive metathesis rule (Flemming 1996) by which clusters of voiceless unaspirated stops become aspirated in combination with an *h* originating after a following vowel. The stem of Cherokee 'speak' is *hne³g,* but in (15d) the *h* of this stem metathesizes over the *a* of the prefix *ga-*, producing initial *k-* (the orthography writes voiceless unaspirated stops with "voiced" symbols and voiceless aspirated stops, phonemically sequences of unaspirated stops plus *h,* with "voiceless" symbols).

Thus, in the Cherokee dictionary, almost all verbs are listed under the letters *a, g, k,* and *u.*[21] The choice of the third-person form, while arbitrary, seems appropriate, first because all verbs, even those treated as subjectless in some languages—such as *a¹ga²sga* 'rain'—include one of these prefixes, and second because Cherokee seems to be a language in which verbs have no distinct citation "name."[22]

4.2. In the San Lucas Quiaviní Zapotec (SLQZ) language, pronominal markers are not prefixed, but verbs in all types of constructions must occur with one of seven "aspect" prefixes, which mark aspect, tense, and mood or modality. In making the SLQZ dictionary, I initially experimented with listing verbs in an unprefixed bare stem form, but this was not acceptable to my collaborator, Felipe H. Lopez, or to other native

---

20. Although Feeling and Pulte 1975 is an excellent (if too brief!) dictionary, I feel that its representation of tone with superscript numbers could be improved on (Munro 1996).

21. Some verbs are listed with initial prepronominal prefixes.

22. In my own work, I found that my Cherokee teacher Virginia Carey, when asked for the translation of an English verb (either bare or with infinitival *to*), might respond with one of the third-person subject forms in the text, with an imperative, or with some other inflected form. There seemed to be no conventional citation form.

speakers and in fact proved not to be feasible, since in a number of verb forms stems coalesce with the aspectual prefix, making identification of the unprefixed stem difficult, and many verbs have suppletive stems in different aspects.

In our dictionary (Munro and Lopez et al. 1999), we chose the habitual stem (marked with the prefix *r-*) as the basic entry form for verbs. Almost all verbs occur in the habitual (for those that do not, various other aspectual stems are listed), and the habitual prefix is the most regular of all the aspectual prefixes, all of the others of which have two or more allomorphic variations; further, speakers fairly easily become accustomed to thinking of the habitual as the "name" of a verb.[23] But our decision had a somewhat unfortunate aesthetic consequence: while the principal Cherokee verb entries are almost entirely restricted to just four initial letters, as discussed in section 4.1, all the main entries for SLQZ verbs start with *r*[24] (in fact, the words on well over a third of the pages of the Zapotec part of our dictionary begin with *r*).

In virtually all types of clauses, SLQZ verbs include either a nominal subject (as in (16a)) or one of nineteen pronominal subject clitics, several of which are exemplified for the verb *rzhùu'nny* 'run' in (16b–e).

(16) (a) *R-zhùu'nny bèe'cw.*   'The dog runs.'
           hab-run dog
      (b) *R-zhùu'nny-a'.*   'I run.'
           hab-run-1s
      (c) *R-zhùu'nny-yuu'.*   'You [sg. formal] run.'
           hab-run-2s.form
      (d) *R-zhùu'nny-èb.*   'He [someone who would be addressed
           hab-run-3s.form   formally] runs.'
      (e) *R-zhùu'nny-rëmm.*   'They [animals or children] run.'
           hab-run-3p.anim

Verbs are listed in our dictionary without a pronominal subject, as in (16a).[25]

4.3. Although verbs in some Uto-Aztecan languages (such as Hopi) do not exhibit subject person agreement, many Uto-Aztecan verbs are as highly inflected as those of Cherokee or SLQZ. In his 1571 dictionary

23. All other attested aspectual stems are listed at each main (habitual) entry in the dictionary, and any that exhibit unpredictable allomorphy are cross-referenced. For more about the making of the SLQZ dictionary, see Munro 1996.
24. Or *rr*, for words with the *r-* prefix added to an *r*-initial stem.
25. There are a few exceptions, such as idioms that are used only with certain (primarily expletive?) subjects.

of Classical Nahuatl, one of the first dictionaries of any language of the Americas, Fray Alonso de Molina uses a novel type of entry that combines a bare-stem form with explicit inflectional information, as in the sample entries in (17). (In these examples and others I have added quotes around the definition and English translations and italicized the entries.)

(17) (a) *temi.ni.* 'estar harto y repleto . . . ' ['to be full or replete . . . ']
    (b) *qua.nitla.* 'comer algo' ['to eat something']
    (c) *itotia.nin.* 'bailar, o dançar' ['to dance, or to dance']
    (d) *itta.niqu.* 'hallar lo que se auia perdido, o lo que se procura y busca, o mirar a otro' ['to search for that which had been lost, or that which one wants or tries to find, or to look at another']

The material following the period in the middle of these verb entry forms includes the following morphemes: first-person singular subject *ni-*, 'something' object *tla-*, first-person singular reflexive *nin-*, and third-person singular object *qu-*. Thus the entries succinctly convey the information that the first verb is intransitive, the second transitive (with, typically, an inanimate object), the third lexically reflexive, and the fourth transitive (with a potential animate object). However, the entries are not words: the stems *temi*, *qua*, *itotia*, and *itta* are not used alone, and the elements following them are prefixes, not suffixes. Molina's approach distributes verbs fairly evenly through the dictionary (rather than list almost all of them under *n-*, which would be the result of putting the prefixes listed with the verbs in (17) at the beginning of their words). It is easy for linguists and scholars to learn to use Molina's dictionary, but I do not know how native speakers received it.

4.4. Cahuilla is another Uto-Aztecan language whose verbs generally have pronominal agreement prefixes. Hansjakob Seiler and Kojiro Hioki's *Cahuilla Dictionary* (1979) lists all verbs in a bare-stem style with an initial hyphen, as in (18).

(18) (a) *-čéŋen-* 'to dance; . . . to kick'
    (b) *-kʷáʔ-* 'to eat'

Chem'ivillu' (Let's Speak Cahuilla) (Sauvel and Munro 1980) is a Cahuilla textbook, not a dictionary, but in its vocabulary we use a similar style for verb entries, in which "bare forms" are preceded by *. (As these examples show, we also adopted a keyboardable orthography.)

(19) (a) **chéngen* 'dance, kick'
    (b) **qwá* 'eat'

I do not recall the motivation that led to the use of this *, but it has a mnemonic value for linguists (since these forms are not acceptable as words on their own) and calls to the student's attention the fact that these forms are not affixes (which are written in the textbook with preceding or following hyphens) but stems that need something added. For instance, consider the following actual sentences (in the Sauvel and Munro orthography):

(20) (a) *Ne-chéngen-qa.*   'I am dancing.'
          1s-dance/kick-pres.sg

     (b) *Hem-chéngen-we.*   'They are dancing.'
          3p-dance/kick-pres.pl

     (c) *Pe-n-chéngen-qa.*   'I am kicking him.'
          3s.obj-1s-dance/kick-pres.sg

     (d) *Pe-n-qwá'-qa.*   'I am eating it.'
          3s.obj-1s-eat-pres.sg

Virtually all Cahuilla verbs must have a suffix of some type in almost all types of sentences; in many constructions, like the present duratives shown above, the suffix varies according to the number of the subject. Similarly, almost all Cahuilla verbs have a pronominal agreement prefix (whether or not a noun subject is present). Intransitive verbs with third-person singular subjects, as in (21a), present the only exception to this generalization; transitive verbs with all third-person singular arguments, as in (21b), still have a prefix:

(21) (a) *Chéngen-qa.*   'He is dancing.'
          dance/kick-pres.sg

     (b) *Pe-chéngen-qa.*   'He is kicking it.'
          3s.obj-dance/kick-pres.sg

I have not figured out the best way to list Cahuilla verbs in a user-friendly dictionary. Although the "bare form" approach shown in (19) (and Seiler and Hioki's analogue in (18)) was designed to make things easy for the student, I have learned since 1980 that many speakers are not at all happy to see nonwords like those in (18) and (19) in the dictionary. It is possible that the best course would be to list all verbs in occurring words (which might mean including suffixes like the *-qa* shown in most of the examples above). Thus intransitive verbs could be listed in unprefixed third-person present forms like (21a), and transitive verbs could be listed in *pe-* prefixed forms like (21b). But there would have to be at least four types of verb entries, not two, since some intransitive verbs (such as **múk* in (22a)) occur only with plural subjects, and some transitive verbs (such as **wén* in (22b)) occur only with plural objects:

(22) (a) *Hem-chéx-we.*   'They are sick.'
           3p-be.sick.pl-pres.pl
      (b) *Me-wén-qa.*   'He put them (there).'
           3p.obj-put.pl.obj-pres.sg

The difficulty of such decisions suggests that, where possible, dictionary consumers should be more closely involved in dictionary production. Sometimes understanding the issues involved makes users more tolerant of inevitable shortcomings in the final product.

4.5. The Siouan language Lakhota provides a final example of the difficulty of finding a single basic verb form for certain types of languages. Many different orthographies have been used for Lakhota; I will present the examples below in the orthography of Pamela Munro, Hannah Lefthand Bull Fixico, and Mary Rose Iron Teeth (1999).[26]

The most widely used dictionary of Lakhota is Father Eugene Buechel's (1983). Buechel's dictionary entries consist of an entry verb plus a definition, usually followed by parenthesized forms showing inflection, as in the examples in (23) (respelled, with some definitions shortened):

(23) (a) *aphá* 'to strike or smite' (*awápha, amápha, unkáphapi*)
      (b) *ináxma* 'to hide [intr.]' (*ináwaxma*)
      (c) *itómni* 'drunk' (*imátomni*)
      (d) *kté* 'to kill' (*wakté, makté*)
      (e) *t'á* 'to die' (*mat'á*)
      (f) *thánka* 'large' (*mathánka*)
      (g) *xwá* 'sleepy' (*maxwá*)

These examples reveal some important facts. For example, Lakhota is an active language, with two types of inflection for intransitive verbs (*wa-* marks an 'I' subject for intransitive active verbs; *ma-* marks an 'I' subject for intransitive nonactive verbs) that are also used with transitives (*wa-* is used for a transitive 'I' subject, *ma-* for a transitive 'me' object).[27] (Buechel gives adjectival verbs

26. This is the most recent revision of a set of lessons developed for use in a class on American Indian languages at the University of California, Los Angeles; it contains a vocabulary from which the lexical examples in the text are taken. I have used this orthography even for citing words from Buechel 1983 because the spellings in Buechel are difficult to reproduce typographically and often inconsistent; I am concerned here only with how information is conveyed in the dictionary, not (at this point) with how things are spelled.

27. Lack of space has prevented discussion of similar conjugational issues for each language considered here. The Garifuna examples, for example, revealed that different pronominal affix series are used in different Garifuna constructions. Chickasaw is a language whose inflection works quite similarly to that of Lakhota. And so on. At this point, I am primarily interested in how the dictionary shows that inflection is added in an unexpected position.

an adjective translation, where I would parallel his verbal translations with, for example, 'to be drunk', 'to be large', or 'to be sleepy'; these are full verbs taking all normal verbal inflection.) Moreover, pronominal prefixes like *ma-* and *wa-* may either appear at the beginning of a verb stem (as in (23d–f)) or be infixed (as in (23a–c)), in much the same way that we saw pronominal prefixes infixed in some Tolkapaya verbs in section 3.5.[28]

However, the entries in (23) do not all have the same status as full words (according to my work with two Lakhota speakers). Consider the third-person singular and plural subject forms of the verbs in (24).

(24) (a) *aphé* 'he hits him', *aphápi* 'they hit him'
    (b) *ináxme* 'he hides', *ináxmapi* 'they hide'
    (c) *itómni* 'he is drunk', *itómnipi* 'they are drunk'
    (d) *kté* 'he kills it', *ktépi* 'they kill it'
    (e) *t'é* 'he dies', *t'ápi* 'they die'
    (f) *thánka* 'he is big', *thankíyanpi* 'they are big'[29]
    (g) *xwá* 'he is sleepy', *xwápi* 'they are sleepy'

This small selection of data illustrates that there are three classes of Lakhota verbs. Those whose stems end in vowels other than *a* (e.g., *itómni*, *kté*) may be used alone as complete sentences and form their plurals simply by suffixation of *-pi*. "Nonablaut" verbs ending in *a*, such as *thánka* and *xwá*, work like the first group. "Ablaut" verbs in *a*, such as *aphá*, *ináxma*, and *t'á*, must change their final *a* to *e* in order to form a complete sentence. Note that for *a*- and *e*-final stems of these two groups, neither the singular nor the plural forms in (24) are sufficient to show which group a verb belongs to. Although there are some morphological cues to ablaut status, this feature, like the position of inflection, is relatively unpredictable. (The facts I report here are for women's speech and vary for younger speakers, who, for example, more often mark the plural with *-p* than with *-pi*. However, all speakers, male and female, younger and older, must know which verbs are ablaut verbs.)

These verbs can be used in the *a*-final stem form before many suffixes and clitics, as in (25), but are not used alone.

(25) *Aphá he?*   'Did he hit him?'
    hit Q

When speakers are asked to translate English verbs like the glosses in (23), they sometimes give ablaut verbs in the final *a* form (e.g., *aphá*,

28. Albright 1999 provides a thorough description of the position of Lakhota infixed subject prefixes.

29. *Thánka* has an irregular plural stem. Other Lakhota verbs form their plural in other ways, such as by reduplication.

ináxma) but in my experience more commonly give the ablauted final *e* form (e.g., *aphé, ináxme*). Thus the independent word status of ablaut verbs with final *a* seems to be dubious.

Buechel's style of dictionary entry, then, while using supplementary examples to show the position of inflection, fails to reveal which verbs are ablaut verbs. Munro, Fixico, and Iron Teeth (1999) list a vocabulary of verbs in a way that conveys both the position of inflection and the verb's ablaut status. Our entries for the verbs above are as follows:

(26) (a) *a*phá/é* 'to hit'[30]
      (b) *iná*xma/e* 'to hide'
      (c) *i*tómni* 'to be drunk'
      (d) *kté* 'to kill'
      (e) *t'á/é* 'to die'
      (f) *thánka* 'to be big'
      (g) *xwá* 'to be sleepy'

We use a * to mark the position of inflection just as explained above for Tolkapaya (§2.5), and we write ablaut verbs with a final *a/e*. (The type of inflection is indicated by a parenthesized feature elsewhere in the entry.) This type of entry is thus rather abstract, since * and *"a/e"* are not sounds of Lakhota. This degree of abstraction seems useful, but it remains to be seen whether it would be appropriate for a dictionary to be used extensively by native speakers and other nonacademics.

5. TRANSLATIONS FOR VERB ENTRIES.

5.1. I translated most of the examples above rather deliberately with bare English verbs (*to*-less infinitives), except when quoting infinitival translations from actual dictionaries (in §§4.3–4.5). In general, it seems to be a dictionary maker's choice whether to include *to* with infinitival definitions in dictionaries.

Native English speakers I have worked with often feel that including *to* in definitions seems more dictionary-like, and using the *to* style of verb definition is helpful in that it helps to establish the part of speech of the defined word (since many English words may be used either as nouns or as verbs). I have used *to* in the verb definitions in most dictionaries I have worked on (exceptions are discussed below).

But an infinitival translation may not be appropriate for all types of verb entry words. A comparison of the Chickasaw and Tolkapaya examples (1c)

---

30. As Buechel's third parenthesized item in (23a) shows, the first-person plural *unk-* prefix is prefixed, not infixed, with this verb. Any system will have to display this additional information for verbs with similar paradigms.

and (2d) (repeated below) shows that while 'to sleep' can be an accurate translation for Chickasaw *nosi,* in a Tolkapaya 'want' construction the irrealis suffix *-ha* is needed to convey the infinitive-ness of the 'want' complement: it is not clear whether 'to sleep' is really a good translation for Tolkapaya *smáa.*

(1) (c) *Nosi banna.*   'He wants to sleep.'
          sleep want
(2) (d) *Smáa-ha 'i.*   'He [etc.] wants to sleep.'
          sleep-irr say

I am not sure if there are any constructions in which unsuffixed Tolkapaya verbs may be translated as infinitives, so it is possible that I should reconsider the *to* style of verb entry definition currently used by Munro and Fasthorse (in preparation).

The argument for using *to* for a bare-stem definition, even for a language like Tolkapaya where this translation may never be strictly appropriate, is that a bare stem is used in a variety of contexts and with a variety of affixes, and the *to* form seems like an appropriate (somewhat abstract) "name" for the verb. The situation changes when the dictionary entry form carries affixes with more content than the phonologically induced absolutive that appears with consonant-final verbs in Tolkapaya (§2.5). For example, no *to* is used in the definitions in the dictionaries of Maricopa and Mojave (Gordon, Heath, and Munro in preparation; Munro, Brown, and Crawford 1992), which are languages whose structure is quite similar to that of Tolkapaya—but with a crucial difference. In these languages, verbs appear with a realis aspect suffix, something with a clear noninfinitival meaning (§3.4). This suffix is not retained when the verbs are used in other contexts. Therefore, the abstraction of an infinitival translation does not seem appropriate.

5.2. Similarly, in Feeling and Pulte's Cherokee dictionary (1975), the verb entries are fully inflected present tense verbs with third-person singular subjects (among the most highly inflected verb entry forms I am familiar with). Entirely appropriately, the definitions they use for the examples in (15) (repeated here) are the full translations for these sentences given below.

(15) (a) *Ga²ti̧³ha.*   'He's stabbing him.'
      (b) *A³go²ni̧³ha.*   'He's target practicing.'
      (c) *U¹dlv³ga.*   'He's sick.'
      (d) *Ka̧²ne³ga.*   'He's speaking.'

5.3. San Lucas Quiaviní Zapotec presents a somewhat subtler problem. Consider (16a), repeated below as (27a), and the corresponding plural subject sentence (27b).

(27) (a) *R-zhùu'nny bèe'cw.*   'The dog runs.'
           hab-run dog
      (b) *R-zhùu'nny ra bèe'cw.*   'The dogs run.'
           hab-run pl dog

As these sentences illustrate, the SLQZ habitual verb *r-zhùu'nny*, which has
no pronominal clitic, can be used with any noun subject, whether singular or plural. (Any pronoun subject is indicated with a clitic pronoun, as
in (16b–e). An SLQZ verb must have a subject of some sort, either nominal or pronominal.)

When I first began working on the SLQZ dictionary, I translated entries
like *r-zhùu'nny* with English unaffixed verbs like 'run' (in other words, with
to-less infinitives). And 'run' is one of the translations of the verb (in (27b)).
However, as I later realized, there are two problems with this approach.[31]

First, consider less active verbs,[32] such as

(28) (a) *R-de'ts cotoony*   'The shirt is inside out.'
           hab-be.inside.out shirt
      (b) *R-de'ts ra cotoony*   'The shirts are inside out.'
           hab-be.inside.out pl shirt

The *to*-less infinitive translation for the verb *r-de'ts* would be 'be inside out'.
But unlike the situation with *r-zhùu'nny*, neither sentence in (28) uses such
a translation for the verb. 'Be inside out' is probably not a good translation for an inflected verb whose meaning is explicitly simple present.

The second problem concerns grammatical number. When we began
to prepare Spanish translations for the entries in our trilingual dictionary,
I realized that the differences between the Spanish and English translations of the sentences in (27) (given as (29)) have important consequences for the dictionary:

(29) (a) *R-zhùu'nny bèe'cw.*   'The dog runs. | El perro corre.'
           hab-run dog
      (b) *R-zhùu'nny ra bèe'cw.*   'The dogs run. | Los perros corren.'
           hab-run pl dog

What this suggests is that if indeed we choose 'run' as the dictionary definition of *r-zhùu'nny*, then (since this is the English plural form, as in
(29b)) the corresponding Spanish definition should be 'corren'. But

31. I am particularly grateful to Michael Galant, who helped me to understand the first
problem mentioned here, and to Olivia V. Méndez and everyone else who helped with the
Spanish translations in Munro, Lopez et al. 1999, for contributing to my understanding of
the second.

32. The majority of verbs that are stative in other aspects have an inceptive translation
in the habitual, but this is not always the case.

unlike 'run', which (though paradigmatically plural, for a noun subject) seems somehow neutral and unmarked, 'corren' is very explicitly plural. It does not seem right to define a verb that will most commonly be used with a singular subject with an English (or Spanish) plural verb. Therefore, we decided to define SLQZ habitual verbs in the dictionary with third-person singular simple presents. Therefore, *r-zhùu'nny* is defined as 'runs | corre', and *r-de'ts* as 'is inside out | está al revés'.[33]

5.4. In light of these considerations, Molina's Nahuatl dictionary entries and their translations (such as (17b), repeated below) seem a bit schizophrenic:

(17) (b) *qua.nitla.* 'comer algo' ['to eat something']

Molina exemplifies inflection of the verbs he lists by giving their first-person singular subject forms immediately following the verb stem. From this, one can derive concrete examples of inflected forms like

(30) *Ni-tla-qua.*   'I eat something.'
    1s-something-eat

But Molina's definition in (17b) is a full Spanish infinitive, a highly abstract translation. This seems somewhat unsatisfying.

6. CONCLUSION.   Deciding what form of a verb to enter in a dictionary is very easy for a language such as English (which has truly uninflected verbs). But for many languages, making this decision is very difficult and may raise new problems involving the translation of the entry form. The form of an entry and its translation should harmonize: if the entry is abstract (a true base form, with no inflection), an infinitival translation (even one with *to*) seems appropriate and even desirable, but if the best dictionary entry is an inflected verb, it should probably be translated as closely as possible.

This conclusion calls into question the long-established practice of using *to*-less infinitives (e.g., including *be*) as definitions of basic verb forms in many languages. Such an approach may not always be correct.

---

33. In fact, some verbs restricted to plural subjects do have plural definitions.

CHAPTER FIVE

Multiple Assertions, Grammatical Constructions, Lexical Pragmatics, and the *Eastern Ojibwa-Chippewa-Ottawa Dictionary*

Richard A. Rhodes

1. INTRODUCTION. In this chapter I discuss a class of problems that arose in the attempt to develop accurate and consistent glosses during the making of the *Eastern Ojibwa-Chippewa-Ottawa Dictionary* (*EOCOD;* Rhodes 1985). My intent was to gloss Ojibwe[1] words in such a way that a modestly sophisticated user of the dictionary would arrive at natural-sounding English translations of Ojibwe based straightforwardly on the glosses given. This seems a fairly minimal demand to make of a bilingual dictionary. However, given how thoroughly different Ojibwe lexical structure is from English, the task proved to be quite difficult and required compromises of various sorts, some of which are not altogether satisfactory. The most significant problems are (1) the multiple assertion problem, (2) the constructional meaning problem, and (3) the pragmatic norms problem. I proceed by sketching what each of these problems is and then by explaining how the dictionary was designed and how that design fared in the face of these problems.

2. THE MULTIPLE ASSERTION PROBLEM. Most Ojibwe verbs are structurally types of compounds that assert complex meanings that can often be fully expressed only in multiple English clauses. For example, the typical Ojibwe verb expressing a simple change of state has two parts, one expressing the resultant state and one expressing the causal mode by which the change of state is effected. Thus the Ojibwe sentence and its English translation in (1) are equally pragmatically appropriate to refer

---

1. There are many spellings for this language name, including *Ojibwa, Ojibway, Ojibwe, Chippewa, Chippeway.* Its native pronunciation is ['ŭdʒɪbŭeː].

to a large class of real-world situations. But the English gloss in (1) is much less specific than the Ojibwe.

(1) *Ngii-bkibdoon biiwaabkoons.*[2] 'I broke the wire.' (lit. 'I pulled the wire and broke it.')

ni-	gii=	bak(i)-[3]	bi-	d-	oo-	-n
1PERS	PAST	**broken (of stringlike objects)**	**push/ pull**[4]	INAN STEM	INAN OBJ	AGR

Several observations are in order here. First, the meanings of the two parts of the Ojibwe compound as well as the whole compound itself are equally available for negation: that is, (2) has three distinct possible readings.

(2) *Gaawiin ngii-bkibdoosiin.*   (a) 'I pulled on it, but it didn't break (stringlike object).'
   (b) 'I broke it but not by pulling on it (stringlike object).'
   (c) 'I didn't pull on it or break it (stringlike object).'

gaawiin	ni-	gii=	bak(i)-	bi-	d-	oo-
not	1PERS	PAST	**broken (of stringlike objects)**	**push/pull**	INAN STEM	INAN OBJ

sii-	-n
NEG	INAN OBJ

This means that neither part of the verb is presupposed. Similar phenomena are found in many other, unrelated Amerindian languages, particularly in Hokan, Penutian, and Wakashan. (See the discussions in Jacobsen 1980 for Washo and in DeLancey 1996, 1999, for Klamath and neighboring languages.) William Jacobsen and Scott DeLancey use the term "bipartite stem" to refer to the morphological construction, but I will use the term "multiple assertion" to refer to the semantic phenomenon just discussed, which arises with bipartite stems.

---

2. *biiwaabkoons* 'wire'.

3. Parenthesized vowels are epenthetic.

4. The meaning of this morpheme is approximately 'induce a unidirectional motion over a path that lies entirely within the visual field'. It contrasts with other morphemes that assert back-and-forth motion and ones that assert unbounded unidirectional motion. For accessibility of reading, we use the shorthand gloss 'push/pull'. In some compounds it can be used idiomatically to mean 'tie', as in the examples in (5) below, where we gloss it in that meaning.

Second, because the phenomenon of multiple assertion is very reminiscent of Leonard Talmy's (1985) well-known notion of semantic conflation, it is worth pointing out that it is not the same. Talmy points out that languages differ as to which kinds of information are grouped (conflated) into (relevantly) monomorphemic stems. Talmy's work focuses on motion verbs, which he analyzes as containing six possible parameters, agent, theme, motion, path, manner, and deixis. He asserts that there are two types of languages depending on which of these parameters are conflated and realized in a single morpheme. For example, in the English phrase *run in,* manner and motion are conflated in *run* and *in* specifies the path, but in the Spanish translation of this phrase, *entrar corriendo,* the motion and path are conflated in *entrar* 'go in', and the manner, *corriendo* 'running', is separate. In focusing on these two types of languages, Talmy leaves out a third type, in which there is essential compounding. Ojibwe is of this third type. The translation of 'run in' in Ojibwe is a bipartite stem, a compound of two morpheme complexes[5] as shown in (3).

(3) *Gii-biindgebtoo* 'He ran in'

gii=	*biindige-*			*-batoo-*			*-w*
PAST	enter			run			3SUBJ
biind-	*ig-*	*e-*		*bah-*	*d-*	*oo-*	
in	build-	PROCESS		run	INAN	DUMMY	
	ing			from	STEM	OBJ	

Each conflates motion with another parameter; *biindige-* 'enter' conflates path and motion, while *-batoo-* 'run' conflates manner and motion.

It is exactly this type of compounding that is at the heart of the multiple assertion problem. The consequence is that in general, ordinary Ojibwe usage demands verbs that are more specific than ordinary English usage. Consider the following sentence drawn from one of the texts in the corpus used to create the dictionary.

(4) *Mii dash gii-zhaad widi ezhi-gomnid niw zhiishiiban gii-bbaa-zgigaadeb-*
   naad kina nnaazh go kina gii-dkobjiged iw sabaab.
   'Then he went where those ducks were swimming and went around tying them all by the legs until he had used the whole cord.' (Bl 38.8)[6]

5. As is frequently the case in languages with a high degree of morphological complexity, there are idiomatic combinations of morphemes that function as stable complexes that behave as if they were monomorphemic; e.g., they appear at the same points in structure as single morphemes. Thus *biindgebtoo* 'run in' contains the complex *biind-ig-e-* 'enter' and *zaagbatoo* 'run out' contains the single morpheme *zaag-* 'out' in the same structure slot. The complexes here are thoroughly idiomatic. One can *biindige-* any enclosure; it need not be a building, and *-batoo-* has no sense of running from anything.

6. Citations from Bloomfield (1957) texts are given in the form (Bl text number.sentence number).

Mii	*dash*	*gii-zhaad*	*widi*	*ezhi-gomnid*
EMPH	then	he-went-to	where	they-swim

niw	*zhiishiiban*	*gii-bbaa-zgigaadebnaad*		
those	ducks	he-went-around-tying-their-legs		

kina	*nnaazh*	*go*	*kina*	*gii-dkobjiged*
all	until	EMPH	all	he-used-it-to-tie

iw	*sabaab.*			
that	cord.			

Of interest are the last two verbs, *gii-bbaa-zgigaadebnaad* '[he] went about tying them by the legs' and *gii-dkobjiged* 'he had used it in tying [them]'. As shown in the morpheme-by-morpheme glosses in (5), both Ojibwe verbs are more specific than their English translations in (4) (repeated here) suggest.

(5) (a) *gii-bbaa-zgigaadebnaad* '[he] went about tying them by the legs'

gii=	*bibaa=*	*zag(i)-*
PAST	[go] around	firm

gaade-	***bi**-n=*	*aa-d*
leg	**tie**-AN	AGREEMENTS

   (b) *gii-dkobjiged* 'he had used it in tying [them]'

gii=	*dakw(i)-*	***bi**-d-*	*ige-*	*-d*
PAST	together	**tie**-INAN	INDEF OBJ	3SUBJ

Now someone might claim that a more accurate translation of the relevant portion of (4) should read as in (6).

(6) ' . . . and went about tying them all firmly by the legs until he had used all the cord to tie [them] together.'

But that misses the point that bilinguals almost always translate as in (4) rather than as in (6). That is, the relatively high specificity is the only option in Ojibwe, but it sounds marked in English.

From the point of view of the lexicographer, an important consideration in assembling an accurate bilingual dictionary is to get the norms of usage to match. But the normal Ojibwe verb is a bipartite compound and asserts what in English would require two verbs (and hence two clauses or clause fragments) or at least a verb and an adverb. To get ordinary English-sounding usage, the dictionary will have to surpress, or at least background, part of the asserted meaning of most Ojibwe verbs.

3. THE CONSTRUCTIONAL MEANING PROBLEM. Until relatively recently, it has not been recognized that (morpho)syntactic constructions themselves can bear lexical-like meanings. The work of Charles J. Fillmore,

Paul Kay, and Catherine O'Connor (1988) and Adele Goldberg (1995) makes compelling arguments for this position. For example, Goldberg makes extensive arguments that part of the meanings of the sentences in (7) (from Goldberg 1995: 9) cannot sensibly be assigned to the verbs but actually reside in the constructions.

(7) (a) *He sneezed the napkin off the table.* (cause-motion construction)
     (b) *She baked him a cake.* (benefactive-recipient construction)
     (c) *Dan talked himself blue in the face.* (resultative construction)

Briefly put, the heart of the argument is that *sneeze* and *talk* are not tran-sitive verbs, nor is *bake* ditransitive. The adjustment of transitivity and the meaning associated with it in each case are part of the construction. For example, in (7a) *sneeze* is neither transitive nor a verb of motion. The motion and the transitivity are in the construction: V NP LOC[+path]. *Sneeze* is simply construable as a possible cause of motion. Thus one can say, in the same construction, *They laughed him off the stage,* because one can easily con-strue laughing as causing the motion but not as a motion verb.

This point that constructions can bear meaning is theoretically controversial because most currently popular formal theories treat constructions as purely epiphenomenal and as a result cannot recognize constructional meaning. It should be noted, however, that there are other theories in the literature that recognize constructions can bear meaning independent of the lexical items used in them, namely, Montague grammar, the semantic theory of Anna Wierzbicka (esp. 1988), and the framework articulated by Ray Jackendoff (1990). A brief discussion is provided by Goldberg (1995: 219 ff.), who also gives extensive arguments about constructional meaning in English.

Once it is recognized that constructions can bear meaning, it is not surprising to find that there exist Ojibwe constructions bearing meanings that are expressed in English by lexical means. A particularly clear exam-ple is given in (8).

(8) *Manj go naa ge-kidwaambaanenh.* 'I don't know what I would say.'
     (lit. 'what I would say', a sentence fragment.)

amanj	*go naa*	*ge-*	*ikido-*
whether	EMPH	FUT	say-thus-

w-	*aan-*	*baan-*	*enh*
IRREALIS-	1pers-sg-	preterite-	dubitative

(CONSTRUCTION: subordinating Q-word + dubitative = 'I don't know Q . . . ')

The problem for the lexicographer, then, is how to represent construc-tional meaning in a dictionary entry. I will return to a particularly thorny example later.

4. THE LEXICAL PRAGMATIC PROBLEM.   The third, and, in some ways, most problematic difficulty in preparing a bilingual dictionary for languages as remote from each other as English and Ojibwe is that the normative views of analogous situations are not commensurate. This means that glossing particular words in natural English often obscures rather than elucidates the language-internal logic of Ojibwe. Consider the expression for hunting in Ojibwe, given in (9).

(9) *Giiwse.* 'He's hunting.' (lit. 'He's walking in loops.')
    giiw-   *ose-*   *w*
    curled-   walk-   3PERS

To an English speaker, (9) appears to be utterly idiomatic, the way *by and large* is.[7] But this is not the case at all. To understand this expression, one needs to know that hunting for individual large game animals in the Subarctic involves walking in loops on the downwind side of fresh animal tracks until one has passed the animal and then doubling back in loops until one locates the prey.[8] For this reason, (9) is not completely idiomatic but rather has a transparent logic to a cultural insider—although it is idiomatic in the sense that it cannot now be used in its literal sense outside of highly loaded contexts. That is, the pragmatics of *giiwsed* matches the pragmatics of *hunt,* but the way *giiwsed* means what it means is clear to an Ojibwe speaker and thus the literal meaning is simultaneously available for jokes or literary allusion in a way that is difficult to make clear in a simple dictionary entry.

Now let me turn to a discussion of the problems as I understood them at the time the database underlying the *EOCOD* was created and how that shaped the dictionary. When I was building the dictionary database, I was aware only of the multiple assertion problem, but the attempt to create a database structure that would handle that problem led to the discovery and, to some extent, the understanding of the other two problems. So let me turn to a brief overview of how I structured the database that lay behind the *EOCOD.*

5. THE STRUCTURE AND HISTORY OF THE *EOCOD* DATABASE.   In an attempt to deal fundamentally with the massive structural differences between Ojibwe and English, I designed the structure of the database underlying the *EOCOD* so that the level of equivalence between Ojibwe and English sat relatively high. That is, rather than looking for word equivalences,

---

7. Of course, *by and large* has a semantically sensible history itself, coming from the nautical language of sailing days, but no one now knows that without having looked it up.

8. A very brief description of this method can be found in Rogers and Smith 1981: 133, fig. 3.

I determined to look at phrase or clause level equivalences and then index those equivalences by key words. These key words and their part of speech together served as the citation forms on which entries were based. The very nature of Ojibwe words forced such an approach, in that the vast majority of Ojibwe verbs gloss not into English words but into English phrases. This is obvious even in earlier Ojibwe-English dictionaries, most notably Baraga (1878). So, for example, the entry for *waabshkiiwed* is linked to the following two English entries (only the relevant parts are cited):

> **skin** *n* . . . ;   **have white skin** waabshkiiwed *vai.*
> **white** *aj* . . . ; **be white [in race]**   waabshkiiwed *vai;* **have one's skin turn white** waabshkiiwed *vai;* **have white skin** waabshkiiwed *vai;* . . .

A schematic diagram of the structure of the records in the database that underlies the cited parts of these entries is given in figure 5.1. In figure 5.1 the Ojibwe *waabshkiiwed* is equated to three English phrases: 'be white [in race]', 'have one's skin turn white', and 'have white skin'. At the same time *waabshkiiwed* is indexed by the citation form [waabshkiiwed | *vai*], so that when the citation form is called up, the three glosses are brought up with it, as indicated schematically in figure 5.2. Similarly, as shown in figure 5.3, on the English side, when [white | *aj*] is called up, the English phrases come along with the Ojibwe gloss *waabshkiiwed*.

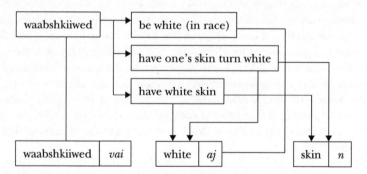

Figure 5.1. Schematic of Links from Ojibwe to English Equivalents.

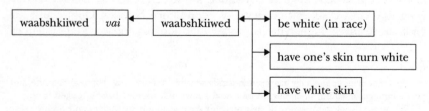

Figure 5.2. Schematic of Links from Citation Form.

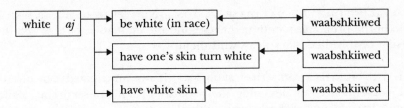

Figure 5.3. Schematic of Links from English Equivalents to Ojibwe.

The software used to implement this structure was a crude (1960s-vintage) relational database system written in Fortran. It was originally designed for maintaining a parts inventory for NASA and had the primary advantage of being in the public domain at a time when relational database technology was young and proprietary systems were expensive. The relational design allowed me to keep the various logically distinct kinds of information in separate files so that the computer would enforce consistency when new data were entered and when corrections in the data were made.

When the data were entirely loaded into the database management system and appropriately corrected, the two halves of the dictionary were created by generating two different reports (in the database sense). One was based on the Ojibwe citation forms and the other on English citation forms. Each report was designed to include the formatting instructions for fonts, paragraph shape, and header information in the TEX typesetting language, and the camera-ready copy was produced by feeding proofread versions of these reports directly to a typesetting machine. In actual practice very little correction needed to be made to the reports.

There were, however, some technical problems, including an important one whose full consequences were not discovered until after the publication of the book. Because the program was designed for doing parts inventory, the amount of information in many individual records was more, and the total number of records was greater in the dictionary application, than in the NASA application. This meant that we overflowed buffers in the system and lost data. But Fortran gives no warning of buffer overflow, so we did not know at what point this happened, nor did we realize the extent of the data lost, which may have run as high as 5 percent. Some corrections were made and many items were restored, but this happened very late in the process and the deadlines prevented a full rechecking of the database. The result is that there are many words in my notes that are missing from the dictionary. These include many words in the glossary to "Chippewa-Ottawa Texts" (Fox, Soney, and Rhodes 1988) and, most unfortunately, the culturally important word (for white Americans at least), *giimoozaabi* 'masked man' (= *Kemosabe*, what Tonto called the Lone Ranger).

6. EVALUATING THE DATABASE DESIGN.   Now let us turn to a discussion of the problems mentioned above and the evaluation of how well the design of this dictionary deals with them.

6.1. THE MULTIPLE ASSERTION PROBLEM.   It was anticipated that one of the consequences of designing the database around phrasal equivalents would be that Ojibwe verbs with multiple assertions would be correctly indexed in the English section of the dictionary under both assertions. However, at the time the database was indexed, I came to be of the opinion that one of the assertions—the one associated with the part of the verb Algonquianists call "the final"—was semantically primary and that the second assertion could be treated in translation as backgrounded in some way. Therefore, although the mechanisms were available for fully indexing both assertions, in fact, the Ojibwe verbs are indexed in the *EOCOD* under only one keyword, reflecting what I believed to be the primary assertion for the purposes of translation. I now believe that this is an incorrect procedure and the forms should be more thoroughly indexed.

Nonetheless, aware of the multiple assertion problem, I developed a system intended to account for the material to be suppressed in translation using square brackets. In the prefatory section of the *EOCOD* is a paragraph discussing the use of square brackets in glosses.

> They are intended to suggest that the material they enclose is parenthetical, redundant, or highly marked (in the linguistic sense) in English usage, but is asserted in Ojibwa.
>   **waabshkiiwed** *vai* be white [in race], have one's skin turn white, have white skin; *pres* **nwaabshkiiwe;** *cc* **e-waa=bshkiiwed, yaabshkiiwed.**
>   (Rhodes 1985: xvi)

In retrospect, this approach was altogether too simplistic for the range of phenomena it was intended to cover. Let me note four distinct cases.

First, the case this device was intended for is multiple assertion in a bipartite stem. In this case both meanings are available to be negated, as in (2) above. But, depending on the particular form, I sometimes used the brackets to mark the information in the first part of the stem as suppressible, as in *maajiiwnaad* 'take s.o. [away]' (*maajii-* 'leaving, away') but more often to mark the information in the second part of the stem as suppressible, as in *jiibhang* 'nudge s.t. [with an instrument]' (*-ah-* 'act with an instrument').

The second case in which I used square brackets is one in which there is an English ambiguity not present in a bipartite stem. An example would be *waabshkiiwed* 'be white [in race]' (*waabishk-* 'white', *-iiwe-* 'have a body'), where the bipartite stem is of a different class (of a type discussed in section 6.2, on constructional meaning). For example, in this class of bipartite stem, the parts are not equally available to negation. The problem in glossing that the brackets were intended to convey is that *waabshkiiwed* can only refer to "white" as a racial term but at the same time to indicate that in the English translation "race" need not be explicitly mentioned.

The third case is that of English ambiguity not supported by any feature of Ojibwe. An example is *gnawaajchigan* 'blaze [on a trail]'. Here there is an entity familiar in both English and Ojibwe, but the English term "blaze" needs to be disambiguated—which the bracketed information does. Again, in general usage, the context will allow the bracketed information to be suppressed.

The fourth case is that of a syntactic property, for example, *naabsing* 'cling to [something]'. In this case, *naabsing* has a syntactic frame that allows (but does not require) a core locative. The use of square brackets here is a matter of inconsistency. In the animate subject form, the brackets are not used, but the syntactic property is indicated with a metalinguistic comment given in italics, *naabshing* 'cling to something *with locative*'. The use of italics is actually the consistent way to express such syntactic properties in this dictionary, although I almost always used the square brackets rather than italics in parentheses to indicate the presence of clausal complements in the syntactic frame, as in *gshkiwezid* 'manage [to do something]'.

The fifth case is that of selectional restrictions. For example, there is a classifier system in Ojibwe such that a form like *naanwaatig* is glossed as 'five [sticks]'. This is a problem in consistency of apparatus because, in general, selectional restrictions are supposed to be represented by italicized material in parentheses, as in *gshkitood* 'earn s.t. (*of money*)'.

As the reader can see, I was wrong about what needed to be covered and how to do it, but unfortunately it took actually making the dictionary to find that out.

6.2. THE CONSTRUCTIONAL MEANING PROBLEM.   At the time the dictionary was made, no one realized that constructions could bear lexical-like meanings. To see how the dictionary fares with this unanticipated problem, let me work through an example. In a well-constructed dictionary, a moderately sophisticated user should be able to look up a word in either side of the dictionary and, on the basis of the information there, construct a reasonable facsimile of a sentence containing that word. So let us look at sentences containing the English word *have*. In the English-Ojibwe section the entry for *have* is as follows:

> **have** *vt* have s.t. yaang *vti;* **have s.t.** (*an.*) yaawaad *vta* **let s.o. have something** bgidnamwaad *vta. M, CL.* (P. 492)

This entry would lead one to believe that the translation of the sentences in (10–12) should all involve *yaang* or *yaawaad*.

(10) Long ago Indians didn't have clocks.
(11) (a) He has two hats.
     (b) Why do you have two ears?
(12) (a) ... , and soon they had a baby.
     (b) She has a son.
     (c) The old woman had five sons.

In fact, this is only true of (10), (11a), and (12a). As one can see from (10'–12') below, (11'b), (12'b), and (12'c) use different constructional means.

(10') *Gaa wii*   *wgii-yaawaa-*   *dbahgii-*   *zhaazhi go*   *Nishnaabeg.*
                     siiwaan   *swaanan*   (Bl 27.1)
       not   they-not-   clock(s)   long ago   Indians
                     have-them

(11') (a) *Niizh*   *wiiwkwaanan*   *wdayaanan.* (Bl S410)
          two   hats   he-**has**-them
      (b) *Wegne-sh*   *wenji-*   *niizhootwageyan?* (Bl 33.4)
          what   for-that-reason- you-**have**-two-**ears**

(12') (a) ... , *gye go*   *mii*   *wiiba*   *gii-yaawaa-*   *binoo-*
                                                 waad   *jiinyan.*
                                                                 (Bl 33.4)
          ... , and   EMPH   soon   they-**had**-him   baby
      (b) *Yaawan*[9]   *wgwisan.* (Bl S151)
          he-**exists**-there   her-son
      (c) *Mndimooyenh*   *sa go naa*   *gii-naanniwan*   *niwi wgwisan.*
                                                             (1R2.2)
          old woman   EMPH   they-**are-five**   those her-sons

The constructions in (11'b), (12'b), and (12'c) are highly specialized. They apply to a subclass of inalienably possessed nominals (cf. especially the difference between (12'a), which does not have an inalienably possessed possessee, and (12'b), which does).

The construction in (11'b) merits further discussion. For body parts, the word-internal construction like that in (11'b) is the normal way of expressing the state of the body part. The enumeration of body parts is

---

9. While it is almost certainly the case that the intransitive stem *yaa-* and the transitive stems *yaam-/yaaw-* are historically related, both the morphological and syntactic properties of these words in synchronic Ojibwe are sufficiently distinct that it would be hard to make a non–ad hoc argument that they are synchronically based on the same stem. The key arguments are (1) that *-am-*, the second morpheme in *yaam-*, cannot be added directly to intransitive roots without some further morphological apparatus converting them to transitive inanimate stems and (2) that intransitive *yaa-* takes a relative root complement (see Rhodes 1990, 1998); transitive *yaam-/yaaw-* does not.

incidental to this construction, which expresses stative notions, such as 'to be X in number'. The core of this morphological construction is a kind of compound. The first part of the compound—in Algonquianist terminology, "the initial"—expresses the state (or in our case the number); the second part—in Algonquianist terminology, "the medial"—expresses the body part; and the whole verb is predicated of the possessor. Thus next to (11'b), we find hundreds of words like the following:

(13) (a) *wiin'zided*   'have dirty feet'
       wiin - (i)zid - e
       dirty - foot - VERB

   (b) *ggaan'gaaded*   'have long legs'
       RED - *ginw - (i)gaad - e*
       RED - long - foot - VERB

   (c) *gzhiibtooged*   'have itchy ears'
       gizhiib - (i)tawag - e
       itchy - ear - VERB

   (d) *giikiijdooskong*   'have a sore elbow'
       RED - *giid - (i)dooskon -g*
       RED - sore - elbow - VERB

   (e) *bookniked*   'have a broken arm'
       bookw -(i)nik - e
       broken - arm - VERB

   (f) *gwaagwaagzhed*   'have grungy skin'
       RED - *gwaag - azh - e*
       RED - grungy - skin- VERB

All of the forms in (13) are from the *EOCOD*, but all are listed in the English half only under the stative, 'dirty', 'long', 'itchy', and so on. It was felt that listing them under the body parts would yield excessively long entries under each body part (and space was, as always in practical lexicography, a serious issue). It did not occur to me until long after publication of the dictionary that there should have been a subsection under the English citation 'have' explaining the construction:

> **have** *vt* **have s.t.** yaang *vti;* **have s.t.** (*an.*) yaawaad *vta* **let s.o. have something** bgidnamwaad *vta. M, CL. To describe a number or state of a body part, as a compound, see under each body part,* e.g., **have two ears** niizhootooged *vai,* **have a broken leg** bookgaaded *vai,* **have a dirty nose** wiinjaaned *vai.*

This would have to be supplemented with extensions to the body part entries, as in the following example based on the entry for 'ear':

> **ear** *n* **my ear** ntawag *ni; As part of a compound to describe states or numbers of ears,* **-she-,** e.g., **have big ears** mmaangshed *vai, or* **-tooge-,** e.g., **have one's ear itch** gzhiibtooged *vai,* **have two ears** niizhootooged *vai.*

Unfortunately, such a solution will not naturally fall out of a dictionary structure like that used to create the *EOCOD*.

6.3. THE LEXICAL PRAGMATICS PROBLEM.   The last area that is problematic for bilingual lexicographers of unrelated languages is pragmatic norms. In the linguistics literature, pragmatics generally refers to matters related to speech acts and politeness (Levinson 1983). Consider the following expressions and their pragmatically appropriate translations.

(14) (a) *Giiwenh.*   'Yeah, right.' (lit. 'so they say')
      (b) *Mii iw.*   'That's it.' (lit. 'that's that')
      (c) *Mii mnik.*   'That's all (of a story).' (lit. 'that's enough')

Until generalizations are available from a deeper analysis of these kinds of usage norms, treating these expressions like idioms will work under the structure of the *EOCOD*. The entry for *giiwenh* includes the ironic usage,

> **giiwenh** *av,* so the story goes, so they say, yeah yeah (*what one says to register disbelief in what someone says*), Ot.

However, it seems to have gone unnoticed that much of what is called usage in language teaching operates under the same general pragmatic principles as politeness and speech act theory, namely, that there are a variety of possible expressions that have, within a certain tolerance, the same reference, and there is a set of norms that select particular expressions as normative such that the use of other expressions entails a different "semantic force." For example, there are numerous clause-level expressions, like (15), which are entirely nominal; that is, they contain no verb at all, where English and other Indo-European languages would require a verb.

(15) *Gegaa go nini wiiyaw.*   'He's almost full grown.' (lit. '[it is] almost the body of a man')

It is, of course, possible to render such clauses in a form containing a verb, as in (15'), but (15) is the normative way of expressing this idea.[10]

(15') *Gegaa go e-gtizid.*   'He's almost full grown.' (lit. 'almost he is full grown')

Most seem to be stative in some sense, but not all. More than that I cannot say at this juncture.

Furthermore, there are expressions treated as idiomatic for the purpose of the dictionary but for which generalizations can be made. It is just that

---

10. It is not clear what the "force" is for (15'), although I suspect it sounds like translation.

this particular type of generalization is not readily reflected in the structure of any dictionary. Consider the following set of Ojibwe words.

(16) (a) *giiwsed*   'hunt' (lit. 'walk in loops') (cf. (9) above)
     (b) *dbahang*   'pay for it/with it' (lit. 'measure it')
     (c) *taaged*   'gamble' (lit. 'put something down for someone')
     (d) *zaaghang*   'go pee' (lit. 'step outside')

What these terms all have in common is that they represent the first (salient) step of an action chain. The first step in traditional large game hunting is to walk in loops. The first step in paying for something is to measure its value. The first step in gambling is to place one's bet. The first step in urinating, at least in the old days, was to step outside. This reference to the first step is conventionalized in Ojibwe. This first came to my attention in the following conversation I once had with one of my language consultants.

A: *Aanii-sh maa gaa-bi-dgoshnan?*   'How did you get here?'
B: *Daabaaning ngii-bi-booz.*   'I drove.' (lit. 'I got in a car
                                       [coming].')

Again, rather than mention the middle section of the action chain, namely, 'I drove', as one would in English, Ojibwe mentions the first step. This exchange shows that the principle of referring to a first step is not just the property of the words in (16), but is, in fact, an active norm in Ojibwe usage in general.

It is not clear to me how to design a dictionary to capture such generalizations, but from the point of documenting them, all the meanings in (16) are cataloged in the *EOCOD*. Thus the design will deal with this class of problem, if only by brute force.

6.4. OTHER UNRESOLVED PROBLEMS.   There are many other problems in the *EOCOD* that the ensuing fifteen years have revealed. Most of these stem, in one way or another, from the lack of syntactic analysis. Since the dictionary was published much work has been done on the syntax of Ojibwe, especially in the syntax of ditransitives and verbs with secondary objects (Rhodes 1991b) and in the syntax of a peculiarly Algonquian construction known as a "relative root" (Rhodes 1990, 1998). The better understanding of these points of syntax would have led to systematic differences in glossing. For example, it is not consistently indicated in the *EOCOD* that forms such as *zhaad* 'go' and *boozid* 'embark, get in a vehicle' license a morphological locative, as in (17). Nor is it indicated that the locative is truly optional in the case of forms like *boozid* but obligatory in the case of words like *zhaad* that contain a relative root (see Rhodes 1990, 1998). Words containing relative roots all share the property that the absence of an overt complement has definite readings for the missing complement and that the understood complement is available as a referent.[11]

(17) (a) (i)   *Jiimaaning gii-boozi.*   'He got **in the canoe.**'
        (ii)   *Gii-boozi*   'He got **aboard.**'
    (b) (i)   *Oodenaang gii-zhaa.*   'He went **to town.**'
        (ii)   *Gii-zhaa*   'He went **there.**'

7. FINAL COMMENTS. By far most of the problems in the *EOCOD* are errors of omission rather than commission. The reason for this arises from the lack of attention in linguistics as a whole to matters of minority languages. To write a fully adequate dictionary for any language is a project measurable, not in man-years, but in man-centuries. It is only with the advent of computers that it has become feasible for a single person to produce a passable dictionary in a mere decade. But even when I had ten years of fieldwork behind me, the funding cycles for such projects were (and still are) too short. The *EOCOD* was produced with a sizable grant from the National Endowment for the Humanities. But that limited the time to three years. The only way to produce a work like the *EOCOD* was to stand on the shoulders of those who went before. Thus I exploited Leonard Bloomfield's (1957) word list and the word list produced by the Odawa Language Project (Piggott and Kaye 1973). But doing so required that all forms be rechecked with language consultants, which was done. In the process, however, subtleties unnoticed by the original collectors still may not appear, especially those that occur infrequently.

11. This is discussed at length in Rhodes 1998. Briefly, if there is no overt locative with *zhaad*, then there is understood to be a definite goal location, best glossed as 'there', and it can be further referred to syntactically.

TWO

Role of the Dictionary in Indigenous Communities

CHAPTER SIX

Issues of Standardization and Community in Aboriginal Language Lexicography

Keren Rice and Leslie Saxon

1. INTRODUCTION.   Aboriginal languages of the Americas typically have just one or two dictionaries representing them, if that. By contrast, the range of English language dictionaries that can be found in an average bookstore is astonishingly large. This range gives an indication of the variety of uses to which dictionaries can be put and the diversity of possible users. In aboriginal communities, where ten dictionaries cannot be supported, hard choices have to be faced in making lexicographic decisions. The prime questions that need to be addressed turn on the audience for the dictionary. The needs, skills, and requirements of First Nations[1] teachers and students are very different from those of professional linguists. What we advocate in this chapter is clarity on the part of dictionary makers concerning who the dictionary is for and dictionary principles suited to the community of anticipated users.

Besides decisions about the type of dictionary to be developed, dictionary makers in aboriginal communities also are commonly faced with issues of orthographic standardization. Concerns range from which symbols should be used and how punctuation should be done to how dialect variation of different kinds should be addressed.

We consider here three lexicographic projects in Athabaskan language communities in Canada, a Dogrib dictionary published in 1996 (Saxon and Siemens 1996) and a Slave dictionary in preparation, both informed in part by a process of orthographic standardization sponsored by the Language Bureau of the Government of the Northwest

---

1. "First Nations" is a term used in Canada for indigenous people. Associated as it is with the political body named the Assembly of First Nations, it is not used of the Inuit.

Territories, and a Kaska dictionary (1997) published by the Kaska Tribal Council, Yukon. We contrast the Kaska dictionary with the other two: it is a truly community-based dictionary, guided closely in its preparation by the wishes of community members. We show how the principles underlying the production of these dictionaries were sensitive to community needs and concerns and at the same time sometimes at odds with commonly accepted lexicographic practices and principles of standardization.

2. ORTHOGRAPHIC STANDARDIZATION IN THE DENE LANGUAGES OF THE NORTHWEST TERRITORIES.   The Dogrib and Slave dictionary projects arose following three years of meetings of language specialists in connection with the Dene Languages Orthographic Standardization Project of the Government of the Northwest Territories (1987–89; see Rice 1989b; Saxon 1990).

The Orthographic Standardization Project itself arose as a consequence of legislation in the Northwest Territories (NWT) that made Dogrib, Slave, and the other aboriginal languages official languages of the NWT: there was an observed need from the point of view of the government for the formulation of standard practices in Dene language writing and for the production of dictionaries that would serve as aids in the standardization process. These dictionaries of course serve other needs and functions in the communities, as reference materials in schools, homes, and offices, as a means for documentation of the language, as a focus for community pride and a sense of achievement, and—in their preparation—as a means to training and employment.

The Orthographic Standardization Project brought together representatives of the five Athabaskan languages of the NWT (Chipewyan, Dogrib, South Slavey, North Slavey, and Gwich'in), linguistic specialists working with these language communities, and employees of the Language Bureau and Department of Education of the government of the NWT. An overriding assumption that the committees began with was the notion that the standardized orthography was to be phonetically based, with each sound represented by a single symbol and each symbol representing one and only one sound. By the end of the three-year period of the project's activities, each of the language committees had prepared technical reports from seven to seventeen pages in length detailing the principles of orthographic standardization arrived at for that language and giving examples of their application. The most important principle, which surfaced in all of the reports in some way, was that conservative forms of speech should be used as the basis for spellings. All of the reports advocated the use of only one spelling per word in some cases of variation while sanctioning spelling variants in other cases. On the issue of "contractions," some language groups recommended the teaching of spellings showing full forms only, while others also sanctioned spellings showing contractions. The workings of these principles are illustrated in the next sections with examples from Dogrib.

3. ORTHOGRAPHIC STANDARDIZATION IN DOGRIB.   Leslie Saxon and Rosa Mantla (1997) outline four principles arising from the Dogrib committee of the Orthographic Standardization Project. It is worthwhile to include them here before considering particular linguistic facts behind the concerns of the committee.

(1) Principles of orthographic standardization
   i. The spelling of words will be standardized: there will be one spelling for any one word.
   ii. The spelling will reflect conservative usage—the speech of elders.
   iii. Spellings will be based on pronunciation and on morpheme analysis.
   iv. Spellings will reflect the full form of a word: contractions and shortened forms will be avoided in spellings.

The first two were foremost in the minds of committee members as they approached their task.

3.1. CONSERVATIVE FORMS OF SPEECH.   Language in the Dogrib speech community naturally shows variation for age. The conservatism of particular variants can be ascertained by comparisons with neighboring languages and by consideration of what count as expected patterns of language change over time. In the Dogrib technical report, two major patterns of age-related phonological variation are discussed: the neutralization of prenasalized stops to plain stops and of the alveopalatal series of consonants to the alveolar place of articulation.

The Dogrib prenasalized stops *mb* and *nd* derive ultimately from Proto-Athabaskan *w and *n (Krauss and Leer 1981; Rice 1989a: chap. 7). For Proto-Northeastern Athabaskan (to which Dogrib belongs), we can reconstruct *m and *n (Ackroyd 1976). With a following nasal vowel the nasal stop is heard. In the context of a following oral vowel conservative speakers of Dogrib use the prenasalized stops. For the majority of current speakers of the language, the prenasalized stops have been simplified to the plain stops, as in (2).

(2) Prenasalized and plain stops in Dogrib
   Prenasalized stop   Plain stop
      mbeh   beh   'knife'

mbò	bò	'meat'
k'ets'embeh	k'ets'ebeh	'swim'
tambàa	tabàa	'shore; along the water'
ndè	dè	'land'
gondaà	godaà	'eye'
nàts'eehndì	nàts'eehdì	'buy'
?ekw'atindeè	?ekw'atideè	'chief'

It is a change in progress, as some speakers retain the prenasalized stops generally while others may retain prenasalization in a few morphemes or words. 'Shore' and 'chief' from the list above, for example, are quite commonly heard with the prenasalized variant even from speakers who do not otherwise use these sounds.

The change represents a partial merger, as there are several loanwords with *b* and many native words with *d* (from Proto-Athabaskan **d*), as exemplified in (3).

(3) Plain stops in Dogrib
bebìa	'baby'
libò	'cup'
libà	'socks'
lìbalà	'canvas'
dii	'this'
dàtłǫ	'how many?'
ts'edè	'eat piece by piece'
sǫnàts'edè	'play'

The technical report dictates that the spellings with <mb> and <nd> should be used in all words for which there is evidence of the variation between prenasalized and plain stops. Words showing the plain consonant without variation should be spelled with <b> and <d>.

The technical report takes the same kind of stance in the matter of the neutralization of the five alveopalatal consonants. This series of consonants, which derive from Proto-Athabaskan palatals, includes plain, aspirated, and ejective stops and voiced and voiceless continuants. The whole series is in the process of shifting to a place of articulation more to the front, following a major trend in the Athabaskan languages at large (Krauss and Golla 1981). This variation is exemplified in (4).

(4) Alveopalatal and alveolar consonants in Dogrib
Alveopalatal	Alveolar	
?agòjà	?agòdzà	'it happened'
ts'ejì	ts'edzì	'breathe'

chǫ	tsǫ	'rain'
seghàįchi	seghàįtsi	'give it to me'
sech'à	sets'à	'away from me'
ts'ìich'è	ts'ìits'è	'to be angry'
nazhaʔeh	nazaʔeh	'sweater'
wek'èts'eèzhǫ	wek'èts'eèzǫ	'know'
shį	sį	'song'
shèts'etį	sèts'etį	'eat a meal'

The report's rule states that the spellings with <j, ch, ch', zh, sh> are to be used in words that show this variation.

The variation and change in progress again represent a neutralization. Words with original alveolar consonants, deriving from plain and rhotacized series of alveopalatal consonants in the protolanguage, are exemplified in (5).

(5) Alveolar consonants in Dogrib

dzę	'day'
yenìįhdzà	'he/she tried it'
tso	'firewood'
ts'ehtsį	'make'
ts'ah	'hat'
ts'eht'è	'cook'
ts'ezeh	'shout'
nàts'ezè	'hunt'
sį	'me'
sǫǫmba	'money'

These sounds are to be spelled with <dz, ts, ts', z, s>, as shown.

In the committee's discussions and deliberations these decisions were not reached easily, for a number of reasons. First, these age-related patterns show geographic correlates as well, such that the conservative patterns are retained more in some communities than in others. Thus the choice of the spelling symbol matching the conservative variant appeared to privilege two of the six communities, along lines, it so happens, that match a political difference.

Second, both of these changes show sociolinguistic variation. Therefore, if standardization of the spellings of words is aimed for, speakers would have to remember which pronunciation to use as a model for spelling, without perhaps being aware that their usage included more than one variant. The issue is heightened by the fact that the consonants involved in these sound changes in progress appear in a very significant proportion of the Dogrib lexicon, in the neighborhood of 20 percent.[2]

Third, both of these changes are neutralizations. Therefore, speakers with the changed segments in their speech could not use their own pronunciation to predict the spelling of a word on the basis of the principle of one sound corresponding to one symbol. Instead, they would either have to have the correct spelling by memory or be able to access other kinds of information that would allow them to choose a spelling, for example, remembering how their mother says the word. Neither of these last considerations amounts to insurmountable difficulties for spellers and readers, but for committee members working before a standardized dictionary existed to refer to, the prospect of arriving at correct spellings according to these methods was daunting.

The fourth consideration went very much to the heart of the difference between spoken language and written text. Many members of the committee were concerned that invaluable information would be lost from a story's telling if the pronunciation variants that the storyteller used were washed over by means of standardized spellings. In the Western tradition, on the contrary, the written text is taken as primary and authoritative in almost all contexts. At the time of the committee meetings no remedy for this vital concern was proposed.

Despite all of these factors, driven essentially by the Western tradition of one spelling per word and the pedagogical argument that reading and writing come easier if words are consistently spelled, committee members went along with the recommendations of Saxon, the professional linguist on the committee.[3]

3.2. OTHER VARIANT PRONUNCIATIONS. Besides the variation in Dogrib in stops and the alveopalatal series, there are many less encompassing sorts of variation involving single phonemes and their allophones, single morphemes and their variants, or variation in word forms. The argument was made in committee discussions that the variation was predictable, so one variant could be chosen for the spelling: from it pronunciations were deducible. This approach was taken in support of the ideal of a single spelling per word.

2. This figure is known because the Dogrib dictionary of 1996 ultimately included two spellings for each of the words with original alveopalatal consonants. The alternative spellings of these words with <dz, ts, ts', z, s> were computer generated and increased the number of entries in the dictionary by approximately the figure cited.

3. The other members of the Dogrib working committee were Lucy Lafferty (chair), Madelaine Chocolate, Harriet Lafferty Paul, Philip Mackenzie, Rosa Mantla, Camilla Nitsiza, Mary Siemens, the late Joe Tobie, Gina Tsetta McLean, and Francis Zoe.

A case involving allophony with *e* will illustrate. This vowel has the basic pronunciation [ɛ], but following the labiovelar continuants it may have a back rounded allophone [ʊ]. The standardization report advocates the spellings <we> and <whe> in these cases, with pronunciations [wɛ] and [wʊ] and [w̥ɛ] and [w̥ʊ] predictable from the spellings.

(6) Allophony of e

Spelling	Pronunciations	
seda	[sɛda]	'for me'
neda	[nɛda]	'for you (sg)'
weda	[wɛda / wʊda]	'for him/her/it'
wemǫ	[wɛmõ / wʊmõ]	'his/her/its mother'
wheda	[w̥ɛda / w̥ʊda]	'he, she, or it is sitting'
whekǫ	[w̥ɛkõ / w̥ukõ]	'it is hot'

The alternative to this treatment would be to adopt the spellings <wo> and <who> for the labialized variants.

A case of allomorphy discussed in the technical report is the second-person singular subject marker, canonically *ne-*. In certain morphological and sociolinguistic contexts this prefix may take the variant form of a nasalized copy of the preceding vowel. The potential for this option is predictable from the unaltered form. Spellings for the two variants are shown in (7); the technical report advocates a standardized spelling with *ne-*.

(7) Allomorphy of *ne-*

Spelling with *ne-*	Alternative	
k'eneda	k'eęda	'you (sg) are walking'
nànetła	nàątła	'you (sg) go'
shènetị	shèętị	'you (sg) are eating'
whenetị	wheętị	'you (sg) are sleeping'
danetło	daątło	'you (sg) dance'

As with the neutralizations discussed in section 3.1, speakers are not necessarily consciously aware of the alternations. If the forms with *ne-* are unrecognized, it is difficult for a writer to choose that form of spelling. Acknowledging the pattern, however, standardization committee members agreed to adopt spellings with canonical *ne-*, keeping to the ideal of representing conservative forms of speech in writing and adopting one spelling per word.

3.3. CONTRACTIONS.   The third issue for standardization of spellings is the question of what to do about "contractions," characteristic of fast speech or casual speech. The allomorphy of *ne-* described in the previous section perhaps falls into this class and certainly does in its origins. Another case is the elision intervocalically of the voiced velar continuant spelled <gh> in postpositional prefixes and stems. Concomitant with the elision is assimilation between the now-contiguous vowels, with shortening tending to occur when three vowel moras would fall together. These patterns are exemplified below.

(8) Elision of *gh*

Full form	Contraction	
segha	saa	'for me'
seghǫʔàh	sǫǫʔàh	'he or she gives me [chunky object]'
ʔeghàlats'eeda	ʔaàlats'eeda	'we are working'
weghàįchi	wàįchi	'give it to him/her'
weghǫènǫ	wǫènǫ	'he or she lost, was beaten in a game'

The recommendation of the technical report is to spell such words in their full forms only.

Another important "contraction" is the deletion of a metrically weak word-inital syllable *ʔe* in words of three syllables or more.[4] The contraction is very well established and is applicable to many words but is not mentioned in the technical report at all. By the principles of that report, however, the noncontracted form would surely be recommended for the written standard. (9) shows a number of examples.[5]

(9) Deletion of *ʔe*

Full form	Contraction	
ʔenįhtł'è	nįhtł'è	'book, paper, mail, bill'
ʔekw'ahti	kw'ahti	'police'
ʔek'aàwi	k'aàwi	'trader, store manager'
ʔek'aèk'ǫ	k'aèk'ǫ	'candle, lamp, electricity'
ʔełexè	łexè	'together, with each other'
ʔek'ètai	k'ètai	'six'
ʔek'èdį	k'èdį	'eight'
ʔekaįhcho	kaįhcho	'it is that big'

In both of these cases, the fact of the contraction is generally well recognized by users of the language, and in very careful speech the contractions are much less likely to be heard, as common as they are in ordinary conversation. These issues and those of section 3.2 were treated

---

4. This is not a fully adequate characterization of the rule as it is too generally stated here. A prefix *ʔe-* in verbs is typically not deleted, as this would inevitably lead to the loss of semantic contrast.

5. The Dogrib dictionary (Saxon and Siemens 1996) followed a recommendation of the technical report that <ʔ> word-initially would not be written except in noun and postpositional stems. Therefore, the full forms of the words with initial ʔ in (9) and other lists will be found in the dictionary with an initial vowel.

by committee members as less vital to the process of orthographic standardization than were the neutralizations of section 3.1. There was less
time spent discussing them, less controversy over the recommendations,
and more ease about the decisions once made. Perhaps the most dis-
comfort arose from the imperative of the idea that each word should have
a single spelling.

4. A DOGRIB DICTIONARY.   When the dictionary appeared in 1996, the
imperative of one spelling for each word had been abandoned—though
not so much as to make the book an attempt to represent all variant forms
of Dogrib words. It gives alternative spellings for many words and, most
strikingly, lists words with conservative alveopalatal consonants twice as
main entries, once with alveopalatal spellings in <j, ch, ch', zh, sh> and
once with alveolar spellings in <dz, ts, ts', z, s>, the latter computer generated in the preparation of the dictionary database.

The change in perspective on the role of the dictionary and the notion
of "standardization" arose in discussions among a working group as the
dictionary was being prepared during the period 1992–96. This group[6]
was influenced by the appearance in 1992 of a preliminary version of the
dictionary edited by Jaap Feenstra, a Summer Institute of Linguistics (SIL)
translator working in the Dogrib communities. Although Feenstra had not
been involved in the standardization committee meetings of the preceding years, the version he edited followed the guidelines of the technical
report, in particular, on the neutralizations of stop consonants and
alveopalatals discussed in section 3.1. The appearance of this edition was
critical to the rethinking that took place subsequently.

The following were recognized as issues not adequately addressed by the
recommendations of the Orthographic Standardization Committee (Saxon
and Mantla 1997). They informed the 1996 revision of the dictionary to
greater and lesser extents.

(10) Factors influencing spellings in Saxon and Siemens (1996)
    i. different usage among elders in different Dogrib communities;
    ii. sociolinguistic variation in the speech of elders, including
       apparent lexical diffusion of phonological changes;
    iii. dialect differences in the Dogrib communities that affect
       underlying representations for words;
    iv. patterns of spelling already established in the Dogrib
       communities;
    v. ease of spelling; and

---

6. The core members of this group were Lucy Lafferty, Jaap Feenstra, Rosa Mantla, Jim
Martin, Mary Siemens, Leslie Saxon, and John B. Zoe.

vi. training requirements for introducing the new spellings and
spelling rules.

These are taken up in the sections that follow.

4.1. GEOGRAPHIC AND SOCIOLINGUISTIC VARIATION. As mentioned
in section 3.1 in connection with the prenasalized stops, there is a notable
geographic division in the Dogrib speech community, with the villages of
Dettah and Ndilo near Yellowknife standing somewhat apart from the four
others (Rae-Edzo, Wha Ti, Gameti, and Wekwe Ti) that lie farther north.[7]
This variation has not been the subject of any significant research effort, but
it is often commented on by linguists working in the area and by speakers
of Dogrib, who notice lexical variation and distinctive patterns with prenasalization and with the consonant *r*. Further, elders' speech also naturally
shows sociolinguistic variation based on the particulars of the speech event.

There is a conflict, then, between the first two standardization principles listed in section 3, the aim for a single spelling for each word and
for the representation in spelling of conservative usage. As conservative
usage itself is not uniform but shows much of the range of variation of
the rest of the speech community, a conflict is inevitable. In the 1996
edition of the Dogrib dictionary, the principle of single spellings was
largely given up in favor of more accurate expression of the variation that
exists in elders' speech. While this decision accords with the principle to
represent conservative usage, it has the added advantage of bringing into
the dictionary spellings that reflect the most common variants used in the
speech community, which are also used by the younger people most likely
to use the dictionary and to be literate in Dogrib.

4.2. REANALYSIS. The principle of single spellings also sometimes conflicts with the principle of morphemic spelling listed in section 3 above.
Conflicts arise when variant pronunciations actually reflect distinct morphological analyses. Looking first at a case in which the two principles are
in harmony, let us consider again *ne-* 'second-person singular' from section 3.2. The form *ne-* is used as a mark of the second-person singular
possessor of nouns, object of postpositions and verbs, as well as verbal subject. Compare (11) with (7) above. With the forms in (11) there is no
variation in usage, unlike what we see with (7).

(11) *ne-* as possessor and object
    nemǫ   'your (sg) mother'
    neyatiì   'your (sg) language, words'

7. Dogrib names for these villages are respectively T'èehdaà, Ndilǫ, Behchokǫ̀, Whatì,
Gamètì, and Wekweètì.

nexè	'with you (sg)'
nets'ǫ	'from you (sg)'
nek'èdì	'he or she is looking after you (sg)'
neghàts'eeda	'we are looking at you (sg)'
k'enehge	'I'm carrying you (sg) [on my back]'
nèwhihtsį	'I made you (sg)'
ne?àh	'you (sg) are eating it'
nejį	'sing (sg)!'

Assuming that spellings are to be morphologically based, choosing the spelling <ne> for the pattern illustrated in (7) is an obvious way to arrive at single spellings to represent the alternation.

There are other cases unlike this one in which variants in pronunciation can be shown to reflect distinct morphological analyses for the words. With them, the two principles come into conflict. The verb 'know' illustrates the issues. In (12) we show two patterns in the singular paradigm of this verb.[8]

(12) Contrasting paradigms for 'know'

Conservative form	Innovative form	
hok'è(r)ezhǫ	hok'èehshǫ	'I know it'
hok'è(n)įzhǫ	hok'èįzhǫ	'you (sg) know it'
hok'è(r)èzhǫ	hok'èezhǫ	'he or she knows it'

The conservative pattern, characterized by a contrast in tone on the prestem syllable as the mark of first versus third person, is indicative of a certain class of stative verbs. The innovative pattern, characterized by *h* in the first-person singular form, is the unmarked imperfective paradigm. Thus the orthographic principles favoring single spellings and spellings based on morphological analysis conflict.

There are several other examples of this type from verb paradigms that could be cited. Other cases come from compound nouns. (For examples and analysis, see Saxon and Siemens 1996; Causley 1996.) There are significant phonological weakenings that occur in the nonhead elements of compounds. Assuming that the weakenings mask the words' etymologies, conservative and innovative pronunciations may well reflect distinct morphological analyses.[9]

---

8. The verb stem initial consonant is subject to variation, being an alveopalatal. This fact is ignored here.

9. The weakening in 'kettle' is the loss of *d;* in 'captain', the weakening of *k'* to *g;* and in 'cardboard box', the reduction of the middle morpheme *wò* from [wò] to [wè], with the latter pronunciation reflecting morphological *wè* (see §3.2). It is not a weakening that we see in '[cow's] milk' but a substitution when the morpheme *?ejïe* evidently ceases to be an analyzable element of the word. The form *ts'e-* is a paradigmatic prefix in verbs used in citation forms and with the gloss 'someone/we [do . . .]' and is our best guess at the source of the innovative form.

(13)   Two forms for compound nouns

Conservative form	Innovative form	
lidìhto	lììhto	'kettle, teapot'
tea+container	?+container	
ts'i k'èdìi dǫǫ̀	ts'i gèdìi dǫǫ̀	'captain of
[boat+driver]+person	[boat+?]+person	a boat'
ʔenįhtł'èwòto	(ʔe)nįhtł'èwèto	'cardboard
[book+skin]+container	[book+?]+container	box'
ʔejiet'oò	(ʔe)ts'eet'oò	'[cow's] milk'
bovine+milk	?+milk	

Here, too, the two principles lead to different approaches to the standardized spellings available for these words.

4.3. ADOPTING SPELLINGS.   Not taken fully into account in the work of the Orthographic Standardization Committee were issues relating to the establishment of newly standardized spellings, with the exception of plans for the compilation of dictionaries. It was recognized that training would be required to introduce and promulgate the new spellings and spelling rules, and in the Dogrib region this was largely carried out through literacy courses at the community level through, among other channels, the Community Teacher Education Program of the Dogrib Divisional Board of Education (1990–96). Saxon produced a number of "technical notes" on Dogrib spelling to assist in the processes of dictionary compilation and literacy and spelling training, dealing with the major phonological alternations that were the subject of the committee's work as well as matters of morphology that impinge on spelling.

It was not calculated that there would be significant resistance at the community level to decisions of the committee, but there was, over the fact of the changes as well as to particulars. Not surprisingly, some proposed changes led to more debate than did others. During dictionary compilation, there was more than one meeting at which the major topic was the spelling for the word for 'Dogrib'. Since the word contains an alveopalatal consonant, this was a source of discussion, as was the fact that its morphological structure would dictate a spelling with a double vowel: Tłįchǫǫ̀.[10] It was decided that a more established spelling, Tłįchǫ, would become the "official" spelling for the dictionary and that this word and this word only would not be shown in the dictionary alternatively spelled with the alveolar consonant <ts>.

10. The final vowel is the realization of the 'possessed noun suffix' on the stem chǫ 'flank, rib'.

Double vowels in fact contributed much to the debate over the promotion of the new spellings. The introduction of many such spellings is the hallmark of the contrast between the 1992 and 1996 editions of the Dogrib dictionary. The items in (14) give a few examples from among hundreds.

(14) Double vowels in Saxon and Siemens (1996)

Spellings from Feenstra (1992)	Spellings from Saxon and Siemens (1996)	
godze	godzeè	'heart'
di dzę	dii dzę̀	'today'
kwìts'ì	kwìts'ìi	'comb'
godo	godoo	'above'

The spellings with double vowels are considered difficult and were for the most part unfamiliar in the community before the work of the Orthographic Standardization Committee, when the attention of many Dogrib educational leaders was first focused on such details of phonological and morphological representation. There are infinitely many minimal sets illustrating the linguistic significance of the contrast: the pairs *gejį* 'they are singing' / *geejį* 'they are afraid' and *whela* 'they are there' / *whelaa* 'the ones which are there' will suffice to show it for our discussion here.[11]

Presentation of this contrast and of its morphological underpinnings has formed the substance of a number of workshops for educators and researchers in the Dogrib region from the early 1990s until the present. The continuing call for instruction is indicative to us of the hold that early orthographic practices have on subsequent developments. This is an important consideration, because it shows that errors or first attempts are not so easily undone.

4.4. SUMMING UP.   The work on the 1996 Dogrib dictionary shows the importance of community involvement in decision making. Although many of the same people were involved both in the development of the standardization principles and in dictionary planning, the contexts of each stage had a significant effect on outcomes. Dictionary planning took place in meetings at the Dogrib schools rather than in meeting rooms of the government. The setting helped to bring out the ideals and practicalities associated with our discussions.

Concerning the difficult issues surrounding choice in spellings, two factors were decisive in determining which spellings would go into the dictionary: the sense that spellings should be accessible from one's own linguistic usage and that a speaker's or writer's linguistic identity should

---

11. The complementizer that serves a relativizing function, illustrated in *whelaa*, lengthens the final vowel in the clause. This is a major source of "double vowels."

not be obliterated in the standardization process. Both of these ideals took precedence over the simplistic assumption that each word could or should be given a unique spelling.

The intended users of the dictionary are the people served by the Dogrib Community Services Board,[12] which sponsored it. The majority of these people are fluent in Dogrib, and it is their writings that will be shaped by the spellings in the dictionary. The vitality of the language is surely a factor in the dictionary's ultimate form: if the language were not actively being used, the same forces for personal identification through language would not be at work.

5. STANDARDIZATION AND LANGUAGES IN THE COMMUNITY SETTING: SLAVE AND KASKA. In this section we examine two other Athabaskan languages, Slave [slevi] and Kaska. The lexicographic issues for these languages are very similar to those discussed for Dogrib—variation in sounds within a speech community is found, creating conflicts for principles of one symbol–one sound and one spelling per word; contractions obscure the full forms, leading to difficulties in the principle of writing full forms only. The Slave situation is complicated by the fact that there are a number of different dialects (or languages, depending on how one looks at things) that fall under the general rubric "Slave." Our focus is on how the interpretation of standardization can affect the kinds of decisions that are made about what is included in a single dictionary. We examine two situations in which quite different decisions were made about what belongs in a dictionary, with a single dialect being represented in one case and several distinct languages in the other, and we attempt to pinpoint some of the reasons why these different choices were made. We begin with a discussion of Slave.

5.1. THE SLAVE SITUATION.

5.1.1. VARIATION IN SLAVE. Slave is defined as a single language by Rice (1989a) based on several criteria, including mutual intelligibility and identity. Earlier linguists (e.g., Howren 1975) defined four distinct languages, Slave, Bearlake, Hare, and Mountain, while the government of the Northwest Territories recognizes two, South Slavey and North Slavey, based to some degree on linguistic and social criteria but determined to a large extent by political factors that are a result of government-defined divisions (e.g., electoral areas). The development of language materials is currently receiving government funding according to

12. This body incorporates the Dogrib Divisional Board of Education, as well as social and health services.

this last classification.[13] In our discussion here we begin by looking at Slave as a whole and then focus on the level called North Slavey.

The four groups defined by Robert Howren (1975) are easily identified on the basis of phonological criteria. The primary difference between these groups was noted by Howren: the development of the Proto-Athabaskan *ts consonant series, as shown in (15), where we see that the *ts series develops differently in each of these groups. (Note that some Slave dialects regularly distinguish a closed front mid vowel and an open front mid vowel. In the orthography, the North Slavey Orthography Standardization Committee decided to use the vowel <e> for the lax one and <ə> for the tense one; this is the orthography used in the discussion of Slave here.)

(15) Regular phonological variation: PA *ts in Slave

South Slavey	Bearlake	Hare	Mountain	
tthe	kwə	fə	pə	'rock'
tth'ih	kw'ih	w'i	p'ih	'mosquito'
thę́	whę́	wę́	fę́	'star'

A few other phonological differences are illustrated in (16). These examples show two ways in which Hare is distinct from the other three groups. First, where verb stems (generally the final syllable of the verb) can carry high tone (marked by an acute accent) in South Slavey, Bearlake, and Mountain, this high tone falls on the prestem syllable in Hare (16a). Second, in many environments, *n develops into [r] rather than [n] in Hare (16b).

(16) Phonological variation in stem tone and *n: unusual properties of Hare

	South Slavey	Bearlake	Hare	Mountain	
(a)	neʔáh	neʔá	néʔa	neʔáh	'you (sg) eat'
	(h)ehk'é	hehk'é	héhk'e	hehk'é	'I shoot it'
(b)	názéh	názə́	rázə	názéh	'she/he hunts'
	nínila	nínila	rírila	nínila	'I placed plural objects'

13. The language that linguists traditionally call Slave is basically identical to the government's term "South Slavey." "North Slavey" is composed of Hare and Bearlake. There are fewer speakers of Mountain in the Northwest Territories, and this group has not fit well into either North or South Slavey, as defined by the NWT government, although it is clearly part of the larger dialect group. Interestingly, Mountain Slavey is included in the Kaska Tribal Dictionary discussed in §5.2. We ignore Mountain in the discussion here. Note the spelling device used for distinguishing between the global term "Slave" (without a final <y>) and the particular term "Slavey."

Not only is there variation between the four major dialect groups, but variation also occurs within a single dialect group, or speech community, similar to that discussed in Dogrib. For instance, in Hare, the types of phonological variation shown in (17) exist. (17a) illustrates variation between a bilabial stop and a rounded velar stop; (17b) shows variation, widespread in Slave, between a glide and a voiced fricative; (17c) demonstrates variation between *x* and *k*, a kind of variation that is restricted to a few lexical items; and (17d) illustrates variation between *i* and *e* in a suffix vowel, another widespread variation in Slave.

(17) Phonological variation within a dialect: Hare
    (a) hịbage   hịgwage   'it is light (in weight)'
    (b) ya   zha   'snow'
    (c) xéhts'ę̨   kéhts'ę̨   'evening'
    (d) t'ǝre   t'ǝri   'girl'

In South Slavey, which is spoken in several geographically widespread communities, there is considerable variation. For instance, some South Slavey dialects have nasal consonants, others prenasalized stops, and still others plain stops; variation is possible even within a particular idiolect. South Slavey parallels Dogrib in this respect. Some examples are given in (18).

(18) Phonological variation within a dialect: South Slavey

Nasal	Prenasalized stop	Plain stop	
goneh	gondeh	godeh	'she/he speaks'
meh	mbeh	beh	'knife'

Much lexical variation is found in South Slavey as well; a small sample showing words from six different South Slavey–speaking communities is given in (19).

(19) Lexical variation within a dialect: South Slavey

Fort Nelson	Liard	Fort Simpson	Providence	Hay River	Alberta	
tehk'ái, dzęlịa	tehk'a	tehk'áa	tehk'áa	dzę	tehk'é	'muskrat'
ịlák'edhi	lák'e	sųlái	sųlái	sųlái	łáhts'eti	'five (things)'
dezonah	dezona, dezhona	dezǫah	dezǫah	ts'údạ, dezǫa	ts'ídoa	'child'
tų́hle	tule	tehmị́e		tehmị́e	xehthéh	'pack'

In (19) we see variation in choice of lexical item both across the South Slavey dialect and within a particular speech community. In addition, some phonological variation is illustrated. Note the form for 'child' in the Liard dialect: as in Dogrib, either the alveolar *z* or the alveopalatal *zh* is possible in this word, depending on the speaker.

As noted above, in the most encompassing interpretation Slave can be identified as a single language based on social and political criteria. No matter how many languages are in fact recognized, considerable diversity is found both between and within speech communities. We focus on the North Slavey group in what follows and look at decision making concerning standardization and dictionaries for that group.

The two dialects that make up North Slavey—Hare and Bearlake—differ significantly. Illustrated above in (15) and (16b) are the development of the Proto-Athabaskan *ts series and of Proto-Athabaskan *n. In addition, these two dialects show other regular phonological correspondences. In Hare, voiceless aspirated affricates spirantize to their voiceless fricative counterparts, as in (20).

(20) Spirantization of voiceless aspirated affricates to voiceless fricatives in Hare

Bearlake	Hare	
tsá	sá	'beaver'
-chile	-shile	'younger brother'
tɬe	ɬe	'lard'

Further, in Hare, the voiceless lateral and labiovelar fricatives do not show voiced-voiceless counterparts parallel to other fricatives but neutralize to their voiced counterpart.

(21) Voicing of lateral and labiovelar fricatives in Hare

Bearlake	Hare	
ɬe	le	'smoke'
wha	wa	'tent pole'

The two dialects also differ in the source of *r*. Both dialects have an [r] phonetically, but in Hare it develops from *n while in Bearlake it develops from *d. The conditioning environments are somewhat complex (see Rice 1989a for discussion).

(22) Development of *r*

Bearlake	Hare	
neshə	reshə	'potato'
ʔerehtɬ'é	ʔedéhtɬ'e	'I write it'

In addition, many lexical differences are found between Bearlake and Hare.

(23) Differences in lexical items: Bearlake and Hare

Bearlake	Hare	
Ɂekwę́	Ɂedǝ	'caribou'
bé	Ɂiyę	'meat'
sǫlái	lák'ǝ	'five'
tehk'ái	dzę	'muskrat'
sahba	bǝre	'trout'

5.1.2. VARIATION AND A DICTIONARY: IMPLICATIONS OF ASSUMP-
TIONS ABOUT STANDARDIZATION.   Now let us consider the implications of this type of diversity for developing a dictionary, given the
assumptions and principles that guided the orthography standardization.
Recall that the orthography standardization committees began their work
with an assumption that the writing system should be phonemically based,
with one sound represented by one symbol and one symbol representing
one sound. In addition, as discussed in section 3 for Dogrib, each of the
committees arrived at a common decision to use one spelling per word
and, in the case of variation, to choose the conservative spelling. Given
the dialect diversity and the assumptions about standardization, one could
imagine at least two possible routes that could be taken in dictionary
development, and these are outlined here. First, it would be possible to
create a dictionary for North Slavey that included both of the major
dialects, and second, it would be possible to create dictionaries for each
dialect separately.

In a common dictionary, given the assumption of one symbol–one
sound, one sound–one symbol, the following types of entries are in order.
(We ignore nonorthographic information that is part of lexical entries,
such as information about category, information about inflection, and
examples.)

(24) fǝ(Hare), kwǝ(Bearlake). rock

However, this format conflicts with the principle of one spelling per word.
We are dealing with essentially the same lexical item here, differing only
by a regular sound correspondence. The major criterion for deciding
between possible spellings of one word, conservative speech, cannot be
used as a mediating factor in cases such as this because conservative
speech cannot be defined in any but a historical way for these two different speech communities. Other types of sound variation where there
are systematic differences between dialects (see (16) above) lead to the
same dilemma: the principle of one spelling per word leads us to seek a
single spelling; the phonemic principle requiring a unique sound-symbol
correspondence demands two spellings, and an appeal to conservative
speech is inconclusive.

Cases of different lexical items, on the other hand, are unproblematic: all lexical items are listed. This leads to some interesting situations as well, as illustrated in (25). Here the word <bé> occurs in both dialects but with different meanings.

(25) (a) ʔįyę (Hare). meat
      (b) bé. meat (Bearlake), food (Hare)

That labeling for dialect is important was evidenced by the Hare dictionary prepared by Rice (1978). In that dictionary, some nouns from the Bearlake dialect were included, based on a word list compiled by Fang-Kuei Li (1929). Hare speakers recognized these words but systematically reacted negatively to their inclusion in the Hare dictionary if they were not labeled for dialect.

A common dictionary leads to problems in making other decisions as well when the criterion of "conservatism" is considered. Taking this criterion strictly, one would be led to write all sounds developing from *n as <n>, as in Bearlake, eschewing the *r* found in Hare (see (16b)). Likewise, one would write verb stem high tones on the verb stem rather than on the prestem syllable (see (16a)). In a strict linguistic sense, these are the conservative choices. However, this is not the case within communities today: the contrasts are clear dialect demarcators, and speakers within a community appeal to their own elders as the indicators of conservative speech, not to those from outside. When discussed in the North Slavey Orthography Standardization Committee, such standardization proposals met with a strongly negative response. Two major reasons were given. First, such standardization obscured dialect differences, making the orthographic representation far removed from the actual speech form. Second, in the absence of models in the community, it would be extremely difficult to learn to write verb stem tones in Hare. For instance, tones would have to be written on verb stems but would be heard as falling on the preceding syllable. Since some preverb stem high tones are lexically part of the stem and others part of the prefix, it is difficult for the Hare speaker to know where the tone should be written without considerable formal knowledge of how to test this linguistically. It is difficult to check it with speakers within the Hare-speaking community as, in general, verb stems do not bear high tones in this dialect. We see echoes of the Dogrib situation in the North Slavey discussions: the principles that follow from general theoretical assumptions do not meet the needs of the community itself.

It is also worth returning to a fact noted for Dogrib: even within a particular speech community, the notion of "conservative speech" is not necessarily particularly well defined. While most of the Slave-speaking communities are long established in terms of the existence of trading posts and churches, it was not until the past fifty years or so that large numbers of people actually moved into the communities more or less on a year-round basis. The current communities are composed of people who until fairly recently came together only at certain times of the year. Thus there can be a number of different "conservative" kinds of speech even within a particular community.

Given the assumptions about sound-symbol correspondences and single spellings, there thus seem to be problems with developing a common dictionary encompassing both North Slavey dialects. Consequently, for North Slavey a decision was made to create different dictionaries for each of the major dialects, and work is ongoing currently on separate dictionaries of Hare and Bearlake. (South Slavey is being treated as a single language for dictionary purposes, and little work is being done on Mountain in the Northwest Territories.) The Hare and Bearlake dictionaries that exist, and those that are in progress, represent the language varieties of a single community or of two fairly homogeneous communities.

The decision to create different dictionaries for different communities fits well with recommendations made concerning standardization of orthography within the overall Slave group. When orthography reform began (see §2), the government established two committees for Slave, South Slavey and North Slavey. These groups met both separately and together, but the assumption from the start was that North and South Slavey were two different languages that could have their own orthographic conventions and would have their own curriculum materials, dictionaries, and the like. The South Slavey group followed this path. In the North Slavey group, however, detailed discussion of a number of different models for standardization of orthography took place, and a decision was made to standardize within communities rather than across communities. (See §5.3 for discussion of the meaning of standardization within a community; see Rice 1995 for discussion of the process used in the North Slavey group.) Once this decision was made, there was little discussion of cross-community cooperation in the development of materials.

5.2. THE KASKA TRIBAL COUNCIL DICTIONARY.   Now let us turn to the Kaska Tribal Council dictionary (1997). Kaska is a language spoken in a number of communities in the Yukon Territory of Canada. The Kaska communities recognize their language as a single language despite dialect diversity. Both phonological and lexical variation is found within Kaska, as within Dogrib and Slave; some examples are given in (26) through (28).

(26) *back legs* (p. 75)

       -ghos   Lower Liard, Good Hope Lake, Frances Lake, Pelly, Ross River

       -ghas   Liard

-ghółé   Ross River
-zézé'   Pelly
-ts'ené'   Frances Lake, Pelly, Ross River

Notice that, as in Slave, there is much variation in choice of word across communities and there can be more than one word used within a community.

(27) *punkwood* (p. 182)
    edénítsuhi   Lower Liard
    denétsu   Good Hope Lake
    edénítsū   Liard, Frances Lake
    edénétsū   Pelly

(28) *muskrat* (p. 64)
    tenusdę   Lower Liard
    tunusdié'   Good Hope Lake, Liard, Frances Lake, Pelly
    tenusdę̌'   Liard

This example, (28), further illustrates that within a single community forms that are basically the same word, with minor phonological variation, can coexist.

Regular phonological correspondences between Kaska dialects are also found. Some are illustrated in (29).

(29) (a) Lower Liard   Others
         itl'át   itl'ét   'cranberries' (p. 13)
     (b) Pelly, Ross River Others
         chą   chǫ   'rain' (p. 14)
     (c) Pelly   Others
         tu'   tū   'water' (p. 16)

(29a) shows that one dialect has *a* while others have *e*; (29b) demonstrates variation between nasalized *a* and *o* and (29c) the variable presence of word-final glottal stops. Kaska is parallel to Dogrib and Slave in terms of the diversity within the group: both phonological and lexical variation exists.

Turning now to the dictionary, the Kaska Tribal Council dictionary is very different from the Slave dictionaries as originally conceived by the orthography standardization committees. It is a topical noun dictionary of a type frequently produced for northern Athabaskan languages, in which words are grouped together by semantic class rather than by alphabetical order. Strikingly, the Kaska Tribal Council dictionary includes not just Kaska, the language that it started with and the language of the title of the dictionary, but also two additional languages, Mountain Slavey and Sekani. These are three distinct languages by all the usual criteria for determining a language, including sociolinguistic, sociopolitical, and linguistic. This dictionary is thus unique in conception. Instead of being restricted to a particular speech community or communities, the dictionary is composed of the languages that make up a particular political unit, three clearly related but nevertheless distinct languages. A typical lexical entry in this dictionary is as in (30).

(30) *muskrat* (p. 30)

tanust'ę́' (tunoost'ę́')[FORT WARE]
tanwust'ą̄ (tunwoost'ą)[FORT WARE]
tanust'á' (tunoost'á')[FORT WARE]
tanust'eā' (tunoost'èa')[FORT WARE]
tenusdę̄[LOWER LIARD]
tenusdié'[GOOD HOPE LAKE]
tenusdę̌'[LIARD]
tenusdié'[LIARD, FRANCES LAKE, PELLY]

dzana[ROSS RIVER]
dzana[MOUNTAIN SLAVEY]

tehk'ā (tehk'a)[FORT WARE]
tahk'a[MOUNTAIN SLAVEY]

his/her muskrat
matunusdié'[GOOD HOPE LAKE]
matenusdę̌'[LIARD]
matenusdié'[PELLY]

1. Kahseh nan ki'ǫ' tū zedlé' gúlīn ekúh tenusdié' nan gunela'. *When earth first appeared, there was only water when muskrat made earth.*[LIARD]
2. Sejōni tenusdié'lá' ts'édāne ma'ējé' kegedetl'ūn tādet'ē dzenēs ts'į́'. Ts'édāne łą́ gutie kuhłā dege. *Old people tie the front feet of a muskrat on a children's shirt for three days so they will really work hard.*[LIARD]

This entry includes the following information. Each word is labeled as to where it is spoken. The first group of words are from Sekani (Fort Ware). They are given in two different orthographies, the Sekani orthography of Hargus (1990) (in parentheses) and a spelling system that is closer to that used for Mountain Slavey and Kaska (Lower Liard, Good Hope Lake, Liard, Francis Lake, Pelly, Ross River). Words of similar phonological shape (cognates) are grouped together. In addition, this dictionary includes example sentences that incorporate cultural content whenever possible, as shown in (30), and short stories providing a setting for each major topic area.

5.3. THE DIFFERENT SITUATIONS.   In the dictionaries described here, we see a continuum of decisions about what is included: a single well-defined dialect, spoken in one or two communities (Hare, Bearlake), a dialect/language with internal diversity (South Slavey, Dogrib), a number of different languages (Kaska/Sekani/Mountain Slavey). In this section we examine some of the reasons that underlie these different choices, focusing on North Slavey and Kaska/Sekani/Mountain Slavey.

5.3.1. VISIONS.   Perhaps the greatest difference between these two situations is related to the times in which the work began and to the source of the vision for the dictionary. The Kaska Tribal Council dictionary is a product of the 1990s. It began as a project on Kaska and grew into a dictionary encompassing the languages of the other groups within the Tribal Council, Sekani and Mountain Slavey. The introduction to the Kaska Tribal Council dictionary states: "This dictionary came together because the vision of the Kaska people was endorsed by the Government of Canada, the Government of the Yukon, and the Government of British Columbia" (p. 1). The introduction stresses that the project was motivated by the Kaska people: "The Kaska vision of their future includes their language and the languages of all the native people in their traditional territory" (p. 1). The dictionary arose out of direction from the chiefs and the speakers of the languages and their sense that one way of aiding the survival of a language is to record the vocabulary of that language along with its cultural context.

The Slave dictionaries began in a rather different way. They began as local projects in the 1960s and 1970s, supervised by linguists and missionaries interested in the language. Further major dictionary work began in the late 1970s and 1980s under the auspices of the federal Department of Indian and Northern Affairs. Linguists were funded to work within communities on dictionaries of the languages of those communities. The early dictionaries thus did not grow out of demands of the community but were externally motivated, if locally based. These linguists set the vision for the work of the standardization committees, for later published dictionaries, and for dictionaries now in progress, and, in fact, issues concerning the scope of the dictionaries in terms of languages were not discussed in any serious way for reasons to be considered further below.

Unpacking this notion of vision, we note two factors. First, in terms of conception, dictionary work has been ongoing in Slave for several decades now, and topical dictionaries at least have been available in several communities for some time. In the Kaska area, on the other hand, the dictionary under discussion represents the first major attempt at a dictionary of Kaska and Mountain Slavey (see Hargus 1990 for a topical dictionary of Sekani).

Second, the work on the Kaska Tribal Council dictionary was initiated by and directed by the Tribal Council. The work on the Slave dictionaries was initiated by missionaries, the government, or linguists, and the work was directed by these people as well.

The decades intervening between the time in which the Slave projects began and the start of the Kaska project have witnessed many changes in the relationship between communities and language professionals, no matter what their background. By and large, projects such as dictionaries were directed by professionals in the 1970s and 1980s. Such externally directed projects would be impossible in many places today. Education, including language education, has increasingly come under the control of aboriginal peoples themselves, thanks to the ascendance of many aboriginal people to positions of power as elected politicians, highly ranked civil servants, and educators employed by government and school boards. Further, the movement toward aboriginal self-government has meant the establishment of a range of educational and social programs under the aegis of tribal councils. Now, rather than the impetus for the development of materials such as dictionaries coming from the outside, it is coming directly from within— from teachers and other community leaders, from students, from interpreters, from people of a younger generation who want to learn their ancestral language. Marking this change, the Kaska Tribal Council dictionary credits three groups of people: the elders who contributed their knowledge of the languages; the Kaska and Sekani professionals who work to provide translation services, teach the language, and promote its development; and the political leaders in the Kaska Tribal Council. While the Slave dictionaries credit the elders who contributed their knowledge, the professionals and the leaders do not receive credit. In the case of the professionals, there were very few such people when these dictionary projects began; in the case of the leaders, their support was generally more passive than active. To put it simply, the Kaska Tribal Cou icil dictionary models the status of work on languages in the 1990s, highlighting increased cooperation within communities and the need for local control. The Slave dictionaries are of an earlier decade when linguists and others set the stage for what they perceived as required. The vision of the missionaries and linguists tended to be a very restricted one, based on traditional linguistic classifications; the Kaska Tribal Council sees the language situation more globally.

5.3.2. STANDARDIZATION.   In addition to vision, a second factor entered into decisions on orthography and dictionary making, namely, standardization. Let us return again to the work of the standardization committees, focusing now on North Slavey.[14] The North Slavey committee discussed in great depth how to define standardization and considered three levels at

14. Rice 1995 gives a fuller treatment of this matter.

which standardization could take place: the regional level (North Slavey), the dialect level (Hare, Bearlake), or the individual level. In all of this discussion, for no level of standardization were the following two principles seriously challenged: (i) the notion of a phonemically based alphabet, with one symbol representing one phoneme, and (ii) the general principle of one spelling per word, with a reliance on conservative speech as the source of standard spellings. What we did not think through at the time is that these two principles are in conflict, with the consequence that attempts to maintain both will necessarily be unsuccessful, no matter what level of standardization is sought.

Standardization at the regional level was defined as follows. We use Bearlake and Hare forms for the purpose of discussion. As discussed in section 5.1, Bearlake and Hare differ systematically in several ways. To take a single example, where the Bearlake dialect generally has *kw*, the Hare dialect usually has *f* instead. The notion of regional-level standardization recommended the development of a common symbol to represent these two sounds, say, <£>. A speaker of Bearlake would pronounce this as [kw] while a Hare speaker would pronounce this as [f]. Regional standardization, though it focused on a common spelling for words that were identical save for regular phonological correspondences, thus involved a step back from the strict notion of one symbol to one sound, allowing a single symbol to be interpreted in more than one way depending on dialect. It did conform to the phonemic principle, in that <£> would have a constant (though different) phonemic value in each of Hare and Bearlake. Regional standardization was seen as having some virtues. For instance, it would facilitate the exchange of materials between communities, allow greater circulation of materials, and be less costly. It would also be beneficial for career development in that teachers would be more easily able to move from community to community throughout the region. On the other hand, transferability of reading skills from English was thought to be problematic. There was also concern about the effect of the writing system on the maintenance of individual dialects and about the greatly increased need for resource and reference materials given the slackening of the principle of one symbol to one sound. While regional standardization was felt to be a worthy goal, the problems associated with it were such that the committee felt it should be rejected.

The second level of standardization, community standardization, involved the development of a single alphabet and spelling system for a particular community. This too had several advantages: it would be easy to distinguish the source community for materials, and transfer to and from English would be more direct, as few novel symbols would be required. On the other hand, it would be difficult for teachers to move from one community to another as they would be called on to learn a new writing system, and it would likewise be difficult for children to move.

Materials would be more costly, and exchange of materials between communities would be more difficult.

Finally, individual standardization meant that a single individual would use a consistent writing system but that within a community, different individuals might differ in how they wrote, reflecting differences in their speech. This system was positively viewed in that little training would be required; the sound-symbol principle would be maintained in its strongest form. In addition, dialect differences are preserved and even individual idiosyncrasies would be recognized. On the other hand, it would be expensive to produce materials, there would be no single established writing system (i.e., spelling) within a community, teachers and students might each write differently, and so on.

The committee's discussions of standardization can be divided into two components, which in fact are at odds with one another: standardization of the alphabet and standardization of spellings. There was general agreement in the committee's deliberations that some version of the one symbol–one sound principle was appropriate—if, for instance, one sees <gw>, it should be pronounced in a single way. However, this decision conflicts with the principle of standardization of spelling, which would promote a single spelling for a particular word based on conservative pronunciation. To take a single example, in Hare it was agreed that the word 'she/he lives' should be written <rágwe>, even though it could be pronounced either [rágwe] or [rábe]. Thus, in reality, the one sound to one symbol principle, while it held for the alphabet, did not hold for spelling, where a single spelling might represent more than one pronunciation.

In attempts to standardize spellings rather than standardize an alphabet, the spellings became more abstract and further removed from something that an individual could learn fairly quickly. Attempts to standardize spellings led, perhaps inevitably, to several things. For instance, it affected the level at which the spelling system was standardized: the community level was chosen rather than the regional level because of the amount of variation beween dialects (which the principle of single spellings did not easily accommodate).

We note that another factor is also involved. There was never serious discussion of abandoning the principle of one symbol to one sound, although the types of standardization of spelling being discussed here suggest this. Basically, literacy for these languages is taught through learning the alphabet or by associating sounds and symbols. A more morphophonemic system was never advocated and in fact was explicitly rejected by the North Slavey standardization committee; thus the writing system is basically a what-you-see-is-what-you-get system, with the spelling being a direct reflection of the pronunciation. Such a system, with spelling mirroring pronunciation, is successful so long as the sound-symbol correspondences are strictly maintained, but it becomes far more difficult when such correspondences are abandoned for whatever reason. In reality, the absence of resources such as dictionaries meant that to a large degree individuals wrote North Slavey the way they spoke, and, given variation within the speech of an individual, even a single word could be spelled in more than one way in a given text.

Different decisions were made in the Kaska situation, where basically the principle of one symbol to one sound is used. In this situation, standardization was defined at a single level, namely, in terms of the alphabet. No attempt was made to standardize the spelling of different pronunciations, either within a particular dialect or across dialects. Thus the Kaska situation invited the inclusion of a number of dialects and languages into a single dictionary in a way the Slave situation did not. The intricacies of dealing with the standardization of spellings in Slave, or even North Slavey, were more than could be handled by the orthography standardization committees, and the goal of a common dictionary was never discussed in any substantial way.

5.3.3. EUROPEAN IDEOLOGIES.   Nancy Dorian, in a searching article on how Western ideologies affected the treatment of aboriginal languages, argues that Europeans brought with them an assumption of standardization:

> Europeans who came from polities with a history of standardizing and promoting just one high-prestige speech form carried their "ideology of contempt" for subordinate languages with them when they conquered far-flung territories, to the serious detriment of indigenous languages. And in addition to a language ideology favoring a single normalized language, derived from the history of national-language standardization in their homelands, Europeans espoused other ideologies that exacerbated their contempt for whatever unstandardized vernaculars they encountered. (1998: 9–10)

We believe that this type of European ideology identified by Dorian was still at work in the 1980s when the orthography standardization committees were meeting and that, at the very base of it, this attitude underlies many of the decisions that were made regarding standardization of spelling. Through our work on the dictionaries, we came to believe that these decisions were wrong, and, in fact, we were often surprised that we could even have countenanced such ideas, given our formal knowledge of language variation and language change.

Perhaps the reason that the standardization committees did not recognize the Eurocentrism of standardization as a goal is that they did not think in terms of favoring "a single normalized language" but rather in terms of ensuring that the speech of the elders, the conservative speakers of the languages, was not lost. It was deemed to be most important that the "real" language be maintained, an idea that entails the judgment that there is something wrong with the language spoken by the younger people—it is somehow not correct—an attitude toward their language held by many of the younger people themselves. The Eurocentric ideal of standardization ended up being couched in terms of wanting to preserve the speech of the elders, thus masking the fact that this was not necessarily the most appropriate goal for dictionary making. It took actual preparation of the dictionaries in collaboration with people in the communities to overcome this ideology and to afford the realization that the goal of normalization is not the only one.

5.4. SUMMING UP.   What is the lesson from this? Most broadly, it is necessary to determine early in the work on the dictionary what the goals of that dictionary are. Who is its audience? Is it primarily for the community or primarily for linguists? These two groups have very different needs, and it is difficult to come up with a single dictionary that meets all of them. Even when the audience is defined as the community, questions remain. Is it a single, fairly homogeneous community (e.g., Hare, Bearlake)? Is it a single dialect with considerable subdialectal variation (Dogrib, South Slavey)? Is it a number of distinct languages (Kaska Tribal Council dictionary)? Until the answers are determined, it is difficult to make much progress.

More specifically, in developing dictionaries it is important to understand just what is meant by standardization. There is quite widespread agreement that standardization of an alphabet is a prerequisite to dictionary work and to developing literacy in a language—it is difficult to support more than one alphabet (except in the limited sense in which we see this for a language like Sekani, as in (30) above). One finds standardization discussed in this way very commonly (see, e.g., Dauenhauer and Dauenhauer 1998; England 1998). Standardization of spellings, on the other hand, is perhaps not appropriate in a dictionary being designed for a community with any internal diversity, where the level of written literacy is rather low and the notion of literacy in the language is quite new.

One must also realize that political considerations are at play in making decisions about dictionaries. The most recent Dogrib and Slave dictionary projects began with government committees; the Kaska was undertaken in a different way. The focus with Dogrib and Slave was on how different the languages are, and from the assumption that different languages have different dictionaries, separate dictionary projects were commenced. With Kaska, the creators of the dictionary did not worry so much about differences but instead decided that a dictionary could serve to bring people together. This ideal, and the (free) choice of spellings based on the principle of one symbol to one sound, allowed the development of a very different type of dictionary.

6. CONCLUSION.   We are not advocating a particular dictionary type. A dictionary could be of single dialects, multiple dialects, single languages, multiple languages; it could be designed for the community member, for the linguist, or, perhaps, for both. What we are advocating is that true involvement of a community must take place in order to determine what a dictionary for community use should be like. Rigidity is not in order, and rules that one establishes at the beginning of a process of making a dictionary must be allowed to change as the dictionary takes on a life of its own. This is perhaps the most important lesson to be learned from all three dictionaries discussed here: what they are now is quite different from what they were when they began.

We are also advocating a relaxation of the principle that spellings must be standardized from the start. Standardized spelling is important in some cases (e.g., placenames often must receive a single spelling), but the imposition of a standardized spelling can inhibit the development of literacy. (We are assuming that literacy is a positive goal; one might question this assumption.) Variations in spelling are a reflection of variations in language, a fact of any language whatsoever. Rather than see dictionaries of First Nations languages as deficient in being unable to reach standardization in spelling, we might view many Western dictionaries as deficient in not recognizing the full range of pronunciations that a word can have but hiding them with a common spelling. Standardization of spelling may emerge in these languages or it may not, depending on many factors, and standardization might be at a community level or at a regional level. Nevertheless, standardization of spelling should not necessarily be taken as a factor in dictionary making. Dictionaries should represent the fullness of what a language is rather than be a straightjacket, turning it into something less than it is.

When we compare these Athabaskan situations with others, we see that standardized spelling is indeed an emergent property. For instance, in early English documents, the spelling is quite reflective of the dialect of English that was being written. Even in contemporary English, spelling of a single word can vary. We see well-known differences between British and American spellings—for example, *gaol/jail, theatre/theater; humour/humor.* Spellings change over time as well. A particularly striking example comes in professional signs in Toronto now found with the spelling *independant* rather than *independent*, certainly an innovation. Thus the notion that standardization of a spelling system is a prerequisite to literacy is a fallacy even in languages such as English, where there has been a longtime focus on developing a standard.

In closing, through our work on dictionaries, we have learned as much about what dictionaries are not as about what dictionaries are. The models from English and other Western languages that we began with in some ways hindered our progress in coming to a decision about what a dictionary for the languages that we were working with should be. The Kaska dictionary was eye-opening in advocating the relaxing of a number of principles. We have discussed the need to understand the context of use with respect to the standardization of orthography, but the same question can be raised concerning many other features of a dictionary: what type of grammatical information must be included; whether examples should be included and, if so, where they should be drawn from; how much encyclopedic content there should be in the definitions; and so on. Each situation will determine which starting principles must be maintained and which should be changed, and that is the challenge of creating a dictionary that will be used over some period of time. This work cannot be done by an outsider or by professionals alone but must involve all of the prospective users of the dictionary in a substantial and meaningful way.

CHAPTER SEVEN

A Dictionary for Whom?

Tensions between Academic and Nonacademic Functions of Bilingual Dictionaries

Leanne Hinton and William F. Weigel

1. INTRODUCTION. The grammars, texts, and dictionaries of Native American languages produced by earlier generations of academic linguists had a straightforward purpose: to document moribund languages before their inevitable extinction. As linguists today, however, we are likely also to want (and in fact are expected) to provide expert assistance to native communities in maintaining and revitalizing their languages. We are usually much better prepared for the first task (documentation) than for the second.

This chapter presents the often differing goals and needs of linguists and communities. We explore possibilities and limitations of the "dual-purpose" bilingual dictionary, intended for both academic and tribal users. We will begin by looking at the range of needs the linguist is likely to find in native communities and then consider how these can be addressed in the development of dictionaries.

2. USES OF DICTIONARIES IN LANGUAGE MAINTENANCE AND REVITALIZATION. The dictionary is a critical reference for language communities involved with language teaching and learning. In bilingual education programs and the newer immersion programs, for example, a dictionary is vital to teachers for curriculum development. For nonspeakers and incipient speakers, the dictionary is important for developing vocabulary. Often the teachers themselves are not fluent speakers and use the dictionary heavily. Since writing systems for small indigenous communities are often relatively new and may have to be learned on one's own without assistance, and may therefore not be fully mastered even by teachers, whether fluent in their language or not, the dictionary can be

an important spelling reference. Furthermore, if the curriculum involves a particular topic (e.g., a section on traditional ceremony), there may be specialized vocabulary relating to that subject that a teacher may want to look up. And, of course, in school, learning how to use a dictionary may be a subject in itself, and children will be using it for various assignments. In communities we have worked in, we find that a dictionary is important even to native speakers, who (since these are moribund languages) may not have used their language for communication for many years and sometimes need the dictionary to remind them of a word.

Not every Native American language is moribund, but languages with great vitality also need dictionaries for many of the uses discussed above. Also, even communities without language teaching programs may nonetheless find that a dictionary of their ancestral language is an important resource. A dictionary is a repository of tribal identity that can be used for a variety of purposes even after the language ceases to be spoken.

3. POINTS OF TENSION BETWEEN LINGUISTIC AND COMMUNITY
   NEEDS FOR DICTIONARIES.

3.1. ORTHOGRAPHY. The first question for a dual-purpose dictionary is what orthographic system is to be used. The use of the International Phonetic Alphabet (IPA) or its Americanist relative is considered standard for linguists; for the sake of linguistic research, it is often argued by linguists that a single phonetic writing system that allows the easy comparison of languages around the world is the ideal to strive for (as outlined in Hinton 1997). Americanists, who have used the Americanist system instead of the IPA for their whole history, have a stake in maintaining their system and have argued for the superiority of the Americanist system with regard to certain orthographic practices. Supporters of the IPA point out that they have the advantage of an official organization that can update the system as needed. But, in any case, the Americanist system and the IPA are converging over time, so that now relatively few symbols differ. In addition to these general points of contention, idiosyncratic orthographic traditions sometimes evolved among scholars of particular languages, language families, or areas.

From the community point of view, both the IPA and the Americanist system have problems. If the community has a standard writing system of its own, it is naturally desirable that this system be used in place of either of the linguistic systems. While some tribal writing systems are perfectly adaptable to the needs of the linguist and are used without question, others present problems. Writing systems such as the Cherokee and Cree syllabaries are especially difficult for linguists to handle, while these are the orthographies that are often preferred by the communities that use them.

A great deal of literature was developed in Humboldt County for Hupa, Yurok, Tolowa, and Karuk in the 1970s and 1980s using UNIFON, an alphabet made up by an employee at Bell Labs in Chicago, adopted by a faculty member (not a linguist) at Humboldt State University, and applied to the languages of California Indians attending classes there. This writing system was strongly disliked by linguists, and became a subject of much heat. That, along with certain important impracticalities of the system, have worked against its continuation, and most of the tribes that were using UNIFON have abandoned it (or are now in the process of abandoning it) in favor of writing systems based on the Roman alphabet. But in the meantime many important materials are written in UNIFON, and many of the last native speakers of these languages are well versed in this system.

The more usual situation among American Indian languages is that there is no standard orthography, and the community wishes to develop one. Linguists are often called in to assist with this development. In that case, too, the phonetic systems are problematic for the community for two main reasons:

1. They offer technological difficulties for people without a great deal of access to high-tech solutions. Typewriters, computers, and the average printing press do not have the special symbols of the IPA. Although fonts can be designed, it takes time, money, and know-how and presents a discouraging barrier to people who just want to get things ready for the next informal class or the coming school year.
2. The phonetic systems do not allow easy application of the reading and writing knowledge of English. Since all community members are bilingual (or monolingual in English) and since they all read and write English, efficiency of learning suggests the development of a writing system that uses this knowledge.

The kind of orthography that is developed naturally by nonlinguists tends to be what Wallace Chafe (pers. com.) calls "folk writing," a system that typically has dashes between syllables and spells each syllable according to English spelling rules. The following are some examples of the folk writing used by a semispeaker of Wukchumne (a.k.a. Wikchamni), a close relative of Yowlumne.

Folk writing	Americanist transcription	
chee	$\check{c}^h ii$	'bone'
ot-ow	$ot^h aw$	'hair'
puh-tuth	$p^h utu\underset{.}{t}$	'body'

From this small sample, it is apparent that this system fails to distinguish the dental stop [t] from the retroalveolar stop [ṭ]. In general, such systems are limited to sounds that are like English, and they tend to miss important distinctions such as glottalized stops or dental versus alveolar places of articulation. Language learners, who often employ such a means of writing as a memory aid, tend to mispronounce their words when reading their own transcription. For native speakers, of course, a limited orthography that misses meaningful sound distinctions would not be much of a problem, for all they need is enough clues to figure out what a given word is. For learners and linguists, however, such an orthography is problematic. Nevertheless, this kind of orthography involves the greatest ease of transfer of English spelling knowledge to the Native language and can become the orthography of preference in a community.

For many languages, linguists and speakers working together have created a kind of compromise orthographic system, one that correctly shows all phonemic distinctions but still caters to the knowledge of English spelling to some extent and avoids special symbols as much as possible, replacing those with digraphs or letters with easy modifications such as capitalization or underlining.

3.2. RELATIONSHIP TO ENGLISH ORTHOGRAPHY. Tribal users of the orthography will usually be native (or at least fluent) English speakers and will almost certainly be more familiar with the spelling of English than with that of any other language. This means, for example, that the linguist's use of the "Spanish" values for vowels is something that the dictionary user must learn. Many tribal orthographies use these values; Navajo, Hopi, Havasupai, and Kumeyaay are just a few of the languages which have adopted them. Long vowels present a problem, especially if written as double vowels, because of the ease of confusion with the idiosyncratic English pronunciation of *ee* and *oo;* but most of the languages just listed use these conventions, and of course the confusion disappears with practice. Some groups, such as the Hualapais, have settled on the use of a colon for long vowels (*e:, o:,* etc.), which avoids the initial confusion of the double-vowel system.

The alternative of using English vowel values presents obvious difficulties, but we will consider some cases in which it seems to have worked. For example, Tlingit uses the following conventions for vowels (Dauenhauer and Dauenhauer 1991).

Tlingit vowels:

Short	*a*	*i*	*e*	*u*
Long	*aa*	*ee*	*ei*	*oo*
IPA	[aː]	[iː]	[eː]	[uː]

For another example, the Puritan missionary John Eliot (the "Apostle to the Indians") developed a spelling system for the Massachusett (also named Wampanoag, or in the modern tribal spelling, Wopanaak) language based on his seventeenth-century English spelling and pronunciation and used it in his famous translation of the Bible. Tribe members continued using the system for both official and personal purposes into the nineteenth century, when the language became extinct (Goddard and Bragdon 1988). Eliot used *ee* to stand for /i/, in keeping with English spelling conventions. For the long high-back vowel /u/, Eliot used an infinity sign (∞), which somewhat resembles *oo*. Since the infinity sign is not on standard keyboards, Ives Goddard and Kathleen J. Bragdon (1988) turned it 90 degrees to write it as an *8*. Both *ee* and *8* are now being used by Wopanaaks in materials developed for language classes aimed at reclaiming their language (Fermino 1998).

3.3. CONSONANT SYSTEMS. The consonants do not present as difficult a problem as vowels, as there is less likelihood of interference from English for people unfamiliar with the system. There are nevertheless two issues that create sticking points during the creation of a community-based writing system: (1) finding unique orthographic representations for sounds not in English; and (2) using letters that have a pronunciation in the heritage language different from that in English.

1. Finding good representations for sounds not in English and yet compatible with the typical keyboard generally means the use of digraphs, diacritics, or unconventional characters. Examples:
   Mayan: the use of 7 for glottal stop in Mayan languages, an orthographic convention developed by Terry Kaufman.
   Tlingit, etc.: the use of *p'*, *t'*, *k'*, etc., for glottalized stops (widespread).
   California: For a voiceless lateral, Hupa chose to use capital *L*, while Yurok chose to use *hl* and Kumeyaay uses *ll*.
2. Letters that have similar but nonidentical pronunciations in English and in a Native American language also create a problem for learners. During the development of the Havasupai writing system, Hinton suggested "t" for the voiceless dental stop but was overruled by the tribal council, which said that people would mispronounce it as alveolar. So a *t* with an extra cross through it (*ŧ*) was settled on instead (Crook, Hinton, and Stenson 1977).

Another case arose when Hinton and native speaker Agnes Vera and her son Matt were designing a practical Yowlumne orthography. Yowlumne has no voiced stops, but the formalist academic literature usually represents the plain/aspirated distinction as *b, d, g* versus *p, t, k*. This is entirely the result of the orthography of Stanley Newman (1944), who provided the most prestigious and influential description of the language. However, it also looks like a reasonable practical solution: it preserves the "one phoneme, one symbol" rule while using only the Latin alphabet. It also seems to make sense phonetically, at least for English speakers, as the two stops series in English contrast in aspiration as well as voicing. Hinton and Vera nonetheless ended up instead using *p, t, k* for the plain stops and *ph, th, kh* for the aspirated. This decision was based on Vera's experience as a teacher of Yowlumne, in which she had found that it helped to prevent her students from voicing the unaspirated series.[1]

Orthographic development is very often mired in politics, with various factions favoring one system over another. Conflicts of this sort may arise from inadequacies of a system that cause some people to desire to abandon it in favor of one that is more adequate, either in terms of representing all (and only) the distinctions present in a language or in terms of being easier to learn or use. As often as not, however, the conflicts may also be based on who uses a particular system. A perfectly adequate writing system may be undesirable to one group of people simply because it is used by another group, or was designed by a person or group whose influence is rejected by others (Crook, Hinton, and Stenson 1977). A linguist developing a dictionary for community use will often become involved in the design of a community writing system or in choosing between competing writing systems that already exist. It is important for linguists to understand the political symbolism of writing systems and to be well versed in the politics of language that are being played out in the community they do research in. It is most important that the linguist be aware of any writing systems that already exist and not add fuel to the fire of factionalism by gratuitously introducing a new writing system to the community when it is not entirely necessary.

3.4. NEW WORDS. Throughout most of the twentieth century, a linguist's goal in producing a dictionary of an endangered language was to produce a record of the language before it disappeared. This is still an important goal of any dictionary, since even in languages that still have lots of speakers, a great deal of vocabulary is lost every generation, especially culturally specific vocabulary that may lose its use when a cultural practice ceases.

Now, however, languages undergoing the process of revitalization have another concern: the creation of new words for modern concepts and practices. Hawaii, for example, has a highly successful immersion school program, in which children are taught from preschool through the twelfth grade in the Hawaiian language. There is such a strong need for new vocabulary to teach such topics as biology, physics, chemistry, and math,

---

1. Hinton had the opposite experience with the Havasupais, who insisted on using *b* and *g* for voiceless unaspirated stops rather than *p* and *k*, because they feared that learners would aspirate these sounds.

not to mention the more elementary subjects, that a lexicon committee has been formed in Hawaii that has monthly meetings specifically aimed at the creation of new vocabulary. The Pūnana Leo Foundation has recently published a dictionary that consists almost entirely of new words (Hale Kuamoʻo and ʻAha Pūnana Leo 1996). This dictionary is in every classroom and is a key resource for teachers.

From the older point of view, such consciously created words (many of them in "Hawaiianized English" and therefore constituting borrowings) might not have much of a place in a linguist's dictionary. But from a present-day community point of view, these are among the most important words in the language, because of their prominence in schools, the main location where Hawaiian is presently used on a daily basis.

3.5. CITATION FORM.   The polysynthetic nature of many Native American languages makes it difficult to decide on the citation form of words. Often there is no basic form of a word that lacks affixation; in many languages the root of a word changes according to case or aspect; and in many languages there are multiple derivational prefixes that would play havoc with alphabetization if included on the word. In the history of Native American scholarship, a root-based dictionary has often been considered ideal, especially for such heavily prefixing languages as Navajo (Young and Morgan 1987) or Blackfoot (Frantz and Russell 1989). However, from the community point of view (and even for a linguist less sophisticated in the language in question), root dictionaries present problems. Let us say that you have a text with a mystery word in it and want to look up the word in the dictionary. If you do not know the word, you may not be able to determine which part of the word the root is. Especially if the word bears a prefix or a changeable root, the dictionary may not be of help in determining what the word is.

In Havasupai there are derivational prefixes as well as inflectional prefixes (the latter mainly for person). In developing a dictionary for community use, it was decided after consultation with Havasupai staff who coauthored the dictionary that derivational prefixes (but not inflectional prefixes) would be included on words and alphabetized according to the prefix. Cross-referencing could guide readers from the prefixed form to the basic root entry and vice versa. It was also decided never to have a "bare root" as an entry—that is, a form that is not a complete word. The basic citation form of verbs was the third-person indicative (bearing a -*g* suffix) and the absolutive noun form (bearing an -*a* suffix on consonant-final nouns and a glottal stop plus echo vowel on the others) (Hinton et al. 1994).

Prefixation is not the only issue. Any sort of morphological complexity can potentially create alphabetization problems. Yowlumne, for example, is exclusively suffixing but exhibits a high degree of root allomorphy, which is conditioned by the suffix attached. Thus the Yowlumne verb meaning 'grow up' may appear in a variety of forms, depending on the suffix:

poohuc'k'a	Imperative
pohoc'on	Durative present
pohc'on	Future
puhc'atinxo	Desiderative

It is possible to derive all of these allomorphs (*poohuc', pohoc', pohc'on, puhc'*) from a single underlying form *puuhc'* and prosodic templates associated with certain suffixes (along with a set of ordered rules or comparable theoretical apparatus), but this type of dictionary entry would be far too abstract to be practically useful: it would not only require mastering some sophisticated phonological theory, but would also require the dictionary user confronting a form like *pohoc'on* to effectively "reverse engineer" the phonology to reach the underlying form *puuhc'* in order to look up the verb.

One approach is to treat each Yowlumne verb as having several "principal parts" instead of a single citation form, in a manner analogous to the Latin and Greek pedagogical traditions. In a context unrelated to lexicography, Charles F. Hockett (1967) suggested as much, claiming that at most three principal parts would be necessary. Although this is not quite true (as the four allomorphs above attest), it will work with the addition of some fairly transparent phonology (such as shortening of long vowels in closed syllables), but this much phonology may defeat the purpose of having principal parts as alphabetizable items.

The often-noted similarity between the morphology of Yokuts and Semitic languages suggests a different approach. One typical widely used Arabic dictionary (Wehr 1976) lists verbs (and various deverbal forms) alphabetically under their underlying consonantal root. Only in those cases in which the root is not recoverable from the form in question is the form listed separately and crossreferenced to the main entry for the root. While Yowlumne verbal roots are not, strictly speaking, consonantal, it is nonetheless true that the only constant across the paradigm of a given Yowlumne verb is the (usually three) consonants of the root. This fact makes the consonantal root the single most readily identifiable marker under which to alphabetize information about the verb. Consonantal root entries actually make more sense for Yowlumne, in that, unlike Arabic, it never employs prefixation, and the root consonants are seldom obscured by phonological processes.

Some version of this approach will be used in the final form of Weigel's Yowlumne dictionary. The most parsimonious format would be to alphabetize the main entry for verbs under a consonantal root citation form, while the entry itself would employ some version of the principal parts approach. However, for community usage, where the users are native English speakers, this approach would seem very alien at first, because it is so different from dictionary organization in English. Community acceptance of this approach could be problematic, despite the fact that it would be relatively easy to learn. Much less economical, yet perhaps preferable to the community, would be to have the root appear in the dictionary in all its forms, with cross-referencing leading to the underlying form.

At least two points should be apparent from this discussion. The choice of the citation form and its role in the dictionary are highly language-specific matters. Thus it is unlikely that a solution for Havasupai or Yowlumne will be directly applicable to other languages. In addition, the choice must be informed by a realistic appraisal of how much grammatical knowledge can be expected of users. Few users will be comfortable with having to command multiple phonological rules or being required to unravel opaque derivational morphology, but in many cases it may be necessary to expect the users to have at least a passive recognition of the basic inflectional affixes in order to be able to segment the affix from its base. Without presuming some such limited knowledge on the part of the user, it is hard to see how a useful dictionary of a morphologically complex language could be designed. Similarly, complexity will usually dictate that the user be acquainted with the organization of the dictionary before trying to use it (although this may merely consist of reading a brief preface such as "How to Use This Dictionary").

3.6. ALPHABETIZATION.   Older linguistic dictionaries sometimes used an alphabetic ordering different from English order. One can frequently find dictionaries that are ordered articulatorily, meaning that the first letter of the dictionary is p.[2] Such a practice is anathema to nonlinguists, and certainly one of the first compromises linguists made when it became clear that communities wanted to use the dictionaries was to put the dictionary in English alphabetical order. Before the advent of the computer, it was not always clear where certain distinct symbols should fall in this order. Where do you put words beginning with glottal stop, for example? The "sort" mechanism on a computer now usually makes

---

2. For example, Stanley Newman's Yokuts (primarily Yowlumne) slip files, as well as the various informally circulated mimeograph word lists based on them, were in "articulatory" order. In fact, Weigel first became aware of the need for a Yowlumne dictionary after hearing linguists complain about the lack of usable, conventionally alphabetized word lists for this language family.

these decisions for us. However, designers should be aware that the sort function in most word-processing and database software is designed to work with ASCII characters and may produce unpredictable results when applied to the special characters or diacritics found in phonetic fonts. Thus, depending on the font and software used, words with an initial glottal stop character may appear as if glottal stop were the first letter of the alphabet, or alphabetically according to the vowel immediately following the glottal stop. Resorting entries by hand is possible, of course, but it is sufficiently tedious and error-prone that it may be a good idea to check out the sorting properties of candidate font/software combinations before committing to them.

Another issue is how to treat digraphs. The English solution is simply to count each letter, even if it is a digraph—so words beginning with *ch* precede words beginning with *ci*. Spanish, however, has a different solution, traditionally treating *ch* as a separate letter for purposes of alphabetization (although this practice is no longer universal). Linguists helping to develop practical alphabets usually want to behave as if a digraph is a single letter, since the digraphs are being used to represent single sounds—so *p'* would have its own section in a dictionary rather than be embedded in the *p* section. On the other hand, this practice can create difficulties for the nonlinguist trying to look up a word.

3.7. BILINGUAL OR MONOLINGUAL?   For two major reasons, it is rare indeed that a linguist needs to consider developing a dictionary that is monolingual in a Native American language. First, if the dictionary is to have an audience of English-speaking academics, their research needs are best met by a dictionary that uses English to explain the meaning and morphology of words and an index alphabetized by English. Second, it is the unfortunate case that most interested tribal users of a dictionary will not be fluent in their language of heritage. Those who are fluent are usually not proficient readers and writers of their heritage language. In the native community, a dictionary is most commonly used (1) as a reference for classroom language curriculum development; (2) as a language learning tool for nonfluent speakers; and, for native speakers, (3) as a tool to help a speaker remember words she or he has not spoken in many years and cannot dredge easily from memory. As virtually all Native Americans are fluent in English, having English translations and an English index is the best way for them to be able to make good use of the dictionary.

However, for a thriving or redeveloping language, a monolingual dictionary can be an important step toward linguistic autonomy. The problem with bilingual dictionaries is that each language is being described in terms of another language; in the case of the subordinate language, there is the danger of conceptual contamination from the superordinate language. Being able to know a language in a way that is independent of one's knowledge of the superordinate language is a worthy goal for communities involved in maintenance and revitalization of their languages, and a monolingual dictionary may be thought of as a kind of political statement of linguistic freedom. While few Native American languages are in a position to make much use of a monolingual dictionary, one language that is ready for such a move is Hawaiian. In the immersion schools, in particular, where the desire is to use the Hawaiian language only (except in English classes, which are also taught there), a dictionary in which a word is in Hawaiian and its definition in English could be thought of as defeating the purpose. As part of the education of their children, Hawaiians might well want them to use monolingual dictionaries.

3.8. ALPHABETIC VERSUS SEMANTIC VERSUS PRAGMATIC GROUPING OF ENTRIES.   There are a number of considerations that come into play in dictionary design for tribal use that have tended to be ignored in the past by linguists writing for the academic world only. An important addition to the dictionary for tribal use is the supplementation of alphabetical listing with organization by semantic category. In school programs, for example, a teacher may wish to have a session about kinship terms, household items, or plants. Such learning by category is obviously desirable in general, but it is essential in some cases, such as kinship terminology, in which there is often no one-to-one meaning correspondence between individual words in the two languages. In such cases the learner must master the new set of terms and their interrelations as a whole.

At least one pictorial dictionary organized on semantic (and pragmatic) principles exists for a Native American language, the *New Oxford Picture Dictionary—English-Navajo* (Oxford, 1990), although it is designed more with the learner of English in mind. Employed alone, this type of listing can make it very frustrating to look up words, but it can be effectively combined with alphabetical listing. The Havasupai dictionary has semantic categories as part of the English-to-Havasupai section. Besides listing all the animals individually according to alphabetical order in the dictionary, the word for "animals" would be in its correct alphabetical location, with a list of all the names for animals (in both English and Havasupai) under it. In any event, it is a good idea to include database fields for semantic and/or pragmatic category. This makes it easy to generate such word lists as separate items or as an appendix to the main dictionary.

For language revitalization, it is often clear that dictionaries of the past have tended to lack some important entries, in particular, idioms and pragmatic information (neither of which are likely to be found in grammars either). One of the first things a learner wants to know is how to greet someone in the target language, for example. An extremely popular item that has been produced lately at the Center for Community Development at Humboldt State University in California is a "phrasebook," now available for Karuk, Hupa, and Tolowa (e.g., Fletcher 1994). The phrasebooks contain useful vocabulary and phrases of interest to language learners. They tell you how to say hello and good-bye, how to count, how to give simple commands like "Eat your dinner." They have vocabulary arranged entirely by semantic categories rather than alphabetically. They are also attractively formatted with many pictures and have the advantage, too, of being pocket-sized, so that they can be carried easily. The practical dictionary designer should consider whether such material would be more appropriate in a separate phrasebook, in addition to the main dictionary (either as an appendix or organized under alphabetized pragmatic categories such as "shopping" or "greetings").

Another issue that comes up often when a tribe is going to use a dictionary for teaching purposes is taboo words. While a linguist's dictionary would almost certainly contain words for "penis," "vagina," "feces," and so on, modern-day Indians usually share the more conservative values of other Americans and feel that it might be inappropriate to have such words in a dictionary that will be sitting out on a table where children might see it. Other words might be sensitive for cultural reasons, such as personal names (if the dictionary would have such a thing) of the dead, or even the word for "dead person" in Karuk. Swearwords of various sorts (if the language has them) might be considered inappropriate for a schoolroom dictionary too. What will be considered taboo (or at least indelicate) cannot be predicted in advance; thus the linguist needs to be sensitive to speaker attitudes during the elicitation process. For example, Weigel's Yowlumne consultants, while not overly prudish about discussing sexual and scatological terminology, evidently found the literal compositional meaning of *kay'win p'otoolo'* ('paintbrush flower') embarrassing and translated it as 'Coyote's backside' rather than the correct 'Coyote's hemorrhoids'.

The solution to the dilemma of thoroughness versus prudishness is often found in creating more than one version of a dictionary. Luckily, with modern databases, a dictionary can be entered in a computer with a field specifying which version of the dictionary a word should or should not appear in, so that some words can be deleted easily for a specific version. With careful design, the database dictionary could be designed for multiple kinds of output—a small dictionary of basic words for children to use; a phrasebook style of dictionary; a teachers' reference dictionary; and a complete, unexpurgated form.

3.9. HOW COMPLETE SHOULD IT BE? Dictionaries are open-ended projects. We know some people who began working on dictionaries as graduate students and have not completed them after a whole career. Because a linguist's professional reputation is at stake, a perfectionist might end up spending many years trying to make a dictionary as complete and error-free as possible. The best and biggest dictionaries (such as the recently published Hopi dictionary [Hopi Dictionary Project 1998]) may take ten or twenty years of full-time work by several people. And tribes, too, want to record every word of their language (an impossibility). Ron Red Elk, a leader in the Comanche language revitalization effort, said that after a year or more of regular "dictionary meetings," an elder asked him when they would finish the dictionary. Ron said, "We will finish the dictionary when you elders stop coming to the meetings, or when there are no speakers left to come" (Red Elk pers. com.).

Certainly no dictionary ever contains the entire language. For one thing, the language keeps adding new words, if there is any life in it at all. There is never a true end point to a dictionary. Of course, it is natural to say that the dictionary should be as complete as possible; but this may mean that it never gets published. The question is, when should one get it out in public?

Tribes need faster results than linguistics does. Unfortunately, dictionaries are often undeservedly considered low-value products for such considerations as promotion and tenure in the academic world. A linguist may feel that the dictionary should be published before a major promotion decision is made, but often the dictionary will become a background project, to be worked on when there is time, and the project may languish for years. Tribes, on the other hand, are interested in dictionaries because they are interested in language maintenance, language teaching, or language revitalization. They want results as fast as possible. They may have a grant to do a dictionary in a limited amount of time. (One linguist we know was once asked by a tribe to do a dictionary for them in two weeks!) More often, they have a need for a dictionary to use in the classroom as soon as possible.

Often, then, tribes and the linguists working with them will decide to compromise between the need for thoroughness and the need for speed by producing multiple versions of a dictionary over time and producing it by photocopy rather than the more final and expensive professional publication (which the linguist may still have in mind for the future). The first edition of the dictionary may be limited to basic vocabulary and may not be completely error-free. Subsequent editions will contain more and more vocabulary, sample sentences, and increasingly well-edited entries. Pamela Munro did this with her Yavapai dictionary, frequently sending copies out to colleagues and Yavapai consultants as the dictionary progressed.

3.10. ISSUES OF AUTHORSHIP, PUBLICATION, COST, COPYRIGHT, AND OWNERSHIP. Hinton recently visited a tribe in the East to give a workshop and was disappointed not to see the linguist there who had been working closely with the tribe on a dictionary. When she asked about it, tribal members told her that they had had a falling out with the linguist over the dictionary, which had just been published. The linguist had originally worked on the dictionary with two elders but over the last year or so had worked closely with a dozen or so other speakers in a newly formed tribal language committee. According to these people, the committee had helped the linguist to make the dictionary much larger than it had been before and had been instrumental in many corrections in the manuscript. The committee had an excellent relationship with this linguist. However, when the proofs arrived, the committee members were disappointed to see that none of them were included as authors (although the two elders were); they were given what they thought was insufficient acknowledgment, and the copyright was in the linguist's name. Furthermore, the committee found many things in the proofs that they felt were errors and should be changed, but, they said, the linguist refused to do so. The committee felt betrayed and was even discussing the possibility of implementing a declaration for approval by the tribal council that their language belonged to the tribe, not to anyone else, and that copyright of books about their language should always be in the tribe's name. They felt that when they worked with a linguist from then on, they would demand a contract that contained many restrictions on publication. The tribe is now starting over with its own dictionary. As the leader of the committee said sadly, "We've all lost out on this. [The linguist] has lost out because now he can't work with us anymore, and we've lost out because now we don't have that linguistic expertise available to us anymore."

This sad story is an illustration of the head-on collision that often takes place between tribes and linguists over the issue of publication. Publication is the lifeblood of an academic career. Linguists have a vital professional self-interest related to publication and must keep in mind a professional audience. Furthermore, linguists' professional reputations are among their greatest concerns and they know that any errors in a publication will be held against them by colleagues. Thus linguists are likely to become quite adamant about, for example, spelling a word in a particular way that may conflict with the opinions of the speakers. (Just because someone speaks a language doesn't necessarily mean that she or he knows how to spell it.) Thus the professional reputation of the linguist (as he or she sees it) is pitted against insistence on ownership of the language by the tribal membership (as they see it).

Publication is the hardest part of the relationship between a linguist and a tribe. Copyright, royalties (if any), authorship, cost, and distribution are all issues that can create rifts. With regard to distribution, for example, the tribe may want a dictionary with distribution limited only to tribal members. They may decide on a dictionary that is not published professionally but is run off in batches at a copy shop for use by the tribe. All these issues need to be worked out in advance of the development of the dictionary. Certainly if the tribe is hiring the linguist as a consultant, the tribe has every right to make the decisions about publication and distribution, although the linguist may decide not to work with the tribe under such restrictions. Unfortunately, both linguists and tribes are often naive about each other's assumptions and do not realize what problems might develop.

It is tempting to suggest that many of these problems, especially the kind of recriminations that Hinton observed, could be avoided by agreeing in advance about all the important details of linguist-tribe collaboration. In unusual cases (e.g., when the tribal organization hires the linguist to create specific learning materials) such an agreement might be appropriate, but more typically the decision to produce a major work like a dictionary can only be made after a solid personal working relationship has developed. Thus it may just be a fact of life that the linguist must often invest considerable time and money before finding out whether such a project is feasible.

Once the decision to produce a dictionary has been made, however, some things can be done to avoid problems. At this point a firm mutual understanding about such matters as ownership, authorship, and editorial control can be reached. It is also essential that before this stage the academic linguist and the tribal language activists have made clear their goals and interests. For example, academics often encounter the belief (among native peoples and elsewhere) that they earn huge royalties on their articles and books. While this may be literally false, linguists should frankly acknowledge their self-interest and the great value of publications to their careers. Similarly, native peoples often consider their ancestral language to be their collective property and thus may find the notion that someone else "owns" the rights to the dictionary outrageous (and perhaps reminiscent of past expropriations). This can make issues of copyright ownership and cost especially thorny. Commercial publishers, even if they do not insist on an assignment of copyright, will normally expect exclusive rights to the material and are likely to price the book well beyond the means of native learners.

One resolution of the problems of ownership and cost is to find an accommodating publisher that will price the dictionary low enough for native users. In other cases, the publisher may be willing to provide a substantial discount for native users or language programs, as the ordinarily quite pricey Mouton de Gruyter did for Richard Rhodes's Ojibwe (Chippewa) dictionary (1985).

The solution providing the greatest flexibility and tribal control is self-publication, and tribes sometimes insist on that. Modern photocopying businesses often provide binding services that allow book-length works to be produced and bound at reasonable prices. Tribes often prefer this also so that they can have control over distribution. For the linguist, however, this may not be the most desirable path: if the work is self-published, the linguist is deprived of the distribution network and prestige of a major publisher, which can be detrimental to one's career.

4. CONCLUSION. We have tried to show here that the planned use of a dictionary may make radical differences in its design. This is not to say, however, that the two audiences we have discussed here—linguists and the native community—are so different that the same dictionary may not be used for both. Most of the dictionaries we have mentioned here are of the utmost use to both audiences. The negotiation that takes place between community and linguist and the resultant ideas that emerge are in fact a very positive influence on linguistic science, and the science of dictionary design is no exception.

CHAPTER EIGHT

Language Renewal and the Technologies of Literacy and Postliteracy

Reflections from Western Mono

Paul V. Kroskrity

1. INTRODUCTION. Although the very definition of a dictionary has historically been viewed as intimately related to a speech community and its socially patterned speech (Zgusta 1971: 197), the current state of many Native American languages—especially those of North America—has necessarily transformed the art and science of dictionary making into a truly sociolinguistic activity. At a time when most of these languages are threatened with extinction and their associated communities are struggling for resources to engage in language renewal efforts (Krauss 1996; Leap 1988), linguists must confront what Nora C. England (1992: 29) has termed "the obligation of linguistic research." One of these obligations, which is most relevant for the present discussion, is to make linguistic resources that are available to speakers of the language (England 1992: 35). While valuable, works aimed more at preservation and documentation of linguistic detail and targeted for professional elites can only seem insensitive to the unprecedented number of communities at this historical moment

I want to gratefully acknowledge the support of many people from the Western Mono and University of California, Los Angeles (UCLA), communities who have made valuable contributions at various stages of the ongoing Mono Language Project. From the Mono community this list includes Annie Anders, Margaret Baty, Lydia Beecher, Melba Beecher, Ida Bishop, Lorraine Bishop, Virgil Bishop, Maggie Cheepo, Ron Goode, Clara Harris, Dan Harris, Margaret Hill, Mary Johnson, Gaylen Lee, Salvina Mayer, Esther Ortiz, Cathy Pomona, Melva Pomona, Frances Sherman, Orie Sherman-Medicine Bull, and Shelby Wesley. From the UCLA community, this list includes Christopher Loether, Jennifer F. Reynolds, Gregory A. Reinhardt, and Karl Teuschl. I want to especially thank Rosalie Bethel for her wisdom, knowledge, energy, and good humor; without her we could not have accomplished anything. Finally, I want to gratefully acknowledge support from the Institute of American Cultures, American Indian Studies Center, UCLA, and the Academic Senate Faculty Research Fund, UCLA.

struggling to combat linguistic obsolescence. But if the twenty-first century poses a uniquely severe challenge to linguistic diversity, as global economic forces continue to bolster the "symbolic capital" (Bourdieu 1991) of "world" languages and diminish that of indigenous languages (Krauss 1996), it also provides new technologies for information manipulation and control. In addition to aiding in the production of conventional print media, computers, the wide array of relevant software programs, and other instruments of "postliteracy" now make possible multimedia works that both continue and extend the role of more conventional indigenous-language dictionaries. This chapter explores the development of both an indigenous language dictionary and a CD-ROM as part of the Mono Language Project—a twenty-year collaboration between members of the Western Mono community and researchers from the University of California, Los Angeles (UCLA), for which I served as project director.

2. THE WESTERN MONO SPEECH COMMUNITY.   Today, Western Mono is an endangered language spoken by members of the Mono community in various central California towns. In communities like North Fork, Auberry, Dunlop, and Sycamore live about 1,500 Mono Indian people (Spier 1978). Within this dispersed community, there are approximately 41 highly fluent speakers and perhaps as many as 100 to 200 people with some knowledge of the language (Hinton 1994: 27–31).[1] Almost all the highly fluent speakers are sixty-five years of age or older. In terms of its genetic-historical classification, Western Mono is a Uto-Aztecan language that is closely related to other neighboring languages of the Numic branch—Northern Paiute, Eastern Mono, and Panamint (Miller 1983).

But Western Mono's status as an endangered language is surely attributable not to its family tree but rather to the hegemonic influence of Spanish and Euro-American invasions. Although a complete appreciation of the impact of these colonial influences in shaping "language ideologies" in contemporary Western Mono communities is beyond the scope of this chapter, it is critically important to mention three interrelated precolonial language-ideological patterns. These, along with the linguistic discrimination of the

---

1. Some younger speakers have knowledge of their ancestral language's grammar and vocabulary, but they often know more than they can say, and this makes it unlikely that they will be able to pass this passive knowledge of the language to the next generation. There are reasons for the relatively high number of self-reported speakers in census and other survey data. Two important reasons are the availability of courses both in and outside of schools, which greatly increases the number of people with some knowledge of the language and the prestige of Native languages for younger speakers, many of whom have adopted the language as an emblem of Mono identity. Western Mono is not alone in experiencing a rebirth of local interest in ancestral languages by Native groups. Indeed, this is happening elsewhere in the state and all over the United States more generally.

colonial period, provide indispensable preparatory background for understanding the relevant historical and cultural factors that informed the dictionary and multimedia efforts within the Mono Language Project and therefore warrant explicit attention. By "language ideology," I mean "the cultural system of ideas about social and linguistic relationships, together with their loading of moral and political interests" (Irvine 1989: 255).

3. LANGUAGE SHIFT AND LANGUAGE-IDEOLOGICAL CHANGE. The three precolonial language ideologies that can be reconstructed as "dominant" (in the sense of Kroskrity 1998) are syncretism, internal diversity, and utilitarianism. Syncretism is a value on taking influence from situations of language contact. Like many California Indian groups (Silver and Miller 1998), the Western Mono communities had very close ties to their neighboring Indian communities. These intertribal relations often included intermarriage and multilingualism. One piece of linguistic evidence that clearly demonstrates this pattern is the Western Mono word *maksi'*. This word, meaning 'co-in-laws', does not exist in any other language to which Western Mono is related. Since this term does not appear elsewhere in either the Numic language branch or, more generally, in the Uto-Aztecan family of languages, it must have been borrowed. The Southern Sierra Miwok language also has the same term, and in that language its structure is not anomalous as it is in Western Mono.[2] These observations make it clear that Western Mono borrowed a Southern Sierra Miwok kinship term and that the reason they borrowed it was because these groups were intermarrying during the precolonial period.

Syncretism is further evidenced in the large inventory of Spanish loanwords that were transmitted to Western Mono through participation in an extensive indigenous network spreading eastward from the coastal missions to the Mono end station created by the natural barrier of the Sierra Nevadas. Another aspect of syncretism is the pervasive multilingualism of the precontact community. With intermarriage and multilingualism pervasive in Mono-speaking communities, it was an unlikely environment to produce a folk one-to-one correlation between specific languages and corresponding ethnic identities such as that which characterized Euro-American "Andersonian (Anderson 1983) linguistic-cultural nationalism" (Silverstein 1996: 127) and the contemporary European nationalist ideologies (Blommaert and Verschueren 1998) with which they are surely homologous.[3]

---

2. The borrowed nature of the word *maksi'* is also suggested by its structure. No indigenous words in the Mono language permit the *ks* consonant cluster. For additional discussion, see also Loether 1997.

3. This "Andersonian" model, which tends to equate linguistic unity and national identity, operates as both a folk and an academic model for understanding language and identity

Speakers of Western Mono recognize many regional dialects, formerly identified with various bands but today identified with the neighboring town. Unlike those of Pueblo Indian groups like the Arizona Tewa (Kroskrity 1993), local ideologies of linguistic differentiation for the Western Mono rarely elevate one regional dialect over another. But regional differences are not the only ones recognized among Mono people. Monos recognize the shaping role of families in creating speech differences in the community. They also recognize and even celebrate individual variation and do not expect all members of the group to conform to a single way of speaking. Just as all members of the community once had their own traditional Mono names and personal songs that they would sing when approaching others, so each person is expected to have his or her own distinctive verbal style.

In addition to honoring variation in this manner, members of the community also emphasize the utilitarian nature of language—language as a tool or a technology. When the Mono community experienced language shift from Mono to English earlier this century, many parents felt it was inappropriate to teach the Native language to their children as it appeared that economic change was necessitating more and more use of English. Several of the oldest members of the community reported that their parents refused to teach them their ancestral languages and rationalized this choice by describing their children as *kumasa-tɨka*, or bread-eaters, who would no longer need a language associated with hunting and gathering and acorn processing activities (like Mono) but would instead require English as the language of the emerging cash economy.[4] This more traditional view of languages as tools as well as the

---

relationships. The folk model is clearly related to homologous European folk models. The academic model, as Silverstein (1996) has argued, has provided many graphic examples of how the language ideology of Euro-American scholars—here the Andersonian model, which represents an uncritical adoption of a folk model—has falsified the linguistic diversity of Native North American speech communities. I share with Silverstein and other linguistic anthropological colleagues a great sense of ambivalence about the work of Anderson (1983). On the positive side, we applaud his acknowledgment of the role of language in the constructivist project of creating communities, national and otherwise, through linguistic products and practices. But on the negative side, we reject his claim that nations-in-the-making must be monolingual communities that "naturally" share a common language. Indeed, this Andersonian precondition appears to be more a product of European and Euro-American language ideologies than a substantiated finding.

4. Unless otherwise indicated, the Mono orthography used in this article is the revised version of Bethel et. al. 1984 currently used by the Mono Language Project. It uses the Roman alphabet but adds three symbols: *ɨ* = a high, central, unrounded vowel; *g* = a back-velar, fricative "*g*"; and ' = glottal stop. In addition, some English orthographic symbols are adapted to Mono: the letter *q* is a back-velar stop, and uppercase vowels at the end of words are voiceless

linguistic discrimination faced by Mono people in the schools and promoted by the federal and state governments played a role in reducing the number of speakers who would pass their language of heritage on to younger generations.

This reconstruction of a precolonial Mono culture of language creates an analytical baseline from which we can see how these patterns have been variously enhanced, reversed, and elaborated in conjunction with both the missions and the state. Despite the fact that the Western Mono represented the easternmost group in the California culture area bounded by the Sierra Nevadas, the influence of the coastal missions of south-central California was considerable and is embodied in the eighty Spanish terms loaned into Western Mono as the end point of a diffusional chain extending from the missions into the Central Valley neighboring tribes like the Yokuts and the Southern Sierra Miwoks (Kroskrity and Reinhardt 1984). Most of these loanwords are nouns reflecting the new material products associated with the missions (e.g., horse, needle, shovel, pistol). The only two verbs that were borrowed are particularly revealing of the Monos' early exposure to the changing political economy of the area. These two verbal loanwords are *tawahani'i-t* from Spanish *trabajar* 'to work' and *tebe'i-t* from Spanish *deber* 'to owe'.

Although such loanwords foreshadowed eventual incorporation—at the bottom—into the imported cash economies associated with Spanish and Euro-American regimes, the Monos at first exploited their marginal location by limiting their participation in these economic systems. Albert Hurtado notes the initial successes of the Mono in incorporating agricultural work into their preexisting seasonal cycle of subsistence activities:

> Even Indians who lived in the mountains relied to some extent on the Fresno River Farm. For example, the Mono Indians worked for white settlers during planting and harvest times, mined gold in the winter and spring, and gathered "the natural products of the mountains" a subagent reported. In addition, the Mono Indians received some food and clothing at the government farm. With all these sources of supply the Monos had "been able to provide themselves with a comfortable living for Indians." (1988: 205)

---

vowels. Though the Mono Language Project uses this orthography, members of the community use a variety of folk approximations such as the one described later in this chapter or in note 5. In addition to these folk efforts is the orthography employed by Gaylen D. Lee, the Mono author of *Walking Where We Lived: Memoirs of a Mono Indian Family* (1998). This system is similar to that used by the project, though it differs in a number of ways, including the representation of vowel length, the nonrepresentation of voiceless vowels, and several other details. The existence of a multiplicity of orthographies and the lack of a perceived need for standardization are definitely traceable to the language-ideological position on internal diversity.

Some Indians, like the Monos, moved constantly from the reservation to private ranches to hunting and gathering grounds, making use of all available opportunities to create a new seasonal round. Other native people chose one survival strategy or another and lived or died with it.

In their movement across reservation boundaries that functioned as "racial barriers" for most Indians (Hurtado 1988: 120), Monos partially and temporarily resisted the local "spectrum of racisms"—including what Étienne Balibar (1991: 39) has termed "exclusive" and "inclusive" racisms. Because their land was so remote, there was no reason for the white population to actively pursue the genocidal practices associated with "exclusive" racism as practiced elsewhere in California. And because Monos themselves controlled their participation in the exploitation associated with "inclusive" racism, the full brunt of economic subordination was temporarily and partially avoided. Still, Western Monos would eventually experience the effects of these projects of racism in its many forms and be represented in the estimated 90 percent loss of California's Indian population from 1769 into the early twentieth century. As Hurtado (1988: v) succinctly summarizes, "This appalling rate of decline resulted from diseases, cultural dislocation, dispersion, and—to a lesser extent—outright homicide."

While Western Monos escaped the most genocidal consequences of their incorporation into the cash economy, they were later subject to the state's ethnocidal practices of legalized indenture of Indian children from 1850 to 1863 (Heizer 1974: 219–26) and, later, compulsory education in schools that prohibited the use of indigenous languages and promoted a castelike racism. In segregated schools attended only by Indians, the physical removal of Indian children saved Euro-American children from their presumably polluting contact. But in the mixed public schools of North Fork, attended by both Monos and local Euro-Americans, white children were encouraged to carry sticks in case they had to come into some type of physical contact with Indians. Even today, some seventy years later, Rosalie Bethel recalls her schoolgirl years with considerable pain because of the stigma associated with being Mono and speaking Mono by the Euro-American population.

Although ethnocidal educational policies did much to link Mono and other indigenous languages to a "stigmatized ethnic identity," often an important factor in cases of language shift (cf. Dorian's 1981 study of East Sutherland Gaelic, Gal's 1979 research on Hungarian speakers in the Austrian community of Oberwart, Kulick's 1992 examination of Gapun language shift), such stigmatizing practices did not and could not dictate English as the language of the home. The utilitarian view of language that associates it with technoeconomic strategies prompted many multilingual parents to make English the language of the home because of its enhanced utility in a continually more encompassing cash economy.

One of the current speakers of Western Mono, now in her seventies, described the linguistic situation as she was growing up in the following manner:

> I was still a girl when my mother stopped speaking Mono in our home. When I asked her why, she said, "You young people will not live as we did. We needed our language as a way of finding food and living from the land. But you are now becoming 'bread-eaters' (*kumasa-tika*). You will need to know how to make money to buy things at the store. The new man's language is what you will need."

In this view, Mono was associated with increasingly obsolete subsistence strategies and English with the new forms of economic participation that would most promote survival. This, coupled with the lack of a strong association between the Mono language and a specific ethnic identity and a value on linguistic borrowing in its many forms, provided an indigenous language-ideological basis that did not offer significant resistance to the spread of English in Mono homes.

It is of course wrong, as Dan Kulick (1992) has recently indicated, to assume that parental decisions are the main cause of language shift. Such a view assumes that parents are overly agentive and in complete control of their linguistic resources, and it ignores the role of the peer group. Kulick (1992: 278) is also wise to attend to the role of unintended consequences in interpreting the role of parents in language shift. Parental intentions are often misdirected or misread by the younger generation. This may have been the case with the Western Mono, where many of our consultants felt that their parents were "ashamed" of their Native language because they did not actively promote it in their homes. Parental practices that were more likely attributable to an older culture of language were often misread as compliance with school policy as part of a total conversion affecting home, school, and peer group.

Today the language shift is almost complete in that English now performs virtually all the functions once performed by Western Mono. The one domain in which Mono language and song persist is in Native religious activities, where Mono is strongly preferred. But the lack of a vital ancestral language has not led to a collapse of the Western Mono community. Mono people are such not by virtue of speaking an ancestral language but by participation in Native activities—festivals, funerals, and assisting family and friends within the group. The language is viewed as significant but not any more so as a cultural resource than a knowledge of basket making or plant use. This, at least, was the state of affairs when I began the Mono Language Project in 1980 and organized workshops with community members in which we, at the request of Ms. Bethel, produced a dictionary of Western Mono designed for community members.

Three interrelated developments seem to signal a new day for Mono as a symbol of Mono cultural identity: (1) its incorporation in "language and culture" (Palmer 1988) programs in the schools; (2) its symbolic role in the battle for federal recognition; and (3) the Native American Languages Acts of 1990 and 1992. All these promote a rethinking of local linkages between a language of heritage and an ethnic identity. It is now fashionable for Mono people to call themselves *Nium*, using the Native self-designation as a loanword into local English.[5] Local schools have used a combination of federal funds and local moneys to create Mono "language and culture" classes for all students. These classes are not designed to restore fluency to the community but for the purpose of familiarizing Mono and other children with important cultural vocabulary (kin terms, food names, placenames) and linguistic routines (like greetings and closings). These terms are explicitly linked to Mono culture and identity and represent curriculum innovations on the basis of improving the self-image of Indian students. Students who receive these lessons certainly get a message from their early classroom experience very different from the one gotten by Rosalie Bethel and her generation.

On another front, Western Monos have been one of many California Indian tribes to seek federal recognition. The rigorous criteria that must be met by candidates for recognition do not explicitly mention languages, but they do mention the need to demonstrate maintenance of cultural continuity. Thus even a partial reversal of language shift—a kind of linguistic "tip" (Dorian 1989) in the direction of the indigenous language—even if it approximates the limited goals of so-called language-and-culture renewal programs, represents a development of great personal and political significance for many members of the Western Mono community.

4. THE MONO LANGUAGE PROJECT.   Against this backdrop, members of the Mono community initiated what was to become a long-term project involving UCLA linguistic anthropology personnel including myself. Using her niece, Orie Sherman-Medicine Bull, then a graduate student in film and television, as a contact person, Rosalie Bethel, a North Fork Mono elder with special expertise in the Western Mono language, inquired whether I had any interest in helping her to systematically write and record her ancestral language. Ms. Bethel had learned her ancestral language from her monolingual mother and had added to this knowledge through her participation in a network of knowledgeable elders from the Western Mono area. For approximately ten years prior to the Mono

---

5. This word is reproduced from a poster used to advertise the Annual Mono Indian Days celebration in summer 1997. It is not written in the Mono Language Project Orthography (where it would be rendered *Niimi*).

Language Project, which began in 1981, Ms. Bethel had dutifully recorded words from the Mono language on index cards. Using an idiosyncratic folk orthography that did not consistently distinguish vowels and that represented the same consonant sound in several alternative ways, Ms. Bethel had nevertheless produced a rudimentary form of what was to become the first Western Mono dictionary. Although her transcriptions lacked phonological accuracy and systematicity, they provided a key resource for the recollection of these forms through elicitation, recording, and the use of an orthography that was generally recognized by Americanists and used in the Smithsonian Institution's multivolume reference work, *Handbook of North American Indians.*

At the time I met Ms. Bethel, I had no previous research experience in California Indian communities, but I had already completed a dissertation based on almost two years of fieldwork on Arizona Tewa—a Kiowa-Tanoan language currently spoken on First Mesa of the Hopi Reservation in northeastern Arizona (Kroskrity 1977). Having taught at UCLA for several years, I was interested in developing a good working relationship with a California Indian community that might serve as a more local research home for me and my students, one that might prove more hospitable than the notoriously difficult Pueblo societies I had previously researched. I had heard that California Indian languages were generally far more moribund than any of the Pueblo and Apachean cultural groups with which I was familiar from my research in the Native American Southwest. But I had never performed research in a community where there were not ancestral language speakers in every generation and in which there were not children growing up with that language. This situation suggested the immediate importance of a dictionary project that would seek to produce linguistic products of value not only to researchers but to community members as well. Since no dictionary of Western Mono had been compiled, it was an easy project to justify in terms of both descriptive linguistics and the Mono community's interest in cultural resource management.

In its early stages, the Mono Language Project resembled a cultural exchange program. Ms. Bethel came to UCLA in 1981 for the winter quarter and became the key consultant for a field methods class of students who were both training and contributing new materials for the descriptive goals of the project. Later, that summer, several student researchers and I went up to North Fork to conduct additional research and to engage a broader segment of the community in linguistic workshop meetings. These meetings were designed to convey the goals of the project, present preliminary results (such as sample pages of dictionaries and standardized orthographies), gather new information, and get community feedback on our accomplishments and our persisting problems. From this ongoing dialogue of native speakers and community leaders, on the one hand, and linguistic anthropologists, on the other, several versions of a dictionary designed for use by community members were planned and produced. The first of these, *A Practical Dictionary of Western Mono* (Bethel et al. 1984), contained about two thousand annotated and exemplified entries written in the initial project orthography. It also contained an English finder's list that complemented the basic Mono-to-English organization of the dictionary. This dictionary also featured a guide to pronunciation and a very brief introduction to Mono grammar. In addition, it contained many tables of words in various semantic domains and a story written in the project orthography. The second edition, produced in 1993, was a revised, slightly expanded, and corrected version that presented entries in a revised orthography. The third edition of the dictionary, which is currently in process, is a slightly expanded version that incorporates new vocabulary encountered in development of narrative materials used in the current multimedia phase of the Mono Language Project.

Before and after each of these editions, the UCLA linguistic team met with community representatives to get a sense of local interests and how these would affect use and acceptance of the dictionary materials. Though our meetings always produced an enthusiastic response from Mono people from North Fork and Auberry from the very beginning of the project in 1980, there is evidence today, as the Mono Language Project completes a CD-ROM of ancestral language performances, that enthusiasm for Western Mono is on the rise even as the specter of language death looms nearer. But although the people we met—mostly elders and some of their younger kinsmen—were enthusiastic about the preservationist aspects of the project, they continuously alerted us to potential difficulties of doing community-based applied lexicography. In the remainder of this section I want to analyze five of these difficulties, connecting this discussion both to the preceding section on local language ideologies and to the following section, which describes the relationship of the mulimedia phase to the earlier dictionaries, moving from ancestral language "literacy" to "postliteracy."

4.1. WHOSE LANGUAGE? The first difficulty was summarized in a frequently asked question, "Whose language will go down in the dictionary as the right way to say things?" Literacy practices within the Mono community were confined to English language sources since there was almost no previous tradition of indigenous language literacy. Ancestral language literacy practices were confined to a single activity—reading signs. Within the community, for example, Western Mono appeared in street signs like "Tuuhoot," the term for 'deer', or signs in public build-ings like the Sierra Mono Museum, where the bathroom was labeled "Quitah-Nobee," using a nonstandard and inconsistent folk orthography. Western Mono people knew that they spoke English somewhat differ-ently from how they wrote it, and they brought to the Mono Language Project this sense of prescriptivism regarding orthographies and dic-tionaries. Furthermore, they knew that within their speech community there were speech differences correlated with both regional and age variation. How would this be accommodated? Since speakers from North Fork and Auberry showed some linguistic differences, almost exclusively in minor differences of pronunciation, they expressed concern that any dictionary entry somehow acknowledge this variation. Example (1), below, demonstrates how we confronted this problem in our represen-tation of the word *mutsipI-* 'flea'.

(1) mutsipI NOUN
"flea"
Example: PukU nehe ewa-kU mutsipi-ge-tU.
"The dog has a lot of fleas."
Sociolinguistic Note: Auberry pronunciation: mujipI

By annotating entries alphabetized by their North Fork Mono repre-sentations with the Auberry forms, we avoided presenting the North Fork forms as the prescriptively correct ones. Even though North Fork [ts] and Auberry [j] are in regular phonological correspondence and could be described with a general rule of dialect variation, community mem-bers strongly preferred the word-by-word treatment as a form of overt acknowledgment of the variation. Similarly, community members who attended the dictionary workshops also encouraged us to take an inclu-sive stance on age-based and stylistic variation. Those speakers of Western Mono who were familiar with English language dictionaries experienced them not only as insensitive to regional variation but also as prescrip-tively limited in stylistic range. Rather than make the dictionary a repos-itory of forms used only by the elders for the purpose of polite com-munication, speakers wanted the dictionary to reflect a broader range of usage within their community. Although they acknowledged attrition in actual use, they encouraged us to include slang forms and vocabulary items from semantic domains of the body, because, as they often said, "people have a need to be talking about these things." Examples (2) and (3) are among the entries that were reshaped to better approximate community specifications.

(2) k<del>i</del>nA NOUN
   1) semen; 2) *(slang)*, bastard, "jerk-off" [insultingly negative]
   Example: Puku-na ah-k<del>i</del>na-na n<del>i</del><del>i</del> a-boni-t.
   "I saw the dog's semen."
   K<del>i</del>nA!
   (You) bastard!
   Mahu k<del>i</del>nA.
   That one is a bastard.

(3) tsede NOUN
   1) butt, buttocks; 2) anus
   Example: I-wana' t<del>i</del>-tsede-maakU na-dona-t.
   "My little brother was stung on his butt."

This question of styles produced significant debate and discussion in the workshops. Some speakers suggested that the larger society might view such words as coarse and inappropriate, but the majority of those attending the workshops successfully argued that the dictionary was "for the community" and that existing Mono words "were there for a purpose that should be respected and included." Although those community members advocating hypermodesty were defeated in this decision, they were successful in convincing others that only the first of the two senses of *tsede*, in (3) above, should be exemplified. In general, however, the prescriptivism that many Mono people associated with English dictionaries (especially the ones they experienced in their own primary and secondary educational institutions) was usually tempered by the indigenous language ideology that emphasized internal diversity.

4.2. ACCESS TO THE INDIGENOUS LANGUAGE.   The second difficulty our project experienced was connected to what Lenore A. Grenoble and Lindsay J. Whaley (1998: 52) have described as "the community's access to the indigenous language and culture." Very few Mono families had a fluent speaker, and very few Monos had even a superficial familiarity with how their ancestral language was pronounced. This lack of access to speech models at home placed a heavy burden on reference tools like the Western Mono dictionary as well as on the practical orthography used to represent local pronunciation. In meetings, speakers encouraged us to use orthographic symbols that were close to English because they were familiar with how to pronounce them. Thus in the second edition of the dictionary, we used "ts" to replace the affricate "c" since such a representation was more "natural" for speakers who were not accustomed to Americanist orthographies but rather conditioned to the Roman alphabet of English. While such changes produced satisfactory results for community members, we ran into greater difficulties attempting to represent phonemes (and allophones) of

Western Mono, which could not be so readily captured by an English-based orthography. Fortunately, only two additional symbols needed to be created: *i̵*, or "barred i" (a high, central, unrounded vowel), and *g* (represented by either overstriking or underlining the letter *g*, a back-velar, voiced fricative). These sounds were especially difficult to represent in a "guide to pronunciation," and they contributed to a sense of frustration among some nonspeakers that the dictionary was beyond their comprehension. Because they had neither ready access to native speakers nor to an established tradition of Native language literacy instruction, many people wanted the dictionary to be more self-explanatory, especially in matters of pronunciation. Apart from phonology, most Mono people, as second-language learners of their ancestral language, also did not have native-speaker discourse models. Lacking local models of narrative or other genres, they needed "text-building" strategies that would demonstrate cohesion and coherence beyond the exemplary sentences we used to illustrate each lexical entry in the dictionary.

4.3. INFLUENCE OF ENGLISH.   Complementary to the preceding factor, the third difficulty was traceable to the Mono community's "access to the majority language" (Grenoble and Whaley 1998: 52), especially insofar as matters of literacy are concerned. In contrast to the lack of a tradition of Native language literacy, virtually all Mono people were literate in English. So powerful was literacy in English for community members that they relied heavily on this experience in attempting to evaluate proposed Native language orthographies and literacy products. As mentioned above, orthographies needed to be as closely modeled on that of English as possible. Since most Mono people were native speakers of English and knew English phonology, there was always the problem of attempting to approach Mono pronunciation through English. Because the two languages have many sounds in common, certainly some knowledge could be successfully extended to Mono. But in the cases of new symbols, like *i̵*, most Mono-as-a-second-language speakers tended to pronounce this vowel like the back and rounded vowel /u/ of their native English. Community members also suggested that Western Mono dictionaries include a guide to pronunciation for each lexical entry on the model of many popular English dictionaries. But this attempted reliance on popular phonetic representations that were conventional in popular reference dictionaries of English was based on an unfounded assumption that such a system could accommodate all the sounds of Western Mono.

The community's fluency in English also influenced the representation of foreignisms from English. Because all speakers knew English better than any other source language, they were almost always aware of English loanwords whereas those from other languages, like Spanish, often escaped popular attention. This is important, because this awareness, coupled with a new sense of competition from English and all its hegemonic resources, has produced a rethinking of the formerly dominant language ideology of syncretism. This is explored below.

4.4. FOREIGNISMS. The fourth difficulty emerged in debates over the inclusion of foreignisms in the dictionary. In general, Western Mono people wanted the dictionary to reflect the syncretic values of the community and its borrowing from other indigenous languages such as Southern Sierra Miwok as well as colonial languages such as Spanish and English. Examples (4–6) illustrate this trend:

(4) maksi' NOUN
   "in-laws" (used both to greet people and to refer to them)
   Example: I-waksi'-a nɨɨ a-boni-t.
      "I see my in-laws."
   Cultural Note: This word is borrowed from Southern Sierra Miwok.

(5) tawahani'i- VERB (Intransitive)
   "to work"
   Example: I-nawa tawahani'i-dɨ.
      "My father is working."
   Cultural Note: This word is borrowed from Spanish *trabajar.*

(6) tuubizi NOUN
   "quarter, $.25"
   Example: I-nawa-tsi' tuubizi-na i-giya-t.
      "My dear father give me a quarter."
   Cultural Note: This term is a borrowing from English based on the
      expression "two bits."
   Connections: See also pobizi "fifty cents."

   Older speakers in the community tended to include all loanwords in accord with the syncretic practices that are representative not only of Western Mono dominant language ideologies but also of aboriginal California more generally (Silver and Miller 1998). But some younger speakers targeted more "transparent" English loanwords like *apɨkatsɪ* 'apricots' and *apa'ni* 'apple' for exceptional puristic treatment, arguing that Mono people should have their own word for such things. This contestation of the formerly dominant syncretic language ideology is clearly related to other changes in the community, including a rethinking of language and identity relationships.

   Such noninstitutionally driven purism resembles other movements in its responsiveness to the symbolic domination of standardized, national languages. Writing about such puristic movements, Manfred Henningsen (1989: 31–32) detects a critical linkage: "The politics of purity . . . originates in a quest for identity and authenticity of a cultural Self that feels threatened by the hegemonic pressure of another culture." But such movements for the Western Mono are not just expressions of an overdue response to linguistic discrimination by the dominant society or evidence that Mono utilitarianism is necessarily giving way to an ideology that recognizes the expressive functions of language: they are also a new strategy for teaching and learning threatened Native American languages. In Hinton's (1994: 243) description of the master-apprentice program approach to language renewal, she lists "Eight Points of Language Learning" (for both teachers and apprentices). Teachers are instructed: "Don't use English, not even to translate." Apprentices are also instructed not to use English, "not even when you can't say it in the language. Find other ways to communicate what you want to say." Thus this type of dyadic, ancestral language "immersion" program provides an important, self-conscious alternative language ideology to more traditional syncretic practices by muting English in favor of fortifying Western Mono.

4.5. RENEWAL OR ABANDONMENT. The fifth and final difficulty emerged in what might be described, following Nora Marks Dauenhauer and Richard Dauenhauer (1998: 62), as a gap between "verbally expressed goals" that advocate language renewal and "unstated but deeply felt emotions and anxieties" that actually advocate abandonment of indigenous language and/or culture. As in other Native American communities (Dauenhauer and Dauenhauer 1998; Leap 1991), there is considerable diversity of opinion within Mono communities regarding the general goals of language renewal and the importance of promoting literacy in the indigenous language. While there is definitely widespread support for the preservationist aspects of language renewal, the community displays considerable division about taking serious steps in the direction of language renewal.

Many elders, for example, express a concern for the need to keep the language alive and advocate Native language literacy programs and language and culture classes "for the young people." But while many of these elders are often willing to contribute to the research and development of language renewal materials, many do not feel comfortable with the novelty and irony of having to learn how to write a language in which they are orally proficient. Similarly, many younger adults voice great concern over ancestral language attrition but cannot find the time, amid the struggles of everyday work and family life, to do more than purchase Native language materials, vowing "to get to them someday." Since many, if not most, young adults do not know Western Mono, the prospect of learning a new language that is very different from English is daunting. Even those elders who possess a great deal of expertise on nonlinguistic Native culture may be uncomfortable with playing the role of a learner in a language and culture class. For such knowledgeable yet linguistically nonfluent elders, language renewal may be welcomed in principle, but insofar as these programs have the potential of equating linguistic knowledge with cultural authority, they may actually be feared. By prioritizing linguistic knowledge, such programs may be viewed as a means of validating the authority of fluent elders while minimizing that of the nonfluent.

Fortunately in most Western Mono communities, the utilitarian language ideology exhibited by most elders does not especially valorize the ancestral language in such a way that would rank mastery of this symbolic technology above other forms of Native expertise. Thus most Western Mono elders do not find language renewal activities to be sites of contestation of their authority. But this is more problematic for younger members who have learned, following the message of the schools and other institutions representing the nation-state, to view language as intimately tied to cultural and personal identities. Among such younger members, this change leads to a privileging of indigenous language expertise above other nonlinguistic forms of cultural expertise and the new possibility of using linguistic knowledge and fluency as emblems of Western Mono ethnic identity.

To conclude this section, it is useful to observe the ways in which Native language literacy programs interact with both formerly dominant language ideologies within the community and those that are currently contended. Syncretism, internal diversity, and utilitarianism have certainly influenced the dictionary phase of the project as well as the form of literacy materials. But perhaps the single most important difficulty presented by the introduction of literacy materials is the relative lack of Native experts who can model such linguistic details as pronunciation of "barred i" or exemplify narrative performance of traditional stories. This is, of course, a strength of multimedia.

5. THE WESTERN MONO AND POSTLITERACY. The Western Mono community is now beginning a postliterate phase of ancestral language development in its experiments with multimedia and CD-ROM technology. Though I began to emphasize video recording of traditional stories, conversation, and personal narratives in 1991 as a means of expanding future editions of the dictionary with new vocabulary and providing the basis for future bilingual text collections, using the project orthography, I did not realize the potential of new media until I saw Brenda Farnell's CD-ROM of Native American storytelling, *Wiyuta: Assiniboine Storytelling with Signs* (1993). When, in summer 1996, Farnell hosted and organized a summer institute at the University of Iowa on developing multimedia projects for threatened Native American languages, I assembled a team of coauthors who attended the workshop, made new media, digitized

existing media, and otherwise began the creation of a CD-ROM for the Western Mono community. Including me, the team also consisted of Rosalie Bethel, the Mono elder who had been most instrumental in the creation of ancestral language literacy materials, and Jennifer F. Reynolds, then an advanced UCLA graduate student, specializing in Mayan language communities in Guatemala. Farnell, assisted by Joan Huntley and her staff at Second Look Computing, taught participants, including ourselves, how to make multimedia projects. After finishing the one-month course at the institute, the academic authors of the CD-ROM returned to UCLA where they completed the project, made it completely cross-platform, and began the testing stage that precedes publication. Following Rosalie Bethel's suggestion, the CD-ROM was titled *Taitaduhaan: Western Mono Ways of Speaking.*

Taitaduhaan, meaning 'our language' in the Western Mono language, is an interactive CD-ROM designed to be informative, useful, and entertaining to a wide range of users who have an interest in learning more about this California Indian people by seeing, hearing, and understanding four performances of traditional and contemporary verbal art in the Native language (with translation). The CD-ROM is "interactive" because readers/users select (through simple clicking operations of a mouse or touchpad) the types and levels of information they want or need to understand the performances. Because the CD-ROM can be navigated in a variety of ways, it can better serve a variety of audiences. And because the performance features of oral traditions, such as tone of voice, facial expression, gesture, rhythm, and volume, are not effectively captured by print media, these authentic performances by a knowledgeable elder are most effectively represented in their fullness by this new medium. In sum, this new computer technology provides the best possible means of appreciating Native oral traditions both for their own sake and for the purpose of learning more about these embattled but persistent Native cultural communities.

Because the CD-ROM provides both a general appreciation of California Indian verbal art forms and a detailed analysis of the language of performance, it meets the needs of a broad range of community members, including teachers as well as learners. The CD-ROM is a valuable tool for both community groups and individuals to gain a closer familiarity with their indigenous languages and oral traditions. Very important, it addresses the need for Native models of speaking by making available a highly fluent native speaker who can exemplify Mono pronunciation and embody Mono discursive performances. The CD-ROM allows individuals to hear and practice sounds by hearing and seeing examples of words and sentences in which all the sounds of the language can be identified. Readers/users need only have minimal computer literacy to run the CD-ROM as it is a self-contained product that always provides HELP menus and prompts to those who need guidance regarding either the correct use of buttons or the explanation of specialized vocabulary used in language analysis or cultural explanation. Educational institutions—both within and outside the Western Mono community—from junior high school to university graduate programs would also use this resource as a way of combating the lack of pedagogical materials on the Western Mono and, more generally, on all Native Americans in California, especially the dearth of audiovisual materials that represent their oral traditions.

Organizationally, the CD-ROM begins with a title screen containing a photograph of Mono Indian baskets while a lively gaming song is sung. As the song continues, timers automatically open "credit" and "purpose" screens that identify the authors and the goal of introducing Mono Indian language and culture to audiences both within and outside of the Mono community. As the song ends, the main menu screen appears, offering four performance selections and two background selections. The background choices are represented by two gray buttons marked COMMUNITY and LANGUAGE. Pushing the first of these buttons reveals a menu of options to learn more about the community through an introductory text, photographs, maps, and a brief biographical sketch of Rosalie Bethel, the Mono elder who performs on the CD-ROM. Pushing the LANGUAGE option reveals a menu of options including seeing and hearing examples of all the pronunciation units of the language as well as language maps and language-family trees that locate the Mono language in linguistic history and geography.

The main menu choices involve four performances: two stories, "Coyote Races Mole" and "Wee'mu'" (a Mono bogeyman figure), a prayer, and a lyrical song for children. The user can choose to navigate each of these performances in two distinct ways. One choice is to "play" the selection from start to finish with synchronized English subtitles. The other is to "examine" each of these performances sentence by sentence. In this mode each sentence appears in a text box containing the Mono language sentence; a detailed, morpheme-by-morpheme translation; and a free translation. Many words and phrases appear in red, and when these are clicked on by the user they reveal additional linguistic and cultural explanation. These additional expansions take a variety of forms. Most often, they produce an onscreen text box.

Example (7) reproduces the text box that automatically appears in screen 15 of the story "Wee'mu'." The item in bold is red in the CD-ROM both to call greater attention to it and to color code it as "interactive" and thus clickable with mouse or touchpad.

(7) Onnoho yaisi mannoho yaisi uhu-bo' na'atsi'
qadu'u hii-paa naqadogi'i-t tïbiiha-qatï-t.
Then and here and that-EMPH boy
NEG anything-OBL listen-TNS play-sit-TNS.
'And then that boy here who didn't listen kept on playing.'[6]

Users can access more information about the highlighted forms by clicking on them. When they do so, an explanatory screen appears:

> This verb, *-qatï-t*, literally means 'to sit' but when used as the second verb of a verb + verb compound, it conveys the specific meaning of 'to keep on V-ing' such as the example here, *tïbiiha-qatï-t* 'to keep on playing'.

In addition to explanatory text boxes, interactivity can also take the form of a movie. At the conclusion of the performance of "Prayer," Rosalie Bethel uses a discourse particle that can serve as concluding formula. In the Examine mode, users can thus select further explanation by clicking on this word:

(8) Prayer Screen #11
   11. MannohO.
     there
     There it is. (It is done.)

Doing this results not in a text box but in a brief movie consisting of a "talking head" shot of Bethel explaining the cultural use of the term as a concluding formula for certain verbal genres.

Readers who seek more details about the structure of *Taitaduhaan* may want to examine a more in-depth analysis of this product (Kroskrity and Reynolds forthcoming). But this sketch of the CD-ROM is sufficient to suggest critical features of its organization and the ways in which it both solves some problems and introduces others. Although it may be somewhat premature to definitively assess the impact of multimedia as an extension of the Native literacy program on the basis of the Mono case, where CD-ROMs have only been experimentally used and not fully implemented in a variety of educational settings, I provide some preliminary conclusions below.

6. CONCLUSIONS.   My conclusions consist of observations of three significant contributions and one potential problem that can be associated with

---

6. Gloss abbreviations used in the examples are the following: EMPH = emphatic particle; NEG = negative; OBL = oblique case marker; TNS = unmarked tense-aspect suffix (a default choice), V = verb. This is only a small subset of the total inventory of grammatical glosses used in the examples of the CD-ROM.

multimedia work in the context of language renewal and as a complement to more conventional community-based lexicography. The most important contribution is the increased access to fluent speakers who are often relatively unavailable in communities where language shift to English is almost complete. Although there is no substitute for actual interaction with a fluent native speaker, multimedia can provide an approximation of the model for speaking that is produced by native speakers in face-to-face interaction.

In addition to providing an outstanding means of capturing some of the most transcriptionally elusive qualities of an oral tradition—prosody, volume, rhythm, facial expression, body orientation and movement— multimedia CD-ROMs offer a uniquely appropriate medium for introducing, or explaining by example, local orthographies.

At the Western Mono community meetings where orthographies were discussed, a frequent complaint was the difficulty of reading Native language terms and sentences in an orthography that was so like English orthography that it often invited mispronunciation in the direction of English. The "Guide to Pronouncing Mono Words" in *Taitaduhaan* illustrates every orthographic symbol used in the final version of the orthography developed during the Mono Language Project. This feature helps the user to understand, through the video and audio of brief, illustrative movies featuring Rosalie Bethel pronouncing Native terms, each orthographic symbol to be exemplified. The symbols include both those that are already familiar to Mono people because of their literacy in English and the few new symbols created to accommodate Western Mono phonology.

Perhaps the best example of the value of having a visual component comes in the form of the movie that is played when the user selects the vowel "barred i": *ɨ*. This vowel is—in articulatory phonetic terms—a high, central, unrounded vowel. In English, nonfront vowels tend to be pronounced with lip rounding, and because most Monos know English better than they know Mono, this frequently occurring vowel is often pronounced as if it were an English [u]. But seeing Rosalie Bethel pronounce words with *ɨ*, such as the example *ɨya* 'sore', provides a visual corrective, since it clearly demonstrates that this vowel, unlike English [u], is pronounced without lip rounding.

Thus different kinds of video and audio can be used in creative ways on a CD-ROM to more accurately represent and teach American Indian languages. From presenting the aesthetics of the oral tradition to representing the phonetics of ancestral language pronunciation, this medium has important educational implications for teachers and learners alike.

A second and very significant contribution of multimedia is the appeal to the Western Mono community through the language ideology of utilitarianism. Western Mono people have been attracted to new technologies, and a writing system and a technology of representation associated with computers are very appealing to Mono people who share this language ideology and general pragmatic emphasis in nonlinguistic culture (Loether 1993). As Elizabeth A. Brandt (1988: 326) has observed of other Native American communities, the association of an ancestral language with new multimedia, computer technologies is a source, for most Native people, not only of pride but also of a sense of inclusion, on a more equal footing, in contemporary developments. Rather than associate their ancestral languages exclusively with the past, the technological representation of these languages conveys a powerful sense of compatibility with both the present and the future, which is clearly important in boosting the symbolic capital of the Native language. Children who use computer technologies to access their ancestral language also exercise valuable technological skills that have a definite value in the job market. These connections are appreciated by community members, especially because a major thrust of language renewal has been directed toward school-age children. It is, of course, interesting to observe that one of the great appeals of postliterate technologies, to community members, is their capacity to capture and reframe the beauty of the preliterate, oral tradition.

The third contribution of multimedia is its compatibility with the Mono syncretic project. Even though all the performances by Rosalie Bethel are exclusively in the Mono language, in accord with the goal of providing the best possible models for learning the indigenous language, most of the performances contain syncretic features. The story "Coyote Races Mole," for example, contains an explanatory conclusion designed just for novice hearers (Kroskrity 1999). The Mono Prayer is a public prayer that intertwines traditional and Christian imagery and diction. Finally, the "Blue Jay Song" is a new, lyrical song genre for children. Since traditional songs for the Western Mono contain only vocables but no true words (Loether 1993), this performance represents a musical innovation that synthesizes a Euro-American children's song genre with Western Mono language and culture. Thus, in an important way, multimedia works can effectively embody the "revised syncretism" of the contemporary Western Mono community by avoiding English but still displaying performances that represent a synthesis of Mono and Euro-American cultural patterns.

Although multimedia work can represent a valuable extension of Native American dictionary projects, it may also introduce new dilemmas. Because dictionaries and their component entries are decontextualized literacy products that rely heavily on the activity of Native readers, they deemphasize, to some extent, the human source of the linguistic information. This relative erasure of the source person is in stark contrast to the immediacy of multimedia products in which the voices and images are audibly and visibly connected to actual people. While this is clearly a strength of multimedia work, it imposes a problem for communities, such as the Western Mono, that embrace internal diversity. One person, even a highly fluent elder like Rosalie Bethel, cannot represent regional, gender, generational, and other forms of diversity. But unlike the more decontextualized products of literacy that permit, even encourage, a detachment of words from individual speakers in an effort to create a shared linguistic resource, multimedia works like *Taitaduhaan* present the performed language in such a highly contextualized manner that they may appear more like the speaker's words than those of the community. Certainly at this point in the project, before full-scale implementation, this is more an anxiety than a reality. Just as literacy products must be reframed in literacy events, so, too, the parents and teachers who use these postliterate technologies and present them to novice others will reframe them in ways that are crucial not only for their reception but also for their successful incorporation in language renewal programs. As a complement to the literate technology that enables dictionary making, the early returns from the Mono Language Project strongly suggest that multimedia will play a valuable role as one of several resources that Native American communities will need in their continuing struggle for language renewal.

THREE

Technology and Dictionary Design

CHAPTER NINE

An Interactive Dictionary and Text Corpus for Sixteenth- and Seventeenth-Century Nahuatl

Una Canger

1. THE UNIQUE STATUS OF NAHUATL AMONG LANGUAGES OF THE AMERICAS. Among the world's languages, only a few were documented and recorded as comprehensively in the sixteenth and seventeenth centuries as Nahuatl. By 1645 Nahuatl had been described in at least five grammars, and in 1571 Fray Alonso de Molina published an expanded version of a Spanish-Nahuatl, Nahuatl-Spanish dictionary, containing more than forty thousand entries. The corpus of texts in Nahuatl from that same period is, both in kind and in quantity, equally impressive and gives it a unique position among the indigenous languages of the Americas. The Copenhagen Nahuatl Dictionary Project (CoNDiP) brings together the lexicographic comprehensiveness of Molina with the contextual usages of the words as found in the texts. The organization of CoNDiP and our application of the dramatic new possibilities in lexicography provided by computers are the focus of this chapter. But first a few words about the abundant corpus of Nahuatl documents and their significance are called for.

The Nahuatl texts are abundant. They represent a great variety of types and genres, comprising historical accounts and chronicles, myths, and poetry pertaining to pre-Columbian culture; and colonial-period administrative documents and Christian devotional texts, such as catechisms, moral dialogues, confessionaries, and stories about the saints. Some of the texts were written by indigenous people who had learned writing and Latin in schools established by the Spaniards shortly after the conquest. Others were collected by Spanish friars. Most of the historical accounts

The project described here has been supported by the Carlsberg Foundation.

and chronicles have no known authors or compilers, but among the important texts we also find the work of an early indigenous historian, Chimalpahin Quauhtlehuanitzin (1958, 1997).

The work of Fray Bernardino de Sahagún, who strove to bring together material for his *Historia general de las cosas de Nueva España* (General History of the Things of New Spain, 1570), provides a major source of information. With the help of young bi- or trilingual Aztecs he visited wise and knowledgeable elders in various towns and collected information in Nahuatl on all aspects of the culture, including detailed descriptions of animals, plants, and other natural phenomena. His organized and edited version of this material is known as the *Florentine Codex*. It consists of twelve volumes, beautifully composed in two columns, Nahuatl and Spanish, and with numerous colored drawings (Sahagún, 1579 [1950–82]). It is undoubtedly the most frequently cited source on all aspects of Aztec culture. Some of the original source material for the *Florentine Codex* is also preserved (Sahagún 1997).

In their desire to convert the indigenous people to Christianity, the friars felt a great need to speak and to be understood. They found that it was easier for them to learn the indigenous languages than it was for the Indians to learn Spanish. Consequently, in part because of the friars' insistence that Nahuatl be used also in official matters and in part because Nahuatl had functioned as a lingua franca already before the arrival of the Spaniards, it continued to be widely used, both practically and officially, all through the sixteenth century and well into the seventeenth (see Heath 1972). As a consequence, there is, in addition to literary texts and historical records of preconquest events, an abundance of documents in or from local archives: land documentation, testaments, municipal documentation, petitions, and correspondence. The literature written in the Nahuatl language from the sixteenth and seventeenth centuries thus represents a rich source for the study of Aztec culture—the political and social system, religion, ethics, and so on—as well as for the study of the Nahuatl language itself.

However, Nahuatl from the sixteenth century is not an easily understood language, and the documents, many of which are written in a highly elaborated style with metaphors and other figures of speech, were hidden away in archives for centuries. Scholars rediscovered the texts and the tools with which to gain access to them only toward the end of the nineteenth century. The first half of this century saw German publications of many of the important texts with translations and discussions of their content (Eduard Seler, Walter Lehmann, Gerdt Kutscher, Günter Zimmermann). During the second half of the twentieth century, scholars from the United States, Mexico, and France (e.g., Arthur J. O. Anderson, John Bierhorst, Charles E. Dibble, Jacqueline Durand-Forest, Angel

María Garibay K., James Lockhart, Miguel León-Portilla, Alfredo López Austin, Susan Schroeder) have added tremendously to the wealth of bilingual publications of Nahuatl texts from the sixteenth and seventeenth centuries.

A profound understanding of the significance of Nahuatl texts and the desire to produce a lexicographic tool that, in terms of word entries and information, would go beyond that of Molina and make its users better equipped for reading and interpreting the many texts has led us in Copenhagen to initiate the Copenhagen Nahuatl Dictionary Project.

This presentation of CoNDiP is organized in the following way: after a brief, informative description of the basic aim and structure of CoNDiP, I expound the lexicographic merits and subsequent achievements made possible by advances in electronic technology; then I discuss the problems we have been faced with in producing CoNDiP, some of which are common to all types of lexicographic work and some specific to the new kind of situations created by the computer; and finally, I give a short account of the history of CoNDiP.

2. BRIEF DESCRIPTION OF CoNDiP. The primary and basic aim has been to make the abundant Nahuatl text material immediately available with as little interpretation as possible, to avoid the inevitable personal bias that befalls any translator. In preparing CoNDiP, we have had in mind both scholars working with Aztec culture and those who are interested more specifically in the Nahuatl language.

CoNDiP is above all a computer-based compilation, organization, and analysis of words from sixteenth- and seventeenth-century Nahuatl texts; it exploits the advantages of the computer and is at variance with the traditional dictionary form to the extent that it can in no way be converted into one or more printed books. Thanks to the electronic medium and the organization of CoNDiP, there is no limit to the amount of material (texts, words, and comments) that can be entered continuously into the system, with no end point, only updated versions.

CoNDiP consists of three permanently and concurrently interactive components: a word dictionary, a root dictionary, and a text component; the links between the elements of these three components form the backbone of the system (see fig. 9.1). The typical entry in the CoNDiP word dictionary contains what would be expected in a traditional dictionary: the entry word, grammatical information, and a gloss. In addition, it displays the root(s) contained in the word in the order in which they occur as well as example sentences from texts. A window for comments written by the compilers as well as by the users also appears. The root(s) given in a word entry are linked to entries in the root dictionary. In this the typical root entry includes the entry root, a gloss, and a list of all the

WORD ENTRY

WORD	class	Eng. GLOSS
gram.inf.		Sp. GLOSS
ROOT(S)		
EXAMPLE SENTENCES/(COMMENT)		
....		
....		

ROOT ENTRY

ROOT	Eng. GLOSS
	Sp. GLOSS
(COMMENT)	
...	
WORDS containing the root	
...	
...	

TEXT

Standardized form
...
...
Paleography
...
...
Translation
...
...

Figure 9.1. Interactive Components of CoNDiP.

words that contain the given root; the root dictionary also provides the possibility for comments on the individual root. The interactiveness of the program is realized in the two-way links between words and roots. The example sentences in the word entries come from the text corpus. Every word in the text corpus is, with its full sentence, linked to its word entry in the word dictionary; and in the text component, texts are divided into numbered sentences, given in paleography,[1] in a standardized version, and with a translation.

The user may look up a word, a root, or a text, including page or folio number, and may naturally profit from the links to move around between the components. In the present version of CoNDiP, the user may not add comments or entries; it is possible, however, to lift out of the system a word entry, a root entry, or the entire list of roots.

Eventually the text component will comprise the relevant sixteenth- and seventeenth-century texts in Nahuatl. We have included Molina's 1571 dictionary as a text; this means that every entry has, in the form of "sentences," all the entries from Molina's Spanish-Nahuatl and Nahuatl-Spanish sections that contain the word in question. Since it is entered as a text, it is possible to jump directly to the text component in order to see the preceding and following entries in Molina's dictionary by scrolling up and down in it. The Molina text is given only in paleography.

The basic structure of CoNDiP was developed in the late 1980s, and the interactive components and the windows for comments were all created in a DOS framework. CoNDiP has not yet been rewritten for a Windows format. Additional features and options, some more closely related to traditional lexicographic aspects and some beyond the normal possibilities of a dictionary, are discussed in the following sections.

3. LEXICOGRAPHIC MERITS OF CoNDiP.

3.1. ALPHABETICAL ORDER OBLITERATED. Words and roots are nowhere in CoNDiP organized in any alphabetical order. They are numbered chronologically according to when they were entered into the program. This number is covert, however, and is of no significance to the user, who accesses a word entry simply by typing the word or by going from the root dictionary or the text component, and accesses a root entry through the word dictionary link or by typing the root. The great advantages of this complete obliteration of alphabetical ordering—radical as it may seem in a dictionary—may not be immediately obvious.

The first advantage is that the dictionary has been representative from the start, in that the first version was not limited to words beginning with certain letters of the alphabet, and when expanded it is expanded evenly over the alphabet. An obvious problem with the obliteration of alphabetical ordering is that one cannot check the words just above or below in

---

1. Among Nahuatl scholars the term "paleography" refers to the exact rendering of a text from a manuscript, as opposed to any standardization or transcription of the text.

the alphabet, but the inclusion of Molina's dictionary and the easy access to word lists in the root dictionary should remedy this loss.

The second advantage is of an entirely different nature. It has to do with Nahuatl orthographies in general, since alphabetical ordering is in no way a straightforward matter in Nahuatl lexicography. In the sixteenth century, orthography was generally not as consistent as it is today. We find a great deal of variation in choice of letters in Spanish texts from the period. Similar orthographic inconsistencies are found in the Nahuatl texts, and they correspond partly to variation in Spanish writing but stem also from phonological differences in the two languages, differences that caused the Spaniards problems. It is a question both of underdifferentiation (Nahuatl distinguishes long and short vowels and has a postvocalic glottal stop, traditionally called *saltillo*, both unknown features in Spanish) and of overdifferentiation (Spanish has five vowels versus four in Nahuatl).

As a result of differing traditions in the writing of Nahuatl and of recent attempts at an orthographic systematization, the alphabetical order in extant dictionaries varies frustratingly. Because all these dictionaries contribute to our understanding of the language, scholars who work with sixteenth-century texts will constantly consult all of them. But because of their different orthographies and above all because of their different alphabetical order, it takes a tremendous amount of practice, and one really has to mind one's p's and q's to consult them successfully.

The choice of problematic letters and their critical order as found in the major dictionaries and in J. Richard Andrews's (1975) grammar are charted below. Table 9.1 gives the critical letters (keyed to the phonemes in the leftmost column) that are used in the dictionaries. In general I have included only those found in word-initial position. Certain intricacies, such as the writing of /w/ and /k^w/ in syllable-final position, are thus not included in the tables. ([ ], / / and < > are used according to the traditional conventions for phonetic, phonemic, and orthographic symbols, respectively.) No significance should be attributed to the vertical order of the phonemes/letters in table 9.1. Table 9.2 displays the ORDER-ING of words according to initial letters in the selected sources (not all the letters of the alphabet are included; <a>, <e>, and other letters that in all the sources are identical and appear in the same place in the alphabet have been left out). Here the vertical order of the letters represents the alphabetical order found in the dictionaries; the phonemic column is the rightmost because it has only an auxiliary function. Thus in Molina's dictionary, for example, we find words beginning with <ca before those that begin with <ça>, those beginning with <ça> before those that begin with <ce>, and so on. The notations <ca, ça> and <co, ço> in the column under "Siméon" are explained below under (1). A comparison of the two

TABLE 9.1. Choice of Letters in Major Nahuatl Dictionaries

Phon	Molina 1571	Siméon 1885	Campbell 1985	Andrews 1975	Karttunen 1983	Bierhorst 1985
/k/	c/_a,o,C,#	c/_a,o,C,#	c/_a,o,C,#	c/_a,o,C,#	c/_a,o,C,#	c/_a,o,C,#
	qu/_i,e	qu/_i,e	qu/_i,e	qu/_i,e	qu/_i,e	qu/_i,e
/s/	c/_e,i	c/_e,i	c/_e,i	c/_e,i	c/_e,i	c/_e,i
	ç/_a,o	ç/_a,o	z/_a,o	z/_a,o	z/_a,o	z/_a,o
	z/_C,#	z/_C,#	z/_C,#	z/_C,#	z/_C,#	z/_C,#
/č/	ch	ch	ch	ch	ch	ch
/kʷ/	cu/_e,i	cu/_e,i	cu/_e,i	cu/_e,i	cu/_e,i	cu/_e,i
	qu/_a	qu/_a	qu/_a	cu/_a	cu/_a	cu/_a
/¢/	tz	tz	tz	tz	tz	tz
/w/	v	u	u	hu	hu	hu
/y/	y	y	y	y	y	y
/i/	i	i	i	i	i	i
/o/	o,v	o,u	o	o	o	o
/'/	-	-	-	h	h	h

TABLE 9.2. Order of Letters in Word-Initial Position
in Major Nahuatl Dictionaries

Molina 1571	Siméon 1885	Campbell 1985	Andrews 1975	Karttunen 1983	Bierhorst 1985	Phon
ca	ca,ça	ca	ca	ca	ca	/ka,(sa)/
ça						/sa/
ce	ce	ce	ce	ce	ce	/se/
ch	ch	ch				/č/
ci	ci	ci	ci	ci	ci	/si/
co	co,ço	co	co	co	co	/ko,(so)/
ço						/so/
			ch	ch	ch	/č/
			cua	cua	cua	/kʷa/
cue	cue	cue	cue	cue	cue	/kʷe/
cui	cui	cui	cui	cui	cui	/kʷi/
			hu	hu	hu	/w/
i,y	i,y	i	i	i	i	/i,(y)/
qua	qua	qua				/kʷa/
que	que	que	que	que	que	/ke/
qui	qui	qui	qui	qui	qui	/ki/
t	t	t	t	t	t	/t/
tl	tl	tl	tl	tl	tl	/λ/
to	to	to			to	/to/
tz	tz	tz	tz	tz	tz	/¢/

(continued)

TABLE 9.2.   *(continued)*

Molina 1571	Siméon 1885	Campbell 1985	Andrews 1975	Karttunen 1983	Bierhorst 1985	Phon
va,ve,vi	ua,ue,ui	ua,ue,ui				/wa,we,wi/
vC	uC					/oC/
		y	y	y	y	/y/
		z	z	z	z	/s/

tables reveals that there is broad agreement concerning choice of letters in the dictionaries and that it is in the ordering of the letters that they differ, creating difficulties for those who continually consult them.

We can see the scope of the difficulties by looking at the seven crucial problems below.

1. Molina (1571) and Siméon (1885) agree on rendering the phoneme /s/ before /a/ or /o/ as <ç>, but whereas Molina gives all the words that begin with <ca> (/ka/) before those beginning with <ça> (/sa/), Siméon alphabetizes according to all the letters in the words, thereby giving at first a few that begin with <ca>, then some with <ça>, then more with <ca>, and so on. The two lexicographers differ in the same way in the case of words beginning with <ço>. The more recent sources avoided this problem by choosing to write <z> for /s/ before /a/ and /o/.

2. There is some disagreement as to where to place words beginning with <ch> (/č/). Molina, Siméon, Campbell (1985), and Bierhorst (1985) intermingle them with words beginning with <c>; Andrews (1975) and Karttunen (1983) place them in a separate section after all the words that begin with <c> for /k/ and /s/.

3. Before /a/, the phoneme /kʷ/ is written <qu> by Molina, Siméon, and Campbell; Andrews, Karttunen, and Bierhorst write <cu>. As a consequence, words beginning with /kʷa/ are found in different places in the two groups of sources. They all agree on writing <cu> for /kʷ/ before /e/ and /i/. /kʷ/ does not occur before /o/.

4. In agreement with Spanish tradition in the sixteenth century, Molina and Siméon use both <i> and <y> for the consonant phoneme /y/, placing words beginning with /y/ in the section with words that begin with /i/. All later sources reserve the letter <i> for the vowel phoneme /i/ and the letter <y> for the consonant phoneme /y/.

5. The phoneme /w/ divides the sources differently: Molina writes it with the letter <v>, Siméon and Campbell prefer <u>; Andrews, Karttunen, and Bierhorst use <hu>. One thus has to look for words beginning with /w/ in totally different places in the sources.

6. The sources disagree on how to handle words that begin with the letter <t>, which may represent just /t/ or, followed by <l> or <z>, two other phonemes, namely, /λ/ and /¢/. Only Andrews and Karttunen establish three distinct sections, one for each of the three phonemes. The others simply organize words beginning with the letter <t> alphabetically.

7. Saltillo was generally not indicated in the texts from the sixteenth and seventeenth centuries. It is not found in Molina, Siméon, or Campbell—the latter two being derived from the first. Andrews, Karttunen, and Bierhorst, however, write it with the letter <h> and include it in the alphabetic ordering. The saltillo does not occur word initially, so it is not included in table 9.2, and the problems this additional letter creates are limited.

3.2. SEVERAL ORTHOGRAPHIES. Eliminating the alphabetical order in CoNDiP does not solve all the problems created by the diversity of orthographic standards. Scholars who work with Nahuatl texts from the sixteenth and seventeenth centuries have a variety of motives and backgrounds and therefore also different preferences as to orthography; some are more linguistically inclined than others, who generally prefer the words to be written the way they find them in the texts and who see no need for the linguist's exotic symbols or for an indication of saltillo and vowel length. This situation can be easily and elegantly taken care of on a computer.

CoNDiP offers the user the option of three different alphabet standards that we call (1) sixteenth-century orthography (ORT); (2) the normalized version (NOR); and (3) transcription (TRA). The selected alphabet standard is given in root entries, in word entries, and in the standardized version of the texts; it does not operate within comments, where we normally use sixteenth-century orthography. This selection of one of the three alphabet standards is in no way definitive; one can shift between them at will.

SIXTEENTH-CENTURY ORTHOGRAPHY most closely resembles the orthography we find in the documents, but it is consistent. A given form is always and everywhere written in the same way.

THE NORMALIZED VERSION differentiates short and long vowels: /a/ versus /ā/, /calli/ 'house' versus /cālli/ 'raven'; and an apostrophe indicates saltillo, for example, /ta'tli/ 'father'. A capital vowel indicates that we have no information about vowel length or a possible saltillo: for example, /kAntli/ 'cheek' stands for /kantli/ or /kāntli/, and /¢IwAktli/ 'a plant' stands for /¢iwaktli/, /¢īwāktli/, /¢i'waktli/, or /¢i'wāktli/.

Some letters in NOR differ in a few contexts from ORT:

ORT	NOR	
quiqua	quicua	'eats it'
açaca	āzaca	'carry water'

TRANSCRIPTION is the standard that least resembles what we see in the documents. In TRA every phoneme is represented by only one symbol, the same one in all contexts.

The following list exemplifies the differences between standardized sixteenth-century orthography and our transcription.

ORT	TRA	
chantli	čānλi	'home'
cactli	kakλi	'sandal'
quenin	kēnin	'how'
quiqua	kikʷa	'eats it'
quicuepa	kikʷepa	'turns it'
neuctli	nekʷλi	'honey'
çan	san	'only'
cecec	sEsēk	'cold'
nez	nēs	'appeared'
nezque	nēske'	'appeared (pl.)'
tlacatl	λākaλ	'man'
tzatzi	¢a'¢i	'shouts'
huehuetl	wēwēλ	'drum'
huauhtli	wawλi	'amaranth'

TRA is the master orthography in which roots, words, and texts are entered into the program and from which the two other orthographies are mechanically derived. The system is sensitive to the three alphabet standards and responds differently depending on the standard in operation. TRA is prim and recognizes only the correct spelling with letters that belong in TRA; it will not recognize, for example, <tl> and <ch>. This strict requirement does not include vowel length and saltillo unless these features are the only indication of a distinction between two or more words. Thus if, for example, one wants to look up /kīsa/ and types it with a short *i*, the correct entry will appear. However, in the case of word pairs that differ only as to vowel length or saltillo, for example, /toka/ 'follow' and /tōka/ 'bury', only the form typed with correct vowel length will appear. In ORT both words will appear in a suggestion list. And here the tolerance is limited only by potential ambiguities. The word <çacatl> 'grass', for example, can successfully be looked up in any one of the following ways: *sakatl, sacatl, zacatl, zakatl, çacatl, çakatl, sakaλ, sacaλ, zacaλ, zakaλ, çacaλ, çakaλ.* Thus ORT gives much more leeway than TRA for looking up roots and words, and TRA offers more information, which, however, is of interest to fewer users.

Occasional Spanish loanwords appear in the Nahuatl texts. These are dealt with according to other rules.

3.3. INSIGNIFICANCE OF GLOSSES.   Since the aim of CoNDiP is to give immediate and comprehensive access to occurrences of words in texts and thereby to encourage new and more well-founded interpretations, the English and Spanish glosses in the word entries lose their importance. This appraisal of the supplied glosses is supported by the immediate access to complete entries from Molina's dictionary. As a consequence, little effort has been spent on finding the absolutely "right" glosses. In keeping with this view, only little space is allocated for glosses. In fact, only after sufficient text material has been entered would it make sense to work out detailed glosses on the basis of those texts.

The same is true of the text translations. We allow ourselves to stay close to the original, both syntactically and lexically. We also introduce a kind of methodical consistency that leads to somewhat awkward and rigid English. However, we adhere to this consistency because it makes the translating process more appropriate for our demands and because it offers information to the user. Furthermore, since the text in all its versions—paleography, standardized, and translation—is divided into sentences, each sentence should, if at all possible, have a meaningful translation that is sufficiently independent of that of the preceding and following sentences. We avoid the traditional dilemma for any translator, namely, striking a balance between being true and close to the original and producing a text acceptable in the target language.

No function for looking up words through the English or Spanish glosses is implemented. However, a more general search function allows the user to search for an English or Spanish gloss.

4. ACHIEVEMENTS.   Some of the possibilities permitted by the electronic medium go well beyond the limits of the traditional book format, as discussed below.

4.1. FULL TEXTS.   The first overwhelming advance is the possibility of having an almost endless number of full texts next to the word entries. That the meanings of words are best understood through their use is the obvious reasoning behind this central feature of CoNDiP. In good traditional dictionaries, words are exemplified by illustrative phrases or sentences—in the best cases, by genuine text sentences. In CoNDiP the use of words is illustrated not only by a few examples but also, ideally and eventually, by the sentences in a comprehensive corpus of sixteenth- and seventeenth-century Nahuatl texts in their full context. The inclusion of full texts and, above all, the linking of these texts to the word entries in the dictionary are cardinal features of CoNDiP. For a quick assessment the reader may look at the list of occurrences of a given word in the narrow context of the sentence, but for every occurrence, there is direct access to the full text in the text component.

4.2. MORPHOLOGICAL ANALYSIS.   During the initial phase of CoNDiP, the first ten to thirty pages of text were subjected to quite a bit of experimentation. Our experiments addressed two distinct areas. The first had to do with the presentation of the texts and how they should appear in the text component and how the text sentences should be displayed in the word entries. This involved both the precise configuration of the screen in the two components and decisions about alphabet standards. The second dealt with the adaptation of texts for their entry into the program and with the crucial linking of what we call a WORD FORM to a word as found in the entry of a dictionary. In this second area, our discussions and decisions were dictated not by pedagogical considerations but by the structure of the Nahuatl language and the inconsistent orthography found in the documents. To establish a morphological analysis that will support the mechanical linking of inflected words to dictionary words is an overwhelmingly complex task for any language, and that Nahuatl is a polysynthetic language with a rich inflectional system employing prefixes, suffixes, compounding, and noun incorporation only adds to the complexity of that task.

A mechanical linking of word forms to dictionary entries was not intended in the first phase of CoNDiP. But even for manual linking, the preparation of texts still involved two connected sets of critical tasks: (1) interpreting the inconsistent orthography found in the texts and (2) producing a morphological analysis. The two are interconnected in that the saltillo (generally not indicated in the texts) and other crucial phonological features play a significant role in the morphology. This has required much debate and work. I discuss some of the details of the two connected sets of tasks.

Simple inconsistences in the orthography involve, for example, the variable use of several letters for a vowel, /i/ or /o/, and a consonant, /y/ or /w/. Thus <i, y, j> can represent /i/ and /y/; <o, u, v> can represent /o/ and /w/. This situation is further complicated by the fact that there is no phonetic distinction between /ia/ and /iya/ or between /oa/ and /owa/. Wherever the syncretism can be resolved, the resolution is based on morphological evidence (see Canger 1980: chap. 1). In the *Florentine Codex*, the word /yōli/ 'he lives' is found in the following variants: <ioli, iuli, yoli>; /yālwa/ 'yesterday' has four orthographic variants: <ialoa, ialhoa, yaloa, yalhua>; and / īwiyān/ 'calmly' has twelve: <ihuiian, iuiian, iuijan, iujian, ivi-ian, ivijan, jujian, jviian, yuiyan, yujian, yviyan, yvjian>.

This rich orthographic variation is crucial when looked at from the perspective of how to correlate an orthographic variant with an analyzed word form. The readings of a word like <quioaliaoaloaia> /Ø-ki-wāl-yawaloā-ya-'/(3.S-3SG.O-DIR.towards-surround-IMPF-PL) 'they surrounded him' can be used as an example of the complexity; it gives 406 possible readings.

The interplay between problems of phonology and morphology can be illustrated by a few examples:

(1) <tlaqua>   (a) /λa-kʷa/   'he eats'
                 (b) /λa-kʷa-'/   'they eat'
                 (c) /λa-kʷa'/   'he ate'

(2) <tlaquatiuh> (a) /λa-kʷa'-ti-w/   'he goes away while eating'
                      NONREF.O-eat-LIGATURE-go
                  (b) /λa-kʷā-tīw/   'he goes to eat'
                      NONREF.O-eat-DIR.away

The three analyses of ambiguous <tlaqua> in (1) are explained by the fact that saltillo functions in some tenses as a marker of plural of subject, and some verbs, for example, /kʷa/ 'eat', have two stems, one ending in a vowel and one in saltillo. The two analyses of <tlaquatiuh> involve (2a), a composite construction with the stem found also in (1c), and (2b), a directional suffix /tīw/ added to a third stem form of the verb 'eat', /kʷā/. In both cases, arguments for the correct analysis will come from the context.

The precise analysis needed for the linking of word forms in texts with words as they appear in the dictionary thus yields a valuable by-product, namely, the comprehensive morphological analysis of word forms in the texts. In preparing the texts, word forms must be analyzed into morphemes and the morphemes are marked as STEMS, DERIVATIONAL AFFIXES, and INFLECTIONAL AFFIXES. Stems (in many cases identical with roots, see §5.1) are marked by a preposed hyphen, derivational affixes by a preposed equal sign, and inflectional affixes by a plus sign.

(3) +ti+k-itti=ti'+ke'   'we showed it to him'
    1PL.S-3O-see-CAUS.PERF-PL.S

Reduplication serves a number of functions in Nahuatl (see Canger 1981), for example: 'plural' of nouns, /koyō-λ/ 'coyote', /kō-koyo-'/ 'coyotes'; 'distributive', /in-ča'-čān ō Ø-ya'-ya'-ke'/ (3PL.P-DISTR-home past 3S-DISTR-GO.PERF-PL.S) 'they went, each to his own home'; 'repetitive', /Ø-šamā-ni/ 'it breaks', /Ø-ša-šama-ka/ 'it breaks in many places'. Some of these functions form part of the inflectional system, and in other cases they belong either in the productive derivational system or among fossilized derivational affixes (see §5.5). In addition to being marked as inflectional or derivational, these prefixes also receive a special mark, ≈, for reduplication:

(4) +≈kō-koyo+'   'coyotes'
    PL-coyote-PL

(5) =≈ka-kala=ka   'clank'
    REP-sound-INTR

In the present version of CoNDiP this morphological analysis is displayed overtly in TRA; in NOR, only stems are marked as such:

(3) TRA   NOR
    +ti+k-itti=ti'+ke'   tik-ittiti'ke'   'we showed it to him'
    1PL.S-3O-see-CAUS.PERF-PL.S

But the combination of alphabet standard and morphological analysis can obviously be separated completely, allowing the user to have any possible combination of the two options.

The declared intention of forcing as little interpretation of the texts as possible on the user may seem to be disregarded in the comprehensive morphological analysis manifested in the transcription. However, the interpretation exhibited in the transcription never conceals the unadulterated ambiguous original, because whatever alphabet standard the user selects, a paleographic version of the text will always appear alongside the analyzed one. The only analysis applied in the paleography is a division of the text into words and sentences. While the division into words is fairly uncontroversial, the identification of clauses is the result of a syntactic analysis that may be questioned, but it is overt and has no concealed consequences, and some division of the text is necessary for purely practical purposes.

The consistent morphological analysis has in fact made the linking partly mechanical. The analyzed text is typed in manually, but subsequently the system, beginning from the first word of the text, suggests the word entry to which that word form is to be linked. I accept it or—in the cases when the suggestion is not correct—I find the correct one, link, and go on to the next word.

For entering Molina's dictionary, we went a little further. A multifaceted program was written that interprets the orthography, provides morphological analyses of a given word, and identifies the dictionary word to which it should be linked. Inflected word forms in Molina's dictionary are limited to a few standardized ones, so as a "text" it is naturally not as complex and demanding as any regular text would be. It is the plan, however, to expand this first pilot parsing program with the goal of creating a tool to aid the user in analyzing inflected word forms. It will handle the same two separate problems: giving a reading to the orthography and identifying and marking the morphemes. Given the profusion of word forms that present multiple readings, the parsing program will in many cases provide suggestions rather than give final analyses. A final and fully developed parsing program will also serve in entering new texts.

4.3. COMMENTS AND OPEN DISCUSSIONS.   Another advantage of the electronic medium is the possibility of comments and open discussions about every word and root. The almost unlimited capacity of the computer today is being exploited in CoNDiP in the concept of comments on entries of individual words and roots. Furthermore, the comments are thought of as a forum for discussions. Wherever called for, my arguments for the phonological interpretation, for a gloss, for root identification, and so on, appear in the form of comments. Others may provide added information or disagreement with my analyses or may contribute with comments on other entries. Such reactions will be entered; if there is more than one comment on a word or root, these are organized chronologically.

4.4. LIST OF WORDS WITH A SHARED ROOT.   Our understanding of the semantics is not only improved through the many text examples. The root entries, which include a list of words containing the given root, provide a better grasp of the basic meaning, history, or etymology of a word.

The word /¢ak^{w}a/, for example, is traditionally translated by 'close', but /ā-¢ak^{w}a/ 'stop water', /i'īyō-¢ak^{w}a/ 'suffocate', and /e'ēka-¢ak^{w}a/ 'protect against the wind' suggest that the meaning is rather 'block (off)'. Precisely this grouping of words around their roots is also found in Campbell's dictionary (1985). He reorganized the material from Molina's Nahuatl-Spanish dictionary in entries according to what he calls "main morphemes," a concept that roughly corresponds to our concept of root.

5. PROBLEMS HANDLED BY CoNDiP.   I have already commented on a number of problems related to the way Nahuatl was written in the sixteenth century. In our work with CoNDiP we have naturally encountered many other problems of different types. I shall touch on a few of these, some well known in traditional lexicography and some tied to the medium and organization of CoNDiP. They deal with (1) the delimitation of certain words; (2) the inclusion of productively derived words; (3) sources for saltillo and vowel quantity; (4) the concept of the root and homonymy in roots; (5) the distinction between derivation and inflection; and (6) the organization of the word lists and texts.

5.1. DELIMITATION OF WORDS.   In describing how texts are handled in CoNDiP, I have said that the division into words may be less controversial than that into sentences; in many cases the wealth of easily identifiable prefixes and suffixes provides an easy solution. However, there are cases of disagreement among Nahuatl scholars as to what a word is, and the handwritten texts provide little guidance in word division because what we recognize as spaces seem to appear randomly. An example of such disagreement is /ō/ indicating 'past'. Traditionally it is considered a prefix; however, according to a general phonological rule, it does not belong to the verb form. The prefix for third-person singular object has two variants, /ki/ and /k/; the distribution of the two is related to a simple rule that allows only the following syllable types: V, CV, VC, CVC. In other words, Nahuatl has no word-initial or word-final consonant clusters. When the prefix for third-person singular object is the first prefix in a verb and precedes a consonant, it has the form /ki/: /Ø-ki-k^{w}a/ 3SG.S-3SG.O-eat 'he eats it'. If the verb begins with a vowel or the prefix in question is preceded by another prefix that ends in a vowel, the other variant, /k/, appears: /Ø-k-a'si/ 3SG.S-3SG.O-reach 'he reaches it', /ni-k-k^{w}a/ 1SG.S-3SG.O-eat 'I eat it'. Now, if the element /ō/ 'past' precedes the prefix in question, it does not influence the choice of variant: /ki/ occurs, hence /ki/ is in word-initial position and /ō/ is a separate word: /ō Ø-ki-k^{w}a'/ PAST 3SG.S-3SG.O-eat.PERF 'he ate it', not */ō-Ø-k-k^{w}a'/. Another argument supporting this analysis is that the particle /iw/ 'thus' and a few other particles occasionally appear between /ō/ 'past' and the verb.

A case in which other considerations come into play is /a'/, a morpheme indicating negation. It occurs most frequently in the word /a'-mo/ 'no, not' and with pronominals and various particles, /a-yāk/ 'no one', /a'-ʎe/ 'nothing', and so on. However, /a'/ also occurs attached to a noun or a verb, and here we distinguish between cases in which /a'/ functions as a separate word from those in which it clearly forms part of a word, for example:

(6) (a) /ni-n-a'-ʎāsa/   'I am fighting death'
        1SG.S-1SG.REFL-neg-let.go
    (b) /a' ō ni-k-nek/   'I did not want it'
        neg past 1SG.S-3SG.O-want

In (6a) /a'/ is preceded by the personal prefix for subject, whereas in (6b) it precedes the prefixes as well as the particle /ō/ 'past'. Whether /a'/ in /ni-n-a'-ʎāsa/ should be analyzed as an inflectional element or whether the word should be considered a compound is an entirely different question.

Our general principle is that wherever there is no clear evidence in favor of considering /a'/ as forming part of a word, it is analyzed as a freestanding particle. This kind of decision has certain consequences that have played a role in our debates. It is a question of recognizing either the free variant or the attached variant of /a'/ as the unmarked one. If the attached variant is considered the unmarked one, we would have to establish a great many words beginning with /a'/, the list of words in the entry for /a'/ in the root dictionary would be very long, and every word would be exemplified by few sentences in the word dictionary. But if the free variant is chosen as the unmarked one, fewer words would have to be established, and many uses of /a'/ would be exemplified in its entry in the word dictionary.

5.2. INCLUSION OF PRODUCTIVELY DERIVED WORDS.   Decisions about whether to include words that are productively derived (a strategy that may lead to unfortunate results; cf. Malkiel's (1962) "ghost words") cause no problems for CoNDiP since all words that occur in a text, including in Molina's dictionary, must be given separate entries. If they have not been found in texts, they have no entry.

5.3. SOURCES FOR SALTILLO AND VOWEL QUANTITY.   Problems involving decisions about saltillo and vowel quantity are not new. They have been dealt with by those of us who have tried to establish a systematic phonemic way of writing sixteenth-century Nahuatl. This has been done most comprehensively by Andrews (1975), Launey (1979, 1986), Karttunen (1983), and Bierhorst (1985). The material available for establishing vowel quantity and the occurrence of saltillo are above all from Carochi (1645), who not only indicates saltillo and vowel length but also occasionally discusses these features. In addition to this cardinal work, we have a few other sources from the seventeenth century and some vocabularies of several quite distinct contemporary dialects from the second half of the twentieth century. The scholars mentioned, who have established their own word corpus and rules for assigning length to the vowels, are not in perfect agreement. The disagreements may be a result of varying access to the sources and also of differing interpretations of the sources. I do not expect uniformity in the phonology of the dialectally and socially diversified Nahuatl spoken by millions of people in the sixteenth and seventeenth centuries. For CoNDiP, we have a practical attitude toward these details of phonology: saltillo and vowel length are included wherever we have information about these features. If our information about them is not straight out of Carochi's grammar, we list our sources of information in a comment on the root. As already mentioned, if we have no information from these sources for some word, we indicate this explicitly by writing the vowels in question with a capital letter. As for vowel quantity that forms part of the inflectional and derivational system, we have established a consistent set of rules, based on phonological analysis and on Carochi's explicit comments.

5.4. THE CONCEPT OF THE ROOT.   In traditional dictionaries, an entry generally subsumes several or many inflected word forms; and one form for each word class is selected to represent all the inflected forms. For modern European languages, the infinitive is the form of the verb that appears in dictionaries, and according to a firmly cemented tradition, this form subsumes all the possible inflected forms of the verb. In this sense the infinitive is an abstraction. The number of inflected forms subsumed under the dictionary form obviously depends on the morphology of the language. This tradition relates to the abstract concept of the "word" that is well established in European culture.

The stem or root is a form that plays a role in traditional lexicography. It is a form that does not appear in isolation in spoken or written texts and is in fact the linguist's construct. Roots in general represent a greater degree of abstraction than dictionary words and are mostly further removed from word forms. It has been mentioned that the purpose of the root dictionary is to compile all the words that contain a given root, assuming that such a compilation will be useful in studies of the derivational system of the language and will give insight into Nahuatl semantics. In the establishment of roots in CoNDiP, we have tried to reconcile three factors or requirements: (1) a certain consistency in the morphological analysis; (2) a view to what may be in keeping with the expectations of the various users of CoNDiP; and (3) some considerations for our knowledge about the history of Nahuatl.

The desire for consistency is a requirement in morphological analysis in general, but we have not adhered strongly to any specific model of morphological analysis and have given priority sometimes to processes and sometimes to items. There are cases in which our consistency results in words that include a stem form different from that of the root. For the words /k-itki/ 'he carries it', /λa-tki-λ/ 'belongings', and /itko/ 'people carry it', we have a root that, according to the word, appears in different shapes (*itki, tki, itk*). Here we choose the longest form (*itki*) to represent the root.

Simple nouns provide another example. Most simple nouns occur in three morphological contexts (1) as unpossessed nouns with a so-called absolutive suffix (-λi/C_, -li/l_, -λ/V_); (2) as possessed nouns, either with a possessive suffix (-wi/C_, -w/V_) or with no suffix; and (3) with no suffix, as the first element in a compound.

UNPOSSESSED		POSSESSED	COMPOUND	
okič-λi	'man'	ī-okič-wi	okič-ēwa	'attack bravely' (man-rise)
siwā-λ	'woman'	ī-siwā-w	siwā-tōtol-in	'turkey hen' (woman-turkey)
kaši-λ	'bowl'	ī-kaš	kaš-peč-λi	'plate' (bowl-bed)
naka-λ	'meat'	ī-nak	naka-ok^wil-in	'maggot' (meat-worm)
šōči-λ	'flower'	ī-šōči-w	šōči-k^wāl-li	'fruit' (flower-good)

The roots we have established for these examples are /okič/ 'man', /siwā/ 'woman', /kaš/ 'bowl', /naka/ 'meat', and /šōči/ 'flower'. The determining criteria have been the form of the root found in compounds and the desire to recognize only three variants of the absolute suffix for the 'singular' (-λi, -li, -λ). The consequence of this decision is that not all stem forms are identical with the root; thus the word /kašiλ/ consists of a variant of the absolute suffix, /λ/, and a stem, /kaši/, that differs from the form that we establish as the root, /kaš/.

A more intricate case involves regular sets of derived verbs: an intransitive verb in /-wi/, a transitive one in /-oa/, and an applicative one in /-lwia/.

INTRANSITIVE	TRANSITIVE	APPLICATIVE	
i'λaka-wi	i'λak-oa	i'λaka-lwia	'damage'
pe¢i-wi	pe¢-oa	pe¢i-lwia	'shine'
poli-wi	pol-oa	pol-wia	'disappear'

The rules that govern the derivation of the transitive and the applicative forms in these sets are fairly simple (see Canger 1980: chaps. 3, 4), but they were not productive in the sixteenth century, so in this case the identification of the root involves the history of the language. And the user who knows only the transitive verb of one of these sets, for example, /poloa/, cannot with certainty predict the root, /poli/. Here considerations for a historically plausible analysis outweigh consistency and transparency of the morphological analysis. As a consequence, it is in general simpler to enter the root dictionary through the word dictionary precisely because a root represents a hard-to-describe abstraction that has its origin in previous stages of the language.

Although it can be a problem to find the phonological shape of a root that ties together a great family of disparate words and satisfies the stipulated ambitions, there are cases in which one is required to decide, often on shaky semantic grounds, whether to establish one or two roots. The question of how to deal with true homonymy is probably not very different for our kind of dictionary than for traditional dictionaries. Should we enter /toma-λ/ 'tomato' and /tomā-wa-k/ 'thick, fat' under one root (according to one analysis, the stem-final vowel is lengthened before the suffix /wa/), or is this a case of two homonymous roots? Campbell (1985) and others believe the two words share one root. However, the only argument I can find in support of this interpretation is the semantic imagination of those scholars, and that seems insufficient. Consequently, in CoNDiP they are registered under two different roots.

An even trickier problem involves near-homonyms resulting from lack of information about vowel quantity and saltillo. For this, Carochi provides help. He has a list of near-homonyms, differing only in vowel length or saltillo. In this list he mentions "Tēma nic, 1. larga, echar maiz, trigo, reales, &c. téma nic 1. breue₂ bañar en temazcal, assar en hornillo, ò barbacoa" (Carochi 1645: 128). But, in fact, the situation is not completely clarified by this information; a third root is involved, /tēmi/ 'swell, be filled', that is homonymous with an intransitive verb, /tēmi/ 'lie together (cats, dogs, corn, gourds)', which is based on the same root as Carochi's first verb. We thus have the following sets:

				BASIC ROOT MEANING
1.	intr.	/tēmi/	'lie together (cats, corn, gourds)'	(involves discrete entities)
	tr.	/tēma/	'pour (corn ...)'	
2.	tr	/tema/	'heat in oven, bathe in temazcal'	(involves heat)
3.	intr.	/tēmi/	'swell, be filled'	(involves liquid or fill)
	tr	/tēmi-tia/	'fill'	

These sets display partial phonological overlap and reveal causes for semantic problems. Because the basic meanings of the roots have not been recognized, 'pour' and 'be filled', as well as 'bathe' and 'fill with liquid', have been paired and have thereby created confusion.

5.5. DERIVATION AND INFLECTION.   The distinction between derivation and inflection plays the same role in CoNDiP as in traditional dictionaries: a derived word has its own dictionary entry, whereas inflected words are subsumed under one unifying entry in some inflected form based on a conventional choice. The only difference is that the dictionary word in CoNDiP is without inflectional affixes; this decision is based on the widespread use of inflectional prefixes in Nahuatl. One exception to this principle is the singular, nominal, absolutive suffix, which is the only inflectional affix that will appear in dictionary words. Thus the transitive verb 'eat' is given as /kʷa/, a nontext form, whereas the word for 'house' appears with the absolutive suffix, /kal-li/, a perfectly common word form.

Now, the distinction between inflection and derivation is in general not clear-cut (see Anderson 1985), but our notation requires that we categorize affixes as inflectional or derivational precisely because the distinction is decisive for whether a word gets its own entry or is identified as an inflected word form to be registered under a dictionary word. For example, the diminutive suffix, also used as an honorific suffix, in Nahuatl is

---

2. tēma nic, first [vowel] long, throw corn, wheat, coins, etc. téma.nic. first [vowel] short, bathe in sweat bath, roast in small oven, or [in] earth oven.

categorized as inflectional; as an appropriate consequence, all sentences containing *Moteucçoma* and *Moteucçomatzin* appear in one list in the entry for /mo-tēkʷ-sōma/ as /mo-tēkʷ-sōma+¢in/ represents an inflected form of /mo-tēkʷ-sōma/. Likewise, the directional prefixes /wāl/ 'toward' and /on/ 'away from' are considered inflectional.

It gets more complicated when an affix functions sometimes as an inflectional affix and sometimes as a derivational one; and certain affixes in Nahuatl seem to work that way. For example, possessed nouns are marked for the person and number of the possessor: /no-kaš/ (1SG.P-bowl) 'my bowl'; and person and number of both subject and object are marked on the verb with prefixes: /ni-k-kʷa/ (1SG.S-3SG.O-eat) 'I eat it'. When the object is nonreferential, one of two prefixes, /λa/ 'nonreferential, nonhuman object' or /tē/ 'nonreferential, human object', appears: /ni-λa-kʷa/ (1SG.S-NONREF.NONH.O-eat) 'I eat', /Ø-tē-miktia/ (3SG.S-NONREF.HUM.O-kill) 'he kills'. This persistent marking of a verb as transitive is retained also when verbal nouns are derived from transitive verbs. Thus 'the act of crying', from the intransitive verb /čōka/, is /čōki-lis-λi/, whereas 'the act of eating', from the transitive verb /kʷa/, is /λa-kʷā-lis-λi/ and no other object prefix can here be exchanged for /λa/. The 'nonreferential, nonhuman object' object prefix participates in the derivation process and is therefore marked as a derivational affix: /=λa-kʷā=lis+λi/. An alternative analysis would categorize the prefixes /tē/ and /λa/ as derivational in all occurrences and claim that they detransitivize transitive verbs.

In other cases certain inflected forms are lexicalized; a relational noun /wān/ 'with' is constructed with possessive person prefixes, /no-wān/ 'with me' or /ī-wān mo-siwā-w/ (3SG.P-with 2SG.P-woman-P) 'with your wife', where /ī/ refers to /mo-siwā-w/. Occasionally this word is used with the third-person singular prefix with the meaning 'and', the reference then being at best vague, and I consider this use a lexicalization. In such cases the possessive prefix is therefore marked as a derivational affix, /=ī-wān/. The same word form is thus sometimes an inflected form (in this case found in the entry /wān/) and in others a dictionary word (in this case found in its own entry /ī-wān/).

5.6. ORGANIZATION OF WORD LISTS AND TEXTS. In the word list of a given root entry we typically find three kinds of words: simple words, derived words, and compounds. Because of the delight in derivation and compounding characteristic of Nahuatl speakers, most roots are found in more than twenty-five words and many in well over one hundred. These words are listed in the root entry, but I have not found any natural and consistent way of organizing these lists because of a number of obvious criteria that intercross and compete. Until now the ordering has been based on some intuitive arrangement: first the simple words, then other words derived from them, then compounds and derivations formed from simple compounds, and at last proper names and toponyms. And within the wealth of compounds, the semantically more concrete have in general been placed before the semantically more abstract, but no absolute consistency is possible.

Text sentences in word entries give rise to similar problems. Should we order them according to texts, first all the sentences from one text, then from another, and so on? Or should we give the user the option of seeing only the first ten sentences from each text? Another possibility is to let users choose any of these options individually.

6. THE HISTORY AND PROPOSED FUTURE OF CoNDiP. The problems outlined here involve practical considerations not only for a computer-based dictionary but also for the linguistic analysis of the Nahuatl language.

6.1. PREHISTORY. A small-scale dictionary project preceded CoNDiP. When I began to teach Classical Nahuatl in the early 1970s, I soon became aware of the quality of Horacio Carochi's *Arte* (1645). His truly linguistic description, his unique notation of vowel quantity and saltillo, and his great fund of examples, word forms, and long sentences (see Canger 1997) are astounding. In 1975–76, with the help of three students, I compiled the Nahuatl words from his examples in the old-fashioned way: with filing cards and pencil. The material was then organized alphabetically according to roots so that a root was given in its phonemic shape, and under such a root all occurrences in Carochi's grammar of words containing the root were listed in their original form and with page references. It was typed up and mimeographed (Adrian, Canger, et al. 1976). This Carochi vocabulary gives the reader easy access to all the occurrences of a given word in their original form and to the words sharing the same root.

When computers entered the scene in the 1980s, the need to construct some kind of computer-based text dictionary for an expedient zipping around between texts and various types of well-organized information became more and more pressing. The decisive factor was, however, the appearance of Michael Thomsen, a rare student from computer science who combined an interest in the language and culture of the Aztecs with a profound appreciation of the details of philology. He became familiar with our Carochi vocabulary, and we began to discuss my dreams of a grand-scale dictionary project. Over the years CoNDiP has grown out of our discussions. Every decision has resulted from thorough debates between the two of us. Only the actual programming has been Thomsen's responsibility alone but always in agreement with the desired layout; and the linguistic aspects of the project have been my responsibility.

6.2. THE PILOT PROJECT.   In summer and early fall 1988 our discussions about how such a dictionary should be organized became more specific. Funded by the Danish Research Council of the Humanities, I went to the annual meeting of the American Anthropological Association in Phoenix, Arizona, in November to present our ideas. The purpose of that presentation was to inform scholars who might have an interest in the project and to involve them in discussions about the principles. We wrote up a proposal and applied to the Carlsberg Foundation for financial support in order to secure Thomsen's participation in the pilot project. Carlsberg deemed the proposal worthy of support, and in December 1988 actual work on the pilot project was begun.

As it turned out, during the first half year, we spent much more time working on the analysis of texts than we had planned, but at all times the debates about analysis and preparation of texts involved the perspective of the whole project. By March 1989 we had prepared the first twenty to thirty pages of text; from then on, we deliberately focused on just a few pages at a time, because we had learned that the principles were constantly being revised. In April 1989 we sent the first report to fifty scholars in Mexico, Guatemala, the United States, Canada, France, Germany, and Denmark.

By the time we received reactions to the first report, we were well into revisions and into the actual programming. The paleography, the transcription, and the English translation of the texts were checked and rechecked for consistency and fortuitous errors. The roots and words were written on cards so as to facilitate the testing of the program and of the interrelationship between the components when they were finally to be entered. The entering of the roots and words from the first short texts became a long process that led to numerous improvements of the program. In late June, while our ideas of how to shape and present the results of the pilot project became clearer and more concrete, we wrote to a limited group of scholars asking them to serve as special critics of the pilot project.

Details in the program were still being revised, and we realized that whatever results the pilot project would lead to, they would not be final; but in the end we put an arbitrary stop to the revisions, tried to tidy up the most conspicuous inconsistencies and blunders, and entered the first short texts. The program worked smoothly and satisfactorily on the small test corpus. In October 1989 we sent out the second and final report on the pilot project.

6.3. SECOND PHASE.   The second phase was begun in 1992. It consisted primarily of adding more material, more words and roots, and more text but also of minor adjustments of the program.

In January 1993 a full-fledged version with a great many new details and options was sent out. The basic structure was unchanged, and the addition of more words and new texts created no significant problems. A natural next step was consequently to approach a task we had discussed over the years, namely, entering all of Molina's dictionary, and that has been the last goal this far.

Our ambitions have been a thoroughly worked-out system, deliberate decisions, and a high degree of precision. The system works very smoothly, and the results are highly satisfactory. Immediate plans for the future involve the entering of more texts and, above all, making CoNDiP available on the Internet.

The abundance of Nahuatl texts and the great interest among scholars in a better understanding of these texts were the incentives for starting CoNDiP, but it has become increasingly clear to us that the model created for the Nahuatl language and these texts from the sixteenth and seventeenth centuries would be useful and instructive if applied to all other languages.

CHAPTER TEN

What's in a Word?

The Whys *and* What Fors *of a Nahuatl Dictionary*

Jonathan D. Amith

1. LEXICOGRAPHY AND THE DOCUMENTATION OF THE SPOKEN WORD.   Harold
Bloom, in beginning one of his essays, states that "the word *meaning* goes
back to a root that signifies 'opinion' or 'intention,' and is closely related to
the word *moaning.*" And he later mentions that "freedom, in a poem, must
mean freedom of meaning, the freedom to have a meaning of one's own"
(Bloom 1985: 1, 3). This rebellious drive for new meaning is not, of course,
the exclusive domain of the poet, nor is new meaning a simple outgrowth
of personal will and private design. Particularly in the languages of societies
with an extended tradition of literacy, meaning is also part of a social system that generates popular texts and seductive jingles while preserving anti-
quated texts and a classic tradition. Undoubtedly related to this emphasis
on (and, of course, availability of) written texts is the fact that the Western
lexicographic tradition, as exemplified by studies in philology and etymology, considers variations in meaning more a temporal than a spatial or social
phenomenon.[1] In societies dominated by print media, the modern lexicographer thus becomes a rather hapless figure, entrusted with the Sisyphean

It has been a pleasure to work with Bill Frawley, Ken Hill, and Pam Munro, who were kind
enough to invite me to participate in this volume even though my work on Nahuatl lexicography and linguistics is still mostly unpublished. Their attention to details and insightful suggestions have helped this essay considerably and saved me from numerous embar-
rassments. I would also like to thank my friends and colleagues José Antonio Flores Farfán,
Donna Perry, and Roberto Zavala for their critical readings of earlier versions. All the preceding, however, are absolved of any responsibility for the errors or inconsistencies that
remain. The fault for these lies with the usual suspect. The latest version of the Nahuatl
Learning Environment can be found at http://www.ldc.upenn.edu/nahuatl.

　　1. The temporal variations, however, are often those of very long-term linguistic shifts.
For an innovative approach to semantic change over short time periods that uses a cognitive and prototype approach to meaning, see Geeraerts 1997.

task of documenting the never-ending and now seldom forgotten linguistic creativity of literate others. Yet alongside this exacerbating and increasingly futile quest for completeness there is another tendency—that for purity of form and orthodoxy of meaning. Lexicography, therefore, often becomes a sort of institutionalized antipoetics. New meanings (in Bloom's term, "moanings") are sanctioned by a self-styled board of *parole*[2] (in certain countries a nationally certified "academy"), an increasingly besieged gatekeeper determining which individual utterances may enter "the prison-house of language," a collective abstraction of both structure and meaning.[3]

For lexicography, therefore, literacy—or perhaps better put, a tradition of the printed word—clearly matters.[4] An early focus on the "great divide" between orality and literacy, and on the autonomy of literacy as an independent variable affecting a wide range of social and cognitive activities, has been deservedly critiqued by researchers in a variety of fields, including social anthropology, sociolinguistics, cultural psychology, rhetoric, folklore, and history.[5] The point is not that societies with a written tradition present a more homogeneous linguistic community but that the printed text often represents a secularization and standardization of language that filters *parole* before it even reaches the lexicographer's desk.[6] Dictionary makers, however, have perhaps been less concerned than other linguists

2. An editor at Merriam-Webster once told a friend of mine, who had offered as a neologism a new and previously undocumented inflected form of a word, that a word usage found only once was idiosyncratic but found twice was idiomatic. Though perhaps somewhat overstated, the editor's assertion, a rather free adaptation of the legal adage that "twice makes a custom," certainly brings to the fore one key problem in lexicography: the number of independently documented occurrences needed to substantiate a valid dictionary entry. In the same vein, for a short sketch on neologisms in English-language dictionaries, see Schoen Brockman (1999), who gives *fuggedaboudit* as a word "[on] the waiting list, pending more evidence," of the *Oxford American Dictionary*.

3. The term is taken from Jameson (1972), who notes, in reference to Saussure's dichotomization of *langue* and *parole*, that "thus, at one stroke, all purely articulatory matters, all questions of local accent, mispronunciation, personal style, are eliminated from the new object under consideration, becoming themselves problems for a different science, that of the *parole*" (p. 26).

4. Linnel (1982, 1988) explores the impact of literacy and writing on linguistics. According to Linnel (1988: 47), it was Vološinov who in the early part of this century (before 1930) had suggested it was the work of linguists and philologists on written texts in foreign languages that had necessitated the construction of dictionaries, with their standard definition presupposing that lexical meanings can be given in terms of a fixed configuration of semantic features. See also the collection of articles in Frawley 1981.

5. This list of fields is that presented by Besnier (1995: 3), who, in his introduction, cites the relevant literature, particularly that which constituted a critical response to the works of Goody, Havelock, and Ong. For a similar critical response, see also Street 1984, 1988, and Street's other works cited in Street 1988.

6. For a notable and impressive exception to common lexicographic practice in English, see Cassidy and Hall 1985–.

with the different ways in which written and nonwritten languages relate to the particular problems that are the topic of their research. Recognizing this, one linguist, Ragnar Rommetveit (1988: 15), has referred to the "written language biases within various branches of semantics," a bias that becomes clear not only in any quick glance at textbooks and theoretical treatises on semantics but in much of the literature on lexicography as well.[7] In general, then, little work has been done on what may be loosely considered *comparative lexicography*, the ways in which the structure and content of dictionaries (and the lexicon/grammar interface) can and should be adapted to the particularities of specific cases—speech communities, lexical corpora, and target audiences.

These particularities, clearly, go far beyond the simple fact of whether the documented language is written or spoken. Much more basic and problematic is the task of identifying or determining the language community that serves as the source of lexical data and the reading or listening community that is the target of the lexicographic project. Secret languages, the specialized lexicons and grammars of rituals and initiation, the esoteric language of religion, verbal dueling, and an innovative poetics of expression as well as a rote poetics of tradition[8] all belie any facile claims of a unified language source group, even in communities that at first glance appear closed and cohesive.[9] Returning somewhat to Bloom's metaphor for meaning, what a field lexicographer hears when he or she enters a community that speaks an undocumented or little-documented language is often a harrowing cacophony, a perplexing admixture of sound and meaning that in the best of circumstances can be associated with particular registers, contexts, or social groups but in the worst seems distressingly idiosyncratic, located at the edge of what some would call "correct" and "incorrect" speech. Eventually these puzzles are "resolved"— in my experience first according to form (phonology and orthography), then according to function (morphosyntax and grammar), and finally (and most fastidiously) according to meaning (semantics and lexicon), the three essential elements of a lexicographic representation.

7. This is apparent in even the most cursory review of the proceedings of the various EuroLEX conferences, as well as in "state-of-the-art" collections on formal semantics (Lappin 1996).

8. Poetics, from this perspective, involves a highly formalized structure of discourse that is oriented not to breaking new semantic ground but to encapsulating a static, at times highly ritualized, form. Thus Berman (1983: 59) notes in regard to early legal traditions that "the dramatic and poetic qualities of Germanic law were associated with the plasticity of its substance. . . . The expression of legal rules in poetic images helped to stamp them on the memory," adding that "the earliest Irish law was expressed in the form of poetry."

9. See the bibliographies in the review articles by Cicourel (1985) and Chafe and Tannen (1987).

If the fragmented nature of the "linguistic community" is one source of uncertainty, the diversity of the potential readership of a lexicon is another. Both factors must be considered in dictionary design, the first more in regard to input, the latter in regard to output. In the case of Nahuatl—considering its function in the colonization and conversion of New Spain and its present role as the principal linguistic icon of Mexican national identity promoted by the nation-state and popularly endorsed in much of central Mexico and among the Chicano community in the United States—the groups that might use a dictionary (linguists, historians, anthropologists, theater and dance troupes, heritage language speakers, and simply the curious, as well as native speakers) would perhaps be more diverse than those groups that would wish to access similar material for other native languages of Latin America.[10] A particularly challenging aspect of Nahuatl lexicography, therefore, is to create a basic corpus that can be used to generate material (through electronic manipulation of the original input) that would be of use to readers as diverse as comparative linguists, on the one hand, and native speakers, on the other.

With such a variety of language sources and pedagogical ends, and trying to meet many needs in a single text, lexicography at times threatens to become a bottleneck, a constricted space of lexical representation that has resulted from standardized materials and narrowed goals. One reaction to this situation is exemplified by the increasing tendency to specialization within the lexicography of major languages: native-speaker dictionaries, collocational dictionaries, monolingual learners' dictionaries, bilingual learners' dictionaries, translators' dictionaries, visual dictionaries, dictionaries (mono- and bilingual) of particular terminologies, explanatory combinational dictionaries, among many others.[11] Although such a fragmented approach provides an inappropriate model for the lexicography of less documented languages—if simply because, given the limited resources (human and financial) for such endeavors, there is little chance of funding for the independent development of such specialized tools—it does suggest that there is an underlying centrifugal force that constantly threatens to pull apart any effort to construct a single "jack-of-all-trades" lexicon.

Another solution (and that undertaken for the Nahuatl material that I have studied) involves a methodology that takes advantage of electronic media to store vast amounts of material in an open-ended database constructed in a flexible and multilevel format. In essence this approach

---

10. Recently, in fact, I have been contacted by prisoners who wish to learn Nahuatl (as well as by department of corrections officials who want to know what prisoners have been writing) and by an individual who wanted the Nahuatl word for "eternal life" added to a tattoo on his back.

11. Snell-Hornby (1990: 232), for example, suggests that bilingual dictionaries should, like their monolingual counterparts, become "increasingly user-specific."

accepts and indeed embraces the inherent centrifugality of lexicography; for this reason it concentrates not simply on defining and delimiting but on building structures that will link together the very many facets of meaning, particularly those that involve the articulation of syntax and semantics.[12] Though dealing with an entirely different range of materials (those from dominant Western languages), several lexicographers have already suggested the direction such an approach might take. Beryl T. Atkins, for example, calls for theoretical linguists "to devise a typology of vocabulary items and a parallel typology of defining strategies suited to each" (1992–93: 26), and others, noting the promise of electronic reference works, have claimed the need for "an almost total restructuring of the way in which [words] are treated in lexicography" (Atkins, Kegl, and Levin 1988: 110).[13] Still others have stressed the study of syntagmatic over paradigmatic relations and have questioned the appropriateness of the word as the primary unit of analysis and presentation, calling for a greater attention to collocation (e.g., Cop 1990; Meyer 1990).[14] Additional shifts in focus should also be considered. It seems clear that in the best of circumstances studies of indigenous, nonwritten languages should be constructed more along the lines of an encyclopedia or "cultural dictionary" than according to the model of a bilingual translators' dictionary with its focus on substitutability of target language for source language terms. Care might also be taken to situate words within semantic and morphosyntactic categories that would prove useful to determining both meaning and

12. The importance of using electronic databases to relate lexical semantics to syntactic behavior is suggested by Pustejovsky, who states, for example, that "it will soon be difficult to carry out serious computational research in the fields of linguistics and N[atural] L[anguage] P[rocessing] without the help of electronic dictionaries and computational lexicographic resources" (1995: 5). See the reference to Dixon 1984 in note 42 below.

13. The original citation has "verbs" instead of "words." With this change, the full quote presents a position similar to that elaborated in the pages below: "We would argue that if dictionaries are to take a quantum leap rather than simply a series of tottering steps into the future—particularly into a future which holds out the enticing prospect of electronic reference works—then what is necessary is not merely a matter of elaborating or modifying existing entries, but rather an almost total restructuring of the way in which verbs are treated in lexicography. Any given verb participates in only a subset of the possible alternation patterns. However, if a dictionary is to provide comprehensive and consistent information about alternations, these must at least be available to the dictionary designer and to the lexicographer during the process of compilation" (p. 110).

14. Cop, for example, stresses a semasiological (receiving rather than producing texts) approach to collocations that focuses on the collocator rather than the base. In discussing the design of monolingual learners' dictionaries, Rundell (1988: 134) argues for a dictionary design that "rather than treating meaning as central, ... give[s] equal weight to all relevant features, including grammar, style and register, collocational properties, pragmatic and connotative features, relationships of synonymy and hyponymy, contextual and syntagmatic preferences, and so on." Mackin (1978) briefly discusses work on collocations in the *Oxford Dictionary of Current Idiomatic English*.

use. Previously such solutions were unrealizable, given the problem of manuscript length, a prime consideration in printed versions, though a virtually nonexistent factor in electronic publishing (CD-ROMs/DVDs and Web sites). The most practical solution to the tension between a drive toward more complete lexicographic studies and cutbacks in the publishing industry would be to produce the complete lexicographic study in electronic format and issue a reduced, practical synthesis in print that would interface with the former.

This section began with a discussion of meaning and of the persistent tension between lexicography and poetics, between the documentation and the fabrication of meaning. It was suggested that a parallel tension exists between written and spoken discourse, not necessarily between these genres of expression per se, but in regard to lexicographic practice—which tends to the prescriptive when the source is the former, descriptive when the source is the latter. A starting point for a new lexicographic approach to the study of indigenous languages was mentioned: the need to design a dictionary project according to the characteristics of the language and language community studied, the nature of the documentation to be processed or produced with the aid of the dictionary, and the needs of the users who will seek access to the final product. Word DEFINITIONS, in this presentational strategy, provide only one facet (albeit perhaps the most basic) of a multidimensional approach to lexicography and, more generally, to the exploration and learning of a less common language for which oral texts provide the basic data.

The goal of this chapter, then, is not to outline the specific problems that Nahuatl poses for lexicography (although some of these will briefly be mentioned) but to explore the manner in which electronic media can be particularly helpful in dealing with issues of lexicography and semantics that have often been mentioned but, in printed lexicons, are difficult to address. The incipient project that I briefly describe below, the Nahuatl Learning Environment, makes use of Internet technology that not only provides a unique tool for exploring the intricacies of the Nahuatl language, but facilitates the cross-linking of corpus, lexicon, and grammar in a single learning and research environment.[15] One goal

15. This learning environment (now at http://www.ldc.upenn.edu/nahuatl) was made possible by the extraordinary support I received from the Linguistic Data Consortium at the University of Pennsylvania. Mark Liberman, the director, has been supportive of the Nahuatl project from the beginning and has given generously of his time and resources. Steven Bird has been most directly responsible for the current search engine for the on-line dictionary of Ameyaltepec Nahuatl. He spent days adapting his *Hyperlex* program to my material and has given me invaluable advice on computational linguistics and lexicography in general. Brian Robinson of Yale University placed the early grammar lessons and exercises on the Yale server (http://www.yale.edu/nahuatl), wrote the script now being used, and established the CGI links between the lessons and exercises and the lexicon. My sincere thanks to all these individuals.

of this project is to develop a model that joins linguistic research and language pedagogy by providing the grammatical context for using dictionary material while furnishing the appropriate lexical base to operationalize a learned grammar. A more comprehensive and long-term goal is to use electronic and Internet technology to link corpus, lexicon, and grammar so that both specialists and nonspecialists can access primary linguistic data (corpus), semantic interpretation (lexicon), and structural analysis (grammar) and in this way more effectively study and learn a language (see fig. 10.1). At the same time, it will then be possible for others to analyze and critique the interpretations offered by the original researcher. The first two sections below explore how these goals—heuristically approached through a discussion of the complementary goals of research and pedagogy—can be met. The third section briefly discusses the relationship between indigenous-language dictionaries and the indigenous community.

2. RESEARCH: ENTRY DESIGN AND LEXICON STRUCTURE. For just over four and a half years I lived in two neighboring Nahuatl-speaking communities located near the Balsas River in central Guerrero—Ameyaltepec (3 years) and San Agustín Oapan ($1\frac{1}{2}$ years). During this period, I conducted ethnographic fieldwork on intervillage relations and at the same time studied Nahuatl—continually writing down on file cards phrases heard in everyday speech, asking friends about the meaning and use of specific words, and taking notes for a reference grammar. By the end of my fieldwork period I had amassed approximately 20,000 such cards (organized by "headword"), the vast majority documenting phrases I had heard in Ameyaltepec, although approximately 2,000 to 3,000 have words and phrases from San Agustín Oapan. Approximately one hundred hours of recordings from various villages will eventually yield interlinearized textual material that will provide additional lexical and syntactic information and eventually be incorporated into the electronic database as primary source material.

Over the past decade, I gradually began to input the Ameyaltepec phrases into an open-ended database format, a simple text file with field delimiters and separators. Later this data was imported into Shoebox, a program written by JAARS, the software developer associated with the Summer Institute of Linguistics. Shoebox permits both flexible field formats and fonts and rapid searches and filters; it also simplifies export according to style sheets (for publication) or in delimited format (for use with other database search engines). Preliminary fields (see partial list in table 10.1) were established for the following purposes: (1) to input primary lexical material along with English and Spanish translations; (2) to facilitate cross-referencing among entries

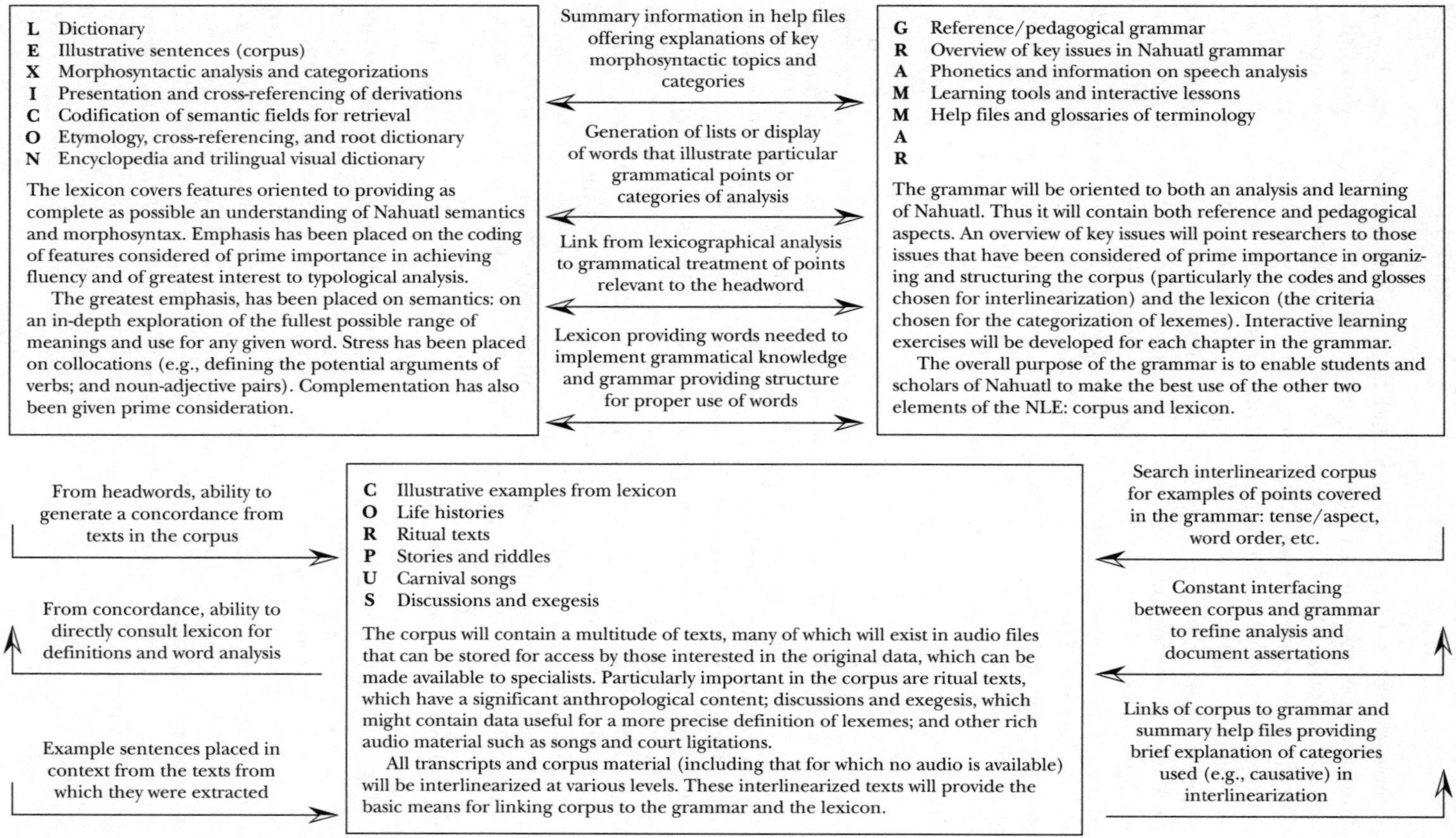

L Dictionary
E Illustrative sentences (corpus)
X Morphosyntactic analysis and categorizations
I Presentation and cross-referencing of derivations
C Codification of semantic fields for retrieval
O Etymology, cross-referencing, and root dictionary
N Encyclopedia and trilingual visual dictionary

The lexicon covers features oriented to providing as complete as possible an understanding of Nahuatl semantics and morphosyntax. Emphasis has been placed on the coding of features considered of prime importance in achieving fluency and of greatest interest to typological analysis.

The greatest emphasis, has been placed on semantics: on an in-depth exploration of the fullest possible range of meanings and use for any given word. Stress has been placed on collocations (e.g., defining the potential arguments of verbs; and noun-adjective pairs). Complementation has also been given prime consideration.

G Reference/pedagogical grammar
R Overview of key issues in Nahuatl grammar
A Phonetics and information on speech analysis
M Learning tools and interactive lessons
M Help files and glossaries of terminology
A
R

The grammar will be oriented to both an analysis and learning of Nahuatl. Thus it will contain both reference and pedagogical aspects. An overview of key issues will point researchers to those issues that have been considered of prime importance in organizing and structuring the corpus (particularly the codes and glosses chosen for interlinearization) and the lexicon (the criteria chosen for the categorization of lexemes). Interactive learning exercises will be developed for each chapter in the grammar.

The overall purpose of the grammar is to enable students and scholars of Nahuatl to make the best use of the other two elements of the NLE: corpus and lexicon.

C Illustrative examples from lexicon
O Life histories
R Ritual texts
P Stories and riddles
U Carnival songs
S Discussions and exegesis

The corpus will contain a multitude of texts, many of which will exist in audio files that can be stored for access by those interested in the original data, which can be made available to specialists. Particularly important in the corpus are ritual texts, which have a significant anthropological content; discussions and exegesis, which might contain data useful for a more precise definition of lexemes; and other rich audio material such as songs and court litigations.

All transcripts and corpus material (including that for which no audio is available) will be interlinearized at various levels. These interlinearized texts will provide the basic means for linking corpus to the grammar and the lexicon.

Summary information in help files offering explanations of key morphosyntactic topics and categories

Generation of lists or display of words that illustrate particular grammatical points or categories of analysis

Link from lexicographical analysis to grammatical treatment of points relevant to the headword

Lexicon providing words needed to implement grammatical knowledge and grammar providing structure for proper use of words

Search interlinearized corpus for examples of points covered in the grammar: tense/aspect, word order, etc.

Constant interfacing between corpus and grammar to refine analysis and document assertions

Links of corpus to grammar and summary help files providing brief explanation of categories used (e.g., causative) in interlinearization

From headwords, ability to generate a concordance from texts in the corpus

From concordance, ability to directly consult lexicon for definitions and word analysis

Example sentences placed in context from the texts from which they were extracted

Figure 10.1. The Nahuatl Learning Environment: Schematic Representation of Links between Elements.

TABLE 10.1. Fields for Ameyaltepec Nahuatl Database Entry

Field Delimiter	Data Input
\w	Headword
\ew and \sw	English/Spanish definition
\ee and \ss	English/Spanish glosses for searching, dictionary reversal, and interlinearization
\cat	Grammatical category and derivational morphology (verb, noun, demonstrative, quantifier; or applicative, causative, denominal, deverbal; e.g., *V-3-d-ca* indicates a derived ditransitive causative; *V-1-b* indicates a basic, underived intransitive)
\com	Schematic part of speech representation for compounds (e.g., *N-V1* indicates noun stem incorporated into an intransitive verb; *V-ka:-V2* indicates a participial verb, ending in *-ka:*, incorporated into a transitive verb)
\mor	Morphological analysis (e.g., *kaltlatla* would be *kal-tlatla* house-burn; *cho:ktia* would be *cho:k(a)-tia* cry-CAUS)
\inf	Verb class for inflectional paradigms, or patterns of noun pluralization and possession
\sem	Semantic field (e.g., *Nat-pl-med* for medicinal plants; *bd* for body parts, *son* for sounds, *tex* for textures)
\p___	Illustrative phrases
\ep__ and \sp__	English/Spanish translations of illustrative phrases
\x___	Various cross-references for roots and the basic stems of derivations
\enc and \snc	English/Spanish cultural and semantic discussions and notes
\nt	Notes and observations for future study or reference

(for instance, by linking base verbs to their causative and applicative forms or by giving stems that can be linked to produce a root dictionary); and (3) to provide fields for the coding of semantic and morphosyntactic categories (such as agentives, colors, and medicinal plants) that clarify meanings while providing data for linguistic and cultural analysis.

The decision as to how to list headword entries is at times fairly straightforward, with several caveats. Intransitive verbs are entered in the least marked form, the third-person singular present indicative. Transitive verbs are recorded by stem, without the object prefix that would be necessary for a well-formed word in Nahuatl, a head-marking language. For various reasons, including their somewhat irregular formations, causatives are given separate entries (e.g., *wetska* 'to laugh' and *wetski:tia* 'to make laugh'), whereas anticausatives, which use the reflexive marker to detransitivize, are not separately listed.[16] In most of these cases relating to transitive and intransitive verbs, there is little difficulty in selecting the proper entry form. The major decision has been to follow tradition and list transitives without any object prefix, resulting in headword entries that are not naturally occurring words.[17]

At other times, however, the determination of entry format and of what words to include is problematic. This is particularly true in regard to incorporation, compounded forms indicating several types of motion, and reduplication.[18] Several criteria are relevant to a decision as to whether to accord a specific form of an incorporated, compounded, or reduplicated word a separate entry. Such words that have been lexicalized or whose meaning is not predictable are listed as headwords; forms whose meaning is covered by highly productive processes described in the grammar are not separately listed. In general an effort has been made to avoid a proliferation of entries and to keep together under one headword variants (such as short- and long-vowel reduplication of verb stems, different possessive markers on a nominal stem) that might provide interesting data for comparison (e.g., the differences between two types of reduplication or possession). An electronic format solves the most basic problem posed by more consolidated entries, since users will be able to employ a search function to find forms (such as *wa:lnemi*, discussed below) that have been listed as senses under a more basic headword (in this case, *nemi*).

Incorporation of certain nominal stems, such as body parts, is highly productive in Nahuatl. The decision of whether to establish a separate entry is

16. Thus one finds both *tlapowi* 'to become open' and *tlapowa* 'to open' as headwords but only *tsakwa* 'to close' and not the anticausative *no-tsakwa* REFL-close 'to become closed'.

17. This format follows that used in many Nahuatl dictionaries, particularly those from the colonial period, and has the weight of tradition behind it. An exception is Brewer and Brewer 1971, which lists transitives with the third-person object prefix *k(i)-*. Note that with intransitives, the third-person subject marker is the zero morpheme; the decision here has been to translate entries with the infinitive, which does not exist in Nahuatl. Below I discuss the utility of changing this format for a dictionary produced especially for native speakers. These points, as well as questions regarding the proper morphophonemic representation for certain stems, can be intensely debated and I have deliberately refrained from touching on all these points. Instead, a brief exposition of problems of entry format and selection associated with incorporation, compounding, and reduplication is offered to acquaint readers with some problems of headword entry design that are particularly prevalent in Nahuatl.

18. Another problem not dealt with here relates to criteria for separate listings of "extrinsically" and "intrinsically" possessed forms (e.g., in regard to *nakatl* 'meat' → *inakaw* 'his meat' and *inakayo* 'his flesh (of the body)'; or in regard to *kahli* 'house' → *ikal* 'his house' and *ikahlo* 'its roof (of a house)'). In general both types of possession are listed under the same headword, though accorded different senses. Only when a *-yo* form exists as a freestanding noun (with an absolutive ending) is it separately entered (e.g., *a:tl* 'water' → *ia:w* 'his water'; *a:yo:tl* 'juice' → *ia:yo* 'its juice'); in these cases each absolutive form is cross-referenced.

usually based on the natural occurrence of a lexeme in the corpus; with few exceptions no effort has been made to produce words that are perfectly well formed but unlikely to occur. Thus *ma:posteki* 'to break one's arm' (*ma:-posteki* 'arm-break'), which is found throughout the corpus, is listed as a headword, whereas the perfectly well formed *mapilposteki* 'to break one's finger' (which did not occur in the corpus, but which any speaker would accept, and which might well occur in a much larger corpus) is not. With incorporation, then, the criteria of inclusion is one of lexicalization, natural occurrence in the corpus, and lack of predictability of meaning.

Nahuatl verb morphology includes a series of elements that tend to indicate some sort of spatial, and occasionally temporal, motion: two prefixes (*on-* and *wa:l-*) and three pairs of suffixes (*-ti/-ki, -to/-ko,* and *-to:ya/-ko:ya*); the first of each pair indicates movement away from a deictic point of reference and the second toward such a point. In general if a verb takes one set (e.g., intraverse motion) it will take the other. In certain cases, however, only one form occurs. Thus *nemi* 'to live', or 'to be present (at a specific location)' occurs as *wa:lnemi* 'to be born'; the past tense is *o:nemiko* 'to have been born'. Here simply a separate sense under the headword *nemi* is given. In another case separate entries are given for *one:wa* 'to depart (away from a deictic reference point)' and *wa:le:wa* 'to come (toward a deictic reference point)'. These forms have been lexicalized: the intransitive verb *e:wa* no longer exists without a directional, and with *one:wa* and *wa:le:wa* the prefixes no longer alter with suffixes in certain tenses and aspects (thus *one:was* 'he will leave' and *o:one:w* 'he left', but compare the alternation in *ontlakwa:s* 'he will go to eat' and *o:tlakwa:to* 'he went to eat').[19]

There is also a series of verbs that appear as suffixes and indicate movement associated with a primary event. For example, *-tasi* refers to an action carried out upon arrival at a particular location away from a deictic reference point: *tlakwa* 'to eat' forms *tlakwatasi* 'to eat upon arriving there'. In general an effort has been made to avoid separately listing these forms of associated motion unless the meaning is not predictable from the component elements. Under this criterion *tlakwatasi* is not accorded a separate entry, but *komo:ntasi* 'to hit the ground with a thud' (derived from the verb *komo:ni* 'to make a booming sound or to thunder') is separately entered; the related form *komo:nteko* 'to hit the ground with a thud (toward a deictic reference point)' is also listed, but users are here pointed to the more common *komo:ntasi*.[20] In other cases in which the meaning of such compounds

19. Nahuatl does not distinguish gender. However, following certain conventions that perhaps should be avoided, I have translated the third-person singular pronoun as 'he'.

20. The endings *-tasi* and *-teko* differ only in terms of deixis; *-teko* indicates an action or event that occurs when the subject arrives at a point toward a deictic reference point (usually the speaker). Thus *tlakwateko* 'he (will) eat upon arriving here'.

might seem idiosyncratic, an example of the relevant form is included under the entry for the principal verb. Thus under *isa* 'to wake up' one finds *isate:wa* 'to suddenly wake up'. With the set of elements described in this paragraph, an effort has been made to avoid separate listings. When meaning is not predictable, however, either a separate entry is given or a separate sense (appropriately marked) is given under the headword.

Finally, there is the problem of reduplication. Reduplicated nouns such as *kakahli* 'canopy' ← *kahli* 'house' and *susuwa:tl* 'effeminate man' ← *suwa:tl* 'woman' are accorded their own entries. Such forms are lexicalized, and their meaning (which involves a metaphoric extension from the nominal base) is not completely predictable. The same pattern of reduplication can be used to indicate toy or play items: *metlatl* 'metate' → *memetlatl* 'toy metate'. This is a productive, though rarely used, construction. Yet to avoid a proliferation of entries, such reduplicated words are not separately listed.[21] Reduplication of adjectives is used mostly to indicate plurality; no separate entries are assigned to these forms.

Unlike the case with nouns, the reduplication of verbal stems is highly productive, a situation that according to the criteria I have established argues against separate listings. In Ameyaltepec, reduplication occurs in two basic shapes: *(C)V-* and *(C)V:-*.[22] Often there is a clear semantic difference between each form:

no:tsa	'to address or call to'	kino:tsa itah[23]	'his father calls to him'
nono:tsa	'to converse with'	kinono:tsa itah	'his father talks to him'
no:no:tsa	'to give advice'	kino:no:tsa itah	'his father counsels him'
teki	'to cut (in a single action)'	kiteki	'he cuts it (i.e., once, all the way through)'
teteki	'to cut (repeatedly)'	kiteteki	'he cuts it (e.g., cloth with scissors)'

21. For convenience, irregular reduplicated plural forms, which are now rare, are separately listed, although the user is simply remitted to the singular. Thus under *ko:koneh* one finds "*pl.*, see *kone:tl*."

22. In many other dialects the first pattern of reduplication is *(C)Vh-* (e.g., *kinohno:tsa*), which in Classical Nahuatl would be *(C)VɁ-(kinoɁno:tsa)*. In Ameyaltepec, word-internal *h* is deleted at the surface level, which leads to problems for interdialectal comparison, some of which are discussed below.

23. Ø-ki-no:tsa-Ø   Ø-i:tah-Ø
    3sgS-3sgO-call-SG.IND   3SGS-3SGPOSS-father-SG.POSSED

te:teki   'to slice'   kite:teki   'he slices it (e.g., bread with a knife)'

One goal in organizing data input into the lexicon is to identify areas of interest to potential users and to structure data entry to facilitate easy retrieval and analysis. Given that the most salient problems will vary among different languages, dictionary design should vary accordingly. In Nahuatl, one particular problem needing research is the range of semantic concomitants to verbal reduplication. Entries into the Ameyaltepec lexicon have therefore been designed to maintain reduplicated forms of a single verb within one entry, providing for easy and rapid comparison between base verbs and both *(C)V-* and *(C)V:-* reduplications.[24] A provisional English-only entry for *no:tsa* exemplifies this organization of data:[25]

> **no:tsa** *(V trans.;* REG. INFLEC. *see* **ki:sa;** ROOT: *no:tsa) applic.* → **no:chilia 1:** (often with prefix *on-* or *wa:l-*) to address or call to *Mitsno:tsa, itlah mits-ihli:sneki.* He's calling you, there is sth he wants to say to you. **2:** to visit or pay a call on *Nikno:stiki:sa mo:stla, a:man xnikaxilia.* I'll pass by and pay a call on him tomorrow, today I don't have time. **3:** to speak to (in the sense of being on good terms with them) *Xne:chno:tsa, ne:xtlawe:lita.* He doesn't speak to me, he hates me. **4:** (*rdp-short*) to carry on a conversation with *Timonono:tsan pa:mpa kwahli timowi:kan.* We talk to each other (a lot) because we get along well. **5:** (*rdp-long*) to give advice to or counsel *Ne:chno:no:tsa nona:n para ma:ka itlah nikchi:was.* My mother gives me advice so that I won't do anything (bad).

At present the underlying field markers of illustrative sentences (not visible in the output but marking the fields in the database) encode certain morphological features of the headword as it occurs in the example phrase. One of these features is reduplication (illustrated below). Here the use of distinct field markers facilitates searches for any illustrative phrase that contains a reduplicated form of the headword:[26]

---

24. When there is significant and unpredictable semantic content to reduplication, the definitions of reduplicated forms are separately numbered (as exemplified with *no:tsa* below), each with a short gloss marking the morphological form being defined (e.g., *rdp-short* for *(C)V-* reduplication and *rdp-long* for *(C)V:-* reduplication).

25. Here, as elsewhere, an English format and translations are given, although Spanish versions also exist. Current plans are for two separate electronic forms of the Nahuatl Learning Environment (including the lexicon), one in Spanish and one in English. Printed versions would also be separate, unless a publisher prefers a fully trilingual (Nahuatl to English and Spanish) lexicon.

26. Thus \ph indicates a simple illustrative phrase; \prs indicates a phrase that manifests *(C)V-* short-vowel reduplication of the verbal headword; and \prl indicates a phrase that

Field delimiter	Illustrative phrase and translation
\ph	*Xne:chno:tsa, ne:xtlawe:lita.*
\eph	He doesn't speak to me, he hates me.
\prs	*Timonono:tsan pa:mpa kwahli timowi:kan.*
\eprs	We talk to each other a lot because we get along well.
\prl	*Ne:chno:no:tsa nona:n para ma:ka itlah nikchi:was.*
\eprl	My mother gives me advice so that I won't do anything (bad).

The employment of distinct delimiters is but a temporary (and unattractive) solution to the problem of accessing particularly salient morphological elements and processes (such as reduplication, directional and purposive motion affixes, certain tense and aspect markers). It is not designed to mark phrases in which a word other than the headword is reduplicated; and it is completely ineffectual in providing a fully searchable text (which could, for example, be used to locate stems or to isolate inflectional morphemes). Only interlinearization would permit such searches (e.g., a search for *rdps* or *rdpl* on the \morph line below would isolate *(C)V-* and *(C)V:-* reduplication, respectively):

\ph	*Xne:chno:tsa, ne:xtlawe:lita.*
\morph	x-Ø-ne:ch-no:tsa-Ø Ø-ne:ch-tlawe:l+ita-Ø
\gloss	NEG-3SGS-1SGO-call-SG.IND 3SGS-1SGO-hate+see-SG.IND
\trans	He doesn't speak to me, he hates me.
\prs	*Timonono:tsan pa:mpa kwahli timowi:kan.*
\morph	ti-mo-rdps-no:tsa-n pa:mpa Ø-kwal-li ti-mo-wi:ka-n
\gloss	1PLS-REFL-RDPS-call-PL.IND because 3SGS-good-ABS
	1PLS-REFL-carry-PL.IND
\trans	We talk to each other a lot because we get along well.
\prl	*Ne:chno:no:tsa nona:n para ma:ka itlah nikchi:was.*
\morph	Ø-ne:ch-rdpl-no:tsa-Ø Ø-no-na:n-Ø para ma:ka itlah ni-k-chi:wa-s
\gloss	3SGS-1SGO-RDPL-call-SG.IND 3SGS-1SGPOSS-mother-SG.AL.POSS so.that NEG-IMP something 1SGS-3SGO-DO-SG.FUT
\trans	My mother gives me advice so that I won't do anything (bad).

---

manifests *(C)V:-* long-vowel reduplication of the verbal headword. Subsequent field delimiters indicate English and Spanish translations of each type of phrase. Other phrase delimiters include \pd to mark sentences that manifest the use of a directional and \pti, which is used to mark phrases with an aspectual auxiliary fused to the verb.

Nevertheless, given the immense amount of labor involved in parsing the illustrative phrases in a dictionary of about ten thousand entries (let alone more than one hundred hours of additional texts), a temporary solution to data access is needed. One such solution (expedient though limited) is the use of specialized delimiters for particular categories that are problematic for grammatical or semantic analysis or that might prove most interesting for cross-linguistic comparison. Such a design also facilitates the isolation and export of illustrative sentences so marked.

Another structural mechanism that has been used to facilitate data access is the employment of complex coding within particular fields. As with delimiters, I have adopted an initial approach that might be described as "practical overcoding," in that a single code is used to mark several categorical features that together isolate terms deemed in need of further study. For any printed or screen version, an interface can convert these overspecific codes to shorter "human readable" forms (e.g., *V-1-nondir-wi* for "intransitive verb manifesting nondirected alternation," where the number 1 indicates the number of core arguments, becomes *V intrans.*). Yet the existence of the underlying code will facilitate searches and subsequent determination of the boundaries and internal structure of selected categories and paradigms.

For example, consider that many dialects of Nahuatl manifest a sequence of apparently denominal forms—adjectivals, inchoatives, and causatives— that manifest the endings *-k(i), -ya,* and *-lia,* respectively, on what seems to be a single nominal stem (see table 10.2).[27] This sequence is one of the most complete and regular paradigms in Nahuatl. By coding each member according to grammatical category (*Adj-d, V-1-d,* and *V-2-d*) while identifying the paradigm by a special code (*-k/ya/lia*), it becomes a simple matter to create a system whereby users of the on-line version of the dictionary can "click" on any member of the paradigm and generate either a list of all related forms (e.g., all adjectivals with a morphology similar to that, say, of *yenkwik*), or a complete set of adjectivals, inchoatives, and causatives (displayed in a format similar to that of table 10.2).

Another feature of the data entry structure chosen is that it permits comparison across categories. This tool is especially useful for examining

---

27. See Dixon 1977: 27 ff. for a brief discussion of the relationship between "adjectives" and inchoative and causative verbs. I mention that the stem is apparently nominal because in most present-day dialects of Nahuatl only a few of the stems occur in nominal forms. One such occurrence is *istatl* 'salt', which in denominal forms signifies 'white' (see table 10.2). A few other cases occur: *xokotl* 'plum' and *xokó:k* 'sour or tart'; *yetl* 'bean' and *yetí:k* 'heavy'. Nevertheless, the majority of these adjectival, inchoative, and causative sequences are built on stems that no longer exist in nominal form. Launey (1992: 110) also refers to these adjectivals as denominal.

TABLE 10.2. Examples of a Word-Formation Paradigm in Nahuatl:
Adjectivals, Inchoatives, Causatives

(Nominal) Stem	Adjectival	Inchoative	Causative
*yenkwi	yenkwik ('new')	yenkwiya ('to become new')	yenkwilia ('to make new')
*yema:ni	yema:nki ('soft')	yema:nia ('to become soft')	yema:nilia ('to make soft')
istatl ('salt')	istá:k ('white')[1]	ista:ya ('to become white')	ista:lia ('to whiten')
Database code	Adj-d-k/ya/lia	V-1-d-k/ya/lia	V-2-d-k/ya/lia
Human readable code	Adj. (denominal)	V. intrans.	V. trans.

NOTE: [1]The Nahuatl orthography I have chosen indicates accent only when it does not
fall on the penultimate syllable, as is the case with istá:k.

morphological processes such as noun incorporation, which both creates new lexical items and affects the argument structure of the clause.
Noun incorporation—which has been the topic of much comparative
and typological work, particularly in regard to the semantic roles of
incorporated nouns—can thus be documented at the lexicosemantic
level (by according the incorporated compound an entry as a headword) while being analyzed at both the morphological (as a compound)
and syntactic (according to the valency of the newly formed verb)
levels.[28] Therefore, it would seem desirable to structure lexical entries
so as to provide for the most complete access to the semantic, morphological, and syntactic concomitants of this process. Incorporation has
been and is highly productive in Nahuatl, which for this reason offers
much data on the process. Making primary data available for use and
analysis by linguists is one goal of the present project.[29] A detailed discussion on how incorporation may be represented and analyzed in a
Nahuatl dictionary is beyond the scope of this chapter. Nevertheless, a
few points may be made regarding how the database design of a lexicon
can facilitate exploration of this topic as well as increase our understanding of the semantic range of certain nominal stems. The sample

28. The best overview and overall study of noun incorporation remains Mithun 1984.
Both Mithun (1984: 77 ff.) and Baker (1995: passim) take various examples from Nahuatl.
For a specific study of Nahuatl, see Merlan 1976. For recent studies of incorporation, see
various works in Chappell and McGregor 1996. For a recent review of the subject, see Gerdts
1998.

29. Croft (1990: 4), for example, notes that the removal of primary data from published
typological studies is a serious problem for linguistic research. On-line presentation of this
material should help to solve this problem.

entries below and the brief discussion that follows illustrate the benefits of a system devised to permit multilevel comparison.[30]

a:te:mi *(V intrans.; N+V1;* REG. INFLEC. *see* **ki:sa;** ROOTS: *a:; te:m)* **1:** for a fruit (plum, melon) to become almost ripe (as it 'fills with water') *Kimich a:te:mis un xokotl.* That plum is just about to become ripe. **2:** to become filled with water (a ditch, a hole in the ground) *Yo:a:te:n kwentli.* The furrows have gotten filled with water (e.g., after a heavy summer rain). **3:** to have a swollen belly (a pregnant female) *Un ne:nkah suwa:tl, yo:pe:w a:te:mi, ne:si ye o:stli.* That woman over there, she has a swollen belly, it appears that she is pregnant.

chi:lkwa *(V intrans.; N+V2;* REG. INFLEC. *see* **kwa;** ROOTS: *chi:l; kwa) caus.→* **chi:lkwaltia** to eat chile *Ma:ski pitentsi:n, wel chi:lkwa.* Even though he is small, he can eat chile.

koma:ltlapa:na *(V trans.; N+V2;* REG. INFLEC. *see* **ki:sa;** ROOTS: *koma:l; tlapa:)* to break the clay griddle *(comal)* of *O:ne:chkoma:ltlapa:n; o:kalakiko tlawa:nke:tl, san o:wets.* He broke my clay griddle; a drunk came in, he just fell.

kone:miki *(V intrans.; N+V1;* REG. INFLEC. *see* **ki:sa;** ROOTS: *kone:; miki)* to lose a child in death *Ye ye:xpa o:kone:mik, xwel tlanemi:tia.* This is already the third time that she has lost a child (i.e., that a child has died on her), she cannot keep children alive.

kopaxokonono:tsa *(V trans.; N+V2;* REG. INFLEC. *see* **ki:sa;** ROOTS: *kopa; xoko; no:tsa)* to brag or boast to, particularly about doing sth that one cannot do, or about having sth that one does not have; to talk big to, to promise something to and not deliver *Te:kopaxokonono:tsa, xtlah kipia.* He brags to people, he doesn't have anything (i.e., property, money, etc.).

kwilxi:ni *(V intrans.; N+V1;* REG. INFLEC. *see* **ki:sa;** ROOTS: *kwil; xi:)* to get covered with maggots or worms *Yo:kwilxi:n nonakaw, a:man xok wel nihkwa:s.* My meat got covered with maggots, now I won't be able to eat it anymore.

panwetsi *(V intrans.; N+V1;* REG. INFLEC. *see* **ki:sa;** ROOTS: *pan; wetsi)* **1:** to reach the summit (of a hill or mountain, of a high building) *Wekapan, xwel tipanwetsis.* It's high, you won't be able to reach the top. **2:** *(fig.)* to become wealthy; to attain power *Panwetsis, momo:stla tekiti wan xkaman tlai.* He'll do very well, he works every day and never gets drunk.

suwa:kochi *(V intrans.; N+V1;* REG. INFLEC. *see* **ki:sa;** ROOTS: *suwa:; kochi)* to sleep with a woman *Mo:stla nisuwa:kochis, a:man nikochis san nose:lti.* Tomorrow I'll sleep with a woman, today I'll just sleep by myself.

tla:kamiki *(V intrans.; N+V1;* REG. INFLEC. *see* **ki:sa;** ROOTS: *tla:ka; miki)* to die like a man (i.e., bravely) *O:tla:kamik, xcho:kaya, san nochi o:kiyo:wih.* He died like a man, he didn't cry, he bore up under everything.

---

30. Note that this "multilevel comparison" is not simply a search on two fields. Rather, it involves the initial coding of a single feature (in this case, valency) in two fields that represent different levels of analysis: morphological and syntactic.

TABLE 10.3. Noun Incorporation in Ameyaltepec Nahuatl

search \cat *for*	search \com *for*	Type of Incorporation Selected For	Example
V-1	N-V2	Type I (Mithun 1984) "saturating" (Launey 1998)	*nichi:lkwa* 'I eat chile'
V-2	N-V2	Type II (Mithun 1984) "modifying" (Launey 1998)	*ne:chkoma:ltlapa:na* 'he breaks my clay griddle'

Incorporation may occur on intransitive (*V1*), transitive (*V2*), or ditransitive (*V3*) verbs. With transitive and ditransitive verbs, the nominal stem may be in a patient relationship to the main verb, reducing its valency in forming the new lexical item (cf. the intransitive *chi:lkwa* above, derived from the noun stem *chi:l-* 'chile' incorporated into the transitive verb *kwa* 'to eat').[31] With verbs of any valency, however, "the case role vacated by the incorporated nouns may be occupied by another argument, leaving the valency of the verb unchanged" (Mithun 1984: 859). In such cases the "modifying" relationship of the incorporated noun to the verb (either intransitive or transitive) may be quite varied—adverbial, locative, and comitative, among others.[32]

One key aspect of noun incorporation, therefore, is its effect on argument structure. For headwords, this can be determined by comparing the valency of the verb with no incorporated noun to that of the incorporated form. In the Nahuatl lexicon of Ameyaltepec, this is accomplished by simultaneously searching in the fields \cat (which gives the valency of the new lexical item) and \com (which gives the valency of the verb to which the noun has been incorporated). In table 10.3, the compound *koma:ltlapa:na,* like *tlapa:na* from which it is derived, is a transitive verb (i.e., the incorporation of *koma:l-* 'clay griddle' does not affect valency), whereas *chi:lkwa* is an intransitive derived through compounding from the transitive kwa 'to eat'.

The ability to search for roots along with shifts in valency will enable users of the Nahuatl dictionary to determine how the incorporation of any particular noun stem affects the valency of a particular verb. The

31. This is Mithun's (1984) Type I incorporation, which Launey (1998: 5), along with others, refers to as "saturating incorporation."

32. For a brief discussion of these relationships in Nahuatl, see Launey 1998. A quite common relationship, particularly when the incorporated noun is a body part, is one that has been called "possessor raising": the incorporated noun is a possessed subject (intransitive) or object (transitive), and the possessor is raised to subject (of an intransitive) or object (of a transitive). For a discussion of the term "possessor raising," see Chappell and McGregor 1996.

TABLE 10.4. Incorporation of *koma:l-* with Ameyaltepec Nahuatl Verbs

Noun Stem	Transitive Verb	Intransitive Compound	Transitive Compound
koma:l-	*chi:wa* 'to make'	*koma:lchi:wa* 'he makes clay griddles'	*ne:chkoma:lchi:wilia* 'he makes clay griddles for me'
koma:l-	*tlapa:na* 'to break'	———	*ne:chkoma:ltlapa:na* 'he breaks my clay griddle'

noun stem *koma:l-* provides a case in point as to how the nature of incorporation may vary according to verb (see table 10.4).

At one level the dictionary reveals that, unsurprisingly, making clay griddles (*koma:lchi:wa*) is a culturally salient activity (and thus glossed by an intransitive verb that is a distinct lexical item), whereas breaking clay griddles is not (given the absence of an intransitive lexeme, **koma:ltlapa:na*, *koma:ltlapa:na* exists only as a transitive verb, the result of "possessor raising," in which a possessor is encoded as primary object: *kitlapa:na nokoma:l* 'he breaks my griddle' → *ne:chkoma:ltlapa:na* 'he griddle-breaks me'). At another level the contrast between *ne:chkoma:lchi:wilia* and *ne:chkoma:ltlapa:na* reveals that the affectedness of someone who has his or her clay griddle broken is greater than that of one who has a griddle made. In both cases, *ne:chkoma:lchi:wilia* and *ne:chkoma:ltlapa:na*, the noun stem is incorporated. However, *koma:lchi:wilia* is an applicative of *koma:lchi:wa* "an intransitive predicate denoting a unitary concept," whereas with *koma:ltlapa:na* incorporation (like that which often occurs with body parts) vacates a case role, here filled by the adversely affected possessor.[33] The structure of the database (which includes a field for the stems that make up any given word) facilitates the extraction of this and similar information on incorporation and compounding.

As noted, in many instances incorporated elements are in some modifying or adverbial relationship with the verb. As the examples given above illustrate, in Nahuatl these relationships are highly variable and include some that are interesting in comparative perspective (e.g., *nikwilxi:ni*, lit. 'I [am] worm-scattered', where the subject is the location at which an event involving the incorporated noun occurs; and *panwetsi*, lit. 'on-fall', in which the incorporated element is a relational noun). An initial understanding of the semantics of incorporation is facilitated by an electronic version of a lexicon that has been structured

33. The citation, and this perspective in general, is based on Mithun 1984.

so as to permit rapid retrieval of the pertinent cases. However, researchers may also be interested in determining the connotations of particular stems that enter into a modifying relationship with a verb. To illustrate, one example given above is *kopaxokonono:tsa,* literally, 'to converse with someone like a *kopaxokotl* tree', a tree known to flower but not come to fruit. People who brag, who talk big, are like the *kopaxokotl* in that they promise "fruit" that is never delivered. Although here the metaphor involves a very specific cultural understanding that would need to be explained in the lexicon, in many cases this would not be true. Thus, for example, the metaphoric extension that establishes the meaning of *tla:kamiki* 'to die bravely' is not as obscure, although it is definitely a culturally specific interpretation of the implications of "man." Moreover, a user who so wishes could generate a list of all words that contain the root *tla:ka* 'man' and thus determine the semantic range of the connotations of this root. Indeed, a search function could easily be developed that would automatically list all words containing the roots (or any single root) of any given headword.

This first section has explored the research implications of a lexicographic project. I have suggested several ways in which project design can help attain certain scholarly goals. The inclusion of reduplicated *CV-* and *CV:-* verb forms (with both definitions and example sentences; see example of *no:tsa* above) under an unreduplicated headword was proposed as a means to facilitate comparison between such forms and thus promote an understanding of the semantics of reduplication. Likewise, by setting up separate field delimiters for illustrative sentences containing a reduplicated version of any given headword, users can easily retrieve all entries that have examples of short- or long-vowel reduplication (a system that would become obsolete after interlinearization). A positive side effect of this organization is the reduction in dictionary size, as measured by the number of headwords.[34] A second aspect of dictionary design oriented to contributing to linguistic research was the coding of morphological and syntactic information, thus facilitating retrieval of certain morphosyntactic phenomena. The case of noun incorporation was mentioned. Other codes

34. The positive aspects of this effect, I think, are well worth contemplating. A dictionary of a polysynthetic language runs a great risk of "overdocumenting" lexical items. This can easily occur with body-part incorporation and it would be easy to elicit hundreds of entries documenting such words. Likewise, Nahuatl has many endings indicating associated and purposive motion that can form "new words" from almost all verbs (e.g., *cho:ka* 'he cries' and *cho:katiw* 'he goes along crying'; *wetska* 'he laughs' and *wetskatinemi* 'he goes around laughing'; and *tlakwa* 'he eats' and *tlakwatiwetsi* 'he eats in a hurry'). With only a few semantic limitations, *-tiw, -tinemi,* and *-tiwetsi,* as well as some half dozen other verbal suffixes of associated motion, can combine with almost any verb. Few of these combinations have been accorded a separate entry in the Ameyaltepec Nahuatl lexicon.

were either only briefly alluded to (e.g., some semantic codes such as *bd* for "body parts") or not mentioned (e.g., *N-ag* for "agentive nouns").

The basic premise offered above is that filtered lexical information (i.e., a lexicon that can be manipulated and searched according to multiple criteria) and the corpus of texts from which a lexicon is constructed constitute primary linguistic data that should be made available in electronic format to scholars and others. Clearly, the targeting of those elements that might prove most useful for comparative or typological analysis or that are most salient for an understanding of the language being documented is not a trivial problem. It must be based on an awareness of general research interests in the field and how a particular language might provide information relevant to these interests. Just as clearly, establishing a format for accessing certain morphosyntactic features (e.g., statistical documentation of word order in example sentences or text corpora) is much more time-consuming and difficult than others (e.g., the generation of a list of causative verbs). Yet the possibilities of significantly advancing linguistic understanding through the widespread availability of electronic versions of lexicographic databases and their associated text corpora should serve to encourage their development and diffusion.

3. PEDAGOGY: TRANSLATION AND LEARNING THROUGH LEXICON AND GRAMMAR.   Dictionaries of indigenous languages of the Americas are, almost perforce, "bilingual": the source language (headword) is the indigenous language (the L_2 of most users) and the target language is the Western (often colonial) language (the L_1 of most users). Given this format, these dictionaries are best suited to passive use, oriented to the translation of received indigenous-language texts by nonnative speakers. The bilingual format is ill suited to the production of source (indigenous) language texts and of limited use for either the reception and translation of texts in the Western language or for the production of such texts by speakers of the indigenous language.[35] Given that the bilingual language format of these dictionaries (with the target language being L_1 for most users) is clearly more by default than by design, it might be appropriate to ask how the traditional structure of such dictionaries can be modified so as to provide the most benefit to the greatest number of users.[36] In this section two uses

35. This use is problematic, although the remarkable *Hopi Dictionary* (Hopi Dictionary Project 1998), with its exhaustive English-Hopi Finder List (pp. 801–60) of perhaps some seven thousand English words, goes a long way toward facilitating such an application.

36. The relationship among source and target language, on the one hand, and L_1 and L_2, on the other, has considerable effect on the strategies employed for defining source language terms. Thus Meyer (1990: 178) notes that "for L_2-L_1 use, explanatory equivalents may be used when there is no precise equivalent in the TL, since the user's native-speaker

are explored: translation of received texts in the indigenous language and learning of the indigenous language.

3.1. TRANSLATION AND STRATEGIES OF DEFINITION. The nature of the documentation to be processed with the aid of a Nahuatl dictionary is a key variable affecting project design. Nahuatl presents an almost unique case among languages native to the Americas in that a tradition of written documentation in this language—including grammars, lexicons, colonial texts, and chronicles—began almost five hundred years ago: the first Nahuatl grammar (Olmos 1547) was contemporary with the earliest grammars of French and English, and a mid–sixteenth-century dictionary (Molina's, in 1571) remains one of the great achievements in the lexicography of indigenous languages of the Americas. Nahuatl was used in the administration and proselytization of indigenous peoples, resulting in a profusion of materials—documents from imperial archives, native-language chronicles, and religious texts—that have been an important source for the study of the colonization and conversion of indigenous peoples in New Spain. Therefore, among the goals of Nahuatl lexicography should be that of providing a reference work capable of aiding in $L_{2(\text{Nahuatl})} \rightarrow L_{1(\text{Spanish/English})}$ translation and interpretation of a wide range of textual material. This orientation to the decoding rather than the encoding of language, to the reception rather than the production of texts, is a primary factor that should influence the project design and presentation of Nahuatl lexicographic materials.

That decoding occurs in the native language of the translator offers considerable protection against infelicitous phrasing of translated items and permits some concession, as is the case with passive dictionaries, to the standard criteria of substitutability for the construction of bilingual translation dictionaries. Many words in a Nahuatl dictionary may, of course, simply be "translated" and not defined. Such a situation would occur, for example, with *pa:mpa* 'because' and *me:stli* 'moon'. Undoubtedly, translation is

---

intuition can help him come up with a translational equivalent which best fits into the TL context; for L_1-L_2 use, however, translational equivalents are more desirable, which means that the lexicographer must anticipate all possible TL contexts and their corresponding TL equivalents." Meyer also notes, in general, that a major weakness of bilingual dictionaries is "an attempt to serve $L_1 \rightarrow L_2$ and $L_2 \rightarrow L_1$ users simultaneously" (p. 177). These weaknesses are divided into two broad categories: "weaknesses which impede the user's selection of a TL equivalent for a source language (SL) items ... [and] weaknesses which impede the user's combination of a TL item, once correctly selected, with other TL items in context" (p. 175). There has been much work on bilingual dictionaries, particularly by Mary Snell-Hornby and Ladislav Zgusta, but little that has been specifically oriented to indigenous languages. For an exception, see Bartholomew and Schoenhals 1983.

also highly appropriate for communicating the referents of certain highly specific lexical terms, such as plant and animal names (here one may think of plant guides in which, particularly for "speakers" of the restricted discourse of Linnaean classification, the genus and species names provide the best unambiguous code for recognizing the meaning of vernacular terms). Yet, despite the functional goal of providing a translators' dictionary, with almost all words of a language such as Nahuatl for which no "backup" monolingual dictionary exists, in general it would be best to offer explanatory constructs (as opposed to substitutable "synonyms") of headword entries and to rely on the native-speaker proficiency of the dictionary user to accommodate the most felicitous word or short phrase into the target language translation.

The lack of "backup" monolingual dictionaries, or sometimes even any other adequate bilingual tool for the understanding of meaning in an indigenous language, places a heavy burden on definitions and the semantics, broadly conceived, of a lexicographic project. Even when a primary focus is on the translation of received texts, there is a need for careful definition of many culturally specific terms or of words for which the "equivalents" of source and target language do not overlap. For example, even though 'bird' and 'leg' would be correct glosses for *to:to:tl* and *ikxi:tl*, respectively, the English translations should include the clarifications that *to:to:tl* refers only to small birds (as is the case with Spanish *pájaro* as opposed to *ave*) and that when referring to animals, *ikxi:tl* signifies only the back legs (the front legs of animals are its "arms," *matli*). Care must always be exercised in providing the caveats and distinctions that result from incomplete overlap or equivalence between the terms of each language. Target language synonyms and substitutable lexemes may be offered, but the general strategy should be to present a more elaborate definition and place greater responsibility on the user or translator to supply the most adequate target language word. The ideal structure of the indigenous-language dictionary, therefore, should be a hybrid between a bilingual dictionary (with the target language being the native language of the user) and a translated monolingual dictionary (in which extreme care is given to the precise meaning and use of specific terms and proper formation of collocations is of prime concern).[37]

Considering the wide-ranging and serious responsibilities of an indigenous language dictionary to fully document meaning and the general inadequacy of a translational model, the best definitional strategy is one that embraces three primary facets of word use and meaning: the

37. On the utility of combining elements of a monolingual learners' dictionary and a bilingual dictionary in one text oriented to learning a second language, see Kharma 1985. See also Magay 1988 on bilingual learners' dictionaries.

semasiological, the onomasiological, and the syntagmatic.[38] The first starts from the sign (the word) and tends to present meaning as word dependent. The second starts from a shared semantic content and groups together words that share meaning. The third approach, syntagmatic, "goes beyond the individual sign and focuses on the combinational aspects of the words" (Svensén 1993: 18). These three approaches do not represent separate aspects of meaning but instead are divergent paths to achieve an understanding of the complexity of meaning as it applies to specific words and groups of words. The necessity of combined use of all three strategies can be illustrated through a discussion of the appropriate definitions and descriptions of *koto:ni* and its transitive form *koto:na*[39] (see the entries below as well as fig. 10.2).[40]

> **koto:na** (*V trans.;* REG. INFLEC. see **ki:sa;** ROOTS: *koto:;* SEM accepts intensifier *te-;* APPLIC. *koto:nilia*) **1:** to snap (sth long that can be stretched or pulled, such as a strap or rubber band) *Xkoto:na un i:loh!* Break off that thread! (e.g., by pulling on it hard or biting it after having finished sewing sth) **2:** to pull apart or pull off into pieces, to shred (e.g., chile, or an onion, etc.) *Xko:koto:na chi:hli para kwaltias tli:n titlakwa:s, ma koko:ya!* Shred some chile (pulling it apart with your fingers and, implicitly, adding it to the

---

38. Approaches to these aspects of meaning and lexicographic strategies are present in much of the literature on the subject. For a concise presentation of these three approaches, see Svensén (1993: 17 ff. and passim).

39. In the Ameyaltepec Nahuatl dictionary, entries have been marked according to various classes. For example, verbs are distinguished among those that form a morphologically marked causative (e.g., *wetska* 'to laugh' and *wetski:tia* 'to make laugh'), those that form a morphologically marked anticausative (e.g., *tsakwa* 'to close' *trans.* and *notsakwa* 'to close' *intrans.*), and those that show an unmarked (or nondirected) alternation between intransitive and transitive (e.g., *koto:ni* and *koto:na*). These categories should help users to better anticipate meaning and will prove useful for typological research. The above distinctions are based on Haspelmath 1993.

Note, as indicated in the entry, that the verb *koto:ni/a* accepts the use of the intensifier *te-* (e.g., *tekoto:ni* 'to suddenly snap'). The verbs that accept this prefix have been marked in the lexicon and seem to belong to a certain semantic type. The Nahuatl dictionary being elaborated will mark these morphosyntactic properties and then discuss word groups (including semantic types) in a separate section.

40. The schematic representation in figure 10.2 illustrates some, but not nearly all, of the annotation conventions and search functions associated with word entries. The verb *koto:ni* has only one stem, and for this reason the entry has no morphological information. However, a form such as *kechkoto:na*, 'to snap or break the neck of', would be coded *N-V2* (noun incorporated into a transitive verb) and would have both *kech* and *koto:* listed as roots. And the entry for the transitive form *koto:na* would reference the ditransitive applicative *koto:nilia* as part of a cross-referencing system that points to morphologically marked derivations such as applicatives and causatives. Not represented in the diagram, though an important part of the Learning Environment, are links, particularly for words such as nouns, to extended cultural information (e.g., medicinal plants would link to illustrations and explanations of their use).

food) so that what you're eating tastes better, so that it becomes spicy hot! **3:** to divide up, particularly in order to distribute or apportion to various persons; to take off a section or portion of *Ma tihkoto:natin notla:l, nikte:makas tlakotipan!* Let's go to fraction off (by measuring, marking, and titling) a portion of my land, I'm going to give about half away! **4:** to end or break off (sth such as a custom or practice, or litigation, particularly acts or processes that take place and continue over long periods of time) *O:kikoto:n plei:toh, xok o:kinek kinenemi:lti:s.* He broke off the suit, he didn't want to pursue it any longer. NOTE: For both the transitive and intransitive forms, the intensifier *te-* is used only when referring to the snapping of an object such as a band, rope, or strap but not to the dividing of land, or ending of litigation, etc.

koto:ni (*V intrans.*; REG. INFLEC. see **ki:sa;** ROOTS: *koto:;* SEM accepts intensifier *te-*) **1:** to snap (sth long that often can be stretched or pulled, such as a strap or rubber band) *Xok kixi:ko:s, ye kokoto:nis. Xtla:lili mejó:r se: yewan ye:nkwik!* It won't bear up anymore, it is about to snap apart in pieces. Better put on one that is new! **2:** to fragment, to break apart in isolated portions (e.g., a brook that during the dry season dries up, leaving strings of poorly connected ponds; or clouds that become scattered and broken up by the wind *O:tsi:tsikiliw moxtli, yo:kokoto:n, kas yeye:kakiawis.* The cloud cover has ripped open here and there, it's come apart, there is a chance a driving hard rain will start to fall. **3:** (for sth, such as a pattern of behavior, a tradition or custom, or litigation) to cease to occur *Yo:koto:n, xok kitla:lian bake:ros.* It's stopped, they don't stage the dance called *vaqueros* anymore. **4:** (for a lineage or family) to end *O:koto:n i:nelwayo, nika:n xok kipia a:kin ke:n kita.* His family line has come to an end, he doesn't have any relatives here anymore. See **posteki.**

The Nahuatl verb *koto:ni* accepts a series of subjects that seem to have several characteristics in common: they can be snapped (straps) or pulled apart (clouds, onions) and include events or situations that "stretch" through time (litigation, customs, kinship relations). The transitive form of the verb, *koto:na,* typically takes a volitional animate agent acting on an object, most of which can also function as the subject of the intransitive *koto:ni.* Yet the overlap between subjects of the intransitive and objects of the transitive is by no means complete. The water of a brook can be the subject of the intransitive yet not the object of the transitive (given that the fragmenting of the water into ponds is the result of a natural process: the drying up of the landscape during the winter months); in a reverse manner, land can be the object of the transitive (*Kikoto:nas i:tla:l* 'He will break up his land') but not the subject of the intransitive. Clouds can be either subject or object, although speakers tend to prefer the oblique expression of agentivity (*O:kokoto:n moxtli ika o:yeye:kak* 'The clouds became scattered as a result of the wind' rather than a transitive form *O:kikoto:n moxtli yeye:katl* 'The wind broke up the clouds').

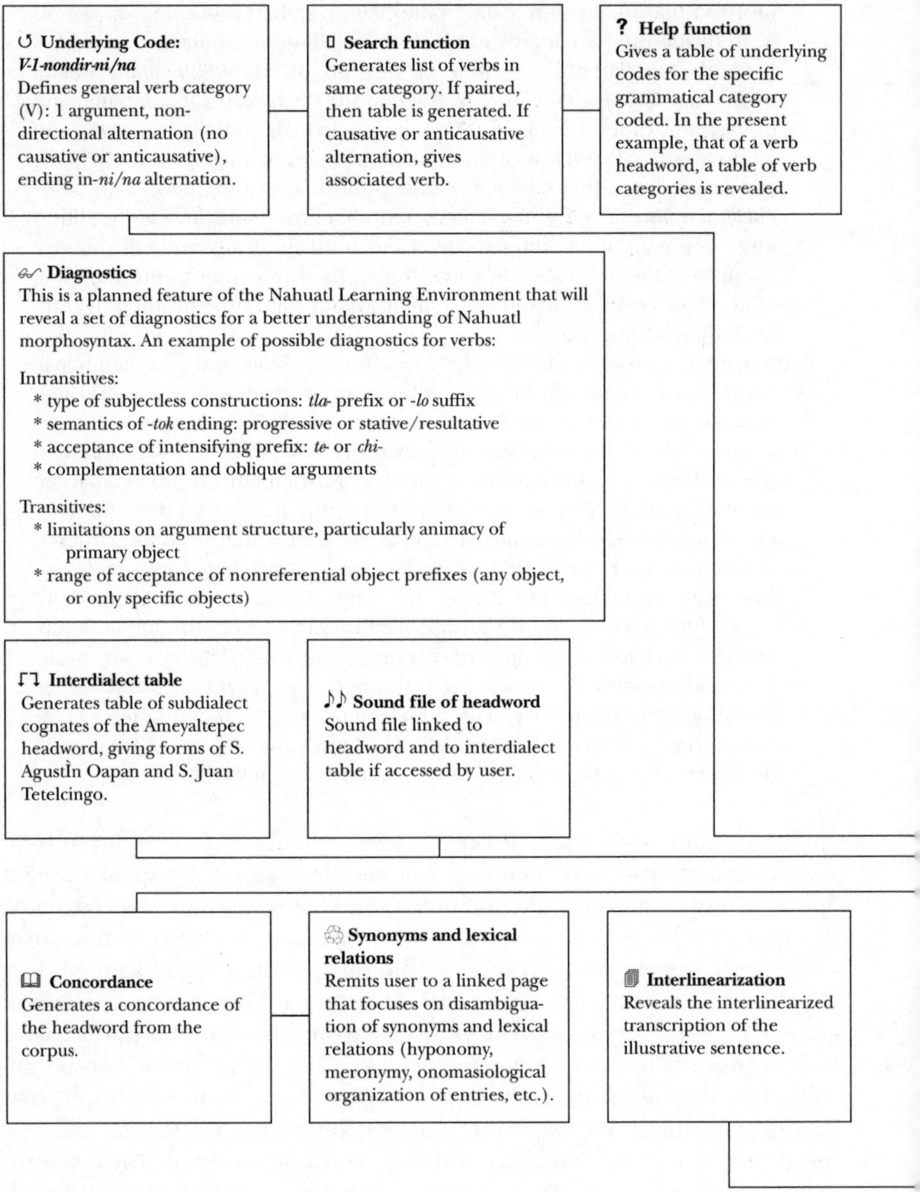

↻ **Underlying Code:**
V-1-nondir-ni/na
Defines general verb category (V): 1 argument, non-directional alternation (no causative or anticausative), ending in-*ni/na* alternation.

▯ **Search function**
Generates list of verbs in same category. If paired, then table is generated. If causative or anticausative alternation, gives associated verb.

? **Help function**
Gives a table of underlying codes for the specific grammatical category coded. In the present example, that of a verb headword, a table of verb categories is revealed.

⌇ **Diagnostics**
This is a planned feature of the Nahuatl Learning Environment that will reveal a set of diagnostics for a better understanding of Nahuatl morphosyntax. An example of possible diagnostics for verbs:

Intransitives:
* type of subjectless constructions: *tla-* prefix or *-lo* suffix
* semantics of *-tok* ending: progressive or stative/resultative
* acceptance of intensifying prefix: *te-* or *chi-*
* complementation and oblique arguments

Transitives:
* limitations on argument structure, particularly animacy of primary object
* range of acceptance of nonreferential object prefixes (any object, or only specific objects)

⌐⌐ **Interdialect table**
Generates table of subdialect cognates of the Ameyaltepec headword, giving forms of S. Agustìn Oapan and S. Juan Tetelcingo.

♪♪ **Sound file of headword**
Sound file linked to headword and to interdialect table if accessed by user.

▱ **Concordance**
Generates a concordance of the headword from the corpus.

⟳ **Synonyms and lexical relations**
Remits user to a linked page that focuses on disambiguation of synonyms and lexical relations (hyponomy, meronymy, onomasiological organization of entries, etc.).

▤ **Interlinearization**
Reveals the interlinearized transcription of the illustrative sentence.

Figure 10.2. The Nahuatl Learning Environment (Lexicon): Schematic Representation of Verb Entry.

✿ **Cross-references of stem**
All
Derivational forms
Nominal incorporation
Participial compounds

↺ **Underlying Code:** *te-*
Defines underlying code, if used.
Te- is an intensifier that occurs with
certain verbs, apparently those
that indicate a sudden action
that harmfully affects a subject or
object.

① **Derivational cross-references**
Links to other entries that are derivations from
the headword of the active entry.

② **Nominal incorporation**
Links to forms with same stem and an
incorporated noun. Possibility to select valence-
reducing or modifying incorporation.

☐ **Search function**
Generates list of words in the
same semantic field as headword;
in the present case all verbs that
accept the intensifier prefix *te-*.

③ **Participial incorporation**
Links to forms in which a participial form of the
headword is incorporated into a compound or in
which a compound has a participial form of
another verb incorporated into headword.

? **Help function**
Gives a table of underlying codes
for semantic fields: sounds,
smells, plants, flowers, shapes,
animals, ritual language, stars,
textures, kinship terminology, etc.

♦♦ **Inflection tables**
This will generate tables of verb inflection based
on general paradigms for regular verbs and pre-
elaborated tables for irregular verbs (such
morphology for Nahuatl is fairly simple). For nouns
a similar function will be used to give possessive
paradigms.

koto:ni (*V intrans.*; REG. INFLEC. see **ki:sa**; ROOTS: *koto:*; SEM accepts intensifier *te-*) **1:** to
snap (sth long that often can be stretched or pulled, such as a strap or
rubber band *Xok kixi:ko:s, yekokoto:nis, xtla:lili mejó:r se: yewa:n ye:nkwik!* ♪♪
It won't bear up any more, it is about to snap apart in pieces, better put
on one that is new! **2:** to fragment, to break apart in isolated portions
(e.g., a brook that during the dry season dries up, leaving strings of
poorly connected ponds; or clouds that become scattered and broken
up by the *O:tsi:tsikiliw moxtli, yo:kokoto:n, kasyeye:dakiawis* ᔆᴶ. The cloud cover
has ripped open here and there, it's come apart, there is a chance a
driving hard rain will start to fall. **3:** (for sth, such as a pattern of
behavior, for example a tradition or custom, or litigation) to cease to
occur *Yo:koto:n, xok kitla:lian bake:ros.* It's stopped, they don't stage the
dance called *vaqueros* anymore. **4:** (for a lineage or family) to end
O:koto:n i:nelwayo, nika:n xok kipia a:kin ke:n kita. His family line
has come to an end, he doesn't have any relatives here anymore. See **posteki.**

linked sound file

subdialect variation
(San Juan
Tetelcingo)

⟳ Link to discussion
disambiguating
near synonyms.

The contrast between possible subjects of intransitive *koto:ni* and objects of transitive *koto:na* demonstrates that whereas the latter include all potential objects that can be affected ("snapped" or "fragmented") by the volitional action of an agent, the former includes only those that can (but do not necessarily) suffer this change of state without the intervention of an agent.[41] Thus with an argument such as 'land', the verb *koto:na* cannot "detransitivize," since 'land' cannot become fragmented without human volitional action. For the fragmentation of 'land', when no agent is specified or known the transitive is used with a reflexive marker (in this case *no-* '3sg') indicating a type of impersonal passive: *O:nokoto:n i:tla:l* 'His land has been split up'; here there is an implication of agentivity that is lacking in the underived intransitive. This use of the reflexive marker is completely predictable from the grammar. Note, however, that with *koto:na* a reflexive marker can also be used with an animate subject. In this case (since, in effect, an animate cannot be the patient of a verb meaning 'to snap', as might be suggested by a reflexive form) the verb acquires a new sense: 'to break loose (from a tether or other object that can snap)'. This meaning requires that the action of the subject be carried out with little control while at the same time affecting an implied object (the tether) in a way that benefits the subject: *O:nokoto:n noburroh, o:choloh* 'My donkey broke free (from its tether), it ran away'. This use of the reflexive (as opposed to its function with a passive meaning) must be lexically marked and, therefore, accounted for in an entry that relates the possible argument structures of the transitive verb *koto:na* to its meaning.[42]

As the present case demonstrates, the "agent-oriented meaning component" of a verb, a component that affects semantics and the set of possible subjects and objects of intransitives and transitives, is not inherent in the verb itself. Rather, it is an aspect of meaning that emerges from word

---

41. The verb *koto:ni* manifests many characteristics of what have been called "unaccusative verbs"; see the early article by Perlmutter (1978) and more recently Levin and Rappaport Hovav (1995), who cite much of the literature. Haspelmath (1993) discusses the implications of "agent-oriented meaning components"; Levin and Rappaport Hovav (1995: esp. chap. 3) explore this issue further.

42. It is possible that a recognition and encoding in the lexicon of certain "semantic types" might facilitate the representation of types of argument structures. In this regard note Dixon (1984: 594), who suggests the implications of semantic types for understanding "general patterns of correlation between semantic and syntactic properties." A similar perspective on the relation of semantics to syntax is set forth in the analysis of verb entries (through a case study of *bake*) by Atkins, Kegl, and Levin (1988). They stress the significance of lexical semantic theory for lexicographic practice in noting that "a theory of lexical organization is needed in order to provide the context for building the entry. And it is the lack of theory in the semantic-syntactic interdependency area that makes . . . dictionary entries less than adequate" (p. 100).

combinations and, more generally, syntactic behavior.[43] Thus even within a basically semasiological approach, dictionary entries should take care to represent potential combinatory (syntagmatic) sequences and note the semantic implications of such collocations. With verbs this will often mean a discussion of potential subjects of intransitives and potential objects of transitives, although the implications for verb meaning of complements and adjuncts should be kept in mind. With attributive adjectives a combinational approach would involve potential collocations with nouns. However, in all cases, to aid users in extrapolating from the few collocators given in the definition to other potential combinations, care must be given to discuss the common denominators that link these bases.[44]

In addition to semasiological and syntagmatic considerations, a third approach to meaning that should be incorporated into a dictionary is onomasiological. The nature of this approach can be illustrated by its treatment of collocations. Whereas the semasiological approach departs from the collocator (e.g., asking for the possible objects of *koto:na*), the onomasiological approach departs from the base (e.g., asking what one can do to land, *tla:hli*).[45] An electronic database format can be of immense help in articulating a semasiological and onomasiological approach to collocations. With verbs, for instance, a field of potential subjects and objects can be created and a search function developed that would generate possible collocators for any given base. Thus under words like *koto:na* 'to divide up (a field)', *pupwa* 'to clear (a field)', *to:ka* 'to plant (a field)', *o:melia* 'to plow (a field) a second time before planting', and *ye:kpuwa* 'to replant (a field) where the first seeds did not sprout', the word *tla:hli* would be listed in a field dedicated exclusively to collocation bases. An entry under *tla:hli*

43. A similar aspect of meaning occurs with a typical unaccusative verb such as *break*, which is considered unaccusative in its intransitive form. Thus, although one may have "He broke the vase" and "The vase broke," with other arguments only a transitive or an intransitive use, but not both, is acceptable: "He broke his promise" but ?"His promise broke"; and ?"He broke his voice"; but "His voice broke." Levin and Rappaport Hovav (1995: 105) give the former example (with *promise*) and suggest that intransitive subjects are a subset of transitive patients. However, as the second example (with *voice;* cf. the Nahuatl example with *brook*) demonstrates, there are also cases of intransitive subjects that cannot be encoded as the objects of transitive verbs even though they are patients.

44. This factor is related to what Mel'čuk (e.g., 1996) refers to as lexical inheritance. See the article by Grimes in this volume. Also pertinent in this regard is Apresjan's (1992–93: 80) concept of lexicographic types, which he defines as "a group of lexemes having a number of properties in common that are sensitive to the same or similar sets of linguistic rules—morphological, syntactic, prosodic, semantic, etc. . . . Every lexicographic type should be treated in the dictionary in a unified way." Both Mel'čuk and Apresjan have dealt with verbs of emotion; see Mel'čuk and Wanner 1996 and Apresjan 1992. See also Dixon 1984.

45. See the discussion in Cop 1990.

in an onomasiological section of the dictionary could then present and analyze information on combinational patterns.

More important, an onomasiological approach also pays particular attention to shades of meaning that distinguish near-synonyms; in this sense it focuses on words that are in a paradigmatic, not syntagmatic, relation. Thus in a resource such as *Merriam-Webster's Collegiate Dictionary*, one finds that entries for *procrastinate, lag, loiter, dawdle*, and *dally* all point to *delay*, where a concise explanation is offered of the differences in meaning among these words. Dictionaries of indigenous languages have generally neglected this facet (disambiguation) of lexicography, a failure that is unfortunate given that such distinctions, presented in a consolidated explication, are key to understanding the subtleties of meaning that would otherwise be difficult, if not impossible, to grasp. The Ameyaltepec Nahuatl dictionary currently being elaborated will include a supplementary section that explores meaning differences of closely related words, including those that can be grouped according to fairly delimited, and often overt, semantic fields. Thus a discussion of definitions might center on words that describe different textures, different ways of hardening (e.g., the differences between verbs such as *tepi:tsiwi, kuhpistia, kuhpitsiwi*, and *kuhtia*, all having to do with hardening or stiffening), or various ways of walking. Other patterns of interlexical relations, particularly hyponymy and meronymy, would also be explored.[46] Presentation would include sets of related words within relatively salient categories such as medicinal plants, colors, smells, and sounds.[47] Still other sets would focus on activities (such as house building, cooking, farming) and objects (e.g., a house, a plow, a plant) and the different verbs and nouns associated with these particular events and objects. This onomasiological facet of the lexicographic project will provide key information on collocators associated with specific bases, on shades of meaning distinctions among near-synonyms, and on words related within given semantic fields. It will be combined with a more formal approach to categories based on the codification of word morphology (e.g., of causative verbs, which could thus be easily extracted from the lexicon). In conjunction these two approaches will provide a more complete understanding of Nahuatl than would emerge from a presentation based strictly on headwords.

This subsection has explored the way in which a basic function of a Nahuatl lexicon as a passive translators' dictionary should be expanded to embrace a greater sensitivity to the semantic complexity of the language.

46. For an overview of interlexical relations, see Cruse 1986.

47. For example, one could mark verbs that refer to animal sounds (e.g., *cho:ka, nanalka, nokwi:katia, tlayowa, tlapi:tsa*) and then in an onomasiological section on animal sounds group animals into categories according to the verbs used to indicate their respective sounds.

Indeed, the primary focus of an indigenous language dictionary should be on semantics, and extreme care should be taken to develop all aspects of meaning as fully as possible. Deficient explanations impoverish the dictionary and do a great injustice to the richness of expression in indigenous languages. Users should be able to provide the appropriate translational equivalent in their native language; but without a detailed exposition of meaning they will be unable to reinterpret or account for many usages that they are bound to encounter in their philological studies. It was suggested that the problem of meaning be broached from three directions—semasiological, onomasiological, and syntagmatic—in order to provide a multidimensional semantic perspective. These approaches move a translators' dictionary into the realm of a learners' dictionary, at least in regard to the dichotomization between a dictionary's role in the reception as opposed to the production of texts. It is to this problem of learning (of producing texts or utterances) and to the indigenous dictionary's role in pedagogy that I now turn.

3.2. LEARNING AND THE STRATEGIES OF TEACHING. Over the past decade, as lexicographers have realized that "language learning imposes its own requirements on the format of a dictionary" and that "traditional dictionaries for general use are not particularly suitable for the purpose of learning, especially a new language," increasing attention has been paid to the development of what is called a "learners [*sic*] dictionary"(Svensén 1993: 24).[48] The driving force behind these dictionaries, which have been elaborated for most of the "major" languages of the world, is to provide students of a given language with an additional tool for language acquisition. The philosophy behind these efforts, however, is one that runs almost contrary to that which should guide lexicographers of indigenous languages. The learners' dictionaries, in effect, presuppose a teaching environment and a fairly elaborate infrastructure of pedagogical tools. Moreover, in molding monolingual native-speaker dictionaries so that they meet both the needs and the abilities of nonnative speakers, learners' dictionaries implement changes (an abridged format in terms of number of headwords and information included, as well as a carefully delimited definitional terminology) that would be unacceptable in a serious lexicographic project on an indigenous language, which would stress completeness of coverage and exhaustive analysis (e.g., etymological, word class, etc.). The problem facing lexicographers of indigenous languages is, therefore, somewhat the mirror image of a problem that has challenged lexicographers of major languages. Simplified dictionaries of

48. For a critical review of the literature, see Dolezal and McCreary 1999.

major languages are the result of an abundance of economic and human resources, whereas simplified dictionaries of indigenous languages (many of which are better described as vocabularies) are most often the result of a scarcity of economic and human resources.[49] And whereas the former comprise dictionaries adapted to an extant learning environment, the latter are often elaborated in a pedagogical vacuum.

The Nahuatl Learning Environment has been designed in part to respond to the problems mentioned in the preceding paragraph. This project aims to join together a lexicon (a brief sketch of which was given earlier), a user's guide to the lexicon, a reference grammar with a pedagogical orientation, and interactive lessons for language learning.[50] By combining research and learning tools, it will provide a corpus of material useful to beginning students as well as expert scholars; it makes available primary linguistic data for research while organizing it in such a manner as to achieve didactic goals; it links a dictionary with a user's guide and grammar so that learning a language and vocabulary go hand in hand; and it establishes an interactive language course that makes full use of a lexicon and reference grammar that otherwise would be used mostly by specialists. The Nahuatl Learning Environment, therefore, seeks to solve a major problem in the study and learning of lesser-taught languages by providing the grammatical and pedagogical context for a dictionary while furnishing the appropriate lexical base for students to practice and implement the language skills they learn through a grammar. Key to this approach is the conviction that printed and electronic media are compatible, not conflicting, forms of representation and diffusion. When possible, even a published work such as a reference grammar should be available electronically so that it may be linked to a lexicon and to annotated primary linguistic data (such as interlinearized texts), thus providing a more comprehensive approach to the study of a given language.[51]

A case was already made for presenting the results of lexicographic projects in indigenous languages in electronic format, although this should by no means preclude the publication of printed material. Several benefits of the former have already been mentioned: the possibility of including large amounts of material that, because of the costs of

---

49. Atkins (1992–93: 9), for example, estimates that "a one-volume collegiate dictionary compiled from scratch will take over 100 person/years of work, and cost up to four million dollars."

50. Target-language material of the Nahuatl Learning Environment is bilingual (English and Spanish), although below only English examples are given (see note 25).

51. The importance of linking primary data to typological studies is mentioned by Croft (1990): see note 29.

publication, would otherwise be unavailable; and the ability of electronic formats with detailed coding to accommodate the research interests and priorities of a wide range of scholars. Another advantage is the facility of linking to the appropriate headword or text much additional material: illustrative material, ethnographic descriptions and data, and sound files (pronunciation guides and minimal pairs, example sentences, types of music described by certain entries, ritual texts). Equally significant is the possibility of using an electronic format to provide an easily accessible user's guide, with help files and a glossary as well as a tutorial for incipient users on how to best extract and exploit the multiple levels of information contained in the lexicon.[52] Lexicographic and semantic data on Nahuatl is of interest to a wide range of people and care should be taken to ensure that they will be able to make full use of the material available. That most similar lexicons have been developed with little pedagogical concern (both in the sense of language teaching and in regard to making the indigenous language dictionary more user-friendly) has undoubtedly adversely limited the potential audience for many lexicographic resources. Two examples should suffice to demonstrate the value of linking learning to the lexicon through electronic media.

One characteristic of Nahuatl that lends itself to a pedagogical use of an electronic lexicographic database is the morphological complexity of words (in terms of both derivational processes and compounding). To teach this aspect of Nahuatl, users can be taken through a short tutorial that would include both a discussion of Nahuatl word formation (such as the manner in which nominal stems can be joined together or incorporated into verbs) and a guide to using Steven Bird's *Hyperlex* search engine to explore this aspect of Nahuatl morphology.[53] By embedding hypertext links with the correct queries into the HTML tutorial text, students who encounter difficulties in defining the parameters of a given search they are requested to perform can easily activate the search engine. This will generate the appropriate list or table of entries, followed by the *Hyperlex* query box with the appropriate data. Table 10.5 is a small sample of a

52. For a user's guide to specific learners' and students' dictionaries in English, see Underhill 1980. Such materials seems to be lacking for many indigenous-language dictionaries, although it is perhaps here that they are most needed. Terms that linguists and other academics might take for granted (*incorporated noun, causative, applicative, stative*) are quite opaque to the majority of people.

53. The processes described below, as indeed the entire electronic format of the Nahuatl lexicon, is made possible by Steven Bird's *Hyperlex* search engine, which he generously adapted to the Nahuatl data I have been working with. Again, through their expertise and generosity, both he and Mark Liberman of the Linguistic Data Consortium have made this project possible. Bird's *Hyperlex*2 should be working by mid-2002.

TABLE 10.5. Sample Result of Morpheme Search on *a:-* 'water'

Morphemes	Words
a:	**a:tl** (*N basic*) **1:** water **2:** (*rel.*) fontanel, soft spot on a young child's head **3:** (*-yo*) juice, nectar (of a fruit or vegetable) **4:** (*-yo*) broth (of a cooked dish such as beans, chicken)
a:; i:	**a:tli** (*V intrans.*) to drink water and, by extension, other (nonalcoholic) beverages **a:tli:tia** (*V trans.*) to give (sb) water or, by extension, other (nonalcoholic) beverages to drink
a:; xi:x	**a:xi:xa** (*V intrans.*) **1:** to urinate on **2:** (*refl.*) to urinate **3:** (*fig.*) to excrete a liquid (e.g., as a tree does sap) **a:xi:xaltia** (*V trans.*) to cause to urinate **a:xi:xtli** (*N deverbal*) urine **i:a:xi:x burroh** (*N complex*) a type of mushroom that often grows on donkey dung
a:; xi:x; -eh	**a:xi:xeh** (*N derived*) person who always has to urinate, who urinates a lot (same as *a:xi:xpal*)
a:; -yo:	**a:yo:tia** (*V trans.*) to add water to (sth, particularly foods being boiled such as beans or sauces)
a:; -yo:; ki:sa	**a:yo:ki:sa** (*V intrans.*) to ooze or secrete a liquid (particularly in reference to the pus or liquid of an infection)
a:; -yo:; wa:tsa	**a:yo:wa:tsa** (*V trans.*) (*refl.*) to lose one's bodily fluids

table generated onscreen by searching for all words that include the stem *a:* 'water'. The actual query is illustrated in a reconstructed screen shot (fig. 10.3).

The facility with which complex queries to *Hyperlex* can be embedded in HTML texts on-line is not only useful for tutorials; in addition, it offers an extremely powerful tool for linking lexicon and grammar into a single learning environment. Queries can be embedded in the electronic text of a reference grammar to permit the extraction of relevant information and paradigms from the lexicon (which can be continually updated) or other primary linguistic data (such as interlinearized texts). For example, in a section of the grammar on causative verbs, students can be offered three types of supplementary learning tools: a short, 100- to 200-word, summary explanation of causativity; a table generated by *Hyperlex* of all causative verbs, their meanings, and derivations; and an interactive lesson teaching the formation and analysis of causative constructions. The same material could be easily accessed from the other (lexicographic) direction. Thus a student working with the lexicon who encounters a causative verb could automatically activate the same short summary explanation of causativity, move to the relevant chapter in the reference grammar, generate a list or

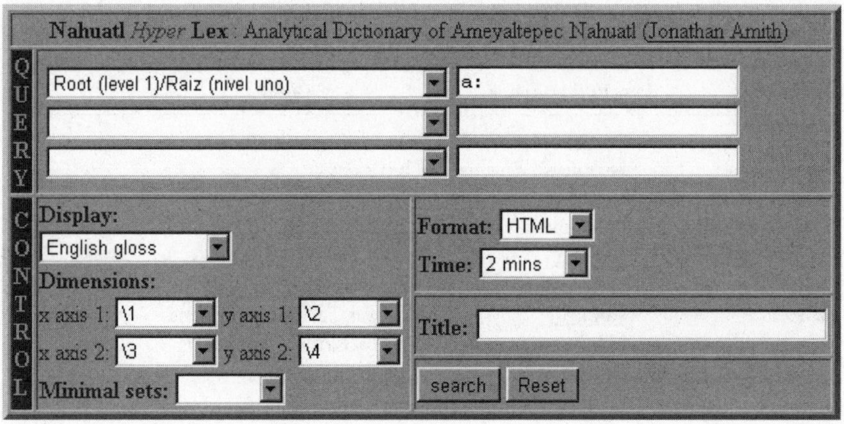

Nahuatl *Hyper* **Lex** : Analytical Dictionary of Ameyaltepec Nahuatl (Jonathan Amith)

QUERY

Root (level 1)/Raiz (nivel uno) ▼ | a:

CONTROL

Display:
English gloss ▼

Format: HTML ▼
Time: 2 mins ▼

Dimensions:
x axis 1: \1 ▼ y axis 1: \2 ▼
x axis 2: \3 ▼ y axis 2: \4 ▼

Title:

Minimal sets: ▼

search   Reset

Figure 10.3. Query Used to Generate Table 10.5.

table of verbs similar to the causative verb on the screen, and practice the formation and analysis of these types of verbs through an interactive lesson on the topic.

The benefits of linking grammar and lexicon can be further exemplified by the treatment accorded intransitive verbs. Most Nahuatl intransitives can be grouped into one of three major formal classes: (1) CAUSATIVE ALTERNATION: those that manifest a basic intransitive form and a morphologically marked causative derivation (e.g., *cho:ka* 'to cry' and *cho:ktia* 'to make someone cry'); (2) ANTICAUSATIVE ALTERNATION: those that have a basic transitive form and a morphologically marked intransitive (e.g., *tsakwa* 'to close', *notsakwa* 'to become closed'); and (3) NONDIRECTED ALTERNATION: those that show minor variation and little evidence for determining the direction of the derivational process (e.g., *chaya:wi* 'to become dispersed', *chaya:wa* 'to disperse or scatter').[54] Each type has been coded in the lexicon; phonological characteristics permit further differentiation. In the chapter on intransitives, one of the tables lists various patterns manifested by verbs showing nondirected alternation (see table 10.6). In the electronic version of the grammar, hypertext queries (see fig. 10.4) have been embedded at the intransitive form of each pair. When readers activate the link at any specific location, *Hyperlex* generates tables of similarly patterned verbs. For example, activating the query embedded at *poliwi* generates a table of all verbs

54. The classes are directly based on a typology proposed by Haspelmath (1993); see note 40. The vast majority of Nahuatl verbs manifest either causative or nondirected alternation.

TABLE 10.6. Intransitive and Transitive Verb Pairs:
Nondirected Alternation

Transitivity	Present Indicative	Gloss
Intrans.	poliwi	he (it) gets lost
Trans.	ki-polowa	he loses it
Intrans.	toma:wi	he gets fat
Trans.	ki-toma:wa	he fattens it
Intrans.	koto:ni	it snaps
Trans.	ki-koto:na	he snaps it
Intrans.	kaxa:ni	it (e.g., a knot) loosens
Trans.	ki-kaxa:nia	he loosens it (a knot)
Intrans.	totomi	it gets untied
Trans.	ki-totoma	he unties it

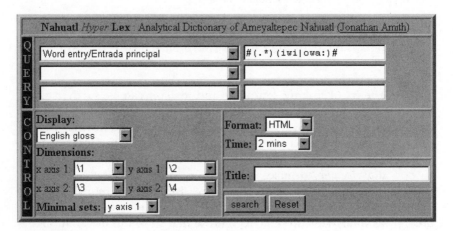

Figure 10.4. Query Used to Generate Table 10.7.

that manifest the same *-iwi/-owa* alternation (see table 10.7). This type
of automatic search can be linked to any point covered in the grammar.

If dictionaries teach the meanings of words, they do not teach the
meaning of language. And if grammars teach structure, they do not teach
content. In isolation each tool is destined to remain a blunt instrument
for learning and a dull device for communication. For many potential
users of the dictionary, carefully elaborated morphosyntactic information
will remain a mysterious code unless a concerted effort is made to explain
and explore the significance of these data. For all the effort that might
be made to present collocations, without a background in grammar, dictionary users will be unable to produce even the simplest of sentences.

TABLE 10.7. Sample of Verbs Manifesting *-iwi/-owa* Variation
(reconstructed screen shot)

Stem	*-iwi*	*-owa*
a:pach	**a:pachiwi** (*V intrans.*) to get covered with water, to become submerged in water	**a:pachowa** (*V trans.*) to submerge in water, to dunk in water
a:tots	**a:totsiwi** (*V intrans.*) to become watery (a mixture, of sth to which water is commonly added)	**a:totsowa** (*V trans.*) to add water to (a mixture, making it more watery)
chi:mal	**chi:maliwi** (*V intrans.*) to spread out in a circle (a stain, the houses at the edge of a town as it grows)	**chi:malowa** (*V trans.*) to spread or flatten out in a circle
chikipe:l	**chikipe:liwi** (*V intrans.*) to split open or burst apart	**chikipe:lowa** (*V trans.*) to split open lengthwise (e.g., a pig after being slaughtered)
chikino:l	**chikino:liwi** (*V intrans.*) to become crooked or bent in places	**chikino:lowa** (*V trans.*) to make crooked or bent

Nor, without a lexical base from which to depart, will students of a grammar be able to apply even a small portion of the knowledge they might have gained. The Nahuatl learning project attempts to make use of electronic formats to link lexicon, grammar, and corpus in a single learning environment. Rather than a learners' dictionary strictly for students interested in language acquisition, it seeks to create a pedagogical tool that can use a linguistically complex and semantically rich text to draw students and scholars into the language. Hopefully it will provide a model for future work in this direction.

4. LEXICOGRAPHY AND THE LANGUAGE COMMUNITY.   In the previous pages I have noted three major categories of users, their concerns, and the textual material they would be dealing with. These are scholars interested in the comparative or lexicographic value of a Nahuatl dictionary, translators interested in the decoding and translation of received (and mostly historical) texts, and students interested in acquiring proficiency in spoken Nahuatl. The needs of these users may be met through the presentation of analytical fields for certain types of morphosyntactic and phonological material, more expanded areas oriented to textual interpretation that would include a cultural and contextually based semantics, and learning tools meant to create tools for the productive and active use of grammar and lexicon. However, another group of potential users

should be considered: native speakers of Nahuatl who wish to use the material as a bilingual learners' dictionary for Spanish or as a source of Nahuatl material that might be used in a village school. The simplest way to deal with this potential conflict of interest is to grab the bull by the horns and simply state what is an unfortunate truth: the goals of linguistics, translation, and learning Nahuatl are often not aligned with many of the goals of indigenous speakers. Indeed, if research into the lexicosemantics of indigenous languages is to benefit native speakers at all, a conscious effort must be made to work with communities of speakers.[55] Here I limit my comments to the ways in which an electronic database format facilitates the manipulation and export of data into a printed medium that can better serve native speakers' needs.

Such a product requires considerable effort to transform the printed output into a text that accommodates specific requirements of the language community. For example, it is important to provide a bilingual text that both departs from Nahuatl into an L_2 target language (oriented to the production of texts in Spanish) and one that departs from Spanish into an L_1 target language (oriented to the reception and interpretation of texts in Spanish). In both instances the material used in constructing the lexicon should be resynthesized in more accessible form. Some of the necessary changes, such as an orthography more in accord with Spanish conventions and the elimination of analytical fields of specialized information, could be accomplished through electronic manipulation of the primary data.[56] In the case of Nahuatl, work with native speakers will perhaps reveal whether certain decisions regarding headword entry should be changed. It may be decided that the obligatory object pronoun for

55. For this and other suggestions, see Jeanne 1992. Much work has been done to make linguistic research more responsive to the language goals of native speakers of indigenous languages. Particularly noteworthy is the work of the American Indian Languages Development Institute (AILDI) at the University of Arizona and Nora England's work with the Proyecto Lingüístico Francisco Marroquín in Guatemala. Robert Laughlin's work with Tzotzil speakers in Chiapas also stands out, as does that of Ofelia Zepeda with Tohono O'odham and the AILDI, and that of the Hopi Dictionary Project in elaborating the previously mentioned *Hopi Dictionary* (1998). See also the various essays in Hale 1992a.

56. I have not discussed orthographic conventions that I have chosen to use or the rationale behind the decisions taken. However, all of these conventions can be changed by fairly simple "search and replace" operations should a different perspective be adopted or, as I suggest here, should it be decided that slight variations in orthography might better suit the needs of different target audiences. Related to this issue (as well as to the question of standardization) is another one that is of particular importance but that I have not discussed here. This is the issue of "interdialectal lexicography," an extremely pressing problem for work in indigenous languages. Electronic databases can solve some of the problems that confront lexicographers who wish to work among language variants that are close but distinct (such as that of two nearby communities). For the Balsas River basin, this might involve

transitive verbs should be represented; if so, a choice must be made between one specific marker (the third person *k(i)-*) or two nonreferential markers (*te:-* for humans and *tla-* for nonhumans). Many of these changes can be made rapidly if a database format was used originally. Other changes must be more carefully contemplated and more laboriously implemented. Headwords must be carefully selected for inclusion; reduplicated forms might be accorded their own entries, and the same might be decided for irregular plurals and certain inflectional forms of verbs. If indeed a learners' dictionary is the goal, illustrative sentences should be selected or elaborated for their pedagogical value, and collocational and syntagmatic relations should be made as clear as possible. If a finders' list is utilized, care should be taken that it represents a basic vocabulary in the national language.

In this section I have briefly discussed the inadequacy of academic syntheses of indigenous lexicons, no matter how well intentioned, for addressing the communicative needs of the native speaker community in the dominant colonial language. I suggested that research material be restructured and a true bilingual learners' dictionary, in a much more traditional sense, be developed for use by native speakers of the language academics study. Yet at the same time, respecting the wishes and privacy of individual speakers, when possible the primary data of linguistic research should also be made available to the community. The utility of this material to promote the teaching and preservation of an indigenous language still as alive and vibrant as Nahuatl should not be minimized. Nor should its value in promoting pride in the indigenous language and culture, and thus indirectly helping language maintenance, be discounted.

5. CONCLUSION.   I began this chapter with a brief discussion of the difference between spoken and written languages as it affects lexicography and suggested that the dictionary tools and resources that have dominated the Western tradition (particularly their focus on written texts and its general orientation to increased specialization) are not altogether appropriate for work in indigenous languages. There are various reasons for this: the implications of the use of oral data for the elaboration of a

---

work in the neighboring villages of Ameyaltepec, San Juan Tetelcingo, and San Agustín Oapan (which, for example, respectively manifest *otli*, *ótlí*, and *ohtle* for 'road'). Electronic manipulation can solve some of the problems of phonological and lexical variation, particularly in the ability of this medium to provide the necessary cross-links and to store and manipulate the vast amounts of data that would be involved in such a comparative lexicographic project.

lexicon, the specific characteristics of the language being documented, the types and needs of users who will access the dictionary (from linguists to historians to members of the speech community), the responsibility of a lexicographer of an indigenous language to provide the greatest flexibility and range of use for the final product, and the value of presenting cultural and encyclopedic information in the dictionary definitions.

The two key elements of the project presented here are a multifaceted approach to meaning (semasiological, onomasiological, and syntagmatic) and the utilization of electronic media to link corpus, lexicon, and grammar in a mutually reinforcing research and learning environment. In the realization of both goals, an electronic format is particularly appropriate. Certainly, the bottom line of a lexicon is the breadth and depth of its definitions, and particular attention to semantics is necessary to convey the full richness of the language being studied. Yet regardless of the care and precision that might go into dictionary preparation, much will be lost if corpus and grammar are not integrated into a system of lexicographic representation. An electronic structure permits the establishment of direct links between these three elements. These links reflect the way in which research involves a constant triangulation between data, definition, and structure in order to develop adequate semantic and morphosyntactic understanding. By developing tools that permit others to re-create this process, at the same time making available primary data and the tools for additional analysis (such as parsed texts and examples, cross-referencing, and so on), both further research and debate are encouraged and language learning becomes a more integrated experience.

CHAPTER ELEVEN

The Comparative Siouan
Dictionary Project

David S. Rood and John E. Koontz

1. INTRODUCTION. The project we describe is the preparation of a dictionary of Comparative Siouan, that is, a reconstruction and cognate list of the vocabulary and, necessarily, much of the morphology of the language that was the ancestor of the modern Siouan languages. (See Rood 1979 for a survey of Siouan studies as they stood before the Comparative Siouan Dictionary project.) The Comparative Siouan Dictionary (CSD) is now in an advanced state of preparation, except for introductory essays and a phase of final cleanup editorial work, though it has now been about twenty years since we first conceived of the idea. This chapter describes the history of the project, including its conceptual history, the use of computers, the funding history, and the evolution of methodology as we moved from paper to computers and learned to work together as a team. Some of the specific linguistic results of the work have been published by Rankin, Carter, and Jones (1998).

The Siouan family consists of fifteen to eighteen documented languages in three major subgroups (see fig. 11.1); the exact number of languages depends on whether one classifies some of them as dialects or as separate languages. They are (1) the Missouri River Siouan group, Crow and Hidatsa; (2) the Central Siouan group, subdivided into Mandan and a large grouping called Mississippi Valley Siouan, comprising Dakotan[1]

---

1. Dakotan is a neologism intended to serve as a term for the subgroup as a whole (Dakotan) in contrast to the Santee-Sisseton and Yankton-Yanktonais version of the native name for the ethnicity (Dakhota or Dakota), which is often applied to the Santee-Sisseton dialect specifically. For a discussion of Dakotan dialectology, see Parks and DeMallie 1992. Santee-Sisseton is commonly known as Santee or Dakhota or Dakota. Yankton-Yanktonais is traditionally grouped erroneously with Assiniboine and Stoney as Nakota or Nakoda. Teton is also known as Lakhota or Lakota.

Proto-Siouan

Missouri River Siouan

Crow

Hidatsa

Central Siouan

Mandan

Mississippi Valley Siouan

Dakotan

Santee-Sisseton

Yankton-Yanktonais

Teton

Assiniboine

Stoney

Hočąk-Chiwere

Winnebago (Hočąk)

Chiwere (Iowa-Oto-Missouria)

Dhegiha

Omaha-Ponca

Kansa (Kaw)

Osage

Quapaw (Arkansas)

Southeastern Siouan

Biloxi

Ofo

Tutelo

Figure 11.1. Siouan Language Family.

(which includes the dialects Santee-Sisseton, Yankton-Yanktonais, and Teton
and the languages—or dialects, depending on one's point of view—Stoney
and Assiniboine), Winnebago-Chiwere (Winnebago or Hočąk and Chiwere
or Ioway-Otoe-Missouria), and Dhegiha (Omaha-Ponca, Osage, Kansa, and

Quapaw); and (3) the Southeastern Siouan group (also called Ohio Valley), Biloxi, Ofo, and Tutelo.[2]

2. OVERVIEW OF THE PROJECT.   Dictionaries are notoriously time-consuming projects, typically the work of lifetimes, or at least professional lifetimes, and this in a discipline where the collaborative work needed to pile up man-years is rare and unusual. Comparative dictionaries are particularly demanding, because they require expertise in more than one language and introduce their own elaborate machinery for correlating and glossing the forms compared. In the CSD project we have been fortunate in having to deal with only ten or twenty languages, but unlucky in having to face multiple orthographies for most of them, including ad hoc ones, and older phonetically based systems.

To reduce the task to manageability, the CSD project at the Center for the Study of the Native Languages of the Plains and Southwest (CeSNaLPS, or the Plains Center) adopted three expedients:

· First, there would be three principal editors—Robert L. Rankin, Richard T. Carter, and A. Wesley Jones—plus a project manager, David S. Rood.

· Second, interested graduate assistants—primarily Jule Gomez de Garcia and John E. Koontz—would be employed.

· Third, given Rood's interest in computer applications in linguistics, it was determined that computers should be used.[3]

The rest of this chapter describes the way in which we worked, grew, and changed. We begin with some additional background.

3. PRECURSORS.   Like any major project, this one had a number of precursors.

3.1. THE SIOUAN LANGUAGES ARCHIVE.   The first precursor was the Siouan Languages Archiving Project. In the early 1970s Rood predicted

2. Hočąk is usually known as Winnebago. The Wisconsin Winnebagos prefer the native name Hočąk, which is also spelled Hocak. Hochank, Hochunk, and Hochangara are other variants. Chiwere, used as a synonym or cover term for Iowa-Oto-Missouria, is a spelling variant of Jiwere or Jiwele, the native name of the Oto. Oto is also spelled Otoe; Iowa is also spelled Ioway. Dhegiha is also spelled Ȼegiha in the turn-of-the-century orthography of the Bureau of American Ethnology. It is an Omaha-Ponca word meaning 'local, one of this group'. It is used by linguists to refer to the whole group of Dhegiha languages. Kansa is also spelled Kansas, Kaw, Konze, or Kanze. The Quapaw are also known as the Arkansas.

3. In addition, Koontz had a background in computer science and Jones was an enthusiastic user of the new personal computers. Koontz was inspired by a course on the use of computers in linguistics that had been offered a few years previously by visiting professor Robert Hsu of the University of Hawaii.

that computers would be an important research tool in linguistics in the future and that the only way to capitalize on this for Siouan languages would be to have our resources, that is, grammars, dictionaries, and text collections, in a form that the computers could manipulate.

At that time computers were giant machines—at the University of Colorado a series of Control Data Corporation systems—housed in air-conditioned buildings and accessed by mysterious people in white coats, who took packages of punched cards from you at a window and, if you were lucky, returned a printout and your cards a few hours or even days later. If you made a programming or data encoding error, you then had to repeat the process, of course, but the iterative refinements of procedures that now take a few minutes took weeks.

We (Rood and colleague Allan R. Taylor) did not know that if we had waited a few years it would have gotten so much easier, so we began to transfer to punched cards the information in the books we wanted to search and to carry box after heavy box of cards down four flights of stairs in Woodbury Hall for transport to the University Computer Center and back (about a six-mile round trip), over and over again.

The results were functional but ugly. The sixty-four-character proprietary Control Data Corporation character set contained only uppercase Roman letters, digits, and a few punctuation marks. This imposed the need to represent many characters with digraphs, trigraphs, and so on, including such simple things as uppercase characters. The standard English lowercase Roman characters were represented by the uppercase characters of the set, the uppercase characters by characters preceded by a plus, acute accents by an asterisk following the character, raised n by an $'N$ following a character, and so on, as in (1). Each character and diacritic encountered in encoding the documents had its own representation. The system employed is defined by Rood (1981).

(1) +DAK'HO*TA = Dak'o'ta, representing Dakhóta
    +UMA'N*HA'N = Uma$^{n'}$ha^n, representing Umáha

Still, by the end of the project we had all the material for the extinct languages and much of the material on the other languages in machine-searchable form (Rood 1981). Now it was time to put it to use.

3.2. THE WORKSHOP ON COMPARATIVE SIOUAN.   A second preliminary step was taken in summer 1984. With support from the National Science Foundation (NSF) and the National Endowment for the Humanities (NEH) we—here primarily Rood—gathered together a group of people who had been working on various Siouan languages[4] and asked them to think about ways we could advance Siouan studies cooperatively, without duplicating efforts. We concluded (among other things) that a comparative project was in order, and we learned that Carter and Rankin were already working independently on comparative Siouan databases (using handwritten slip files), each with the idea that he would someday compile a comparative dictionary. At the workshop they agreed to merge their files and transfer the information to "cognate set sheets," single-page compilations from various languages of forms that looked like they might constitute a cognate set. This work was undertaken at the workshop. The resulting sheets were passed from person to person, with the idea of filling in more possible forms from various additional sources not yet consulted by Rankin or Carter.

At the end of the workshop the participants divided themselves into teams to execute various follow-up projects. The first of those was to be the comparative dictionary, based on the workshop slips, and the editors designated were Carter, Rankin, and Jones. Rood was given the task of overseeing the project and finding funding for it, which kept him busy writing grant proposals for the next couple of years. None of the other projects we planned at that time—a revised bibliography, a collection of grammatical sketches, and a collection of papers—have yet been started, the dictionary having taken all our attention until now.[5]

4. THE FIRST FEW YEARS.   During the next three years, the cognate set sheets were passed from editor to editor. First Carter took them home and sorted through them, dividing some sets into two or three or merging sets that seemed to be duplicates. Then Rankin, spending a sabbatical year in Boulder, did the same thing. Finally Jones, in Bismarck, got a turn at adding Hidatsa and Crow material and scrutinizing the others' work. During this period, Graczyk and Koontz added various slips, which were sent to the dictionary editors, or commented further on existing slips. In summer 1989, after one failed attempt, we received funding from the NEH for the project and began the long series of summer meetings and winter tasks that are summarized in table 11.1 below. The story hereafter involves parallel developments in computational technology, our

---

4. Carter (University of Manitoba), Jones (University of Mary), Rankin (University of Kansas), Rood (organizer) (University of Colorado), Patricia A. Shaw (University of British Columbia), and Paul Voorhis (Brandon University), with Allan R. Taylor (University of Colorado) and Josephine White Eagle (MIT) part of the time, and (then) graduate students Randolph Graczyk (University of Chicago), John E. Koontz (University of Colorado), and Willem de Reuse (University of Kansas). Ray Gordon (SIL) also visited briefly.

5. Paul Voorhis did complete a manuscript sketch grammar of Catawba for the projected volume of grammatical sketches of Siouan languages.

TABLE 11.1. Chronology of the Dictionary

Date	Funding	Methodology
1984–85	Workshop NEH, NSF[1]	Slip files to cognate sheets.
1986–89	none	Copying cognate sheets (paper shuffling).
July 1989	NEH[2]	First use of computer database program.
1990–91	NEH, APS, CU	Continue as above.
July 1991	Extension; new grant denied	Everyone on a computer; daily file merging; everyone doing different languages.
Summer 1992	New NEH grant[3]	Printouts, everyone on same page, data entry later.
Summer 1993	NEH-2 continued & supplemented	Working together on one computer; "finished" about 25% of database.
Summer 1994	Supplement from NEH	All on one computer; about 84% of database acceptable to all.
Summer 1995	Squeezed supplement	Finished last 16% and went through all of it again.
Fall 1995ff	none	Database exchanged for proofing and cleanup; formatting and indexing programs
1999ff	none	Copy editing using formatted printed copies of the database.
200?	none	Final printed product?

NOTES: [1]NEH: RD-20477-84; NSF: BNS 8406236.
[2]NEH: RT-21062-84.
[3]NEH: RT-21238-91.

understanding of Proto-Siouan, and our evolution of various techniques for cooperative editing.

4.1. THE FIRST COMPUTERIZATION. We originally thought we could do the entire job in three years, although the NEH would agree only to support us for two. Skeptical about meeting their expectations, we nevertheless plunged gleefully into the work. It is hard to remember now what computer technology and tools were like in those days, but as the computationally supported part of the project began in 1989, there were only a couple of database programs available to us that seemed appropriate, and neither of them was quite what we needed (see §6.3 below).

In spite of this handicap, we finally chose the program that seemed to be the lesser of two evils (askSam) and hired Jule Gomez de Garcia (at the University of Colorado) to start entering the cognate set sheets, using a brand-new IBM PC/AT with a huge 20-megabyte hard drive, a major advance over the computer center visits and the roomful of cabinets of punch cards of a few years earlier.[6]

The first two years, the editorial team assembled annually in Boulder for several weeks each summer. During those first summer meetings, we continued to use the cognate set sheets as our working tools, since interactive computing was still not feasible. The editors sat around a big table and discussed the contents of the sheets one by one. They appointed a scribe to write down their results, so that Gomez de Garcia could then transfer the new decisions to the database.

4.2. THE COMPUTER ENVIRONMENT.

4.2.1. DOS AND THE CHARACTER SETS.   The computers employed in the project from the very first PC/AT on have all been independent (non-networked) DOS systems. The ones in service currently run in Microsoft Windows 95, but the project continues to operate primarily in DOS windows.

The main impact of using DOS has been that DOS supports as its only native character set the 256-character IBM extended ASCII set, while the project employs well over 256 characters, many of them not included in this set. This has never been a real limitation because throughout the time of our work the technology to stretch this DOS limitation has been available. Still, we have spent considerable time setting up this technology and maintaining it, and we have always been limited within this technology to seeing a single character set at a time on the screen, though we could print as many as we needed on the same page.

Under DOS, the character set problem must be resolved for each combination of display device and application. The two display devices in question have been the EGA/VGA[7] series of graphics cards (and suitable attached monitors) and the Hewlett-Packard LaserJet series PCL[8] (non PostScript LaserJet) printers and compatibles, mainly the Plains Center's[9] now quite venerable HP LaserJet II.

The details of solving the character problem under DOS need not detain us here, because they are obsolete under modern versions of

---

6. Simultaneously, Rood acquired an IBM PC/AT with a 30-megabyte hard drive for use as an editorial tool with the *International Journal of American Linguistics*. The Department of Linguistics at the University of Colorado already had a pair of similar machines for its own use.

7. Enhanced Graphics Adapter/Video Graphics Array.

8. Printer Control Language.

9. The Plains Center is the name by which the University of Colorado's Center for the Study of the Native Languages of the Plains and Southwest (CeSNaLPS) is commonly known.

Microsoft Windows, which support TrueType fonts for display and print-ing. Suffice it to say that we use the Duke Language Toolkit to create the EGA/VGA screen fonts, and the Summer Institute of Linguistics (SIL) program Keyswap to redefine keyboards. We use the SIL Premier Fonts and now the SIL Legacy Fonts packages to create printer fonts, and we use the SoftCraft Font Solution Pack (primarily the Laser Fonts package) to generate Microsoft Word printer drivers for the HP LaserJet II and sup-plement the features of the SIL font tools. The SIL packages can make Microsoft Word printer drivers, but the Laser Fonts package is (or was) much more adept at this.

Given the evolution of Microsoft Windows in its various versions and the development of TrueType fonts for use with it, a more satisfactory solution today would be to use the SIL Encore Fonts package to create Windows and printer fonts and the SIL-promoted TavulteSoft Keyboard Manager tool to define keyboards. In the Microsoft Windows environment it is possible to see more than one font at a time on the screen as well as on paper, in any application that supports the use of Windows fonts and printing.

4.2.2. INFORMATION AND DATABASE COORDINATION. For the bulk of the project, some members did not have access to e-mail, and none of the project computers at the University of Colorado were networked in any significant sense before late 1997. The lack of e-mail access for some of the members made collaboration during the academic year difficult, but the teaching loads and other research of the editors prevented most academic year CSD activity during nonsabbatical years anyway.

A more serious problem has been the lack of file-sharing facilities. All exchanges of files took place by diskette, though it sometimes took some ingenuity to fit the database onto a diskette. Various file compression and archiving tools have been used in this capacity. All these problems have been rendered obsolete now by the general availability of Internet-based e-mail, ftp file transfer, the Web, and larger removable media.

5. FURTHER EVOLUTION. As the work progressed, we found that we needed more and more time, and, of course, we kept running out of money, too. The first grant was supplemented by the American Philosophical Society and by the University of Colorado and given a time extension, but in 1991 we were forced to apply for a second grant. Our first application was denied, because we were not doing "salvage" linguis-tics, which seemed to demand all the available funding for Native Amer-ican projects at the time. But the second time we successfully argued that we had all done our part in that arena and were now ready to make use of some of what we had helped to salvage. The second grant, supple-mented in 1993 and extended twice, saw us through to where we are now.

We had to make concessions to get the supplement, such as accepting reduced indirect cost reimbursements and doing without honoraria for the summer workshops for the last two years.

During this period, there was a distinct evolution in the way we processed the growing and maturing database. At first the cognate set sheets contained essentially guesses, and to a considerable extent the early effort involved splitting, lumping, and rearranging sets. Then came a period when we concentrated on expanding the contents of the sheets, at which point each editor undertook to work with subgroups of languages, for example, Jones with Crow and Hidatsa, Carter with Mandan, Dakotan, and some of the Southeastern languages, and Rankin with the others. John Koontz also contributed to this effort for the Winnebago and Chiwere groups.

During our summer meetings in this period, each of us had his own computer and the three editors worked independently on the database, though the files were merged at the end of each day so that everyone had a newly updated version the next day. Those sessions involved long periods of silent clicking and page flipping, interspersed with questions and discussion about what was being discovered.

Off and on during this period we were able to add new chunks of data, too; these included new forms from Chiwere elicited by Louanna Furbee and her colleagues, from Osage by Carolyn Quintero, and additions from continuing fieldwork on Crow by Randolph Graczyk and on Mandan by Carter. We also made use of archive searching of Winnebago and Chiwere material by Gomez de Garcia and of Omaha-Ponca material by Koontz.

Gradually, in fact imperceptibly at the time, we switched away from finding new forms to discovering new sound correspondences, and it was during this period, too, that the editors discovered big differences of opinion on how to represent certain features of the protolanguage. Eventually they agreed on some compromise representations, but not without intense (and often repeated) argument. There were times when we wondered whether the team would survive the controversy, but the editors' loyalty to the project ultimately overcame their loyalty to their own preferences. Naturally, the potential for this kind of disagreement becoming fatal is a danger for this kind of project; in our case it has proved surmountable.

As the database matured, the effort to bring forms from the individual languages into established and growing cognate sets changed to one of examining the sets from top to bottom for consistency in sound correspondence. At first when this point was reached, the editors found themselves most comfortable with multiple copies of printouts of the computer database. These they discussed at length and scribbled on, after which the scribbles were converted to database amendments by Jule Gomez de Garcia. Then, in summer 1993, they discovered that they could work directly on the computer by clustering around a single screen and discussing what they saw, changing and fixing it then and there. We thus witnessed a very fine-grained evolution from pure paper to machine copies of paper to separate copies of machine entries to single, interactive entries. From here, that looks impressively logical and systematic, but in fact it was just a way of growing, and unplanned growing at that.

Summer 1995 saw us using up the very last pennies of our grant money, but at the same time we found we had a nearly finished dictionary. The painfully slow process of looking at each set carefully together, which had covered 25 percent of the database one year (1993), an additional 60 percent the next (1994), and the last 15 percent in the third year, accelerated so fast that in the third year the editors finished their examination of the database and also went through the whole collection a second time. Now they were happy with their results and Koontz was able to write computer programs for formatting and indexing that could be rerun on the database at will. This has freed us to edit from formatted material, a definite psychological plus, without fearing that we were creating new problems for the final product. Eight years of cooperation (counting the workshop), instead of the originally envisioned two or three, have finally come near to paying off. Unfortunately, the close examination of the database entailed in formatting it for printing has revealed the presence of numerous minor inconsistencies in form.

6. THE DATABASE.

6.1. CONSTRUCTION.   As stated in section 3.2, initially the CSD database was based on the combined slip files of Carter and Rankin, with consideration directed to the published reconstructions of Matthews and others, including to some extent the early work of Wolf, though this work is difficult to collate with more recent work.[10] We supplemented this material with

- observations from specialists in particular languages, for example, Randolph Graczyk for Crow and Josephine White Eagle for Winnebago;
- extensive examination of some newly rediscovered correspondences like *R ("funny r") (cf. Dorsey 1885);
- attempts to find sets involving unusual segmental sequences found in some of the languages (like Dakotan gw or Ioway-Otoe dw); and
- searches for culturally and ethnotaxonomically relevant vocabulary.

---

10. We were also given access to the unpublished work of Terrence Kaufman but decided not to consult it because of the various philological and other problems of working with the unpublished notes of a living individual without his direct involvement.

These are all standard techniques and for the most part were carried out manually.

We did not attempt the technique of back-construction, in which, using known or postulated sound changes, all possible predecessors of forms in various languages are constructed and collated mechanically, looking for matches that will then be evaluated under human intervention. This would best be done at the root level in languages with the kind of morphological structure that Siouan languages have, and we lacked extensive root lists to which to apply this technique.

We did, however, have access to the computer files from the Siouan Language Archiving Project. These included a large number of texts in certain of the languages and several dictionaries. We were able to use these in several ways.

First, and most simply, we were able to do computerized searches of the materials for particular languages to fill in gaps in our data. For example, Koontz has searched the Dorsey (1890, 1891) texts extensively to fill in the gaps in the Omaha-Ponca data. We have also searched for unusual segmental sequences or interesting morphological structures.

Second, we needed to find a way to identify the verb roots that were hiding behind any of several instrumental prefixes, since the roots are often cognate but do not occur with the same prefixes from language to language. For example, take the PSi form *-xuxe* 'to break brittle things'. The cognates in the daughter languages occur with various instrumental prefixes, for example, Hidatsa *núxuxxe* 'break by hand', Lakhota *naxúye* 'break by stepping on', Winnebago *booxúxux* 'break something brittle by blowing'. So we culled from several large, representative dictionaries in the Siouan Archives all the instrumental derivative entries that we could identify automatically by shape. These were first folded at the root initial to facilitate sorting by root initials and then manually collated by Jones (see Jones 1991), leading to his discovery that a large portion of the underlying roots of instrumental stems fall into families of related forms such that stems of the structure $C_1C_2VC_3$ seem to display a very old complex structure in which C_1 and/or C_3 may have constituted separate morphemes added to the C_2V root. We refer to the nonroot morphemes as root extensions and in the database (not in the final dictionary) use the purported root and extensions to keep apart sets with similar glosses.

6.2. FORM.   We maintain our dictionary as a form of database.[11] In effect, the database is a computerized slip file. It does not look like a

---

11. Much of Koontz's thinking on this can be traced to the work of Hsu, though some of the same principles are reiterated in the SIL Shoebox manual. Hsu's work has been particularly influential in the lexicography of Pacific and Native American languages.

printed dictionary in this format, but it is easy to find one's way around in and edit. We derive printed reports, including the final printed dictionary, from this form using various software tools. Part of the database entry for 'dog' is given below.[12]

GLOSS[dog
GRAMCAT[N
SEMCAT[Anml
ENTHIST[GdeG 11-29-89
CHGHIST[done 06-20-90
CHGHIST[. . .
\PSI[*wi-šúke
OTHREC[. . .
PCH[. . .
PMV[*šúkE
PDA[*šúkA
LA[šúka | 'dog' C
DA[†šúka | "suŋ´-ka" | 'dog' R-450a
ST[súga | 'dog' PAS
PWC[*šúųke
. . .

CH[šúŋe | 'horse' Marsh
WI[šúųk | 'dog, horse' KM-3005
WI[šúųgník | 'puppy' KM-3002
PDH[. . .
PSE[. . .
COM[This ancient term has been adapted in historical times . . .

Key to fieldnames (not all exemplified): GLOSS gloss; GRAMCAT grammatical category; SEMCAT semantic category; ENTHIST entry (keying) history; CHGHIST change history; PSC Proto-Siouan-Catawban; PSI Proto-Siouan reconstruction; OTHREC other reconstructions; PCH Proto-Crow-Hidatsa; CR Crow; HI Hidatsa; PMA Pre-Mandan; MA Mandan; PMV Proto-Mississippi Valley; PDA Proto-Dakotan; LA Lakota (Teton); Da Dakota (Santee); SV Sioux Valley; YA Yankton; YS Yanktonais; AS Assiniboine; ST Stoney; PWC Proto-Winnebago-Chiwere; CH Chiwere (Ioway-Otoe); IO Ioway; OT Otoe; MO Missouria; WI Winnebago; PDH Proto-Dhegiha; OP Omaha-Ponca; PO Ponca; OM Omaha; KS Kansa; OS Osage; QU Quapaw; PSE Proto-Southeastern; TU Tutelo; SP Sapony; PBO Proto-Biloxi-Ofo; Bl Biloxi; OF Ofo; PCA Proto-Catawban; CA Catawba; WO Woccon; OTHLGS Other language (families); COM Comment. Key to source abbreviations (partial): C Richard Carter; R Robert Rankin; PAS Patricia Shaw; (Gordon) Marsh; KM Kenneth Miner.

12. For this chapter, the figures and lists were recoded using our three current Microsoft Windows ANSI-based character sets, which we call Standard Siouan, James Dorsey, and Dakotanist. These are implemented as TrueType fonts. In the actual database we use a single modified DOS Enhanced ASCII character set we call Siouan Dictionary. Siouan

It might seem simpler to maintain the data in the form of a final document, that is, as a word processor or desktop publisher file, or in some form of application-independent markup, for example, SGML or HTML, but that approach commits one to at least a particular final structure and generally also to a particular formatting scheme, depending on the factorability of formatting schemes in the application chosen. It may be possible, but difficult, to convert from this structure and formatting scheme to others, whether for primary use or merely to obtain some auxiliary report. Moreover, conversion between formatting schemes often results in the loss of some or all of the formatting. Thus maintaining the database in final report form commits one in some degree to a particular structure and a particular formatting of it, which can be awkward in a ten- to twenty-year project. Apart from this, report formats are seldom optimal for computerized data retrieval.

The form of database we selected for our efforts is called informally a textbase (see askSam Systems 1991: 2). Textbases are an extension of the standard tabular conception of a database to more freely formatted textual data. Although they have been applied to such tasks as organizing legal briefs, contact notes, and recipes, they are particularly useful for dictionaries and other linguistic work.

As in a standard database, the basic unit of data is a record, which is subdivided into fields. In the illustration for 'dog' above, for example, the record represents the cognate set 'dog'. Most of the fields represent cognate forms. The fields represent reconstructions, comments, notes on the editing process, and so on. Thus the LA field is a cognate Lakota (Teton) form for 'dog', and the PDA field is the Proto-Dakotan reconstruction based on the various Dakotan forms, while COM is a general comment by the editors. The key field is GLOSS, the English gloss.

In spite of these similarities, there are some differences between databases and textbases. Databases require the existence of a unique key or indexing field. Textbases do not. Textbase keys are typically ordered, but they need not be unique. This permits, for example, two records representing descriptions of two homophones, or, in our case, multiple records for reconstructions with the same gloss. In some extreme cases of textbases, there are no keys and even the record structure may be missing. The extreme cases usually arise with treatment of running texts as databases.

Dictionary is implemented both as an EGA/VGA screen font and as a Hewlett-Packard Laser-Jet printer bitmap font.

The Siouan Dictionary character set lacks some characters that we need. In the database these are represented with digraphs, like *a.* for *ą*. In printing, both the Siouan Dictionary character set and the digraphs are mapped to several different modified ASCII bitmap fonts, including the Siouan Dictionary bitmap font mentioned above. Some additional fonts are required to achieve the typographic requirements of the dictionary apparatus.

Another difference is that standard databases permit only a fixed set of fields in a record, while textbases permit an arbitrary number of fields in each record. Usually the set is similar from record to record, but a field can be omitted if there is no information to include in it, or a new field added, if something new turns up. In principle each record may have a unique set of fields. In the context of a dictionary, fields relevant to a particular kind of lexical entry can be included in that kind of entry but omitted in others. A Siouanist can include reflexive derivatives with verbs but omit them with nouns. By extension, fields for which the data are missing can also be omitted. Thus, in a comparative dictionary, there need be no reflex field for a language that does not participate in that cognate set. If a given language has no cognate for *wi-šúke, no field for that language appears.

Fields may also be repeated. This allows multiple definitions or multiple examples. Because of these two extensions, the name of the field must typically be included with each instance of the field, to identify the type of field. Thus the illustration for 'dog' has two WI fields for two (related) Winnebago stems including cognates for *wi-šúke.

Standard databases usually require fixed-length, fixed-form fields, whereas textbases permit arbitrary-length, variable-form fields. Thus there is no arbitrary limit on the length of a definition or an example. Cognate citations can be as long as needed, as can comments.

Textbase data fields can have internal structuring called subfields. Our citation fields consist in principle of the following:

• a standard orthography phonological form, in many cases necessarily deduced from a subphonological source recording;

• the source recording itself in the original orthography, if it differs from the standard form;

• the gloss from the source; and

• a reference to the source.

In support of the subfield structure, remarks on a given citation should be placed in an accompanying field, not intermingled arbitrarily with the material just listed. Unfortunately, we arrived at this last principle after the fact, and we have always had a great deal of difficulty adhering to the other stipulations. The subfields are nicely divided with | characters, but in our original scheme we relied on the dagger marking deduced standard forms and the quotation marks around source forms and glosses to impose the structure. It would probably have been a good idea to write a program to critique and/or heuristically correct the format of citation fields and to have encouraged the editors to run it at intervals. In fact, Koontz runs something like this as part of the formatting process, but this is too late in the processing to be optimal.

Returning to the illustration of 'dog', the first DA (Dakota) field there represents a deduced standard form *šúka*, recorded "šuŋ'-ka," meaning 'dog', in the Riggs dictionary (1890: 450, col. a). In practice we might early on have recorded only the deduced standard form, omitting the source form and/or the gloss and/or some or all of the reference.

Apart from failing to adhere to our standards, we overlooked one further refinement and, since thinking of it, have debated its merits. We should perhaps have devised some sort of scheme to delimit the parts of forms being compared. To some extent this is obvious, but not marking it explicitly may cover some imprecision in our thinking in some sets and may pose difficulties for readers less familiar with Siouan morphology. Its absence also makes it difficult to use programs to extract tables of sound correspondences. On the other hand, it would be particularly awkward in forms where cognate pieces are discontinuous or where syncope or cluster simplification has distorted the picture of a particular language. Likewise problematic, the obvious schemes for delimiting this sort of thing present difficulties for simple searching programs aimed at forms not instrumented in this way (see §7.1.2 for more details).

The issue of what to use as a key is a very real one in a comparative dictionary database. For a long time we made do with brief glosses, the problem being that the same set or an overlapping one was often lurking somewhere else under a different gloss. It was also sometimes difficult to keep sets pure in terms of phonological correspondences. This latter problem was solved by Jones, who, in the course of his root extension work (see details in §6.1), devised a scheme for representing the phonology of the root in terms of its core and extensions. This helped considerably in sorting out phonologically similar sets, but probably the only way to remove overlapping sets systematically is to have a complete set of indices of where the cited forms occur and refer to these continuously. In fact, some sort of automated identification of problem sets ought to be possible, given the indices.

6.3. THE SOFTWARE.   After considering several textbase systems on the market in the late 1980s and one devised with considerable effort by Jones, called SiouxAnn, we selected one called askSam, mostly because it was the only one that seemed relatively friendly to user-defined character sets. It turned out to have several egregious faults, including a strange and (for us) unusable scripting and report-generating tool and a peculiar two-level system of records that interacted with fixed lengths for the lower level of record. Nevertheless, it did permit searches restricted to fields; it did permit the use of user-defined character sets; and although we have long since abandoned it, its traces still remain. In particular, we label fields with labels of the form "label[". The trailing "]" following the field was optional, and we have always omitted it.

We have since replaced askSam with several text editors. This is the approach recommended for use with Lexware by Hsu (1985). All these editors are "programmer's editors," characterized mainly by such features as

· being willing to edit any size file that can be stored on the system;

· ability to edit more than one file at a time;

· availability of pattern-based searching; and

· some sort of scripting language for encapsulating editing procedures.

We have used mainly products called Brief and the Sage Programmer's Editor. Some of us prefer one and some the other.

It should be noted that in the meantime the SIL has introduced a system called Shoebox, now available in a Windows version.[13] This is a textbase system for linguists, and had it been available when we began we would certainly have used it. It labels fields with labels of the form \label, following the conventions of the SIL's Standard Format for textbases, and has a host of features of use to a linguist. In fact, Koontz has been covertly using it in one way or another since it first came out, always converting the textbase to Standard Format first before doing any work with it:

```
\gl dog
\gc N
\sc Anml
\enh GdeG 11-29-89
\chh done 06-20-90
\chh . . .
\psi |SS *wi-šúke
\or . . .
\pch . . .
\pmv |SS *šúkE
\pda |SS *šúkA
\la |SS šúka |GL dog |SC C
\da |SS ³LB{z}šúka |BA šuŋ´-ka |GL dog |SC R-450a
\st |SS šúga |GL dog |SC PAS
\pwc |SS *šųùke
    . . .
\ch |SS šúŋe |GL horse |SC Marsh
\wi |SS šúųk |GL dog, horse |SC KM-3005
\wi |SS šųųgník |GL puppy |SC KM-3002
\pdh . . .
```

13. In spite of the availability of Shoebox, we suspect that text editors will remain an important tool in projects such as the CSD.

\pse ...

\com This ancient term has been adapted in historical times ...

...

SIL Standard Format does not have a particular practice for marking subfields, but several of the tools SIL provides use notations like |xx{...} to label and delimit use of a zone in which the character format named xx is to be used. As subfields generally have their own distinctive character formatting, this notation is pressed into service in the CSD to represent subfields. However, to save keystrokes and simplify searching subfields with tools not aware of Standard Format conventions, subfields are generally marked |xx ... in the CSD textbase. Certain single-character subfields use a variant of the more restrictive notation; for example, ^xLB{z} represents |LB{z}, which selects the dagger character out of the Lexbats (special lexicographical symbols) character set. The use of "^x" in lieu of "|" is a trick to prevent these notations from being processed at the wrong time.

6.4. PRINTING THE DATABASE.   To print a simple verbatim copy of the database in our DOS environment requires either the use of a word processor or manual installation of fonts in the printer. None of the textbase systems we have used do printing using user-defined fonts. Most do no printing at all. Because the SIL has been making it easy to use Microsoft Word for DOS as a linguistic tool throughout this period, this has been our printing tool of choice, though other expedients have been used from time to time. We started out with version 4.0, and are currently using versions 5.5 and 6.0. Printing is achieved by exporting the textbase to a text file or by appropriating the existing textbase file, if that is stored in text form. This file is then imported into Microsoft Word, formatted using the Siouan Dictionary font, and printed.

More elaborate reports have always required, unfortunately, the intervention of a programmer. This intervention permits extracting, modifying, and rearranging fields and selecting particular fonts for use with individual subfields or individual characters. The approach we have used has been to

· export the textbase from the textbase program;

· convert the textbase to an intermediate format with a script written in the Mortice-Kern Systems (MKS) Toolkit version of AWK for DOS. AWK is a Unix-derived scripting language, strong on pattern matching and character processing (see Aho, Kernighan, and Weinberger 1988);

· convert the intermediate format into a Microsoft Word for DOS file with one of a series of minor SIL tools, currently CTW; and

· print the resulting file with Microsoft Word for DOS.

This omits several steps required by perverse behavior on the part of one or the other of the applications, and the whole process is too complex to go into in detail in this context, but some general observations on the conversion process and the intermediate format are in order.

What the SIL conversion tools do is convert a Standard Format textbase into a Microsoft Word for DOS file. Unfortunately, for simplicity, the textbases to be converted are assumed to be of a special kind configured to facilitate the specification of the Microsoft Word report format. These format-specifying textbases are not laid out on anything like the data-organizing principles used in laying out the CSD textbase. In the CSD textbase, records represent a set of compared forms, with each field providing a citation for one of the forms, or a comment on it, or a reconstruction. In a format-specifying textbase, the fields correspond instead to paragraphs of the report, and certain specially delimited strings within the fields correspond to stretches of text that are printed with special typefaces and type variants. The conversion script or program that we supply converts the field structure of the CSD textbase into the field structure of the format-specifying textbase and preserves or adds delimiters for parts of fields that need special formatting. See figure 11.2 for an example of the 'dog' record restructured as a format-specifying textbase.

In the form shown in figure 11.2, the fields are \DG (dictionary gloss), \DH (dictionary header), \DA (dictionary article), and \DC (dictionary

\DG |RG{286|RG{.}}{tab}|HW{dog} |GI{N}|RG{,} |GI{Anml}

\DH Original GdeG 11-29-89|RG{:' changed done 06-20-90|RG{;} . . .

\DA |LG{psi}{#}|SS{*wi-šúke}

\DA |FW{cf|RG{.}} . . . |RG{;} . . . |LG{pch} . . . |RG{ų} |LG{pmv}{#}|SS{*šúkE} |RG{ų}

   |LG{pda}{#}|SS{*šúkA} |RG{ų} |LG{la}{#}|SS{šúka} |GL{dog} |SC{rtc} |RG{ų}

   |LG{da}{#}|SS{|LB{z}šúka} |BA{šuŋ'-ka} |GL{dog} |SC{R-450a} |RG{ų}

   |LG{st}{#}|SS{šúga} |GL{dog} |SC{PAS} |RGų |LG{pwc}{#}|SS{*š{ú,}ųke} |RG{ų} . . .

   |LG{ch}{#}|SS{šúŋe} |GL{horse} |SC{Marsh} |RG{ų} |LG{wi}{#}|SS{šúųk}

   |GL{dog|RG{,} horse} |SC{KM-3005}|RG{;} |LG{wi}{#}|SS{šųųgník} |GL{puppy}

   |SC{KM-3002} |RG{ų} |LG{pdh} . . . |LG{pse} . . .

\DC This ancient term has been adapted in historical times . . .

Figure 11.2. 'Dog' Record Restructured as a Format-Specifying Textbase.

comment), instead of the individual citations of previous illustrations. In fact, the citations are run together in a single \DA field, representing a single paragraph. The citation fields of the textbase become subfields of this paragraph, each in the |xx{. . .} notation, and they are separated from each other within the paragraph with bullets (|RG{ʉ}) introduced by the formatting program. The |RG{. . .} character formatting notation selects the "regular" DOS ASCII character set, while |SS{. . .} selects the Standard Siouan character set, |BA{. . .} selects the BAE (or Dorsey) character set, and so on.

The AWK scripts that convert the CSD textbase to the format-specifying version also introduce standard abbreviations. For example, C as an abbreviation for (Richard T.) Carter is replaced by rtc.

The {#} notations in this form of the database are used in connection with the generation of citation indices. Figure 11.3 is the final report, albeit still at a draft stage of development.

286.   **DOG** N, Anml

Original GdeG 11-29-89; changed done 06-20-90; . . .

PSI *wi-šų́ke

cf. . . .· PCH . . . · PMV *šų́kE · PDA *šúkA · LA šų́ka *dog* RTC · DA †šų́ka śuŋ'-ka *dog* R-450A ·

ST sų́ga *dog* PAS · PWC *šų́ʉke · . . . · CH šų́ŋe *horse* MARSH · WI šų́ʉk *dog, horse* KM-3005;

WI šʉʉgnį́k *puppy* KM-3002 · PDH . . . · PSE . . .

This ancient term has been adapted in historical times . . .

Figure 11.3. Final Report.

An essential component of this formatting process is the Microsoft Word style sheet, a file describing a set of section, paragraph, and character formats that the word processor permits users to apply to a word processor file. Each section, paragraph, and specially formatted character string within a paragraph is annotated with the name of the style that applies to it, and changing the style's definition in the style sheet file changes every piece of text annotated with that style name. In the SIL scheme of format-specifying textbases, the names of the fields match the names of the desired paragraph styles in a style sheet. For example, \DG fields are printed with the DG, or Dictionary Gloss, style.

Strings within a paragraph needing special formatting are delimited with sequences like |xx{yyy}, where *yyy* is the string and *xx* is the name of a character format in the style sheet; for example, in the \DG field the |HW{dog} sequence refers to the HW, or Headword, character style, which involves small bold capitals in the SIL Sophia sans serif font (cf. earlier illustrations).

More recently, SIL has turned its attention to this problem in the Windows context, and we now have two tools for converting from data textbases to Microsoft Word for Windows files, or, actually, to application-independent interchange files in Microsoft Rich Text Format (RTF), which can then be conveyed into Microsoft Word for Windows or any other program that accepts RTF files. Shoebox for Windows can even do a certain amount of printing itself now. The two formatting tools are called Multi-Dictionary Formatter and SF Converter. The former is restricted by the particular set of data textbase field labels it insists on. Its scheme of labels simply does not work for synchronic analyses of many American languages, let alone for comparative dictionaries. The latter, however, is probably flexible enough to replace many features of the conversion scripts that the CSD project has been employing, though not all.

Note that a number of new script writing tools are also now available for the PC, including freeware versions of Perl (Siever, Spainhour, and Patwardhan 1999) and Tcl/Tk (Ousterhout 1994). For some time there has also been a freeware version of AWK from the GNU software project.

7. CONCLUSION.

7.1. SOLVED AND CONTINUING COMPUTER PROBLEMS.   Some of the problems we encountered have been solved—greatly reduced or essentially eliminated—by improvements in the general computing environment, though we have not yet adopted all of these. This is particularly true of our character set problems and the twin issues of personal communications and file access (see §4.2). Some of the problems we encountered have known solutions that have not been materially facilitated by developments since the project began but are still within reason with a little work (see §§6.3, 6.4). There are, however, some computing problems we encountered that are only beginning to be solvable or have not yet been solved. We will try to summarize them here.

7.1.1. FILE SHARING PROBLEMS.   The project involved five or more workers simultaneously, at four or more sites during the academic year. While the technology of editing shared files is well understood and used in many commercial applications, our lack of networking technology has consistently prevented us from simultaneous editing of a single, centralized set of files. Although file sharing networks with record-based locking have existed throughout the period in which we have been working on the CSD, they are only now beginning to be a standard part of Windows computing and to appear in academic computing outside of computer department experiments. As far as we know, none of the linguistic textbase software mentioned above supports such file sharing anyway. In the absence of file sharing at this level, we shipped diskettes by mail and divided the database into zones[14] that only one person was allowed to edit. In practical terms we have never managed to get a zone through more than one person during an academic year. During summer meetings, the editors mostly worked on the entire file as a committee.

Another sort of collaboration that better networking might have fostered would be some sort of automated conformance checking of the databases during off-hours by a conformance authority.

Note that even with record-based file locking, there are some procedural questions that must be addressed. There is no point in carefully locking others out of a record while one edits it, if one of these others will be deleting the now modified and unlocked record tomorrow. And what should be done if two editors wish to lock overlapping sets of records for separate purposes? A certain coherence and noncollision of agendas must be maintained, and this can probably only be achieved on a spiritual plane more or less separate from computing. The best computing itself can manage in this sphere is to keep an automated change log and provide facilities for backing out of conflicting changes.

7.1.2. PATTERN MATCHING PROBLEMS.   It has already been mentioned that there is a potential for mechanisms indicating what parts of forms are being compared to interfere with searching. It is hard to search for *wasabe* if there are brackets ensconced around the *sabe:* *wa[sabe]* or separators between the components: *w.a.s.a.b.e* or *wa-sab-e*. A similar problem can occur as a result of interference from subfield or character formatting codes like |*xx{yyy}*|. And the same problem occurs with respect to diacritics, which cannot be easily omitted. So searching for *wasabe* will not work if the form in the database is *wasábe* or *wasǫbe*. In a more general fashion, even differences in segments can get in the way. Why shouldn't *wasabe* match *wasape,* and so on? In fact, the truth is that linguists can easily find uses for much more powerful searching tools than currently exist. Shoebox has taken some steps in this direction, by allowing the definition of sets of characters, but not enough, and specialized solutions for linguists are less useful than they might be if they are restricted to particular applications and not available in all applications on a system.

7.2. EVALUATING THE EXPERIENCE.   Before we conclude, we want to comment on two more topics: the concept of team editing and the barriers

---

14. It almost goes without saying that we have also not used any of the standard programming project tools for version control.

to final printing and dissemination of this magnificent product. As most readers probably know, the construction of a dictionary by a team, while normal for such projects as the standard reference dictionaries for European languages, is unusual for "exotic" languages. Naturally, the images of all the disasters of committee-created monsters spring readily to mind. However, in this case there seemed to be no other way to follow up on the 1984 workshop to ensure that we would some day get a dictionary, since both Rankin and Carter, the initiators of the work, had the reputation of waiting until everything was perfect before sharing anything with the rest of us.

In the CSD project, Rankin and Carter are the main lexicographers. Jones was added because of his background in historical linguistics and his crucial knowledge of the northern languages, which were unknown to the rest of us. Koontz was added to the project because of his long-standing interest in the reconstruction of the morphology of the family and because of his computer expertise.

Rood's role is pretty exclusively that of administrator and overseer— fund-raiser, red-tape cutter, and, once in a while, umpire. The personalities of the team members make or break the ability of the team to succeed, and the project manager will always be grateful for the willingness of this team to compromise for the sake of the project. Jones has never complained to Rood about anything, and although both Carter and Rankin have strong opinions about how to reconstruct certain phenomena, they have been able to come to compromises that allow the project to move ahead. Whenever there is a disagreement that does not permit compromise, both sides of the story are told at the relevant entry in the dictionary. Amazingly, there are not very many of those. We should probably emphasize that we are reporting results here; Rood was not usually in the same room in which the discussions that led to the compromises took place, but he never saw any blood, though there were sometimes some scowls.

A major strength of the team concept is the depth of the knowledge that informs the final decisions. Without Jones's specialized understanding of Hidatsa and Crow and his interest in working on their relationships with each other and the rest of the family, we would have had little hope of giving those languages their proper place in the reconstructions. Rankin knows Dhegiha equally deeply, and Carter's specialized knowledge of Mandan and Dakotan fills in details on that end. Both Carter and Rankin have worked extensively with the Southeastern languages to the extent that their documentation permits, and Koontz added not only Omaha-Ponca but also some understanding of Winnebago to the group. Thus we covered the family; no one working alone could have done this much in this length of time. So, if we were asked whether this approach is wise and workable, we would have to answer a resounding "Yes, if . . ."

It is certain that the results of this project are here sooner and stronger because of the multiple contributions from the team.

Naturally, there have been other contributions, mentioned above, but the integration of these contributions remains the achievement of the editors. Finally and importantly, we need to emphasize that Jule Gomez de Garcia has played a major role at various points in this project, although she was nominally hired for data entry. For at least two years, she continued her work without any pay whatsoever when the funding was low, and in many cases her skill in following the garbled directions of the editors saved us lots of time and backtracking. We have saved this mention of Jule's special contributions until last so it will be remembered.

So why hasn't the Comparative Siouan Dictionary been published yet? We have mentioned the perfectionist traits of the editors, and these tendencies will require a fair amount of further editing. Rood still needs to write an introduction and sketch of Siouan structure. The presentations at various Siouan and Caddoan conferences over the past two decades, though, constitute a start toward those introductory chapters, and the polishing and cleaning continue on the plains of Colorado, Kansas, Nebraska, and North Dakota. We are fairly confident that "Carter, Jones, Rankin et al." will be available for your perusal early in the new millennium.

FOUR

Specific Projects
and Personal Accounts

CHAPTER TWELVE

Writing a Nez Perce Dictionary

Haruo Aoki

A dictionary does not suddenly appear out of the clear blue sky. Behind the printed pages are the lexicographers who wrote them, and they have their own views on language, which are closely associated with their linguistic history. As the dictionary writer's experience is bound to leave some imprint on his work, I should summarize my language experiences, which can be characterized by two major themes: collection and use of many dictionaries in a multilingual and multidialectal environment; and sensitivity to the social and linguistic barriers in doing fieldwork and organizing lexical information for dictionaries.

1. AUTHOR'S LINGUISTIC HISTORY.   I was born in 1930 in the port town of Kunsan, on the west coast of the Korean peninsula, a colony of Japan until 1945. In the 1930s about 60 percent of Kunsan's population was Korean and 40 percent Japanese. I was born and raised in the section of the town where Korean and Japanese small store owners lived along with some Chinese silk merchants and one Russian tailor. I heard all these languages but spoke Japanese. At home many of the major dialect types of Japanese were spoken. My grandfather spoke the Osaka dialect. My grandmother spoke a dialect of the island of Shikoku. My father spoke the outlandish dialect of Nagasaki, and my mother spoke a refined dialect of western Honshu. Much of our dinner conversation was about different names in Japanese dialects for the same thing. At school we spoke Standard Japanese, which served as a lingua franca for children who had different dialects spoken at home.

In 1945, when World War II was over, all the Japanese had to leave Korea, and I finished high school in Nagasaki Prefecture and majored in English at Hiroshima University. On graduation in 1953, I was selected as a Fulbright Scholar and studied at UCLA (M.A., English) and Berkeley (Ph.D., linguistics).

2. DICTIONARY EXPERIENCE. The first dictionary I owned was a small (about 5 × 7 inches), one-inch-thick Japanese language dictionary I received as an award from Kunsan Elementary School when I finished the sixth and last year. I did not use it very much except to check the accuracy of my cursive style in writing Chinese characters.

The second dictionary I had was an English-Japanese dictionary that my parents bought for me when I entered Kunsan Middle School, where I started my first classes in a foreign language. This was my first bilingual reference work. It had entry or headwords in conventional English spelling, followed by the pronunciation, in the familiar square brackets, in the International Phonetic Alphabet mostly following Daniel Jones (in 1942 few dictionaries in Japan recorded American pronunciation), word classes such as nouns and verbs, and glosses in Japanese. I used this dictionary more than the first but not very heavily, because the glossary appended to our English textbooks was sufficient for most of the dictionary work.

Courses in Chinese classics in middle school meant I had to use Chinese-Japanese dictionaries. The one I used had a triple look-up system: by pronunciation, by the shape of the Chinese character, and by its meaning. My copy was well worn before the end of the first year from my efforts to read selections from Confucius and Mencius.

At college I started to use monolingual English dictionaries, just to get practice in reading definitions in English. I bought one written by a Japanese lexicographer and later obtained a copy of the *Concise Oxford Dictionary* pirated somewhere in Southeast Asia; it was the only kind available in Hiroshima in the late 1940s. To satisfy the undergraduate foreign language requirement, I took French and German, but the dictionaries I had to buy for these courses were not substantively different from the bilingual dictionaries I was already familiar with.

Sanskrit courses I had at Berkeley required a novel use of dictionaries or of procedures before looking things up in a dictionary. In a Sanskrit text there are long strings of words glued together by sandhi rules, and they have to be separated into words before one can find them in a dictionary. What was involved in ungluing was basically the reverse application of procedures that glued the words together. Sanskrit provided a chance to think about lexicographic organization in a language with a touch of polysynthesis, where the most expedient linguistic unit to be dealt with was not coterminous with the word.

My interests expanded to a few etymological dictionaries, such as Akiyasu Tōdō's *Kanji Gogen Jiten* (Chinese Etymological Dictionary), which is in reality a study in the interrelationship of graphemes and word families, and Julius Pokorny's *Indogermanisches etymologisches Wörterbuch* (Indo-European Etymological Dictionary).

Berkeley courses in Native American languages gave me a chance to use dictionaries of these languages and weigh advantages and disadvantages of different approaches. I found dictionaries with abstract notations, which are the fruits of careful and involved analysis, useful when accompanied by phonetic notations that are closer to the actual pronunciation.

Then, as my teaching and research continued, my dictionary holdings began to diversify. They included a multiple-volume dictionary of modern Japanese, another set of volumes organized by historical period, and a third set of dialect words accompanied by linguistic atlases of Japan. I came to favor dictionaries with citations from various genres of literature and historical records. I also came to notice shortcomings in some of the dictionaries. For example, even a fairly large dictionary such as the twenty-volume *Nihon Kokugo Daijiten* (Big Dictionary of Japanese [Tokyo: Shōgakukan, 1972–76]) had the frustrating feature of not providing internationally useful frames of reference such as the scientific names for biological items and chemical formulas for traditional substances. I never made a list of features that an ideal dictionary should contain. But I would not be surprised if various sources of frustration in my earlier experience with dictionaries had some influence on what I did later.

3. FIELDWORK.   While I was a graduate student at Berkeley (1958–65), I took courses in Native American languages and a two-semester field method course and worked as a research assistant for Professor Mary R. Haas, Director of the Survey of California and Other Languages. The assistant's work involved typing Hans J. Uldall's Nisenan notes and Edward Sapir's notes on Takelma.

In 1960 Dr. Merle W. Wells, Archivist of the Idaho Historical Society in Boise, came to Berkeley to look for a linguist to record native languages of Idaho, which included the Nez Perce language. Haas asked me if I wanted to study Nez Perce. I was not sure if I was good enough for the job, and I consulted Professor William F. Shipley and fellow students Shirley Silver, Catherine Callaghan, Wick Miller, and Allan R. Taylor, and with their encouragement, I decided to take on the work. After the spring semester of 1960 ended, I drove to Boise, then on to Lewiston.

Usually, fieldwork means gathering data in the field as in sociology and anthropology. But in linguistics the fieldwork situation is a bit different in that it requires, more like language classes, long hours of contact with a few teachers.

At Lapwai, where the Nez Perce tribal offices are located, I was introduced to a ninety-one-year-old elder, but he had a hearing problem. Next,

I was introduced to another man in his seventies, but he had too many things to do and summer was the time to do them. Then I was told to come up the Clearwater River and search for teachers in the Kamiah-Kooskia area. The name Harry Wheeler was mentioned, and I drove to his home at Stites. He had had a stroke and needed the assistance of his wife, Ida, in getting around and also to repronounce words that he could not enunciate clearly because of his stroke-induced speech impediment.

During my search for language teachers in Lapwai and Kamiah, the two Nez Perce population centers in Idaho, I learned that it was impossible to find someone who could drop everything for three months in the summer to teach their language to a beginner. The young and able-bodied people were busy working, and the elderly had health problems.

I wrote to Haas in Berkeley describing the difficulty I was having finding teachers and asking for her opinion on the advisability of working with two teachers at once since the arrangement would eat up the budgeted allowance faster than planned. Until I received her authorization, I decided to study with both Harry and Ida but at the half schedule of four hours a day (although there were difficulties even with this arrangement). Harry and Ida's second son fought Japanese in the Philippines, and judging by the way our topics of conversation went, it was clear that Harry regarded me as the enemy who shot at his son. In contrast, Tim, his son and a veteran of the Pacific war, greeted me with a firm handshake and a ready smile.

In 1960 we had no battery-operated tape recorder, and there was no electricity at Harry's house at Stites. So I picked a motel in Kooskia, closest to his house, and provided taxi service between Kooskia and Stites before and after our sessions. After the first session I started copying Nez Perce words and the English glosses on 3 × 5 cards: *ná:qc* and 'one' on a card and another card with the same entry. I alphabetized the first card by Nez Perce and the second set by English gloss. Thus the Nez Perce–English and English–Nez Perce dictionary was born in a hot motel room in Kooskia, Idaho.

I was concerned that four hours a day might not be enough to get the work done. However, in the first ten minutes, I piled up a healthy number of questions to resolve: for example, the extent and operation of vowel harmony, numeral classifiers, sound symbolism (Aoki 1994b), and the quinary system; and exploration of a six-way contrast of velars and postvelars.

Two weeks into the fieldwork the Wheelers decided to go to Talmaks, a Presbyterian summer camp, which was to last for two weeks in the tribal pine forest near the town of Cragmont. Harry's father had been one of the first ordained Nez Perce Presbyterian ministers. I already had spent nine days looking for a teacher and could not afford two more weeks of no work. So I decided to go also.

Talmaks turned out to be a version of a "sun dance," which is a summer ceremony observed among the native peoples of the Plains consisting of usually eight days of ritual smoking, fasting, and penance through self-torture. The ceremony was modified by missionaries, who were unhappy with certain features of the original practice. The two-week-long gathering had an aspect of social reunion free from the frequent interference of the workplace. One of these social visits from Harry's old acquaintances gave me a glimpse of tribal politicking.

There was a tribal elder who was reported to have translated a *Webster's* English language dictionary into Nez Perce. He was older than Harry, and Harry told me that when he was a boy at the Indian boarding school dormitory, this older boy used to beat him up whenever Harry spoke Nez Perce. The English language was "the language" of the boarding school, and the teachers enforced the "English only" policy by corporal punishment administered by themselves and by the deputized older students. This elder paid Harry a visit and told him that I was a Japanese spy trying to steal the Nez Perce language for the next war. The story of the Navajo "code talkers'" contribution to victory in World War II was understandably widespread among Native Americans and was in the background of this man's allegation.

Fortunately for me, after the first two weeks of work Harry had arrived at the conclusion that I had little to do with the war with Japan, and I had not shot at his son. Harry said he told this man that he was wrong, that I was not a Japanese spy, and that he was going to keep on helping me learn the Nez Perce language regardless of his objections. This summer camp gave me many opportunities to witness signs of jealousy and factional infighting and also made me realize how important it is to find a teacher who is impartial and aware of the significance of the fieldwork to preserve the Nez Perce language.

In the second summer, Harry's failing health and greater involvement with religious activities necessitated that I look for another teacher. Again I was fortunate that Mrs. Elizabeth P. Wilson decided to teach me. I would get up in the morning and drive from my motel to her house on the outskirts of the town of Kamiah, Idaho. Typically, we would work together until noon and then she would invite me to have lunch with her. After lunch, she made phone calls to her friends and I looked over my notes in the tepee pitched in her front yard. Then we worked together until five o'clock.

This routine was punctuated by various other activities. We traveled to Musselshell to dig camas and camped for days. After the morning's digging, she cleaned camas as I asked her questions about words and their meanings. She was well aware of the pitfalls of one-to-one translations. Typically, we would come across a Nez Perce word and spend some time pinning down its correct pronunciation. Then she would give an English equivalent. Finally, she would ask me to come up with some synonyms for that equivalent until she picked a few candidates that were more or less close to the Nez Perce original. Talk about a "walking dictionary"!

She was half Nez Perce, and some jealous members of the tribe tried to spread the rumor that "full-blooded" members have better knowledge of things Nez Perce. She paid no attention to such rumors and continued to preserve the Nez Perce side of her cultural heritage as few others did. For example, although a growing number of her tribal friends relied on the local supermarket supplies, she was one of the dwindling number of people who still harvested camas and made dried meat. So I dug camas, helped her bake it in an earth oven, helped her cut up deer meat into thin strips, and tended the fire while we smoked deer meat in the tepee.

When I was transcribing and translating the coyote stories, Mrs. Wilson used to invite her lady friends and me to dinner. I was asked to read my transcription. At that time there were not many television sets in homes in the area, and my reading provided the evening's entertainment for her guests—and a marvelous opportunity for me to spot my mistakes, which often supplied more seeds for amusement. Pretty soon I knew, by the guests' laughs, when I had inadvertently mispronounced something and said a dirty word. Later I checked these words with other teachers and entered them in the file.

4. USER PROJECTION. Dictionaries take different forms depending on the expected user. If the users know the language, probably they need no dictionary to speak the language. For thousands of years speakers of Nez Perce and languages ancestral to it managed beautifully without a dictionary. In languages such as Chinese and English, with writing conventions not closely related to actual pronunciation, people use dictionaries to make sure they have the correct radicals or to check the spelling. Since there is no long-standing orthographic convention in Nez Perce, there is little need for a native speller's dictionary unless it is to remember a word that one has forgotten.

Because of these conditions of use, for a native speaker the gloss of an entry may even be a picture. For example, in an English–Nez Perce dictionary (1) and Nez Perce–English dictionary (2), we could have entries as follows:

(1) mushroom n.
(2) n. mushroom

But if the user is not a speaker of Nez Perce, a more helpful device is needed. This is all the more important today because a steadily decreasing number of the Nez Perce people are native speakers.

After my stay among the Nez Perce speakers I gathered that even among the people who are legally members of the tribe, the number of native speakers was declining at an accelerated speed. Under these circumstances a dictionary should not be a gathering of pictures and mnemonic scratchings. Information should be given fully, and if it erred, it should be on the side of redundancy and obviousness. Thus *Webster's New World Dictionary* (Third College Edition) is intended for native as well as nonnative speakers of English, but even this dictionary, under 'see', for example, explicitly gives *saw*, *seen*, and *seeing*, as under 'potato', it provides -*toes* as the plural ending.

As I assessed the situation, two points became obvious. First, I needed to furnish information that was as exhaustive as possible. Second, I wanted to make the material accessible to a wide range of people. The users would not necessarily be linguists. They were more likely to be tribal members, historians, anthropologists, screenwriters, and interested ordinary people. Thus I wanted to keep linguistic terms to a minimum and avoid unfamiliar and pedantic-sounding terms, even if they were more accurate and descriptive.

There is another matter related to this: the choice of symbols to represent esoteric sounds. I thought that because none of the previous dictionaries gave detailed information on the Nez Perce pronunciation, a new work should provide this. Even if not all users needed precise information on pronunciation, I wanted it to be available for people who did. I therefore decided to identify each sound by using Americanist phonetic symbols. If, as a result, some user is annoyed by the array of symbols such as *k*, *q*, *k'*, and *q'*, that person can choose to pronounce all of them using the *k*-sound in *king* (known as speaking Nez Perce "with a white man's accent"). In effect, this is all that previous dictionaries enabled a nonnative speaker to do, and it should be fine, so long as one is aware that what he is doing is omitting phonetic distinctions.

5. GATHERING THE MATERIAL.

5.1. EVERYDAY LEXICON.
At first, I gathered lexical items by association. Harry and Ida Wheeler went through names of animals that they could think of one day, plants the next day, and so forth. At the same time I kept on revising earlier analyses in phonetic, morphophonemic, morphological, syntactic, semantic, and pragmatic areas. Subsequent data gathering covered basic vocabulary used in daily conversations. I also recorded words used in talking to babies and small children.

5.2. NONEVERYDAY LEXICON.
One question I faced was how to handle expressions that, though not found in everyday conversation, did occur in legends and statements of folk beliefs. One example is the pair *ʔiscilépetis* and *ʔisciqótqot*.

These words are found in one folktale recorded by Phinney (1934: 314) and Aoki and Walker (1989: 55 ff.). They are words used in a Nez Perce oral narrative by Coyote when he is flying with the Goose brothers. When he wants to fly lower, he uses the first word, and when he wants to gain altitude, he utters the second. Those of us who are not Coyote are not likely to use these words every day.

A somewhat different example is the following pair: (3) contains a third-person subject and is found in everyday conversation, but (4), which contains a first-person subject, is not.

(3) *hé:t'ilpse*   I am crazy ("It makes me crazy")
(4) *ʔé:t'ilpse*   ("I make him/her crazy")

The Nez Perce tradition is that the spirit of the dead causes insanity. Thus unless you are dead, you cannot say (4). I decided to include information like this in the dictionary.

In 1966 and 1967, Deward E. Walker made a tape recording of Nez Perce coyote stories by two master storytellers, Sam Watters and Elizabeth Wilson. I transcribed the tape, and Elizabeth Wilson was vital in preparing the translation, which was published in 1989 as *Nez Perce Oral Narratives*. This constituted the first group of myth vocabulary added to the data for the dictionary.

5.3. REEXAMINING EARLIER DATA.   The first recorded encounter of Nez Perce people with Euro-Americans is the 1804 meeting with Lewis and Clark. The first century of contact produced a handful of grammars and a dictionary. The second century produced an excellent collection of folktales by Archie Phinney (1934).

I went over all of the mythological texts in Phinney's 488-page *Nez Percé Texts* (1934) and checked the pronunciation (Phinney did not consistently mark glottalized nasals, liquids, and semivowels) and other related forms. When an item was no longer recognized by my teachers, I simply recorded these items exactly as given by Phinney. Fortunately, these were not numerous, no more than twenty morphemes. Considering the non-everyday nature of these lexical items, the low figure testifies to how little of the language's lexicon was lost between 1930 (Phinney collected his material in 1929 and 1930; see 1934: vii) and the 1960s among knowledgeable speakers.

Next, I examined the only Nez Perce dictionary in print, the 1895 *Dictionary of the Numipu or Nez Perce Language, Part I, English–Nez Perce* (part 2 of this work, presumably Nez Perce–English, never materialized: see Schoenberg 1966: 14, 38). On the title page the author is given as "a Missionary of the Society of Jesus, in the Rocky Mountains." Schoenberg (1966: 37) identified this missionary as Anthony Morvillo (1895). While

Phinney's collection of folktales is a Columbia University M.A. thesis prepared under Franz Boas, Morvillo's dictionary is a missionary tool with a heavily Latin framework. Indeed, his Nez Perce grammar published four years earlier is titled *Grammatica Linguae Numipu* (1891) and is written in Latin. The words in this dictionary required more extensive phonetic checking (Morvillo did not mark the distinction between glottalized and nonglottalized consonants). When a word was not recognized by any of my teachers I simply quoted it verbatim.

6. ORGANIZATION OF THE DICTIONARY.

6.1. PHYSICAL CONSIDERATIONS. The material to be included in the dictionary was considerable. At a draft stage the total number of double-spaced pages with numerous handwritten insertions exceeded two thousand. First, I wanted the dictionary to be in one volume, if possible; multiple-volume dictionaries are unwieldy. Second, considering that some of the users might be tribal elders (and my own eyesight was not getting any better) and that some phonetic symbols had small diacritic marks, I wanted to make the fonts as large as possible. Third, I wanted to use a heavy grade of paper. My copy of Morvillo's dictionary had yellowed pages with dark brown edges, and the paper had become so brittle that I had to be extremely careful in turning pages. Fourth, if possible, I wanted the dictionary to be hardcover. I did not think the binding of a paperback volume of more than one thousand pages would last. So I checked with the University of California Press, asked about the limit of page numbers for a volume to satisfy these conditions, and mentioned that the price should be set as low as possible. I was told that the number of pages was about 1,200 and the estimated price was about $70. Within these limits, I decided to use the largest possible font. My heart fell when the dictionary was published four years later and the price was set at a whopping $135.

6.2. FORMAT. There are certain ingredients commonly found in all bilingual dictionaries: the headword in the target language, designation such as noun, verb, and so forth (usually abbreviated *n, v,* etc.), and the gloss in a language more familiar to the user. There are also related words, noun forms for verbs, verb forms for nouns, forms with different prefixes or suffixes. For the benefit of those who were working on dictionaries under the Survey of California and Other Indian Languages, William F. Shipley wrote a style sheet in the 1960s outlining where to place what, down to how many spaces between what entries. In a word, the Shipley format is an "airy" one. Well-defined indentations mark the hierarchy of the subentries. I followed the practice, which was negatively reviewed by some (Bright 1994) and favorably by others (Kroeber 1995).

6.3. HEADWORD.   What unit to select for headwords is an important issue in a dictionary of a polysynthetic language, especially when there are prefixes in the system, as in Nez Perce. It was clear that selecting a word or a minimum free form, as in English dictionaries, fails to assemble related forms in one place. So I decided to place morphemes as the headwords.

6.4. GRAY AREAS.   Even with this focus on morphemic headwords, I encountered a number of difficulties with entries. The following are Nez Perce numbers:

ná:qc	one	ʔoylá:qc	six
lepít	two	ʔuyné:pt	seven
mitá:t	three	ʔoymátat	eight
pí:lept	four	k'úyc	nine
pá:xat	five	pú:timt	ten

While this appears to be a partial quinary system (base five, reusing the numerals at six), I saw little advantage in adhering strictly to the principle of morpheme-as-headword. By considering the second parts of 'six', 'seven', and 'eight' as variants of 'one', 'two', and 'three' respectively, we might reduce the number of headwords, but we then put entries for 'one' and 'six', for example, under one headword, thus creating a large and heterogeneous entry. In these cases I made multimorphemic headwords and cross-referenced them: ʔoylá:qc cross-referenced to ná:qc.

6.5. CITATIONS.   I used four sources to illustrate headwords, providing sentential examples: Phinney 1934, field notes 1960–70, Aoki 1979, and Aoki and Walker 1989. For conversational examples, the field notes and a part of Aoki 1979 were useful. Phinney 1934, a part of Aoki 1979, and Aoki and Walker 1989 yielded examples of usage in coyote stories.

6.6. PERIPHERAL ENTRIES.   Besides the basics of Nez Perce headwords and English gloss, I tried to incorporate information on word history when available. Since there was no modern published dictionary of Sahaptin, Nez Perce's sister language, during the time of my dictionary preparation, I made use of preliminary versions of *Sahaptin Animal Terms* and *Sahaptin Plant Terms* compiled by Eugene S. Hunn (which later appeared as appendices in Hunn et al. 1990) and his *Nch'i-Wána* (The Big River) (Hunn et al. 1990). I made no pretense of making an exhaustive or extensive study. Occasionally I included forms in other neighboring languages for comparison, as I had done previously (Aoki 1975).

I was not sure glosses like 'guardian spirit' were sufficiently informative to the user unfamiliar with the Nez Perce culture. I tried to add ethnographic information and in some cases, such as camas baking, line drawings to provide visual aids. I prepared line drawings, ranked them in order of priority, and filled blank spaces at the end of a letter.

For the names of plants and animals, I tried to cite scientific names. I thought I should be extra careful in this area, because I was raised in cities and in a different part of the world. I decided to include illustrations in case the users were as unfamiliar with the flora and fauna of the Nez Perce country as I was.

In cases of small plants, I collected the specimens, placed them in my notebooks, and asked for identification at the university herbarium at Berkeley. For large trees, I was fortunate to have as a teacher Archie Lawyer, a native speaker with an M.A. in forestry from the University of Idaho. For animals and birds, I showed regional illustrated guidebooks to Harry Wheeler, who had hunting experience. For fish names, Eugene Wilson, a son of Mrs. Wilson and an avid fisherman, provided information. Alan G. Marshall shared his ethnobotanic and ethnozoological notes with me.

Scientific names are not the answer to everything. Some plant and animal designations reflect semantic domains that sometimes combine scientific categories and sometimes cut across different families. In these cases 'any prickly plant' and 'animals with paws', while appearing nonscientific and imprecise, struck me as the more accurate glosses. In addition, I entered comments on the uses that plants were put to, when such information was available.

7. SPELLING AND POLITICS. In a language that has many speakers, the question of what single individual has the ultimate last word on the language does not arise. If someone proposed a law stating that all studies of the Japanese language, including dictionary writing, should be examined and approved by the "Japanese Language Person," appointed by the Prime Minister, or by the Emperor of Japan, the chance of his being taken seriously would be slim. But I was to find out that the situation with Nez Perce was different.

In 1962 I sent an offprint of my first article, "Nez Perce and Northern Sahaptin: A Binary Comparison" (Aoki 1962), to the Chairman of the Nez Perce Tribe. The addressee did not respond, but a member of the tribe named Slickpoo wrote and mentioned that he did not like the Americanist phonetic symbols that I used. I wrote back and said I would wait for the tribe's writing system. My *Nez Perce Grammar* was completed in 1965, but it was not published until 1970, after a fruitless wait for the tribal recommendation of an orthographic system.

After completing the grammar, I published *Nez Perce Texts* in 1979. These were stories I collected during my work with Harry Wheeler, Ida Wheeler, and Elizabeth Wilson.

I then began work on the materials that were eventually published as *Nez Perce Oral Narratives* in 1989. In this case Deward Walker had tape-recorded coyote stories in 1966–67, and I did the translations, checking the accuracy with Elizabeth Wilson. When I had completed the transcription and interlinear English translations for these stories, the Tribe asked me to make the free English translation available to its publication project. This became a basis for *Nu Mee Poom Tit Wah Tit (Nez Perce Legends)*, published in 1972 by the Tribe. In the book's introduction, there is the following discussion of the writing system used in the volume.

> The method used to write the occasional Nez Perce words appearing in these legends has been developed by Allen P. Slickpoo, a member of the Nez Perce tribe. It is a practical method quite similar to the earlier missionary methods. Although Slickpoo's method does not yet present all the significant distinctions found in the language, such as glottal stops, it does provide an easily used method of pronouncing words which would otherwise be difficult for English speakers. Vowel sounds employed in the Slickpoo method are /i/, /e/, /a/, /u/, and /o/. Because some vowels in Nez Perce are long, some words contain sounds written as /ee/, /oe/, or /ah/. In such cases the second letter signifies that the vowel sound is held for about twice the length of the short version of the vowel. Consonant sounds used in the Slickpoo method are /p/, /t/, /ts/, /k/, /h/, /kh/, /hk/, /l/, /m/, /n/, /s/, /w/, and /y/. They generally resemble the English sounds rendered by the same symbols with the exceptions of /hk/ and /kh/. The /hk/ represents what linguists call a dorso-post-velic trill and to the uneducated ear sounds somewhat like a person clearing his throat. A softer version of the /hk/ is the /kh/, a sound linguists describe as a dorso-velic spirant. It is heard in the German word for I, *ich*. As an aid to pronunciation, Slickpoo also uses hyphens to divide Nez Perce words into more easily pronounced syllables. (Nez Perce Tribe 1972: xvii)

The 1972 introduction also states: "The tribe has not officially adopted a method of writing or spelling the language, which is rapidly becoming unknown among younger members of the Tribe" (p. xviii). There was no mention that more than half of *Nu Mee Poom Tit Wah Tit* was based on my work, and there was likewise no acknowledgment of Mrs. Wilson's involvement.

Because there was no officially adopted method of writing Nez Perce and the "practical method" used in the above tribal publication did not "present all the significant distinctions found in the language" (Nez Perce Tribe 1972: viii), I thought it was my responsibility to adopt a system that represented all the significant distinctions in the Nez Perce language. The work that provided the basis of *Nu Mee Poom Tit Wah Tit* was published with the transcription in the Americanist phonetic symbols and interlinear English translation as *Nez Perce Oral Narratives,* under the coauthorship of Walker and myself in 1989. Similarly, the *Nez Perce Dictionary* adopts the same transcription system. My reason for using the Americanist phonetic symbols is quite simple and straightforward; it is possible to convert phonetic symbols to any "practical" spellings, but conversion in the reverse direction is not possible, and we lose important information in the process.

Tribal reaction to the 1994 dictionary may be glimpsed from the following transcript of National Native News of Alaska Public Radio (APR) Network aired on May 17, 1994.

> *Steve Heimel of APR:* The good news is there's now a dictionary of the Nez Perce language. The bad news is that one of the few remaining speakers of Nez Perce says the author should have talked to him. He says the dictionary is flawed. John Masters of KBSU Boise reports.

> *John Masters:* Allen Slickpoo, Sr. says the dictionary contains many inaccuracies and could be confusing to young Nez Perce. For the past 34 years, Professor Emeritus Haruo Aoki of the University of California at Berkeley worked on the 1200 page dictionary, a project he began in 1960 by taping interviews with the tribal elders. Slickpoo says that Aoki made mistakes that could have been corrected if he had let someone from the tribe review the book before it was published.

> *Allen Slickpoo:* He more or less had kind of a different perception of what he was hearing from the people and consequently a lot of the words that he uses in his dictionary we have found to be in error.

> *Masters:* Slickpoo says neither Aoki nor the tribe have been in contact with one another to correct those errors. He says tribal members have not yet decided if they will use the book in Nez Perce schools.

> Reporting from Boise, I'm John Masters.

Since I did not have an opportunity to talk to John Masters, I would like to state a few relevant facts and figures. First, in 1960 my teachers were in their sixties, seventies, and eighties, at least a generation older than the current senior tribal members in 1994. Second, I consulted many more than just one member of the Nez Perce Tribe; if anyone took the trouble to read the preface of my dictionary, he or she would have counted ten teachers and, all told, forty-two members of the Nez Perce Tribe, including Al Slickpoo, who contributed.

What is noteworthy here is that three people, Steve Heimel of Alaska Public Radio Network, John Masters of KBSU Boise, and Al Slickpoo of the Nez Perce Tribe, passed judgment on a dictionary apparently without even reading the preface, which is only one page long. It is also noteworthy that words that had been alive and in use thirty years previously were now perceived as "errors" by the Tribal Ethnographer, an appointment that presumably would reflect a high level of knowledge of the tribal culture.

8. TECHNOLOGY AND DICTIONARIES. Dictionary writers' work is limited or expanded by the technology available to them. The way I started my fieldwork in 1960 probably did not differ much from the way the nineteenth-century Christian missionaries did, by way of pen and ink on paper. One major advantage I had was a magnetic tape recorder; a typewriter was another.

After 3 × 5 slips filled one, then two, and eventually ten file boxes, I looked into the possibility of using a personal computer, but the slow development of the capability to handle phonetic symbols in early models caused me to wait until the 1980s. Using a custom-made daisywheel in a mechanical printer and a customized conversion table in the word processor program called Volkswriter, I inputted the transcribed texts and produced the 630 camera-ready pages of *Nez Perce Oral Narratives* (Aoki and Walker 1989). Next, I inputted the lexical slips, which included forms from my field notes and those from Phinney (1934) and Aoki (1979). Electronically stored, the information was now available for computer manipulation. I cut up the texts and used them to illustrate the headword. Now it was not necessary to input the English–Nez Perce dictionary portion. Copying and pasting produced the English–Nez Perce index, and unlike the Nez Perce–English section, the work on the index took only two weeks. The PC had only 640 Kb, and the whole dictionary was on twenty 5-inch floppy disks.

Future dictionaries could add dimensions of time, color, and sound. Besides still photographs, moving pictures and animations can be used to illustrate verbs of motion, building of structures, and the working of contraptions. Visual aids combined with sound can create moving pictures to illustrate, for example, how to make elk whistles, prepare venison for smoking, bake camas in an earth oven, and tan deer hide. Various dance steps and movements might be illustrated by line drawings and by film strips of dancers. Audio buttons in a dictionary might provide pronunciation of headwords and furnish examples of how citations sounded as recorded by senior speakers, as well as traditional chants and songs. The incorporation of sound and moving pictures, already available on CDs for thriving languages, strikes me as particularly important in reference works for endangered languages and especially to keep the interest of young learners, who are carriers of the language to the future.

Compared to thirty years ago, someone starting a new dictionary of the Nez Perce language today would have a heretofore undreamed-of abundance of technology available. By contrast, what has become scarce is source material to work on, as the amount of language in actual use continues to decline.

CHAPTER THIRTEEN

On Publishing the *Hopi Dictionary*

Kenneth C. Hill

1. INTRODUCTION. The Hopi dictionary database corpus was closed in May 1996 after more than ten years' work. I submitted a camera-ready copy of the dictionary (Hopi Dictionary Project 1998) to the University of Arizona Press in spring 1997, in time for release in the fall. The dictionary—a massive work, consisting of 900 pages, in three columns, in 7-point type, with nearly 30,000 Hopi entries[1] and some 7,500 English-to-Hopi finder items, plus a grammatical sketch and end papers and illustrations—was advertised at $85 per copy.

The press release caused a great stir in the Hopi community. Leigh J. Kuwanwisiwma,[2] Director of the Hopi Tribe's Cultural Preservation Office (CPO), immediately challenged the Press to suspend publication until various questions could be resolved. The biggest problem for the CPO was that access to the dictionary was to be permitted to non-Hopis. The dictionary had already been printed (though the printed sheets were not yet cut and bound), but the University of Arizona Press halted the manufacturing process until some meeting of minds might be achieved.

I had known clouds were on the horizon (see below), and I had not alerted the Press to them. I thought (foolishly, in retrospect) that once the dictionary was produced, as a fait accompli, complications would be minimal. How wrong I was.

---

1. There is a total of 29,394 entries, of which 23,994 are "main entries"; the rest are "cross-reference entries."

2. = Ku.**wan**.wi.siw.ma. I provide standardized (dictionary) spellings for Hopi names as needed. As a guide for pronunciation, I boldface the stressed syllable and separate the syllables with periods.

This is an account of the experience of getting the Hopi dictionary published. The story is from my own records and from my own point of view, and my memory may be somewhat selective. I hope I have not unfairly mischaracterized anything regarding the University of Arizona Press or the Hopi Tribe or any individual.

2. BACKGROUND. Hopi suffers greatly from the loss of younger speakers. Many youngsters growing up in the Hopi world are learning English rather than Hopi as their first language. The reasons for this are various and are much the same as the reasons other indigenous languages are in decline; these reasons do not need to be reviewed here in any detail, being common to almost all indigenous communities in the face of culturally, economically, and communicationally dominant languages, especially in our modern society of mass communication. But, as is the case with many other communities similarly afflicted with language loss, many senior members of the Hopi community, concerned about the problem, yearn for some way to counter this tendency.

The Hopi Dictionary Project was formed under the idea that a comprehensive dictionary of the Hopi language, presented as a serious reference work, might motivate Hopis to recognize their language as one of respectable status among the written languages of the world. Such a dictionary would also provide the scholarly community with a much-desired linguistic resource.

Hitherto, Hopi has not been a written language except by scholars. Early efforts by ethnographers and linguists, and by Hopi individuals, were various and often confusing. Lexical studies had been of limited scope, failed to represent important phonological features, and contained serious inaccuracies (e.g., Voegelin and Voegelin 1957; Albert and Shaul 1985; Seaman 1985).

Although literacy in Hopi was minimal in 1985 when we first put the project together, Hopi orthography had achieved a certain stability over the previous couple of decades through a New Testament translation (American Bible Society 1972), the publication of various folkloric collections, and a variety of technical linguistic studies. For the dictionary, we had to expand the existing spelling system to include marks for falling tone (grave accent), exceptional stress (acute accent),[3] and hiatus between consonant groups that might otherwise be understood as units (i.e., *k.w* = /kw/ but *kw* = /k^w/, *t.s* = /ts/, *ts* = /t^s/). The glottal stop is represented by the apostrophe. In Hopi spelling, *u* represents the high back unrounded vowel [ɯ], that is, the vowel represented as

3. Grave accent plus acute accent on the same vowel is represented as circumflex accent; e.g., *mansâltsoki* (man.**sâl**.tso.ki) 'apple tree'.

i ("barred *i*") in most Uto-Aztecan studies, and *ö* represents the low front rounded vowel [œ].

3. ORIGINS OF THE PROJECT. The dictionary was conceived as both a scholarly reference work and as a tool to be used in efforts to revitalize the use of the Hopi language. The project came out of the Bureau of Applied Research in Anthropology at the University of Arizona (BARA), at the time under the direction of Carlos G. Vélez-Ibáñez.[4]

It was Vélez-Ibáñez who brought me into the project. He told me in fall 1985 of earlier attempts on the part of BARA to secure funding for a Hopi dictionary project from the National Endowment for the Humanities (NEH) that had failed (but apparently just barely) and urged me to try to put things together such that the NEH would fund such a project. I succeeded (even though it is painfully clear now that what I knew then was pathetically short of what I needed to know to get the dictionary accomplished). The project was funded by the NEH beginning in July 1986.[5]

My principal colleagues in the project at BARA were Emory Sekaquaptewa[6] and Mary E. Black. Ekkehart Malotki, at Northern Arizona University (Flagstaff), along with the late Michael Lomatuway'ma[7] and, later, Michael's widow, Lorena, also contributed to the project. Sekaquaptewa is a native speaker of Hopi and a member of the University of Arizona faculty. He also sits as a judge on the Hopi appellate court. Every spring semester Sekaquaptewa offers a course, "Hopi Language in Culture," in the Department of Anthropology.[8] Black is an experienced librarian and a longtime student of Hopi and coresearcher with Sekaquaptewa. Malotki is Professor of Languages at Northern Arizona University. He had published Hopi folklore in volumes containing Hopi stories in bilingual form (Talashoema 1978; Malotki and Lomatuway'ma 1984; Malotki 1985) and had also published two important theoretical monographs (Malotki 1979, 1983). He had compiled a working Hopi lexical file of some sixty thousand file slips and shared information from this file with the dictionary project and provided many new examples as he did additional fieldwork. Michael and

4. Now Dean of the College of Humanities, Arts, and Social Sciences, University of California, Riverside.

5. Grant no. RT-20713-86, renewed as NEH RT-21344.

6. = Si.**kya**.kwap.ti.wa.

7. = Lo.**ma**.tu.wa'y.ma. Some earlier spellings of Hopi, including American Bible Society 1972 and Malotki's works prior to the dictionary project, wrote <y'> for 'y. Etymologically and derivationally, -'y- is a reduction of -'i-.

8. In recent years, as more and more Hopi students attend the University of Arizona, Sekaquaptewa has been making a special effort to have them gain literacy in their own language. Of course, for Anglos, the course is mainly focused on gaining an understanding of an exotic grammatical system and of Hopi culture.

Lorena Lomatuway'ma were his sources of information on Hopi for the duration of the project.

I am a linguist mainly focused on Uto-Aztecan languages, having worked intensively with Tohono O'odham (Papago), Nahuatl (Aztec), and Serrano, and less so with Cahuilla, Gabrielino, and Huichol.[9] I came into the project with a serious interest in lexicography, which necessarily includes an interest in recording the minutiae of the facts of a language. As a pilot study for the Hopi dictionary, I compiled a preliminary dictionary of Serrano based on the file slips I had assembled for my dissertation (Hill 1967).[10] I started the beginnings of the Hopi dictionary based on the vocabulary of the teaching materials Sekaquaptewa was using in his course.

I was responsible for all technical aspects of the project, including software selection, database design, ways of dealing with a project based in different places (the University of Arizona at Tucson and Northern Arizona University at Flagstaff), plus typesetting and graphics.[11] I made the final decision regarding the form of each entry as well as the end matter.

Too many American indigenous languages have been represented in dictionary form as meager word lists. Even the most copious dictionaries of indigenous languages do not have the "look" of familiar English-language commercial dictionaries.[12] An appearance like that of a serious English-language desktop dictionary would signify language respectability to a community already literate in English (and the Hopi community is exactly that). Thus the printed appearance of the dictionary was an important concern.

The Hopi Dictionary Project was funded by the NEH division committed to materials access. This required that any publication from our project would necessarily be made accessible to the public at large. In this

9. Hopi is a member of the Uto-Aztecan language family. It is supposedly an isolate within the family, or at least within Northern Uto-Aztecan, but it is remarkably similar in many features to Serrano, on which I did my dissertation (Hill 1967).

10. Over the past few years, as I have gone back to review the Serrano material in light of the understanding I have gained from work on the dictionary, I have come to understand how very limited my ideas had been regarding Serrano.

11. Ken Gary, of San Diego, California, contributed many line drawings, the Arizona State Museum allowed access to photographs in their collection, and some book publishers allowed access to published illustrations. Many illustrations were scanned from physical objects, either items I collected in the field or cultural items that Sekaquaptewa made available to me. I learned a lot about computer graphics during the late period of the project.

12. E.g., Laughlin 1975; Thompson and Thompson 1996; Young and Morgan 1987. These dictionaries are excellent contributions with respect to the documentation of the languages involved, but their format is quite off-putting for the nonspecialist user, or at least the format makes the language look "exotic" with regard to the expectations of the nonlinguist dictionary user.

spirit, the project was able to generate matching funds from a variety of sources. Without additional funding the project would have foundered.

4. SOME CULTURAL CONSIDERATIONS.   We took great care that no dictionary entry or illustrative sentence should in any way compromise the Hopis' sense of religious propriety. Thus, for example, the dancers who appear in the sacred space in the plaza are throughout referred to as "kachinas," with no secular explanation. The names of myriad kachinas[13] are given in the dictionary, but the names in themselves are public knowledge. The dictionary exposes no content of any ritual. No sacred object is illustrated or described. Even though Sekaquaptewa, one of the senior editors, is a native speaker of Hopi and is involved with Hopi ceremonial life, sometimes there were items of this nature that he had to submit to our "usage panel" (see below) for review. All comments from the panel were taken seriously. As a consequence, we are confident that the dictionary contains no information in violation of Hopi ritual standards.

Further, in line with Hopi cultural prescriptions, we have backgrounded authorship. Within Hopi culture individuals are not supposed to seek personal aggrandizement. Accordingly, the cover and title page attribute authorship to the Hopi Dictionary Project. Advertising lists the authorship only as the Hopi Dictionary Project. Only later, in an internal page among the introductory materials, is the editorship spelled out, along with a list of other contributors to the volume, such as is done with commercial dictionaries.

5. THE PROJECT GOES AHEAD.   The project officially began July 1, 1986, with the onset of NEH funding. Soon after the initiation of funding, Vélez-Ibáñez called a news conference at which it was announced that any royalties from the sale of the dictionary would be turned over to the Hopi community. We worried that the Hopi community might believe that outsiders were out to make unfair monetary gain from Hopi culture. Thus we made it clear from the start that for us the dictionary was a scholarly venture and that nobody wanted to make money off the Hopis.[14] Eventually, the project was able to identify the Hopi Foundation, a charitable organization devoted to Hopi education, as an appropriate recipient of royalties.

13. The dictionary contains 367 "kachina" entries. Although some of them are synonyms, the large number attests to a cultural exuberance.

14. In our original grant proposal to the NEH, we expressed "the intention to use any early royalties resulting from the publication of the Dictionary to help support the subsequent publication of a reduced, practical dictionary for use in Hopi schools." But we soon recognized that, with a work of this sort, the expectation of "early" royalties is highly unrealistic.

The project was clear in its contact with the Hopi community all along that the dictionary would be an intellectual resource to be shared with interested scholars, whoever they might be. Matching funds, to be generated from private, that is, nongovernmental, sources, were required by our NEH funding. Such funds, of course, were dedicated to making a dictionary that would be available to the general public. It is doubtful if any of the private funders would have agreed to fund a dictionary that they would be restricted from seeing.

As the project got under way, there was a lot of productive interchange between the project and various Hopi Tribal entities and individuals. A joint venture of the project and the Hopi Health Department,[15] the *Handbook of Hopi Anatomical Terms* (Hopi Health Department 1988), was published in 1988. All the technology and much of the vocabulary involved originated within the project. The Health Department correctly gave the project and its editors full credit. The vocabulary of the *Handbook* is incorporated in the dictionary with appropriate acknowledgments. In 1989 the project was consulted by the Office of Hopi Lands to establish a consistent spelling for Hopi placenames. This was in connection with an important legal case trying to establish what the traditional Hopi connections were within lands in the western part of the Navajo Reservation.[16] The placename information was shared with the CPO.

As the project went along, various specialized printouts of dictionary entries were made for the CPO (which included the occasional Anglo researcher), and a few times a full interim printout of the dictionary was provided. The specialized printouts dealt with subjects such as agriculture, botany, geology, geography, and traditional games.

The project, through Sekaquaptewa's personal contacts, set up a usage panel of senior men. At first the panel volunteered their work. That is, they worked for no pay, just for the satisfaction that they were working with a project that might help their grandchildren's generation keep the Hopi language. Later they were paid under contract from the University of Arizona. When that funding ran out—during a time when I, as project director, was working full time at zero percent salary[17]—the CPO facilitated

15. Leon Nuvayestema (= Nu.**va**.yes.ti.ma), Director.

16. The "Navajo" Reservation, by a 1934 executive order, was set up "for the Navajos and such other Indians already located thereon" (Sekaquaptewa, pers. com.). Because the Hopis and the San Juan Paiutes had a presence there, the legal question about their claim on the land had arisen. The matter has yet to be resolved.

17. Mary Black was supported by emergency funding arranged by Vélez-Ibáñez; without emergency funding she would have to have left the project. Sekaquaptewa and Malotki remained on their regular university salaries. I was able to stay on because of personal resources.

the panel's work.[18] Still later, with renewed funding, the project was able to pay the panelists again, under contract from the University of Arizona, partly out of NEH funds and partly out of a grant to the project for that special purpose by the Wenner-Gren Foundation.

In summer 1991, with the full cooperation of the CPO, I presented the Hopi Dictionary Project at the Smithsonian Institution's Festival of American Folklife on the Mall in Washington, D.C. The CPO was represented at this event. The Hopis seemed pleased that knowledge about the dictionary was being made available to the thousands of people who attended. The publicly circulated statement on the dictionary included the information that it was being developed "in an effort to preserve and revitalize this important Southwestern language as well as to provide a scholarly reference for students of Native American languages." No Hopi objection to this purpose statement was offered. The Washington Hopi Representative (i.e., lobbyist)—himself a Hopi—expressed considerable sympathetic interest in the project.

The project was frequently visited at its headquarters at BARA by representatives of the Hopi community: teachers, judges, researchers, and Tribal officials: once by then Tribal Chairman Vernon Masayesva[19] along with members of his staff, a couple of times by the Director of the Office of Hopi Lands, and several times by Kuwanwisiwma.

The Tuba City high school, on the Navajo Reservation and adjacent to the westernmost community of the Hopi Reservation, Moencopi,[20] has both Navajo and Hopi students. Arizona has a foreign-language requirement for high school students; the only languages offered in the high school were Spanish and Navajo. Hopi parents wanted the curriculum expanded to include the teaching of Hopi. The high school principal consulted the project regarding getting the Hopi language into the curriculum there.

6. TROUBLES ON THE HORIZON. The Tuba City high school was not able to introduce the Hopi language into the curriculum. If a Hopi course were to be offered, under Arizona law, it would have to be available to any interested student. The idea that a non-Hopi might be able to study Hopi was unacceptable to some Hopi parents. The plan to offer Hopi instruction was abandoned.

In the mid-1990s the Native American Graves and Repatriation Act of 1990 became an issue:

18. We have no record of any financial arrangements for that work.
19. = Ma.**sa**.yes.va.
20. = Mùnqapi (= **Mùn**.qa.pi).

In a letter sent to a number of museums in 1994, Vernon Masayesva, chairman and CEO of the Hopi Tribe, formally states the tribe's interest in all published or unpublished field data relating to the Hopi, including notes, drawings, and photographs, particularly those dealing with religious matters. Chairman Masayesva additionally requests the immediate closing of these records to anyone who has not received written authorization from the Hopi Tribe (Brown 1998: 194).[21]

In 1994 Kuwanwisiwma called a meeting having to do with indigenous intellectual property rights. Feeling pressed with dictionary work, I did not attend, believing that the meeting would simply be confrontational and nonproductive.

7. THINGS COME TO A HEAD.   In late July 1997 I received a letter from Kuwanwisiwma expressing dismay regarding the advertising of the soon-to-be-released Hopi dictionary. He expressed several concerns: (1) the question of copyright: "at a minimum . . . a joint copyright [with the Hopi Tribe] should have been considered"; (2) the question of the representation of the Hopi consultants in the contractual relationship with the publisher, basically the question of "informed consent" to publish a dictionary that would be a "commercial product and made available to a wider audience of non-Hopis"; (3) the question of the allocation of royalties. He wanted the Hopi Health Department and the CPO, both of which had contributed to the project, to be included as beneficiaries. He objected to any efforts to "sell the Hopi language" and expressed dismay at the list price of $85 for the dictionary. His letter insisted that we "hold off on any printing, advertisement and distribution of this dictionary until these questions are discussed and resolved."

The Press immediately suspended production, awaiting developments. I responded to Kuwanwisiwma's letter, mentioning that copyright with the University of Arizona Board of Regents was strictly a legal technicality, that royalties were to be turned over to the Hopi community, and that every

---

21. Brown goes on to report:

The Hopi initiative was soon followed by a declaration issued by a consortium of Apache tribes demanding exclusive decision-making power and control over Apache "cultural property," here defined as "all images, text, ceremonies, music, songs, stories, symbols, beliefs, customs, ideas and other physical and spiritual objects and concepts" relating to the Apache, including any representations of Apache culture offered by Apache or non-Apache people (Inter-Apache Summit on Repatriation 1995: 3). This broad definition of cultural property presumably encompasses ethnographic field notes, feature films (e.g., John Ford's *Fort Apache*), historical works, and any other medium in which Apache cultural practices appear, whether presented literally or as imaginative, expressionistic, or parodic embellishments of concepts with which Apache identify (1988: 194).

effort had been made to keep the price of the volume to a minimum. I also expressed the belief that he would be pleased when he saw the final version of the dictionary.

8. THE MEETING IN PHOENIX.   After this interchange, there was a meeting in Phoenix on August 26, 1997, attended by myself, Sekaquaptewa, and Black, representing the dictionary project; by Stephen F. Cox, Director, and Christine Szuter, Editor, representing the University of Arizona Press;[22] by a representative of the Hopi Tribal Chairman's office; and by Kuwanwisiwma and nine other individuals who were introduced as representatives of a cross section of the Hopi community.

It was soon apparent that all the Hopi representatives invited to the meeting wanted to suppress publication of the dictionary if it were to be made available to non-Hopis. The issues raised earlier in Kuwanwisiwma's letter were raised again and again. The representatives repeatedly used technical terms such as "intellectual property rights," "informed consent," and "reciprocity" and the expression "sell the Hopi language." Kuwanwisiwma even claimed that one of the project's foremost panelists had agreed with him that the dictionary should be kept from non-Hopis.[23]

There were a number of other contentious points raised at the meeting, the main one being that the Hopi language is something that should be kept secret from all non-Hopis: Hopi is unique among the languages of the world—completely unlike English or other indigenous American languages. It belongs solely to the Hopis. It comes out of the unique history of the Hopi clans and is part of their privileged clan inheritance.

As "intellectual property," the Hopi language should remain under the control of some body authorized by the Tribe. At the meeting I understood this argument to mean that to get the dictionary published, each and every speaker (or at least everyone who had interacted with project personnel) was expected to be on record stating that their "intellectual property rights" were not being violated by the publication of the dictionary. Since the Hopi language was devised by no individual, living or dead, but solely by linguistic evolution within a whole community, the legal notion of an "intellectual property right" within American jurisprudence seems inappropriate.

22. Cox has since retired, and Szuter is the new Press Director.

23. Sekaquaptewa told me later that this was almost certainly in response to a leading question (Sekaquaptewa is a trained and experienced jurist). The panelist in question, Herschel Talashoema (Ta.**las**.ho.yiw.ma), has been a participant in publications available to the world at large (Talashoema 1978, 1993) and was well aware while working with the project that the dictionary was to be published both as a scholarly work and as a contribution to the needs of the Hopi community.

The "money" question arose many times. The dictionary makers, it was said, were unfairly trying to gain a lot of money from the linguistic knowledge of the Hopis. We explained several times that any royalties would be minimal and many years off and, in any case, would be consigned to the Hopi Foundation, not to the dictionary compilers. No one was prepared to believe us. Why should anyone be doing all this work if not to get rich off the Hopis? The idea of scholarship for its own sake was not a possibility acceptable to the representatives.

But designating royalties to the Hopi Foundation was not good enough. The royalties should go to the CPO. However, it would be unlawful to send royalties directly to that office since it is an entity fully funded by the Hopi Tribe. An outside organization such as the University of Arizona can contract with the Hopi Tribe itself but not with any of its secondary entities. Eventually it was agreed that half of any royalties should be assigned to the Hopi Foundation and half to the Hopi Tribe government.

Questions were raised that the knowledge of the Hopi contributors to the dictionary was being used without their "informed consent." That every one of the panelists had signed a contract for their work with the University of Arizona was not sufficient evidence to convince the representatives that the panelists knew what they were doing.

The representatives also demanded to inspect our contract with the NEH. We explained that no such contract existed, that one applies for funding under explicitly stated guidelines and that on receipt of funding the guidelines apply. In our case there was the explicit promise that we were to make the dictionary available to the public.

It was repeatedly stated that, in principle, there was no problem with publishing the dictionary, but if it were to be published, it should be made available only to Hopis. And a couple of representatives said that Hopis should not have to pay for it.

Some speakers said that publishing just about anything about Hopi culture was harmful. One woman claimed that the publication of a description of how to make piki (*piiki*), the Hopi wafer-thin corn "tortilla," was destructive. She mentioned that her daughter, on finding that the manner of making piki was described in a book, said that she therefore had no obligation to learn how to do that: it was all in the book. The same woman, on hearing that Sekaquaptewa was offering a Hopi language course at the University of Arizona, challenged: "Who authorized it?"

9. AFTER THE MEETING IN PHOENIX.   Cox responded with a letter (September 30, 1997) to Ferrell H. Secakuku,[24] Chairman of the Hopi

24. = Si.**kya**.ku.ku.

Tribe, replying to Kuwanwisiwma's concerns. He reiterated many of the points made in my letter of July 30. He pointed out that the Hopi Dictionary Project was careful to recognize the help of everyone who worked on the project and asked for advice regarding any omissions.

As for "informed consent," he noted that for the duration of the project, participants "have made a full and earnest attempt to inform everyone who participated in the project of their plan to publish the book."

Regarding copyright: "Copyright law protects the dictionary as a particular written expression—from the way it is organized to the way particular definitions are composed—from unwarranted copying. Copyright law is not meant to govern the use of any language, whether English, Japanese, or Hopi."

He recognized "that the Hopi language developed through the unique experience of the Hopi people" and went on to promise that the Press would include the acknowledgment in the front matter of the dictionary: "Everything in this dictionary derives from the deep historical experience and cultural knowledge of the Hopi people, however imperfectly their knowledge may be represented here."

He pointed out, regarding the availability of the dictionary, that the Press had committed to giving the Chairman of the Hopi Tribe twenty-three copies of the book to distribute to Hopi schools and Tribal Council members. Further, he promised that the Hopi Tribe could purchase additional copies directly from the Press through various arrangements at a 40 percent discount.

Regarding the question of access of non-Hopis to the dictionary, he noted that it was the mission of the Press, "as publishers of scholarly books, to publish responsible books for serious readers" and that the Press expected that the non-Hopi purchasers of the dictionary would be primarily scholars of linguistics and university libraries.

Royalties would be divided equally between the Hopi Foundation and the Hopi Tribal government. The Hopi Dictionary Project participants individually would receive no financial benefit from the publication of the book.

This letter went unanswered for some months because of political changes at Hopi.

On October 16, 1997, the CPO sent out a publicly circulated memorandum in which it was noted that the CPO's Cultural Advisory Team opposed the sale of the dictionary. Further, the CPO asked that the Hopi Tribe recognize the right of individual Hopis to "be independently represented by legal counsel if the Hopi Tribe is unable to or unwilling to contest the publication and sale of this dictionary."

There was no doubt in my mind, on receipt of this memorandum, that the publication of the dictionary was seriously threatened. Cox, however, was not disheartened and pressed on.

Also, during this time there was considerable independent activity on the part of the office of the Vice President for Research at the University of Arizona, exploring various avenues of possible compromise with the Hopis. Even though this effort seemed to threaten to muddy the water, it was clear that the university was taking the question of the publication of the dictionary quite seriously.

On February 23, 1998, the new Tribe Chairman, Wayne Taylor, Jr., responded to Cox apologizing for the delay in communications (political matters at Hopi had been in transition for several months). He specified two proposals: (1) that there might be a transfer of copyright to the Hopi Tribe and (2) that the Hopi Tribal Council would purchase all the printed dictionaries.

On March 5, 1998, after considerable discussion with the dictionary staff, Cox answered. It would be arranged that the copyright and all remaining inventory would be transferred to the Hopi Tribe on January 1, 2008. Cox also promised 23 free copies to the Hopi Tribal government and agreed to provide the Tribe with 500 copies at half price, noting, however, that this would result in a loss of nearly $10,000 to the Press. Of the press run of 1,500 copies, 21 copies would be reserved for the compilers, 50 copies for reviewers, 50 copies to be distributed among federal and state officials, the Arizona Board of Regents, and Press officials, and, significantly, "150 copies to fill orders on hand for the dictionary; 1,206 copies to fill anticipated orders." He reminded the Chairman that the University of Arizona Press is a not-for-profit publisher and that its books are priced accordingly.

Cox's proposal was accepted. On May 14, 1998, I received word from the Press that one of the first copies of the dictionary was being made available to me. I got it the next day. Immediately thereafter, a Hopi book-seller, Alph Secakuku,[25] bought multiple copies, wanting to beat the rush. Several of Sekaquaptewa's Hopi students received their own copies to show to their family and friends in the Hopi community.[26]

Since the dictionary's release I have heard absolutely no complaint about its publication. Now the entire first printing of 1,500 copies has sold out with only minimal advertising and the dictionary is going on to a second printing. The reviews I have seen (Bright 1999; McLaughlin 1999; Whiteley 1999; Dakin 2000) appeared only after the decision was made to issue the second printing.

25. Brother of former Chairman, Ferrell H. Secakuku.
26. Sekaquaptewa paid for those dictionary copies. It was his belief that once people saw our product they would not find it threatening but interesting and potentially useful. He was right.

10. SHOULD I HAVE BEEN WORRIED? In Sekaquaptewa's view, the opinions expressed by Kuwanwisiwma and the representatives at the meeting in Phoenix were not representative of the Hopi community. But, at least as I understood matters and as they had to be dealt with practically, Kuwanwisiwma was in a position of considerable power.

Once the dictionary was published, Malotki admonished me that I should have had much more faith in the University of Arizona. He suggested that the university simply would not abandon the results of a project the size of ours (more than $1 million of sponsored research plus contributions of faculty time and facilities). My own view of university priorities is more jaundiced. I have seen large-budget items abandoned that seemed to me to be more important to a university's future than the publication of the dictionary.

Further, there remain some feelings at Hopi against works such as the dictionary, not all of which were represented at the meeting in Phoenix. Some Hopis hold that if the Hopi language dies out and along with it all the ceremonial aspects of Hopi culture, so be it. That would signal an appropriate judgment from the spirit world that to the extent that the Hopis have fallen away from their past (virtuous) ways, they are unworthy and deserve the loss of their language and culture. Another view expressed by some Hopis is that since the Hopi language was not written traditionally, it should never be written.

All in all, I feel we were fortunate, in the end, that the University of Arizona Press remained steadfast and that we achieved publication of the dictionary.

CHAPTER FOURTEEN

Writing a User-Friendly Dictionary

Catherine A. Callaghan

1. INTRODUCTORY REMARKS. The guiding principle behind the lexicographer's work should be the Golden Rule; the author should ask what kind of dictionary he or she would want if forced to look up words in an unfamiliar language. Ease of reference and completeness of data are overriding principles. I am assuming the reader is a scholar with at least a minimal knowledge of linguistic terms. In my experience, all scholars labor under time constraints. Each precious hour spent deciphering a cumbersome alphabetical order is time wasted. I discuss the problems of devising a more general reference book for native speakers later in this chapter.

2. INTRODUCTION AND GRAMMATICAL SKETCH. The introduction to the dictionary should focus on cultural and historical information concerning speakers and include a bibliography. If the dictionary resulted from personal fieldwork, proper acknowledgment to consultants is necessary. If a dictionary derives from another scholar's field notes, the lexicographer should acknowledge this fact in a subtitle or consider making the fieldworker a coauthor. All abbreviations should be carefully defined either before or after the introduction, and the organizational principles underlying the entries should be spelled out.

A brief grammatical sketch is necessary to aid the reader in segmenting entries. The phonological section of this sketch should consist of a brief statement of the allophones of each phoneme, with reference to the closest English equivalent to aid the nonlinguist. Morphophonemes and morphophonemic rules should include examples. The morphological section should focus on basic nominal and verbal inflection plus the most common types of derivation. Tables and paradigms are especially helpful in the case of agglutinative or fusional languages, along with numerous illustrative examples.

Because theoreticians rarely become lexicographers, most dictionaries are essentially theory-neutral rather than venues for demonstrating prowess in handling the latest theoretical approach. I consider this tendency admirable. For one thing, such approaches quickly go out of fashion and would make the dictionary difficult to read for future generations of linguists. In the case of endangered languages, the dictionary may be the only modern data source of its kind available and should be accessible to as many people as possible.[1] In other words, it should be a complete reference source for books of a more specialized kind, such as dictionaries for native speakers or language learners.

3. ARRANGEMENT OF ENTRIES.   Entries should be arranged in alphabetical order according to the Roman alphabet, with additional symbols following the letter they most closely resemble. For example, č should follow c, ə should follow e, and so on. The advantage of this alphabetical order in terms of ease of reference greatly outweighs its disadvantages. Purists who think such an order unscientific or illogical should remember that the Roman alphabet is imprinted in our subconscious. Even if they are personally able to handle another order, such as labial stops followed by dental stops, followed by velar stops, followed by series of spirants, and so on, access is greatly slowed for large numbers of readers, including many linguists. I belong to this latter group, and I have wasted many valuable hours struggling with this type of ordering, which also renders the dictionary inaccessible altogether for nonlinguists.

Old word lists are frequently ordered semantically. This order was supposed to facilitate cross-linguistic comparison by allowing a reader quick access to potential cognates that had undergone meaning shifts, such as 'foot' to 'leg'. If such lists are of any length, one quickly wastes time trying to remember where the numerals are located or whether 'wing' and 'egg' count as body parts, food, or animal terms. Any advantage conferred by being able to compare 'foot' in one language quickly with 'leg' in a related language soon disappears.

It is especially deplorable when unpublished word lists are automatically published however the author chose to order them. I have never understood this practice or why modern editors feel they must honor the cumbersome choices of their predecessors. Reordering the entries as I have described might initially require more time, but future ease of reference makes this investment well worth the effort. In one case, I

---

1. Margaret Langdon (1996) has made these points eloquently, especially in regard to grammars.

reordered an entire list for my personal use. If the editor had done this chore, I and others would have saved considerable time.

4. ENTRIES AND SUBENTRIES.   The proper composition of entries and subentries is the hardest problem facing the lexicographer, and no single solution will fit all languages. I have been fortunate in my own research in that the Miwok and Costanoan languages have few prefixes except for easily segmentable pronominal prefixes in some languages, and even these could be considered proclitics. The philosophy I outline here has worked for me, and I describe it in the hope that it will aid others in choosing a framework for their dictionaries.

Entries consist of stems and affixes. Affixes should be written morphophonemically, with a statement of their allomorphs and distribution under the main entry, along with examples of words illustrating each allomorph. Each allomorph should also be listed elsewhere in proper alphabetic order and cross-referenced to the main entry.

A family of derivationally related stems should be listed under its simplest member. The main stem plus an inflectional affix, if any, would constitute a word. Part of speech and meaning (or meanings) should follow.

Complex stems should be listed in alphabetic order under the main entry, along with the part of speech, including the derivational category (causative, reflexive, etc.).

Example sentences can illustrate the range of meaning of each entry and subentry. Complete sentences are usually preferable to phrases, as there is less ambiguity.

Both main entries and subentries should be written phonemically. Many people argue for a morphophonemic transcription for the main entry, but that would require readers to carry morphophonemic rules in their heads when using the dictionary to look up words in texts. For similar reasons, I would not require that a main entry should necessarily consist of a root. The grammatical synopsis should help the reader to extract roots from these stems when necessary.

Stems that include derivational prefixes pose a special problem. I suggest that such stems be listed as subentries under a main entry, parallel to the treatment of stems with derivational suffixes. In English, the words *conceive, deceive, perceive,* and *receive* should be listed in that order under *-ceive,* with the hyphen indicating that the stem (or root) in question never occurs without a prefix.[2]

If the item is a known loanword, its source should be stated. It is especially important to flag loanwords from other aboriginal languages.

---

2. I have used the traditional spelling of English examples instead of phonemic transcription, which of course would be used in the type of dictionary I am describing.

Entirely too much genetic classification is proposed without first carefully sifting out such loans.

Plant and animal terms should be identified by genus and species if possible, but I have discovered the hard way that such identification is difficult for amateurs. Fortunately, C. Hart Merriam (1979) obtained wildlife terms in several central California Indian languages early in this century. While his phonetics were deplorable, his species identifications were largely accurate. Since he also gave the popular names, I could reelicit these terms in target languages and jog the consultant's memory with an approximate pronunciation if he or she failed to recall the item.

5. EXAMPLE ENTRIES AND DISCUSSION.   The following entries are from the *Northern Sierra Miwok Dictionary* (Callaghan 1987).[3] To facilitate discussion, I have segmented the morphs and included a morpheme-by-morpheme translation of example sentences.

5.1. SUFFIXES.

-aj- ns meaning obscure. Found in the names of plants, birds, insects, fish, animals, secretions, lake, field, shadow, and measles.

{-wa-} as, ns, and vs negative. {-wa-} is -wa- ~ -a- after -sHe-?- 'past tense'[4] (plus augment) and -wa- elsewhere. {-wa-} always follows augmented stems.

huŋe·-se-?-a-t. I didn't sit down: 'sit-past tense-aug.-neg.-I'
ne·?i· kawa·ju-?-wa-?. This is not a horse: 'this is horse-aug.-neg.-nom.'

5.2. WORDS.

cy·my- iV and tV (1) to climb (2) to ride (a horse, car)
cy·my-m mol·a-j. I'm climbing a white oak: 'climb-I white oak-obj.'
cy·my-· kawa·j-yj. He's riding a horse: 'ride-he horse-obj.'

3. Northern Sierra Miwok is a central California Indian language. *j* is [y], and *y* is [ɨ], *c* is [č], and · indicates length, which functions as a consonant for canonical purposes. //H// designates length when canonically permissible. In this regard, permitted syllable canons are CV and CVC, where C is any consonant (including ·) and V is any vowel. //Y// is *u* ~ *o* if the vowel of the preceding syllable is *u* or *o*. Otherwise, //Y// is *y*.

Abbreviations of Miwok languages are given in note 5. Additional abbreviations now follow: ns = noun suffix, as = adjective suffix, vs = verb suffix, aug. = augment, neg. = negative, nom. = nominative, iV = intransitive verb, tV = transitive verb, N = noun, adv. = adverb, obj. = objective, loc. = locative, all. = allative, dir. = directed action, impers. = impersonal, agent. = agentive, DU = recorded by Donald Ultan, PU = Proto Utian (Miwok-Costanoan), PCo = Proto Costanoan, PMis = Proto Sierra Miwok, PMie = Proto Eastern Miwok, PMiw = Proto Western Miwok, PMi = Proto Miwok, (J) = Jackson Valley dialect of Plains Miwok, (L) = Lockford dialect of Plains Miwok.

4. In this entry in Callaghan 1987: 241, -*sHe*- is incorrectly glossed as 'negative'.

cy·my-· le·ka-j. He's climbing on that tree: 'climb-he tree-obj.'
cy·my-· miš·i·n-ym. He's riding in a car: 'ride-he car-loc.'
cym-pa- tV dir. to climb after someone
　　cym-pa-t. He's climbing after me: 'climb-after-me'
cymy-n·a- N impers. agent. stepladder: 'something to climb on': 'climb-
　　impers. agent.'
cymyʔ-·a- N ladder: 'climb-ns'
cy·myʔ-·ajny- iV to ride around: 'ride-around'

5.3. DISCUSSION. -*aj* probably does not have full morphemic status, and it sometimes has a slightly pejorative connotation. Historically, it probably spread through the language by analogy. Examples are *py·laj-y-* 'field', *ṭiw·aj-y-* 'yellowhammer', and *ʔitkaj-y-* 'tears'.

//-sHe-// 'past tense in negative constructions' is *-se-* after consonants and *-s·e-* after vowels, since //H// represents length only when canonically permissible. An augmented stem consists of a stem plus *-ʔ*. Note that *-ʔ* is also the marker of the nominative case.

The examples under these entries were designed to illustrate their range of meaning. Since Northern Sierra Miwok is highly agglutinating, I thought it unnecessary to segment these examples by morph and provide a morpheme-by-morpheme translation, as I have done here, but in hindsight, I wish I had made the dictionary even more user-friendly by doing so.

cy·my- originally meant 'to climb', but by extension, it has acquired the meaning 'to ride' as well, which is logical, since one climbs onto a horse and into a car. The example sentences illustrate the range of meaning and also the fact that -j~-yj (objective case) follows the noun designating what is climbed on or into.

Rigid consistency would have forced me to segment the stem as *cy·m-y-*, since //-Y-// (-*u*- ~ -*o*- ~ -*y*-) is a stem formative suffix on verbs ending in a consonant. But if a monosyllabic verbal stem would result, historical evidence favors considering *y* part of the stem. Where two analyses are possible, I favor the one that best accords with history, in part because it facilitates internal reconstruction as well as the reconstruction of Proto Miwok and, ultimately, Proto Utian.

cy·my- 'to climb, ride' is a Long Stem verb. In *cym-pa-* 'to climb after someone', *cym-* is Stem 2b of a Long Stem whose final vowel is *y*, and this stem type is automatic before *-pa-* 'directed action'. *-n·a-* 'impersonal agentive' follows Stem 2 (CVCV-) in *cymy-n·a-* 'stepladder', and *-·a-* 'noun formative suffix' follows Stem 2a (CVCVʔ-) in *cymyʔ-·a-* 'ladder'. *-·ajny-* 'around' also follows this latter stem in *cymyʔ-·ajny-* 'to ride around'. A raised dot (·) lengthens the preceding consonant in these examples. We see that even a reasonably complete dictionary entails extensive morphological analysis of the language.

A summary of stem types and their distribution appears in the "Grammatical Synopsis" in the *Northern Miwok Dictionary* (Callaghan 1987). In addition to making my analysis accord with history, I have labeled the stems as closely as possible to the systems used by L. S. Freeland (1951), L. S. Freeland and Sylvia M. Broadbent (1960), and Broadbent (1964), so that interested readers will not have to rely on a concordance. I recognize an additional major stem type (Stem 5), and it was necessary to divide Freeland and Broadbent's Stem 2 into three subtypes (Stem 2, Stem 2a, and Stem 2b).

I have followed the Northern Sierra Miwok–English section with an English–Northern Sierra Miwok section, which should be used as an index to the first part. In defining words, I use the infinitive to refer to English verbs for reasons of clarity. Hence 'climb, to' is defined as *cy·my-*, *ʔetu·m-u-*. A reader would have to look up both words to learn that *ʔetu·m-u-* means specifically to climb a hill or a mountain. Subentries are so labeled. For example, 'climb after someone, to' is defined as *cympa-* under *cy·my-*.

I wish to emphasize that I am using examples from my Northern Sierra Miwok dictionary to illustrate my points only because I am familiar with it, not because I consider it the best example for contemporary lexicographers. It does not hold a candle to some of the dictionaries being produced today. An example is Haruo Aoki's elegant, detailed *Nez Perce Dictionary* (1994a), which includes illustrations and photographs and is nearly thirteen hundred pages long.

6. THE ROLE OF THE COMPUTER.   Material for the *Northern Sierra Miwok Dictionary* was gathered during short field trips over a period of thirty years. For a long time, I faithfully typed my field notes onto slips in the field or shortly thereafter, but as academic responsibilities grew, I was unable to do so, especially since I was simultaneously gathering material for a Plains Miwok dictionary (Callaghan 1984).

Rightly or wrongly, I did not computerize until a research assistant wrote software allowing for special symbols to appear both in the printout and on the screen. Unfortunately, this breakthrough came too late to aid in compiling the *Northern Sierra Miwok Dictionary*.

Subsequent advances in computer technology now allow field-workers to compile a dictionary in the field, revising it in progress. Linguists should keep alphabetization current for ease of reference, even if it is initially more time consuming. Needless to say, the computer now enables the lexicographer to produce dictionaries that are much more complete and elegant.

7. COMPARATIVE DICTIONARIES.   I am in the process of compiling a comparative Miwok dictionary, using a format similar to the one outlined

above for the dictionary of a contemporary language. Each main entry consists of a stem reconstructed at the deepest possible level. Reconstructible derivatives appear under the main entry, which need not be the simplest reconstructible stem, only the one whose time depth is greatest.[5]

7.1. EXAMPLE ENTRIES.

PMi *-aj ns a sequence found in names of plants, birds, insects, fish, field. It does not have full morphemic status, but it has been active in analogical reformations. In Plains Miwok, -e- 'nominalizer' sometimes follows, resulting in the sequence -a·je-.

PMis *lapi·saj N fish, trout

PMis *melŋaj N yellow jacket. Probably cognate with **PMiw** *mé·nani 'yellow jacket'.

PMis *py·laj N flat place, field, valley. It is cognate with **PCo** *pire 'land, earth, < **PU** *py(·)la 'land, earth, ground, field'.

Mil pódwaj N snake. Probably from Hill Patwin porwan 'snake' (DU) with analogical reformation.

PMie *ṭisi·naj N ant

  PMis *ṭisi·naj N ant

  Mip tisi·naj (J), tisi·na·je- (L) N ant

PMie *ṭiw·aj N yellowhammer. Cognate with **PCos** *ṭiwak 'yellowhammer' < **PU** *ṭiw(·)a ... 'yellowhammer'.

PMie *walak·aj N flat tule

---

5. On the basis of lexical items, structural similarities, and sound correspondences, the Miwok languages can be grouped as follows, allowing for reconstruction at different time depths.

  I. Eastern Miwok (Mie)
    A. Sierra Miwok (Mis)
      1. Northern Sierra Miwok (Mins)
      2. Central Sierra Miwok (Mics)
      3. Southern Sierra Miwok (Miss)
    B. Plains Miwok (Mip)
    C. Bay Miwok (Miba)
  II. Western Miwok (Miw)
    A. Coast Miwok (Mic) (Coast Miwok may have been a single language with divergent dialects.)
      1. Bodega Miwok (Mib)
      2. Marin Miwok (Mim)
    B. Lake Miwok (Mil)

The Miwok family is related to the Costanoan languages, once spoken along the coast of California from San Francisco south to Big Sur. There is increasing evidence for genetic relationship between Utian (Miwok-Costanoan) and Yokuts (Callaghan 1997). Any wider genetic affiliations are speculative.

PMis *čy·my- iV and tV to climb
  Miss cy·my- iV and tV to climb, to ride
  Mics cy·my- iV to climb
  Mins cy·my- iV and tV to climb, to ride
  PMis *čym·e-č ~ *čym·y-č adv. south. Originally, this word probably meant 'south southeast' along the orientation of the Sierra Nevadas, which would explain its association with words meaning 'climb'.
    Miss cym·e-c adv. (?) and N south
    Mics cym·e-c adv. in the south
    Mins cym·y-c adv. south
  PMis *čym·e-to- N all. south, southerner, south language. This is an example of a noun inflected with a locational case being used also for a person or group living in that location.
    Miss cym·e-to- N all. south, southerner, Yokuts person or language
    Mics cym·e-to- N all. a southerner
    Mins cym·e-to- N. all. a southerner, a West Point Indian, a Tuolumne Indian

7.2. DISCUSSION.   PMi *-aj includes the comparative evidence for the earlier assertion that -aj lacks full morphemic status and spread through the Miwok languages by analogy. Most telling are Costanoan cognates for 'yellowhammer' and 'field' that lack -aj, also Mil *ṗódwaj* 'snake' from Hill Patwin *porwan* 'snake'. This item was included because it illustrates the analogical spread of -aj, even into loanwords.

The entry under PMis *čy·my- 'to climb' includes the forms in Sierra Miwok languages underlying the reconstruction. The meaning 'to ride' is not cited for the protoform, which presumably antedates the introduction of the horse. PMi *čym·e-č 'south' is a derivative form with an adverbial suffix, PMis *-č, which is cognate with Mil -c and Mip -c, both markers of the objective case.

Normally, I did not include reconstructions of inflected forms of nouns and verbs in this dictionary except in illustrative paradigms and examples. However, PMis *čym·e-to- 'south, southerner, south language' is an instance of a noun in the allative case being reinterpreted in some contexts as a simple noun referring to a person from a certain place, or even as the language spoken there. Consequently, it counts as a derivative form.

8. TEACHING DICTIONARIES.   I was disappointed when I discovered that interested Indians were unable to use my dictionaries. The orthography was an impediment, as was the arrangement of derived stems under the main entry. When asked to prepare Northern Sierra Miwok teaching materials, I devised what I considered the least confusing orthography, which I will present here.

Users of teaching dictionaries are typically familiar only with English spelling and English dictionaries. A useful orthography should be as close to English as possible while maintaining necessary phonemic contrasts. Each symbol and digraph should be carefully described in terms of the closest English equivalent in the introduction, along with illustrative examples. During language classes, students should be required to read the introduction, since people customarily skip this important section of dictionaries and textbooks.

Northern Sierra Miwok has six vowels, *a, e, i, o, u,* and *y* [ɨ], which can be either long or short. The consonantal phonemes are *p, t, ṭ, c* [č], *k, ʔ, s, h, m, n, ŋ, w, l,* and *j* [y], all of which can be long or short (I have omitted marginal phonemes). As mentioned above, length is indicated by a raised dot (·).

In teaching materials, the values of *a, e, i, o, u* should be defined with reference to their closest English equivalent, followed by an appropriate example. Long vowels and long consonants should be written double, but the word "long" should never be used in a description of a sound, since English language dictionaries have thoroughly confused readers in this regard. "Dragged out" is a more effective phrase. The following descriptions and examples were taken, with modification, from Callaghan and Bibby (1985).

> *a* sounds like the *a* in f*a*ther. h*a*ŋgi' "roundhouse"
> *aa* sounds like the *a* in f*a*ther (dragged out). p*aa*pa' "grandfather"

"y" is not an acceptable symbol for [ɨ], but neither is "ɨ" because it resembles "i" too closely. "ə" is more tolerable, especially because it now appears in some English dictionaries.

Plains Miwok has a seven-vowel system, with two central vowels. If I were writing a teaching dictionary for this language, I would use "ʌ" to indicate the mid central unrounded vowel.

> *ə* sounds like the *e* in plac*e*s. m*ə*lli "to sing"
> *əə* sounds like the *e* in plac*e*s (dragged out). t*əə*kema' "spider web"

c [č] should be written *ch.* If *š* is a phoneme, it should be written *sh,* and *ŋ* should be written *ng.* Technical terms like "aspiration" should be avoided in descriptions of sounds. *ʔ* is also a confusing symbol, since it resembles a question mark too closely. For glottal stop, I use the apostrophe (').

Examples should be included, even where the sound and symbol are the same as in English. I explain that double consonants are pronounced the same as single consonants except that they are dragged out. Digraphs should also be doubled to indicate length.

> ' sounds like a "clipped" passage of air before a vowel and a "catch" at the end of a word. 'ache' "grandchild"

t is formed by pressing the tip of the tongue against the upper teeth without a puff of air. Between vowels and after *n*, *t* sometimes sounds like
the *d* in *d*og. *t*aman "north", su*t*uu*t*u "to stretch"
ch sounds like the *ch* in *ch*ur*ch* without a puff of air. Between vowels, *ch* sometimes sounds like the *j* in *j*ust. *ch*uku' "dog"
h sounds like the *h* of house. *h*ewe' "dry"
ng sounds like the *ng* in si*ng*. hu*ng*e' "fog"
y sounds like the *y* in *y*es. *y*angnge "to go to sleep"

There is no adequate substitute for *ṭ*. *tr*, *T*, and *d* will all lead to mispronunciation. Since students tend to omit the subscript dot, special drills
are necessary. The teacher should point out that *ṭ* represents a sound that
differentiates words, and it is as important to place the dot under it as it
is to dot the *i*'s and *j*'s in English. These statements also apply to *ṣ*, which
is phonemic in some dialects of Central Sierra Miwok.

ṭ is formed by curling the tip of the tongue behind the alveolar ridge (the
ridge behind the front teeth). Between vowels and after *n*, *ṭ* sometimes
sounds like the *d* in *d*og. *ṭ*ayṭi' "blue jay", heṭeeyə "to see"

The convention among linguists of using exclusively lowercase letters
is also confusing. Sentences and proper nouns should start with capital
letters, as in English. *cy·my·le·kaj* 'he's climbing on that tree' would be
rewritten as *Chəəməə leekay. Yaa'itya'iitə'* 'Evening Star'.

Of course, the order of all words should be alphabetical as it is in
English dictionaries, whether the words are based on simple or derived
stems. *ch* should follow *b* (*a* in the case of Northern Sierra Miwok, since
the language lacks *b* except in loanwords), *ə* should follow *e*, *ng* should
follow *n*, and *ṭ* should follow *t*. Glottal stop (') should either precede or
follow all other letters. Nouns are cited in the nominative case.

9. CONCLUDING REMARKS.   No one set of recommendations will fit dictionaries of all languages, as they vary typologically. In some instances,
orthographic conventions for scholarly dictionaries may suit teaching dictionaries with little or no modification. In other cases, an adequate popular orthography already exists. The important thing for the linguist is to
adopt conventions that are easy to apply and use and that are acceptable
to students of the language.

CHAPTER FIFTEEN

The NAPUS (Native American Placenames of the United States) Project

Principles and Problems

William Bright

1. INTRODUCTION.   This chapter is in part the story of my ongoing involvement with the field of American Indian placenames and in part a progress report on the current project, known as NAPUS, to which my involvement has led me. I have dabbled in name studies over the years (e.g., Bright 1984), but it was only after retirement from teaching that I undertook more extensive work on toponomy—revisions of George Eichler's *Colorado Place Names* (1977) and E. G. Gudde's book on California (1969). Now I have undertaken a new, five-year project for the University of Oklahoma Press: a large, comprehensive dictionary of the origins of U.S. placenames, used in English, which have American Indian origins. (I include here origins in Latin America, e.g., terms like *coyote*, borrowed through Spanish from Aztec.) The aim is to produce a work that will consolidate data from existing publications on the topic but also add authoritative etymological information based on current field research by anthropological linguists. A consulting editorial board of ten linguists, each responsible for particular native language families or cultural areas, has been appointed; but I also solicit and welcome input from all interested toponymists, local experts, and tribal scholars. A prospectus that has been published in the journal *Names* and elsewhere is shown in (1).

(1) NATIVE AMERICAN PLACENAMES OF THE UNITED STATES
    to be published by the University of Oklahoma Press

This is to announce the preparation of *Native American Placenames of the United States* (NAPUS), a large reference book in dictionary format, to be published by the University of Oklahoma Press. The work is to be prepared under the editorial direction of William Bright, of the University of Colorado, during the period 1997–2002, and is planned for publication in 2003.

GOAL. The emphasis in the book will be on the origins of U.S. place-names, used in English, which derive from Native American languages. The aim is to produce a work which is responsible to existing placename scholarship, but which will provide authoritative etymological information based on current linguistic research.

CONTENT. Among published reference works on American placenames, there are a few which cover the entire U.S., and many devoted to particular states; but in general these do not give special attention to Native American names. A handful of books deal with Native names in particular states, but all existing works are grounded primarily in historical and literary research. The aim of NAPUS is to supplement such materials by drawing on published and unpublished research by linguists who specialize in Native languages, in order to create a volume which will be comprehensive and definitive for the entire nation.

THE EDITOR. William Bright is Emeritus Professor of Linguistics and Anthropology, UCLA, and Professor Adjoint of Linguistics, University of Colorado, Boulder. His specialties include anthropological linguistics, sociolinguistics, and American Indian languages. In the field of toponymy, he has authored a book on *Colorado Place Names* (1993), has edited a special issue of the journal *Names* on American Indian placenames (1996), and most recently has prepared a revised 4th edition of E. G. Gudde's *California Place Names* (1998).

EDITORIAL BOARD. The Editor will be joined in the preparation of the volume by a board of Consulting Editors who are outstanding researchers in the field of Native American linguistics. These scholars will take responsibility for language families and/or areas in which each has expertise. The following have agreed to serve:

Wallace Chafe, Linguistics, University of California, Santa Barbara, CA (Iroquoian, Caddoan)
Ives Goddard, Anthropology, Smithsonian Institution, Washington, DC (Algonquian)
Jane H. Hill, Anthropology, University of Arizona, Tucson, AZ (O'odham, Southwest)
Kenneth C. Hill, Tucson, AZ (Hopi, Southwest)
Lawrence Kaplan, Alaska Native Language Center, University of Alaska, Fairbanks, AK (Eskimo-Aleut)
James Kari, Alaska Native Language Center, University of Alaska, Fairbanks, AK (Athabaskan)
M. Dale Kinkade, Linguistics, University of British Columbia, Vancouver (Salish, Northwest)
John McLaughlin, English, Utah State University, Logan, UT (Uto-Aztecan)
Marianne Mithun, Linguistics, University of California, Santa Barbara, CA (Iroquoian)
Pamela Munro, Linguistics, University of California, Los Angeles, CA (Yuman, Muskogean, Southeast)
David Pentland, Linguistics, University of Manitoba, Winnipeg (Algonquian)

Robert Rankin, Linguistics, University of Kansas, Lawrence, KS (Siouan, Plains)

CONSULTANTS. Information regarding particular languages and areas will be obtained by consultation with a large number of native speakers, linguistic specialists, and onomastic scholars throughout the nation. The participation of all interested parties is welcomed!

2. MATERIALS.   No comprehensive work of the type I propose has been carried out up to now, but four main kinds of published information are especially relevant to the project.

2.1. GNIS.   My basic inventory of terms will be drawn from the Geographical Names Information System (GNIS), the digital database of placenames that is available on the Internet from the U.S. Board on Geographic Names. However, I do not mean to include every possible Indian name that occurs in that database or on available maps. Some entries in the GNIS or on maps are erroneous; or they refer to long-vanished railroad sidings where no one ever lived, or otherwise have neither significant historical associations nor modern currency. What I would like to include are the names that people are likely to encounter—in books, on maps, or on the land—and about which they are curious. The other sources that I will list below will help me decide what names to include.

2.2. U.S. PLACENAME DICTIONARIES.   Another source consists of placename dictionaries of the United States as a whole, such as those by George R. Stewart (1970) and Kelsie Harder (1976); these give some information about the best-known names, such as *Chicago* and *Oklahoma*; but because they try to cover placenames of every type, they cannot devote much attention to lesser-known names.

2.3. REGIONAL PLACENAME DICTIONARIES.   Still another source consists of placename dictionaries of individual parts of the United States, such as well-known state placename books; good examples are Byrd Howell Granger's (1983) work for Arizona and Lewis A. McArthur's (1992) for Oregon. However, these books vary in the attention they give to names of Native American origin. A problem with both these types of dictionaries is that most of the compilers had little specialist knowledge about American Indian languages and often were not able to make use of existing linguistic resources on those languages. As a result, the information that all these sources provide on placenames of Indian origin is likely to be somewhat deficient.

2.4. REGIONAL INDIAN PLACENAME DICTIONARIES.   A final source comprises a relatively limited number of volumes devoted specifically to placenames of Indian origin in particular areas of the United States, such as the excellent volumes published by Virgil Vogel for Illinois (1963), Iowa (1983), Michigan (1986), and Wisconsin (1991). (Other relevant works include Beauchamp 1907; Donehoo 1928; Huden 1962; Kenny 1961; Pukui, Elbert, and Mookini 1974; Rydjord 1968.) These works are usually quite comprehensive for the areas they cover, and in some cases they have been prepared by scholars with considerable sophistication in American Indian linguistics; I can especially mention the older books by William Alexander Read on Louisiana (1927), Florida (1934), and Alabama (1937, rev. 1984) and the very recent work on names of the Navajo Reservation, by Alan Wilson (1995).

3. PROCEDURES.

3.1. THE DATABASE.   My current procedure begins with consolidating material from sources of all these types into a single computerized database. Most of this work has been completed in 2000 and 2001. A sample printout from that file can be seen in (2). These data are "raw" in the sense that they have multiple sources, which sometimes contradict each other, and are unedited.

(2) **BALLY; BOLLY; BULLY** (CALIF, Bright 1998) [bal′ē, bol′ē, bōol′ē] all occur. Wintu *buli* 'mountain' forms part of the names of several mountains in northern California. In Wintu, Bully Choop means 'mountain peak'; Winnibulli is 'middle mountain', and Yolla Bolly is 'snow mountain'.

BALUKAI (ARIZ, Wilson 1995) MESA: Baalók'aa'í ¶ baa - *near it, alongside it* ¶ lók'aa' - *reeds* ¶ Reeds near it or alongside it. The mesa, west of Salina (Tsé Lání), is 20 miles in length from north to south, and is separated from Black Mesa (Dziłíjiin) on the north by Burnt Corn Wash (Naadą́ą́' Díílid).

BANNOCK (CALIF, San Bernardino Co., Gudde/Bright 1998) [ban′ək]. From the name of a Numic Indian tribe in Idaho, *pannákwatï* (*HNAI* 11: 306). The term was changed by folk etymology to "Bannock," after a kind of Scottish flapjack much used by early traders and settlers. ¶¶ (WYO, Teton Co., Urbanek 1988) FALLS. Named for the western Indian tribe who once roamed here in Gallatin Range, but was finally placed on a reservation in Idaho. Bannock Peak, 10,323, YNP: named for Bannock Indians who entered Yellowstone Park in 1877.

BANTAM (CONN, Trumbull 1881) (*-om, -um*), *Bantaham,* etc.: a name given to the place at which Litchfield was settled; afterwards, to 'The Great Pond' and river in that township. This name does not appear in the Indian deed of the territory, 1715–16, but the order of Court, May, 1719, authorizes the settlement of "a place called *Bantam*"; and in the first deed recorded in Litchfield town records, May, 1719, the plantation is called *Bantaham.* "Bantam river" was so denominated in 1720, but the pond, in the early records, is simply 'the Great Pond.' The Rev. Azel

Backus (ms. Hist. of Bethlem, 1812) states that "*Shippaug* or Great Pond was the Indian name of Litchfield pond and gave the name to the river." ¶ If *Bantaham* or *Bantam* is of Indian origin—which is nearly certain—it must be a corruption of *peäntam* (Narr. *peyaun 'tam*) 'he prays' or 'praying,' a word used to designate a Christian Indian; and it may have been an appellation of the local sagamore, or of Weramaug, the sachem of New Milford. As a place-name, it is analogous to *Nonantam*, i.e., 'he blesses', the village in which Eliot's first Indian converts were gathered. **BASHI** (ALA, Read 1984) [bash'ī] 1. A creek flowing into the Tombigbee from the east. 2. A village which takes its name from that of the creek; recorded on the Smith map, 1891. ¶ *Bashai C.* La Tourrette, 1844. ¶ *Bashi* may be from Choctaw *bachaya*, "line," "row," "course"—hence Line Creek. { . . . }

3.2. COMPREHENSIVE BIBLIOGRAPHY.   Concurrently with this compilation, I have also compiled a unified computerized bibliography of all my published sources; (3) is a sample printout.

(3) Badenoch, Alex. 1976. Past and Present place names and post offices of Forest County, Pennsylvania. [s.l.]: Forest Press. 52 p. {Worldcat Pennsylvania}

Baile, Laurel Elizabeth. 1974. The origins of many Tulsa County place-names [S.l.: s.n.] 15, [3] leaves. "A winter term project for Oberlin College, Oberlin, Ohio." Reproduced from typescript. {Worldcat Oklahoma}

Bakeman, Mary. 1991. Minnesota places: now and then. St. Paul, MN (P.O. Box 16069, St. Paul 55116-0059): Minnesota Genealogical Society. 6, 56 p. {Worldcat Minnesota}

Baker, Jim. 1973. How our counties got their names. Worthington, Ohio: Pioneer Press Service. [94] p. {Worldcat Ohio}

Baker, Ronald L. 1995. From Needmore to Prosperity: Hoosier place names in folk history. Bloomington: Indiana University Press. 371 p. {Indiana, have}

Baker, Ronald L., & Marvin Carmony. 1975. Indiana place names. Bloomington, Indiana Univ. Press. xxii, 196 p. ¶ 2271 names in this study, with a brief section on pronunciation and on classification of names. ¶ Review: Donald Zimmer, Indiana magazine of history 72:360–61, Dec. 1976; Arthur F. Beringause, Names 24:216, Sept. 1976. {Sealock Indiana}

Ballard, Edward. 1900. Geographical names on the coast of Maine. Washington, DC: United States Coast Survey. 19 p., 30 cm. {Worldcat Maine}

Barbour, Philip L. 1967. Chickahominy place names in Captain John Smith's True relation. Names 15:216–27. ¶ Deals with the Indian nomenclature of the Chickahominy River basin in 1607. The guest editor of this issue, Hamill Kenny, raises several questions, p. 225–26. {Sealock Virginia}

Barbour, Philip L. 1971. The earliest reconnaissance of Chesapeake Bay area: Captain John Smith's map and Indian vocabulary. Virginia magazine of history and biography 79:280–302. ¶ Bibliography: p. 283–84. ¶ The Indian place-names recorded by Smith in his writings and on his map are listed, roughly located, and analyzed where possible. Most are in the language called Powhatan. Names are mainly in Virginia and Maryland, with a few in Delaware and Pennsylvania. {Sealock Maryland}

Barge, William D. 1936. Illinois place names. Journal of the Illinois State Historical Society 29:189–311. {Illinois, Callary 1985:74}

Barnes, Arthur M. 1948. Pronunciation guide to Iowa place names. Iowa City: State University of Iowa, School of Journalism. 2, 8, 8 leaves; 28 cm. {Worldcat Iowa}

Barnes, Arthur M. 1959. Pronunciation guide to names of places and state officeholders in Iowa. Prepared in cooperation with the Iowa Radio-Telegraph News Association. 2d ed. Iowa City, State Univ. of Iowa. 12 p. {Sealock Iowa}

3.3. ASSIGNMENT TO CONSULTING EDITORS.   The next major part of the project, which began in 1999, was to send relevant portions of my database, on diskette, to my ten consulting editors, asking for input derived from their personal knowledge of various languages and from information they obtain from consultants as mentioned above.

3.4. CONSOLIDATION AND EDITING.   As the consulting editors return such input to me, I am consolidating the entire body of data and editing it to create entries for the final dictionary. A sample printout of some California placenames, illustrating a possible format that those entries may take, is shown in (4).

(4) **Bannock** (Calif., San Bernardino Co.) [ban'ək] From the name of a Numic Indian tribe in Idaho, *pannákwatï* (*HNAI* 11:306). The term was changed by folk etymology to "Bannock," after a kind of Scottish flapjack much used by early traders and settlers (Gudde/Bright).

Bohemotash (Calif., Shasta Co.) [bō hē´mə tash] From Wintu *bohema thoos*, lit. 'big camp' (Shepherd).

Bolinas (Calif., Marin Co.) [bō lē´nəs]. A map of 1834 has the word "Baulenes" on the peninsula which now includes Bolinas Point, Duxbury Point, and the town of Bolinas. The name *Baulenes*, possibly from a Coast Miwok word of undetermined meaning, probably referred to the Indians who inhabited the region (Gudde/Bright).

Bollibokka (Calif., Shasta Co.) [bol ē bok'ə] Apparently from Wintu *buli* 'mountain' and *phaqa* 'manzanita' (Shepherd).

Bully Choop (Calif., Shasta & Trinity Cos.) [bŏŏl ē chŏŏp´]. Represents Wintu *buli č'uup* 'mountain peak', from *buli* 'mountain' and *č'uup* 'sharp point, awl' (Shepherd). The name has sometimes been folk-etymologized as "bullet shoot."

Buriburi (Calif., San Mateo Co.) [bûr ē bûr'ē, byōō rē byōō'rē]. Mentioned in mission records of 1798. From a Costanoan name, perhaps related to Rumsen *purris* 'needle' (Harrington; Callaghan).

Cabazon (Calif., Riverside Co.) [kab'ə zon]. The name of a Cahuilla Indian chief who lived in this area in the 1860s; from Spanish *cabezón* 'big head'. (Gudde/Bright)

Cachuma (Calif., Santa Barbara Co.) [kə chōō' mə]. From Span. *Aquitsumu,* borrowed in turn from Chumash *'aqitsu'm* 'sign' (Applegate 1975:27).

Cahto (Mendocino & Humboldt Cos.) [kã'tō]. From Northern Pomo *khaṭo* 'lake', containing *khá* 'water' (Oswalt).

Cahuenga (Calif., Los Angeles Co.) [kə hung'gə, kə weng'gə]. Documented in Spanish from 1802. From Gabrielino *kawé'nga* (Munro); possibly cognate with Luiseño *qawíinga* 'at the mountain', from *qawúcha* 'mountain', and Cahuilla *qáwinga'* 'at the rock', from *qáwish* 'rock'.

Cahuilla (Calif., Riverside Co.) [kə wē'ə]. The place name, first recorded in the 1830s as Cagüilla, is the Spanish and English name of the Cahuilla Indian tribe (Takic family). The tribal name is sometimes thought to be from Cahuilla *qáwiy'a* 'leader, chief'; but in fact it is borrowed from local Spanish *Cahuilla* 'unbaptized Indian'; this term, used in Mission days, was itself apparently derived from an extinct language of Baja California (Bright 1977). As a geographical term, the name was used in 1859 for the valley northeast of the San Jacinto Mountains, with the spelling Cohuilla; in 1873 with the spelling Coahuila; and with similar spellings on all maps published before 1891 (Gudde/Bright). Cf. also Coachella.

4. QUESTIONS FROM THE DEVIL'S ADVOCATE.   When I submitted my proposal for this project to the University of Oklahoma Press, they naturally sent it for evaluation to two referees. The evaluation of one was entirely positive; the other also made some favorable comments, but in addition raised important questions, to which the press asked me to respond. I think of this evaluator as the "Devil's Advocate," since his questions were challenging and forced me to think hard about some problems. Some very basic questions raised by him follow.

4.1. "WHY HASN'T ANYONE DONE ANYTHING LIKE THIS EVER BEFORE?" The suggestion, of course, is that it has not been done because it might be impossible. I can think of several possible answers to this question. One is that most people working in the field have been writing for local audiences, frequently defined in terms of state university presses or state and county historical societies; and their ambitions have been correspondingly restrained. Another point is that local writers who have studied regional toponymy have generally not had access to the research methods of American Indian linguistics or to the bibliographical resources available in that field; this is a major respect in which I hope to contribute something new. Finally, a possible reason why there has been no American Indian placenames volume to date is that, if one thinks of a totally comprehensive and perfect work, the job is indeed too daunting for anyone to undertake. But that is not what I have in mind. I am proposing a large reference work, but not necessarily the largest or most complete that could ever be published. I want to finish this in my lifetime! This is related to a second question—

4.2. "WILL YOU SETTLE ALL THE PROBLEMS?" The referee asks whether I would "repeat the thousands of errors already in print"—or if, rather, I would "settle all the problems of Amerind topoynymics." Both of these are extreme statements. Of course, I will not knowingly repeat old errors. Of the errors already in print, it is clear that many have resulted from ignoring available knowledge of American Indian languages; with the help of linguist colleagues, I feel confident of resolving many such problems—as I have already done for Colorado and California. But especially in eastern states, where many native languages have been long extinct, some problems can never be solved with certainty; in such cases I can only cite etymologies suggested by earlier writers, adding appropriate qualifiers such as "perhaps." I will always prefer to admit a gap in knowledge rather than to offer unqualified speculations like some that have appeared in print. Given these limitations, I believe that I can produce a new and useful type of reference work.

4.3. "WHAT TO PUT IN?" Finally, the referee asks: "How will you decide what to put in, and what to leave out?" The problem has of course been faced by earlier collectors of Indian-related toponyms, especially by Vogel—whose Wisconsin dictionary, for instance, casts a very wide net and classifies names under chapter headings such as "Tribal names," "Personal names," "Names from fauna," "Names from flora," and so on. Yet such all-inclusive compilations contain some fairly uninteresting items; for example, many states have an "Indian Creek," perhaps so named because someone arrived there and encountered an Indian, or a group of Indians, or an Indian village. But the name carries little information of a cultural or historical sort. The general question remains: What are the criteria for inclusion?

5. A TYPOLOGY AND ITS ELABORATION. While I was thinking about criteria for including or excluding materials from the NAPUS project, and pondering possible typologies for that purpose, Grant Smith had the kindness to send me a copy of his recent article, "Amerindian Place Names: A Typology Based on Meaning and Form" (1996). I was delighted to find that he had come up with criteria for classification that were extremely

useful for my purposes. However, as I considered how my data could be classified in terms of Smith's typology, I also began to think of ways in which his typology could be elaborated and possibly supplemented. So I would like to review Smith's system here and add my own observations. I hasten to emphasize that I am not trying to criticize or supersede Smith's proposal, but only to offer comments that may prove relevant to further discussion. My view of typologies, I would emphasize, is that they should never be carved in stone; they have value only to the extent that they are helpful in research, and any proposed typology needs to be tested in terms of its continuing usefulness.

Smith's categories, then, are as follows.

5.1. "AMERINDIAN ORAL NAMES" are defined as "those terms presumably used in Amerindian languages to designate places" (Smith 1996: 55). I have two comments on this category.

5.1.1. ORAL VERSUS WRITTEN LANGUAGES. Some Native American languages are now frequently written; they have official, standardized orthographies, and materials are published in them. An example is Navajo, and the official orthography is used in the book by Wilson (1995) that I have already mentioned. This fact makes the term "oral" seem inappropriate for this category; I suggest instead something like "AMERINDIAN TRADITIONAL NAMES," meaning all the names traditionally used, in situ, by American Indian languages of the past or present. Of course, some such names have also come to be used in English, such as *Chicago* or *Tucson*. But as defined here, the category comprehends an immense number of names—tens of thousands, at the very least—that have never entered English usage; indeed, only a relatively small number of them have been recorded, typically by anthropologists, under the heading ETHNOGEOGRAPHY. Exemplary works of this genre are T. T. Waterman's *Yurok Geography* (1920, for a tribe of California) and Eugene S. Hunn's *Nch'i-wána, "The Big River": Mid-Columbia Indians and Their Land* (Hunn et al. 1990). Several American Indians have told me that their tribes need research on their native placenames and have asked whether I will be able to help them. I agree that such work is important, and I have in fact done such research for the Karuk tribe in California. But unfortunately the NAPUS project will not be able to address this need. Since the scope of NAPUS is very broad in one sense, namely, that of covering the entire United States, it has to be limited in another sense, namely, to those Indian placenames that have entered English usage.

5.1.2. ENGLISH < INDIAN < EUROPEAN. A problem that occasionally arises is that we are not sure whether an ostensible Indian placename may have a European source. For instance, *Galice* is the name of an Athabaskan Indian tribe, a settlement, and a creek in Oregon, and it is explained by McArthur (1992) as a French surname. However, in the 1950s the last surviving speaker of the Galice language told the anthropologist Harry Hoijer that the name represented an Indian pronunciation *galiis* of the English word *Kelly's;* that is, the settlement was named after a miner called Kelly. To the extent that this latter etymology may be valid, then we have the possibility of a placename that has an Indian history, although its ultimate source is European.

5.2. "INDIGENOUS DERIVATIONS" are defined by Smith (1996: 56) as "terms derived from languages indigenous to the geographic areas in which they are used by Eng. speakers." This clearly includes a large number of the placenames to be covered by NAPUS. But several subcategories can be distinguished, each with its own type of motivation.

5.2.1. As already mentioned, some terms are genuine native placenames, borrowed into English and still used in situ, such as *Chicago* or *Tucson.*

5.2.2. Some are names of prominent Indian individuals, such as *Seattle* or *Spokane.*

5.2.3. Some are derived from other words of local Indian languages, for example, *Chittamo* (Wisc.), from Ojibwe *ajidamoo* 'red squirrel'. It should be noted, however, that the English word *chipmunk,* found in placenames both of Wisconsin and other states, is itself derived from the same Ojibwe word. In the case of a particular place called *Chipmunk Rapids,* we may not be able to tell whether the name is based directly on Ojibwe or on the English word.

5.2.4. A special category consists of placenames in which white explorers evidently interpreted Indian generic terms as if they were specific, and adapted the Indian terms into English accordingly. Thus in 1844, when John C. Frémont's party first saw Lake Tahoe, they asked a Washo Indian what it was called, and the Indian said, *dá'aw* 'a lake'; this was written down in English as *Tahoe.* In 1877, in the same area, the Wheeler surveying party asked another Washo to identify a California mountain, and the Indian said, *dalá'ak* 'a mountain'; this became *Mount Tallac.*

5.3. "PIDGIN DERIVATIONS" are "derived or borrowed from Amerindian-based pidgins (i.e., mixed languages) developed to facilitate contact between the indigenous people and European immigrants" (Smith 1996: 57). Many cases involve the Chinook Jargon, a trade language of the Pacific Northwest, containing elements of several Native languages, especially Chinookan and Salishan, as well as French and English. Again some subcategories can be distinguished.

5.3.1.   A name may come from the pidgin, which in turn takes it from a native language. Thus the word *Skookum,* occurring in many northwestern placenames, represents the Chinook Jargon for 'strong, powerful', borrowed in turn from a Salishan language.

5.3.2.   A name may come from the pidgin but have its ultimate origin in a European language. Thus the word *Siwash,* again occurring in many northwestern placenames, represents the Chinook Jargon word for 'Indian', borrowed from French *sauvage.*

5.4.   "TRANSFERRED DERIVATIONS"   are defined as "terms that have been borrowed into English or French and then applied as placenames outside the geographic regions of the languages from which they have been borrowed" (Smith 1996: 59). These are very common and will constitute a large body of the data included in NAPUS. Again some subcategories can be distinguished.

5.4.1.   Common nouns used in English are often carried from one region to another, for example, *Teepee Flats* (Wash.) uses the Siouan term *tipi* 'house', which is native to the Great Plains. The *Pogonip,* a frequently foggy hillside overlooking Santa Cruz (Calif.), is an application of a word that English speakers in the Great Basin had borrowed from Numic *pakï-nappi* 'fog'.

5.4.2.   Transferred placenames are common, for example, *Milwaukee,* transferred from Wisconsin to Oregon, and *Chicago,* as applied to *Port Chicago* in California, were originally Algonquian placenames.

5.4.3.   Some names are locally thought to be of Indian origin but actually have European origins: thus *Calumet* (Ill., Mich.), understood as a word for 'Indian pipe', is borrowed by English from a Norman French dialect word for 'pipe', related to Standard French *chalumeau* 'type of flute'. Such a word, then, does not actually have an Indian origin, but was applied as a placename because of its Indian cultural associations.

5.5.   "PSEUDO-AMERINDIAN TERMS"   are defined as "imaginative imitations of presumed Indian speech or coinages usually interpreted as such" (Smith 1996: 60). Again there are subcategories.

5.5.1.   Complete inventions sometimes are found. An example is *Lake Itasca,* the Minnesota origin of the Mississippi River; the name was coined by Henry R. Schoolcraft, who also gave imaginary Indian names to several counties in the state of Michigan. In the case of *Itasca,* he took letters from an intended, but ungrammatical, Latin phrase: *veritas caput,* supposed to mean 'true head(waters)'. (Cf. Vogel 1991; better Latin would be *verum caput.*)

5.5.2.   Some supposed Indian names are those that were originally given currency by literary works, especially in Henry Wadsworth Longfellow's *Hiawatha.* An example was the word *Hiawatha* itself, now found as a placename in many states. In this case the name was not originally fictitious; it was borne by a famous Iroquois leader in New York State, but apparently the poet liked the sound of it and applied it to the hero of his epic, who was supposed to be an Algonquian of the Great Lakes area.

5.6. "TRANSLATIONS"   are defined by Smith as "English terms that are presumed to be literal translations of indigenous place names, descriptions, or associations, or of symbolic features in Amerindian legends" (1996: 61). We may perhaps distinguish two varieties.

5.6.1.   One type consists of what linguists call "calques" (derived from a French term meaning 'a tracing or copy'). Thus the *Medicine Bow Mountains* (Colo., Wyo.) are thought to translate a Shoshone term, referring to a bow used for magical purposes; *Pipestone Lake* (Wisc.) is supposed to translate an Algonquian word for a type of stone from which the Indians made pipe bowls. However, in most such cases it is difficult to confirm the original Indian name of the place; whites could have simply adapted "medicine bow" and "pipestone" as common nouns, from Indian usage, and later applied them as placenames.

5.6.2.   Some cases have still more dubious origins. A widespread name like *Badger Creek* is sometimes assumed on very little evidence (e.g., by Vogel) to represent a translation of an Indian name. A particular stream may or may not have had an Indian name meaning 'badger creek'; but if it was frequented by badgers, it was very likely to be given such a name in English. If a name has no clearly documented Indian association, either linguistic or cultural, I am reluctant to include it in the coverage for NAPUS.

5.7. "ADOPTED EUROPEAN NAMES"   are defined as "commemoratives and possessives of [the names of] indigenous people who have adopted European names" (Smith 1996: 62). In this category falls a placename like *Adams* (Mass.), named for an otherwise obscure Indian with that family name. However, other types of adopted names may be of greater linguistic or historical interest.

5.7.1. Some names reflect cases in which English has borrowed an Indian personal name, which was borrowed in turn from a European language; an example is *Lolo* (Mont.) from a Salish personal name *Lolo,* from French *Laurent.* A somewhat more complex case is *Stanislaus* (River and County, Calif.), an English adaptation of *Estanislao,* the Spanish baptismal name of an Indian who became famous for his successful raids on Spanish missions.

5.7.2. Other names are calques; thus *Black Hawk, Big Foot* (Wisc.) are translations of the names of Algonquian leaders.

5.7.3. In some cases it must be recognized that placenames are of ambiguous Indian origin. For instance, is *St. Germain* (Wisc.) named after the French soldier Jean-François St. Germain, who arrived in the area in the seventeenth century, or after one or more of his mixed-blood descendants who have lived in Wisconsin ever since?

5.8. ENGLISH < SPANISH/FRENCH < INDIAN. In addition to Smith's (1996) categories, it is possible to suggest two others. Some placenames are borrowings from Spanish or French common nouns which are in turn borrowed from native languages. We can recognize the following categories.

5.8.1. Some placenames are borrowed through Spanish or French, but ultimately come from Indian languages of the same area, for example, *Abalone Point* (Calif.), from Cal.Sp. *aulón(es),* from Rumsen *aulon.*

5.8.2. Some placenames are transferred, through Spanish or French, from some other colonized area, for example, *Temescal Canyon* (Calif.) < Mex.Sp. *temazcal* 'sweathouse', from Aztec *temazcalli.* A possible example involving French is *Muskellunge* (Mich., Wisc.), from the English name of a type of fish resembling a pike, from French *maquinonge,* from Ojibwe *maashkinoozhe* 'evil(-looking) pike'.

5.8.3. Some names involve transformation via folk etymology in Spanish or French, based on an earlier Indian name; thus *Temetate Creek* (Calif.) takes its name from the Mexican Spanish word *temetate* 'stone grinding-slab', ostensibly from Aztec *temetlatl;* but this is probably in fact a reworking of the original Chumash placename, which was *stemeqtatimi,* of unknown meaning. Another example is *Canadian River* (Colo., Okla.), from Sp. *canadiano,* seemingly from the name of the country *Canada* (transmitted through French but originally Iroquoian); however, the name is probably in fact a reshaping of Caddo *káyántinu',* the name of the nearby Red River.

5.8.4. Some names, borrowed by English through Spanish or French, are specifically derived from American Indian placenames in areas outside the United States; this is then a special category of TRANSFER placenames, of two types as follows.

5.8.4.1. Names borrowed through Spanish from Latin America include placenames such as *Mexico* and *Lima.*

5.8.4.2. Names borrowed from French Canada include familiar ones like *Quebec* and *Ontario.* These names require some special attention, however, as most of them come from Iroquoian or Algonquian languages that are spoken in both Canada and the United States; there may therefore be doubt in some cases as to whether a name was first borrowed on the U.S. or the Canadian side of the border.

5.9. HYBRID INDIAN NAMES   are those coined from parts of two or more other names, one or more of which are of Indian origin. The motive for such coinages is usually that the place is located in or near the sites whose names are represented in the hybrid; examples are *Texarkana* (Tex., Ark.) and *Clackamette* (Ore., from *Clackamas* and *Willamette*). Such names of course have no motivation in American Indian culture or history. They may be candidates for inclusion in NAPUS, however, because of their interest as curiosities or because they may occasionally be mistaken for genuine Indian names.

6. CONCLUSION.   As regards the question of what should ultimately be included in NAPUS, I feel no urgency to reach a final decision. I have begun with the motto, "Put in everything," on the principle that it is easier to take things out than to put them in. However, thinking about Grant Smith's (1996) typology has been very helpful to me in formulating some tentative criteria. The final NAPUS compilation should clearly include placenames, used in English, that have actual etymologies in American Indian languages; I believe it should also include those that have associations with American Indian history and culture—either historically valid or locally believed. In short, it should include the names people interested in American Indian traditions might look up in a book such as NAPUS.

CHAPTER SIXTEEN

Alonso de Molina as Lexicographer

Mary L. Clayton and R. Joe Campbell

1. INTRODUCTION: HISTORY OF THE MOLINA DICTIONARIES AND RELATIONSHIP TO OTHER NAHUATL DICTIONARIES. Fray Alonso de Molina, a Franciscan who went to New Spain as a boy (most probably before 1530)[1] and is reported to have learned Nahuatl from his Indian playmates, wrote three bilingual dictionaries of Nahuatl (Nah) and Spanish (Sp). The second and third of these, published in 1571, are even now, some 430 years later, the primary dictionaries for the Nahuatl language and the mainstay for anyone undertaking the study of this language, especially as it was spoken in early colonial times.

Molina did not write the first known vocabulary of Nahuatl. That distinction belongs to Fray Andrés de Olmos, who wrote a small lexicon, appended to his *Arte de la lengua mexicana*.[2] That vocabulary includes both Spanish-Nahuatl and Nahuatl-Spanish but totals only some two thousand

We would especially like to thank Ladislav Zgusta for his generosity in providing encouragement and advice, both specific and general, on various aspects of this chapter. We have benefited greatly from discussions with him on a number of points. He has seen this chapter only in its final form and of course bears no responsibility for any errors that it may contain. We would also like to thank Ricardo Salvador and Frances Karttunen for their comments on *cacao*, and Barbara Santos for her work on figure 16.1. Finally, we express our appreciation to the Reference Department, University of Illinois at Urbana–Champaign Library, for help with the Olmos reference.

1. See Zulaica 1939 and M. León-Portilla 1970 for attempts to piece together Molina's biography.

2. Fray Andrés de Olmos' *Arte de la lengua mexicana*, or *Arte para aprender la lengua mexicana* dates from 1547. It was unpublished until the nineteenth century. For an edition that includes the vocabulary, see Olmos 1547 [1985]. Note that *la lengua mexicana* 'the Mexican language' is Nahuatl. See Hill and Hill 1986 for extensive discussion.

items,[3] and in any case, the version of his *Arte* containing the vocabulary (six manuscripts survive) was not published until 1985.

Molina's first dictionary, *Aqui comiença vn vocabulario en la lengua castellana y mexicana,* was published in 1555.[4] This first published lexicon of the Nahuatl language, accessed through the Spanish source language, was the first published dictionary of any Amerindian language. It is neither small nor amateurish. This is a very substantial work, to this day surpassed in size only by each part of Molina's own second dictionary and by Rémi Siméon's 1885 work.[5] It is a work showing a surprising degree of linguistic sophistication, as will become apparent below. It was never republished,[6] undoubtedly because of the appearance of the 1571 dictionaries, and so today exists in only a few rare book collections. In 1571 Molina published in one volume both a much-expanded Spanish-Nahuatl dictionary and a new Nahuatl-Spanish dictionary, under the titles *Vocabulario en lengua castellana y mexicana* and *Vocabulario en lengua mexicana y castellana.* Even these works did not reappear in print until the latter half of the nineteenth century, when they were published in Germany by Julius Platzmann (in 1880) in an "edición facsimilaria," which was intended to remain rigidly faithful to the first edition, including the rather few typographical errors. Unfortunately, the 1880 edition introduced a number of new errors, the most frequent being a misreading of *u* and *n.* It is the Platzmann edition that is available today in facsimile as republished by Porrúa in 1970 under the title *Vocabulario en lengua castellana y mexicana y mexicana y castellana,* with a preliminary study by Miguel León-Portilla, and reprinted several times since. A true facsimile of the 1571 works was published in 1944 by Ediciones Cultura Hispánica. The two 1571 works are often referred to as "the first part" and "the second part," but, in fact, apparently only with the Porrúa edition were they given a unified title page.

Below is a listing of the number of entries[7] in each of these dictionaries, along with the number of Nahuatl equivalents for the two

3. We count 2,062 total entries, many of the Sp>Nah entries with more than one Nahuatl equivalent, and have no explanation for the paleographer's claim (Olmos 1547 [1985]: 12) that places the total at 1,178.

4. For a fuller account of the publication history of the dictionaries and a discussion of Molina's bibliography in general, see A. León-Portilla 1988 as well as Zulaica 1939 and M. León-Portilla 1970.

5. Siméon 1885 is based largely on these two dictionaries, but it also includes vocabulary from other classical sources. Note that it is only Nahuatl-to-French.

6. Zulaica (1939: 103) reports: "Hay una edición facsimilar hecha en los Estados Unidos por Julius Bieu, aunque sin la portada a dos tintas." WorldCat database lists a photolithographic reproduction by Julius Bien, dated 1850. The only copy in the WorldCat list is held by Georgetown University.

7. These numbers are based on our databases, and though they should be very close, they may not be exact because of an occasional format problem in the database.

Spanish-to-Nahuatl dictionaries. By comparison, the Spanish-to-Latin dictionary of Antonio de Nebrija (2d ed., 1516) is approximately 15,600 words.

	Spanish entries	Nahuatl equivalents
Molina 1555 Sp>Nah	13,866	29,742
Molina 1571 Sp>Nah	17,410	37,433

Nahuatl entries in Molina 1571 Nah>Sp: 23,625

In addition to its place as the preeminent Nahuatl dictionary, the 1571 work has served as a source for modern lexical works, the first of which was Siméon (1885). In the twentieth century Frances Karttunen used it as the primary source for her Spanish glosses in *An Analytical Dictionary of Nahuatl* (1983), and R. Joe Campbell's *Morphological Dictionary of Classical Nahuatl* (1985) analyzes the noninflectional morphology of Molina's Nahuatl-Spanish dictionary.

Molina left us no commentary on his lexicographical aims, assumptions, and methodology. Representing his views on dictionary making, we have only the *prólogos* 'prefaces' and *avisos* 'notes [to the reader]' that precede each of his three dictionaries, and the dictionaries themselves. A close look at these products in fact provides a variety of interesting hints on how he went about creating these monumental bilingual Nahuatl and Spanish dictionaries and how he interpreted the task of the lexicographer. In addition, we can examine the dictionaries that he probably had at hand in an attempt to determine to what extent his work was original and to what extent it simply followed contemporary practices. In this chapter, we consider these various sources of information as we examine Molina's point of view and his practices in various aspects of the lexicographer's craft.

We will refer to Molina's dictionaries as follows:

Sp>Nah55:   Molina 1555, Spanish to Nahuatl only. *Aqui comiença vn vocabulario en la lengua castellana y mexicana*

Sp>Nah71:   Molina 1571, Spanish to Nahuatl. *Vocabulario en lengua castellana y mexicana*

Nah>Sp71:   Molina 1571, Nahuatl to Spanish. *Vocabulario en lengua mexicana y castellana*, published with the above.

Citations of entries are given with folio and column numbers. Sp>Nah55 is not divided into columns.

A central question to be addressed in considering both the form and the content of Molina's dictionaries is his debt to Antonio de Nebrija, the Spanish lexicographer and grammarian whose Latin-Spanish dictionary and Spanish grammar (*Arte*) appeared in 1492, followed by his Spanish-

Latin dictionary in 1495 and the second edition of this in 1516. It has been pointed out by a variety of authors[8] that Nebrija's work was available as a model to New World lexicographers. Doris Bartholomew (1991: 2697) claims that Molina "acknowledged his debt to Nebrija in his Spanish-Aztec[9] dictionary in 1555." In fact, the only mention we find of Nebrija in that work is Molina's third note to the reader in which he points out that he gives Spanish verbs in the infinitive, as does Nebrija. In the preface to the Nahuatl-Spanish dictionary of 1571, Molina mentions that he, like Nebrija, has produced a pair of dictionaries. Finally, in the second note to the reader in that preface, he mentions that he follows the alphabetical order of Nebrija, apparently meaning the alphabetical order of the Latin-Spanish dictionary. Bartholomew also mentions that Nebrija was used as a word list,[10] and Karttunen (1988, 1991, 1995) has suggested that the Nebrija dictionary was actually used as an elicitation list by the missionary-friars in the development of their dictionaries of New World languages. We will examine this claim carefully with regard to Molina's lexical works in what follows and will conclude that to the extent that Molina was influenced by Nebrija, that influence was more subtle and far less direct than one might have expected.

We know that Molina had access to Nebrija's *Arte* and one or more of the dictionaries, though we cannot be sure which. An inventory was mandated in July 1572 of all of the possessions of the Colegio de Santa Cruz de Tlatelolco (García Icazbalceta 1892: 255–57), where Molina was *guardián* of the convent. The inventory includes the library—a total of some sixty books including four Bibles and two New Testaments. Among the books are four copies of Nebrija's *Arte de gramatica,* two *"vocabularios"* of Ambrogio Calepino, and three dictionaries by Nebrija that are identified simply as *"Vocabularios de Antonio de Librija."*[11] Both the Latin-first and the Spanish-first dictionaries of Nebrija would almost surely have been called *vocabularios* by the inventory makers, as were the Calepinos, which

8. For statements on this topic, see, e.g., Bartholomew 1991; McQuown 1991; Haensch 1990. Since completion of this chapter, we have become aware of Hernandez Hernandez 1993, but we have not been able to examine this work.

9. "Aztec" as a language name = Nahuatl.

10. The only Nahuatl dictionary we are aware of that is based on Nebrija's word list is Ayer ms. 1478 in the Newberry Library, an anonymous sixteenth-century Spanish-Latin-Nahuatl dictionary based directly on Nebrija 1516. Clayton is preparing a Nahuatl alphabetical dictionary, a morphological dictionary, and a monograph based on this work, along with an edition of the manuscript. See Clayton 1989.

11. Librija = Nebrija.

were Latin or Latin-polyglot dictionaries.[12] *Vocabulario* was not only part of a specific title of one form of the Spanish-first dictionary but a generic term as well, and it is clear from the inventory list that its makers were less interested in bibliographical documentation than in roughly identifying the various possessions of the school. There were other books owned by the school that occurred in duplicate copies. Thus we know only that Nebrija was represented in their library. We do not know whether the vocabularies were Latin-Spanish, Spanish-Latin, or both, or in what edition(s).

2. THE PREFACES: GENERAL PHILOSOPHY.   Each of Molina's three dictionaries contains a preface that has little to do with the respective dictionary beyond giving the rationale for its creation. However, each preface is followed by notes to the reader that in fact constitute a useful guide to particular aspects of the dictionaries. They also discuss very insightfully certain linguistic issues to which we will return below. Both prefaces and notes are identical in Sp>Nah55 and Sp>Nah71 except for a very few words and for the twelfth note of the former, which refers the reader to last-minute additions to the 1555 dictionary, which are given in an appendix. The combination of preface and notes gives us a sense of Molina's purpose and a look at his linguistic acuity.

Nebrija's prefaces, though not much more relevant to his dictionaries, are quite different from Molina's. While Nebrija gives biographical information and boasts at some length of his own importance in the world of letters, Molina discusses the sin of pride and its punishments, including in particular the pride of those who constructed the Tower of Babel and their punishment in the fragmentation of language and the resulting disruption in human communication. This brings Molina to the necessity of communication with the loca' people. To quote from his preface:[13]

> What greater harm can there be against human nature and inclination, being naturally [according to the words of Aristotle] fond of conversation and company, than that they should lack the principal medium for human interaction, which is a common language? . . . This harm and disadvantage we have experienced ourselves in this land, where, given that Christian piety inclines us to benefit these natives both in temporal and in spiritual matters, the lack of the language impedes us. And it is no small disadvantage that those who are to govern and rule them, and put everything in good order and provide

12. The name of Ambrogio Calepino (b. 1435 or 1440, d. 1510 or 1511) became synonymous with Latin and polyglot dictionaries—at least 165 editions before 1600. First published in 1502, his own work usually bore the title *Ad Librum* or *Dictionarium*. See Labarre 1975. Without exception, the title pages of the 211 editions that Labarre lists between 1502 and 1779 are in Latin.

13. The English translations from the prefaces and notes to the reader are ours.

them justice, remedying and fixing the grievances which they receive, do not have mutual understanding with them, but rather that the reason and justice which they have are relinquished to the good or bad intentions of the Nahuatl-speaker or interpreter. (Molina 1555, 1571, preface, unpaginated)

He continues, with reference to the relief of the Spanish people when their king, "el Inuictissimo Cesar," Charles I of Spain, Charles V of the Holy Roman Empire, learned to speak Spanish without the intermediary of interpreters: "because many times, although the water be clean and clear, the pipes through which it passes make it cloudy." The main necessity and urgency for understanding with *los naturales* 'the natives' is the missionaries' goal of bringing them salvation:

> For if in temporal matters, where what is at stake is only property, honor and physical life, it is so beneficial for those who are to rule and govern the natives to have a mutual understanding with them, how much more necessary is it in spiritual matters, where what is at issue is no less than the life of the soul and its salvation or perdition? (Molina 1555, 1571, preface, unpaginated)

In this regard, Molina's attitude seems very similar to that of Bernardino de Sahagún, his colleague who collected the texts that have come to be known as the *Florentine Codex* (Sahagún 1579 [1950–82]), and who, in the name of saving souls, worked as a linguistic anthropologist. For while Molina tells us—and, we are sure, truly believed—that the purpose of the dictionary was to communicate with Nahuatl speakers in order to convert them to Christianity and to administer the sacraments to them, he simultaneously delighted in the strangeness and ingenuity of the language, as we see in the following excerpts from his prefaces:

> [W]hen I published the vocabulary of the Mexican language the first time, . . . I had no other intent than to begin to open a path, in order that in the course of time and with the diligence of other more lively minds, there would be an on-going discovery of the limitless mine (so to speak) of words and manners of speaking which this very copious and clever Mexican language has. And . . . since then, some years have passed, and in this time other words have continued to offer themselves to me anew [of the many which remain and will always remain to be put in]. (Molina 1571, 2d preface, unpaginated)

> I have learned it through a little use and exercise, and this cannot entirely uncover the secrets which there are in the language, which is so full, so elegant and of such cleverness and subtlety in its metaphors and expressions as those who practice it will come to know. (Molina 1555, 1571, preface, unpaginated)

These attitudes show through in the apparent delight with which Molina constructs some of his entries, as we will see below.

Some of Molina's notes to the reader will be discussed throughout this chapter as they become relevant. Here we condense the remaining ones, by their number in the Molina text, followed by our comments, because they illustrate the variety of linguistic matters to which he gave his attention.

From the Spanish-to-Nahuatl dictionaries:

> 1. Some Spanish words used in entries are rare or not actually used, but they make clear the properties of Nahuatl. For example *abaxador,* in order to clarify *tlatemouiani,* which in good Spanish means 'one who lowers something'.

Thus he "invents" a Spanish word with an agentive suffix to illustrate the agentive suffix *-ni* in Nahuatl. (*abaxador* = mod Sp *abajar* 'to lower' + *-dor* agentive suffix).

> 2. Where words occur in more than one dialect form, or different words are used, he will first give the word used in Tetzcoco and in Mexico, and then the words from other areas.

However, he does not identify which words are not from the preferred dialects.

> 3. Nahuatl verbs are given in first-person singular present indicative if there is one, otherwise in the third person. Spanish verbs are in the infinitive.
>
> 5. All the different words which there are to signify a single thing, which in Latin we call synonyms, will be separated with a period. And granted, the general meaning of all of these is the same, but in particular some are applied and said of some things, of which one could not say the others which are placed here. For example, 'to help': *nitepaleuia. nitenanamiqui. nitenanquilia.* The first is said of one who helps another in his necessities, works, and illnesses. The second is said of one who helps someone who is actively doing something, such as someone who is lifting from the ground some stone or large log, etc. The third is said of one who helps at mass. . . . Also it is said of one who helps to work the land of his neighbor, etc. And in this way there are many of this type, which are clarified much better in the second vocabulary which begins in the language of the Indians.

This is a noteworthy statement important for what it says about Molina's insights into meaning. But even more noteworthy is the fact that this statement occurs not only in the preface to the 1571 Spanish-to-Nahuatl dictionary but also in his 1555 work. Apparently at that time he already had in mind, and perhaps in preparation, the Nahuatl-as-source-language dictionary.

> 6. Spanish words derived from verbs, such as nouns and adverbs will be placed with the verbs that they are derived from if these agree in their first syllables, but they will be alphabetized in the normal way if they do not.

7. In Nahuatl, *u* is sometimes written for *o* and *o* for *u*, because the Indians use them variably in their pronunciation.

9. There are many words in the language which do not mean anything by themselves, but combined with others, they mean something. Thus, *c*, *qui*, which do not mean anything, but placed in front of a verb they indicate that the action of the verb passes to something else. And in Spanish we say 'a Pedro, a Juan'. *Pedro nictlaçotla.* I love Pedro.

10. Due to a lack of verbal nouns in the language, sometimes these are replaced with the preterite of the verb, or by other tenses, and when adverbs are lacking, they are replaced by verbal nouns in *-liztli* followed by the particle *-tica;* e.g., *teoyeuacatiliztica* 'escasamente', 'stingily'.

With regard to note 10 above, one should notice that it is the final word that is the adverb. *Teoyeuacatiliztli* is an abstract deverbal noun 'stinginess'.

11. Only the numbers which are the most common in Spanish are placed in the alphabetical order in order to give notice that they are to be found at the end of the vocabulary where they are given in numerical order. Numbers are placed there because their way of counting is very different and it is necessary to give some rules to understand the differences.

13. [note 12 in 1571] Some of these notes will not be understood by those who do not know Latin, because they are founded on the art of grammar. But they are placed here because for those who understand, they will provide light in order to better know how to use the verbs and what is derived from them.

And from the Nahuatl-to-Spanish dictionary of 1571:

4. The Indians do not speak of parts of the human body in the singular and the absolutive as Spanish does, but rather in the plural and always with the possessive prefix before them. For example, to say *maitl,* which means 'hand', they say *toma,* which means 'our hand'. . . . And for this reason, they are placed this way in this vocabulary, in order to follow their manner of speaking; however they are also given in the absolutive.

5. Some phrases and complete sentences are put into the dictionary because even though this practice seems to exceed the limits of a vocabulary, these expressions are very important to know and difficult to construct. And for the same reason some reverential verbs are placed in the dictionary as well.

8. Most verbs in Nahuatl make frequentatives by reduplicating their first or second syllable.

Nebrija's prefaces do not provide the variety of linguistic comments that Molina's do, but the preface to the Latin-Spanish dictionary does include a discussion of changes in vocabulary that accompany changes in the real world and the lack of congruence between Spanish and Latin with regard to what can be said with one word. Nebrija also provides an account of a quite modern-looking system of usage labels such as *novum* and *graecum*. There is also a substantial exposition of Latin verb construction types and a list of abbreviations for a classification of Latin verbs. The only guidance for dictionary usage given in the preface of the Spanish-to-Latin dictionary is the list of the alphabetical order used.

We see, then, that Molina has gone far beyond Nebrija in making various issues of language structure as well as his lexicographic practice explicit to the reader.

3. BACK MATTER; METALANGUAGE.

3.1. NUMERALS.   Both Sp>Nah dictionaries have a separate component dedicated to numerals following the vocabulary list. This account is what one might expect to find in a grammar. (And in this regard, it should be remembered that Molina's grammar did not appear until 1571.) These twelve folios (in three and a half folios in the larger-format double columns of the 1571 edition) provide an explanation of the base-twenty number system as well as a description of the system of number- classifiers, for example, "In order to count hens, eggs, cacao, prickly-pear fruit, tamales, Spanish loaves of bread, vessels, seats, fruit, beans, gourds, turnips, jicamas, melons, books or round and cylindrical things . . . " (Molina 1555: f251r). He also enumerates such compounds as ordinal numbers and 'another two . . .', 'two by two . . .', 'one of ten . . .', 'three times . . .', and so on. A note in each of the three prefaces explains the need for this component and refers the reader to it. The second edition provides a slightly longer list of numbers in two paragraphs and adds four additional short paragraphs.

3.2. METALANGUAGE.   Molina's metalanguage is a mixture of Spanish and Latin, by which he communicates to the reader a variety of types of information about Nahuatl in a format that places function over form.

3.2.1.   The most frequent device that Molina uses is the letter *s* ("long *s*") followed by a period, meaning 'that is to say'. Twelve times in Sp>Nah55 and nine times in Sp>Nah71 he spells this out: Latin *scilicet*, which he spells correctly in Sp>Nah71 but consistently spells incorrectly, probably as he pronounced it, as *silicet*, in Sp>Nah55. The following entry is an example of his occasionally free style:[14]

---

14. Unless otherwise noted, our translations represent the Spanish of Nebrija or Molina without regard to our opinion of the appropriateness of the relationship between the Spanish and Latin or Spanish and Nahuatl, respectively. We translate these other languages only when their meanings are directly relevant to the discussion. We usually transcribe

Acarrear piedras. ni, teçaca. acento breue. y assi de los de mas, SILICET acarrear madera, trigo &c. Sp>Nah55 f4r
'to haul rocks. *ni, teçaca.* short accent. and so on for the rest, that is to say,
to carry wood, wheat, etc.'

What he has done here is explain his use of *y assi de los de mas* (mod Sp
y así de los demás). We return to the remainder of this quotation in section 4.4.2.1. In the Nahuatl, Molina uses the abbreviation *i.* in the same
way as *scilicet*. We assume it abbreviates *id est*.

3.2.2.   Also illustrated in the above quotation is Molina's use of *y assi de
los de mas* (*y así de los demás*) 'and in that way with the rest'. In the 1571
dictionaries he also uses the equivalent Latin expression *et sic de alijs* (or
in one case, *et sic de similibus*). Sp>Nah55 contains only *y assi de los de mas*
(12) while Nah>Sp71 contains only *et sic de alijs* (35). Sp>Nah71 contains
both, and in the largest number (35 of the Spanish, 19 of the Latin). While
we count only a few entries with this notation in Sp>Nah55, in Sp>Nah71
the use of the device has grown to 54 occurrences. The reason for Molina's
greatly increased use of these two expressions is not hard to find: given
that one cannot possibly put all compound forms, much less all syntactic
constructions, in the dictionary, they provide Molina with a ready means
of exemplifying the structures of the language for the reader and guiding
him in the formation of items not actually in the dictionary—a way of illustrating what he saw as the elegance, cleverness, and subtlety of Nahuatl.
Consider the examples below, which take the following form:

Literal entry from Molina
Entry with English translation of Spanish and the Nahuatl for the sub-
stitutable item italicized.
Nahuatl morphology
Literal translation of Nahuatl morphemes.

Carne de venado.   maçanacatl.   ET SIC DE SIMILIBUS. Sp>Nah71 f25r1
'Deer meat.   *maça*nacatl.   AND SO ON FOR SIMILAR THINGS.'
maça nacatl
'deer-meat'

---

literally the authors' conventions for use of the letters *i, j, y, u, v* but do not indicate the
difference between *s* and "long *s*." In some cases, we regularize word division in both languages and irrelevant minor spelling deviations for the benefit of the reader. Thus examples for which there are references to both Sp>Nah dictionaries may in fact differ in such
trivialities as spacing or a missing *n*. Where we do translate Nahuatl, our translations are
roughly morpheme by morpheme, with brackets enclosing translations of morphemes
requiring more than one English word. In some cases, a more detailed morphology is possible but not relevant to the discussion.

This example not only gives the reader the word for 'meat', but it exemplifies for him how to use it in constructions denoting particular kinds of meat, with the assurance that the one given is typical for the group.

Figura de quatro angulos. nauhcampa nacace machiyotl. Y ASSI DE LOS DE MAS.

Sp>Nah71 f62v2

'Figure with four angles. *nauh*campa nacace machiyotl. AND SO ON WITH THE REST.'

nauh- cam- pa   nacaz[15] e   machiyotl
'four- place- toward ear-   [one-who-has]   sign'

Here Molina differs from Nebrija, who maintains separate entries for every shape from three angles to eleven in order to give their Greek equivalents. Molina's abbreviation by means of example and metalanguage allows the reader to construct the words for other figures on his own.

Hazia la cibdad de mexico. *mexicopa. mexicopauic.* ET SIC DE ALIJS.

Sp>Nah71 f70r1

'Toward the city of Mexico. *mexicopa. mexico*pauic. AND SO ON FOR THE OTHERS.'

mexico- pa   mexico -pa   -uic
'Mexico-toward'   'Mexico-toward-direction'

In this entry the headword *hazia* 'toward' corresponds to the Nahuatl postposition *pa*, which Molina demonstrates in context, explaining to the reader that anyplace else could be substituted for *Mexico* in the example phrase.

Sostituto ser de alguno, o puesto en su lugar, conforme al oficio que tiene
como de tlatoani. nite, tlatocatilia. De calpixqui. nite, calpixcatilia. Y ASSI
DELOS DEMAS. Sp>Nah71 f110v2
'To be substituted for someone, or to be put in his place, depending on the
office which he has such as tlatoani. nite, *tlatoca*tilia. From calpixqui:
nite, *calpixca*tilia. AND SO ON FOR THE OTHERS.'

ni-te,   tlatoca-ti- lia.   ni-te,   cal- pix- ca-   ti- lia
'I- someone, ruler- be-cause.' 'I- someone, house-keep-[one-who]-be-cause'

(The Nahuatl actually means 'to cause someone to be a ruler', and so on. Molina's example is not the most propitious, since idiosyncratically the *tlatoca* of the compound does not occur in the uncompounded form *tlatoqui* and substitutes the similar agentive noun *tlatoani*, formed from the present rather than the preterite stem.)

---

15. *c* before a front round vowel becomes *z* when the vowel is deleted.

Notice that in this last example what Molina has actually placed in the dictionary is a particular use of a Nahuatl construction (preterite agentive noun plus intransitive denominative verb suffix *-ti* plus causative suffix *-lia*), keyed to the Spanish headword *sostituto* 'substituted'. The suffix combination means 'to cause to become' or 'to cause to be like', and the reader may fill in whatever noun he wishes, based on Molina's examples.

3.2.3.   Molina uses the Latin phrase *per metaphoram* 'by metaphor' and various abbreviations of it to indicate the inclusion of metaphorical equivalents in addition to other Nahuatl equivalents, or sometimes as the only equivalent(s). Four examples follow.[16] For reasons of space, we will translate only the Spanish and the metaphors rather than all of the Nahuatl equivalents.

> Esconder algo. nitla, tlatia. nitla, ynaya. nitla, yyana. ET PER METAPHORÃ. pet-latitlan, ycpaltitlan nitlaaquia. ycpaltitlan nitlacalaquia. Sp>Nah71 f57v2-58r1
>
> 'To hide something . . . AND METAPHORICALLY . . . (1) . . . (2) . . .'

(1)   petlatitlan, icpaltitlan nitlaaquia.

| petla- | ti- | tlan, | icpal-ti- | tlan | ni-tla- | aqui- a. |

'[reed-mat]-ligature-place, seat- ligature-place   I- something-enter-cause.'
'I put something under a reed mat, a seat.'

(The modern *icpalli, equipal* in Mexican Spanish, is a leather-covered chair whose seat is a cylindrical drumlike stand, with the inside hollow, though usually visible through slats.)

(2)   icpaltitlan nitlacalaquia.

| icpal-ti- | tlan | ni-tla- | cal- | aqui- a. |

'seat-ligature-place I- something-container-enter-cause.'
'I put something under an *equipal.*'

> Cruel persona. cocole. tlauele. & PER METAPHORAM. tequani. Sp>Nah55 f58r
>
> 'A cruel person. *cocole. tlauele.* AND METAPHORICALLY *tequani.*'

te-   qua-ni
someone-   eat-[one-who]

---

16. Verbs in Nahuatl entries are given in the form "prefixes, verb" in the Sp>Nah dictionaries, "verb. prefixes" in the Nah>Sp dictionary. Where the meaning of the Nahuatl is relevant to the discussion, the English glossing of the Nahuatl should enable the reader to follow the structure of the entry.

(Literally a someone-eater, a carnivorous animal or a poisonous animal such as a spider. The identical entry appears in Sp>Nah71 but without the designation of metaphor.)

> Caer engraue delicto. nin, atoyauia. nino, tepexiuia. METAPHO.
> Sp>Nah71 f22v2 (in Sp>Nah55 f39v as 'Caer engran delito')
> 'To fall into serious crime. *nin, atoyauia. nino, tepexiuia.* METAPHOR-
>   ICAL'
> 'I throw myself into a river.' 'I fall over a cliff.'
> nin, atoyauia. nino, tepexiuia.

> ni-n[o],   atoya-uia.   ni-no,   tepexi-   uia.
> 'I-myself, river-[apply-to].   I- myself, [high-place]-[apply-to]'

(These verbs appear in Nah>Sp71 but are provided only in their literal meanings.)

3.2.4. LABEL-LIKE COMMENTS.   Although Molina does not employ a for-mal system of labels, he does use notations of various types on an ad hoc basis. For example, in a variety of items, he includes the information that certain words or expressions are used only by women, or (less frequently) by men. The most obvious examples of these are kinship terms and related words. For example:

> Desposarse. nino, manepanoa. nino, namictia. teoyoticaninonamictia. [Y EL
>   VARON DIZE.] nino, ciuauatia. [Y LA MUGER DIZE.] ninocchotia.
> 'To be wed . . . [AND THE MAN SAYS.] *nino, ciuauatia.* [AND THE WOMAN SAYS.]
>   *ninocchotia.'* where *ciuauatia* is 'to make oneself one who has a woman'
>   and *occhotia* is 'to take a husband'. Sp>Nah71 f43r2

However, there are a few cases in which the meaning is affective, and he is giving us the equivalents of modern descriptive labels.

> Bien esta, otorgando. maiui. yequalli. Y LAS MUGERES DIZEN. xiço. xiçoti.
> Sp>Nah71 f19v2
> 'It's ok, authorizing. . . . AND THE WOMEN SAY. *xiço. xiçoti.'*

> Xiço. bien esta, otorgando. Y ES HABLA DE SOLAS LAS MUGERES. Nah>Sp71
> f159r1
> '*Xiço.* It's ok, authorizing. AND IT IS SPEECH ONLY OF WOMEN.'

Molina also uses grammatical labels such as *aduerbio* 'adverb' (quite fre-quent) and *pronombre* 'pronoun' (occasional).

3.2.5. Molina also specifies whether Nahuatl equivalents apply to animate or inanimate subjects in one Spanish entry in Sp>Nah55 and two in Sp>Nah71.

Quedo estar, DE COSAS ANIMADAS. ni, tlamattica. ni, pactica. ni, tlamatcaca.
  Y DELAS YNANIMADAS DIZĒ. tlamattimani, tlamatcamani. Sp>Nah55 f206r,
  Sp>Nah71 f100v1
  'To be quiet, OF ANIMATE THINGS. . . . AND OF INANIMATE THINGS THEY SAY . . .'

Sin cuento. amo çantlapoualtin. DIZESE DE COSAS ANIMADAS. Y DE INANI-
  MADAS. amoçan tlapoualli. Sp>Nah71 f109v1
  'Without number. . . . IT IS SAID OF ANIMATE THINGS. AND OF INANIMATE ONES
  . . .'

In both cases, Molina gives verb forms in the first person for the animates,
in third person for the inanimates.

3.2.6.   Molina uses two means of cross-referencing one entry word to
another: *busca* 'see' and *lo mismo es que* 'it is the same as . . .' and slight
variants of this, once in its Latin equivalent *idem est quod* in Sp>Nah71.
These two expressions are used only 32 times in Sp>Nah55. In
Sp>Nah71, we count 22 occurrences of *lo mismo es que* but well over
300 of *busca*. The two seem to serve the same function. In Nah>Sp71,
with only two exceptions, *lo mismo es que* is used exclusively, more than
450 times.

Below we give a variety of examples with commentary, since we think
that these provide a vivid picture of Molina's meticulous attention to a
variety of issues.

Guerrero. LO MESMO ES QUE guerreador. Sp>Nah55 f134r, Sp>Nah71 f67r2
  'warrior. IT IS THE SAME AS "warrior".'

Metalanguage identifies a Spanish synonym, which is the immediately
preceding entry word with four Nahuatl equivalents.

Amo nonnocaqui. LO MESMO ES QUE amo ninocaqui. Nah>Sp71 f5v1
  '*amo nonnocaqui*. IT IS THE SAME AS "*amo ninocaqui*".'

The insertion of the directional prefix *-on-* gives quite a different look
to the verb. Molina equates *ni-on-no-caqui* 'I-directional-myself-hear' with
ni-no-caqui 'I-myself-hear'. The effect of this directional on meaning is
minimal and hence the *lo mesmo es que*. The entire phrase means something like 'I don't pay attention'.

Tlayuua. LO MESMO ES QUE anochecer, o hazer escuro. Pre. otlayuuac.
  Nah>Sp71 f122v1
  '*tlayoua*. IT IS THE SAME AS "for night to fall", or "to become dark". preterite
  otlayouac.'

In this case, Molina seems to have forgotten that he is in the Spanish
target-language field for a Nahuatl entry word. All he needs is the Spanish equivalents *anochecer, hazer escuro*. The *lo mesmo es que* is misplaced.

Tlaquimiloqui. LO MESMO ES QUE tlaquimiloani. Nah>Sp71 f134r2
'*tlaquimiloqui.* IT IS THE SAME AS "*tlaquimiloani*".'

The entry word and the word to which Molina equates it are both deverbal agent nouns, the entry word formed on the past, the other on the
present: 'something-[a-wrap]-[apply-to]-[past-agent]', 'something-[a-wrap]-
[apply-to]-[present-agent]'.

Teputzcomonia. nite. LO MISMO ES QUE tepotzcomonia. Pre. oniteteputz-
comoni. Nah>Sp71 f103v1
'*teputzcomonia. nite.* IT IS THE SAME AS "*tepotzcomonia*". preterite *oniteteputz-
comoni.*'

In this way Molina acknowledges two different spellings, probably sig-
naling variant pronunciations, for the entry word, due to the fact that
Nahuatl has only one rounded vowel phoneme.

Acechar. BUSCA asechar. Sp>Nah71 f2v2
'to be a look-out. SEE *asechar.*'

Molina refers the reader to a variant spelling of the Spanish word
because of the incipient loss of distinction between the two front sibilants
in New World Spanish. Errors of this type are rare in Molina. The modern word is *acechar.*

3.2.7. Latin *vel* 'or' occurs in both Spanish and Nahuatl to offer alternatives. To the best of our knowledge, Spanish *o* 'or' occurs only in Spanish. Alternatives may occur in both source and target language and
between grammatical components in Nahuatl as well as between equivalents. The first example shows both Spanish *o* and Latin *vel* in the same
Spanish equivalent.

Quemman. Algunas vezes, atiempos, O a ratos. VEL. aque hora? pregun-
tando. Aduer. Nah>Sp71 f88v2
'sometimes, at times, OR occasionally, OR at what time? interrogative.'

Aquedar el ganado. nite VEL nitla, yacatzacuilia. Sp>Nah71 f12v2
'to detain cattle. I-someone OR I-something, nose-close-benefactive.'

Exercitarme en armas, VEL simile. nino, yeyecoua. nino, mamachtia.
Sp>Nah71 f61v2
'to practice with weapons, OR [something] similar.' (where *simile* is also
Latin)

Agosto mes. lo mismo. UEL. yc chicuei metztli ycexiuitl. Sp>Nah55 f1or
'August, month. the same. OR the eighth month in a year.'

The availability of alternatives allows Molina the descriptive style of
entry construction that he favors.

4. CONTENT.   In describing and evaluating Molina's dictionaries, a variety of issues of macrostructure, language, and semantic content converge in such a way that it would be difficult to discuss them separately, and thus we take them up under this general heading.

4.1. INSIDER/OUTSIDER: MOLINA'S VIEWPOINT.   As we will see below, Molina's vocabulary usage places him comfortably in the early colonial Mexican world. His knowledge of Nahuatl vocabulary and the culture in which it is based tells us that he was in close and familiar contact with its speakers, and we see from his prefaces that he wrote the dictionaries to help the Spaniards meet the needs of these speakers, and, in particular, to help his fellow missionaries bring them the Christian faith. Yet even he maintained, as we might expect, something of the point of view of an outsider. Although much of what appears in the dictionaries applies to the world in general, no small number of entries report native customs, environment, and material culture. These entries impart something of the flavor of an anthropological work here and there. We think we see a tendency, though no more than that, to use third-person plurals with reference to 'them' in contrast to the impersonal *se* in reference to 'people in general'. For example, *caracol grande de agua con que tañen. tecciztli. atecocoli.* Sp>Nah55 f44r 'large sea snail or conch which they play [as a musical instrument]' uses the third person 'they play' rather than the impersonal 'is played, one plays'. The entry *caña de çahumerio que chupan los indios, o cosa embeuida. tlachichintli.* Nah>Sp71 f117r2 'cane of aromatic substance that the Indians puff or something which is drunk' actually shows *los indios* as the overt subject of *chupan* 'they suck, puff'. Compare these with *casa desierta o desamparada, que no se habita. ça iuhticac.* Nah>Sp71 f14v2 'deserted house which is not inhabited' (not *casa desierta . . . que no habitan* 'deserted house which they do not inhabit'); also *canto que se canta a otro. tecuicatiliztli.* Sp>Nah55 f43r 'a song which is sung to someone else' (not *canto que cantan a otro* 'a song which they sing to someone else').

Molina's more direct references to the New World and its people take several forms. The entries for *chilli* illustrate three ways of referring to the New World:

> Axi pimienta dela tierra. chilli. Sp>Nah55 f3or
> '*aji*, pepper of the [this] land.'
> Axi o pimienta desta tierra. chilli. Sp>Nah71 f17v2
> '*aji* or pepper of this land.'
> Chilli. axi. o pimienta de las indias. Nah>Sp71 f21r1
> '*aji* or pepper of the Indies.'

The people themselves he calls *indios* 'Indians', or in the prefaces, *los naturales* 'the natives':

> Tlaxaxauaniliztli. alaridos que dã los moros y LOS YNDIOS enla guerra.
> Nah>Sp71 f145v1
> 'cries which the Moors and THE INDIANS make in war.'

> Camisa que vsan LAS YNDIAS. uipilli. Sp>Nah55 f42r
> 'shirt which THE INDIAN WOMEN wear.'

> India tlaca. gente DELAS YNDIAS. Nah>Sp71 f39r1
> 'people OF THE INDIES.'

A somewhat more ambiguous entry, though we think he is referring only to the indigenous peoples of New Spain, is

> Nueua españa tlaca. LA GẼTE, O LOS NATURALES DELA NUEUA ESPAÑA.
> Nah>Sp71 f74r2
> 'THE PEOPLE OR THE NATIVES OF NEW SPAIN'

4.2. LANGUAGE: AMERINDIAN BORROWINGS; NAHUATL IN SPANISH AND SPANISH IN NAHUATL. Molina shows an easy and nonpuristic outlook in his language use. In some cases, probably without realizing it, he incorporates Amerindian vocabulary, both Nahuatl and Caribbean, in his Spanish, and likewise he is readily accepting of Spanish borrowings into Nahuatl. In his prefaces, Molina discusses the difficulties of dealing with new concepts both in Nahuatl and in Spanish and points out the need for circumlocutions in both languages and for Spanish borrowings, both literal and adapted, in Nahuatl. Interestingly, he does not mention borrowings INTO Spanish, of which he has a number.

> The third point involves a difficulty and not a small one: that we have many things that they were not familiar with nor were aware of. And for these things they did not have and still do not have their own words. And on the other hand, the things which they had which we lacked in our language cannot easily be communicated by precise and exact words. And thus in order to understand their words as well as to clarify our own, sometimes long circumlocutions and round-abouts are necessary. (Preface Sp>Nah55, unpaginated)

> Eighth Note
> Where *lo mesmo* or *idem* is placed after the Romance [Spanish], one is to understand that the natives do not have another suitable word in their language, but rather that they use the same one that we have literally. And other times from our Romance and their language they form their nouns or verbs by varying or changing something of our Romance and their language, or mixing the one language with the other. For example, Ninocalças-copina, descalçome las calças.

I-myself-*calças* (pants)-remove 'I take off my pants.'[17] (Preface Sp>Nah55, unpaginated)

We see from these quotations and from Molina's practice that his focus is on functional communication. He is not concerned with artificial puristic standards for either language.

4.2.1. BORROWINGS IN SPANISH.

4.2.1.1.   Molina's Spanish and also the Nahuatl that he reports show the effects of cultural exchange on both languages by midcentury. In the first place, it is interesting to see the easy incorporation of non-Nahuatl Amerindian words in his Spanish. We note the following: *axi* 'hot pepper', *batata* 'potato', *cacique* 'cacique', *canoa* 'canoe', *huracan* 'hurricane', *maguei* 'maguey, agave', *maiz* 'maize, corn', and *tuna* 'prickly-pear fruit, tuna'. These appear in the Spanish of the dictionaries as easily as do words of French or Arabic origin, though in smaller numbers.[18] By contrast, Nebrija (1495) has only the word *canoa,* and we are aware of no other Amerindian borrowings in his 1516 revision.

4.2.1.2.   It is interesting to note that these words serve both in the source-language Spanish and the target-language Spanish as the counterparts of Nahuatl words, resulting in entries that have Amerindian equivalents for Amerindian headwords. However, not one of these words occurs in the Nahuatl field of any of the dictionaries. Following is a nonexhaustive list.[19]

> TUNA. nochtli. cierta fruta conocida. Sp>Nah71 f115r2
> 'TUNA. *nochtli.* a certain known fruit.'
> Nochtli. TUNA, fruta conocida. Nah>Sp71 f72v1
> '*nochtli.* TUNA, a known fruit.'
> MAGUEI. metl. Sp>Nah71 f80v1
> 'MAGUEY. *metl.*'
> Metl. MAGUEI. Nah>Sp71 f55v1
> '*metl.* MAGUEY.'

17. Although *descalçar,* as in modern Spanish, normally meant 'to take off one's shoes' (*calçado*), it is clear from Molina's usage in the dictionaries that here he means literally to remove one's *calças* 'pants, trousers'.

18. Perhaps all that is surprising in this list is that these words were so well rooted in Spanish and accepted by Molina by the mid-sixteenth century. They are now such a part of mainstream culture that all but one of them (*ají*) occur in the *American Heritage Dictionary of the English Language.*

19. The majority of these words occur in Sp>Nah55 as well as the 1571 dictionaries but do not appear in this list because they are not headwords there.

BATATA. fruta conocida. camotli. Sp>Nah71 f19r1
'POTATO, a known fruit. *camotli.*'
Camotli. BATATA, rayz comestible. Nah>Sp71 f12r2
'*camotli.* POTATO, an edible root.'
AXI o pimienta desta tierra. chilli. Sp>Nah71 f17v2, similar Sp>Nah55 f30r
'AJÍ or pepper of this land. *chilli.*'
Chilli. AXI o pimienta de las indias. Nah>Sp71 f21r1
'*chili.* AJÍ or pepper of the Indies.'
MAIZ seco en maçorcas. centli. cintli. Sp>Nah71 f8ov2
'dry CORN on cobs. *centli. cintli.*'
Cintli. maçorcas de MAYZ secas y curadas. Nah>Sp71 f22v1
'*cintli.* ears of dry and cured CORN.'
Centli. maçorca de MAYZ curada y seca. Nah>Sp71 f18r1
'*centli.* an ear of cured and dry CORN.'
Tlaolli. MAYZ desgranado, curado y seco. Nah>Sp71 f130r1
'*tlaolli.* shelled CORN, cured and dry.'

And finally, Molina has at least two entries in which actual NAHUATL borrowings appear as Spanish entry words alongside their Nahuatl etyma in an equivalent relationship.

PETACA, hecha como caxa de cañas. petlacalli. Sp>Nah71 f95v2
'SUITCASE, made like a reed container. *petlacalli.*'
TAMEME, que lleua carga. tlamama. tlameme. Sp>Nah71 f111v1
'PORTER who carries a load. *tlamama. tlameme.*'

4.2.1.3. But while the above examples are directly involved in equivalent relationships, the majority of instances of Amerindianisms, from Nahuatl as well as from other languages, are merely part of the Spanish text. For example:

Çoço. nitla. ensartar cuentas, AXI, flores, o cosas semejantes. preterito. onitl-açoçoc. Nah>Sp71 f24v2
'to string beads, AJÍ, flowers, or similar things.'

Cercar la heredad de espinas, o de puyas de MAGUEY. nitla, uitzteca. nitla, uitzquetza. Sp>Nah71 f34r2
'to surround land with thorns or with MAGUEY points.'

Caxcara de granada o TUNA o cosa semejante. euayotl. Sp>Nah55 f46v
'peel of pomegranate or PRICKLY-PEAR FRUIT, or something similar.'

And with Nahuatl borrowings in the Spanish:

Echar CACAO de vna XICAL a otra para que haga espuma. naquetza. nachiua. Sp>Nah55 f91 (*cacao* perhaps < Nah *cacahuatl*, though Spanish may have received it from some other language.[20] *xical* < Nah *xicalli*)
'to pour CACAO from one GOURD CUP to another so that it makes foam.'

Centlaquechcuitl. vna espiga de trigo, de CHIA, o de cosa semejante.
Nah>Sp71 f18r1 (*chia* < Nah *chia* or *chiya* 'chia' [as in "chia pet"])
'a head of wheat or of CHIA, or something similar.'

Hundir se o abollar se el atabal o *petaca* por se auer asẽtado sobre ella.
pachiui. Sp>Nah55 f143r (*petaca* < Nah *petlacalli* < *petlatl* 'reed mat' and
calli 'house, container')
'for a drum or suitcase to collapse or get dented because of someone's having sat on it.'

4.2.1.4. Some of the Nahuatl borrowings into Spanish are taken literally
from Nahuatl. Others have been assimilated to various degrees into the
Spanish phonological and morphological system. In only one case have
we found a Nahuatl borrowing that has been absorbed into a compound
in Spanish. The following examples show two Spanish correspondences
for Nah *chilatl* 'chili-water':

Agua de axi. chilatl. Sp>Nah55 f1ov, Sp>Nah71 f6r1
Aguachil o agua de axi. chilatl. Sp>Nah71 f6r2
Chilatl. aguachil, o agua de axi. Nah>Sp71 f2ov2

Sp *agua de axi* is literally 'water of *ají*'. The other form, *aguachil,* is more
interesting. It is a Spanish compound from Sp *agua* 'water' and Nah *chilli*
'chili pepper', using a Spanish pattern of compounding parallel to the
Spanish compound *aguamiel* 'water sweetened with honey', from *agua* and
miel 'honey'. This borrowing apparently did not survive.

The list of Nahuatl words that we have found that appear as borrowings in Spanish follows, with the forms of the borrowings and number of
occurrences of each given for each dictionary.

Nahuatl word	Sp>Nah55	Sp>Nah71	Nah>Sp71
auacatl 'avocado'	—	aguacates 1	—
cacauatl 'chocolate bean'	cacao 14	cacao 18	cacao 35
cacaxtli 'carrying frame'	—	—	cacaxtle 1
cactli 'shoe'	—	—	cacles 6
camotli 'sweet potato'	—	—	camotes 2
chilli 'chili pepper'	—	-chil 1	-chil 1
	—	chilli 3	chilli 14
	—	chili 1	—

20. The question of the origin of Sp *cacao* is a complicated one that is outside the scope
of this chapter. Nah *cacauatl* 'chocolate bean, cacao' was borrowed into Spanish as *cacahu-
ate* and *cacahuete* 'peanut' from Nah *tlalcacauatl.*

chi(y)a(m)- 'chia'	chia 6	chia 9	chia 14
icpalli 'leather chair'	icpal 1	—	—
mecapalli 'headstrap'	—	mecapalli 4	mecapalli 2
	—	mecapal 6	—
petlacalli 'reed box'	petaca 1	petaca 3	petaca 1
pinolli 'pinole'	—	pinolli 1	pinolli 5
	pinol 1	pinol 4	pinol 1
tamalli 'tamale'	tamalli 1	—	tamalli 1
	—	—	tamal 1
	—	tamales 6	tamales 4
tameme 'porter'	—	tameme 4	tameme 10
temazcalli 'sauna'	—	temazcalli 1	temazcalli 5
tequiyotl 'work, tribute'	—	tequios 1	tequio 2
	—	tequiuh 1	—
toçan 'mole, gopher'	—	—	toçan 2
	—	—	tuçan 1
tomatl 'tomatillo'	tomatl 1	tomatl 1	tomatl 1
	—	tomates 1	tomates 2
xicalli 'gourd cup'	—	xicalli 1	xicalli 1
	xical 1	xical 3	xical 4
	xicala 2	xicala 2	xicala 2
xilotl 'tender ear of corn'	—	xilotl 1	—
xitomatl 'tomato'	—	—	xitomatl 1

The most apparent generalization that can be made from this list is that borrowings are less frequent in Sp>Nah55. Whether the borrowings to come had not yet fully taken root in Spanish or whether Molina was for some reason still reluctant to use them, we cannot know. The Spanish of Nah>Sp71 shows a slightly lower percentage of assimilated borrowings (50%) than do the Sp>Nah dictionaries (62.5%). Beyond these points, it is difficult to generalize.

The most assimilated of Molina's borrowings is the Nahuatl compound *petlacalli* 'reed-mat covered box' from *petlatl* 'reed mat' and *calli* 'house, container'. This word, 'suitcase' in Mexican Spanish, occurs with various meanings in other modern dialects. Spanish has borrowed the internal *tl* as *t* and has dropped not only the absolutive *-li* suffix but the stem-final *l* as well, giving *petaca* from *petlacalli*. This is the only form in which Molina borrows this word.

More generalized types of adaptation to Spanish phonology are apparent from this list, as are several unassimilated borrowings. Nouns ending in *-atl* normally give *-ate* in Spanish, whereas words in *-lli* give final *-l*, with the normal Spanish plural in *-es*. In addition to showing both this pattern and its unassimilated form, *xicalli* appears idiosyncratically in all three dictionaries as *xicala*, which is the precursor of modern Spanish *jícara* 'calabash, bowl, pot'.

4.2.1.5.   On a few occasions, a Nahuatl word is quoted or reported in Spanish as a foreign term:

> Axuia. nitla. vntar o embixar algo con cierto vnguento que se llama axin.
> preteri. onitlaaxui. Nah>Sp71 f1or2
> '*Axuia. nitla.* to spread or paint something with a certain ointment which is
> called *axin.* preterite *onitlaaxui.*'

4.2.1.6.   Finally, in a small number of cases (twenty-one, with a few other cases being ambiguous), when a headword or an equivalent was needed in Spanish for a Nahuatl object that did not correspond to one in Spanish, an analogy was drawn to a similar object in Spanish, noting that the one in question was 'from the/this land'. For example:

> Tañer trompeta dela tierra. ni, quiquiçoa. Sp>Nah55 f231v, Sp>Nah71
> f111v2
> 'to play a trumpet of the land. *ni, quiquiçoa.*'

> Axin. cierto vnguento desta tierra. Nah>Sp71 f1or1
> '*Axin.* a certain ointment of this land.'

And thus foreign objects could be related to known ones even without the need for borrowings.

4.2.2.   Spanish borrowings into Nahuatl, both assimilated and unassimilated, occur in greater variety and number than do borrowings from Nahuatl into Spanish and, largely because of the nature of Nahuatl morphology, are far better integrated into the language than are Nahuatl borrowings into Spanish. Molina explains in note 9 of the Nah>Sp71 preface that the natives use words composed of both languages "which compounds are so used that they do not say them in any other way and for this reason we must also use them in the same manner that they do."

4.2.2.1.   Molina (preface, quoted in §4.2 above) uses the indications *lo mismo* or *lo mesmo* (the older form of the word) or Latin *idem*, all meaning 'the same', to indicate that the Indians use the Spanish word by itself. It is clear that he means by this nothing more than uncompounded borrowing, because there are almost NO occurrences of simple Spanish words occurring as Nahuatl equivalents, beyond the notations mentioned above, while there is an abundance of Spanish borrowings in Nahuatl compounds, some of them also occurring as *lo mismo* in their simple form. There is apparently little of interest to be said about the distribution of *mismo* versus *mesmo* to indicate borrowings. *Lo mismo* outnumbers *lo mesmo* by two to one and occurs as a higher percentage of the total in Sp>Nah71 than in Sp>Nah55. *Idem* occurs only twice, both in Sp>Nah71.

Some of the borrowings that are so indicated are:

Angel. lo mismo. Sp>Nah55 f18v
'Angel. the same.'

Colchon. lo mismo. vel. quachpepechtli. Sp>Nah55 f48r, Sp>Nah71 f27r1
'Cushion. the same. or blanket-[flattened-surface].'

Azeyte. lo mismo. Sp>Nah55 f30r, Sp>Nah71 f18r1
'Oil. the same.'

4.2.2.2. SPANISH BORROWINGS IN COMPOUNDS AND CONSTRUCTIONS.
Azeite 'oil', was a common borrowing in Nahuatl (25 occurrences in the
three dictionaries). In addition to the above occurrences as *lo mismo*, we
see adjacent to them in the dictionaries the following compounded
entries in which the Spanish word is overt.

Azeytera. azeyte contontli. chiama contontli. Sp>Nah71 f18r1, (Sp>Nah55
f30r first equivalent only)
'Oil dispenser. oil pot-small. chia-water pot-small.'

Azeytero que lo vende. azeyte namacac. chiamanamacac. Sp>Nah55 f30r,
Sp>Nah71 f18r1
'Oil-man who sells oil. oil sell-[one-who]. chia-water-sell-[one-who].'

Some other Spanish words that occur embedded in Nahuatl compounds are illustrated below. We present these examples not as entries
but rather with the illustrated compound first in standardized spelling,
followed by its Spanish counterpart, Nahuatl morphological analysis, and
English translation.

almendrasazeite. azeite de almendras. Sp>Nah71 f18r2
almendras-azeite 'almond-oil', 'oil from almonds.' (Sp *almendras* 'almonds',
aceite 'oil')

This is an interesting compound in that both halves are Spanish borrowings, compounded in the normal Nahuatl pattern.

cahuallo ipan icpalli. silla de cauallo o mula. Sp>Nah55 f226r, Sp>Nah71
f109r2, Nah>Sp71 f12v2
cahuallo i-pan icpalli 'horse its-on seat', 'saddle of a horse or mule' (Sp *caballo*
'horse')

ni, cahuallosillaana. desensillar bestia. Sp>Nah55 f76r, Sp>Nah71 f41r1
ni, cahuallo-silla-ana. 'I, horse-seat-grasp', 'to unsaddle a horse' (Sp *caballo*
'horse', *silla* 'seat, saddle')

The verb *ana* has as its incorporated object a Nahuatl compound noun
consisting of two borrowed Spanish nouns.

ni, cahuallocaccopina. desherrar bestia. Sp>Nah55 f76v, Sp>Nah71 f41r2,
Nah>Sp71 f12v2
ni, cahuallo-cac-copina 'I, horse-shoe-remove', 'to unshoe a horse'

The verb is preceded by its incorporated direct object, a noun-noun compound, *cauallo-cactli,* of which the first element is Sp *caballo* 'horse'.

ni, cãdelayacacotona. despauilar candela. Sp>Nah55 f79v
ni, candela-yaca-cotona 'I, candle-nose-cut' 'to trim a candle wick' (Sp *candela*
'candle')

seboocotl. candela de sebo. Sp>Nah55 f42v, Sp>Nah71 f24r1
sebo-ocotl 'tallow-[pine-torch]', 'candle of tallow' (Sp *sebo* 'tallow')

Molina's spacing for words in both languages is not entirely consistent.
But in addition to this, he shows a tendency to separate compounds containing borrowings in cases where he would be less likely to write entirely
native compounds as separate words. For example, 'beeswax candle' is *xico-
cuitlaocotl* 'bee-excrement-[pine-torch]', but he writes the above-mentioned
'tallow candle' as *sebo ocotl* even though its structure is the same.

Religious vocabulary represents about 25 percent of the total borrowed
word types. We mention one example below.

icualanilitzin dios. yra de dios. Nah>Sp71 f42-1
i -cualani -li[z]-tzin dios 'his-[become-angry]-ness-honorific God', 'the wrath
of God' (Sp *dios* 'god')

4.2.2.3.   There was a parallel in Nahuatl for the *de la tierra, desta tierra*
device in Spanish. This alternative to borrowings from Spanish was the liken-
ing of the Spanish concept to be borrowed to something similar in Nahuatl
with the designation *castillan* 'Castile-place' (with the *ll* pronounced long as
in Nahuatl, not as [y] or [ʎ] as in Spanish). For example, *ajo* 'garlic' was borrowed as *lo mismo* in Sp>Nah55. In Sp>Nah71, this had become *Aio. lo mismo.
vel. castillan xonacatl.* 'Garlic. the same, or Castile-place onion.' Sp>Nah71
f7v1. 'Leek' occurs as *Puerro. lo mismo. vel uey castillan xonacatl.* 'the same, or
large Castile-place onion.' Sp>Nah55 f204r, Sp>Nah71 f99v1. It also occurs
as *Puerro. castillan xonacatl.* 'Leek, Castile-place onion.' Sp>Nah71 f97v2. *Sar-
dina arẽcada pece conocido. castillã michuatzaltepitõ.* 'Herring, a known fish.
Castile-place fish-dried-small-dimin' occurs in both Sp>Nah55 f221v, and
Sp>Nah71 f107v1. *Trigo. castillan tlaulli.* 'Wheat. Castile-place shelled corn.'
also occurs in both Sp>Nah55 f238r and Sp>Nah71 f115r1. Molina uses this
device a total of forty-five times in Sp>Nah55, fifty-three times in Sp>Nah71,
sometimes accompanied by *lo mismo* or another equivalent.[21]

21. For an account of Spanish borrowing in Nahuatl, see Karttunen and Lockhart 1976;
Karttunen 1985.

4.3. THE QUESTION OF THE NEBRIJA ELICITATION LIST. The question of whether Nebrija's dictionary served as an elicitation list for Molina requires a close comparison of the content and form of the respective Spanish components of Nebrija (we use the fuller 1516 edition for this purpose) and Molina's original Spanish-to-Nahuatl dictionary of 1555.

To determine the degree of incorporation of Nebrija's word list into Molina 1555, we alphabetized[22] the dictionaries together and made a careful comparison of all entries beginning in Sp *ca-* (except for *caz-* and *caç-*, because of a technical problem). This count was part of a broader comparison of the content of all three Molina dictionaries and Nebrija 1516, so all four dictionaries were sorted together, with Nah>Sp71 being sorted Spanish-first like the others. The resulting file consisted of a total of 2,566 entries within this alphabetical range. This sample included 755 entries from Nebrija 1516 and 534 from Molina 1555.

The problem of determining what are and are not the "same" entries in two dictionaries is more complicated than one might imagine. Naturally, we discounted differences in spelling and spacing. In addition, because we suspected that claims of Molina's dependence on Nebrija have been overestimated, we took a very broad interpretation of "same" to give this claim the fairest consideration possible. For example, the following pairs of Spanish items were classified as representing "the same entry":

Nebrija	Molina
cachorro can pequeño.	cachorro perro.
caer como quiera.	caer generalmente.
caldereria lugar.	caldereria do se hazen.
cãpesino cosa de tal cãpo.	campesino.
cangilon vaso de barro.	cangilon.
carnero dõde echã los huessos.	carnero de muertos.
cayda o caymiento.	cayda generalmente.

4.3.1. Using this definition of "same entry," we counted 545 entries in Nebrija 1516 alone, 324 entries in Molina 1555 alone, and 210 entries shared by both dictionaries. See figure 16.1.

Thus we see that if we assume Molina was in fact borrowing from Nebrija, he took only 27.8 percent of Nebrija's entries to incorporate into his own dictionary, where they form 39.3 percent of his word list. It should be recalled that these numbers are based on a very broad interpretation of

22. All of our programming is done by Campbell in a DOS/Windows environment, using Catspaw SPITBOL, a string-processing language related to SNOBOL4, and Opt-Tech Sort. For purposes of searching and sorting, all Nahuatl entries carry a regularized spelling in addition to their original spelling.

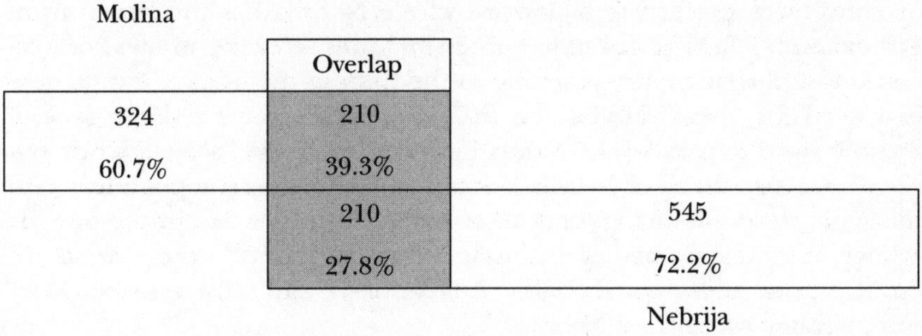

Molina

	Overlap	
324	210	
60.7%	39.3%	
	210	545
	27.8%	72.2%

Nebrija

Figure 16.1. Comparison of Molina 1555 and Nebrija 1516.

"same." A narrower interpretation of identity would have resulted in an even smaller intersection of the two vocabulary lists. Furthermore, since the first edition (1495) of Nebrija's Spanish-to-Latin dictionary was published only sixty years before the first edition of Molina's, a substantial intersection in the two sets of entries is to be expected simply by virtue of the fact that these are both Spanish word lists compiled little more than half a century apart. It seems to us that the differences between the two dictionaries are greater than what one would expect from changes in the Spanish lexis over this short period, even allowing for the difference in milieu and the upheaval brought about by the conquest of the New World.

This is not to say, however, that we do not think Molina consulted Nebrija's dictionary in one form or another and integrated entries from it. The following two entries, for example, seem too similar to attribute to chance.

Carne de membrillo. cydonites, ę. Neb16 f18r2
Carne de membrillo. necutlanelolli membrillo. Sp>Nah71 f25r1
'meat of the quince'

Caudillo. busca en capitan, &c. Neb16 f19r1
Caudillo. busca capitan. Sp>Nah71 f25v4
'Leader. See *capitán*.'

Both of these entries were added in the 1571 edition, where there are rather few new entries that correspond to entries from Nebrija. In the first case, this is the only entry in either dictionary in which *carne* refers to the meat of a fruit, and in both cases, the fruit is quince. In the second case, no equivalent for *caudillo* is given, but in each dictionary, the reader is referred to the word *capitán*.

4.3.2.   A number of cases of lack of agreement in lexical content are due to Molina's choosing a hyperonym where Nebrija gives hyponyms, or conversely, preferring hyponyms where Nebrija has the hyperonym. For example, Nebrija has nine entries for *carne* referring to meat of various kinds, plus one entry referring to the flesh of the quince, but no general word for 'meat'. Molina, on the other hand, wants a single general Spanish word to parallel the Nahuatl word *nacatl* 'meat', although one can certainly construct all of Nebrija's entries in Nahuatl by compounding with this basic word. Molina ignores all of Nebrija's entries except the one for quince and makes his own simple entry for meat: *carne. nacatl.* In Sp>Nah71 he adds *carne de hombre* 'human flesh' and *carne de venado* 'venison', neither taken from Nebrija.

Likewise in another case of choosing the hyperonym, Molina wants only one entry for the word *carro* 'wagon or cart' and does not put that in until Sp>Nah71, cross-referenced to *carreta* 'wagon or cart', while Nebrija has no general *carro* but has no less than SEVEN more specific entries, all of which Molina rejects.

On the other hand, it is Molina who prefers hyponyms in the case of *caracol*. Both Molina and Nebrija have *caracol de escalera* 'spiral staircase'. Beyond this, Nebrija has only simple *caracol* 'snail, conch'. Molina, wanting hyponyms to distinguish several types of univalve shells, has four entries for *caracol,* all of them with limiting glosses in Spanish and with different Nahuatl equivalents: *caracol como los de España* 'conch or snail like those in Spain', *caracol grande de agua con que tañen* 'large sea snail that they play [as a musical instrument]', *caracol largo* 'long snail', and *caracol muy chico* 'very small snail'.

Similarly, Nebrija has two entries for *cabezudo* 'having a large head': *cabeçuda cosa con cabeça* 'headed, something having a head' and *cabeçudo hombre* 'a man with a large head'. For Molina, apparently the second of these is insufficient and the first is unnecessary since it is the hyperonym for the new entries that he makes. He omits both, and for *cabeçudo hombre* he substitutes four more specific entries: *cabeçudo de cabeça ancha* 'having a wide head', *cabeçudo de cabeça larga* 'having a long head', *cabeçudo de gran cabeça* 'having a large head', and *cabeçudo porfiado* 'big-headed, stubborn', each with a different Nahuatl equivalent or equivalents.

4.3.3.   Not all differences between the word lists result from the choice of hyperonym/hyponyms. In addition to such examples, and independent of hyperonym/hyponym relationships, we see examples such as *cavar* 'to dig' and related nouns and adjectives: Nebrija has twelve entries for these items. Molina incorporates only ONE of these in Sp>Nah55 but introduces seven of his own. He adds eight more in Sp>Nah71, including the rather picturesque *Cauar la tierra o escaruarla con el pie, estando hablando con otro* 'to dig at the earth or scratch it with the foot, [while] standing talking with someone'.

This example serves to introduce an important aspect of Molina's approach to dictionary building that he shares with Nebrija, and we shall return to it after a brief excursus on the modern bilingual dictionary.

4.3.4. Modern lexicography suggests that since one uses a bilingual dictionary quite differently and for different purposes, depending on whether one is going out of one's native language or into it, it is best to compose separate dictionary pairs, active (or encoding) and passive (or decoding), for native speakers of each language used in a bilingual dictionary.[23] If such a plan is not feasible, it is at least necessary to attend to the different uses to which the two halves of a dictionary will be put: where the user will be going from the known to the unknown, where from the unknown to the known. In the case of the Molina dictionaries, we have seen that he did not have the intention of serving native-speaking Nahuatl users. Furthermore, in the case of Nebrija's dictionaries, there were no native speakers of Latin whose interests might be accommodated, so we might expect the dictionaries of both authors to serve as active bilingual dictionaries in the Spanish-first dictionaries and as passive bilingual dictionaries in the case of the Latin-to-Spanish and Nahuatl-to-Spanish dictionaries. Thus we might expect them to closely match our assumptions concerning the form of modern bilingual dictionaries. But, in fact, neither Nebrija nor Molina had fully worked out the concept of the active bilingual dictionary. One would expect that an active bilingual dictionary (native > foreign, encoding) would base its word list on the needs of the source language: what the things are that one might need to express (considering the level of completeness of the dictionary) rather than what the available concepts are in the target language, because the active dictionary is where the speaker of a language goes to find out how to put his thoughts, of necessity phrased in the language that he knows best, into the foreign language. Yet the forms of many of the Spanish lemmata in these dictionaries and therefore the Spanish word lists themselves seem to be driven not by the source language but rather by their respective target languages.

4.3.5. SPANISH ENTRY WORDS AS DRIVEN BY THE TARGET LANGUAGE. We illustrate the claims of the above paragraph first by citing verbs with adverbs or prepositional phrases in Nebrija's Sp>Lat dictionaries. These are present not because they are lexicalized in Spanish—in fact, some of them do not even make a great deal of sense—but because they represent

---

23. For the typology of bilingual dictionaries, see Zgusta 1971: 298–307; Kromann, Riiber, and Rosbach 1984, 1991.

his translations of the corresponding Latin verbs with prefixes, which he apparently thought the user should be able to access directly through both dictionaries. Thus, for example, for the Spanish verb *caer* 'to fall', Nebrija offers three entries requiring different Latin equivalents:

> caer como quiera. cado -is, cecidi. 'to fall in general'
> caer resbalando o deslizandose. labor -eris. 'to slip and fall'
> caer subitamente. ruo, -is. labo, -as. 'to fall suddenly'

In addition to these, he provides separate entries for the first verb compounded with Latin prefixes *con-, re-, de-, sub-, in-,* and *ob-* as well as the derived frequentative verb *casito, -as, -avi* 'to fall often'.

> caer a menudo. casito, -as, -avi. 'to fall often'
> caer juntamente. concido, -is, concidi. 'to fall together'
> caer otra vez. recido, -is, recidi. 'to fall again'
> caer de arriba. decido, -is, decidi. 'to fall from above'
> caer abaxo. succido, -is, succidi. 'to fall downwards'
> caer en alguna cosa. incido, -is, incidi. 'to fall on or into something'
> caer muriendo. occido, -is, occidi. 'to fall dying'

In the case of the second verb, he has entries for compounds with *sub-* and *de-, in-, ad-, con-, dis-,* and *re-*.

> caer assi de arriba. sublabor, -eris. delabor, -eris. 'to fall in this way from above'
> caer assi en otra cosa. illabor, -eris. 'to fall in this way on something else'
> caer assi hazia otra cosa. allabor, -eris. 'to fall in this way toward something else'
> caer assi juntamente. collabor, -eris. 'to fall in this way together'
> caer assi en diversas partes. dilabor, -eris. 'to fall in this way in various pieces, to fall apart in this way'
> caer assi otra vez. relabor, -eris. 'to fall in this way again'

It is not hard to see that all of these entries are present in the Spanish dictionary only because they have lexicalized equivalents in Latin. In a more modern dictionary, one might expect a single entry for *caer* with its various Latin equivalents being glossed or exemplified in such a way that the user could find the one he wanted within the entry, or with a nest of explanatory Spanish entries and their equivalents.

Returning now to the above-mentioned entry in Sp>Nah71 *Cauar la tierra o escaruarla con el pie, estando hablando con otro* 'to dig at the earth or scratch it with the foot, [while] standing talking with someone', we see that it is similar in spirit to Nebrija's *caer* entries listed above. That is to say, Molina provides the entry solely because there is a "one-word" Nahuatl equivalent for it (*nitla, icxipopoxoa.* 'I-something-foot-repeatedly-soften')[24] that he wishes to place in the Spanish-first dictionary, even though the resulting Spanish entry is not a lexicalized concept in Spanish.

Some extreme cases of this practice occur in Sp>Nah71. Not only are these not lexicalized Spanish expressions, but they are not even individual nonlexicalized items. From the perspective of the whole entry, each one looks like a Nahuatl entry word with two or three Spanish equivalents but turned around so that the Spanish equivalents come first.

> Abuela, liebre, o tia hermana de abuelo. citli. Sp>Nah71 f2r2
> 'Grandmother, hare, or aunt, sister of a grandparent.'
> Cuñado de hombre, o massa para hazer pan. textli. Sp>Nah71 f33r2
> 'A man's brother-in-law, or dough for making bread.'

The first of these, a most unlikely Spanish entry, obviously exists because all three of these Spanish concepts share the same Nahuatl form *citli*. It seems clear that the first and third are in fact the same kinship term from the Nahuatl perspective, while the second, 'hare', may have a separate origin or may be a metaphorical extension of the other two. Both *liebre* and *tia* have their own entries, but neither of these includes the other words.

The second entry, consisting of two unrelated Spanish phrases, is similarly incongruous. What the two phrases have in common is that their Nahuatl equivalents are homographs. They differ in vowel length, which Molina does not spell. The four entries for *massa* (mod Sp *masa*) in the same dictionary deal only with flour. Since this Spanish-Nahuatl dictionary was published together with the Nahuatl-Spanish dictionary, our first thought was that Molina might be making efficient, if misguided, use of his "card file." But no, the Nah>Sp side has *Textli. cuñado de varon, o massa de harina.* Nah>Sp71 f112v2, where *varon* 'male' is more careful than *hombre* 'man, person' for this kinship definition, and *harina* without further clarification should be 'wheat flour'. These corresponding entries in the two parts of the dictionary have equivalent but slightly different Spanish, and there is no way to know whether, being fluent in both languages, Molina simply wrote out the definitions separately without checking them one against the other or whether he revised one based on the other.

---

24. It is difficult to establish with certainty which "words" are lexicalized units in Nahuatl. Given the structure of the language, with its "sentence-words" and its propensity for complex compounds and derivations, many such forms are productive forms that technically do not belong in a dictionary. However, a number of them have acquired conventionalized meanings that are not identical to the sum of their parts. See section 4.4.2.2 for a discussion of this issue.

The practice of constructing lemmata to meet the needs of the target language not only affects the form of individual entries, but as a result determines the eventual macrostructure of the dictionary (thence many of the differences between the word sets of Nebrija and Molina). By way of illustration, consider the following entries for *arder* 'to burn' in Sp>Nah55. These six Spanish lemmata have a total of eleven Nahuatl equivalents, with only one word appearing more than once. Since the word list itself is the issue, we do not include the Nahuatl. (By comparison, Nebrija gives three entries, *arder* 'burn', *arder mucho* 'burn a lot', and *arder con huego* 'burn with fire [flames]', also determined by his choice of target-language equivalents.)

> Arder quemarse. 'to burn, to burn up'
> Arder o dar luz la candela. 'for a candle to burn or give light'
> Arder echando llama. 'to burn, shooting out flames'
> Arder la tierra de calor. 'for the land to burn with heat'
> Arder la cabeça de dolor. 'for the head to burn with pain'
> Arder la cabeça del sol o huego. 'for the head to burn from the sun or from fire'

Molina chooses these particular restrictions on the meaning of *arder* in order to match them to the particular Nahuatl equivalents that he wants to accommodate. These entries have their origin not in the source language but in the target language and thus resemble Spanish equivalents in a passive (decoding) Nahuatl-Spanish dictionary, but with access through Spanish. These separate entries have the effect of teasing apart individual senses of the Spanish word in question and providing each of these with Nahuatl equivalents. One would otherwise expect more general Spanish entry words, with meaning dealt with by separating and disambiguating the Nahuatl equivalents within the target-language field of the entry.

While this practice of including target-language concepts in the source-language word list may sometimes be necessary and desirable, both of the authors under discussion carry it to a surprising extreme. If what a speaker is required to look up is not words in his native language but "meanings" (turned into lemmata) corresponding to target-language lexical items for which there is no source-language lexicalized counterpart, how would he know that these particular Spanish entries are possible things to "mean"?[25] This habit of including entry words in the Spanish dictionaries that are in fact lemmata constructed to accommodate target-language lexical items results in the user having to do more "shopping around" for the form he

---

25. Zgusta (1971: 309–10) discusses the occasional necessity for source-language entries which must be based on the semantic content of the target language and ways of making such entries accessible to the user.

needs than he would in a modern dictionary. But, on the other hand, Molina has in this way provided a rich characterization of the Nahuatl lexis even in the Spanish source-language dictionaries.

This, then, is both the primary similarity between Nebrija and Molina and the main reason for the differences in their word lists: whether Spanish to foreign language, or foreign language to Spanish, all of these dictionaries look "outward" toward the foreign language (which Molina refers to simply as *la lengua* 'the language'). Since Nebrija's dictionaries and Molina's have greatly divergent "other" languages, it is not surprising, given their philosophy of dictionary building, in which the foreign language is the focal point of both the source-language and target-language dictionaries, that their Spanish word sets are diverted in different directions.

We could say that Molina's dictionaries all give the impression of being "Nahuatl dictionaries" regardless of the language of access. Indeed, his comments in the preface to Nah>Sp71 suggest that this was his intent. Here, he makes reference to "when I published the vocabulary of the Mexican language the first time," in effect telling us that he in fact saw the Spanish-to-Nahuatl dictionary as a vocabulary of Nahuatl. And in note 6 of this preface, he says:

> [T]he Spanish of the words of the language [in order to better understand their meaning] are to be sought in this vocabulary which begins in the Mexican language, inasmuch as in it they are better clarified than in the one which begins in Spanish. And the reason for this is because each word of the language could be better revealed separately in the already mentioned second vocabulary than in the first. (Molina 1571, 2d preface, unpaginated)

Thus it appears that Molina sees his job primarily as clarifying Nahuatl words in Spanish rather than as facilitating translation INTO Nahuatl, regardless of the direction of the dictionary.

4.4. EXAMINATION OF EACH COMPONENT LANGUAGE.   From the above conclusion that Molina saw all of his vocabularies as first and foremost vocabularies of Nahuatl, it follows that the fundamental typological division in the dictionaries would not be between source language and target language but between foreign language (Nahuatl) and native language (Spanish), and indeed this is clearly the case. For example, some grammatical information is given for Nahuatl as both the source language and the target language, but in neither case is it given for Spanish. Likewise, there is a strong tendency for the Nahuatl of entries in both the source and the target side to be simple and lemmalike and for the Spanish of both sides to be wordy and definitional. Although there are, of course, differences between source and target use of each language, these are secondary to their similarities, which we will discuss first.

4.4.1. THE SPANISH SIDE OF ENTRIES, WHETHER FIRST OR SECOND.

4.4.1.1. SPANISH SPELLING. Although in the present context there is no reason to discuss the Spanish spelling system, we will point out a few idiosyncracies in Molina's usage.

Two archaic spellings that Molina uses are *nrr* for *nr* and *nss* for *ns*. In earlier Spanish, *rr* had represented the trilled *r*, even when this occurred in initial position and after *n*; however, by the sixteenth century this spelling was no longer the norm. While *ss* continued to spell the voiceless /s/ in intervocalic position in the sixteenth century, the cluster *ns* was spelled with one *s*. The modern *nr* and *ns* spellings were the ones Nebrija used even in the first edition (1495) of his Spanish dictionary sixty years before Molina's first dictionary. The archaic spellings are the norm in Sp>Nah55, but their numbers drop to near zero in the 1571 dictionaries.

Another conservative trait is the lack of initial *h* where it represents Latin *h*. This *h* had been lost when it ceased to be pronounced, probably during the first century B.C.E. Spanish developed a new *h* when Latin *f* in initial position became *h*. When this *h* also ceased to be pronounced and the two thus fell together as zero, the Latin *h* was reintroduced etymologically in the spelling of a number of words. These words are represented in Molina in the modern way with their Latin *h*'s, except when they occur as headwords. In that case, Molina follows tradition—also Nebrija's tradition—and spells the words without *h*. Thus *onra* 'honor' as headword but *honra* and related words within entries, and the same for *ombre / hombre* 'man' and *ora / hora* 'hour'. The ONLY spellings without the *h* are in headword position, and sometimes even these are spelled and alphabetized with the *h*.

On the other hand, the reintroduction of clusters that had been lost in the history of Spanish resulted in what have come to be known as "learned clusters." Spellings with these are of more recent origin than spellings showing cluster simplification. We see these in Molina's work in such pairs as *santo / sancto* 'saint', and groups of related words involving pairs such as *presuncion / presumpcion* 'presumptuousness' and *cativar / cap-tivar* 'to capture'. These three pairs of words, along with words related to them, show a clear progression from the simplified clusters in Sp>Nah55 to the competing reintroduced clusters in Nah>Sp71. On the other hand, *codicia / cobdicia* 'greed' shows a pattern contrary to the others, with a preponderance of the clusters in the two Spanish dictionaries and an even balance of reduced forms and clusters in Nah>Sp71. This is because the *bd* was not a prestige Latin cluster that could be reintroduced but rather an intermediate stage that was in decline during the sixteenth century. It shows the more recent form, with the cluster simplified, in Nah>Sp71. We show our results below.

	Sp>Nah55	Sp>Nah71	Nah>Sp71
presun..	3	0	3
presump..	0	3	19
cativar	5	10	0
captivar	0	1	20
santo	12	2	1
sancto	1	16	25
cobdicia	8	14	12
codicia	0	0	12

It is clear that each word takes its own history, favoring one form or the other almost exclusively in any one dictionary, a remarkable fact when one considers that the words are scattered throughout the dictionaries, not all alphabetized together in headword position. The overall pattern for the learned clusters is that Nah>Sp71 has the highest proportion of the reintroduced clusters while Sp>Nah55 has the most normally developed forms.

Molina's dictionaries show at least two kinds of spellings in Spanish that show the influence of Nahuatl bilingualism. As Molina mentions in his prefaces, *o* and *u* are variants of the same phoneme in Nahuatl and spellings are quite random. In a handful of cases, substitution of *u* for *o* has spilled over into Spanish. *Furtuna* appears for *fortuna* in the entry *bienes de furtuna. tlatquitl* (Sp>Nah71 f19v2). In no fewer than six entries, *codicia* 'greed' and its derivatives are spelled *cudicia* and alphabetized with the other *cu*'s in Sp>Nah71 f32v2. Spellings for *azotea* 'balcony, roof' are distributed as shown below.

	Sp>Nah55	Sp>Nah71	Nah>Sp71
azotea	1	3	3
azutea	2	2	0

Another, somewhat more pervasive, influence of Nahuatl is seen in the spelling of Spanish /sk/ clusters. While the precursors of modern Castilian Spanish /θ/ (spelled *z*, *ç*, and *c* before *i* and *e*) were heard by both Spaniards and Nahuatl speakers as (near-) equivalents of the Nahuatl /s/, the Castilian apico-alveolar /s/ was associated with the Nahuatl /š/, spelled *x*. Since the Spanish of this period had a /š/ phoneme of its own, this caused a merger of Spanish /s/ and /š/ as Nahuatl /š/ in borrowings into Nahuatl, though the Spanish *s* spelling was occasionally maintained. We see what appears to be the same merger of Spanish /s/ with /š/ when the cluster /sk/ occurs in the environment of back vowels. This was not a Spanish pattern of merger. In fact, in Latin American Spanish the /s/ phoneme merged with the precursors of /θ/ to give the modern Latin American /s/.

		Sp>Nah55	Sp>Nah71	Nah>Sp71
/moska-/	mosca-	9	7	0
	moxca-	2	4	13
/maska-/	masca-	1	0	0
	maxca-	6	12	12
/kaska-/	casca-	4	3	0
	caxca-	10	22	20
/kasko-/	casco-	0	0	0
	caxco-	2	3	13
/kosko-/	cosco-	0	0	0
	coxco-	0	2	6

Examples of these spellings are *moxca* for *mosca* 'fly', *maxcara* for *mascara* 'mask', *caxcabel* for *cascabel* 'jingle bell', *caxco* for *casco* 'helmet, cask', *coxcorron* for *coscorron* 'a blow'. We found no instances of this phenomenon in clusters of *s* with *p* or *t*.

4.4.1.2. MOLINA'S SPANISH "DEFINITIONS" IN BOTH HALVES. Although a number of Molina's Spanish entries are simple words, many are phrases or even lengthier descriptions or explanations. In many such cases, it would be difficult or impossible to distinguish between source-language phrases and target-language phrases, because all of the Spanish parts seem to define or explain the Nahuatl regardless of whether Spanish is the source language or the target language.

Consider the following Spanish counterparts for the Nahuatl word *ayotzoyacatl:*

Calabaça pequeña y tierna, cogida por sazonar y curada al sol, para comer entre año.
'small and tender gourd, picked in order to ripen and cured in the sun, in order to eat [it] during the year.'

Calabaça cogida sin sazon para curarla al sol, y guardarla para comer la guisada entre año.
'gourd picked without ripening in order to cure it in the sun, and keep it to eat it cooked during the year.'

These are both fine definitions or explanations for *ayotzoyacatl*, though a bit encyclopedic, and one would not be surprised to find them as Spanish explanations for *ayotzoyacatl* in the target-language side of a Nahuatl-Spanish dictionary, which in fact is where the second one is located

(Nah>Sp71 f3v2). The first one is the source-language lemma or entry word corresponding to *ayotzoyacatl* in Sp>Nah71 f23r1.

Or consider the following Spanish counterparts for Nah *cochtlaza. nite:*

> Adormecer a alguno con encantamiento, o en otra manera assi.
> 'to put someone to sleep with a spell, or by some similar means.'

> Adormecer a alguno con encantamiento, para robarle su hazienda.
> 'to put someone to sleep with a spell, in order to rob him of his property.'

As in the first pair, the second example is the target-language equivalent for the Nahuatl word in Nah>Sp71 f23r2, while the first is the source-language entry from Sp>Nah71 f4v2. Both resemble explanations in the target-language field far more than headword lemmata.

One of the most flagrant examples we have found of this "flipping" of what would appear to be a passive Nahuatl-Spanish entry so that the Spanish precedes is the following entry, which has *tlapictli* as its Nahuatl equivalent:

> Armario pequeño o agujero hecho en la pared para poner algo. tlapictli.
>   Sp>Nah55 f23r
> 'small closet or hole made in the wall in order to put something [there].'

Also in this regard, one particular verb that seems to have caught Molina's imagination is *cuecueyoca,* the frequentative of *cueyoni* 'seethe'. We cite the relevant Spanish entries below.

> Bullir los gusanos o peces enel agua o cosa assi. Sp>Nah55 f37r
> 'for worms or fish in the water to seethe.'

> Bullir las hormigas pulgas o piojos o cosas semejantes. Sp>Nah55 f37r
> 'for ants, fleas, lice or similar things to seethe.'

> Reluzir las piedras preciosas o los peces dentro del agua conel mouimiento
>   que hazen o el ayuntamiento delas hormigas o las lagunas y campos o
>   gentes ayuntadas por el mouimiento que hazen. Sp>Nah55 f212r,
>   Sp>Nah71 f103v1
> 'for precious stones to sparkle, or for fish to sparkle in the water with the
>   movement that they make, or a congregation of ants, or the lakes and
>   fields or people grouped together, due to the movement that they make.'

> Relumbrar o reluzir, o bullir y heruir los piojos, pulgas, gusanos, hormigas
>   enel hormiguero, la gente enel mercado, o los peces enel agua.
>   Nah>Sp71 f25v2
> 'for something to shine, or sparkle, or seethe and boil, such as lice, fleas,
>   worms, ants in the anthill, or people in the market, or fish in the water.'

Molina considered it a matter of some interest that Nahuatl has a verb that expresses the movement of such diverse objects as fields of grain in the wind, bodies of water when disturbed, schools of fish, closely packed groups of insects or even people, and also the apparent movement of light on gemstones. It is important to remember that only the last of these entries is technically for the purpose of "defining" the Nahuatl. The others, which occur in the Spanish source-language dictionaries, are complex lemmata in place of headwords, constructed for the purpose of illustrating the various facets of this verb for the Spanish-speaking user. These entries show clearly that Molina's aim was the elucidation of the Nahuatl lexis rather than the more utilitarian provision of a correspondence list between the two languages.

Another noteworthy feature of Molina's Spanish is his tendency to provide very fine specific examples. We illustrate with two entries from Nah>Sp71:

Tlahneuia. nicno. tomar vna cosa por otra, pensando que era suya la capa, siendo de otro, o pensando que hablaua con Pedro, no siendo el sino otro. &c. Prete. onicnotlahneui. Nah>Sp71 f120v1
'to mistake something for something else, thinking that the cape was one's own, it being actually someone else's, or thinking that one was talking with Pedro, it not being him but someone else, etc.'

Tlachialia. nite. atalayar, o mirar si viene alguien para auisar alos que estan haziendo algo, y no querrian que los viesse nadie. P. onitetlachiali. Nah>Sp71 f117r1
'to be a look-out, or watch out to see if anyone is coming in order to inform those who are doing something and who would not want anyone to see them.'

In both of the above cases, Molina has given in the target-language Spanish not only a definition of the Nahuatl verb but also a clear and concrete example from which the reader should be able to generalize.

As the above paragraphs illustrate, most meaning discrimination is accomplished not in the Nahuatl field but in the glosses that refine the meaning of the Spanish entry word, or of the Spanish equivalent. For the source-language Spanish, these carefully honed lemmata can then be paired with quite specific Nahuatl equivalents. Consider the case of *aguzar* and its related entries (Sp>Nah71 f6v1):

Aguzar punta o ser el primero o delantero de los que caminan, o de los que estan puestos en orden. nitla, yacauitzoa. nitla, yacachiqui. nitla, yacatia.
'to sharpen a point or be the first or front one of those who are walking, or of those who/which are placed in order. I-something-nose-[thorn-become-cause]. I-something-nose-scrape. I-something-nose-[have-cause].'
Aguzada punta. tlayacauitzolli. tlayacachictli.
'a sharpened point. something-nose-thorn-become-past-[passive-nominal-ize]-absolutive. something-nose-scrape-[passive-nominalize]-absolutive.'

Aguzarse assi. yacauitzaui.
'to be sharpened like this. nose-thorn-become.'
Aguzar dar filo. busca afilar.
'to sharpen, give an edge. see *afilar*.'
Aguzadera piedra. tlatentiloni.
'sharpening stone. something-lip-[have-cause]-passive-[agent-present].'
Aguzador. tlatentiani. tlatenti.
'sharpener. something-lip-[have-cause]-[agent-present]. something-lip-[have-cause]-[agent-past].'

Note that for the second verb *aguzar*, Molina refers the reader to another lexical item, even though this one contains a clear explanatory gloss and he could have given a Nahuatl equivalent in this entry. The reason seems to be that he has just worked his way through several entries relating to sharpening points, and although he follows this entry, which has to do with sharpening an edge, with two other entries related to edges, the more exact term is *afilar*. The reader is referred to those entries where he finds (f5r2):

Afilar cosa de hierro. nitla, tentia. nitla, tenitztia.
'to put an edge on something of iron. I-something-lip-[have-cause]. I-something-lip-obsidian-[have-cause].'
Afilar espada o cosa de dos filos. nitla, necoctentia. nitla, necoc tenitztia.
'to put an edge on a sword or something with two edges. . . . '
Afilada cosa
'a sharpened thing'
Afilador
'one who sharpens'
Afiladura
'the act or result of sharpening'

This extended example shows the attention to meaning that gives rise to Molina's extended Spanish entries, whether in the source language or in the target language. This and the previous examples illustrate well Molina's approach to lexicography. We see once again the primacy of the Nahuatl lexis in both source- and target-language Spanish. Even where Spanish is the source language and should be providing headwords, the entries are frequently molded to the needs of Nahuatl. These Spanish entries are better crafted not for searching out how to SAY something but for finding explanations of what something MEANS—except, of course, that that end is much better served through the Nah>Sp dictionary, as Molina himself observes. This is not a phrasebook for sixteenth-century tourists. On the other hand, as a volume to be studied for the acquisition of Nahuatl vocabulary, it provides the Spanish-speaking user with well-drawn portraits of Nahuatl words, regardless of the language of access.

4.4.2. THE NAHUATL SIDE, WHETHER FIRST OR SECOND.

4.4.2.1. SPELLING.   Molina's spelling is, by sixteenth-century standards, surprisingly regular. He did not attempt to represent vowel length orthographically and only occasionally spelled the glottal stop.[26] However, it is clear from the combination of Molina's remarks and his practice that these omissions were not a result of ignorance. In the seventh note in the preface to Nah>Sp71, Molina tells the reader,

> [T]here are some ambiguous verbs and nouns which are differentiated by the different accents that they have, with which they change their meanings; and other times, without making these different accents, the meanings of the verbs and nouns change, and then one must discover their meanings from the contexts in which they are used. (Molina 1571, 2d preface, unpaginated)

By "accents," he is undoubtedly referring to vowel length, and possibly to glottal stops as well. There is also one reference to vowel length in the text itself.

> Acarrear piedras. ni, teçaca. acento breue. y assi de los de mas, silicet acarrear madera, trigo &c. Sp>Nah55 f4r 'to haul rocks. ni, teçaca. short accent. and so on for the rest, that is to say, to carry wood, wheat, etc.'

Molina's remark *acento breve* 'short accent' is intended to explain his (correct) analysis of the verb as *ni-* [*te-çaca*] 'I stone-carry' with an embedded object *tetl* 'stone', rather than as *ni-te,* subject prefix followed by object prefix 'I-someone', in which the *te* would have a long vowel /e:/. Unfortunately, this is all we hear from Molina on the topic of vowel length, but the two comments are enough to assure us that it was not the case that he could not hear it.

Information on glottal stops is sparse but indicates clearly that their omission is a matter of choice. We count a total of 141 occurrences of the glottal stop, representing thirty-three different morphemes. The words most frequently spelled with the glottal stop are *uehca* 'far' (26), various compounds of *pahtli* 'medicine' (16), and forms of *ihtoa* 'say' (18) and of *ihmati* 'to be skilled' (15). Others total fewer than ten each. Fifty-four of these words occur in Sp>Nah55, seventy-four are in Sp>Nah71, and only thirteen are in Nah>Sp71. These figures do not represent the quantity of information that we wish Molina had provided us, but they do assure us that he heard the glottal stops. One has the impression that he intended not to write them but that occasionally they slipped through.

---

26. Where the glottal stop is spelled in Nahuatl, the tradition is to spell it with *h*, regardless of whether the pronunciation is a glottal stop or [h], as in a number of modern dialects (and, we might assume, some sixteenth-century dialects as well).

We might also mention that the earliest dictionary not infrequently neglects to spell word-final *n,* which was weakly pronounced in some dialects, if at all. Most of these have been inserted in the 1571 dictionaries.

4.4.2.2.   The Nahuatl components of these dictionaries, unlike the Spanish, consist primarily of translational equivalents, or what appear to the outsider to be translational equivalents, for their Spanish counterparts. The extended explanations and descriptions of the Spanish side do not occur in Nahuatl. However, this statement must be tempered with the knowledge that the languages are very different and that one can say a great deal in a single word in Nahuatl. This brings us to a central question in the lexicography of such languages: what exactly belongs in their dictionaries? One might think that this question might be more appropriately discussed in section 6 on the Nah>Sp dictionary, but since in a large number of cases Spanish lemmata are constructed for the very purpose of calling forth a particular Nahuatl equivalent (in effect, the headword of a Nahuatl-as-source-language entry), it seems more relevant to discuss the topic not in terms of headwords but simply in terms of the Nahuatl component of the dictionary.

Nahuatl is frequently described as being composed of "sentence-words," in which pronominal prefixes for subjects and objects, as well as adverbs, possessed postpositions, and object nouns, can be incorporated preceding the verb in the same "word" with it. We are thus confronted with situations in which it is difficult to know what are lexicalized units and what are simply productive, freely substitutable formations corresponding to sentences in other languages. Clearly, one cannot put all of the sentences in the dictionary. Yet to give only morphemes, stems, or short primary words leaves much of the ingenuity of the language hidden and much of its lexis unaccounted for. Molina surely considered this question. His response, readily apparent in the Nahuatl inventory of the dictionaries, is predictable in light of his goal of tapping the "limitless mine . . . of words and manners of speaking which this very copious and clever Mexican language has." Or to look at it from a different perspective, the Spanish components of his dictionaries do not consist only of lexical units, so why should the Nahuatl components have such a limitation?

Although the dictionaries have a much higher percentage of Nahuatl entries that are translational equivalents of the corresponding Spanish than Spanish entries that can substitute for their Nahuatl counterparts, many of these from the Nahuatl perspective are technically more than minimal lexical units. For example, Molina lists twenty-three words in which a noun is compounded with *namacac* 'sell-preterite', meaning 'one who sells', for example, water, chia oil, salt, fish, medicine, charcoal, people, hens, wine, wax. This list, taken from Campbell (1985), is arbitrary and freely extendable.

Other words that are composed of more than one morpheme are equally clearly NOT free forms but rather lexicalized units that are not productive compounds or are otherwise unpredictable. For example, *cuitlatl* 'excrement, secretion' combines with nouns for various body parts to form predictable compounds, but it also combines with the word for 'bee' to form *xicocuitlatl* 'beeswax' and with the word for 'god' to form *teocuitlatl* 'gold, silver'. These two cases are unarguably lexicalized compounds that require representation in dictionaries. Intermediate between these two extremes are cases which appear to be conventionalized but may or may not also represent their component parts—or may simply appear conventionalized to us but to the native speaker of classical Nahuatl may have been recognized and produced as the sum of their parts.

For example, the verb *xeliui* (intransitive form) means 'to split' and occurs in intransitive, transitive, and benefactive forms. The uncompounded transitive verb *xeloa. nitla* means 'I split wood, separate out cattle, or divide or separate something', and the uncompounded benefactive *xeluia. nitetla* means 'to share, divide (among) or apportion'. Compounded with the noun (as adverb) *maitl* 'hand', we see transitive and benefactive forms as defined below. Literally, 'I hand-split something' and 'I hand-split something for someone'.

> maxeloa. nitla. [transitive] apartar con las manos la gente para passar entre ella, o apartar las yeruas y cañas o cosas semejantes, para hender por ellas. Sp>Nah71 f11v2
> 'to divide [a group of] people with one's hands in order to go between them, or to divide brush or cane or similar things, in order to go through them.'

> maxelhuia. nitetla. [benefactive] hazer camino a otro, hendiendo por medio del cañaueral o del yeruaçal crecido y alto. Sp>Nah71 f69v2
> 'to break a path for someone, dividing a canefield or a high and overgrown field of weeds.'

We think it is clear that the compounded forms do not just mean 'to do the meaning of the uncompounded forms with one's hands'. They involve specifically the gesture of extending one's arms, hands together, and then separating them to force something apart. Whether these compounds are limited to this specific meaning is less certain. These examples illustrate the fact that compounds may vary over a wide range from productivity to lexicalization. Molina's judgment was that many such words have a place in a bilingual dictionary despite their derived and even nonlexicalized nature, and we agree.

5. THE SPANISH-TO-NAHUATL DICTIONARIES.

5.1. MICROSTRUCTURE: PREFIXES IN NAHUATL. Molina addresses the question of verbal structure in the fourth note to the reader:

Because it is very necessary to know what is the substance of the verb and what is the pronoun or particles which are placed before it, in order to use well the verbs and verbal nouns which are derived from them, a comma will be placed so that one knows that what is put after it is the substance and body of the verb and what is before it is the pronoun or particles that are prefixed to the verb. But although there is a division between the verb and the particles, everything is to be pronounced together. (Molina 1555, 1571, preface, unpaginated)

Molina's first dictionary is the first that we know of to address this issue. His solution to the problem is both effective and minimally disruptive, since he leaves the prefixes in their normal position while separating them from their verbs. Separation of verbal prefixes is far more complete in Sp>Nah71 than in Sp>Nah55. None of the dictionaries succeeds in separating all of the prefixes, and some outright errors can be found: *niteçaca* 'I haul stones' is incorrectly divided as *nite, çaca* in Sp>Nah71 f2v2 even though it was correctly divided in Sp>Nah55 (see example above, §4.4.2.1). The *te-* in this case is not the nonspecific human object prefix but the noun *tetl* 'stone'. And *ni, qualtoca* 'to go to visit someone' in all three dictionaries should be *nicual, toca* (i.e., ni-c-ual, toca, 'I-it/him-[direction-toward] follow').

5.2. MACROSTRUCTURE.

5.2.1. ALPHABETICAL ORDER.

Molina and Nebrija use the same order of initial letters (*a, b, c, ç, ch, d, . . .*), but their internal order differs. For Nebrija, *c, ç,* and *ch* are three entirely separate letters. *Aça* follows *acu* and is followed by *ace, aci, aço. Ach* comes next, before *ad.* For Molina, *ç* is separate only in the sense that *c* and *ç* between the same two letters are not intermingled, but they occur as a subset of the *c*'s, in the order *aca, aça, ace, ach, acl, aco, aço, acr, acu, açu, ad.* Neither *ç* nor *ch* has a separate place in Molina's internal alphabetical order.

In initial position, Nebrija organizes *g* phonemically, with all /g/ preceding all /ž/ (spelled *ge, gi* > mod Sp /x/). Molina allows the two phonemes to mingle in strictly alphabetical order *ga, ge, gl, go, . . .* Nebrija places *agui* /agi/ after *aga* and before *ago.* Molina places *agui* /agi/ strictly alphabetically, after *agud,* and actually splitting /aguž/, which is also spelled *agui* or *aguj.*

Both authors place *y* with *i* both initially and internally, combining the vowel *i* with the consonant *y* /y/ (both of which they call *i vocal*) but separating it from /ž/ (>modern /x/), spelled *i,j,* called *i consonante.*

Both authors also treat *ll* (/ʎ/ or /y/) and *rr* (trill) as separate letters, that is, phonemically, in initial position, but order them alphabetically rather than phonemically internally: *ali, all, alm, arq, arr, art.*

Because they were alphabetizing by hand, items can be found in both authors that do not follow their apparent patterns of alphabetization. Also, both authors violate their rules of order in order to group related words together (see §5.2.2).

5.2.2. NEST-TYPE GROUPS.   The specificity of entries mentioned in section 4.3.5 above results in another characteristic of both the Nebrija and the Molina dictionaries. Where a modern dictionary might have nests, there are instead groups of entries requiring cross-referencing information or repetition of parts of a preceding entry.

Since entries are very narrow semantically, related words are also narrow, for example, words derivationally related to a verb such as the agent, the past participle used as noun or adjective, or the adverb. Instead of treating such related words in nests within the verb entries, or alternatively, in separate entries (but with the greater variety of equivalents associated with the main verb), Nebrija and Molina give, for example, a narrowly defined verb, then entries for each of the words derivationally related to this main entry. These related words are formally separate entries but frequently anaphorically related (e.g., *tal* 'such a', *desta manera* 'in this way', *assi* 'thus') to the first entry (or related in a "chain" to the immediately preceding entry). In this way the authors go through all of the forms related to one sense, then pick up the next sense and repeat the process. The resulting configuration might be termed "external nests," since they resemble items nested in one entry, except that the "organization" is AMONG entries, not WITHIN them. One might say that the basic unit in these dictionaries is not the individual entry but the resulting groups of entries, especially since the anaphoric references prevent many individual entries from standing on their own.[27] We give an example from Sp>Nah71 f32v1. We translate the entire passage below the original:

> Cubrir con rescoldo y brasas membrillos. cebollas, &c. paraque seasen. nitla, nexpachoa. nitla, nextoca.
> Cubierta cosa assi. tlanexpacholli. tlanextoctli.
> Cubrimiento tal. tlanexpacholiztli. tlanextocaliztli.
> Cubridor desta manera. tlanexpachoani. tlanexpachoqui. tlanextocac. tlanextocani.
>   . . .
> Cubrir al que esta durmiendo. nite, quentia.

---

27. This factor is an unwelcome complication for handling such data by computer, since the antecedent in each case must be given its own field and "dragged along" to make the entry comprehensible; e.g., Molina 1555 has eight entries of the form *caydo assi* (mod Sp *caído así*) 'fallen in this way', each of which had to be related to a DIFFERENT entry for *cayda* 'a fall (in a certain way)'.

Cubridor tal. tequentiani.
Cubrimiento assi. tequentiliztli.

To cover onions, quinces, etc. with embers in order for them to roast.
I-something-ashes-press. I-something-ashes-bury.
Thing covered in this way. something-ashes-press-[passive-nominalize]-abso-
lutive. something-ashes-bury-[passive-nominalize]-absolutive.
Such a covering. something-ashes-press-nominalize-absolutive. something-
ashes-bury-nominalize-absolutive.
A coverer of this type. something-ashes-press-[agent-present]. something-
ashes-press-[agent-past]. something-ashes-bury-[agent-present]. some-
thing-ashes-bury-[agent-past].
. . .

To cover the one who is sleeping. I-someone-cover-apply.
Such a coverer. someone-cover-apply-[agent-present].
A covering in this way. someone-cover-apply-nominalize-absolutive.

5.3. CONTENT: CHANGES FROM SP>NAH55 TO SP>NAH71. To determine the relationship of the earlier Sp>Nah dictionary to the later one,
we analyzed 300 consecutive entries from Sp>Nah55, which were sorted
along with the same range of entries from the other dictionaries. These
were from the same *ca-* range discussed in section 4.3.1 above. The count
of these items shows that 272 of them are carried over into Sp>Nah71,
while 28 are not. Of these 28, 17 are numbers, several of which are also
represented in the numeral section at the end of the dictionary, leaving
only 11 entries that appear to have been abandoned. However, a close
look at some of the apparently missing entries shows that in several cases
some other change took place that had the effect of "hiding" the entry
without actually deleting it. For example, in at least one case, two Spanish entries were conflated into a more general one that carried the Nahuatl equivalents of both of the earlier entries. In other cases, the Spanish entry was so changed that it appears in our accounting as the loss of
a Sp>Nah55 entry and the addition of a new entry in Sp>Nah71. Thus it
appears that very nearly all of the content of Sp>Nah55 was carried over
into Sp>Nah71 in one form or another.

   A more interesting view of the development of Sp>Nah71 is obtained
by examining the two dictionaries to see how Sp>Nah71 relates to its pred-
ecessor (see table 16.1). A count of 300 consecutive entries in Sp>Nah71
shows that 52 of them did not appear in Sp>Nah55. Of the remaining
248 entries, 152 are exact matches while one matches in Spanish but not
in Nahuatl. In 74 entries the Spanish occurs in both Sp>Nah71 and
Sp>Nah55 but has been altered in some way, though the Nahuatl remains
the same. Both languages have been changed in 21 entries. We see then
that in this sample, Sp>Nah71 contains 21 percent more entries than

TABLE 16.1. Comparison of Spanish Entries of Sp>Nah71 and Sp>Nah55

		Matching Entries		Altered Entries	
		Sp & Nah	Sp only	Sp & Nah	Sp only
Entries in Sp>		match	matches	altered	altered
Nah71	300				
In Sp>Nah55	248	152	1	74	21
Not in Sp>					
Nah55	52				

Sp>Nah55, and of those entries that occur in both dictionaries, 38 percent have been modified. Of the 300 entries counted, 49 percent are either new in Sp>Nah71 or revised from Sp>Nah55.

Some stylistic improvement in Sp>Nah71 is worth mentioning. The style is more natural, less telegraphic. Entry words are more likely to be separated from their clarifying or limiting glosses by a comma and/or by transitional words, *assi como* 'such as'. There is also a greater tendency to use definite articles in ways that are natural for Spanish, whereas such articles were not infrequently suppressed in Sp>Nah55.

5.4. SPANISH DICTIONARIES: CONCLUSIONS.   Since Nahuatl lexicography existed only in unpublished form until the publication of Sp>Nah55, even the existence of that work was a great advancement for the field. Molina's treatment of verbs was an especially important innovation. His 1571 Sp>Nah dictionary expanded the word set and improved and refined the content of entries.

6. THE NAHUATL-SPANISH DICTIONARY.

6.1. MICROSTRUCTURE.   The second of Molina's 1571 dictionaries, the first Nahuatl-to-Spanish dictionary beyond the simple word list of Olmos, required Molina to use some ingenuity in indicating the Nahuatl headwords, given that Nahuatl is a prefixing language and one would not want all of the verbs alphabetized under the first-person prefix *ni-*. As we saw above in section 5.1, Molina had already recognized the advantage to the user of separating inflectional prefixes from verb stems. So in Nah>Sp71 it was a simple matter to transpose this already separated material so that it followed the verb. In his third note to the reader in the preface, he lays out this entry structure, along with information on preterite placement:

> The active verbs in this language are never pronounced nor found absolute, as in Spanish we say *amar, enseñar, oir,* etc., but rather they are always accompanied by pronouns or particles which denote the person who undergoes and who performs [the action], thus *nitetlaçotla, nitemachtia, nitlacaqui,* etc. And

because putting such particles where they are pronounced and used, it would
be impossible to give order to the vocabulary, and also not everyone would
understand what was the body of the verb and which were the particles which
accompany it—Because of this, I have the verbs in this order: first I put the
body of the verb itself, and then the pronoun or particle which belongs to it,
taking it off the front and putting it after it; and then its Spanish, together
with its preterite, because so many and so diverse are its endings that in the
Arte it would not be possible to give enough rules for all of the preterites
without a lot of work. And for the most part in this Vocabulary, verbs are given
with their particles in the first-person singular, and sometimes with the third.
(Molina 1571, 2d preface, unpaginated)

Nominalizations of verbs in Nahuatl keep the object prefixes of the
verbs from which they are derived, and these prefixes Molina does not
remove. Deverbal nouns do not have objects if they are derived from
intransitive verbs or from single-object verbs that have been passivized.
These deverbal nouns are thus located in the dictionary alphabetically
adjacent to their respective verbs, while deverbal nouns having object prefixes are alphabetized according to the respective prefix. For example:

verb and nominalization		Molina's form
nimiqui	'I die'	miqui, ni
miquiliztli	'death'	miquiliztli
nitemictia	'I kill someone'	mictia, nite
temictiliztli	'act of killing someone'	temictiliztli

If one analyzes the nouns as $[[\text{prefix(es)-verb}]_V\text{-nominalizing-suffix}]_N$,
i.e., $[[\text{te-micti(a)}]_V \text{-liz}]_N$ (note that *-tli* 'absolutive' is an inflectional noun
suffix), there is logic in the way Molina handles the differences between
nouns and verbs with regard to their prefixes. There may, however, be a
question of whether the reader's best interests are served by this decision,
as verbs are thus separated from their transitive nominalizations.

Molina's insight in Sp>Nah55 that prefixes should be separated from
verbs and the natural development to move them in order to expose the
verb stem to alphabetical order in Nah>Sp71 was a very important innovation in Nahuatl lexicography.

6.2. MACROSTRUCTURE: ALPHABETICAL ORDER.   In the second note
to the reader in the preface to Nah>Sp71, Molina tells us that since
Nahuatl lacks certain letters of the alphabet, it seemed to him that he
was not obligated to follow exactly the alphabetical order of other vocabularies, which he describes as "putting the words successively, with all of
their first letters tied to the order of the alphabet." He considered revising this order by placing together all of the spellings for /k/ (*ca, cl, co,*
. . .) followed by *ç*, which spells /s/ in Nahuatl, and then *ch* /č/. He

also considered putting words with the initial affricate /t^s/ among the
ç's because they "go along with the pronunciation of ça . . . ," by which
he probably meant that the fricative release corresponds to Spanish ç
rather than to s, therefore the missionaries' spelling tç or tz. But he concluded that the most accurate solution would be:

> to inter-weave all words in their own place, keeping the usual order of the
> alphabet . . . 'so that all of the Mexican words are to be sought in this vocab-
> ulary in the same manner as the Latin ones, and from Romance[28] are
> sought in the *Vocabulario* of Antonio [de Nebrija], through the same alpha-
> betical order; that is to say, c before a, c before e, c before h, c before i, etc.,
> and the same order will be kept in the third and fourth letters that follow
> these.

6.3. CONTENT. As one might expect, certain changes in the character
of the entries are required by the reversal of source and target languages,
although, as we have observed, the differences between the two resulting
dictionaries are not as great as one might expect.

6.3.1. We saw in section 4.4.1.2 that Molina's Spanish descriptions are
expansive and definitional in both source-language and target-language
position. We see numerous entries in which the target-language Spanish
is not necessarily more detailed but broader in its collection of details
because Molina has gathered from the Sp>Nah dictionaries the various
Spanish counterparts for a given Nahuatl word and has placed all of these
together where the Nahuatl word is the headword.

Consider the crafting of the Spanish for the entry word *pitzauac*, an
adjective meaning 'thin, narrow'. The Spanish-first dictionaries each
contain three entries that are paired with *pitzauac*. Sp>Nah55 and
Sp>Nah71 are so similar that we can use the entries from the latter for
this example.

> Angosta cosa,[29] assi como tabla, heredad, pared, adobe, camino o cosa seme-
> jante. pitzauac, amopatlauac. Sp>Nah71 f1ov1

28. "Demanera, que todos los vocabloe [*sic*] Mexicanos se han de buscar eneste Vocabulario, assi como los latinos y de romance se buscan enel Vocabulario del Antonio por el
mismo orden del Abece, conuiene a saber, C. ante a. C. ante e. C. ante. h. C. ante. i. &c.
Y el mismo orden se guardara enlas terceras y quartas letras que despues destaes [*sic*] se
siguen." The passage "como los latinos y de romance" is not entirely clear. It is tempting to
think that he meant to refer only to Nebrija's Latin-to-Spanish vocabulary, since in fact it is
the only one that is alphabetized in the way he describes here. The Spanish-to-Latin word
list is alphabetized, as was described above, rather like Molina's Spanish-to-Nahuatl list.

29. Like Nebrija, and probably following his example, Molina signifies that a word is an
adjective by giving it in its feminine form, modifying the feminine noun *cosa* 'thing'.

'A thin thing, such as a board, parcel of land, wall, adobe brick, road, or something similar.'

Delgada cosa assi. [assi = Delgadez de cosas largas y rollizas. pitzauacayotl]. pitzauac, pitzactic, pitzactli. Sp>Nah71 f37r2
'a thin thing of this type.' [this type = thinness of long and round things].

Enxuto hombre. vacqui, pitzauac. Sp>Nah71 f56v1
'lean man.'

In Nah>Sp71, Molina gathers the Spanish of these three entries and extends it to compile a fuller list of nouns to which this adjective might be applied. The resulting list provides an evocative explanation of the meaning of the Nahuatl word.

Pitzauac. cosa delgada, assi como varas, pilares, colunas, sogas y cosas largas y rollizas, o el camino, el viento delgado y sotil, los frisoles pequeños, lantejas, o cosas semejantes. Nah>Sp71 f82v1
'a thin thing, such as sticks, pillars, columns, ropes, and long and round things, or a road, a light and subtle breeze, small kidney beans, lentils, or similar things.'

Molina lists *cueponi, ni* under the following Spanish entries in each of the Sp>Nah dictionaries:

brotar o abrirse las flores 'for flowers to come out or open' Sp>Nah55 f36v, Sp>Nah71 f21r2
estallar rebentando 'to explode bursting' Sp>Nah55 f118r, Sp>Nah71 f6or2
luzir o resplandecer 'to shine or gleam' Sp>Nah55 f158r, Sp>Nah71 f79r2
luzir con piedras preciosas 'to shine with precious stones' Sp>Nah55 f158r Sp>Nah71 f79r2
rebentar sonando 'to burst with a noise' Sp>Nah55 f209r, Sp>Nah71 f102r

In Nah>Sp71, Molina has added illustrative subjects to these verbs, arriving at the following list:

dar estallido el hueuo, o la castaña quando la asan, o abrirse y abrotar la flor, o la rosa, o resplandecer alguna cosa. Nah>Sp71 f26r2
'for an egg to burst, or a chestnut when they roast it, or for a flower or a rose to open and burst forth, or for something to gleam.'

In addition to gathering the various Spanish entries into the Nah>Sp target language, Molina not infrequently adds an explanatory gloss, sometimes but not always based on the details of the Nahuatl—rather in the spirit of an etymological explanation. For example, in Sp>Nah71, Molina has the following entry:

Nadador que nada. tlamaneloani. tlacxiuitequini. Sp>Nah71 f88r1
'a swimmer who swims. something-hand-stir-[agent-present]. something-foot-beat-[agent-present].'

When the Nahuatl words become the entry words in Nah>Sp71, he feels obligated to add the details that in one case the swimmer is using his hands, in the other, his feet.

> Tlamaneloani. nadador con las manos. Nah>Sp71 f125v2
> 'something-hand-stir-[agent-present]. a swimmer with his hands.'
> Tlacxiuitequini. nadador tal. [tal = con los pies] Nah>Sp71 f120r2
> 'something-foot-beat-[agent-present]. such a swimmer [such = with his feet].'

A look at a number of entries from the Spanish-first dictionaries compared with their corresponding entries in Nah>Sp71 indicates that Molina not only combined the Spanish entries in the target-language field of Nah>Sp71 but also extensively rewrote them. Despite the differences arising from the rewriting, he appears to have worked from the earlier dictionaries. That is to say, he had some way of collecting the various Spanish entries that shared a given Nahuatl equivalent.

6.3.2. COMPARISON OF SPANISH IN NAH>SP71 WITH THAT OF SP>NAH71. Given Molina's philosophy of dictionary building, that is, his willingness to let both the active and the passive dictionary "favor" Nahuatl, even though this makes the two dictionaries look very much alike except for their language of access, one might expect that he would simply reverse the two languages of the first 1571 dictionary to obtain the second, allowing, of course, for the division of the Nahuatl field into separate equivalents for purposes of alphabetization as headwords. However, a short sample indicates that this was not his method.

A count of 300 consecutive[30] occurrences of the Spanish in entries from Nah>Sp71 compared with the corresponding Spanish entries from Sp>Nah71 yields the results shown in table 16.2. We see that in 131 (44%) of the 300 items, the Spanish of Nah>Sp71 is not in Sp>Nah71 at all (on the "loose interpretation" of "same" set up earlier). This is due in part to the "gathering" we spoke of above, which integrates the Spanish of two or more entries from the Sp>Nah dictionaries. Of the 169 entries in which Nah>Sp71 has (loosely) the same Spanish as Sp>Nah71, 84 (50%) match Sp>Nah71 in their Spanish, although only 73 (43%) of these are truly paired, since in the remaining 11 (7%) the Nahuatl has been altered. In the other 50 percent, Molina made some alteration, sometimes only trivial, in the Spanish used in Nah>Sp71, showing that he did not, in fact, engage in a mechanical transfer of source language to target language.

---

30. Sixteen entries in this range, all number terms, were omitted from this count. They are present in Sp>Nah55 and Nah>Sp71 but absent in Sp>Nah71 because of an apparent change in Molina's opinion of what types of numerical terms should be included in the word list.

TABLE 16.2. Comparison of Spanish Entries of Nah>Sp71 and Sp>Nah71

		Matching Entries		Altered Entries	
		84		85	
Nah>Sp71 entries counted:	300	Sp & Nah match	Sp only matches	Sp & Nah altered	Sp only altered
Entries shared with Sp>Nah71	169	73	11	18	67
Entries not shared with Sp>Nah71	131				

We have already seen examples of Spanish from Nah>Sp71 that dif-
fered from the Spanish-first dictionaries by having been gathered and
combined from several Spanish entries with additional embellishments.
For a case of more trivial though extensive rewriting, consider the Spanish
for *chipaua* 'to become clean, clear'. In Sp>Nah55 f5r, the Spanish is
aclararse qualquiera licor 'for any kind of liquid to become clear'. In the
two 1571 dictionaries we see the following:

> aclararse y asentarse qualquiera licor que estaua turbio y rebuelto. chipaua.
> yectia. Sp>Nah71 f3r2
> 'for any kind of liquid which was cloudy and unsettled to become clear and
> to settle out.'

> chipaua. pararse limpio, o pararse clara el agua turbia, o purificarse algo.
> pre. ochipauac. Nah>Sp71 f21r1
> 'for cloudy water to become clean or clear, or for something to become
> purified.'

In Sp>Nah71, Molina has augmented his earlier gloss *qualquiera licor.* The
relationship of the Spanish of Nah>Sp71 to that of the other dictionaries is an interesting one: although they mean very much the same thing,
of the eleven words in the Nah>Sp and the ten words in the Sp>Nah,
they have only the adjective *turbio* and the *clar-* root of *aclararse, clara* in
common. It is as if Molina wrote the Spanish afresh with no reference to
what he had done earlier, though we have seen other cases in which the
Spanish of the target language draws together, with or without additional
material, the entries of the Spanish source-language entries.

We see less extensive, though more substantial, changes in the entries
below, all of them in the direction of making the Spanish target language
even more definitional than it had been as source language, usually by
adding synonyms and/or paraphrases:

> For *tepuzapaztli. tepoz-apaztli* 'copper-bowl'
> Spanish source language: *caldera.* Sp>Nah55 f40v, Sp>Nah71 f23r2 'large
> vessel'

Spanish target language: *caldera de cobre, bacia o paila.* Nah>Sp71 f103v2
'copper cauldron, basin or frying pan'

In the Spanish-first dictionaries, there are simple one-word equivalents. In Nah>Sp71, Molina adds description and alternatives. It is also noteworthy that Molina does not put *cobre* 'copper' into his Spanish until Nah>Sp71, even though it is in Nebrija's entry for *caldera* and even though it literally translates the Nah *tepoz-*.

> For *tepuzquacalalatli. tepoz-qua-calalatli* 'metal-head-helmet'
> Spanish source language: *capacete de hierro.* Sp>Nah55 f43v, Sp>Nah71 f24v1 'iron helmet'
> Spanish target language: *capacete de hierro, o celada armadura dela cabeça.* Nah>Sp71 f104r1 'iron helmet; or helmet, armor for the head'

> For *temimilquatzaccayotl. te-mimil-qua-tzac-ca-yotl* 'stone-cylinder-head-[close-off]-nominalizer-ness'
> Spanish source language: *capitel de coluna.* Sp>Nah55 f44r, Sp>Nah71 f24v1 'capital of a column'
> Spanish target language: *capitelde coluna de piedra redonda.* Nah>Sp71 f97v1 'capital of a column made of round stone'

6.3.3. COMPARISON OF MOLINA'S NAHUATL INVENTORIES.   To compare the Nahuatl inventories of the three dictionaries, we used Campbell's databases in which spelling and spacing have been standardized and prefixes stripped in a consistent way, thus drawing together numerous words that were not identical in their dictionary forms. While it is not likely that we have achieved total consistency in spelling or spacing, the results of this comparison may be taken as roughly indicative of the relationships among the dictionaries. Further refinements to the database will, of course, decrease differences among the dictionaries. It should be noted that we use the term "word" to include simple, compounded, and derived words as well as phrases used in equivalents or in entries. Our sample comprises the range of equivalents and entry words in initial *pa-* and initial *po-*, including all and only those words that are alphabetized with these initials after the above-mentioned adjustments. For the Spanish-to-Nahuatl dictionaries, all instances of a word in the Nahuatl equivalents are included. This procedure gave us 3,090 total tokens belonging to 1,113 types, distributed in the three dictionaries as follows:

	Sp>Nah55	*Sp>Nah71*	*Nah>Sp71*
tokens	1,016	1,322	752
types	716	897	721

Numbers for the latter dictionary are, of course, quite different from the Spanish dictionaries because they represent headwords and not equivalents. It is important to remember that this sample is so small (3.2–3.5% of tokens) that it is only approximate for the corpus as a whole. In the remainder of this section, we will discuss only word types, not tokens.

In this sample, a few Nahuatl words appear uniquely in each of the three dictionaries. In Sp>Nah55 there are 35, in Sp>Nah71 169, and in Nah>Sp71 152. Sp>Nah55 shares 29 Nahuatl words with Nah>Sp71 that are lacking in Sp>Nah71.

Some other statistics for the Nahuatl types in this sample follow:

in the Spanish dictionaries only	392
intersection of the Spanish dictionaries	651
union of the Spanish dictionaries	961
in Sp>Nah55 and not Sp>Nah71	64
in Sp>Nah71 and not Sp>Nah55	246
in the 1571 dictionaries only	398
intersection of the 1571 dictionaries	540
union of the 1571 dictionaries	1,078
in Sp>Nah71 and not Nah>Sp71	357
in Nah>Sp71 and not Sp>Nah71	181
union of all three dictionaries	1,113
intersection of all three dictionaries	463

The question most often raised involves the relationship of the Nahuatl corpus of Nah>Sp71 to that of Sp>Nah71. One cannot consider just the relative sizes of the two dictionaries, because the Spanish dictionary, where the Nahuatl is found in the equivalents, naturally includes a higher ratio of tokens to types. Nor can one simply subtract the number of types in the Nahuatl dictionary from that of the Spanish dictionary, because each dictionary contains words missing from the other. A more insightful approach is to examine the nonintersecting subsets of each dictionary in terms of their relationship to the union of words in the two dictionaries. The union of Nahuatl words in the two 1571 dictionaries consists of 357 words that are only in Sp>Nah71, 540 words in the intersection of the two dictionaries, and 181 words that are only in Nah>Sp71. We see then that one-third (33.1%) of the words in the two dictionaries do not appear in the second half, whereas only about half that number (16.8%) fail to appear in the first. But one should not assume from these numbers that Sp>Nah71 is a gold mine of lexical information not found in Nah>Sp71. There are, of course, interesting lexical items in one or both Spanish dictionaries that are not in the Nahuatl dictionary. For example, from the Spanish dictionaries only we have the following:

pacyotl. trama de tela. Sp>Nah55 f237r, Sp>Nah71 f114v1 'woof or weft of fabric'

pacyoacaltontli. lançadera de texedor. Sp>Nah55 f152v, Sp>Nah71 f76v2 'weaver's shuttle'

çan pactaliztli. ocio por ociosidad. Sp>Nah55 f182v, Sp>Nah71 f89v2 'idleness'

pactani. saluo de peligro. Sp>Nah55 f221r, Sp>Nah71 f107r2 'safe from danger'

However, the preponderance of cases of nonoccurrence in Nah>Sp71 is a result of Molina's inclusion of predictable Nahuatl phrases and derived forms in the Spanish dictionaries that he did not feel the need to include in the Nahuatl dictionary. For example, *nitla, paccaihiyohuia* 'to be patient, have patience' occurs in all three dictionaries, but *anitla, paccaihiyohuia* 'to be impatient' occurs only in Sp>Nah55 f147v and Sp>Nah71 f74v1, where it translates *ympaciente ser.* Although some negatives of words or phrases do occur in Nah>Sp71, they are predictable, and thus many such items are to be found only as equivalents in one or both Spanish dictionaries.

Similarly, *ni, pachichihua* 'to compound medicines' occurs in all three dictionaries. But the derived abstract and agentive nouns occur only in Sp>Nah71:

pachichihualiztli. composicion tal. Sp>Nah71 f28r2 'such compounding'
pachichihuani. componedor desta manera o boticario. Sp>Nah71 f28r2 'one who compounds in this way, apothecary'

Tlapactli 'washed or fulled' appears in all three dictionaries; but the phrase *ayamo tlapactli ichcatomitl* 'dirty wool' occurs only in Sp>Nah55 f152v and Sp>Nah71 f76v2.

Occasionally a non-co-occurring item in the passive dictionary is offset by another one in the active dictionary. For example, the following two items appear only in the Spanish dictionaries:

noyollo pachihui. satisfazerme de algo. Sp>Nah71 f107v1 contentarse, satifazerse [*sic*]. Sp>Nah55 f54r
my-heart (it)-settles 'I am satisfied, content'
amo noyollo pachihui. descontentarse de algo. Sp>Nah55 f73v, Sp>Nah71 f39v2
neg. my-heart (it)-settles 'I am discontent'

But they are matched by the following similar item, which occurs only in Nah>Sp71:

pachiuhtica noyollo. estar contento y satisfecho mi coraçon. Nah>Sp71 f78v2
settle-past-ligature-[be-in-the-act-of] my-heart 'I am content, satisfied'

There are also words or phrases that are appropriate only for the Nahuatl dictionary. For example, *pacxixitli* Nah>Sp71 f79r1 is glossed simply as *cierto paxaro* 'a certain bird' and thus does not appear in the Spanish dictionaries.

Molina's awareness of the differences in function between passive and active dictionaries seems greater with regard to the Nahuatl content than with regard to the Spanish. We have seen that his Spanish tends to be definitional in both equivalents and headwords, in keeping with the intended function of all three dictionaries. And in this regard he seems not to distinguish clearly between passive and active dictionaries. Yet we see numerous differences between the inventory of Nahuatl in equivalents as opposed to headwords, suggesting that in fact Molina's disregard for the active/passive distinction in the Spanish of his dictionaries may have been by choice rather than by oversight.

6.4. NAHUATL DICTIONARY: CONCLUSIONS.   Molina's Nahuatl dictionary follows from, but is different from, his Spanish dictionaries. It would be interesting to be able to determine where in the history of these three dictionaries the Nah>Sp71 fits. From the fact that it is last in order it does not necessarily follow that it was the last written, especially when we consider that already in 1555 Molina speaks of such a dictionary and may even have had it in progress. However, the fact that so many entries show that he had access to the Spanish dictionaries suggests that it was finished late in the total process, regardless of when it was begun.

7. CONCLUSION.   Molina was driven by the compound aims of bringing the Christian faith to the Indians and exposing and explicating the ingenuity of the Nahuatl language. His work was even less mechanical than one might have expected considering the limitations under which he worked. Thus we note that he did not simply carry over Sp>Nah55 to Sp>Nah71, nor did he reverse Sp>Nah71 to arrive at Nah>Sp71 (or vice versa). What is equally clear is that the differences between the dictionaries are not random. Molina had some way of seeing his trail, of handling words as individual entities in each language rather than only as inseparable lists on paper. He could modify, refine, augment, and reorganize. One has only to see the contents of Nah>Sp71 sorted by Spanish alongside the contents of Sp>Nah71 and Sp>Nah55 to realize that, although he did not have 3 × 5 cards and shoeboxes to store them in, he must have had something functionally comparable. It is entertaining to imagine what his resources and facilities might have been. Did he use paper or the more available but much bulkier *amate* bark paper? Did young Indian students spend their afternoons cutting the material to his specifications? Pre-hard-disk dictionary making is space consuming. In the spare environment of the convent, what kind of area was allocated for the

endeavor? Whatever the answers to these questions might be, we can see that Molina had a clear goal, which he accomplished exceedingly well from the point of view of the passive dictionary of Nahuatl, perhaps slightly less successfully from the perspective of the active dictionary, given the arrangement and apparent aims of the Spanish-first dictionaries.

Although there were changes and advances from one dictionary to another, these show attention to detail and are not as major as we had expected at the outset of our study. To a surprising degree, the consideration and maturation of the concepts that underlie these works took place before the writing of Sp>Nah55. And although Molina almost surely availed himself of some form of Nebrija's dictionary, he certainly did not adopt it as an elicitation list. The two dictionaries show a surprisingly low degree of congruence considering their proximity in time. We attribute this limitation of shared Spanish entries between Molina's Spanish-to-Nahuatl dictionary and Nebrija's Spanish-to-Latin dictionary primarily to the fact that both of them are bilingual dictionaries in which Spanish is NOT the "language of interest." It is in fact Nebrija's and Molina's response to their respective target languages in which their greatest similarity lies. Molina merits our admiration, not for having availed himself of Nebrija, but for having done so with such temperance and judiciousness and for having seen the need to go far beyond Nebrija's example in the construction of entries. In contrast to Nebrija, Molina provides not simpleminded equivalences but, through example and description, finely drawn characterizations of the lexis of a language of which J. Richard Andrews (1975: x) has said: "Nahuatl is an exotic language. It is not just foreign like Spanish, German, or Russian; it is strangely foreign."

In the preface to Nah>Sp71, Molina, with reference to having written the Nahuatl-Spanish dictionary, refers to "this other Vocabulary which begins with the Mexican language, which has cost me a labor which Our Lord knows and those who understand can imagine" (Molina 1571, 2d preface, unpaginated).

Those of us "who understand" because we also have labored at constructing dictionaries probably do not REALLY understand, never having done so under the conditions in which Molina worked: having no computers, tape recorders, electric lights, or 3 × 5 cards and working with writing instruments that must be continually replenished and a library of fewer than sixty titles, most of them irrelevant to the task at hand.

We can, and should, marvel at the success of Molina's dedication—apparent in the fact that his dictionary is still the central resource of Nahuatl scholars more than four hundred years after he wrote it—his linguistic sophistication, and his astute craftsmanship as a lexicographer.

BIBLIOGRAPHY

Ackroyd, Lynda
 1976   Proto-Northeastern Athapaskan: Stem-initial consonants and vow-
          els. M.A. thesis, University of Toronto.

Adrian, Karen, Una Canger et al.
 1976   *Diccionario de vocablos aztecas contenidos en el* Arte de la lengua
          mexicana *de Horacio Carochi.* Copenhagen: Institute of the Sociol-
          ogy of the Indigenous Religions, Languages, and Cultures of
          America, University of Copenhagen.

Aho, Alfred V., Brian W. Kernighan, and Peter J. Weinberger
 1988   *The AWK Programming Language.* Reading, Mass.: Addison-Wesley.

Albert, Roy, and David Leedom Shaul
 1985   *A Concise Hopi and English Lexicon.* Philadelphia: John Benjamins.

Albright, Adam
 1999   The productivity of infixation in Lakhota. Paper presented at the
          annual meeting of the Linguistic Society of America.

American Bible Society
 1972   *God Lavayiyat aṅ Puhuvasiwni.* New Testament, King James
          Version. New York: American Bible Society.

Anderson, Benedict
 1983   *Imagined Communities: Reflections on the Origins and Spread of
          Nationalism.* London: Verso.

Anderson, Stephen R.
 1985   Inflectional morphology. In *Language Typology and Syntactic Descrip-
          tion.* Vol. 3: *Grammatical Categories and the Lexicon,* ed. Timothy
          Shopen, 150–201 Cambridge: Cambridge University Press.

Andrews, J. Richard
   1975   *Introduction to Classical Nahuatl.* Austin: University of Texas Press.

Aoki, Haruo
   1962   Nez Perce and Northern Sahaptin: A binary comparison. *International Journal of American Linguistics* 28: 172–82.
   1970   *Nez Perce Grammar.* University of California Publications in Linguistics 62. Berkeley and Los Angeles: University of California Press.
   1975   The East Plateau linguistic diffusion area. *International Journal of American Linguistics* 41: 183–99.
   1979   *Nez Perce Texts.* University of California Publications in Linguistics 90. Berkeley and Los Angeles: University of California Press.
   1994a   *Nez Perce Dictionary.* University of California Publications in Linguistics 122. Berkeley and Los Angeles: University of California Press.
   1994b   Symbolism in Nez Perce. In *Sound Symbolism,* ed. Leanne Hinton, Johanna Nichols, and John J. Ohala, 15–22. Cambridge: Cambridge University Press.

Aoki, Haruo, and Deward E. Walker, Jr.
   1989   *Nez Perce Oral Narratives.* University of California Publications in Linguistics 104. Berkeley and Los Angeles: University of California Press.

Apresjan, Jurij D.
   1992   Systematic lexicography. In *EURALEX '92 Proceedings,* vol. 1, ed. Hannu Tommola et al., 3–16. Tampere, Finland: Department of Translation Studies, University of Tampere.
   1992–93   Systemic lexicography as a basis of dictionary-making. *Dictionaries* 14: 79–87.

askSam Systems
   1991   *askSam Reference.* Version 5. 2d printing. Perry, Fla.: askSam Systems.

Atkins, Beryl T.
   1992–93   Theoretical lexicography and its relation to dictionary-making. *Dictionaries* 14: 4–43.

Atkins, Beryl T., Judy Kegl, and Beth Levin
   1988   Anatomy of a verb entry: From linguistic theory to lexicographic practice. *International Journal of Lexicography* 1: 84–126.

Avilés, Alejandro, Ken Hale, and Danilo Salamanca
   1988   Insubordinate complements in Miskitu. Manuscript, Massachusetts Institute of Technology, Department of Linguistics.

Baker, Mark C.
   1988   *Incorporation: A Theory of Grammatical Function Changing.* Chicago: University of Chicago Press.
   1995   *The Polysynthesis Parameter.* Oxford: Oxford University Press.

Balibar, Étienne
1991   Racism and nationalism. In *Race, Nation, Class: Ambiguous Identities*, ed. Étienne Balibar and I. Wallerstein, 37–67. London: Verso.

Baraga, Frederick
1878   *A Dictionary of the Otchipwe Language*. 2d ed. Reprint 1966, 1973. Minneapolis: Ross & Haines.

Bartholomew, Doris
1991   Lexicography of the languages of the Mesoamerican Indians. In *Wörterbücher/Dictionaries/Dictionnaires*, ed. Franz Josef Hausmann, Oskar Reichmann, Herbert Ernst Wiegand, and Ladislav Zgusta, 2697–2700. Berlin: Walter de Gruyter.

Bartholomew, Doris A., and Louise C. Schoenhals
1983   *Bilingual Dictionaries for Indigenous Languages*. Mexico City: Instituto Lingüístico de Verano.

Beauchamp, William M.
1907   *Aboriginal Place Names of New York*. Albany: New York State Museum.

Berman, Harold J.
1983   *Law and Revolution: The Formation of the Western Legal Tradition*. Cambridge, Mass.: Harvard University Press.

Besnier, Niko
1995   *Literacy, Emotion, and Authority: Reading and Writing on a Polynesian Atoll*. Cambridge: Cambridge University Press.

Bethel, Rosalie, Paul V. Kroskrity, Christopher Loether, and Gregory A. Reinhardt
1984   *A Practical Dictionary of Western Mono*. North Fork, Calif.: Sierra Mono Museum.

Bierhorst, John
1985   *A Nahuatl-English Dictionary and Concordance to the CANTARES MEXICANOS with an Analytic Transcription and Grammatical Notes*. Stanford: Stanford University Press.

Bittner, Maria
1994   *Case, Scope, and Binding*. Dordrecht: Kluwer.

Blommaert, Jan, and Jef Verschueren
1998   The role of language in European nationalist ideologies. In *Language Ideologies, Practice and Theory*, ed. Bambi B. Schieffelin, Kathryn A. Woolard, and Paul V. Kroskrity, 189–210. New York: Oxford University Press.

Bloom, Harold
1985   The breaking of form. In *Deconstruction and Criticism*, ed. Harold Bloom et al., 1–37. New York: Continuum.

Bloomfield, Leonard
1957   *Eastern Ojibwa: A Grammatical Sketch, Texts, and Word List.* Ed.
        Charles F. Hockett. Ann Arbor: University of Michigan Press.

Bourdieu, Pierre
1991   *Language and Symbolic Power.* Cambridge, Mass.: Harvard University
        Press.

Brandt, Elizabeth A.
1988   Applied linguistic anthropology and American Indian language
        renewal. *Human Organization* 47: 322–29.

Brewer, Forest, and Jean G. Brewer
1971   *Vocabulario mexicano de Tetelcingo, Morelos: Castellano-mexicano,
        mexicano-castellano.* Mexico City: Instituto Lingüístico de Verano.

Bright, William
1984   Place names of American Indian origin. In *American Indian Lin-
        guistics and Literature,* ed. W. Bright, 63–75. Berlin: Mouton.
1993   *Colorado Place Names.* Boulder, Colo.: Johnson. (Revision of
        Eichler 1977.)
1994   Brief notices. *Language in Society* 23: 619–20.
1998   *1500 California Place Names: Their Origin and Meaning.* Berkeley:
        University of California Press. (Revision of Gudde 1969.)
1999   Review of Hopi Dictionary Project 1998. *Language in Society* 28:
        481–83.

Brinton, Daniel
1895   The Matagalpan linguistic stock of Central America. *Proceedings of
        the American Philosophical Society* 34: 403–15.

Broadbent, Sylvia M.
1964   *The Southern Sierra Miwok Language.* University of California Publi-
        cations in Linguistics 38. Berkeley and Los Angeles: University of
        California Press.

Brown, Michael F.
1998   Can culture be copyrighted? *Current Anthropology* 39: 193–206.

Buck, Carl Darling
1949   *A Dictionary of Selected Synonyms in the Principal Indo-European Lan-
        guages: A Contribution to the History of Ideas.* Chicago: University of
        Chicago Press.

Buechel, Rev. Eugene, S.J.
1983   *A Dictionary—Oie Wowapi Wan of Teton Sioux (Lakota-English:
        English-Lakota/Lakota-Ieska: Ieska-Lakota).* Ed. Rev. Paul Manhart,
        S.J. Pine Ridge, S. Dak.: Red Cloud Indian School, Inc., Holy
        Rosary Mission.

Callaghan, Catherine A.
1984   *Plains Miwok Dictionary.* University of California Publications in

Linguistics 105. Berkeley and Los Angeles: University of
California Press.

1987   *Northern Sierra Miwok Dictionary.* University of California Publications in Linguistics 110. Berkeley and Los Angeles: University of
California Press.

1997   Evidence for Yok-Utian. *International Journal of American Linguistics*
63: 18–64.

Callaghan, Catherine A., and Brian Bibby

1985   *Northern Sierra Miwuk [sic] Language Handbook.* Carmichael, Calif.:
San Juan Unified School District.

Campbell, Lyle

1979   Middle American languages. In *The Languages of Native America,*
ed. Lyle Campbell and Marianne Mithun, 902–1000. Austin:
University of Texas Press.

Campbell, Lyle, Terrence Kaufman, and Thomas C. Smith-Stark

1986   Meso-America as a linguistic area. *Language* 62: 530–70.

Campbell, R. Joe

1985   *A Morphological Dictionary of Classical Nahuatl: A Morpheme Index
to the* Vocabulario en lengua mexicana y castellana *of Fray
Alonso de Molina.* Madison, Wisc.: Hispanic Seminary of
Medieval Studies.

Canger, Una

1980   *Five Studies Inspired by Nahuatl Verbs in -oa.* Travaux du cercle lin-
guistique de Copenhague 19. Copenhagen.

1981   Reduplication in Nahuatl, in dialectal and historical perspective.
In *Nahuatl Studies in Memory of Fernando Horcasitas,* ed. Frances
Karttunen, 29–52. Texas Linguistic Forum 18. Austin: University
of Texas, Department of Linguistics.

1997   El *Arte* de Horacio Carochi. In *La descripción de las lenguas
amerindias en la época colonial,* ed. Klaus Zimmermann, 59–74.
Berlin: Ibero-Amerikanisches Institut.

Carochi, Horacio

1645   *Arte de la lengua mexicana con la declaracion de los advebios della.*
Mexico City: Juan Ruyz.

Carter, Richard T., A. Wesley Jones, Robert L. Rankin, et al.

N.d.   Comparative Siouan dictionary. Manuscript.

Cassidy, Frederic G., chief ed., Joan Houston Hall, assoc. ed.

1985–   *Dictionary of American Regional English.* Cambridge, Mass.: Belknap
Press of Harvard University Press.

Causley, Trisha

1996   Morphological obfuscation in Dogrib nominal compounds. Ph.D.
generals paper, University of Toronto.

Cayetano, E. Roy
1993 *The People's Garifuna Dictionary.* Dangriga, Belize: National Garifuna Council.

Chafe, Wallace, and Deborah Tannen
1987 The relation between written and spoken language. *Annual Review of Anthropology* 16: 383–407.

Chappell, Hilary, and William McGregor
1996 Prolegomena to a theory of inalienability. In *The Grammar of Inalienability: A Typological Perspective on Body Part Terms and the Part-Whole Relation,* ed. Hilary Chappell and William McGregor, 3–30. Berlin: Mouton de Gruyter.

Chappell, Hilary, and William McGregor, eds.
1996 *The Grammar of Inalienability: A Typological Perspective on Body Part Terms and the Part-Whole Relation.* Berlin: Mouton de Gruyter.

Chimalpahin Quauhtlehuanitzin, Domingo de San Antón Muñón
1958 *Das* Memorial breve acerca de la fundación de la ciudad de Culhuacan. Aztekischer Text mit deutscher Übersetzung von Walter Lehmann und Gerdt Kutscher. Quellenwerke zur alten Geschichte Amerikas aufgezeichnet in den Sprachen der Eingeborenen; Bd. 7. Stuttgart: W. Kohlhammer.
1997 *Codex Chimalpahin. Society and Politics in Mexico Tenochtitlan, Tlatelolco, Texcoco, Culhuacan, and Other Nahua Altepetl in Central Mexico. The Nahuatl and Spanish Annals and Accounts Collected and Recorded by Don Domingo de San Antón Muñón Chimalpahin Quauhtlehuanitzin.* Ed. and trans. Arthur J. O. Anderson and Susan Schroeder. 2 vols. Norman: University of Oklahoma Press.

Cicourel, Alan
1985 Text and discourse. *Annual Review of Anthropology* 14: 159–85.

CIDCA (Centro de Investigaciones y Documentación de la Costa Atlántica)
1985 *Miskitu Bila Aisanka. Gramática misquita.* Managua.
1998 *Diccionario del miskito.* Manuscript. Managua.

Clark, Eve, and Herbert Clark
1979 When nouns surface as verbs. *Language* 55: 767–811.

Clayton, Mary L.
1989 A trilingual Spanish-Latin-Nahuatl manuscript dictionary sometimes attributed to Fray Bernardino de Sahagún. *International Journal of American Linguistics* 55: 391–416.

CODIUL/UYUTMUBAL
1998 *Diccionario del ulwa (sumu meridional).* Manuscript. CIDCA/Massachusetts Institute of Technology, Department of Linguistics.

Constenla Umaña, Adolfo
N.d.   Elementos de fonología comparada de las lenguas Misumalpas.
            Manuscript. University of Costa Rica.

Conzemius, Edward
1929   Notes on the Miskito and Sumu languages of eastern Nicaragua
            and Honduras. *International Journal of American Linguistics* 5:
            57–115.

Cop, Margaret
1990   The function of collocations in dictionaries. In *BudaLEX '88 Pro-
            ceedings,* ed. Tamás Magay and J. Zigány, 35–46. Budapest:
            Akadémiai Kiadó.

Coward, David F., and Charles E. Grimes
1995   *Making Dictionaries: A Guide to Lexicography and the Multi-Dictionary
            Formatter.* Version 1.0. Waxhaw, N.C.: Summer Institute of Linguistics.

Craig, Colette
1985   Indigenous languages of Nicaragua of Chibchan affiliation. *Estudios
            de lingüística chibcha* 4: 47–55. San José: Programa de Investigación
            del Departamento de Lingüística de la Universidad de Costa Rica.

Craig, Colette, and Ken Hale
1992   A possible Macro-Chibchan etymon. *Anthropological Linguistics* 34:
            173–201.

Creamer, Thomas
1989   Shuowen Jiezi and textual criticism in China. *International Journal
            of Lexicography* 2: 176–87.

Croft, William
1990   *Typology and Universals.* Cambridge: Cambridge University Press.

Crook, Rena, Leanne Hinton, and Nancy Stenson
1977   The Havasupai writing system. In *Proceedings of the 1976 Hokan-
            Yuman Languages Workshop,* 1–16. University Museum Studies 11.
            Carbondale: Southern Illinois University.

Cruse, D. A.
1986   *Lexical Semantics.* Cambridge: Cambridge University Press.

Dakin, Karen
2000   Review of the Hopi Dictionary Project 1998. *International Journal
            of American Linguistics* 66: 398–402.

Dauenhauer, Nora Marks, and Richard Dauenhauer
1991   *Beginning Tlingit.* Juneau: Sealaska Heritage Foundation.
1998   Technical, emotional, and ideological issues in reversing
            language shift: Examples from southeast Alaska. In *Endangered
            Languages: Language Loss and Community Response,* ed. Lenore A.
            Grenoble and Lindsay J. Whaley, 57–98. Cambridge: Cambridge
            University Press.

Davis, Daniel W., and John S. Wimbish
   1993   *Integrated Data Management and Analysis for the Field Linguist. The Linguist's Shoebox: User's Manual.* Version 2.0. Waxhaw, N.C.: Summer Institute of Linguistics.

DeLancey, Scott
   1996   The bipartite stem belt: Disentangling areal and genetic correspondences. In *Proceedings of the Twenty-second Annual Meeting of the Berkeley Linguistics Society. Special Session on Historical Issues in Native American Languages,* ed. David Librik and Roxanne Beeler, 37–54. Berkeley: Berkeley Linguistic Society.
   1999   Lexical prefixes and the bipartite stem construction in Klamath. *International Journal of American Linguistics* 65: 56–83.

Dixon, R. M. W.
   1977   Where have all the adjectives gone? *Studies in Language* 1: 19–80.
   1984   The semantic basis of syntactic properties. In *Proceedings of the Tenth Annual Meeting of the Berkeley Linguistics Society,* ed. C. Brugman and M. McCaulay, 583–95. Berkeley: Berkeley Linguistic Society.

Dolezal, Fredric Thomas, and Don R. McCreary
   1999   *Pedagogical Lexicography Today: A Critical Bibliography on Learners' Dictionaries with Special Emphasis on Language Learners and Dictionary Users.* Tübingen: Niemeyer.

Donehoo, George P.
   1928   *A History of the Indian Villages and Place Names in Pennsylvania.* Harrisburg: Telegraph Press.

Dorian, Nancy
   1981   *Language Death.* Philadelphia: University of Pennsylvania Press.
   1989   *Investigating Obsolescence: Studies in Language Contraction and Death.* Cambridge: Cambridge University Press.
   1998   Western language ideologies and small-language prospects. In *Endangered Languages: Language Loss and Community Response,* ed. Lenore A. Grenoble and Lindsay J. Whaley, 3–21. Cambridge: Cambridge University Press.

Dorsey, James O.
   1885   On the comparative phonology of four Siouan languages. *Smithsonian Institution, Annual Report for 1883,* 919–29. Washington, D.C.: Government Printing Office.
   1890   *The Cegiha Language. Contributions to North American Ethnology VI.* Washington, D.C.: Government Printing Office.
   1891   Omaha and Ponka letters. *Bureau of American Ethnology Bulletin* 11: 1–127. Washington, D.C.: Government Printing Office.

England, Nora C.
   1992   Doing Mayan linguistics in Guatemala. *Language* 68: 29–35.

1998   Mayan efforts toward language preservation. In *Endangered Languages: Language Loss and Community Response*, ed. Lenore A. Grenoble and Lindsay J. Whaley, 99–116. Cambridge: Cambridge University Press.

Eichler, George
1977   *Colorado Place Names.* Boulder, Colo.: Johnson. (Revised as Bright 1993.)

Farnell, Brenda
1993   *Wiyuta: Assiniboine Storytelling with Signs.* Austin: University of Texas Press.

Feeling, Durbin, and William Pulte
1975   *Cherokee-English Dictionary* (by Durbin Feeling; ed. William Pulte) with Outline of Cherokee Grammar (by William Pulte and Durbin Feeling). Tahlequah: Cherokee Nation of Oklahoma.

Feenstra, Jaap
1992   *Tłįchǫ Yati Enįhtł'è/Dogrib Dictionary.* Rae-Edzo, NWT: Dogrib Divisional Board of Education.

Fermino, Jessie Little Bear
1998   Wampanoag language reclamation project: First steps to healing the circle. Paper presented at the V Encuentro de Lingüística en el Noroeste, Hermosillo, Universidad de Sonora.

Fillmore, Charles J., Paul Kay, and Catherine O'Connor
1988   Regularity and idiomaticity in grammatical constructions: The case of *let alone. Language* 64: 501–38.

Finer, Daniel
1985a   *The Formal Grammar of Switch-Reference.* New York: Garland.
1985b   The syntax of switch-reference. *Linguistic Inquiry* 16: 35–55.

Flemming, Edward
1996   Laryngeal metathesis and vowel deletion in Cherokee. In *Cherokee Papers from UCLA,* ed. Pamela Munro, 23–44. UCLA Occasional Papers in Linguistics 16. Los Angeles: UCLA Department of Linguistics.

Fletcher, Jill Sherman
1994   *Now You're Speaking Hupa.* Humboldt, Calif.: Hoopa Valley Tribe.

Fox, Francis X., Nora Soney, and Richard A. Rhodes
1988   Chippewa-Ottawa texts. In *An Ojibwe Text Anthology,* ed. John D. Nichols, 33–68. Text+ Series–Number 2: Studies in the Interpretation of Canadian Native Languages and Cultures. London: University of Western Ontario.

Frantz, Donald G., and Norma Jean Russell
1989   *Blackfoot Dictionary of Stems, Roots, and Affixes.* Toronto: University of Toronto Press.

Frawley, William
1987   *Text and Epistemology.* Norwood, N.J.: Ablex.

Frawley, William, ed.
1981   *Linguistics and Literacy.* New York: Plenum Press.
1992–93 Forum on theory and practice in lexicography. *Dictionaries* 14: 1–159.

Freeland, L. S.
1951   *Language of the Sierra Miwok.* Memoir 6 of the *International Journal of American Linguistics*/Indiana University Publications in Anthropology and Linguistics.

Freeland, L. S., and Sylvia M. Broadbent
1960   *Central Sierra Miwok Dictionary with Texts.* University of California Publications in Linguistics 23. Berkeley and Los Angeles: University of California Press.

Gal, Susan
1979   *Language Shift: Social Dimensions of Linguistic Change in Bilingual Austria.* New York: Academic Press.

García Icazbalceta, Joaquín
1892   Códice de Tlatelolco. In *Códice Mendieta: Documentos franciscanos, siglos XVI y XVII,* vol. 2: 241–77. Nueva colección de documentos para la historia de México, 1886–92, vol. 5. Mexico City: Imprenta de Francisco Díaz de León.

Geeraerts, Dirk
1997   *Diachronic Prototype Semantics: A Contribution to Historical Lexicology.* Oxford: Oxford University Press.

Gerdts, Donna B.
1998   Incorporation. In *The Handbook of Morphology,* ed. Andrew Spencer and Arnold M. Zwicky, 84–100. Oxford: Blackwell.

Gillette, Jeffrey W.
1986   *Duke Language Toolkit.* Version 2.20. Duke Language Learning Project. Durham, N.C.: Duke University.

Goddard, Cliff
1998   *Semantic Analysis: A Practical Introduction.* Oxford: Oxford University Press.

Goddard, Ives, and Kathleen J. Bragdon
1988   *Native Writings in Massachusett.* Memoirs of the American Philosophical Society, vol. 185, pt. 2. Philadelphia: American Philosophical Society.

Goldberg, Adele
1995   *Constructions: A Construction Grammar Approach to Argument Structure.* Chicago: University of Chicago Press.

Gordon, Lynn
    1986   *Maricopa Morphology and Syntax.* University of California Publications in Linguistics 108. Berkeley and Los Angeles: University of California Press.

Gordon, Lynn, Pollyanna Heath, and Pamela Munro
    In preparation   *A Maricopa Dictionary.*

Granger, Byrd Howell
    1983   *Arizona's Names: X Marks the Place.* Tucson, Ariz.: Falconer.

Green, Thomas
    1992   Covert clause structure in the Miskitu noun phrase. Manuscript. Massachusetts Institute of Technology, Department of Linguistics.

Green, Thomas, and Ken Hale
    1998   Ulwa, the language of Karawala, eastern Nicaragua: Its position and prospects in modern Nicaragua. *International Journal of the Sociology of Language* 132: 185–201.

Grenoble, Lenore A., and Lindsay J. Whaley
    1998   Toward a typology of language endangerment. In *Endangered Languages: Language Loss and Community Response,* ed. Lenore A. Grenoble and Lindsay J. Whaley, 22–54. Cambridge: Cambridge University Press.

Grimes, Joseph E.
    1964   *Huichol Syntax.* The Hague: Mouton.
    1990   Inverse functions in the lexicon. In *Meaning-Text Theory: Linguistics, Lexicography, and Implicatives,* ed. James Steele, 350–64. Ottawa: University of Ottawa Press.
    1996   Lexical functions across languages. In *Lexical Functions in Lexicography and Natural Language Processing,* ed. Leo Wanner, 103–13. Amsterdam: John Benjamins.

Grimes E., José, Pedro de la Cruz Avila, José Carrillo Vicente, Filiberto Díaz, Román Díaz, Antonio de la Rosa, and Toribio Rentería
    1981   *El huichol: Apuntes sobre el léxico.* Technical Report No. 5 to the National Science Foundation. Ithaca, N.Y.: Department of Modern Languages and Linguistics, Cornell University. [Available as ERIC microfiche ED 210 901.]

Gudde, Erwin G.
    1969   *1000 California Place Names.* 3d ed. Berkeley: University of California Press. (Revised as Bright 1998.)

Haensch, Günther
    1990   Spanische Lexikographie. In *Wörterbücher/Dictionaries/Dictionnaires,* ed. Franz Josef Hausmann, Oskar Reichmann, Herbert Ernst Wiegand, and Ladislav Zgusta, 1738–67. Berlin: Walter de Gruyter.

Hale, Ken
1989   The causative construction in Miskitu. In *Sentential Complementa-
         tion and the Lexicon: Studies in Honour of Wim de Geest,* ed.
         D. Jaspers et al., 189–205. Dordrecht: Foris Publications.
1991a   Misumalpan verb sequencing constructions. In *Serial Verbs: Gram-
         matical, Comparative and Cognitive Approaches,* ed. Claire Lefebvre,
         1–35. Amsterdam: John Benjamins.
1991b   El ulwa, sumo meridional: Un idioma distinto? WANI, 11. Mana-
         gua.
1992a   On endangered languages and the safeguarding of diversity. *Lan-
         guage* 68: 1–3.
1992b   Subject obviation, switch reference, and control. In *Control and
         Grammar,* ed. R. Larson et al., 51–77. Dordrecht: Kluwer.
1994   Preliminary observations on lexico-semantic primitives in the
         Misumalpan languages of Nicaragua. In *Semantic and Lexical Uni-
         versals: Theory and Empirical Findings,* ed. Cliff Goddard and Anna
         Wierzbicka, 263–83. Amsterdam: John Benjamins.

Hale, Ken, and Abanel Lacayo
1988   *Vocabulario preliminar del ulwa (sumu meridional).* CIDCA/CCS–
         Massachusetts Institute of Technology.

Hale Kuamo'o and 'Aha Pūnana Leo
1996   Mā amaka Kaiao. Hale Kuamo'o-Kikowaena 'ō lelo Hawai'i. Hilo:
         Hale Kuamo'o Hawaiian Language Center, University of Hawaii
         at Hilo.

Halpern, Abraham
1947   Yuma IV: Verb themes. *International Journal of American Linguistics*
         13: 18–30.

Hancher, Michael
1996   Illustrations. *Dictionaries* 17: 79–115.

Harder, Kelsie
1976   *Illustrated Dictionary of Placenames: US and Canada.* New York: Van
         Nostrand Reinhold.

Hardy, Heather K.
1979   Tolkapaya syntax: Aspect, modality, and adverbial modification in
         a Yavapai dialect. Ph.D. dissertation, University of California, Los
         Angeles.

Hargus, Sharon
1990   The Fort Ware Sekani topical dictionary. Manuscript.

Haspelmath, Martin
1993   More on the typology of inchoative/causative verb alternations. In
         Causatives and Transitivity, ed. Bernard Comrie and Maria Polinsky,
         87–111. Amsterdam: John Benjamins.

Hausmann, Franz Josef, Oskar Reichmann, Herbert Ernst Wiegand, and
Ladislav Zgusta, eds.
1990–91   *Wörterbücher/Dictionaries/Dictionnaires.* Vols. 1 and 2 (1990), vol. 3
(1991). Berlin: Walter de Gruyter.

Heath, G. R.
1927   *Grammar of the Miskito Language.* Herrnhut: F. Lindenbein.
1950   Miskito glossary, with ethnographic commentary. *International
Journal of American Linguistics* 16: 20–34.

Heath, Shirley Brice
1972   *Telling Tongues. Language Policy in Mexico: Colony to Nation.* New
York: Teachers College Press.

Heizer, Robert F.
1974   *The Destruction of California Indians.* Lincoln: University of
Nebraska Press.

Henningsen, Manfred
1989   The politics of purity and exclusion. In *The Politics of Language
Purism,* ed. B. Jernudd and M. Shapiro, 31–52. Berlin: Mouton
de Gruyter.

Hernandez Hernandez, Esther
1993   Estudios sobre el lexico en el 'Vocabulario en lengua castellana y
mexicana y mexicana y castellana' (1571) de fray Alonso de
Molina. (Vols. 1 and 2). Ph.D. dissertation, State University of
New York at Albany. Dissertation Abstracts.

Hill, Jane H., and Kenneth C. Hill
1986   *Speaking Mexicano: Dynamics of Syncretic Language in Central Mexico.*
Tucson: University of Arizona Press.

Hill, Kenneth C.
1967   A Grammar of the Serrano Language. Ph.D. dissertation,
University of California, Los Angeles.

Hinton, Leanne
1994   *Flutes of Fire: Essays on California Indian languages.* Berkeley, Calif.:
Heyday Press.
1997   Survival of endangered languages: The California master-apprentice program. *International Journal of the Sociology of Language* 123:
177–91.

Hinton, Leanne, Members of the Bilingual Education Program, and the
Havasupai Community
1994   *A Dictionary of the Havasupai Language.* Supai, Ariz.: Havasupai
Tribe.

Hockett, Charles F.
1967   The Yawelmani basic verb. *Language* 43: 208–22.

Holt, Dennis
  1975   The development of the Paya sound system. Manuscript. Univer-
            sity of California, Los Angeles, Department of Linguistics.

Hopi Dictionary Project
  1998   *Hopi Dictionary/Hopìikwa Lavàytutuveni: A Hopi-English Dictionary
            of the Third Mesa Dialect.* Tucson: University of Arizona Press.

Hopi Health Department
  1988   *Handbook of Hopi Anatomical Terms.* Kykotsmovi, Ariz.: Hopi Tribe.

Howren, Robert
  1975   Some isoglosses in Mackenzie-drainage Athapaskan. In *Proceed-
            ings: Northern Athapaskan Conference, 1971,* vol. 2, ed. Annette
            McFayden Clark, 577–618. Ottawa: National Museums of
            Canada.

Hsu, Robert
  1985   *Lexware Manual: Computer Programs for Lexicography Developed at the
            University of Hawaii.* Edition 1.5. Manoa: University of Hawaii
            Department of Linguistics.

Huden, John C.
  1962   *Indian Place Names of New England.* New York: Museum of the
            American Indian, Heye Foundation.

Hunn, Eugene S., with James Selam and Family
  1990   *Nch'i-wána, "The Big River": Mid-Columbia Indians and Their Land.*
            Seattle: University of Washington Press.

Hurtado, Albert L.
  1988   *Indian Survival on the California Frontier.* New Haven: Yale Univer-
            sity Press.

Inter-Apache Summit on Repatriation
  1995   Inter-Apache policy on repatriation and the protection of Apache
            cultures. Manuscript.

Irvine, Judith
  1989   When talk isn't cheap: Language and political economy. *American
            Ethnologist* 16: 248–67.

JAARS, INC.
  2000   *The Linguist's Shoebox: Tutorial and User's Guide.* Waxhaw, N.C.:
            Summer Institute of Linguistics.

Jackendoff, Ray
  1990   *Semantic Structures.* Cambridge, Mass.: MIT Press.

Jacobsen, William
  1967   Switch-reference in Hokan-Coahuiltecan. In *Studies in Southwest-
            ern Ethnolinguistics,* ed. Dell Hymes and W. E. Bittle, 238–63. The
            Hague: Mouton.

1980   Washo bipartite verb stems. In *American Indian and Indoeuropean Studies: Papers in Honor of Madison S. Beeler,* ed. Kathryn Klar, 85–99. The Hague: Mouton.

Jameson, Fredric
1972   *The Prison-House of Language: A Critical Account of Structuralism and Russian Formalism.* Princeton, N.J.: Princeton University Press.

Jeanne, LaVerne Masayesva
1992   An institutional response to language endangerment: A proposal for a Native American Language Center. *Language* 68: 24–28.

Jeanne, LaVerne Masayesva, and Ken Hale
1998   Transitivización en hopi. Paper presented at the V Encuentro de Lingüística en el Noroeste, Hermosillo, Universidad de Sonora.

Jones, A. Wesley
1991   The case for root extensions in Proto-Siouan. In *Proceedings of the 1990 Mid-America Linguistics Conference,* 505–17. Lawrence: Department of Linguistics, University of Kansas.

Kang, Myung-Yoon
1987   The Miskitu ending -*i* and VP complementation. Manuscript. Massachusetts Institute of Technology, Department of Linguistics.

Karttunen, Frances
1983   *An Analytical Dictionary of Nahuatl.* Austin: University of Texas Press. (2d ed., Norman: University of Oklahoma Press, 1992.)
1985   *Nahuatl and Maya in Contact with Spanish.* Texas Linguistics Forum 26. Austin: University of Texas at Austin, Department of Linguistics and Center for Cognitive Science.
1988   The roots of sixteenth-century Mesoamerican lexicography. In *Smoke and Mist: Mesoamerican Studies in Memory of Thelma Sullivan,* ed. J. Kathryn Josserand and Karen Dakin, 545–59. Oxford: B.A.R. International Series 402.
1991   Nahuatl lexicography. In *Wörterbücher/Dictionaries/Dictionnaires,* ed. Franz Josef Hausmann, Oskar Reichmann, Herbert Ernst Wiegand, and Ladislav Zgusta, 2657–61. Berlin: Walter de Gruyter.
1995   The roots of sixteenth-century Mesoamerican lexicography. In *Cultures, Ideologies, and the Dictionary: Studies in Honor of Ladislav Zgusta,* ed. Braj B. Kachru and Henry Kahane, 75–88. Tübingen: Max Niemeyer.

Karttunen, Frances, and James Lockhart
1976   *Nahuatl in the Middle Years: Language Contact Phenomena in Texts of the Colonial Period.* University of California Publications in Linguistics 85. Berkeley and Los Angeles: University of California Press.

Kaska Tribal Council
1997   *Guāzgi K'ügé'/Our Language Book: Nouns. Kaska, Mountain Slavey and Sekani.* Kaska Tribal Council.

Kenny, Hamill
1961   *The Origin and Meaning of the Indian Place Names of Maryland.*
        Baltimore: Waverly.

Kharma, Nayef N.
1985   Wanted: A brand-new type of learner's dictionary. *Multilingua* 4:
        85–90.

Kilpatrick, Alan
1997   *The Night Has a Naked Soul: Witchcraft and Sorcery among the West-*
        ern Cherokee. Syracuse, N.Y.: Syracuse University Press.

Kilpatrick, Anna Gritts, and Jack F. Kilpatrick
1966a   Chronicles of Wolftown: Social documents of the North Carolina
        Cherokees, 1850–1862. *Bureau of American Ethnology Bulletin* 196:
        1–111.
1966b   Eastern Cherokee folktales: Reconstructed from the notes of Frans
        M. Olbrechts. *Bureau of American Ethnology Bulletin* 196: 379–447.

Kilpatrick, Jack F., and Anna Gritts Kilpatrick
1965   *The Shadow of Sequoyah: Social Documents of the Cherokees,*
        1862–1964. Norman: University of Oklahoma Press.

Krauss, Michael
1996   Status of Native American language endangerment. In *Stabilizing*
        Indigenous Languages, ed. G. Cantoni, 16–21. Flagstaff: Northern
        Arizona University.

Krauss, Michael, and Victor Golla
1981   Northern Athabaskan languages. In *Subarctic.* Vol. 6 of *Handbook*
        of North American Indians, ed. June Helm, 67–85. Washington,
        D.C.: Smithsonian Institution Press.

Krauss, Michael, and Jeff Leer
1981   *Proto-Athapaskan ỹ and the Na-Dene Sonorants.* Fairbanks: Alaska
        Native Language Center.

Kroeber, Paul D.
1995   Review of *Nez Perce Dictionary. Language* 7: 634.

Kromann, Hans-Peder, Theis Riiber, and Poul Rosbach
1984   Active and passive bilingual dictionaries: The Shcherba concept
        reconsidered. *LEXeter '83 Proceedings,* ed. R. Hartmann, 207–15.
        Tübingen: Niemeyer.
1991   Principles of bilingual lexicography. In *Wörterbücher/Dictionaries/*
        Dictionnaires, ed. Franz Josef Hausmann, Oskar Reichmann,
        Herbert Ernst Wiegand, and Ladislav Zgusta, 2711–28. Berlin:
        Walter de Gruyter.

Kroskrity, Paul V.
1977   Aspects of Arizona Tewa language structure and use. Ph.D.
        dissertation, Indiana University.

1993   *Language, History, and Identity: Ethnolinguistic Studies of the Arizona*
           Tewa. Tucson: University of Arizona Press.
1998   Arizona Tewa kiva speech as a manifestation of a dominant lan-
           guage ideology. In *Language Ideologies, Practice and Theory,* ed.
           Bambi B. Schieffelin, Kathryn A. Woolard, and Paul V. Kroskrity,
           103–23. New York: Oxford University Press.
1999   Language ideologies, language shift, and the imagination of a
           Western Mono community: The recontextualization of a coyote
           story. In *Language and Ideology,* ed. Jef Verschueren, 270–89.
           Antwerp: International Pragmatics Association.

Kroskrity, Paul V., and Gregory A. Reinhardt
1984   Spanish and English loanwords in Western Mono. *Journal of Cali-*
           fornia and Great Basin Anthropology, Papers in Linguistics 4: 107–38.

Kroskrity, Paul V., and Jennifer F. Reynolds
Forth-   On using multimedia in language renewal: Observations from
coming   making the CD-ROM *Taitaduhaan.* In *Manual of Language Revital-*
           ization, ed. Kenneth L. Hale and Leanne Hinton. Orlando, Fla.
           Academic Press.

Kulick, Don
1992   *Language Shift and Cultural Reproduction.* Cambridge: Cambridge
           University Press.

Labarre, Albert
1975   *Bibliographie du Dictionarium d'Ambrogio Calepino.* Baden-Baden:
           Éditions Valentin Koerner.

Landau, Sidney
1984   *Dictionaries: The art and craft of lexicography.* New York: Scribners.

Langdon, Margaret
1996   Lessons from the field: A retrospective. Paper presented at the
           annual meeting of the Linguistic Society of America, San Diego,
           California.

Lappin, Shalom, ed.
1996   *The Handbook of Contemporary Semantic Theory.* Oxford: Blackwell.

Laughlin, Robert M.
1975   *The Great Tzotzil Dictionary of San Lorenzo Zinacatán.* Smithsonian
           Contributions to Anthropology 19. Washington, D.C.: Smithsonian
           Institution Press.

Launey, Michel
1979   *Introduction à la langue et la littérature aztèques. Tome 1:*
           (Grammaire). Paris: L'Harmattan.
1986   Catégories et opérations dans la grammaire nahuatl. Thèse
           présentée à l'Université de Paris-IV pour l'obtention du Doctorat
           d'État.

1992   *Introducción a la lengua y a la literatura náhuatl.* Mexico City: Universidad Nacional Autónoma de México.
1998   Compound nouns vs. incorporation in classical Nahuatl. Manuscript.

Leap, William
1988   Applied linguistics and American Indian language renewal: Introductory comments. *Human Organization* 47: 283–90.
1991   Pathways to Indian language literacy building on the Northern Ute Reservation. *Anthropology and Education Quarterly* 22: 21–41.

Lee, Gaylen D.
1998   *Walking Where We Lived: Memoirs of a Mono Indian Family.* Norman: University of Oklahoma Press.

Lehmann, Walter
1920   *Zentral-Amerika, Teil I, Die Sprachen Zentral-Amerikas in ihren Beziehungen zueinander sowie zu Sud-Amerika und Mexiko.* Berlin: Dietrich Reimer.
1938   *Die Geschichte der Königreiche von Culhuacan und Mexiko.*
[1974] Aztekischer Text mit Übersetzung von Walter Lehmann. Quellenwerke zur alten Geschichte Amerikas, aufgezeichnet in den Sprachen der Eingeborenen. Bd. 1, Stuttgart and Berlin. Bd. 2, um ein Register vermehrte und berichtigte Auflage, herausgegeben von Gerdt Kutscher, Stuttgart.

León-Portilla, Ascención H. de
1988   *Tepuztlahcuilolli: Impresos en náhuatl: historia y bibliografía.* Mexico City: Universidad Nacional Autónoma de México.

León-Portilla, Miguel
1970   Estudio preliminar. In *Vocabulario en lengua castellana y mexicana y mexicana y castellana,* by Alonso de Molina (1571), xiii–lxiv. Mexico City: Porrúa.

Levin, Beth, and Malka Rappaport Hovav
1995   *Unaccusatives: At the Syntax-Lexical Interface.* Cambridge, Mass.: MIT Press.

Levinson, Stephen C.
1983   *Pragmatics.* Cambridge: Cambridge University Press.

Li Fang-Kuei
1929   Hare stem list. Manuscript.

Li, Yafei
1991   On deriving serial verb constructions. In *Serial Verbs: Grammatical, Comparative and Cognitive Approaches,* ed. Claire Lefebvre, 101–35. Amsterdam: John Benjamins.

Linnel, Per
1982   *The Written Language Bias in Linguistics.* Linköping: Department of Communication Studies.

1988   The impact of literacy on the conception of language. In *The Written World: Studies in Literate Thought and Action,* ed. Roger Säljö, 41–58. Berlin: Springer-Verlag.

Loether, Christopher
1991   Verbal art among the Western Mono. Ph.D. dissertation, University of California, Los Angeles.
1993   *Niimina ahubiya:* Western Mono song genres. *Journal of California and Great Basin Anthropology* 15: 48–57.
1997   Yokuts and English loanwords in Western Mono. In *The Life of Language: Papers in Honor of William Bright,* ed. Jane H. Hill, P. J. Mistry, and Lyle Campbell, 101–22. The Hague: Mouton de Gruyter.

Longacre, Robert
1985   Sentences as combinations of clauses. In *Language Typology and Syntactic Description.* Vol. 2: Complex Constituents, ed. Timothy Shopen, 235–86. Cambridge: Cambridge University Press.

Loughridge, R. M., and David M. Hodge
1890   *English and Muskogee Dictionary.* St. Louis, Mo.: J. T. Smith. (Reprint Okmulgee, Okla.: Baptist Home Mission Board, 1964.)

Mackin, Ronald
1978   On collocations: Words shall be known by the company they keep. In *In Honour of A. S. Hornby,* ed. Peter Strevens, 149–65. Oxford: Oxford University Press.

Magay, Tamás
1988   On some problems of the bilingual learner's dictionary. In *ZüriLEX '86 Proceedings,* ed. Mary Snell-Hornby, 171–77. Tübingen: A. Francke Verlag.

Malkiel, Yakov
1962   A typological classification of dictionaries on the basis of distinctive features. In *Problems in Lexicography,* ed. Fred W. Householder and Sol Saporta, 3–24. *International Journal of American Linguistics.* Pt. 2/Indiana University Research Center in Anthropology, Folklore, and Linguistics Publication 21. Bloomington.

Malotki, Ekkehart
1979   *Hopi-Raum: Eine sprachwissenschaftliche Analyse der Raumvorstellungen in der Hopi-Sprache.* Tübingen: Gunter Narr Verlag.
1983   *Hopi Time: A Linguistic Analysis of the Temporal Concepts in the Hopi Language.* Berlin: Mouton.
1985   *Gullible Coyote. Una'ihu: A Bilingual Collection of Hopi Coyote Stories.* Tucson: University of Arizona Press.

Malotki, Ekkehart, and Michael Lomatuway'ma
1984   *Hopi Coyote Tales—Istutuwutsi.* Lincoln: University of Nebraska Press.

Marx, W. G., and G. R. Heath
1961   *Diccionario miskito-español, español-miskito.* Tegucigalpa: Imprenta Calderón.

Mason, John A.
1939   Los cuatro grandes filones lingüísticos de México y Centroamérica. In *Actas del XXVII Congreso de Americanistas,* 282–88.
1940   The native languages of Middle America. In *The Maya and Their Neighbors,* ed. Clarence L. Hay, 52–87. New York: Appleton Century Company.

McArthur, Lewis A., ed.
1992   *Oregon Geographic Names,* 6th ed. Portland: Oregon Historical Society Press.

McCawley, James
1992–93   How to achieve lexicographic virtue through selective and judicious sinning. *Dictionaries* 14: 120–29.

McIntosh, Juan B., and José Grimes E.
1954   *Niuqui 'iquisicayari: Vixárica niuquiyári, teivári niuquiyári hepáïsita; Vocabulario huichol-castellano, castellano-huichol.* Mexico City: Instituto Lingüístico de Verano en cooperación con la Dirección General de Asuntos Indígenas de la Secretaría de Educación Pública.

McLaughlin, John E.
1999   Review of Hopi Dictionary Project 1998. *Anthropological Linguistics* 41: 252–53.

McQuown, Norman A.
1991   Lexikographie der Mayasprachen. In *Wörterbücher/Dictionaries/Dictionnaires,* ed. Franz Josef Hausmann, Oskar Reichmann, Herbert Ernst Wiegand, and Ladislav Zgusta, 2661–70. Berlin: Walter de Gruyter.

Mel'čuk, Igor' A.
1988   Semantic description of lexical units in an Explanatory Combinatorial Dictionary: Basic principles and heuristic criteria. *International Journal of Lexicography* 1: 164–88.
1996   Lexical functions: A tool for the description of lexical relations in a lexicon. In *Lexical Functions in Lexicography and Natural Language Processing,* ed. Leo Wanner, 37–102. Amsterdam: John Benjamins.

Mel'čuk, Igor' A., and Leo Wanner
1996   Lexical functions and lexical inheritance for emotion lexemes in German. In *Lexical Functions in Lexicography and Natural Language Processing,* ed. Leo Wanner, 209–78. Amsterdam: John Benjamins.

Mel'čuk, Igor' A., and Aleksandr K. Žolkovsky
1984   *Tolkovo-kombinatornij slovar' sovremennogo russkogo jazyka: Opyty semantiko-sintaksičeskogo opisanija russkoj leksiki* (Explanatory-Combinatorial Dictionary of Modern Russian: Semantico-Syntactic

Studies of Russian Vocabulary). Vienna: Wiener Slawistischer Almanach.

Mel'čuk, Igor' A., Aleksandr K. Žolkovsky, Nadia Arbatchewsky-Jumarie, Léo Elnitsky, Lidija Iordanskaja, and Adèle Lessard
1984   *Dictionnaire explicatif et combinatoire du français contemporain.*
[and later] Recherches Lexico-Sémantiques 1 and following volumes. Montréal: Les Presses de l'Université de Montréal.

Merlan, Francesca
1976   Noun incorporation and discourse reference in modern Nahuatl. *International Journal of American Linguistics* 42: 177–91.

Merriam, C. Hart
1979   *Indian Names for Plants and Animals among California and Other Western North American Tribes* (assembled and annotated by Robert F. Heizer). Ballena Press Publications in Archaeology, Ethnology and History 14. Socorro, New Mex.: Ballena Press.

Meyer, Ingrid
1990   Interlingual meaning-text lexicography: Towards a new type of dictionary for translation. In *Meaning-Text Theory: Linguistics, Lexicography, and Implications,* ed. James Steele, 175–270. Ottawa: University of Ottawa Press.

Microsoft
1993   *Microsoft Word: User's Guide.* Version 6.0. Seattle, Wash.: Microsoft Corporation.

Miller, Wick R.
1983   Uto-Aztecan languages. In *Southwest,* ed. A. Ortiz, 113–24. *Handbook of North American Indians* 10. Washington, D.C.: Smithsonian Institution Press.

Milroy, Lesley
1987   *Language and Social Networks.* 2d ed. Oxford: Basil Blackwell.

Mithun, Marianne
1984   The evolution of noun incorporation. *Language* 60: 847–94.

Molina, Fray Alonso de
1555   *Aqui comiença un vocabulario en la lengua castellana y mexicana.* Mexico City: Juan Pablos. (Microfilm from the Newberry Library.)
1571   *Vocabulario de la lengua mexicana compuesto por el P. fray Alonso de*
[1880] *Molina,* published by Julio Platzmann, edición facsimilaria. 2 vols. in 1. Leipzig: B. G. Teubner.
1571   *Vocabulario en lengua castellana y mexicana por el R. P. fray Alonso de*
[1944] *Molina de la Orden del Bienaventurado Nuestro Padre San Francisco.* Obra impresa en México, por Antonio de Spinola[*sic*] en 1571 y ahora editada en facsímil. (Includes the *Vocabulario en lengua mex-*

icana y castellana with separate title page). Madrid: Ediciones Cultura Hispánica.

1571 *Arte de la lengua mexicana y castellana por el Reverendo Padre fray*
[1945] *Alonso de Molina de la orden de San Francisco.* Obra impresa en México por Pedro Ocharte, en 1571 y ahora reproducida en facsímil de original facilitado por D. Antonio Graiño. Colección de incunables americanos siglo XVI. volumen VI. Madrid: Ediciones Cultura Hispánica.

1571 *Vocabulario en lengua castellana y mexicana y mexicana y castellana.*
[1970] Mexico City: Antonio de Spinosa (with a preliminary study by Miguel León-Portilla). Mexico City: Porrúa.

Morvillo, Anthony
1895 *A Dictionary of the Numipu or Nez Perce Language* (by a Missionary of the Society of Jesus, in the Rocky Mountains. Part I, English–Nez Perce). Montana: St. Ignatius' Mission Print.

Munro, Pamela
1981 Mojave *k* and *m*: It ain't necessarily so. In *Proceedings of the 1980 Hokan Languages Workshop,* ed. J. E. Redden, 124–29. *Occasional Papers on Linguistics* 9. Carbondale: Southern Illinois University.
1996 Making a Zapotec dictionary. *Dictionaries* 17: 131–55.
1997 The Garifuna gender system. In *The Life of Language: Papers in Honor of William Bright,* ed. Jane H. Hill, P. J. Mistry, and Lyle Campbell, 443–61. The Hague: Mouton de Gruyter.
2000 The leaky grammar of the Chickasaw applicatives. In *Proceedings of the Chicago Linguistic Society* (36-1), ed. Arika Okrent and John Boyle, 285–310. Chicago: CLS.

Munro, Pamela, Nellie Brown, and Judith G. Crawford
1992 *A Mojave Dictionary.* UCLA Occasional Papers in Linguistics 10. Los Angeles: UCLA Department of Linguistics.

Munro, Pamela, and Molly Star Fasthorse
In preparation *Tolkapaya Yavapai: A Dictionary.*

Munro, Pamela, Hannah Lefthand Bull Fixico, and Mary Rose Iron Teeth
1999 Ten lessons in Lakhota. Manuscript.

Munro, Pamela, and Lynn Gordon
1990 Inflectional ablaut in the River languages. In *Papers from the 1989 Hokan-Penutian Workshop. University of Oregon Papers in Linguistics* 2, ed. S. DeLancey, 69–86. Eugene: University of Oregon.

Munro, Pamela, and Felipe H. Lopez, with Olivia V. Méndez, Rodrigo Garcia, and Michael R. Galant
1999 *Di'csyonaary X: tëe'n Dìi'zh Sah Sann Lu'uc (San Lucas Quiaviní Zapotec Dictionary/Diccionario zapoteco de San Lucas Quiaviní).* Chicano Studies Research Center Publications. Los Angeles: UCLA, Chicano Studies Research Center.

Munro, Pamela, and Catherine Willmond
1994   *Chickasaw: An Analytical Dictionary.* Norman: University of
        Oklahoma Press.

Nebrija, Elio Antonio de
1492   *Lexicon hoc est dictionarium ex sermone latino in hispaniensem, inter-*
[1979] *prete Aelio Antonio Neprissensi.* Ed. Germán Colón and Amadeu-J.
        Soberanas. Barcelona: Puvill-Editor.
1492   *Vocabulario español-latino.* Facsimile ed. Madrid: Real Academia
[1951] Española.
1516   *Vocabulario de romãce en latin hecho por el doctissimo maestro Antonio*
        de Nebrissa nuevamẽte corregido & augmẽtado. Microfilm. Hispanic
        Society of America.
1516   *Vocabulario de romance en latín. Transcripción crítica de la edición*
[1973] *revisada por el autor (Sevilla, 1516) con una introducción.* Ed. Gerald
        J. MacDonald. Madrid: Editorial Castalia.

Newman, Stanley
1944   *The Yokuts Language of California.* Viking Fund Publications in
        Anthropology 2. New York: Viking Fund.

Nez Perce Tribe
1972   *Nu Mee Poom Tit Wah Tit (Nez Perce Legends).* Lipwai: Idaho's Nez
        Perce Tribe.

Nichols, John D., and Earl Nyholm
1995   *A Concise Dictionary of Minnesota Ojibwe.* Minneapolis: University of
        Minnesota Press.

Norwood, Susan
1993   El sumu, lengua oprimida—habilidades lingüísticas y cambio
        social: Los sumus. *Wani* 14: 53–64.
1997   *Gramática de la lengua sumu.* Managua: CIDCA-UCA.

Olmos, Andrés de
1547   *Arte de la lengua mexicana y vocabulario.* Ed. Thelma Sullivan and
[1985] René Acuña. Mexico City: Instituto de Investigaciones Filológicas,
        Universidad Nacional Autónoma de México.
1547   *Arte de la lengua mexicana: Concluido en el convento de San Andrés de*
[1993] *Ueytlalpan, en la provincia de la Totonacapan que es en la Nueva*
        España, el 1 de enero de 1547. Edition, introductory study, translit-
        eration, and notes by Ascención Léon-Portilla and Miguel León-
        Portilla. Madrid: Ediciones de Cultura Hispánica; Instituto de
        Cooperación Iberoamericana.

Ousterhout, John K.
1994   *Tcl and the Tk Toolkit.* Reading, Mass.: Addison-Wesley.

Palmer, Gary B.
1988   The language and culture approach in the Coeur d'Alene Lan-
        guage Preservation Project. *Human Organization* 47: 307–17.

Parks, Douglas, and Raymond DeMallie
1992   Sioux, Assiniboine, and Stoney dialects: A classification. *Anthropological Linguistics* 34: 233–55.

Perlmutter, David
1978   Impersonal passives and the unaccusative hypothesis. In *Proceedings of the Fourth Annual Meeting of the Berkeley Linguistic Society*, 157–89. Berkeley: Berkeley Linguistic Society.

Phinney, Archie
1934   *Nez Perce Texts*. New York: Columbia University Press.

Piggot, Glynn, and Jonathan Kaye
1973   *Odawa Language Project: Second Report*. Toronto: Centre for Linguistic Studies, University of Toronto.

Platero, Paul
1974   The Navajo relative clause. *International Journal of American Linguistics* 40: 202–46.
1982   Missing noun phrases and grammatical relations in Navajo. *International Journal of American Linguistics* 48: 286–305.

Pukui, Mary Kawena, Samuel H. Elbert, and Esther T. Mookini
1974   *Place Names of Hawaii*. 2d ed. Honolulu: University Press of Hawaii.

Pulte, William, and Durbin Feeling
1975   Outline of Cherokee grammar. In *Cherokee-English Dictionary*, by Durbin Feeling, ed. William Pulte, 235–355. Tahlequah: Cherokee Nation of Oklahoma.

Pustejovsky, James
1995   *The Generative Lexicon*. Cambridge, Mass.: MIT Press.

Rankin, Robert L., Richard T. Carter, and A. Wesley Jones
1998   Proto-Siouan phonology and grammar. In *Proceedings of the 1997 Mid-America Linguistics Conference*, ed. Xingzhong Li, Luis Lopez, and Tom Stroik, 366–75. Columbia: Linguistics Area Program of the University of Missouri–Columbia.

Read, William Alexander
1927   *Louisiana Place-Names of Indian Origin*. Baton Rouge: Louisiana State University Press.
1934   *Florida Place-Names of Indian Origin and Seminole Personal Names*. Baton Rouge: Louisiana State University Press.
1937   *Indian Place-Names in Alabama*. Baton Rouge: Louisiana State University Press. (2d ed., rev. by J. M. Macmillan. Tuscaloosa: University of Alabama Press, 1984.)

Rhodes, Richard A.
1985   *Eastern Ojibwa-Chippewa-Ottawa Dictionary*. Trends in Linguistics, Documentation 3. Berlin: Mouton.

1988   Ojibwa politeness and social structure. In *Papers of the Nineteenth Algonquian Conference,* ed. William Cowan, 165–74. Ottawa: Carleton University.

1989   'We are going to go there.'—Positive politeness in Ojibwa. *Multilingua* 8: 249–58.

1990   Relative root complements. Paper presented at the 29th Conference on American Indian Languages, New Orleans, November.

1991a   Lexicography of the languages of the North American Indians. In *Wörterbücher/Dictionaries/Dictionnaires,* ed. Franz Josef Hausmann, Oskar Reichmann, Herbert Ernst Wiegand, and Ladislav Zgusta, 2691–96. Berlin: Walter de Gruyter.

1991b   Ojibwa secondary objects. In *Grammatical Relations: A Cross Theoretical Perspective,* 401–14. Palo Alto, Calif.: Stanford Linguistics Association.

1998   Clause structure, core arguments, and the Algonquian relative root construction. Belcourt Lecture, University of Manitoba, 20 March.

Rice, Keren
1978   *Hare Dictionary.* Ottawa: Northern Social Research Division, Department of Indian and Northern Affairs.

1989a   *A Grammar of Slave.* Berlin: Mouton de Gruyter.

1989b   *A Manual for Spelling, Word Division, and Punctuation for North Slavey.* Yellowknife, NWT: Language Bureau, Ministry of Culture and Communication, Government of the Northwest Territories.

1995   Developing orthographies: The Athapaskan languages of the Northwest Territories, Canada. In *Scripts and Literacy: Reading and Learning to Read Alphabets, Syllabaries and Characters,* ed. Insup Taylor and David R. Olson, 77–94. Dordrecht: Kluwer Academic Publishers.

Riggs, Steven R.
1890   *A Dakota-English Dictionary.* Ed. James Owen Dorsey. Washington, D.C.: U.S. Geological Survey of the Rocky Mountain Region. (Reprint 1968, Minneapolis, Minn.: Ross & Haines.)

Rogers, Edward S., and James G. E. Smith
1981   Environment and culture in the Shield and Mackenzie borderlands. In *Subarctic.* Vol. 6 of *Handbook of North American Indians,* ed. June Helm, 130–45. Washington, D.C.: Smithsonian Institution Press.

Rommetveit, Ragnar
1988   On literacy and the myth of literal meaning. In *The Written World: Studies in Literate Thought and Action,* ed. Roger Säljö, 13–40. Berlin: Springer-Verlag.

Rood, David S.
1979   Siouan. In *The Languages of Native America,* ed. Lyle Campbell and Marianne Mithun, 236–98. Austin: University of Texas Press.

1981   *User's Handbook for the Siouan Languages Archives.* Bound
            typescript. Department of Linguistics, University of Colorado.

Rundell, Michael
    1988   Changing the rules: Why the monolingual learner's dictionary
            should move away from the native-speaker tradition. In *Zürilex
            '86 Proceedings,* ed. Mary Snell-Hornby, 127–38. Tübingen: A.
            Francke Verlag.

Rydjord, John
    1968   *Indian Place-Names: Their Origin, Evolution, and Meanings, Collected
            in Kansas from the Siouan, Algonquian, Shoshonean, Caddoan,
            Iroquoian, and Other Tongues.* Norman: University of Oklahoma
            Press.

Sahagún, Bernardino de
    1579 [1950–82]   *Florentine Codex, General History of the Things of New Spain.*
            Ed. and trans. Arthur J. O. Anderson and Charles E. Dibble. In
            13 parts. Monographs of the School of American Research,
            Santa Fe, New Mex. Santa Fe and Salt Lake City: School of
            American Research and University of Utah.
    1979   *Códice florentino.* MS 218–220 of the Palatina collection of the
            Biblioteca Medicea Laurenziana. Facsimile ed. 3 vols. Florence:
            Giunti Barbera and the Archivo General de la Nación.
    1997   *Primeros memoriales.* Paleography of Nahuatl and English transla-
            tion by Thelma D. Sullivan. Norman: University of Oklahoma
            Press.

Salamanca, Danilo
    1988   Elementos de gramática del miskito. Ph.D. dissertation,
            Massachusetts Institute of Technology.
    1998   Morphological alternations in Miskito verbs: Miskitu-k/w/b.
            Manuscript. Massachusetts Institute of Technology, Department
            of Linguistics.

Sauvel, Katherine Siva, and Pamela Munro
    1981   *Chem'ivillu' (Let's Speak Cahuilla).* Los Angeles and Banning, Calif.:
            UCLA American Indian Studies Center, and Malki Museum
            Press.

Saxon, Leslie
    1990   Technical report on the Dogrib standard orthography. Department
            of Culture and Communication, Government of the Northwest
            Territories, in a supplement to the Report of the Special Commit-
            tee on Aboriginal Languages, 8–18.

Saxon, Leslie, and Rosa Mantla
    1997   On standardized forms of Dogrib spellings. Paper presented at
            the Athapaskan Language Conference, University of Oregon,
            Eugene.

Saxon, Leslie, and Mary Siemens
1996   *Tłįchǫ Yatiì Enįhtłè/A Dogrib Dictionary.* Rae-Edzo, NWT: Dogrib Divisional Board of Education.

Schoen Brockman, Elin
1999   Word for word/neology. *New York Times, Week in Review,* August 22, 1999, 7.

Schoenberg, Wilfred P., S.J.
1966   *Jesuit Mission Presses in the Pacific Northwest.* Portland, Ore.: Champoeg Press.

Seaman, P. David
1985   *Hopi Dictionary.* Northern Arizona University Anthropological Paper No. 2. Flagstaff: Department of Anthropology, Northern Arizona University.

Seiler, Hansjakob, and Kojiro Hioki
1979   *Cahuilla Dictionary.* Banning, Calif.: Malki Museum Press.

Shaterian, Alan W.
1983   Yavapai phonology and dictionary. Ph.D. dissertation, University of California, Berkeley.

Siever, Ellen, Stephen Spainhour, and Nathan Patwardhan
1999   *Perl in a Nutshell: A Desktop Quick Reference.* Sebastopol, Calif.: O'Reilly & Associates.

SIL (Summer Institute of Linguistics)
1988   *Keyswap: A Keyboard Enhancer for the IBM-PC* (Version 1.2) and *Keydef: A Screen-oriented Keyboard Definer* (Version 1.0). Dallas: Summer Institute of Linguistics.
1990   *SIL Premier Font System.* Dallas: Summer Institute of Linguistics.
1994a   *Glyph Catalog.* Dallas: Printing Arts Department, Summer Institute of Linguistics.
1994b   *SIL Encore Fonts.* Dallas: Summer Institute of Linguistics.
1994c   *SIL Legacy Font System.* Dallas: Summer Institute of Linguistics.

Silver, Shirley, and Wick R. Miller
1998   *American Indian Languages: Cultural and Social Contexts.* Tucson: University of Arizona Press.

Silverstein, Michael
1996   Encountering language and the languages of encounter in North American ethnohistory. *Journal of Linguistic Anthropology* 6: 126–44.

Siméon, Rémi
1885   *Dictionnaire de la langue nahuatl ou mexicaine.* Paris: Imprimerie Nationale. (Reprint, with a preface by Jacqueline de Durand-Forest. Graz: Akademische Druck- u. Verlagsanstalt, 1963.)

Sinclair, J.
1987   *Collins COBUILD English Language Dictionary.* London: Collins.

Smith, Grant
1996   Amerindian place names: A typology based on meaning and form. *Onomastica Canadiana* 78: 53–64.

Snell-Hornby, Mary
1990   Bilingual dictionaries—Visions and revisions. In *BudaLEX '88 Proceedings,* ed. Tamás Magay and J. Zigány, 207–15. Budapest: Akadémiai Kiadó.

SoftCraft
1988   *Laser Fonts User's Manual.* Version 4/5. Madison, Wisc.: SoftCraft, Inc.
1989   *Font Solution Pack User's Guide.* Version 2. Madison, Wisc.: SoftCraft, Inc.

Spier, Robert F. G.
1978   Monache. In *California.* Vol. 8 of *Handbook of North American Indians,* ed. R. F. Heizer, 426–36. Washington, D.C.: Smithsonian Institution Press.

Stewart, George R.
1970   *American Place-Names.* New York: Oxford University Press.

Street, Brian V.
1984   *Literacy in Theory and Practice.* Cambridge: Cambridge University Press.
1988   Literacy practices and literacy myths. In *The Written World: Studies in Literate Thought and Action,* ed. Roger Säljö, 59–72. Berlin: Springer-Verlag.

Svensén, Bo
1993   *Practical Lexicography: Principles and Methods of Dictionary-Making.* Oxford: Oxford University Press.

Talashoema, Herschel
1978   *Hopitutuwutsi. Hopi Tales: A Bilingual Collection of Hopi Indian Stories.* Recorded and trans. Ekkehart Malotki. Flagstaff: Museum of Northern Arizona Press. (Reprint, Sun Tracks 9. Tucson: Sun Tracks and the University of Arizona Press, 1983.)
1993   *Coyote and Little Turtle: Iisaw niqw Yöngösonhoya: A Traditional Hopi Tale.* Ed. and trans. Emory Sekaquaptewa and Barbara Pepper. Santa Fe, New Mex.: Clear Light Publishers.

Talmy, Leonard
1985   Lexicalization patterns: Semantic structure in lexical forms. In *Language Typology and Syntactic Description.* Vol. 3: *Grammatical Categories and the Lexicon,* ed. Timothy Shopen, 57–149. Cambridge: Cambridge University Press.

Thompson, Laurence C., and M. Terry Thompson
1996   *Thompson River Salish Dictionary: nɬeʔkepmxcín.* UMPOL no. 12. Missoula: University of Montana.

Tooker, William W.
1911   *The Indian Place-Names on Long Island and Islands Adjacent.* New York: Putnam.

Tufte, Edward
1983   *The Visual Display of Quantitative Information.* Cheshire, Conn.: Graphics Press.
1990   *Envisioning Information.* Cheshire, Conn.: Graphics Press.
1997   *Visual Explanations.* Cheshire, Conn.: Graphics Press.

Underhill, Adrian
1980   *Use Your Dictionary: A Practice Book for Users of* Oxford Advanced Learner's Dictionary of Current English *and* Oxford Student's Dictionary of Current English. Oxford: Oxford University Press.

Voegelin, Charles F., and Florence M. Voegelin
1957   *Hopi Domains: A Lexical Approach to the Problem of Selection.* Memoir 14 of the *International Journal of American Linguistics*/Indiana University Publications in Anthropology and Linguistics.

Vogel, Virgil J.
1963   *Indian Place Names in Illinois.* Springfield: Illinois State Historical Library.
1983   *Iowa Place Names of Indian Origin.* Iowa City: University of Iowa Press.
1986   *Indian Names in Michigan.* Ann Arbor: University of Michigan Press.
1991   *Indian Names on Wisconsin's Map.* Madison: University of Wisconsin Press.

Voorhis, Paul
N.d.   Grammatical sketch of Catawba. Manuscript.

Walker, Willard
1969   Notes on native writing systems and the design of native literacy programs. *Anthropological Linguistics* 11: 148–66.

Wanner, Leo, ed.
1996   *Lexical Functions in Lexicography and Natural Language Processing.* Amsterdam: John Benjamins.

Waterman, T. T.
1920   *Yurok Geography.* Berkeley: University of California Press.

Weber, David J., H. Andrew Black, and Stephen R. McConnel
1988   *AMPLE: A Tool for Exploring Morphology.* Dallas: Summer Institute of Linguistics.

Wehr, Hans
1976   *A Dictionary of Modern Written Arabic.* 3d ed. Ed. J. Milton Cowan. Ithaca, N.Y.: Spoken Language Services.

Weinreich, Uriel
1966   Explorations in semantic theory. In *Current Trends in Linguistics 3, Theoretical Foundations,* ed. Thomas A. Sebeok, 395–477. The Hague: Mouton.

Whiteley, Peter M.
1999   Review of Hopi Dictionary Project 1998. *Linguistic Anthropology* 10: 659–60.

Wierzbicka, Anna
1972   *Semantic Primitives.* Linguistische Forschungen No. 22. Frankfurt: Athenäum.
1988   *The Semantics of Grammar.* Amsterdam: John Benjamins.
1996   *Semantics: Primes and Universals.* Oxford: Oxford University Press.

Williamson, Janis S.
1987   An indefiniteness restriction for relative clauses in Lakhota. In *The Representation of (In)definiteness,* ed. Eric Reuland and Alice ter Meulen, 168–90. Cambridge, Mass.: MIT Press.

Wilson, Alan
1995   *Navajo Placenames.* Guilford, Conn.: Audio-Forum.

Wimbish, John S.
1990   *Shoebox: A Data Management Program for the Field Linguist.* Version 1.2. Indonesia: Summer Institute of Linguistics and Pattimura University.

Young, Robert W., and William Morgan, Sr.
1987   *The Navajo Language: A Grammar and Colloquial Dictionary.* Rev. ed. Albuquerque: University of New Mexico Press.

Young, Robert W., William Morgan, Sr., and Sally Midgette
1992   *Analytical Lexicon of Navajo.* Albuquerque: University of New Mexico Press.

Zgusta, Ladislav
1971   *Manual of Lexicography.* The Hague: Mouton; Prague: Czechoslovak Academy of Sciences.

Zulaica Gárate, Román
1939   *Los franciscanos y la imprenta en México en el siglo XVI, Estudio biobibliográfico.* Mexico City: Editorial Pedro Robredo.

UNIVERSAL RESOURCE LOCATORS

Summer Institute of Linguistics Encore Fonts:
http://www.sil.org/computing/fonts/Encore.html

Summer Institute of Linguistics Keyswap:
http://www.sil.org/computing/catalog/keyswap.html

Summer Institute of Linguistics Linguist's Shoebox:
http://www.sil.org/computing/catalog/shoebox.html

Summer Institute of Linguistics SF Converter:
http://www.sil.org/computing/catalog/sfc.html

TavulteSoft Keyboard Manager (Keyman):
http://www.sil.org/computing/fonts/keyman.html

CONTRIBUTORS

Jonathan Amith is a social anthropologist who has conducted ethnohistorical research on central Guerrero, Mexico, and ethnographic and linguistic fieldwork in two Nahuatl-speaking villages of this region: Ameyaltepec and San Agustín Oapan. He is editor of *The Amate Tradition: Innovation and Dissent in Mexican Art* (1995) and author (with Thomas Smith-Stark) of two articles on the Nahuatl of the Balsas River valley. He is presently working on a lexicon, grammar, and corpus of Nahuatl texts from the Balsas River valley with a grant from the U.S. Department of Education.

Haruo Aoki was a faculty member in the Oriental Languages Department (now the Department of East Asian Languages and Cultures) at the University of California, Berkeley, from 1964 to 1991. He has published *Nez Perce Grammar* (1970), *Nez Perce Texts* (1979), (with D. E. Walker) *Nez Perce Oral Narratives* (1989), and *Nez Perce Dictionary* (1994), all in the University of California Publications in Linguistics series. He is currently consultant for the Nez Perce Section, Language Preservation Program, Colville Confederated Tribes, Nespelem, Washington.

William Bright is Professor Emeritus of Linguistics and Anthropology at the University of California, Los Angeles, as well as Professor Adjoint of Linguistics at the University of Colorado. He has been editor of *Language,* the journal of the Linguistic Society of America; of the *International Encyclopedia of Linguistics;* of the journal *Language in Society;* and most recently of the journal *Written Language & Literacy.* His interests include sociolinguistics, oral literature, grammatology, and onomastics.

Catherine A. Callaghan is the author of four dictionaries of Miwok languages, spoken in central California. She has been Visiting Professor at the University of Hawaii and a faculty member in the Department of Linguistics at Ohio State University. She has received several National Science Foundation grants to pursue her research on Miwok and Costanoan and has published numerous articles on these languages. She is currently revising her Ph.D. dissertation, "Lake Miwok Grammar," so as to trace the development of the language from Proto Miwok.

R. Joe Campbell is retired from teaching Spanish linguistics and grammar, Nahuatl, and the SNOBOL programming language, most recently as Associate Professor at Indiana University. In addition to Nahuatl, his research interests include the dialectology of Chicano Spanish and the Spanish of Jalisco, Mexico. He has carried out fieldwork on Nahuatl in Hueyapan, Morelos; Pómaro, Michoacán; San Agustín Oapan and Ameyaltepec, Guerrero; San Miguel Canoa, Puebla; and northern Puebla. Among his publications are *A Morphological Dictionary of Classical Nahuatl: A Morpheme Index to the Vocabulario en lengua mexicana y castellana of Fray Alonso de Molina* (1985) and a two-volume introduction to Nahuatl grammar (with Frances Karttunen), *Foundation Course in Nahuatl Grammar* (1989). His current work involves the compilation of a dictionary, with morphological analysis, of the vocabulary of Fray Bernardino de Sahagún's *La historia de las cosas de Nueva España* (commonly known as *The Florentine Codex*).

Una Canger is Associate Professor in the Department of American Indian Languages and Cultures, University of Copenhagen, Denmark, where she has been teaching since 1970. She has conducted field studies among Mam speakers in Guatemala and Nahuatl speakers in several communities in Mexico. Among her published works are articles on field methods, linguistic data, aspects of various Nahuatl dialects, and *Five Studies Inspired by Nahuatl Verbs in -oa* (1980). Her current research is on the Nahuatl dialect area called the "Western Periphery" in central and western Mexico.

Mary L. Clayton is Associate Professor of Spanish and Portuguese at Indiana University. In addition to lexicography, her research interests include phonological theory and language change and variation. After initial work in Nahuatl, she turned her attention to Ayer ms. 1478, a trilingual Spanish-Latin-Nahuatl manuscript dictionary, for which she is preparing a Nahuatl alphabetical dictionary, a morphological dictionary, and a monographic study. This work has been supported in part by a National Endowment for the Humanities Research Grant. She has published numerous articles, including (with R. Joe Campbell) "Fray Bernardino de Sahagún's contribution to the lexicon of classical Nahuatl," in *The Work of Bernardino de Sahagún: Pioneer Ethnographer of Sixteenth-Century Aztec Mexico.*

Durbin Feeling served as Cherokee Language Specialist for the Cherokee Bilingual Education Program at Tahlequah, Oklahoma; as news editor for the Cherokee Nation Communication Center; as Director of Adult Education Programs and Cherokee Language Specialist for the Cherokee Nation; as a radio news broadcaster in Cherokee on KGCR Radio in Pryor, Oklahoma; and, most recently, as Tribal Linguist for the Cherokee Nation. Feeling has taught Cherokee at the University of Tulsa and at Rogers State University. His major publications include the *Cherokee-English Dictionary* (1975), (with William Pulte) *An Outline of Cherokee Grammar* (1975), and "The Use of Cherokee in Christian Religious Services," in *Proceedings of the Seventh Annual Native American Language Issues Institute* (1987). He is the author of a large number of curriculum materials.

William Frawley is Dean of the Columbian College of Arts and Science at George Washington University. Prior to that, he was Director of Undergraduate Studies at the University of Delaware, where he was Chair of the Department of Linguistics and Director of Cognitive Science. He has written or edited twelve books and more than fifty papers on language and cognitive science, including *Linguistic Semantics* (1992) and *Vygotsky and Cognitive Science* (1997). He is currently editor in chief of the second edition of the *Oxford International Encyclopedia of Linguistics* and is also on the Editorial Advisory Board for Oxford American Dictionaries. His most recent work is on the computational structure of language disorders, which appears as a target article with continuing commentary in *Computational Intelligence.*

Joseph E. Grimes has been a member of the Summer Institute of Linguistics since 1950, specializing in Huichol of Mexico and, most recently, in Hawaii Pidgin. He was consulting editor of the *Ethnologue* from 1972 to 2000, designing the computer software to convert the database into a book. Until 2000 he was Professor of Linguistics at Cornell University, where he did research on discourse and lexical theory and set up and directed the phonetics laboratory. He has served on the Executive Committee of the Linguistic Society of America and was its representative on the Consortium of Social Science Associations for several years.

Ken Hale taught linguistics in the anthropology departments at the University of Illinois and the University of Arizona. Since 1967 he taught and did research in the Department of Linguistics and Philosophy at the Massachusetts Institute of Technology. His primary research was on the syntax, morphology, and lexical structures of the Pama-Nyungan languages of Australia, the Uto-Aztecan and Athabaskan languages of the southwestern United States, and the Misumalpan languages of Nicaragua and Honduras. He participated in the educational programs of the American

Indian Languages Development Institute (AILDI) and the Navajo Language Academy (NLA).

Kenneth C. Hill was a faculty member at the University of Michigan from 1965 to 1985 and Chairman of the Department of Linguistics from 1977 to 1982. He served as director of the Hopi Dictionary Project, 1985–88, at the University of Arizona. His major publications include (with Jane H. Hill) *Speaking Mexicano* (1986) and the *Hopi Dictionary/Hopi `ikwa Lava`ytutuveni* (editor in chief) (1998). His research is in Uto-Aztecan linguistics.

Leanne Hinton is a Professor of Linguistics at the University of California, Berkeley, and the director of the Survey of California and Other Indian Languages. She has written or edited eight books and more than one hundred articles. Her main field is American Indian languages, within which she has specialized in language and music, sociolinguistics, historical linguistics, and language revitalization. She has written a community-oriented dictionary for the Havasupai language, assisted in the development of a dictionary for Kumeyaay (Northern Diegueño), and served as an adviser for several other community-based dictionaries.

John E. Koontz has been a computer scientist at the National Institute for Standards and Technology since 1977. He was introduced to the computer production of dictionaries by Robert Hsu and to the Siouan languages by Allan Taylor and David Rood. He subsequently became involved in the comparative investigation of the family and in an investigation of the Omaha-Ponca language, for which he is preparing a grammar. He was a participant in the 1984 Comparative Siouan Workshop and has been involved in the Comparative Siouan Dictionary Project from its inception.

Paul V. Kroskrity is Professor of Anthropology and Chair, Interdepartmental Program in American Indian Studies, at the University of California, Los Angeles. His specializes in linguistic anthropology, with an emphasis on Native American languages and cultures. He has conducted long-term fieldwork with the Arizona Tewa, who reside on First Mesa of the Hopi Reservation in northeastern Arizona, and with members of the Mono Indian communities of North Fork and Auberry in central California. He has published many books and articles, including *Language, History, and Identity: Ethnolinguistic Studies of the Arizona Tewa* (1993); (editor) *Regimes of Language: Ideologies, Polities, and Identities* (2000); and (coauthor) *Taitaduhaan: Western Mono Ways of Speaking* (CD-ROM).

Pamela Munro is Professor of Linguistics at the University of California, Los Angeles. She has done fieldwork and published on a number of American Indian and indigenous American languages (especially from the

Yuman, Uto-Aztecan, Muskogean, and Zapotecan families), as well as on the Wolof language of Senegal and UCLA undergraduate slang.

William Pulte worked for the Cherokee Bilingual Education Program in Tahlequah, Oklahoma, from 1971 to 1973 and was project director in 1972–73. He is currently Associate Professor of Anthropology and Director of Teacher Training Programs in Bilingual Education at Southern Methodist University, where he has been a faculty member since 1973. He has received a number of grants for teacher training projects in bilingual education from the U.S. Department of Education, Office of Bilingual Education and Minority Languages Affairs. His research is on Cherokee and bilingual education.

Richard Rhodes is Associate Professor of Linguistics at the University of California, Berkeley. He has an abiding interest in endangered languages. His primary fieldwork is on Ojibwe, which he has been studying for nearly thirty years, but he has also worked with speakers of Métchif, a mixed language of the Canadian plains, and is currently part of a language documentation project in Mesoamerica, where he is working on a dictionary of the Mexican language Sayula Popoluca.

Keren Rice is Professor in the Department of Linguistics and Director of the Aboriginal Studies Program at the University of Toronto. She is the author of *A Grammar of Slave* (1998) and *Morpheme Order and Semantic Scope: Word Formation in the Athapaskan Verb* (2000).

David S. Rood is Professor of Linguistics at the University of Colorado, where he has taught since 1967. He has taught at various Native American teacher training institutes, and in 1998–99 he was a visiting faculty member at the University of Cologne. Since 1980 he has been editor in chief of the *International Journal of American Linguistics.* His research interests are the description and history of Lakhota (Siouan) and Wichita (Caddoan). He has had research grants from the National Endowment for the Humanities and the National Science Foundation, including support for the work in this volume. He is currently receiving support for a multimedia Wichita dictionary from the VolkswagenStiftung, Hannover, Germany.

Danilo Salamanca contributed to the creation and development of the Centro de Investigación y Documentación de la Costa Atlántica (CIDCA) of Nicaragua, a research institution specializing in indigenous matters, where he worked from 1981 to 1995. Since 1996 he has served as a consultant for the foundation and advancement of bilingual education programs for the Miskito people of Honduras. He is the author of *Gramática escolar del Miskito* and *Diccionario Miskito* (2000).

Leslie Saxon is Associate Professor of Linguistics at the University of Victoria, Victoria, Canada, and has also been affiliated with the Dogrib Community Services Board, Rae-Edzo, Northwest Territories. With the help of an advisory group, she and Mary Siemens edited a Dogrib dictionary (1996) for use in Dogrib schools and communities.

William F. Weigel is a Ph.D. candidate in linguistics at the University of California, Berkeley. Most of his research has focused on language shift and language obsolescence, especially in connection with the Yokuts language family.

INDEX

Compositor:	The GTS Companies
Text:	10/12 Baskerville, Times Phonetic IPA
Display:	Baskerville
Printer:	Maple-Vail Manufacturing Group
Binder:	Maple-Vail Manufacturing Group